SCHAUM'S OUTLINE OF

Theory and Problems of

BUSINESS STATISTICS

SCHAUM'S
OUTLINE OF

Theory and Problems of

BUSINESS STATISTICS

Fourth Edition

LEONARD J. KAZMIER

W. P. Carey School of Business
Arizona State University

Schaum's Outline Series

McGRAW-HILL

New York   Chicago   San Francisco   Lisbon
London   Madrid   Mexico City   Milan   New Delhi
San Juan   Seoul   Singapore   Sydney   Toronto

LEONARD J. KAZMIER earned his Ph.D. at Ohio State University, and the bachelor's and master's degrees at Wayne State University, Detroit. He is author or coauthor of several books in management concepts, statistical analysis, and computer applications in business. Editions of these books have been translated into French, German, Italian, Spanish, Portuguese, and Japanese. Professor Kazmier is a charter member of the Decision Sciences Institute, in which he has held several national elective offices. His research interests have included the application of statistical methods for the study of security price changes and securities market volatility. He has taught as a member of the faculty at Wayne State University, the University of Notre Dame, and Arizona State University.

Schaum's Outline of Theory and Problems of
BUSINESS STATISTICS

Excel is a registered trademark of Microsoft.
Minitab is a registered trademark of Minitab, Inc.
Execustat is a registered trademark of PWS-Kent Publishing, Co.

3 4 5 6 7 8 9 10 11 12 13 14 15 16 17 18 19 20 CUS CUS 0 9 8 7 6 5

ISBN 0-07-141080-5

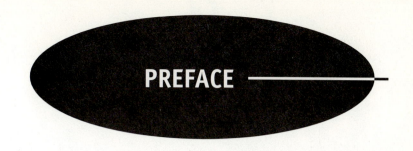

PREFACE

This book covers the basic methods of statistical description, statistical inference, decision analysis, and process control that are included in introductory and intermediate-level courses in business statistics.

The concepts and methods are presented in a clear and concise manner, and lengthy explanations have been minimized in favor of presenting concrete examples. Because this book has been developed particularly for those whose interest is the *application* of statistical techniques, mathematical derivations are omitted.

When used as a supplement to a course text, the numerous examples and solved problems will help to clarify the mathematical explanations included in such books. This Outline can also serve as an excellent *reference book* because the concise manner of coverage makes it easier to find required procedures. Finally, this book is complete enough in its coverage that it can in fact be used as the course textbook.

This edition of the Outline has been thoroughly updated, and now includes computer-based solutions using Excel (copyright Microsoft, Inc.), Minitab (copyright Minitab, Inc.), and Execustat (copyright PWS-Kent Publishing Co.).

LEONARD J. KAZMIER

CONTENTS

CHAPTER 11   Testing Other Hypotheses   197

CHAPTER 12   The Chi-Square Test for the Analysis of
                     Qualitative Data   219

CHAPTER 16   ## Time Series Analysis and Business Forecasting   **296**

CHAPTER 17   ## Nonparametric Statistics   **318**

CHAPTER 18   ## Decision Analysis: Payoff Tables and Decision Trees **336**

Theory and Problems of
BUSINESS STATISTICS

CHAPTER 1

Analyzing Business Data

1.1 DEFINITION OF BUSINESS STATISTICS

Statistics refers to the body of techniques used for collecting, organizing, analyzing, and interpreting data. The data may be quantitative, with values expressed numerically, or they may be qualitative, with characteristics such as consumer preferences being tabulated. Statistics is used in business to help make better decisions by understanding the *sources of variation* and by uncovering *patterns and relationships* in business data.

1.2 DESCRIPTIVE AND INFERENTIAL STATISTICS

Descriptive statistics include the techniques that are used to summarize and describe numerical data for the purpose of easier interpretation. These methods can either be graphical or involve computational analysis (see Chapters 2, 3, and 4).

EXAMPLE 1. The monthly sales volume for a product during the past year can be described and made meaningful by preparing a bar chart or a line graph (as described in Section 2.11). The relative sales by month can be highlighted by calculating an index number for each month such that the deviation from 100 for any given month indicates the percentage deviation of sales in that month as compared with average monthly sales during the entire year.

Inferential statistics include those techniques by which decisions about a statistical population or process are made based only on a sample having been observed. Because such decisions are made under conditions of uncertainty, the use of probability concepts is required. Whereas the measured characteristics of a sample are called *sample statistics*, the measured characteristics of a statistical population, or universe, are called *population parameters*. The procedure by which the characteristics of all the members of a defined population are measured is called a *census*. When statistical inference is used in process control, the sampling is concerned particularly with uncovering and controlling the sources of variation in the quality of the output. Chapters 5 through 7 cover probability concepts, and most of the chapters after that are concerned with the application of these concepts in statistical inference.

1

EXAMPLE 2.   In order to estimate the voltage required to cause an electrical device to fail, a sample of such devices can be subjected to increasingly higher voltages until each device fails. Based on these sample results, the probability of failure at various voltage levels for the other devices in the sampled population can be estimated.

1.3   TYPES OF APPLICATIONS IN BUSINESS

The methods of *classical statistics* were developed for the analysis of sampled (objective) data, and for the purpose of inference about the population from which the sample was selected. There is explicit exclusion of personal judgments about the data, and there is an implicit assumption that sampling is done from a static (stable) population. The methods of *decision analysis* focus on incorporating managerial judgments into statistical analysis (see Chapter 18). The methods of *statistical process control* are used with the premise that the output of a process may not be stable. Rather, the process may be dynamic, with assignable causes associated with variation in the quality of the output over time (see Chapter 19).

EXAMPLE 3.   Using the classical approach to statistical inference, the uncertain level of sales for a new product would be estimated on the basis of market studies done in accordance with the requirements of scientific sampling. In the decision-analysis approach, the judgments of managers would be quantified and incorporated into the analysis. Statistical process control would focus particularly on the pattern of sales in a sequence of time periods during test marketing of the product.

1.4   DISCRETE AND CONTINUOUS VARIABLES

A *discrete variable* can have observed values only at isolated points along a scale of values. In business statistics, such data typically occur through the process of *counting*; hence, the values generally are expressed as integers (whole numbers). A *continuous variable* can assume a value at any fractional point along a specified interval of values. Continuous data are generated by the process of *measuring*.

EXAMPLE 4.   Examples of discrete data are the number of persons per household, the units of an item in inventory, and the number of assembled components that are found to be defective. Examples of continuous data are the weight of a shipment, the length of time before the first failure of a device, and the average number of persons per household in a large community. Note that an *average number* of persons can be a fractional value and is thus a continuous variable, even though the *number* per household is a discrete variable.

1.5   OBTAINING DATA THROUGH DIRECT OBSERVATION VS. SURVEYS

One way data can be obtained is by direct observation. This is the basis for the actions that are taken in statistical process control, in which samples of output are systematically assessed. Another form of direct observation is a *statistical experiment*, in which there is overt control over some or all of the factors that may influence the variable being studied, so that possible causes can be identified.

EXAMPLE 5.   Two methods of assembling a component could be compared by having one group of employees use one of the methods and a second group of employees use the other method. The members of the first group are carefully matched to the members of the second group in terms of such factors as age and experience.

In some situations it is not possible to collect data directly but, rather, the information has to be obtained from individual respondents. A *statistical survey* is the process of collecting data by asking individuals to provide the data. The data may be obtained through such methods as personal interviews, telephone interviews, or written questionnaires.

EXAMPLE 6.   An analyst in a state's Department of Economic Security may need to determine what increases or decreases in the employment level are planned by business firms located in that state. A standard method by which such data can be obtained is to conduct a survey of the business firms.

1.6 METHODS OF RANDOM SAMPLING

Random sampling is a type of sampling in which every item in a population of interest, or *target population*, has a known, and usually equal, chance of being chosen for inclusion in the sample. Having such a sample ensures that the sample items are chosen without bias and provides the statistical basis for determining the confidence that can be associated with the inferences (see Chapters 8 and 9). A random sample is also called a *probability sample*, or *scientific sample*. The four principal methods of random sampling are the simple, systematic, stratified, and cluster sampling methods.

A *simple random sample* is one in which individual items are chosen from the target population on the basis of chance. Such chance selection is similar to the random drawing of numbers in a lottery. However, in statistical sampling a *table of random numbers* or a *random-number generator* computer program generally is used to identify the numbered items in the population that are to be selected for the sample.

EXAMPLE 7. Appendix 1 is an abbreviated table of random numbers. Suppose we wish to take a simple random sample of 10 accounts receivable from a population of 90 such accounts, with the accounts being numbered 01 to 90. We would enter the table of random numbers "blindly" by literally closing our eyes and pointing to a starting position. Then we would read the digits in groups of two in any direction to choose the accounts for our sample. Suppose we begin reading numbers (as pairs) starting from the number on line 6, column 1. The 10 account numbers for the sample would be 66, 06, 59, 94, 78, 70, 08, 67, 12, and 65. However, since there are only 90 accounts, the number 94 cannot be included. Instead, the next number (11) is included in the sample. If any of the selected numbers are repeated, they are included only once in the sample.

A *systematic sample* is a random sample in which the items are selected from the population at a uniform interval of a listed order, such as choosing every tenth account receivable for the sample. The first account of the 10 accounts to be included in the sample would be chosen randomly (perhaps by reference to a table of random numbers). A particular concern with systematic sampling is the existence of any periodic, or cyclical, factor in the population listing that could lead to a systematic error in the sample results.

EXAMPLE 8. If every twelfth house is at a corner location in a neighborhood surveyed for adequate street lighting, a systematic sample would include a systematic bias if every twelfth household were included in the survey. In this case, either all or none of the surveyed households would be at a corner location.

In *stratified sampling* the items in the population are first classified into separate subgroups, or strata, by the researcher on the basis of one or more important characteristics. Then a simple random or systematic sample is taken separately from each stratum. Such a sampling plan can be used to ensure proportionate representation of various population subgroups in the sample. Further, the required sample size to achieve a given level of precision typically is smaller than it is with simple random sampling, thereby reducing sampling cost.

EXAMPLE 9. In a study of student attitudes toward on-campus housing, we have reason to believe that important differences may exist between undergraduate and graduate students, and between men and women students. Therefore, a stratified sampling plan should be considered in which a simple random sample is taken separately from the four strata: male undergraduate, female undergraduate, male graduate, and female graduate.

Cluster sampling is a type of random sampling in which the population items occur naturally in subgroups. Entire subgroups, or clusters, are then randomly sampled.

EXAMPLE 10. If an analyst in a state's Department of Economic Security needs to study the hourly wage rates being paid in a metropolitan area, it would be difficult to obtain a listing of all the wage earners in the target population. However, a listing of the *firms* in that area can be obtained much more easily. The analyst then can take a simple random sample of the identified firms, which represent *clusters* of employees, and obtain the wage rates being paid to the employees of these firms.

1.7 OTHER SAMPLING METHODS

Although a nonrandom sample can turn out to be representative of the population, there is difficulty in assuming beforehand that it will be unbiased, or in expressing statistically the confidence that can be associated with inferences from such a sample.

A *judgment sample* is one in which an individual selects the items to be included in the sample. The extent to which such a sample is representative of the population then depends on the judgment of that individual and cannot be statistically assessed.

EXAMPLE 11. Rather than choosing the records that are to be audited on some random basis, an accountant chooses the records for a sample audit based on the judgment that these particular types of records are likely to be representative of the records in general. There is no way of assessing statistically whether such a sample is likely to be biased, or how closely the sample result approximates the population.

A *convenience sample* includes the most easily accessible measurements, or observations, as is implied by the word *convenience*.

EXAMPLE 12. A community development office undertakes a study of the public attitude toward a new downtown shopping plaza by taking an opinion poll at one of the entrances to the plaza. The survey results certainly are not likely to reflect the attitude of people who have not been at the plaza, of people who were at the plaza but chose not to participate in the poll, or of people in parts of the plaza that were not sampled.

A strict random sample is not usually feasible in statistical process control, since only readily available items or transactions can easily be inspected. In order to capture changes that are taking place in the quality of process output, small samples are taken at regular intervals of time. Such a sampling scheme is called the *method of rational subgroups*. Such sample data are treated as if random samples were taken at each point in time, with the understanding that one should be alert to any known reasons why such a sampling scheme could lead to biased results.

EXAMPLE 13. Groups of four packages of potato chips are sampled and weighed at regular intervals of time in a packaging process in order to determine conformance to minimum weight specifications. These rational subgroups provide the statistical basis for determining whether the process is stable and in control, or whether unusual variation in the sequence of sample weights exists for which an assignable cause needs to be identified and corrected.

1.8 USING EXCEL AND MINITAB TO GENERATE RANDOM NUMBERS

Computer software is widely available to generate randomly selected digits within any specified range of values. Solved Problems 1.10 and 1.11 illustrate the use of Excel and Minitab, respectively, for selecting simple random samples.

Solved Problems

DESCRIPTIVE AND INFERENTIAL STATISTICS

1.1. Indicate which of the following terms or operations are concerned with a sample or sampling (S), and which are concerned with a population (P): (*a*) Group measures called *parameters*, (*b*) use of *inferential statistics*, (*c*) taking a *census*, (*d*) judging the quality of an incoming shipment of fruit by inspecting several crates of the large number included in the shipment.

(*a*) P, (*b*) S, (*c*) P, (*d*) S

TYPES OF APPLICATIONS IN BUSINESS

1.2. Indicate which of the following types of information could be used most readily in either classical statistical inference (CI), decision analysis (DA), or statistical process control (PC): (*a*) Managerial judgments about the likely level of sales for a new product, (*b*) subjecting every fiftieth car assembled to a comprehensive quality evaluation, (*c*) survey results for a simple random sample of people who purchased a particular automobile model, (*d*) verification of bank account balances for a systematic random sample of accounts.

(*a*) DA, (*b*) PC, (*c*) CI, (*d*) CI

DISCRETE AND CONTINUOUS VARIABLES

1.3. For the following types of values, designate discrete variables (D) and continuous variables (C): (*a*) Weight of the contents of a package of cereal, (*b*) diameter of a bearing, (*c*) number of defective items produced, (*d*) number of individuals in a geographic area who are collecting unemployment benefits, (*e*) the average number of prospective customers contacted per sales representative during the past month, (*f*) dollar amount of sales.

(*a*) C, (*b*) C, (*c*) D, (*d*) D, (*e*) C, (*f*) D (*Note*: Although monetary amounts are discrete, when the amounts are large relative to the one-cent discrete units, they generally are treated as continuous data.)

OBTAINING DATA THROUGH DIRECT OBSERVATION VS. SURVEYS

1.4. Indicate which of the following data-gathering procedures would be considered an experiment (E), and which would be considered a survey (S): (*a*) A political poll of how individuals intend to vote in an upcoming election, (*b*) customers in a shopping mall interviewed about why they shop there, (*c*) comparing two approaches to marketing an annuity policy by having each approach used in comparable geographic areas.

(*a*) S, (*b*) S, (*c*) E

1.5. In the area of statistical measurements, such as questionnaires, *reliability* refers to the consistency of the measuring instrument and *validity* refers to the accuracy of the instrument. Thus, if a questionnaire yields similar results when completed by two equivalent groups of respondents, then the questionnaire can be described as being reliable. Does the fact that an instrument is reliable thereby guarantee that it is valid?

The reliability of a measuring instrument does not guarantee that it is valid for a particular purpose. An instrument that is reliable is consistent in the repeated measurements that are produced, but the measurements may all include a common error, or bias, component. (See the next Solved Problem.)

1.6. Refer to Solved Problem 1.5, above. Can a survey instrument that is not reliable have validity for a particular purpose?

An instrument that is not reliable cannot be valid for *any* particular purpose. In the absence of reliability, there is no consistency in the results that are obtained. An analogy to a rifle range can illustrate this concept. Bullet holes that are closely clustered on a target are indicative of the reliability (consistency) in firing the rifle. In such a case the validity (accuracy) may be improved by adjusting the sights so that the bullet holes subsequently will be centered at the bull's-eye of the target. But widely dispersed bullet holes would indicate a lack of reliability, and under such a condition no adjustment in the sights can lead to a high score.

METHODS OF RANDOM SAMPLING

1.7. For the purpose of statistical inference a *representative* sample is desired. Yet, the methods of statistical inference require only that a *random* sample be obtained. Why?

There is no sampling method that can guarantee a representative sample. The best we can do is to void any consistent or systematic bias by the use of random (probability) sampling. While a random sample rarely will be exactly representative of the target population from which it was obtained, use of this procedure does guarantee that only chance factors underlie the amount of difference between the sample and the population.

1.8. An oil company wants to determine the factors affecting consumer choice of gasoline service stations in a test area, and therefore has obtained the names and addresses of and available personal information for all the registered car owners residing in that area. Describe how a sample of this list could be obtained using each of the four methods of random sampling described in this chapter.

For a *simple random sample*, the listed names could be numbered sequentially, and then the individuals to be sampled could be selected by using a table of random numbers. For a *systematic sample*, every *n*th (such as 5th) person on the list could be contacted, starting randomly within the first five names. For a *stratified sample*, we can classify the owners by their type of car, the value of their car, sex, or age, and then take a simple random or systematic sample from each defined stratum. For a *cluster sample*, we could choose to interview all the registered car owners residing in randomly selected blocks in the test area. Having a geographic basis, this type of cluster sample can also be called an *area sample*.

OTHER SAMPLING METHODS

1.9. Indicate which of the following types of samples best exemplify or would be concerned with either a judgment sample (J), a convenience sample (C), or the method of rational subgroups (R): (*a*) Samples of five light bulbs each are taken every 20 minutes in a production process to determine their resistance to high voltage, (*b*) a beverage company assesses consumer response to the taste of a proposed alcohol-free beer by taste tests in taverns located in the city where the corporate offices are located, (*c*) an opinion poller working for a political candidate talks to people at various locations in the district based on the assessment that the individuals appear representative of the district's voters.

(*a*) R, (*b*) C, (*c*) J

USING EXCEL AND MINITAB TO GENERATE RANDOM NUMBERS

1.10. A state economist wishes to obtain a simple random sample of 30 business firms from the 435 that are located in a particular part of the state. For convenience, the firms are identified by the ID numbers 1 through 435. Use Excel to obtain the 30 ID numbers of the sampled firms to be included in the study.

Figure 1-1 presents the Excel output that lists the sampled firms in rows 1 through 30 of the second column. By the very nature of a random sample, your sampled firms will be different. The Excel instructions for selecting the simple random sample of size $n = 30$ for this example are as follows:

(1) Open Excel. Place the integers from 1 to 435 in column A of the worksheet by first entering the number 1 in cell A1. With cell A1 active (by clicking away from and back to A1, for instance), click **Edit → Fill → Series** and open the Series dialog box.

(2) Select the **Series in Columns** button with **Step value** of 1 and **Stop value** of 435. Click **OK**, and the integers 1 to 435 will appear in column A.

(3) To identify the 30 firms to be sampled, click **Tools → Data Analysis → Sampling**. Designate the **Input Range** as $A$1:$A$435, the **Sampling Method** as **Random**, the number of samples as 30, and the **Output Range** as $B$1. Click **OK**, and the IDs of the randomly selected firms will appear in rows 1 through 30 of column B.

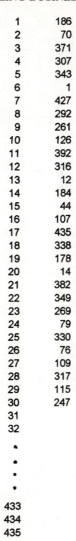

1	186
2	70
3	371
4	307
5	343
6	1
7	427
8	292
9	261
10	126
11	392
12	316
13	12
14	184
15	44
16	107
17	435
18	338
19	178
20	14
21	382
22	349
23	269
24	79
25	330
26	76
27	109
28	317
29	115
30	247
31	
32	
.	
.	
.	
.	
433	
434	
435	

Fig. 1-1   Excel output of a simple random sample.

1.11. A state economist wishes to obtain a simple random sample of 30 business firms from the 435 that are located in a particular part of the state. For convenience, the firms are identified by the ID numbers 1 through 435. Use Minitab to obtain the 30 ID numbers of the sampled firms to be included in the study.

Figure 1-2 presents the Minitab output that lists the sampled firms in rows 1 through 30 of column C2. By the very nature of a random sample, your sampled firms will be different. The Minitab instructions for selecting the simple random sample of size $n = 30$ for this example are as follows:

(1)   Open Minitab. Place the integers from 1 to 435 in column C1 as follows. Click **Calc → Make Patterned Data → Simple Set of Numbers**. Then select **Store patterned data in:** C1 **From first value:** 1 **To last value:** 435 **In steps of:** 1. Click **OK**, and the integers 1 to 435 will appear in column C1.

(2)   To identify the 30 firms to be sampled, click **Calc → Random Data → Samples from Columns**. Then select **Sample** 30 **from column[s]:** C1 and **Store samples in:** C2. Click **OK**, and the IDs of the randomly selected firms will appear in rows 1 through 30 of column C2.

	C1	C2
1	1	425
2	2	256
3	3	403
4	4	322
5	5	349
6	6	124
7	7	395
8	8	315
9	9	334
10	10	381
11	11	72
12	12	100
13	13	236
14	14	303
15	15	253
16	16	213
17	17	34
18	18	365
19	19	58
20	20	300
21	21	10
22	22	83
23	23	211
24	24	279
25	25	416
26	26	311
27	27	325
28	28	110
29	29	275
30	30	179
31	31	
32	32	

.   .   .
.   .   .
.   .   .
.   .   .

433	433	
434	434	
435	435	

Fig. 1-2   Minitab output of a single random sample.

Supplementary Problems

DESCRIPTIVE AND INFERENTIAL STATISTICS

1.12.   Indicate which of the following terms or operations are concerned with a sample or sampling (S), and which are concerned with a population (P): (*a*) Universe, (*b*) group measures called *statistics*, (*c*) application of probability concepts, (*d*) inspection of every item that is assembled, (*e*) inspection of every 10th item that is assembled.
Ans.   (*a*) P, (*b*) S, (*c*) S, (*d*) P, (*e*) S

TYPES OF APPLICATIONS IN BUSINESS

1.13.   Indicate which of the following types of information could be used most readily in classical statistical inference (CI), decision analysis (DA), or statistical process control (PC): (*a*) Questionnaire responses that are obtained from a sample of current members of a professional organization, (*b*) customer ratings of an automobile service department collected monthly, (*c*) investment analysts' ratings of "new and emerging companies," (*d*) wage and salary data collected from a sample of employers in a metropolitan area.
Ans.   (*a*) CI, (*b*) PC, (*c*) DA, (*d*) CI

DISCRETE AND CONTINUOUS VARIABLES

1.14. For the following types of values, designate discrete variables (D) and continuous variables (C): (*a*) Number of units of an item held in stock, (*b*) ratio of current assets to current liabilities, (*c*) total tonnage shipped, (*d*) quantity shipped, in units, (*e*) volume of traffic on a toll road, (*f*) attendance at the company's annual meeting.
Ans.   (*a*) D, (*b*) C, (*c*) C, (*d*) D, (*e*) D, (*f*) D

OBTAINING DATA THROUGH DIRECT OBSERVATION VS. SURVEYS

1.15. Indicate which of the following data-gathering procedures would be considered an experiment (E), and which would be considered a survey (S): (*a*) Comparing the results of a new approach to training airline ticket agents to those of the traditional approach, (*b*) evaluating two different sets of assembly instructions for a toy by having two comparable groups of children assemble the toy using the different instructions, (*c*) having a product-evaluation magazine send subscribers a questionnaire asking them to rate the products that they have recently purchased.
Ans.   (*a*) E, (*b*) E, (*c*) S

METHODS OF RANDOM SAMPLING

1.16. Identify whether the simple random (R) or the systematic (S) sampling method is used in the following: (*a*) Using a table of random numbers to select a sample of people entering an amusement park and (*b*) interviewing every 100th person entering an amusement park, randomly starting at the 55th person to enter the park.
Ans.   (*a*) R, (*b*) S

1.17. For the following group-oriented sampling situations, identify whether the stratified (St) or the cluster (C) sampling method would be used: (*a*) Estimating the voting preferences of people who live in various neighborhoods and (*b*) studying consumer attitudes with the belief that there are important differences according to age and sex.
Ans.   (*a*) C, (*b*) St

OTHER SAMPLING METHODS

1.18. Indicate which of the following types of samples best exemplify or would be concerned with a judgment sample (J), a convenience sample (C), or the method of rational subgroups (R): (*a*) A real estate appraiser selects a sample of homes sold in a neighborhood, which seem representative of homes located there, in order to arrive at an estimate of the level of home values in that neighborhood, (*b*) in a battery-manufacturing plant, battery life is monitored every half hour to assure that the output satisfies specifications, (*c*) a fast-food outlet has company employees evaluate a new chicken-combo sandwich in terms of taste and perceived value.
Ans.   (*a*) J, (*b*) R, (*c*) C

USING COMPUTER SOFTWARE TO GENERATE RANDOM NUMBERS

1.19. An auditor wishes to take a simple random sample of 50 accounts from the 5,250 accounts receivable in a large firm. The accounts are sequentially numbered from 0001 to 5250. Use available computer software to obtain a listing of the required 50 random numbers.

Statistical Presentations and Graphical Displays

2.1 FREQUENCY DISTRIBUTIONS

A *frequency distribution* is a table in which possible values for a variable are grouped into classes, and the number of observed values which fall into each class is recorded. Data organized in a frequency distribution are called *grouped data*. In contrast, for *ungrouped data* every observed value of the random variable is listed.

EXAMPLE 1.   A frequency distribution of weekly wages is shown in Table 2.1. Note that the amounts are reported to the nearest dollar. When a remainder that is to be rounded is "exactly 0.5" (exactly $0.50 in this case), the convention is to round to the nearest *even* number. Thus a weekly wage of $259.50 would have been rounded to $260 as part of the data-grouping process.

Table 2.1   A Frequency Distribution of Weekly Wages for 100 Entry-Level Workers

Weekly wage	Number of workers (f)
$240–259	7
260–279	20
280–299	33
300–319	25
320–339	11
340–359	4
Total	100

2.2 CLASS INTERVALS

For each class in a frequency distribution, the lower and upper *stated class limits* indicate the values included within the class. (See the first column of Table 2.1.) In contrast, the *exact class limits*, or *class boundaries*, are the specific points that serve to separate adjoining classes along a measurement scale for continuous variables. Exact class limits can be determined by identifying the points that are halfway between the upper and lower stated class limits, respectively, of adjoining classes. The *class interval* identifies the range of values included within a class and can be determined by subtracting the lower exact class limit from the upper exact class limit for the class. When exact limits are not identified, the class interval can be determined by subtracting the lower stated limit for a class from the lower stated limit of the adjoining next-higher class. Finally, for certain purposes the values in a class often are represented by the *class midpoint*, which can be determined by adding one-half of the class interval to the lower exact limit of the class.

EXAMPLE 2.   Table 2.2 presents the exact class limits and the class midpoints for the frequency distribution in Table 2.1.

Table 2.2   Weekly Wages for 100 Entry-Level Workers

Weekly wage (class limits)	Exact class limits*	Class midpoint	Number of workers
$240–259	$239.50–259.50	$249.50	7
260–279	259.50–279.50	269.50	20
280–299	279.50–299.50	289.50	33
300–319	299.50–319.50	309.50	25
320–339	319.50–339.50	329.50	11
340–359	339.50–359.50	349.50	4
		Total	100

* In general, only one additional significant digit is expressed in exact class limits as compared with stated class limits. However, because with monetary units the next more precise unit of measurement after "nearest dollar" is usually defined as "nearest cent," in this case two additional digits are expressed.

EXAMPLE 3.   Calculated by the two approaches, the class interval for the first class in Table 2.2 is $259.50 − $239.50 = $20 (subtraction of the lower exact class limit from the upper exact class limit of the class) $260 − $240 = $20 (subtraction of the lower stated class limit of the class from the lower stated class limit of the adjoining next-higher class).

Computationally, it is generally desirable that all class intervals in a given frequency distribution be equal. A formula which can be used to determine the approximate class interval to be used is

$$\text{Approximate interval} = \frac{\left[\begin{array}{c}\text{largest value in}\\ \text{ungrouped data}\end{array}\right] - \left[\begin{array}{c}\text{smallest value in}\\ \text{ungrouped data}\end{array}\right]}{\text{number of classes desired}} \qquad (2.1)$$

EXAMPLE 4.   For the original, ungrouped data that were grouped in Table 2.1, suppose the highest observed wage was $358 and the lowest observed wage was $242. Given the objective of having six classes with equal class intervals,

$$\text{Approximate interval} = \frac{358 - 242}{6} = \$19.33$$

The closest convenient class size is thus $20.

For data that are distributed in a highly nonuniform way, such as annual salary data for a variety of occupations, *unequal class intervals* may be desirable. In such a case, the larger class intervals are used for the ranges of values in which there are relatively few observations.

2.3 HISTOGRAMS AND FREQUENCY POLYGONS

A *histogram* is a bar graph of a frequency distribution. As indicated in Fig. 2-1, typically the exact class limits are entered along the horizontal axis of the graph while the numbers of observations are listed along the vertical axis. However, class midpoints instead of class limits also are used to identify the classes.

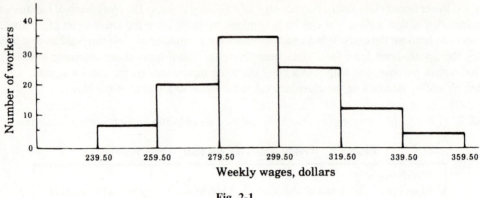

Fig. 2-1

EXAMPLE 5.   A histogram for the frequency distribution of weekly wages in Table 2.2 is shown in Fig. 2-1.

A *frequency polygon* is a line graph of a frequency distribution. As indicated in Fig. 2-2, the two axes of this graph are similar to those of the histogram except that the midpoint of each class typically is identified along the horizontal axis. The number of observations in each class is represented by a dot above the midpoint of the class, and these dots are joined by a series of line segments to form a polygon, or "many-sided figure."

EXAMPLE 6.   A frequency polygon for the distribution of weekly wages in Table 2.2 is shown in Fig. 2-2.

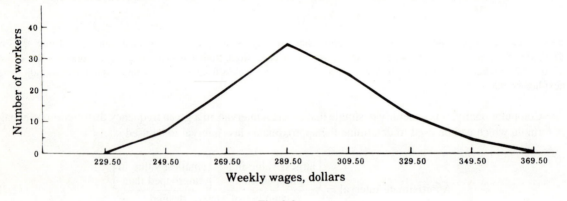

Fig. 2-2

2.4 FREQUENCY CURVES

A frequency curve is a smoothed frequency polygon.

EXAMPLE 7.   Figure 2-3 is a frequency curve for the distribution of weekly wages in Table 2.2.

In terms of skewness, a frequency curve can be: (1) *negatively skewed*: nonsymmetrical with the "tail" to the left; (2) *positively skewed*: nonsymmetrical with the "tail" to the right; or (3) *symmetrical*.

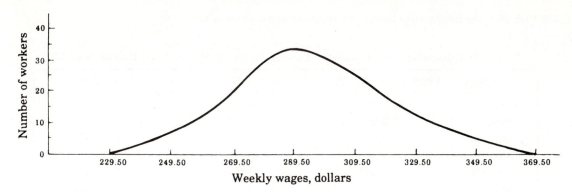

Fig. 2-3

EXAMPLE 8.   The concept of frequency curve skewness is illustrated graphically in Fig. 2-4.

In terms of kurtosis, a frequency curve can be: (1) *platykurtic*: flat, with the observations distributed relatively evenly across the classes; (2) *leptokurtic*: peaked, with the observations concentrated within a narrow range of values; or (3) *mesokurtic*: neither flat nor peaked, in terms of the distribution of observed values.

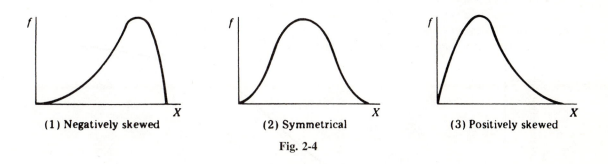

Fig. 2-4

EXAMPLE 9.   Types of frequency curves in terms of kurtosis are shown in Fig. 2-5.

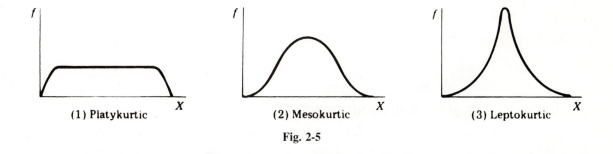

Fig. 2-5

2.5   CUMULATIVE FREQUENCY DISTRIBUTIONS

A *cumulative frequency distribution* identifies the cumulative number of observations included below the upper exact limit of each class in the distribution. The cumulative frequency for a class can be determined by adding the observed frequency for that class to the cumulative frequency for the preceding class.

EXAMPLE 10.   The calculation of cumulative frequencies is illustrated in Table 2.3.

Table 2.3   Calculation of the Cumulative Frequencies for the Weekly Wage Data of Table 2.2

Weekly wage	Upper exact class limit	Number of workers (f)	Cumulative frequency (cf)
$240–259	$259.50	7	7
260–279	279.50	20	$20 + 7 = 27$
280–299	299.50	33	$33 + 27 = 60$
300–319	319.50	25	$25 + 60 = 85$
320–339	339.50	11	$11 + 85 = 96$
340–359	359.50	4	$4 + 96 = 100$
		Total $\overline{100}$	

The graph of a cumulative frequency distribution is called an *ogive* (pronounced "ō-jive"). For the less-than type of cumulative distribution, this graph indicates the cumulative frequency below each exact class limit of the frequency distribution. When such a line graph is smoothed, it is called an *ogive curve*.

EXAMPLE 11.   An ogive curve for the cumulative distribution in Table 2.3 is given in Fig. 2-6.

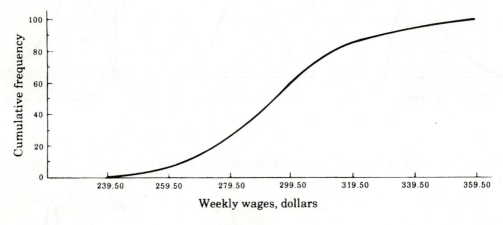

Fig. 2-6

2.6   RELATIVE FREQUENCY DISTRIBUTIONS

A *relative frequency distribution* is one in which the number of observations associated with each class has been converted into a relative frequency by dividing by the total number of observations in the entire distribution. Each relative frequency is thus a proportion, and can be converted into a percentage by multiplying by 100.

One of the advantages associated with preparing a relative frequency distribution is that the cumulative distribution and the ogive for such a distribution indicate the cumulative proportion (or percentage) of observations up to the various possible values of the variable. A *percentile* value is the cumulative percentage of observations up to a designated value of a variable. (See Problems 2.14, and 2.16 to 2.20.)

2.7   THE "AND-UNDER" TYPE OF FREQUENCY DISTRIBUTION

The class limits that are given in computer-generated frequency distributions usually are "and-under" types of limits. For such limits, the stated class limits are also the exact limits that define the class. The values that are grouped in any one class are equal to or greater than the lower class limit, and up to but not including the value of the upper class limit. A descriptive way of presenting such class limits is

5 and under 8

8 and under 11

In addition to this type of distribution being more convenient to implement for computer software, it sometimes also reflects a more "natural" way of collecting the data in the first place. For instance, people's ages generally are reported as the age at the last birthday, rather than the age at the nearest birthday. Thus, to be 24 years old is to be at least 24 but less than 25 years old. Solved Problems 2.21 and 2.22 concern an and-under frequency distribution. Problems 2.28 to 2.31 present Excel and Minitab output that include and-under distributions.

2.8   STEM-AND-LEAF DIAGRAMS

A *stem-and-leaf diagram* is a relatively simple way of organizing and presenting measurements in a rank-ordered bar chart format. This is a popular technique in *exploratory data analysis*. As the name implies, exploratory data analysis is concerned with techniques for preliminary analyses of data in order to gain insights about patterns and relationships. Frequency distributions and the associated graphic techniques covered in the previous sections of this chapter are also often used for this purpose. In contrast, *confirmatory data analysis* includes the principal methods of statistical inference that constitute most of this book, beginning with Chapter 8 on statistical estimation. Confirmatory data analysis is concerned with coming to final statistical conclusions about patterns and relationships in data.

A stem-and-leaf diagram is similar to a histogram, except that it is easier to construct and shows the actual data values, rather than having the specific values lost by being grouped into defined classes. However, the technique is most readily applicable and meaningful only if the first digit of the measurement, or possibly the first two digits, provides a good basis for separating data into groups. Each group then is analogous to a class or category in a frequency distribution. Where the first digit alone is used to group the measurements, the name stem-and-leaf refers to the fact that the first digit is the stem, and each of the measurements with that first-digit value becomes a leaf in the display.

EXAMPLE 12.   Table 2.4 presents the scores earned by 50 students in a 100-point exam in financial accounting. Figure 2-7 is the stem-and-leaf diagram for these scores. Notice that in addition to being able to observe the overall pattern of scores, the individual scores can also be seen. For instance, on the line with the stem of 6, the two posted leaf values of 2 represent the two scores of 62 that are included in Table 2.4.

Table 2.4   Scores Earned by 50 Students in an Exam in Financial Accounting

58	88	65	96	85
74	69	63	88	65
85	91	81	80	90
65	66	81	92	71
82	98	86	100	82
72	94	72	84	73
76	78	78	77	74
83	82	66	76	63
62	62	59	87	97
100	75	84	96	99

Stem	Leaf
5	8 9
6	2 2 3 3 5 5 5 6 6 9
7	1 2 2 3 4 4 5 6 6 7 8 8
8	0 1 1 2 2 2 3 4 4 5 5 6 7 8 8
9	0 1 2 4 6 6 7 8 9
10	0 0

Fig. 2-7 Stem-and-leaf diagram.

2.9 DOTPLOTS

A *dotplot* is similar to a histogram in that a distribution of the data value is portrayed graphically. However, the difference is that the values are plotted *individually*, rather than being grouped into classes. Dotplots are more applicable for small data sets, for which grouping the values into classes of a frequency distribution is not warranted. Dotplots are particularly useful for comparing two different data sets, or two subgroups of a data set. Solved Problem 2.24 includes a dotplot that illustrates the graphical comparison of two subsets of data.

2.10 PARETO CHARTS

A *Pareto chart* is similar to a histogram, except that it is a frequency bar chart for a *qualitative variable*, rather than being used for quantitative data that have been grouped into classes. The bars of the chart, which can represent either frequencies or relative frequencies (percentages) are arranged in descending order from left to right. This arrangement results in the most important categories of data, according to frequency of occurrence, being located at the initial positions in the chart. Pareto charts are used in process control to tabulate the causes associated with assignable-cause variations in the quality of process output. It is typical that only a few categories of causes are associated with most quality problems, and Pareto charts permit worker teams and managers to focus on these most important areas that are in need of corrective action.

EXAMPLE 13.   The refrigerators that did not pass final inspection at an appliance assembly plant during the past month were found to have defects that were due to the following causes: assembly, lacquer finish, electrical malfunction, dents, or other causes. Figure 2-8, from Minitab, is the Pareto chart that graphically presents both the frequency and the relative frequency of each cause of inspection failure. As we can observe, the large majority of inspection failures are due to defects in the assembly and the lacquer finish.

2.11 BAR CHARTS AND LINE GRAPHS

A *time series* is a set of observed values, such as production or sales data, for a sequentially ordered series of time periods. Special methods of analysis for such data are described in Chapter 16. For the purpose of graphic presentation, both bar charts and line graphs are useful. A *bar chart* depicts the time-series amounts by a series of bars.

EXAMPLE 14.   The bar chart in Fig. 2-9 depicts the reported net earnings for a major commercial bank (in $millions) for a sequence of coded years.

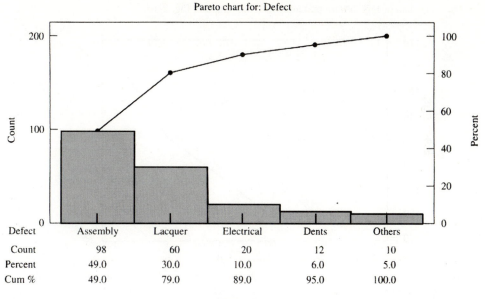

Pareto chart for: Defect

Defect	Assembly	Lacquer	Electrical	Dents	Others
Count	98	60	20	12	10
Percent	49.0	30.0	10.0	6.0	5.0
Cum %	49.0	79.0	89.0	95.0	100.0

Fig. 2-8

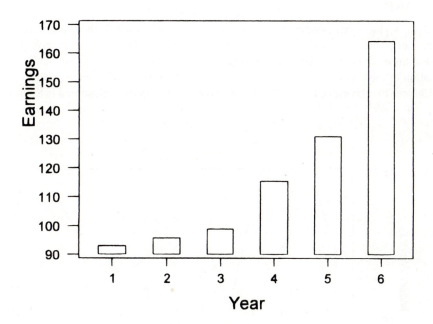

Fig. 2-9   Bar chart.

A *component bar chart* portrays subdivisions within the bars on the chart. For example, each bar in Fig. 2-9 could be subdivided into separate parts (and perhaps color-coded) to indicate the relative contribution of each segment of the business to the net earnings for each year. (See Solved Problem 2.26.) The use of Excel and Minitab to obtain bar charts is illustrated in Problems 2.32 and 2.33.

A *line graph* portrays time-series amounts by a connected series of line segments.

EXAMPLE 15.   The data of Fig. 2-9 are presented as a line graph in Fig. 2-10.

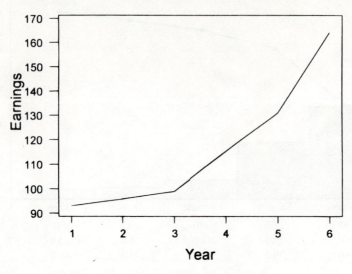

Fig. 2-10   Line graph.

2.12   RUN CHARTS

A *run chart* is a plot of data values in the time-sequence order in which they were observed. The values that are plotted can be the individual observed values or summary values, such as a series of sample means. When lower and upper limits for acceptance sampling are added to such a chart, it is called a *control chart*. The determination of these limits and the use of control charts in statistical quality control is explained and illustrated in Chapter 19. The use of Excel and Minitab to obtain run charts is illustrated in Solved Problems 2.34 and 2.35.

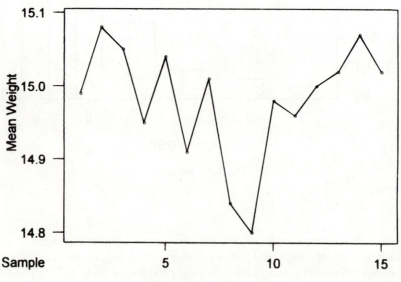

Fig. 2-11   Run chart.

EXAMPLE 16. Figure 2-11 portrays a run chart for the sequence of mean weights for samples of four packages of potato chips taken at 15 different times using the sampling method of rational subgroups (see Chapter 1, Example 13). The sequence of mean weights for the samples was found to be: 14.99, 15.08, 15.05, 14.95, 15.04, 14.91, 15.01, 14.84, 14.80, 14.98, 14.96, 15.00, 15.02, 15.07, and 15.02 oz. The specification for the average net weight to be packaged in the process is 15.00 oz. Whether any of the deviations of these sample means from the specified weight standard can be considered a meaningful deviation is discussed fully in Chapter 19.

2.13 PIE CHARTS

A *pie chart* is a pie-shaped figure in which the pieces of the pie represent divisions of a total amount, such as the distribution of a company's sales dollar.

A *percentage pie chart* is one in which the values have been converted into percentages in order to make them easier to compare. The use of Excel and Minitab to obtain pie charts is illustrated in Solved Problems 2.36 and 2.37.

EXAMPLE 17. Figure 2-12 is a pie chart depicting the revenues and the percentage of total revenues for the Xerox Corporation during a recent year according to the categories of *core business* (called "Heartland" by Xerox), *growth markets*, *developing countries*, and *niche opportunities*.

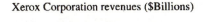

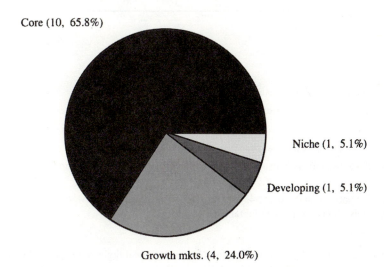

Fig. 2-12   Pie chart.

2.14 USING EXCEL AND MINITAB

Solved Problems 2.28 through 2.37 illustrate the use of Excel and Minitab for obtaining histograms, bar charts, run charts, and pie charts.

Solved Problems

FREQUENCY DISTRIBUTIONS, CLASS INTERVALS, AND RELATED GRAPHIC METHODS

2.1. With reference to Table 2.5,

Table 2.5 Frequency Distribution of Monthly Apartment Rental Rates for 200 Studio Apartments

Rental rate	Number of apartments
$350–379	3
380–409	8
410–439	10
440–469	13
470–499	33
500–529	40
530–559	35
560–589	30
590–619	16
620–649	12
Total	200

(*a*) what are the lower and upper stated limits of the first class?

(*b*) what are the lower and upper exact limits of the first class?

(*c*) the class interval used is the same for all classes of the distribution. What is the interval size?

(*d*) what is the midpoint of the first class?

(*e*) what are the lower and upper exact limits of the class in which the largest number of apartment rental rates was tabulated?

(*f*) suppose a monthly rental rate of $439.50 were reported. Identify the lower and upper stated limits of the class in which this observation would be tallied.

(*a*) $350 and $379

(*b*) $340.50 and $379.50 (*Note*: As in Example 2, two additional digits are expressed in this case instead of the usual one additional digit in exact class limits as compared with stated class limits.)

(*c*) Focusing on the interval of values in the first class,
$379.50 − $349.50 = $30 (subtraction of the lower exact class limit from the upper exact class limit of the class)
$380 − $350 = $30 (subtraction of the lower stated class limit of the class from the lower stated class limit of the next-higher adjoining class)

(*d*) $349.50 + 30/2 = $349.50 + $15.00 = $364.50

(*e*) $499.50 and $529.50

(*f*) $440 and $469 (*Note*: $439.50 is first rounded to $440 as the nearest dollar using the even-number rule described in Section 2.1.)

2.2.   Prepare a histogram for the data in Table 2.5.

A histogram for the data in Table 2.5 appears in Fig. 2-13.

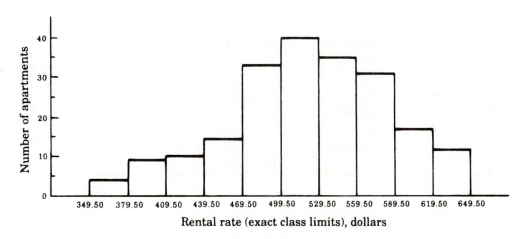

Fig. 2-13

2.3.   Prepare a frequency polygon and a frequency curve for the data in Table 2.5.

Figure 2-14 is a graphic presentation of the frequency polygon and frequency curve for the data in Table 2.5.

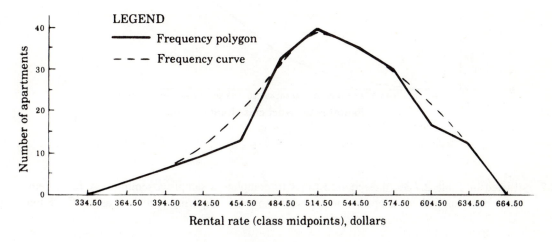

Fig. 2-14

2.4.   Describe the frequency curve in Fig. 2-14 from the standpoint of skewness.

The frequency curve appears to be somewhat negatively skewed.

2.5.   Prepare a cumulative frequency distribution for the data in Table 2.5.

See Table 2.6.

Table 2.6   Cumulative Frequency Distribution of Apartment Rental Rates

Rental rate	Class boundaries	Number of apartments	Cumulative frequency (*cf*)
$350–379	$349.50–379.50	3	3
380–409	379.50–409.50	8	11
410–439	409.50–439.50	10	21
440–469	439.50–469.50	13	34
470–499	469.50–499.50	33	67
500–529	499.50–529.50	40	107
530–559	529.50–559.50	35	142
560–589	559.50–589.50	30	172
590–619	589.50–619.50	16	188
620–649	619.50–649.50	12	200
		Total 200	

2.6 Present the cumulative frequency distribution in Table 2.6 graphically by means of an ogive curve.

The ogive curve for the data in Table 2.6 is shown in Fig. 2-15.

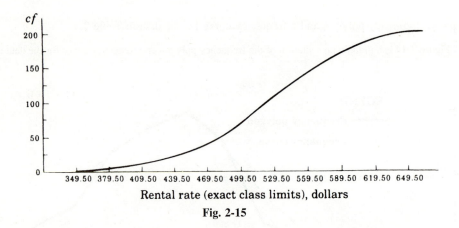

Rental rate (exact class limits), dollars

Fig. 2-15

2.7 Listed in Table 2.7 are the required times to complete a sample assembly task for 30 employees who have applied for a promotional transfer to a job requiring precision assembly. Suppose we

Table 2.7   Assembly Times for 30 Employees, min

10	14	15	13	17
16	12	14	11	13
15	18	9	14	14
9	15	11	13	11
12	10	17	16	12
11	16	12	14	15

wish to organize these data into five classes with equal class sizes. Determine the convenient interval size.

$$\text{Approximate interval} = \frac{\left[\begin{array}{c}\text{largest value in}\\ \text{ungrouped data}\end{array}\right] - \left[\begin{array}{c}\text{smallest value in}\\ \text{ungrouped data}\end{array}\right]}{\text{number of classes desired}}$$

$$= \frac{18 - 9}{5} = 1.80$$

In this case, it is convenient to round the interval to 2.0.

2.8. Prepare a frequency distribution for the data in Table 2.7 using a class interval of 2.0 for all classes and setting the lower stated limit of the first class at 9 min.

The required construction appears in Table 2.8.

Table 2.8   Frequency Distribution for the Assembly Times

Time, min	Number of employees
9–10	4
11–12	8
13–14	8
15–16	7
17–18	3
	Total 30

2.9. In Table 2.8 refer to the class with the lowest number of employees and identify (*a*) its exact limits, (*b*) its interval, (*c*) its midpoint.

(*a*)   16.5–18.5, (*b*) $18.5 - 16.5 = 2.0$, (*c*) $16.5 + 2.0/2 = 17.5$.

2.10. Prepare a histogram for the frequency distribution in Table 2.8.

The histogram is presented in Fig. 2-16.

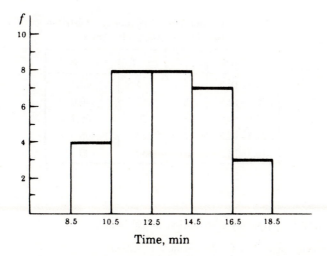

Time, min

Fig. 2-16

2.11. Prepare a frequency polygon and frequency curve for the data in Table 2.8.

The frequency polygon and frequency curve appear in Fig. 2-17.

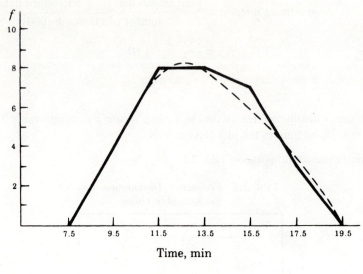

Fig. 2-17

2.12. Describe the frequency curve in Fig. 2-17 in terms of skewness.

The frequency curve is close to being symmetrical, but with slight positive skewness.

2.13. Prepare a cumulative frequency distribution for the frequency distribution of assembly times in Table 2.8, using exact limits to identify each class and including cumulative percentages as well as cumulative frequencies in the table.

See Table 2.9 for the cumulative frequency distribution.

Table 2.9 Cumulative Frequency Distribution for the Assembly Times

Time, min	f	cf	Cum. pct.
8.5–10.5	4	4	13.3
10.5–12.5	8	12	40.0
12.5–14.5	8	20	66.7
14.5–16.5	7	27	90.0
16.5–18.5	3	30	100.0

2.14 Refer to the cumulative frequency distribution in Table 2.9.

(a) Construct the percentage ogive for these data.

(b) At what percentile point is an assembly time of 15 minutes?

(c)   What is the assembly time at the 20th percentile of the distribution?

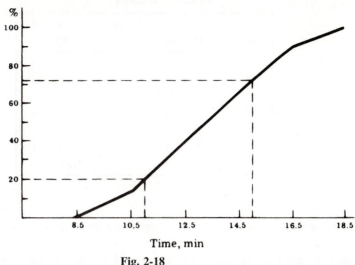

Time, min

Fig. 2-18

(a)   The ogive is presented in Fig. 2-18.

(b)   As identified by the dashed lines in the upper portion of the figure, the approximate percentile for 15 minutes of assembly time is 72.

(c)   As identified by the dashed lines in the lower portion of the figure, the approximate time at the 20th percentile is 11 minutes.

FORMS OF FREQUENCY CURVES

2.15.   Given that frequency curve (a) in Fig. 2-19 is both symmetrical and mesokurtic, describe curves (b), (c), (d), (e), and (f) in terms of skewness and kurtosis.

Curve (b) is symmetrical and leptokurtic; curve (c), positively skewed and mesokurtic; curve (d), negatively skewed and mesokurtic; curve (e), symmetrical and platykurtic; and curve (f), positively skewed and leptokurtic.

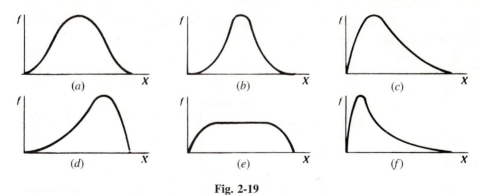

Fig. 2-19

RELATIVE FREQUENCY DISTRIBUTIONS

2.16.   Using the instructions in Section 2.6, determine (a) the relative frequencies and (b) the cumulative proportions for the data in Table 2.10.

Table 2.10   Average Number of Injuries per Thousand Worker-Hours in a Particular Industry

Average number of injuries per thousand worker-hours	Number of firms
1.5–1.7	3
1.8–2.0	12
2.1–2.3	14
2.4–2.6	9
2.7–2.9	7
3.0–3.2	5
Total	50

The relative frequencies and cumulative proportions for the data in Table 2.10 are given in Table 2.11.

Table 2.11   Relative Frequencies and Cumulative Proportions for Average Number of Injuries

Average number of injuries per thousand worker-hours	Number of firms	(a) Relative frequency	(b) Cumulative proportion
1.5–1.7	3	0.06	0.06
1.8–2.0	12	0.24	0.30
2.1–2.3	14	0.28	0.58
2.4–2.6	9	0.18	0.76
2.7–2.9	7	0.14	0.90
3.0–3.2	5	0.10	1.00
Total	50	Total 1.00	

2.17. With reference to Table 2.11, construct (a) a histogram for the relative frequency distribution and (b) an ogive for the cumulative proportions.

(a)   See Fig. 2-20.

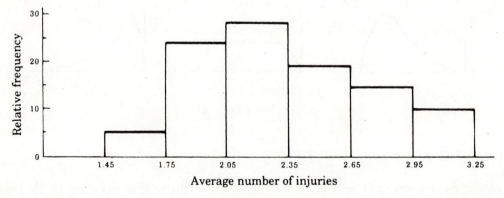

Fig. 2-20

(*b*)   See Fig. 2-21.

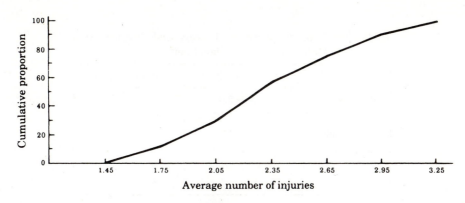

Fig. 2-21

2.18.   (*a*) Referring to Table 2.11, what proportion of firms are in the category of having had an average of at least 3.0 injuries per thousand worker-hours? (*b*) What percentage or firms were at or below an average of 2.0 injuries per thousand worker-hours?

(*a*)   0.10, (*b*)   6% + 24% = 30%

2.19.   (*a*) Referring to Table 2.11, what is the percentile value associated with an average of 2.95 (approximately 3.0) injuries per thousand worker-hours? (*b*) What is the average number of accidents at the 58th percentile?

(*a*)   90th percentile, (*b*)   2.35.

2.20.   By graphic interpolation on an ogive curve, we can determine the approximate percentiles for various values of the variable, and vice versa. Referring to Fig. 2-21, (*a*) What is the approximate percentile associated with an average of 2.5 accidents? (*b*) What is the approximate average number of accidents at the 50th percentile?

(*a*)   65th percentile (This is the approximate height of the ogive corresponding to 2.50 along the horizontal axis.)

(*b*)   2.25 (This is the approximate point along the horizontal axis which corresponds to the 0.50 height of the ogive.)

THE "AND-UNDER" TYPE OF FREQUENCY DISTRIBUTION

2.21.   Identify the exact class limits for the data in Table 2.12.

Table 2.12   Time Required to Process and Prepare Mail Orders

Time, min	Number of orders
5 and under 8	10
8 and under 11	17
11 and under 14	12
14 and under 17	6
17 and under 20	2
Total	47

From Table 2.12,

2.22   Construct a frequency polygon for the frequency distribution in Table 2.13.

Table 2.13   Time Required to Process and Prepare Mail Orders (with Exact Class Limits)

Time, min	Exact class limits	Number of orders
5 and under 8	5.0–8.0	10
8 and under 11	8.0–11.0	17
11 and under 14	11.0–14.0	12
14 and under 17	14.0–17.0	6
17 and under 20	17.0–20.0	2
	Total	47

The frequency polygon appears in Fig. 2-22.

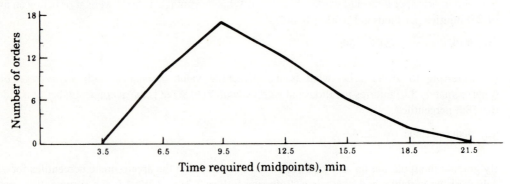

Fig. 2-22

STEM-AND-LEAF DIAGRAMS

2.23.   Table 2.14 lists the high and low temperatures recorded in 40 selected U.S. cities on May 15 of a recent year. Prepare a stem-and-leaf diagram for the high temperatures that were recorded.

Table 2.14   High and Low Temperatures in 40 U.S. Cities

	High	Low		High	Low
Albany, N.Y.	69	39	Las Vegas	94	63
Anchorage	60	47	Los Angeles	76	61
Atlanta	76	46	Memphis	78	51
Austin	82	66	Miami Beach	82	67
Birmingham	76	42	Milwaukee	75	48
Boston	64	53	New York City	74	50
Buffalo	63	44	Palm Springs	93	64
Casper	58	51	Phoenix	94	74
Chicago	76	45	Pittsburgh	67	44

(*Continued*)

Table 2.14   (*Continued*)

	High	Low		High	Low
Cleveland	70	40	Portland, Ore.	70	53
Columbia, S.C.	74	47	Richmond	70	46
Columbus, Oh.	71	40	Rochester, N.Y.	62	42
Dallas	86	68	St. Louis	76	58
Detroit	71	43	San Antonio	81	69
Forth Wayne	76	37	San Diego	69	62
Green Bay	75	38	San Francisco	78	55
Honolulu	84	65	Seattle	67	50
Houston	84	67	Syracuse	63	43
Jacksonville	77	50	Tampa	85	59
Kansas City	72	59	Washington, D.C.	69	52

The stem-and-leaf diagram appears in Fig. 2-23.

```
Stem    Leaf

  5     8

  6     0 2 3 3 4 7 7 9 9 9

  7     0 0 0 1 1 2 4 4 5 5 6 6 6 6 6 6 7 8 8

  8     1 2 2 4 4 5 6

  9     3 4 4
```

Fig. 2-23   Stem-and-leaf diagram for temperature data.

DOTPLOTS

2.24. Table 2.15 presents resting pulse rates for a sample of 40 adults, half of whom do not smoke (code 0) and half of whom are regular smokers (code 1). Use computer software to prepare a dotplot that will facilitate the comparison of the pulse rates for the nonsmokers vs. the smokers in this sample. Interpret the dotplot that is obtained.

Figure 2-24 presents a dotplot in which the two subgroups of people are plotted separately, but using the same scale in order to facilitate comparison. As we can observe by the centering of the respective distributions, the sample of habitual smokers shows they have a somewhat higher pulse rate than the nonsmokers. As indicated by the spread of each subset of data, the smokers are more variable in their pulse rates than are the nonsmokers. Whether such sample differences can be interpreted as representing actual differences in the population will be considered in Chapters 9 and 11, which cover, respectively, estimating the difference between population parameters and testing for difference in population parameters.

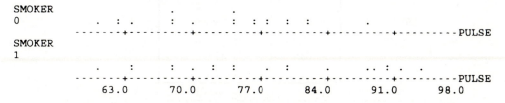

Fig. 2-24   Dotplot for pulse rates.

Table 2.15 Resting Pulse Rates for a Sample of Adults, Ages 30–35

Pulse rate	Habitual smoker? (0 = no; 1 = yes)
82	0
68	0
78	0
80	0
62	0
60	0
62	0
76	0
74	0
74	0
68	0
68	0
64	0
76	0
88	0
70	0
78	0
80	0
74	0
82	0
80	1
90	1
64	1
74	1
70	1
74	1
84	1
72	1
92	1
64	1
94	1
80	1
78	1
88	1
60	1
68	1
90	1
89	1
68	1
72	1

BAR CHARTS AND LINE GRAPHS

2.25. Table 2.16 includes some of the financial results that were reported by an electric power company for six consecutive years. Prepare a vertical bar chart portraying the per-share annual earnings of the company for the coded years.

<table>
<thead>
<tr><th colspan="4">Table 2.16 Per-share Earnings from Continuing Operations, Dividends, and Retained Earnings for an Electric Power Company</th></tr>
<tr><th>Year</th><th>Earnings</th><th>Dividends</th><th>Retained earnings</th></tr>
</thead>
<tbody>
<tr><td>1</td><td>$1.61</td><td>$1.52</td><td>$0.09</td></tr>
<tr><td>2</td><td>2.17</td><td>1.72</td><td>0.45</td></tr>
<tr><td>3</td><td>2.48</td><td>1.92</td><td>0.56</td></tr>
<tr><td>4</td><td>3.09</td><td>2.20</td><td>0.89</td></tr>
<tr><td>5</td><td>4.02</td><td>2.60</td><td>1.42</td></tr>
<tr><td>6</td><td>4.35</td><td>3.00</td><td>1.35</td></tr>
</tbody>
</table>

The bar chart appears in Fig. 2-25.

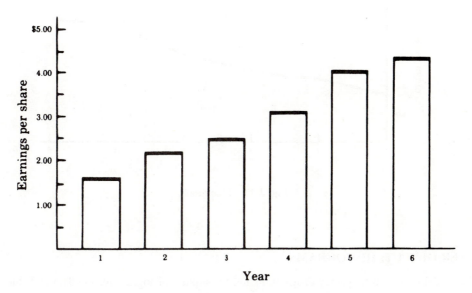

Fig. 2-25 Bar chart.

2.26. Prepare a component bar chart for the data in Table 2.16 such that the division of per-share earnings between dividends (D) and retained earnings (R) is indicated for each year.

Figure 2-26 presents a component bar chart for the data in Table 2.16.

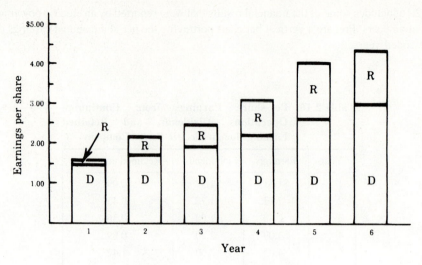

Fig. 2-26   Component bar chart.

2.27.   Prepare a line graph for the per-share earnings reported in Table 2.16.

The line graph is given in Fig. 2-27.

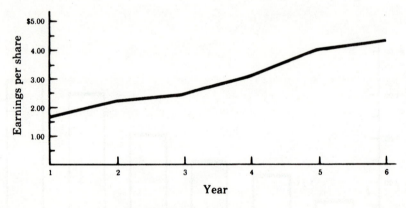

Fig. 2-27   Line graph.

COMPUTER OUTPUT: HISTOGRAMS

2.28.   Use Excel to form a frequency distribution and to output a histogram for the data in Table 2.7, which lists the times in minutes that it took a sample of 30 employees to complete an assembly task.

(*a*)   Describe the type of frequency distribution that has been formed.

(*b*)   Identify the exact class limits (class boundaries) of the first two listed classes.

(*c*)   Determine the size of the class interval.

(*d*)   Identify the midpoint of the second listed class.

Figure 2-28 presents the frequency distribution and histogram that were obtained as the standard Excel output. The output is not particularly reader-friendly in terms of the appearance of the histogram. However, in the next

Bin	Frequency
9	2
10.8	2
12.6	8
14.4	8
16.2	7
More	3

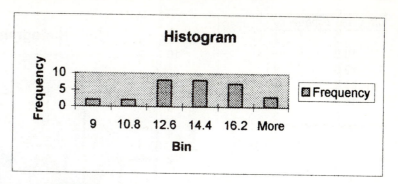

Fig. 2-28   Frequency distribution and histogram from Excel.

Solved Problem, 2.29, we will modify the output so that it is more useful. The measurement listed for each bin of the frequency distribution and associated histogram is the *upper boundary* of the respective class interval, even though it is printed at the middle of each bar of the histogram.

(*a*) As explained in the paragraph above, the style of output is different from historically standard types of output, with upper-class boundaries serving to identify each class.

(*b*) The first listed class includes all listed measurements of 9 minutes or less. The second listed class includes all measurements greater than 9 minutes and less than or equal to 10.8 minutes. Note that this style of output is *not* the same as the "and-under" type described in Section 2.7. If the second class were of the "and-under" type, the class would include all values at or above 9 minutes but *less than* 10.8 minutes.

(*c*) For convenience we refer to the second listed class, for which both class limits are specified. The class interval is: $10.8 - 9.0 = 1.8$.

(*d*) The midpoint is the lower exact limit plus one-half the interval size: $9.0 + (1.8/2) = 9.9$.

The Excel instructions that result in the output presented in Fig. 2-28 are as follows:

(1) Open Excel. Enter the data from Table 2.7 into column A of the worksheet.

(2) Click **Tools → Data Analysis → Histogram** and open the Histogram dialog box. Designate the **Input Range** as $A$1:$A$30 and the **Output Range** as $C$1 (to provide for one column of space between the input and the output).

(3) Click the checkbox for **Chart Output**. Click **OK** and the output will appear as shown in Fig. 2-28.

2.29. Improve the histogram given in Fig. 2-28 by (*a*) increasing the height of the bars, (*b*) substituting "Time,min" for "Bin" as the label for the horizontal axis, (*c*) inserting the specific bin label for the last listed class in place of the default "More," and (*d*) delete the gaps between the vertical bars, since a histogram (as contrasted to the bar chart described in Section 2.11) should have no gaps.

Figure 2-29 presents the improved histogram and associated frequency distribution. The Excel instructions that result in this output are as follows:

(*a*) Increase the height of the chart as follows. Click anywhere on the chart and "handles" appear on the sides and corners. Click on the bottom handle and drag it down to increase the height of the bars.

(*b*) Click on the "Bin" label and type "Time, min" as the replacement.

(*c*) To determine the upper limit of the last class, we note (from Problem 2.28) that the class interval is 1.8. So the upper limit is $16.2 + 1.8 = 18$. Click on the cell of the worksheet that contains the "More" and insert "18."

(*d*) To remove the gaps, double-click on any histogram bar, and the **Format Data Series** dialog box appears. Then click **Option** and in the text box for **Gap width** insert: 0.

2.30. Use Minitab to form a frequency distribution and to output a histogram for the data in Table 2.7, which lists the times in minutes that it took a sample of 30 employees to complete an assembly task.

Time, min	Frequency
9	2
10.8	1
12.6	8
14.4	8
16.2	7
18	3

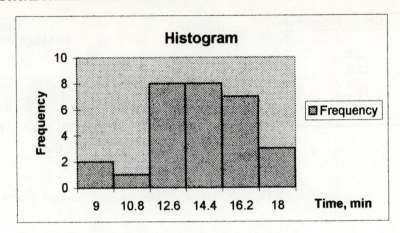

Fig. 2-29 Improved histogram from Excel.

(a) Identify the midpoint of the first class.

(b) Determine the size of the class interval.

Figure 2-30 presents the histogram that was obtained as the standard Minitab output. As implied by the positions of the values for the horizontal axis, the printed values are midpoints.

(a) As explained in the paragraph above, the values printed along the horizontal axis are midpoints. Therefore, the midpoint of the first listed class is 9.0.

(b) By reference to the midpoints of two adjoining classes: $10 - 9 = 1$.

The Minitab instructions that result in the output presented in Fig. 2-30 are as follows:

(1) Open Minitab. Enter the data from Table 2.7 into column C1 of the worksheet.

(2) Click **Graph** → **Histogram**. Under **Graph variables**, on line 1 insert: C1.

(3) Click **OK**.

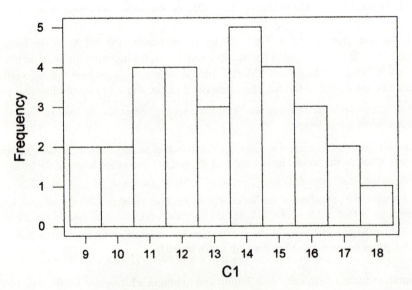

Fig. 2-30 Histogram from Minitab.

2.31. Change the analysis done in Problem 2.30, above, by substituting "Time,min" for C1 as the label for the horizontal axis and by specifying that the midpoint of the first class interval should be set at 10 with a class interval of 2.

(a)   Identify the lower- and upper-class limits for the first class.

(b)   Describe the type of frequency distribution that has been formed.

   Figure 2-31 presents the required histogram. As is true in Fig. 2-30, the values listed along the horizontal axis are class midpoints. Unlike the Excel output given in Figs. 2-28 and 2-29, the class limits are of the "and-under" type, as described in Section 2.7.

(a)   The class limits are at the midpoint plus-and-minus one-half the interval: $10 \pm \frac{1}{2}(2) = 9.0$ and 11.0.

(b)   As explained in the paragraph above, the classes reported are the "and-under" type. Thus, the first listed class contains all measured times between 9 minutes *and under* 11 minutes. By reference to the original data table, we see that the four values in the first class are 9, 9, 10, and 10; the two 11-minute values are *not* included in the tally for this class.

   The Minitab instructions that result in the output presented in Fig. 2-31 are as follows:

(1)   Open Minitab. Enter the data from Table 2.7 into column C1 of the worksheet.

(2)   Click the column-name cell located directly below the C1 column label. Type: Time,min.

(3)   Click **Graph → Histogram**. Under **Graph variables**, on line 1 insert: C1.

(4)   Click **Options** ... and in the resulting dialog box insert 10:18/2 for **Midpoint/cutpoint positions**. The meaning of this specification is that the midpoints for the histogram should range from 10 to 18 with an interval of 2.

(5)   Click **OK**.

(6)   Upon returning to the original dialog box, click **OK**.

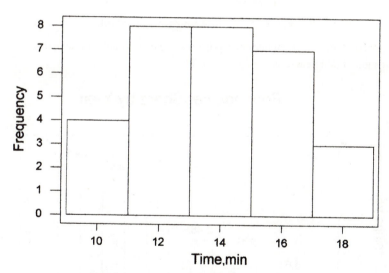

Fig. 2-31   Modified histogram from Minitab.

COMPUTER OUTPUT: BAR CHARTS

2.32. Use Excel to prepare a vertical bar chart portraying the per-share annual earnings of an electric power company for the coded years, as reported in Table 2.16.

   Figure 2-32 is the bar chart obtained using Excel. The instructions that result in the output are as follows:

(1) Open Excel. In cell A1 enter: Year. In B1 enter: Earnings per share.

(2) Enter the coded year and associated values below the respective headings.

(3) Select **Insert → Chart**. Then select **Column** as the **Chart type** and select the first chart subtype (Clustered Column). Click **Next**.

(4) Specify the **Data Range** as $B$1:$B$7 and select **Series in Columns**. Click **Next**.

(5) For **Chart title** enter: Earnings per Share by Year. For **Category (X) axis** enter: Year. For **Value (Y) axis** enter: Earnings per share. Click **Next**.

(6) For **Place chart** select **As new sheet**. Click **Finish**.

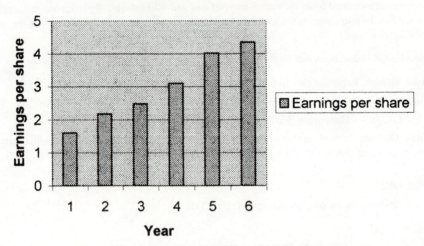

Fig. 2-32   Vertical bar chart from Excel.

2.33.   Use Minitab to prepare a vertical bar chart portraying the per-share annual earnings of an electric power company for the coded years, as reported in Table 2.16.

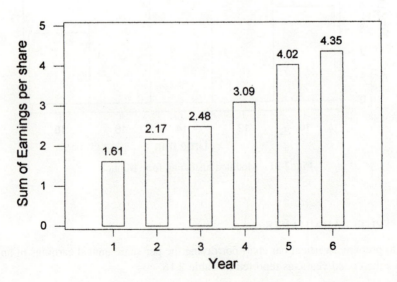

Fig. 2-33   Vertical bar chart from Minitab.

Figure 2-33 is the bar chart obtained using Minitab. The instructions that result in the output are as follows:

(1)   Open Minitab. In the column-name cell directly below C1 enter: Year. Below C2 enter: Earnings per share.

(2)   Enter the coded years and the associated values below the respective headings.

(3)   Select **Graph** → **Chart**. In the **Graph variables** box under **Y** for **Graph 1**, enter C2. Under **X** for **Graph 1** enter C1.

(4)   In the **Data display** box for **Item 1** under **Display**, choose **Bar**. Under **For each**, choose **Graph**.

(5)   Click **Annotation** → **Title**. On line 1 under **Title** type: Earnings per Share by Year. Click **OK**.

(6)   Click **Annotation** → **Data Labels** and check **Show data labels**. Click **OK**.

(7)   Select **Frame** → **Min and Max**. In the table, for **Minimum for X:** enter 0; for **Maximum for X:** enter 7; for **Minimum for Y:** enter 0; for **Maximum for Y:** enter 5.00. Click **OK**.

(8)   Upon returning to the original dialog box again click **OK**.

COMPUTER OUTPUT: RUN CHARTS

2.34.   When a coupon redemption process is in control, a maximum of 3 percent of the rebates include an error of any kind. For repeated rational subgroup samples of size $n = 100$ each, the maximum number of errors per sample thus is set at 3 for the process to be considered "in control." For 20 such sequential samples, the numbers of rebates processed that contain an error are as follows: 2, 2, 3, 6, 1, 3, 6, 4, 7, 2, 5, 0, 3, 2, 4, 5, 3, 8, 1, and 4. Use Excel to obtain a run chart for this sequence of sample outcomes. Based on the chart, does the process appear to be in control?

Figure 2-34 is the run chart obtained by the use of Excel. Based on this chart, it is clear that the process clearly is *not* in control. Not only are many of the observed number of errors above 3, there is great variability from sample to sample. Control procedures need to focus on this variability, as well as the level of errors. (Comprehensive coverage of process control is included in Chapter 19.)

The Excel instructions that result in the chart presented in Fig. 2-34 are as follows:

(1)   Open Excel. Enter the number of errors per sample in column **A**.

(2)   Click **Chart** → **Line** and select the fourth line chart subtype (Line with Markers). Click **Next**.

(3)   Click **Series**. For **Data Range** enter: $A$1:$A$20. Click **Next**.

(4)   For **Chart title** enter: Run Chart from Excel. For **Category (X) axis** enter: Sample. For **Value (Y) axis** enter: No. errors. Click **Next**.

(5)   For **Place chart** select **As new sheet**. Click **Finish**.

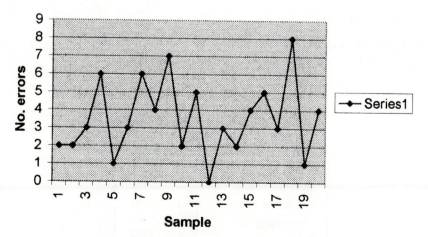

Fig. 2-34   Run chart from Excel.

2.35. Refer to Problem 2.34, above. Use Minitab to obtain a run chart for the sequence of sample outcomes. Based on the chart, does the process appear to be in control?

Figure 2-35 is the run chart obtained by the use of Minitab. Based on this chart, it is clear that the process clearly is *not* in control. Not only are many of the observed number of errors above 3, there is great variability from sample to sample. Control procedures need to focus on this variability, as well as the level of errors. (Comprehensive coverage of process control is included in Chapter 19.)

The Minitab instructions that result in the chart presented in Fig. 2-35 are as follows:

(1) Open Minitab. In the column-name cell directly below C1 enter: No. errors. Then enter the data for the 20 samples below the column name.

(2) Select **Graph → Time Series Plot**. In the **Graph variables** box under **Y** for **Graph 1** enter C1.

(3) In the **Data display** box for **Item 1** under **Display**, choose **Connect**. Under **For each**, choose **Graph**.

(4) Click **Annotation → Title**. On line 1 under **Title** enter: Run Chart from Minitab. Click **OK**.

(5) Click **Annotation → Data Labels** and check **Show data labels**. Click **OK**.

(6) Upon returning to the original dialog box again click **OK**.

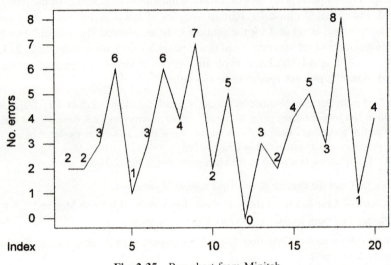

Fig. 2-35   Run chart from Minitab.

COMPUTER OUTPUT: PIE CHARTS

2.36. Table 2.17 reports the portfolio amounts invested in various geographic regions by a global equities mutual fund. Prepare a percentage pie chart to convey this information graphically by the use of Excel.

Table 2.17   Distribution of Investments: Global Equities Fund (in $millions)

U.S. & North America	$231
Japan & Far East	158
Continental Europe	84
United Kingdom	53
Total	$526

The pie chart is presented in Fig. 2-36. The Excel instructions that were used to obtain this output are as follows:

(1) Open Excel. Enter the abbreviated names of the four geographic regions in cells A1–A4 and the respective investment amounts in cells B1–B4.

(2) Select **Insert → Chart**. Select **Pie** as the **Chart type** and select the first subtype. Click **Next**.

(3) For **Data Range** specify $A$1:$B$4. Click **Next**.

(4) For **Chart title** insert: Pie Chart from Excel. For **Data Labels** select **Show label and percent** as the only selection in the dialog box. Click **Next**.

(5) For **Place chart** select **As new sheet**. Click **Finish**.

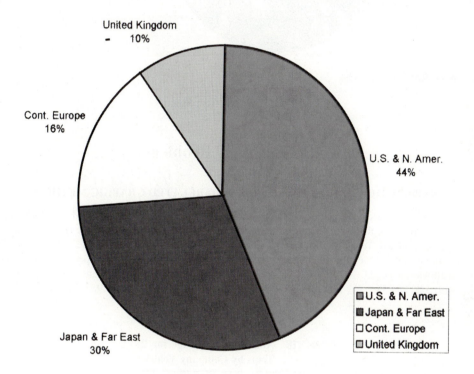

Fig. 2-36   Pie chart from Excel.

2.37. Table 2.17 reports the portfolio amounts invested in various geographic regions by a global equities mutual find. Prepare a percentage pie chart to convey this information graphically by the use of Minitab.

The pie chart is presented in Fig. 2-37. The Minitab instructions that were used to obtain this output are as follows:

(1) Open Minitab. In the column-name cell below C1 enter: Investments, Below C2 enter: $millions.

(2) Enter the abbreviated names of the geographic regions in column C1 and the respective investments amounts in column C2.

(3) Select **Graph → Pie Chart**.

(4) Check **Chart table**. For **Categories in** enter: C1 and for **Frequencies** enter C2.

(5) For **Title** enter: Pie Chart from Minitab. Click **OK**.

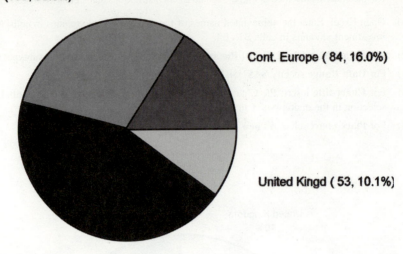

Fig. 2-37   Pie chart from Minitab.

Supplementary Problems

FREQUENCY DISTRIBUTIONS, CLASS INTERVALS, AND RELATED GRAPHIC METHODS

2.38.   Table 2.18 is a frequency distribution for the gasoline mileage obtained for 25 sampled trips for company-owned vehicles. (*a*) What are the lower and upper stated limits of the last class? (*b*) What are the lower and upper exact limits of the last class? (*c*) What class interval is used? (*d*) What is the midpoint of the last class? (*e*) Suppose the mileage per gallon was found to be 29.9 for a particular trip. Indicate the lower and upper limits of the class in which this result was included.
Ans.   (*a*) 34.0 and 35.9, (*b*) 33.95 and 35.95, (*c*) 2.0, (*d*) 34.95, (*e*) 28.0 and 29.9.

Table 2.18   Automobile Mileage for 25 Trips by Company Vehicles

Miles per gallon	Number of trips
24.0–25.9	3
26.0–27.9	5
28.0–29.9	10
30.0–31.9	4
32.0–33.9	2
34.0–35.9	1
Total	25

2.39.   Prepare a histogram for the data in Table 2.18.

2.40.   Prepare a frequency polygon and a frequency curve for the data in Table 2.18.

2.41.   Describe the frequency curve constructed in Problem 2.40 from the standpoint of skewness.
Ans.   The frequency curve appears to be somewhat positively skewed.

2.42. Form a cumulative frequency distribution for the data in Table 2.18 and prepare an ogive to present this distribution graphically.

2.43. Table 2.19 presents the amounts of 40 personal loans used to finance appliance and furniture purchases. Suppose we wish to arrange the loan amounts in a frequency distribution with a total of seven classes. Assuming equal class intervals, what would be a convenient class interval for this frequency distribution?
    Ans. $400

Table 2.19   The Amounts of 40 Personal Loans

$ 932	$1,000	$ 356	$2,227
515	554	1,190	954
452	973	300	2,112
1,900	660	1,610	445
1,200	720	1,525	784
1,278	1,388	1,000	870
2,540	851	1,890	630
586	329	935	3,000
1,650	1,423	592	334
1,219	727	655	1,590

2.44. Prepare a frequency distribution for the data in Table 2.19, beginning the first class at a lower class limit of $300 and using a class interval of $400.

2.45. Prepare a histogram for the frequency distribution formed in Problem 2.44.

2.46. Prepare a frequency polygon and frequency curve for the frequency distribution formed in Problem 2.44.

2.47. Describe the frequency curve constructed in Problem 2.46 in terms of skewness.
    Ans.   The frequency curve is clearly positively skewed.

2.48. Prepare a cumulative frequency distribution for the frequency distribution formed in Problem 2.44 and prepare an ogive curve for these data.

FORMS OF FREQUENCY CURVES

2.49. Describe the following curves in terms of skewness or kurtosis, as appropriate: (*a*) A frequency curve with a tail to the right, (*b*) a frequency curve that is relatively peaked, (*c*) a frequency curve that is relatively flat, (*d*) a frequency curve with a tail to the left.
    Ans.   (*a*) Positively skewed, (*b*) leptokurtic, (*c*) platykurtic, (*d*) negatively skewed

RELATIVE FREQUENCY DISTRIBUTIONS

2.50. Prepare a relative frequency table for the frequency distribution presented in Table 2.20.

2.51. Construct a histogram for the relative frequency distribution in Problem 2.50.

2.52. Referring to Table 2.20, (*a*) What percentage of cutting tools lasted at least 125 hr? (*b*) What percentage of cutting tools had a lifetime of at least 100 hr?
    Ans.   (*a*) 6%, (*b*) 31%

2.53 Prepare a table of cumulative proportions for the frequency distribution in Table 2.20.

Table 2.20 Lifetime of Cutting Tools in an Industrial Process

Hours before replacement	Number of tools
0.0–24.9	2
25.0–49.9	4
50.0–74.9	12
75.0–99.9	30
100.0–124.9	18
125.0–149.0	4
Total	70

2.54. Referring to the table constructed in Problem 2.53, (*a*) What is the tool lifetime associated with the 26th percentile of the distribution? (*b*) What is the percentile associated with a tool lifetime of approximately 100 hr?
Ans.   (*a*) 74.95 hr, $\cong$75 hr, (*b*) 69th percentile

2.55. Prepare the ogive for the cumulative proportions determined in Problem 2.53.

2.56. Refer to the ogive prepared in Problem 2.55 and determine the following values, approximately, by graphic interpolation: (*a*) The tool lifetime at the 50th percentile of the distribution, (*b*) the percentile associated with a tool lifetime of 60 hr.
Ans.   (*a*) Approx. 89 hr, (*b*) approx. 16th percentile

THE "AND-UNDER" TYPE OF FREQUENCY DISTRIBUTION

2.57. By reference to the frequency distribution in Table 2.21, determine (*a*) the lower stated limit of the first class, (b) the upper stated class limit of the first class, (*c*) the lower exact limit of the first class, (*d*) the upper exact limit of the first class, (*e*) the midpoint of the first class.
Ans.   (*a*) 18, (*b*) 20, (*c*) 18.0, (*d*) 20.0, (*e*) 19.0

Table 2.21 Ages of a Sample of Applicants for a Training Program

Age	Number of applicants
18 and under 20	5
20 and under 22	18
22 and under 24	10
24 and under 26	6
26 and under 28	5
28 and under 30	4
30 and under 22	2
Total	50

2.58. Prepare a frequency polygon for the frequency distribution in Table 2.21.

2.59. Use computer software to form a frequency distribution and to output a histogram for the data in Table 2.19, for the amounts of 40 personal loans. Specify that the midpoint of the first class should be at 500 and that a class interval of 400 should be used.

(*a*) Describe the type of frequency distribution that has been formed.

(*b*) Identify the midpoint of the first class.

(*c*) Determine the size of the class interval.

(d)   Identify the lower and upper stated class limits for the first class.

(e)   Determine the lower and upper exact class limits for the first class.

Ans.   (a) and-under frequency distribution, (b) 500.0, (c) 400.0, (d) 200 and 600, (e) 200.0 and 600.0

STEM-AND-LEAF DIAGRAMS

2.60.   Prepare a stem-and-leaf diagram for the daily low temperatures that are reported in Table 2.14, for Problem 2.23. Compare the form of the distribution of daily lows with that of the daily highs, for which the stem-and-leaf diagram is given in Fig. 2-23.

DOTPLOTS

2.61.   Refer to Table 2.15, presented with Problem 2.24, for the resting pulse rates for a sample of 40 adults. Use computer software to obtain a dotplot similar to the one presented in Fig. 2-24.

BAR CHARTS AND LINE GRAPHS

2.62   Table 2.22 presents the annual investment in R&D (research and development) for a sequence of five years by a major aerospace company. Construct a vertical bar chart for these data.

Table 2.22   Annual Expenditures on Research and Development by an Aerospace Company (in $millions)

Year	Amount
1	$751
2	754
3	827
4	1,417
5	1,846

2.63.   Construct a line graph for the R&D expenditures in the preceding problem.

RUN CHARTS

2.64.   When the manufacturing process for AA batteries is in control, the average battery life is 7.5 hours, or 450 minutes. For 10 sequential samples of nine batteries each that were placed in a rack that systematically drains the batteries to simulate everyday battery usage, the sample battery life averages are found to be: 460, 450, 440, 470, 460, 450, 420, 430, 440, and 430 minutes. Prepare a run chart for these sample results.

PIE CHARTS

2.65   The foreign sales for a particular year for a major aerospace company are given in Table 2.23. Construct a percentage pie chart for the revenue from foreign sales according to geographic area.

Table 2.23   Foreign Sales for an Aerospace Company (in $millions)

Europe		$7,175
Asia		7,108
Oceania		1,911
Western Hemisphere		872
Africa		430
	Total	$17,496

CHAPTER 3

Describing Business Data: Measures of Location

3.1 MEASURES OF LOCATION IN DATA SETS

A *measure of location* is a value that is calculated for a group of data and that is used to describe the data in some way. Typically, we wish the value to be representative of all of the values in the group, and thus some kind of average is desired. In the statistical sense an *average* is a *measure of central tendency* for a collection of values. This chapter covers the various statistical procedures concerned with measures of location.

3.2 THE ARITHMETIC MEAN

The *arithmetic mean*, or *arithmetic average*, is defined as the sum of the values in the data group divided by the number of values.

In statistics, a descriptive measure of a population, or a *population parameter*, is typically represented by a Greek letter, whereas a descriptive measure of a sample, or a *sample statistic*, is represented by a Roman letter. Thus, the arithmetic mean for a population of values is represented by the symbol μ (read "mew"), while the arithmetic mean for a sample of values is represented by the symbol $\bar{X}$ (read "X bar"). The formulas for the population mean and the sample mean are

$$\mu = \frac{\Sigma X}{N} \qquad (3.1)$$

$$\bar{X} = \frac{\Sigma X}{n} \qquad (3.2)$$

Operationally, the two formulas are identical; in both cases, one sums all of the values (ΣX) and then divides by the number of values. However, the distinction in the denominators is that in statistical analysis the uppercase N typically indicates the number of items in the population, while the lowercase n indicates the number of items in the sample.

EXAMPLE 1.   During a particular summer month, the eight salespeople in a heating and air-conditioning firm sold the following number of central air-conditioning units: 8, 11, 5, 14, 8, 11, 16, 11. Considering this month as the statistical population of interest, the mean number of units sold is

$$\mu = \frac{\Sigma X}{N} = \frac{84}{8} = 10.5 \text{ units}$$

Note: For reporting purposes, one generally reports the measures of location to one additional digit beyond the original level of measurement.

3.3   THE WEIGHTED MEAN

The *weighted mean* or *weighted average* is an arithmetic mean in which each value is weighted according to its importance in the overall group. The formulas for the population, and sample weighted means are identical:

$$\mu_w \qquad \text{or} \qquad \bar{X}_w = \frac{\Sigma(wX)}{\Sigma w} \qquad\qquad (3.3)$$

Operationally, each value in the group (X) is multiplied by the appropriate weight factor (w), and the products are then summed and divided by the sum of the weights.

EXAMPLE 2.   In a multiproduct company, the profit margins for the company's four product lines during the past fiscal year were: line *A*, 4.2 percent; line *B*, 5.5 percent; line *C*, 7.4 percent; and line *D*, 10.1 percent. The *unweighted* mean profit margin is

$$\mu = \frac{\Sigma X}{N} = \frac{27.2}{4} = 6.8\%$$

However, unless the four products are equal in sales, this unweighted average is incorrect. Assuming the sales totals in Table 3.1, the weighted mean correctly describes the overall average.

Table 3.1   Profit Margin and Sales Volume for Four Product Lines

Product line	Profit margin (X)	Sales (w)	wX
A	4.2%	$30,000,000	$1,260,000
B	5.5	20,000,000	1,100,000
C	7.4	5,000,000	370,000
D	10.1	3,000,000	303,000
		$\Sigma w = \overline{\$58,000,000}$	$\Sigma(wX) = \overline{\$3,033,000}$

$$\mu_w = \frac{\Sigma(wX)}{\Sigma w} = \frac{\$3,033,000}{\$58,000,000} = 5.2\%$$

3.4   THE MEDIAN

The *median* of a group of items is the value of the middle item when all the items in the group are arranged in either ascending or descending order, in terms of value. For a group with an even number of items, the median is assumed to be midway between the two values adjacent to the middle. When a large number of values is contained in the group, the following formula to determine the position of the median in the ordered group is useful:

$$\text{Med} = X_{[(n/2)+(1/2)]} \qquad\qquad (3.4)$$

EXAMPLE 3. The eight salespeople described in Example 1 sold the following number of central air-conditioning units, in ascending order: 5, 8, 8, 11, 11, 11, 14, 16. The value of the median is

$$\text{Med} = X_{[(n/2)+(1/2)]} = X_{[(8/2)+(1/2)]} = X_{4.5} = 11.0$$

The value of the median is between the fourth and fifth value in the ordered group. Since both these values equal "11" in this case, the median equals 11.0.

3.5 THE MODE

The *mode* is the value that occurs most frequently in a set of values. Such a distribution is described as being *unimodal*. For a small data set in which no measured values are repeated, there is no mode. When two nonadjoining values are about equal in having maximum frequencies associated with them, the distribution is described as being *bimodal*. Distributions of measurements with several modes are referred to as being multimodal.

EXAMPLE 4. The eight salespeople described in Example 1 sold the following number of central air-conditioning units: 8, 11, 5, 14, 8, 11, 16, and 11. The mode for this group of values is the value with the greatest frequency, or mode = 11.0.

3.6 RELATIONSHIP BETWEEN THE MEAN AND THE MEDIAN

For any symmetrical distribution, the mean, median, and mode all coincide in value [see Fig. 3-1(*a*)]. For a positively skewed distribution the mean is always larger than the median [see Fig. 3-1(*b*)]. For a negatively skewed distribution the mean is always smaller than the median [see Fig. 3-1(*c*)]. These latter two relationships are always true, regardless of whether or not the distribution is unimodal. One measure of skewness in statistics, which focuses on the difference between the values of the mean and the median for a group of values, is Pearson's coefficient of skewness, described in Section 4.12. The concepts of symmetry and skewness are explained in Section 2.4.

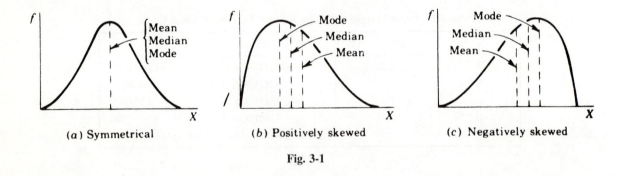

(a) Symmetrical   (b) Positively skewed   (c) Negatively skewed

Fig. 3-1

EXAMPLE 5. For the sales data considered in Examples 1, 3, and 4, the mean is 10.5, while the median is 11.0. Because the mean is smaller than the median, the distribution of observed values is somewhat negatively skewed, that is, skewed to the left.

3.7 MATHEMATICAL CRITERIA SATISFIED BY THE MEDIAN AND THE MEAN

One purpose for determining any measure of central tendency, such as a median or mean, is to use it to represent the general level of the values included in the group. Both the median and the mean are "good" representative measures, but from the standpoint of different mathematical criteria or objectives. The median is the representative value that minimizes the sum of the absolute values of the differences between each value in the group and the median. That is, the median minimizes the sum of the *absolute deviations* with respect to the individual values being represented. In contrast, the arithmetic mean focuses on minimizing the sum of the *squared deviations* with respect to the individual values in the group. The criterion by which the objective is that of minimizing the sum of the squared deviations associated with a representative value is called the *least-squares criterion*. This criterion is the one that is most important in statistical inference based on sample data, as discussed further in the following section.

EXAMPLE 6.   For the sales data that we have considered in the previous examples, the median is 11.0 and the mean is 10.5. The ordered sales amounts are presented in the first column of Table 3.2. The other columns of this table are concerned with determining the sum of the absolute deviations and of the squared deviations of the individual values with respect to both the median and the mean. Note that the sum of the absolute deviations for the median, 20, is lower than the corresponding sum of 21.0 for the mean. On the other hand, for the least-squares criterion, the sum of the squared deviations for the mean, 86.00, is lower than the corresponding sum of 88 for the median. No value that is different from the mean can have a lower sum of squared deviations than the mean.

Table 3.2   Mathematical Criteria Satisfied by the Median and the Mean (Med = 11.0; Mean = 10.5)

X	$\|X - \text{Med}\|$	$\|X - \text{Mean}\|$	$(X - \text{Med})^2$	$(X - \text{Mean})^2$
5	6	5.5	36	30.25
8	3	2.5	9	6.25
8	3	2.5	9	6.25
11	0	0.5	0	0.25
11	0	0.5	0	0.25
11	0	0.5	0	0.25
14	3	3.5	9	12.25
16	5	5.5	25	30.25
Sum	20	21.0	88	86.00

3.8   USE OF THE MEAN, MEDIAN, AND MODE

We first consider the use of these measures of average for representing *population data*. The value of the mode indicates where most of the observed values, such as hourly wage rates in a company, are located. It can be useful as a descriptive measure for a population group, *but only if* there is one clear mode. On the other hand, the median is always an excellent measure by which to represent the "typical" level of observed values, such as wage rates, in a population. This is true regardless of whether there is more than one mode or whether the population distribution is skewed or symmetrical. The lack of symmetry is no special problem because the median wage rate, for example, is always the wage rate of the "middle person" when the wage rates are listed in order of magnitude. The arithmetic mean is also an excellent representative value for a population, *but only if* the population is fairly symmetrical. For nonsymmetrical data, the extreme values (for instance, a few very high wage rates for technical specialists) will serve to distort the value of the mean as a representative value. Thus, the median is generally the best measure of data location for describing population data.

We now consider the use of the three measures of location with respect to *sample data*. Recall from Chapter 1 that the purpose of statistical inference with sample data is to make probability statements about the population from which the sample was selected. The mode is not a good measure of location with respect to sample data because its value can vary greatly from sample to sample. The median is better than the mode because its value is more stable from sample to sample. However, the value of the mean is the most stable of the three measures. As will be introduced further in Section 4.9 and explained fully in Chapter 8, the reason for the relative stability of the sample mean from sample to sample is because it is the measure of location that satisfies the least-squares criterion. Thus, for sample data, the best measure of location generally is the arithmetic mean.

EXAMPLE 7. The wage rates of all 650 hourly employees in a manufacturing firm have been compiled. The best representative measure of the typical wage rate is the median, because a population is involved and the median is relatively unaffected by any lack of symmetry in the wage rates. In fact, such data as wage rates and salary amounts are likely to be positively skewed, with relatively few wage or salary amounts being exceptionally high and in the right tail of the distribution.

EXAMPLE 8. A *random sample* of $n = 100$ wage rates is obtained in a company having several thousand hourly employees. The best representative wage rate *for the several thousand employees* is the sample mean. Although the sample mean is unlikely to be exactly equal to the mean wage rate for the entire population, it will generally be much closer to the population mean than the sample median would be as an estimator of the population median wage rate.

3.9   USE OF THE MEAN IN STATISTICAL PROCESS CONTROL

In Section 2.12 we observed that a run chart is a plot of data values in the time-sequence order in which they were observed, and that the values plotted can be individual values or averages of sequential samples. We prefer to plot averages rather than individual values because any average generally will be more stable (less variable) from sample to sample than are the individual observations. As we observed in the preceding section, the sample mean is more stable than either the median or the mode. For this reason, the focus of run charts concerned with sample averages is to plot the sample means. Such a chart is called an $\bar{X}$ chart, and serves as the basis for determining whether a process is stable, or whether there is process variation with an assignable cause that should be corrected.

EXAMPLE 9. Refer to the run chart in Fig. 2-11 (page 18) of the preceding chapter. This run chart for the sequence of mean weights for samples of $n = 4$ packages of potato chips is typical of the kinds of charts that are prepared for the purpose of statistical process control, as explained and illustrated in Chapter 19.

3.10   QUARTILES, DECILES, AND PERCENTILES

Quartiles, deciles, and percentiles are similar to the median in that they also subdivide a distribution of measurements according to the proportion of frequencies observed. Whereas the median divides a distribution into halves, quartiles divide it into quarters, deciles divide it into tenths, and percentile points divide it into 100 parts. Formula (3.4) for the median is modified according to the fraction point of interest. For example,

$$Q_1(\text{first quartile}) = X_{[(n/4)+(1/2)]} \tag{3.5}$$

$$D_3(\text{third decile}) = X_{[(3n/10)+(1/2)]} \tag{3.6}$$

$$P_{70}(\text{seventieth percentile}) = X_{[(70n/100)+(1/2)]} \tag{3.7}$$

EXAMPLE 10. The eight salespeople described in Example 1 sold the following number of central air-conditioning units, in ascending order: 5, 8, 8, 11, 11, 11, 14, 16. Find the positions of the first quartile and third quartile for this distribution.

$$Q_1 = X_{[(n/4)+(1/2)]} = X_{[(8/4)+(1/2)]} = X_{2.5} = 8.0$$
$$Q_3 = X_{[(3n/4)+(1/2)]} = X_{[(24/4)+(1/2)]} = X_{6.5} = 12.5$$

The position of the first quartile is midway between the second and third values in the ordered array. Since both of these values are 8, the value at the first quartile is 8.0. The value of the third quartile is midway between the sixth and seventh values in the array, or midway between 11 and 14, which is 12.5.

3.11   USING EXCEL AND MINITAB

Computer software is available to determine a variety of measures of average. Solved Problems 3.17 and 3.18 illustrate the use of Excel and Minitab to determine the values of the mean and median for a sample of product assembly times.

Solved Problems

THE MEAN, MEDIAN, AND MODE

3.1. For a sample of 15 students at an elementary-school snack bar, the following sales amounts arranged in ascending order of magnitude are observed: $0.10, 0.10, 0.25, 0.25, 0.25, 0.35, 0.40, 0.53, 0.90, 1.25, 1.35, 2.45, 2.71, 3.09, 4.10. Determine the (*a*) mean, (*b*) median, and (*c*) mode for these sales amounts.

(*a*) $\bar{X} = \dfrac{\Sigma X}{n} = \dfrac{18.08}{15} = \$1.21$

(*b*) $\text{Med} = X_{[(n/2)+(1/2)]} = X_{[(15/2)+(1/2)]} = X_8 = \$0.53$

(*c*) Mode = most frequent value = $0.25

3.2. How would you describe the distribution in Problem 3.1 from the standpoint of skewness?

With the mean being substantially larger than the median, the distribution of values is clearly positively skewed, or skewed to the right.

3.3. For the data in Problem 3.1, suppose that you are asked to determine the typical purchase amount only *for this particular group of students*. Which measure of average would you report? Why?

Note that once we decide to focus only on this particular group, we are treating this group as our *population* of interest. Therefore, the best choice is to report the median as being the typical value; this is the eighth value in the array, or $0.53.

3.4. Refer to Problem 3.3 above. Suppose we wish to estimate the typical amount of purchase in the population from which the sample was taken. Which measure of average would you report? Why?

Because statistical inference for a population is involved, our main concern is to report an average that is the most stable and has the least variability from sample to sample. The average that satisfied this requirement is the mean, because it satisfies the least-squares criterion. Therefore, the value reported should be the sample mean, or $1.21.

3.5. A sample of 20 production workers in a company earned the following net pay amounts after all deductions for a given week, rounded to the nearest dollar and arranged in ascending order: $240, 240, 240, 240, 240, 240, 240, 240, 255, 255, 265, 265, 280, 280, 290, 300, 305, 325, 330, 340. Calculate the (*a*) mean, (*b*) median, and (*c*) mode for this group of wages.

(*a*) $\bar{X} = \dfrac{\Sigma X}{n} = \dfrac{5{,}410}{20} = \$270.50$

(*b*) $\text{Median} = X_{[(n/2)+(1/2)]} = X_{[(20/2)+(1/2)]} = X_{10.5} = \$260.00$

(*c*) Mode = most frequent value = $240.00

3.6. For the wage data in Problem 3.5, describe the distribution in terms of skewness.

With the mean being larger than the median, the distribution can be described as being positively skewed, or skewed to the right.

3.7. With respect to the data in Problem 3.5, suppose you are the vice president in charge of collective bargaining for the company. What measure of average net pay would you report as being representative of all the company workers in general?

Because the sample mean is the highest of the three averages, your inclination might be to report this value. Using this value is highly defensible, given that statistical inference is involved and that the sample mean is the most stable of the estimators that might be used.

3.8. With respect to the data in Problem 3.5, suppose you are the elected president of the employee bargaining unit. What measure of average would you report as being representative of workers in general?

In terms of your bargaining position, you might be inclined to report the mode, or at least the median, rather than the mean. Defense of your choice would rest on identifying the net pay amounts for most people in the sample (for the mode) or on the observation that the sample mean is affected by a few high wage amounts. However, both the median and mode have more variability from sample to sample, and therefore are less stable population estimators than is the mean.

3.9. A work-standards expert observes the amount of time required to prepare a sample of 10 business letters in an office, with the following results listed in ascending order to the nearest minute: 5, 5, 5, 7, 9, 14, 15, 15, 16, 18. Determine the (a) mean, (b) median, and (c) mode for this group of values.

(a) $\bar{X} = \dfrac{\Sigma X}{n} = \dfrac{109}{10} = 10.9 \, \text{min}$

(b) $\text{Med} = X_{[(n/2) + (1/2)]} = X_{[(10/2) + (1/2)]} = X_{5.5} = 11.5 \, \text{min}$

(c) $\text{Mode} = \text{most frequent value} = 5.0$

3.10. Compare the values of the mean and median in Problem 3.9 and comment on the form of the distribution.

Because the mean is smaller than the median, the distribution is somewhat negatively skewed.

THE WEIGHTED MEAN

3.11. Suppose that the per-gallon prices of unleaded regular gasoline are listed for 22 metropolitan areas varying considerably in size and in gasoline sales. The (a) median and (b) arithmetic mean are computed for these data. Describe the meaning that each of these values would have.

(a)   The median would indicate the average, or typical, price in the sense that half the metropolitan areas would have gasoline prices below this value and half would have prices above this value.

(b)   The meaning of the arithmetic mean as an unweighted value is questionable at best. Clearly, it would *not* indicate the mean gasoline prices being paid by all the gasoline purchasers living in the 22 metropolitan areas, because the small metropolitan areas would be represented equally with the large areas in such an average. In order to determine a suitable mean for all purchasers in these metropolitan areas, a weighted mean (using gasoline sales as weights) would have to be computed.

3.12. Referring to Table 3.3, determine the overall percentage defective of all items assembled during the sampled week.

Table 3.3   Percentage of Defective Items in an Assembly Department in a Sampled Week

Shift	Percentage defective (X)	Number of items, in thousands (w)	wX
1	1.1	210	231.0
2	1.5	120	180.0
3	2.3	50	115.0
		$\Sigma w = \overline{380}$	$\Sigma(wX) = \overline{526.0}$

Using formula (3.3),

$$\bar{X}_w = \frac{\Sigma(wX)}{\Sigma w} = \frac{526.0}{380} = 1.4\% \, \text{defective}$$

MATHEMATICAL CRITERIA SATISFIED BY THE MEDIAN AND THE MEAN

3.13. Refer to the sample data in Problem 3.5 and demonstrate that the sum of the absolute values of the deviations is a smaller sum for the median than it is for the mean. Also demonstrate that the sum of the squared deviations is smaller for the mean than it is for the median.

By reference to Table 3.4, we see that the sum of the absolute deviations for the median is 550, which is less than the corresponding sum of 572.00 for the mean. Also, as expected, the sum of the squared deviations of 21,945.00 for the mean is less than the corresponding sum of 24,150 for the median.

Table 3.4　Mathematical Criteria Satisfied for the Pay Data in Problem 3.5
(Med = \$260.00; Mean = \$270.50)

X	$|X - \text{Med}|$	$|X - \text{Mean}|$	$(X - \text{Med})^2$	$(X - \text{Mean})^2$
240	20	30.50	400	930.25
240	20	30.50	400	930.25
240	20	30.50	400	930.25
240	20	30.50	400	930.25
240	20	30.50	400	930.25
240	20	30.50	400	930.25
240	20	30.50	400	930.25
240	20	30.50	400	930.25
255	5	15.50	25	240.25
255	5	15.50	25	240.25
265	5	5.50	25	30.25
265	5	5.50	25	30.25
280	20	9.50	400	90.25
280	20	9.50	400	90.25
290	30	19.50	900	380.25
300	40	29.50	1,600	870.25
305	45	34.50	2,025	1,190.25
325	65	54.50	4,225	2,970.25
330	70	59.50	4,900	3,540.25
340	80	69.50	6,400	4,830.25
Sum	550	572.00	24,150	21,945.00

3.14. Refer to the sum of the squared deviations for the mean as determined in Problem 3.13 above. Demonstrate that no other "typical" value for the group has a lower sum of squared deviations by choosing trial averages of \$270 and of \$271. Note that each of these trial values is equally and just fractionally different from the sample mean of \$270.50, but in opposite directions.

By reference to Table 3.5, we see that these two trial averages have the same sum of squared deviations, 21,950, which is greater than the corresponding sum of 21,945.00 for the sample mean. Any other trial value that has a greater difference from the sample mean, in either direction, would have a still-higher sum of squared deviations.

Table 3.5   Alternative Values Used in Lieu of the Mean in Table 3.4

X	$\lvert X-270\rvert$	$\lvert X-271\rvert$	$(X-270)^2$	$(X-271)^2$
240	30	31	900	961
240	30	31	900	961
240	30	31	900	961
240	30	31	900	961
240	30	31	900	961
240	30	31	900	961
240	30	31	900	961
240	30	31	900	961
255	15	16	225	256
255	15	16	225	256
265	5	6	25	36
265	5	6	25	36
280	10	9	100	81
280	10	9	100	81
290	20	19	400	361
300	30	19	900	841
305	35	34	1,225	1,156
325	55	54	3,025	2,916
330	60	59	3,600	3,481
340	70	69	4,900	4,761
Sum	570	564	21,950	21,950

QUARTILES, DECILES, AND PERCENTILES

3.15. For the data in Problem 3.1, determine the values at the (*a*) second quartile, (*b*) second decile, and (*c*) 40th percentile point for these sales amounts.

(*a*) $Q_2 = X_{[(2n/4)+(1/2)]} = X_{(7.5+0.5)} = X_8 = \$0.53$

   (*Note*:   By definition, the second quartile is always at the same point as the median.)

(*b*) $D_2 = X_{[(2n/10)+(1/2)]} = X_{(3.0+0.5)} = X_{3.5} = \$0.25$

   (*Note*:   This is the value midway between the third and fourth sales amounts, arranged in ascending order.)

(*c*) $P_{40} = X_{[(40n/100)+(1/2)]} = X_{(6.0+0.5)} = X_{6.5} = 0.375 \cong \$0.38$

3.16. For the measurements in Problem 3.5, determine the values at the (*a*) third quartile, (*b*) ninth decile, (*c*) 50th percentile point, and (*d*) 84th percentile point for this group of wages.

(*a*) $Q_3 = X_{[(3n/4)+(1/2)]} = X_{15.5} = \$295.00$

   (*Note*:   This is the value midway between the 15th and 16th wage amounts, arranged in ascending order.)

(*b*) $D_9 = X_{[(9n/10)+(1/2)]} = X_{18.5} = \$327.50$

(*c*) $P_{50} = X_{[(50n/100)+(1/2)]} = X_{10.5} = \$260.00$

   (*Note*:   By definition the 50th percentile point is always at the same point as the median.)

(*d*) $P_{84} = X_{[(84n/100)+(1/2)]} = X_{(16.8+0.5)} = X_{17.3} = \$311.00$

   (*Note*:   This is the value which is *three-tenths* of the way between the 17th and 18th wage amounts arranged in ascending order.)

USING EXCEL AND MINITAB

3.17. Use Excel to determine the values of the mean and median for the data in Table 2.7 (page 22), for the time required to complete an assembly task by a sample of 30 employees. Based on the two values, what kind of skewness, if any, exists for this data distribution? In Problems 2.28 and 2.29, these data were grouped into frequency distributions by the use of Excel, with the associated output of histograms.

Figure 3-2 presents the output of descriptive statistics for these data. As can be observed, the mean assembly time is 13.3 min and the median assembly time is 13.5 min. Because the mean is somewhat smaller in value than the median, there is some degree of negative skewness for the distribution of the values. The meanings of many of the other measures that are reported in the output will be considered in Chapter 4.

The Excel instructions that result in the output presented in Fig. 3-2 are as follows:

(1) Open Excel. In cell Al enter the column label: Assy. Times, min. Enter the data values in column A beginning at cell A2.

(2) Click **Tools → Data Analysis → Descriptive Statistics**. Click **OK**.

(3) Designate the **Input Range** as: $A$1:$A$31.

(4) Select **Labels in First Row**.

(5) Select **Output Range** and insert: $C$1 (to provide for one column of space between the input and the output).

(6) Select **Summary Statistics**.

(7) Click **OK**.

Assy. Times, min.	
Mean	13.3
Standard Error	0.445024
Median	13.5
Mode	14
Standard Deviation	2.437494
Sample Variance	5.941379
Kurtosis	-0.81237
Skewness	-0.00735
Range	9
Minimum	9
Maximum	18
Sum	399
Count	30

Fig. 3-2   Excel output.

3.18. Use Minitab to determine the values of the mean and median for the data in Table 2.7 (page 22), for the time required to complete an assembly task by a sample of 30 employees. Based on the two values, what kind of skewness, if any, exists for this data distribution? In Problems 2.30 and 2.31, these data were grouped into frequency distributions by the use of Minitab, with the associated output of histograms.

Figure 3-3 presents the output of descriptive statistics for these data. As can be observed, the mean assembly time is 13.3 min and the median assembly time is 13.5 min. Because the mean is somewhat smaller in value than the median, there is some degree of negative skewness for the distribution of the values. Q1 and Q3 values in the output are the 1st and 3rd quartiles for the data distribution. The meanings of some of the other measures that are reported will be considered in Chapter 4.

The Minitab instructions that result in the output presented in Fig. 3-2 are as follows:

(1) Open Minitab. In the column-name cell for column C1 enter: Assy. Times, min. Then enter the sample data in column C1.

(2) Click **Stat** → **Basic Statistics** → **Display Descriptive Statistics**.

(3) For **Variables** enter: C1.

(4) Click **OK**.

Descriptive Statistics: Assy. Times, min.

Variable	N	Mean	Median	TrMean	StDev	SE Mean
Assy. Ti	30	13.300	13.500	13.308	2.437	0.445

Variable	Minimum	Maximum	Q1	Q3
Assy. Ti	9.000	18.000	11.000	15.000

Fig. 3-3 Minitab output.

Supplementary Problems

THE MEAN, MEDIAN, AND MODE

3.19. The number of cars sold by each of the 10 salespeople in an automobile dealership during a particular month, arranged in ascending order, is: 2, 4, 7, 10, 10, 10, 12, 12, 14, 15. Determine the population (*a*) mean, (*b*) median, and (*c*) mode for the number of cars sold.
Ans. (*a*) 9.6, (*b*) 10.0, (*c*) 10.0

3.20. Which value in Problem 3.19 best describes the "typical" sales volume per salesperson?
Ans. 10.0

3.21. Describe the distribution of the sales data in Problem 3.19 in terms of skewness.
Ans. Positively skewed.

3.22. The weights of a sample of outgoing packages in a mailroom, weighed to the nearest ounce, are found to be: 21, 18, 30, 12, 14, 17, 28, 10, 16, 25 oz. Determine the (*a*) mean, (*b*) median, and (*c*) mode for these weights.
Ans. (*a*) 19.1, (*b*) 17.5, (*c*) there is no mode

3.23. Describe the distribution of the weights in Problem 3.22 in terms of skewness.
Ans. Positively skewed.

3.24. As indicated by the wording in Problem 3.22, the packages that were weighed are a random sample of all such packages handled in the mailroom. What is the best estimate of the typical weight of all packages handled in the mailroom?
Ans. 19.1 oz

3.25. For the weights reported in Problem 3.22, suppose we wish to describe *only* the weights of the selected group of packages. What is the best representative value for the group?
Ans. 17.5 oz

3.26. The following examination scores, arranged in ascending order, were achieved by 20 students enrolled in a decision analysis course: 39, 46, 57, 65, 70, 72, 72, 75, 77, 79, 81, 81, 84, 84, 84, 87, 93, 94, 97, 97. Determine the (*a*) mean, (*b*) median, and (*c*) mode for these scores.
Ans. (*a*) 76.7, (*b*) 80.0, (*c*) 84.0

3.27. Describe the distribution of test scores in Problem 3.26 in terms of skewness.
Ans. Negatively skewed.

3.28. The number of accidents which occurred during a given month in the 13 manufacturing departments of an industrial plant was: 2, 0, 0, 3, 3, 12, 1, 0, 8, 1, 0, 5, 1. Calculate the (*a*) mean, (*b*) median, and (*c*) mode for the number of accidents per department.
Ans. (*a*) 2.8, (*b*) 1.0, (*c*) 0

3.29. Describe the distribution of accident rates reported in Problem 3.28 in terms of skewness.
Ans. Positively skewed.

THE WEIGHTED MEAN

3.30. Suppose the retail prices of the selected items have changed as indicated in Table 3.6. Determine the mean percentage change in retail prices *without* reference to the average expenditures included in the table.
Ans. 4.0%

Table 3.6   Changes in the Retail Prices of Selected Items During a Particular Year

Item	Percent increase	Average expenditure per month (before increase)
Milk	10%	$20.00
Ground beef	−6	30.00
Apparel	−8	30.00
Gasoline	20	50.00

3.31. Referring to Table 3.6, determine the mean percentage change by weighting the percent increase for each item by the average amount per month spent on that item before the increase.
Ans. 6.0%

3.32. Is the mean percentage price change calculated in Problem 3.30 or 3.31 more appropriate as a measure of the impact of the price changes on this particular consumer? Why?
Ans. The weighted mean in Problem 3.31 is more appropriate (see Example 2 for an explanation).

QUARTILES, DECILES, AND PERCENTILES

3.33. Determine the values at the (*a*) first quartile, (*b*) second decile, and (*c*) 30th percentile point for the sales amounts in Problem 3.19.
Ans. (*a*) 7.0, (*b*) 5.5, (*c*) 8.5

3.34. From Problem 3.22, determine the weights at the (*a*) third quartile, (*b*) third decile, and (*c*) 70th percentile point.
Ans. (*a*) 25.0 oz, (*b*) 15.0 oz, (*c*) 23.0 oz

3.35. Determine the (*a*) second quartile, (*b*) ninth decile, and (*c*) 50th percentile point for the examination scores in Problem 3.26
Ans. (*a*) 80.0, (*b*) 95.5, (*c*) 80.0

3.36. In general, which quartile, decile, and percentile point, respectively, are equivalent to the median?
  Ans.   Second quartile, fifth decile, and 50th percentile point.

COMPUTER OUTPUT

3.37. Use computer software to determine the mean and the median for the data in Table 2.19 (page 41), for the amounts of 40 personal loans.
  Ans.   The mean loan amount is $1,097.40 and the median is $944.50.

CHAPTER 4

Describing Business Data: Measures of Dispersion

4.1 MEASURES OF DISPERSION IN DATA SETS

The measures of central tendency described in Chapter 3 are useful for identifying the "typical" value in a group of values. In contrast, *measures of dispersion*, or *variability*, are concerned with describing the variability among the values. Several techniques are available for measuring the extent of variability in data sets. The ones which are described in this chapter are the *range*, *modified ranges*, *average deviation*, *variance*, *standard deviation*, and *coefficient of variation*.

EXAMPLE 1. Suppose that two different packaging machines result in a mean weight of 10.0 oz of cereal being packaged, but that in one case all packages are within 0.10 oz of this weight while in the other case the weights may vary by as much as 1.0 oz in either direction. Measuring the variability, or dispersion, of the amounts being packaged would be every bit as important as measuring the average in this case.

The concept of skewness has been described in Section 2.4 and 3.6. Pearson's *coefficient of skewness* is described in Section 4.12.

4.2 THE RANGE

The *range*, or R, is the difference between highest and lowest values included in a data set. Thus, when H represents the highest value in the group and L represents the lowest value, the range for ungrouped data is

$$R = H - L \qquad (4.1)$$

57

EXAMPLE 2. During a particular summer month, the eight salespeople in a heating and air-conditioning firm sold the following numbers of central air-conditioning units: 8, 11, 5, 14, 8, 11, 16, 11. The range of the number of units sold is

$$R = H - L = 16 - 5 = 11.0 \text{ units}$$

Note: For purposes of comparison, we generally report the measures of variability to one additional digit beyond the original level of measurement.

4.3 MODIFIED RANGES

A *modified range* is a range for which some of the extreme values at each end of the distribution are eliminated from consideration. The middle 50 percent is the range between the values at the 25th percentile point and the 75th percentile point of the distribution. As such, it is also the range between the first and third quartiles of the distribution. For this reason, the middle 50 percent range is usually designated as the *interquartile range* (*IQR*). Thus,

$$IQR = Q_3 - Q_1 \qquad\qquad (4.2)$$

Other modified ranges that are sometimes used are the middle 80 percent, middle 90 percent, and middle 95 percent.

EXAMPLE 3. The data for the sales of central air-conditioning units presented in Example 2, in ascending order, are: 5, 8, 8, 11, 11, 11, 14, 16. Thus the number of observations is $N = 8$ for these population data. To compute the interquartile range, we first must determine the values at Q_3 (the 75th percentile point) and Q_1 (the 25th percentile point) and then subtract Q_1 from Q_3:

$$Q_3 = X_{[(75N/100)+(1/2)]} = X_{[6+(1/2)]} = X_{6.5} = 12.5$$
$$Q_1 = X_{[(25N/100)+(1/2)]} = X_{[2+(1/2)]} = X_{2.5} = 8.0$$
$$IQR = Q_3 - Q_1 = 12.5 - 8.0 = 4.5 \text{ units}$$

4.4 BOX PLOTS

A *box plot* is a graph that portrays the distribution of a data set by reference to the values at the quartiles as location measures and the value of the interquartile range as the reference measure of variability. A box plot is a relatively easy way of graphing data and observing the extent of skewness in the distribution. As such, it is an easier alternative to forming a frequency distribution and plotting a histogram, as described in Sections 2.1 to 2.3. The box plot is also called a *box-and-whisker plot*, for reasons that will be obvious in Example 4, below. Because of its relative ease of use, the box plot is a principal technique of *exploratory data analysis*, as described in Section 2.8 on stem-and-leaf displays.

EXAMPLE 4. Figure 4-1 presents the box plot for the unit sales data in Example 3. The lower and upper boundary points of the rectangular box in the graph are called hinges and generally are located at Q_1 and Q_3. Thus, based on the quartile values determined in Example 3, the lower hinge is at 8.0 and the upper hinge is at 12.5. The vertical line within the box indicates the position of the median (or Q_2), which is at 11.0. The dashed horizontal lines to the left and right of the box are called whiskers and extend to the "inner fences," which are 1.5 units of the interquartile range in each direction. Thus, the whiskers extend to:

$$Q_1 - (1.5 \times IQR) = 8.0 - (1.5)(4.5) = 1.25$$
$$Q_3 + (1.5 \times IQR) = 12.5 + (1.5)(4.5) = 19.25$$

The "outer fences" in Fig. 4-1 extend to 3.0 units of the interquartile range in each direction from Q_1 and Q_3, or to -5.5 and 25.5 for the lower and upper outer fences, respectively. For this example note that the lower outer fence is at the value of 0 for practical purposes, since negative units of sale are not possible. Any values lying between the inner and outer fences are considered to be mild outliers, while values located beyond the outer fences are extreme outliers. For any outliers, we would investigate whether such values were collected under the same circumstances as the other values, and whether any measurement errors may have occurred. There are clearly no outliers for our small group of eight values, since all the sales values listed in Example 3 are within the inner fences.

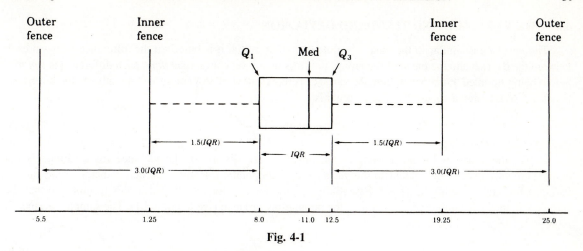

Fig. 4-1

4.5   THE MEAN ABSOLUTE DEVIATION

The *mean absolute deviation*, or *MAD*, is based on the absolute value of the difference between each value in the data set and the mean of the group. It is sometimes called the "average deviation." The mean average of these absolute values is then determined. The absolute values of the differences are used because the sum of all of the plus and minus differences (rather than the absolute differences) is always equal to zero. Thus the respective formulas for the population and sample MAD are

$$\text{Population } MAD = \frac{\Sigma|X - \mu|}{N} \tag{4.3}$$

$$\text{Sample } MAD = \frac{\Sigma|X - \bar{X}|}{n} \tag{4.4}$$

EXAMPLE 5.   For the air-conditioning sales data given in Example 2, the arithmetic mean is 10.5 units (see Section 3.2). Using the calculations in Table 4.1, the mean absolute deviation is determined as follows:

$$MAD = \frac{\Sigma|X - \mu|}{N} = \frac{21.0}{8} = 2.625 \cong 2.6 \text{ units}$$

Table 4.1   Worksheet for Calculating the Average Deviation for the Sales Data ($\mu = 10.5$)

X	$X - \mu$	$|X - \mu|$
5	-5.5	5.5
8	-2.5	2.5
8	-2.5	2.5
11	0.5	0.5
11	0.5	0.5
11	0.5	0.5
14	3.5	3.5
16	5.5	5.5
	Total	21.0

Thus, we can say that on average, a salesperson's unit sales of air conditioners differs by 2.6 units from the group mean, in either direction.

4.6   THE VARIANCE AND STANDARD DEVIATION

The *variance* is similar to the mean absolute deviation in that it is based on the difference between each value in the data set and the mean of the group. It differs in one very important way: each difference is *squared* before being summed. For a population, the variance is represented by $V(X)$ or, more typically, by the lowercase Greek σ^2 (read "sigma squared"). The formula is

$$V(X) = \sigma^2 = \frac{\Sigma(X - \mu)^2}{N} \qquad (4.5)$$

Unlike the situation for other sample statistics we have discussed, the variance for a sample is not computationally exactly equivalent to the variance for a population. Rather, the denominator in the sample variance formula is slightly different. Essentially, a correction factor is included in this formula, so that the sample variance is an unbiased estimator of the population variance (see Section 8.1). The sample variance is represented by s^2; its formula is

$$s^2 = \frac{\Sigma(X - \bar{X})^2}{n - 1} \qquad (4.6)$$

In general, it is difficult to interpret the meaning of the value of a variance because the units in which it is expressed are squared values. Partly for this reason, the square root of the variance, represented by Greek σ (or s for a sample) and called the *standard deviation* is more frequently used. The formulas are

Population standard deviation: $\qquad \sigma = \sqrt{\dfrac{\Sigma(X - \mu)^2}{N}} \qquad (4.7)$

Sample standard deviation: $\qquad s = \sqrt{\dfrac{\Sigma(X - \bar{X})^2}{n - 1}} \qquad (4.8)$

The standard deviation is particularly useful in conjunction with the so-called normal distribution (see Section 4.9).

EXAMPLE 6.   For the air-conditioning sales data given in Example 2 the arithmetic mean is 10.5 units (see Section 3.2). Considering these monthly sales data to be the statistical population of interest, the standard deviation is determined from the calculations in Table 4.2 as follows:

$$\sigma = \sqrt{\frac{\Sigma(X - \mu)^2}{N}} = \sqrt{\frac{86}{8}} = \sqrt{10.75} = 3.3$$

Table 4.2   Worksheet for Calculating the Population Standard Deviation for the Sales Data ($\mu = 10.5$)

X	$X - \mu$	$(X - \mu)^2$
5	-5.5	30.25
8	-2.5	6.25
8	-2.5	6.25
11	0.5	0.25
11	0.5	0.25
11	0.5	0.25
14	3.5	12.25
16	5.5	30.25
	Total	86.00

4.7 SIMPLIFIED CALCULATIONS FOR THE VARIANCE AND STANDARD DEVIATION

The formulas in Section 4.6 are called *deviations formulas*, because in each case the specific deviations of individual values from the mean must be determined. Alternative formulas, which are mathematically equivalent but which do not require the determination of each deviation, have been derived. Because these formulas are generally easier to use for computations, they are called *computational formulas*.

The computational formulas are

Population variance:
$$\sigma^2 = \frac{\Sigma X^2 - N\mu^2}{N} \qquad (4.9)$$

Population standard deviation:
$$\sigma = \sqrt{\frac{\Sigma X^2 - N\mu^2}{N}} \qquad (4.10)$$

Sample variance:
$$s^2 = \frac{\Sigma X^2 - n\bar{X}^2}{n-1} \qquad (4.11)$$

Sample standard deviation:
$$s = \sqrt{\frac{\Sigma X^2 - n\bar{X}^2}{n-1}} \qquad (4.12)$$

EXAMPLE 7.   For the air-conditioning sales data presented in Example 2, we calculate the population standard deviation below by the use of the alternative computational formula and Table 4.3 to demonstrate that the answer is the same as the answer obtained with the deviation formula in Example 6. The mean for these data is 10.5 units.

$$\sigma = \sqrt{\frac{\Sigma X^2 - N\mu^2}{N}} = \sqrt{\frac{968 - 8(10.5)^2}{8}} = \sqrt{10.75} = 3.3 \text{ units}$$

Table 4.3   Worksheet for Calculating the Population Standard Deviation for the Sales Data

X	X^2
5	25
8	64
8	64
11	121
11	121
11	121
14	196
16	256
Total	968

4.8   THE MATHEMATICAL CRITERION ASSOCIATED WITH THE
VARIANCE AND STANDARD DEVIATION

In Section 3.7 we described the least-squares criterion and established that the arithmetic mean is the measure of data location that satisfies this criterion. Now refer to Formula (*4.5*) and note that the variance is in fact a type of arithmetic mean, in that it is the sum of squared deviations divided by the number of such values. From this standpoint alone, the variance is thereby associated with the least-squares criterion. Note also that the sum of the squared deviations in the numerator of the variance formula is precisely the sum that is minimized when the arithmetic mean is used as the measure of location. Therefore, the variance and its square root, the standard deviation, have a close mathematical relationship with the mean, and both are used in statistical inference with sample data.

EXAMPLE 8.   Refer to Table 4.2, which is the worksheet that was used to calculate the standard deviation for the sales data in Example 3. Note that the sum of the squared deviations, 86.00, which is the numerator in the standard deviation formula, cannot be made lower by the choice of any other location measure with a value different from the population mean of 10.5.

4.9   USE OF THE STANDARD DEVIATION IN DATA DESCRIPTION

As established in the preceding section, the standard deviation is used in conjunction with a number of methods of statistical inference covered in later chapters of this book. A description of these methods is beyond the scope of the present chapter. However, aside from the uses of the standard deviation in inference, we can now briefly introduce a use of the standard deviation in data description. Consider a distribution of data values that is both symmetrical and mesokurtic (neither flat nor peaked). As will be more fully described in Chapter 7, the frequency curve for such a distribution is called a *normal curve*. For a set of values that is *normally distributed*, it is always true that approximately 68 percent of the values are included within one standard deviation of the mean and approximately 95 percent of the values are included within two standard deviation units of the mean. These observations are presented diagrammatically in Figs. 4-2(*a*) and (*b*), respectively. Thus, in addition to the mean and standard deviation both being associated with the least-squares criterion, they are also mutually used in analyses for normally distributed variables.

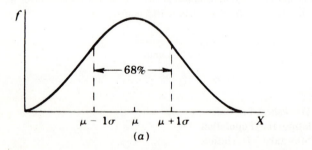

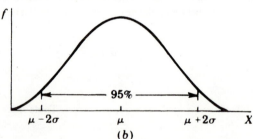

Fig. 4-2

EXAMPLE 9.   The electrical billings in a residential area for the month of June are observed to be normally distributed. If the mean of the billings is calculated to be $84.00 with a standard deviation of $24.00, then it follows that approximately 68 percent of the billed amounts are within $24.00 of the mean, or between $60.00 and $108.00. It also follows that approximately 95 percent of the billed amounts are within $48.00 of the mean, or between $36.00 and $132.00.

4.10   USE OF THE RANGE AND STANDARD DEVIATION IN
STATISTICAL PROCESS CONTROL

As introduced in Section 3.9, the sample mean is used in process control for averages by the construction of $\bar{X}$ charts. In addition to controlling process averages, there is at least an equal interest in controlling process variability. To monitor and control variability, either the ranges or the standard deviations of the rational subgroups that constitute the sequential samples (see Section 1.7) are determined. In either case, the values are plotted identically in form to the run chart for the sequence of sample mean weights in Fig. 2-11 (page 18). Such a chart for sample ranges is called an *R chart*, while the chart for sample standard deviations is called an *s chart*. The construction and use of such charts in process control is described in Chapter 19.

EXAMPLE 10.   Refer to Example 16 and the associated Fig. 2-11 in Chapter 2 (page 18). The run chart in Fig. 2-11 is concerned with monitoring the mean weight of the packages of potato chips. Suppose the values of the ranges for the 15 samples of $n = 4$ packages of potato chips are: 0.36, 0.11, 0.20, 0.13, 0.10, 0.15, 0.20, 0.24, 0.31, 0.14, 0.33, 0.13, 0.11, 0.15, and 0.27 oz. That is, in the first sample of four packages there was a difference of 0.36 oz between the weights of the two packages with the highest and lowest weights, and so forth for the other 14 samples. Figure 4-3 is the run chart for these ranges. Whether any of the deviations of the sample ranges from the overall mean average of all the ranges can be considered as being a meaningful deviation is considered further in Chapter 19.

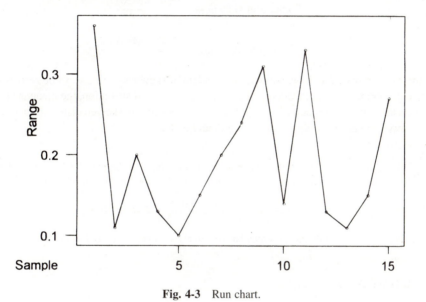

Fig. 4-3   Run chart.

From the standpoint of using the measure of variability that is most stable, the least-squares oriented *s* chart is preferred. Historically, the range has been used most frequently for monitoring process variability because it can be easily determined with little calculation. However, availability of more sophisticated weighing devices that are programmed to calculate both the sample mean and standard deviation has resulted in greater use of *s* charts.

4.11   THE COEFFICIENT OF VARIATION

The *coefficient of variation, CV,* indicates the relative magnitude of the standard deviation as compared with the mean of the distribution of measurements, as a percentage. Thus, the formulas are

Population:
$$CV = \frac{\sigma}{\mu} \times 100 \qquad (4.13)$$

Sample:
$$CV = \frac{s}{\bar{X}} \times 100 \qquad (4.14)$$

The coefficient of variation is useful when we wish to compare the variability of two data sets relative to the general level of values (and thus relative to the mean) in each set.

EXAMPLE 11. For two common stock issues in the electronics industry, the daily mean closing market price during a one-month period for stock A was \$150 with a standard deviation of \$5. For stock B, the mean price was \$50 with a standard deviation of \$3. On an absolute comparison basis, the variability in the price of stock A was greater, because of the larger standard deviation. But relative to the price level, the respective coefficients of variation should be compared:

$$CV(A) = \frac{\sigma}{\mu} \times 100 = \frac{5}{150} \times 100 = 3.3\% \quad \text{and} \quad CV(B) = \frac{\sigma}{\mu} \times 100 = \frac{3}{50} \times 100 = 6.0\%$$

Therefore, relative to the average price level for each stock issue, we can conclude that stock B has been almost twice as variable in price as stock A.

4.12   PEARSON'S COEFFICIENT OF SKEWNESS

Pearson's *coefficient of skewness* measures the departure from symmetry by expressing the difference between the mean and the median relative to the standard deviation of the group of measurements. The formulas are

$$\text{Population skewness} = \frac{3(\mu - \text{Med})}{\sigma} \tag{4.15}$$

$$\text{Sample skewness} = \frac{3(\bar{X} - \text{Med})}{s} \tag{4.16}$$

For a symmetrical distribution the value of the coefficient of skewness will always be zero, because the mean and median are equal to one another in value. For a positively skewed distribution, the mean is always larger than the median; hence, the value of the coefficient is positive. For a negatively skewed distribution, the mean is always smaller than the median; hence, the value of the coefficient is negative.

EXAMPLE 12. For the air-conditioning sales data presented in Example 2, the mean is 10.5 units, the medium is 11.0 units (from Section 3.2 and 3.4), and the standard deviation is 3.3 units. The coefficient of skewness is

$$\text{Skewness} = \frac{3(\mu - \text{Med})}{\sigma} = \frac{3(10.5 - 11.0)}{3.3} = -0.45$$

Thus the distribution of sales amounts is somewhat negatively skewed, or skewed to the left.

4.13   USING EXCEL AND MINITAB

Solved Problem 4.17 presents a set of measures of location and variability using Excel, while Problem 4.18 presents output from Minitab.

Solved Problems

THE RANGES, MEAN ABSOLUTE DEVIATION, AND STANDARD DEVIATION

4.1.   For a sample of 15 students at an elementary school snack bar, the following sales amounts, arranged in ascending order of magnitude, are observed: \$0.10, 0.10, 0.25, 0.25, 0.25, 0.35, 0.40, 0.53, 0.90, 1.25, 1.35, 2.45, 2.71, 3.09, 4.10. Determine the (*a*) range and (*b*) interquartile range for these sample data.

(*a*) $R = H - L = \$4.10 - 0.10 = \$4.00$

(*b*) $IQR = Q_3 - Q_1 = 2.175 - 0.25 = 1.925 \cong \$1.92$
where $Q_3 = X_{[(75n/100)+(1/2)]} = X_{(1.25+0.50)} = X_{11.75} = 1.35 + 0.825 = \$2.175$
(*Note*:   This is the interpolated value *three-fourths* of the distance between the 11th and 12th ordered sales amounts.)
and $Q_1 = X_{[(25n/100)+(1/2)]} = X_{(3.75+0.50)} = X_{4.25} = \$0.25$

4.2. Compute the mean absolute deviation for the data in Problem 4.1. The sample mean for this group of values was determined to be $1.21 in Problem 3.1.

Using Table 4.4, the mean absolute deviation is calculated as follows:

$$MAD = \frac{\Sigma |X - \bar{X}|}{n} = \frac{\$15.45}{15} = \$1.03$$

Table 4.4 Worksheet for Calculating the Mean Absolute Deviation for the Snack Bar Data

X	$X - \bar{X}$	$|X - \bar{X}|$
$0.10	$-1.11	$1.11
0.10	-1.11	1.11
0.25	-0.96	0.96
0.25	-0.96	0.96
0.25	-0.96	0.96
0.35	-0.86	0.86
0.40	-0.81	0.81
0.53	-0.68	0.68
0.90	-0.31	0.31
1.25	0.04	0.04
1.35	0.14	0.14
2.45	1.24	1.24
2.71	1.50	1.50
3.09	1.88	1.88
4.10	2.89	2.89
	Total	$15.45

4.3. Determine the sample standard deviation for the data in Problems 4.1 and 4.2 by using (*a*) the deviations formula and (*b*) the alternative computational formula, and demonstrate that the answers are equivalent.

Table 4.5 Worksheet for Calculating the Sample Standard Deviation for the Snack Bar Data

X	$X - \bar{X}$	$(X - \bar{X})^2$	X^2
$0.10	$-1.11	1.2321	0.0100
0.10	-1.11	1.2321	0.0100
0.25	-0.96	0.9216	0.0625
0.25	-0.96	0.9216	0.0625
0.25	-0.96	0.9216	0.0625
0.35	-0.86	0.7396	0.1225
0.40	-0.81	0.6561	0.1600
0.53	-0.68	0.4624	0.2809
0.90	-0.31	0.0961	0.8100
1.25	0.04	0.0016	1.5625
1.35	0.14	0.0196	1.8225
2.45	1.24	1.5376	6.0025
2.71	1.50	2.2500	7.3441
3.09	1.88	3.5344	9.5481
4.10	2.89	8.3521	16.8100
	Total	22.8785	Total 44.6706

From Table 4.5,

(a) $s = \sqrt{\dfrac{\Sigma(X - \bar{X})^2}{n - 1}} = \sqrt{\dfrac{22.8785}{15 - 1}} = \sqrt{1.6342} \cong \$1.28$

(b) $s = \sqrt{\dfrac{\Sigma X^2 - n\bar{X}^2}{n - 1}} = \sqrt{\dfrac{44.6706 - 15(1.21)^2}{15 - 1}} = \sqrt{1.6221} \cong \$1.27$

The answers are slightly different because of rounding error associated with the fact that the sample mean was rounded to two places.

4.4.   A sample of 20 production workers in a small company earned the following wages for a given week, rounded to the nearest dollar and arranged in ascending order: \$240, 240, 240, 240, 240, 240, 240, 240, 255, 255, 265, 265, 280, 280, 290, 300, 305, 325, 330, 340. Determine the (a) range and (b) middle 80 percent range for this sample.

(a) $R = H - L = \$340 - \$240 = \$100$

(b)   Middle 80% $R = P_{90} - P_{10} = \$327.50 - \$240.00 = \$87.50$
      where $P_{90} = X_{[(90n/100) + (1/2)]} = X_{[18 + (1/2)]} = X_{18.5} = \$325 + \$2.50 = \$327.50$
      $P_{10} = X_{[(10n/100) + (1/2)]} = X_{[2 + (1/2)]} = X_{2.5} = \$240.00$

4.5.   Compute the mean absolute deviation for the wages in Problem 4.4. The sample mean for these wages was determined to be \$270.50 in Problem 3.5.

From Table 4.6, the average deviation is

$$MAD = \frac{\Sigma|X - \bar{X}|}{n} = \frac{\$572.00}{20} = \$28.60$$

Table 4.6   Worksheet for Calculating the Mean
Absolute Deviation for the Wage Data

X	$X - \bar{X}$	$|X - \bar{X}|$
\$240	\$ $-$ 30.50	\$30.50
240	$-$ 30.50	30.50
240	$-$ 30.50	30.50
240	$-$ 30.50	30.50
240	$-$ 30.50	30.50
240	$-$ 30.50	30.50
240	$-$ 30.50	30.50
240	$-$ 30.50	30.50
255	$-$ 15.50	15.50
255	$-$ 15.50	15.50
265	$-$ 5.50	5.50
265	$-$ 5.50	5.50
280	9.50	9.50
280	9.50	9.50
290	19.50	19.50
300	29.50	29.50
305	34.50	34.50
325	54.50	54.50
330	59.50	59.50
340	69.50	69.50
	Total	\$572.00

4.6. Determine the (*a*) sample variance and (*b*) sample standard deviation for the data in Problems 4.4 and 4.5, using the deviations formulas.

With reference to Table 4.7,

(*a*) $s^2 = \dfrac{\Sigma(X - \bar{X})^2}{n - 1} = \dfrac{21,945.00}{20 - 1} = 1,155.00$

(*b*) $s = \sqrt{\dfrac{\Sigma(X - \bar{X})^2}{n - 1}} = \sqrt{1,155.00} \cong \$33.99$

Table 4.7 Worksheet for Calculating the Sample Variance and Standard Deviation for the Wage Data

X	$X - \bar{X}$	$(X - \bar{X})^2$
$240	$-30.50	$930.25
240	-30.50	930.25
240	-30.50	930.25
240	-30.50	930.25
240	-30.50	930.25
240	-30.50	930.25
240	-30.50	930.25
240	-30.50	930.25
255	-15.50	240.25
255	-15.50	240.25
265	-5.50	30.25
265	-5.50	30.25
280	9.50	90.25
280	9.50	90.25
290	19.50	380.25
300	29.50	870.25
305	34.50	1,190.25
325	56.50	2,970.25
330	59.50	3,540.25
340	69.50	4,830.25
	Total	$21,945.00

4.7. A work-standards expert observes the amount of time required to prepare a sample of 10 business letters in an office with the following results listed in ascending order to the nearest minute: 5, 5, 5, 7, 9, 14, 15, 15, 16, 18. Determine the (*a*) range and (*b*) middle 70 percent for the sample.

(*a*) $R = H - L = 18 - 5 = 13\,\text{min}$

(*b*) Middle 70% $R = P_{85} - P_{15} = 16.0 - 5.0 = 11.0\,\text{min}$
   where $P_{85} = X_{[(85n/100)+(1/2)]} = X_{(8.5+0.5)} = X_9 = 16.0\,\text{min}$
   $P_{15} = X_{[(15n/100)+(1/2)]} = X_{(1.5+0.5)} = X_2 = 5.0\,\text{min}$

4.8. Compute the mean absolute deviation for the preparation time in Problem 4.7. The sample mean was determined to be 10.9 min in Problem 3.9.

Table 4.8 Worksheet for Calculating the Mean Absolute Deviation for the Preparation-Time Data

X	$X - \bar{X}$	$\lvert X - \bar{X} \rvert$
5	-5.9	5.9
5	-5.9	5.9
5	-5.9	5.9
7	-3.9	3.9
9	-1.9	1.9
14	3.1	3.1
15	4.1	4.1
15	4.1	4.1
16	5.1	5.1
18	7.1	7.1
	Total	47.0

From Table 4.8,

$$MAD = \frac{\Sigma \lvert X - \bar{X} \rvert}{n} = \frac{47.0}{10} = 4.7 \, \text{min}$$

4.9   Determine the (*a*) sample variance and (*b*) sample standard deviation for the preparation-time data in Problems 4.7 and 4.8, using the alternative computational formulas.

With reference to Table 4.9,

(*a*) $s^2 = \dfrac{\Sigma X^2 - n\bar{X}^2}{n-1} = \dfrac{1{,}431 - 10\,(10.9)^2}{10-1} = 26.99$

(*b*) $s = \sqrt{\dfrac{\Sigma X^2 - n\bar{X}^2}{n-1}} = \sqrt{26.99} \cong 5.2 \, \text{min}$

Table 4.9 Worksheet for Calculating the Sample Variance and Standard Deviation for the Preparation-Time Data

X	X^2
5	25
5	25
5	25
7	49
9	81
14	196
15	225
15	225
16	256
18	324
Total	1,431

USE OF THE STANDARD DEVIATION

4.10. Many national academic achievement and aptitude tests, such as the SAT, report standardized test scores with the mean for the normative group used to establish scoring standards converted to 500 with a standard deviation of 100. Suppose that the distribution of scores for such a test is known to be approximately normally distributed. Determine the approximate percentage of reported scores that would be between (*a*) 400 and 600 and (*b*) between 500 and 700.

    (*a*)   68% (since these limits are within one standard deviation of the mean)

    (*b*)   47.5% (i.e., one-half of the middle 95 percent)

4.11. Referring to the standardized achievement test in Problem 4.10, what are the percentile values that would be reported for scores of (*a*) 400, (*b*) 500, (*c*) 600, and (*d*) 700?

    (*a*)   16 (Since 68 percent of the scores are between 400 and 600, one-half of the remaining 32 percent, or 16 percent, would be below 400, while the other 16 percent would be above 600.)

    (*b*)   50 (Since the mean for a normally distributed variable is at the 50th percentile point of the distribution.)

    (*c*)   84 (As explained in (*a*), above, since 16 percent are above a score of 600, this leaves 84 percent at or below a score of 600.)

    (*d*)   97.5 (Because 95 percent of the scores are between 300 and 700, and one-half of 5 percent, or 2.5 percent, are below 300, the total percentage at or below 700 is 97.5 percent.)

THE COEFFICIENT OF VARIATION

4.12. Determine the coefficient of variation for the wage data analyzed in Problems 4.4 to 4.6.

    Since $\bar{X} = \$270.50$ and $s = \$33.99$,

$$CV = \frac{s}{\bar{X}} \times 100 = \frac{33.99}{270.50} \times 100 = 12.6\%$$

4.13. For the same industrial firm as in Problem 4.12, above, the mean weekly salary for a sample of supervisory employees is $\bar{X} = \$730.75$, with $s = \$45.52$. Determine the coefficient of variation for these salary amounts.

$$CV = \frac{s}{\bar{X}} \times 100 = \frac{45.52}{730.75} \times 100 = 6.2\%$$

4.14. Compare the variability of the production workers' wages in Problem 4.12 with the supervisory salaries in Problem 4.13 (*a*) on an absolute basis and (*b*) relative to the mean level of weekly income for the two groups of employees.

    (*a*)   On an absolute basis, there is more variability among the supervisors' salaries ($s = \$45.52$) than there is among the production workers' weekly wages ($s = \$33.99$).

    (*b*)   On a basis relative to the respective means, the two coefficients of variation are compared. Referring to the solutions to Problems 4.12 and 4.13, we can observe that the coefficient of variation for the hourly wage data (0.126) is about twice as large as the respective coefficient for the weekly salaries (0.062), thereby indicating greater *relative* variability for the wage data.

PEARSON'S COEFFICIENT OF SKEWNESS

4.15. Compute the coefficient of skewness for the snack-bar data that were analyzed in Problems 4.1 to 4.3.

Since $\bar{X} = \$1.21$, Med $= \$0.53$ (from Problem 3.1), and $s = \$1.27$,

$$\text{Skewness} = \frac{3(\bar{X} - \text{Med})}{s} = \frac{3(1.21 - 0.53)}{1.27} = 1.61$$

Therefore the distribution of sales amounts is positively skewed, or skewed to the right.

4.16. Compute the coefficient of skewness for the wage data analyzed in Problems 4.4 to 4.6.

Since $\bar{X} = \$270.50$, Med $= \$260.00$ (from Problem 3.5), and $s = \$33.99$,

$$\text{Skewness} = \frac{3(\bar{X} - \text{Med})}{s} = \frac{3(270.50 - 260.00)}{33.99} = 0.93$$

Therefore the distribution of the wage amounts is slightly positively skewed.

USING EXCEL AND MINITAB

4.17. Use Excel to determine the range, standard deviation, and variance for the data in Table 2.7 (page 22), for the time required to complete an assembly task by a sample of 30 employees. In Problem 3.17 we determined the values of the mean and median for these data by the use of Excel.

Figure 4-4 presents the output of descriptive statistics for these data, which is the same output as obtained in the solution for Problem 3.17. As can be observed, the value of the range is 9 min (which is the difference between the maximum value of 18 and the minimum of 9 min that are reported), the standard deviation is 2.437494, or more simply, 2.4 min, and the variance is 5.941379, or more simply, 5.9. As always, the variance is the squared value of the standard deviation, and thus is expressed in *squared* units. Note that in Excel, as is true for most software, it is the *sample standard deviation* that is reported in the standard output. The reason for this is that this measure of variability typically is used in conjunction with *statistical inference*, rather than simply statistical description. Therefore, the data that are analyzed are usually *sample* data taken from some defined population.

The Excel instructions that result in the output presented in Fig. 4-4 are

(1) Open Excel. In cell A1 enter the column label: Assy. Times, min. Enter the data values in column A beginning at cell A2.

(2) Click **Tools** → **Data Analysis** → **Descriptive Statistics**. Click **OK**.

(3) Designate the **Input Range** as: $$A$1:$A$31.

(4) Select **Labels in First Row**.

(5) Select **Summary Statistics**. Click **OK**.

Assy. Times, min.	
Mean	13.3
Standard Error	0.445024
Median	13.5
Mode	14
Standard Deviation	2.437494
Sample Variance	5.941379
Kurtosis	-0.81237
Skewness	-0.00735
Range	9
Minimum	9
Maximum	18
Sum	399
Count	30

Fig. 4-4   Excel output.

4.18. Use Minitab to determine the range, standard deviation, and variance for the data in Table 2.7 (page 22), for the time required to complete an assembly task by a sample of 30 employees. In Problem 3.18 we determined the values of the mean and median for these data by the use of Minitab.

Figure 4-5 presents the output of descriptive statistics for these data, which is the same output as obtained in the solution for Problem 3.18. The value of the range is determined by subtracting the lowest reported value in the sample from the highest reported value: R = MAX − MIN = 18.000 − 9.000 = 9 minutes. The standard deviation is 2.437, or more simply, 2.4 minutes. The variance is the squared value $(2.437)^2 = 5.939$, or more simply, 5.9. As always, because the variance is the squared value of the standard deviation, it is expressed in *squared* units. Note that in Minitab, as is true for most software, it is the *sample standard deviation* that is reported in the standard output. The reason for this is that this measure of variability typically is used in conjunction with *statistical inference*, rather than simply statistical description. Therefore, the data that are analyzed are usually *sample* data taken from some defined population.

The Minitab instructions that result in the output presented in Fig. 4-5 are

(1)   Open Minitab. In the column-name cell for column C1 enter: Assy. Times, min. Then enter the sample data in column C1.

(2)   Click **Stat** → **Basic Statistics** → **Display Descriptive Statistics**.

(3)   For **Variables** enter: C1.

(4)   Click **OK**.

Descriptive Statistics: Assy. Times, min.

Variable	N	Mean	Median	TrMean	StDev	SE Mean
Assy. Ti	30	13.300	13.500	13.308	2.437	0.445

Variable	Minimum	Maximum	Q1	Q3
Assy. Ti	9.000	18.000	11.000	15.000

Fig. 4-5   Minitab output.

Supplementary Problems

THE RANGES, MEAN ABSOLUTE DEVIATION, AND STANDARD DEVIATION

4.19. The number of cars sold by each of the 10 salespeople in an automobile dealership during a particular month, arranged in ascending order, is: 2, 4, 7, 10, 10, 10, 12, 12 14, 15. Determine the (*a*) range, (*b*) interquartile range, and (*c*) middle 80 percent range for these data.
Ans.   (*a*) 13, (*b*) 5.0, (*c*) 11.5

4.20. Compute the mean absolute deviation for the sales data in Problem 4.19. The population mean for these values was determined to be 9.6 in Problem 3.19.
Ans. $3.16 \cong 3.2$

4.21. From Problem 4.19, determine the standard deviation by using the deviation formula and considering the group of values as constituting a statistical population.
Ans. $3.955 \cong 4.0$

4.22. The weights of a sample of outgoing packages in a mailroom, weighed to the nearest ounce, are found to be: 21, 18, 30, 12, 14, 17, 28, 10, 16, 25 oz. Determine the (*a*) range and (*b*) interquartile range for these weights.
Ans.   (*a*) 20.0, (*b*) 11.0

4.23. Compute the mean absolute deviation for the sampled packages in Problem 4.22. The sample mean was determined to be 19.1 oz in Problem 3.22.
   Ans. $5.52 \cong 5.5$

4.24. Determine the (*a*) sample variance and (*b*) sample standard deviation for the data in Problem 4.22, by use of the computational version of the respective formulas.
   Ans.   (*a*) 45.7, (*b*) 6.8

4.25. The following examination scores, arranged in ascending order, were achieved by 20 students enrolled in a decision analysis course: 39, 46, 57, 65, 70, 72, 72, 75, 77, 79, 81, 81, 84, 84, 84, 87, 93, 94, 97, 97. Determine the (*a*) range and (*b*) middle 90 percent range for these data.
   Ans.   (*a*) 58.0, (*b*) 54.5

4.26. Compute the mean absolute deviation for the examination scores in Problem 4.25. The mean examination score was determined to be 76.7 in Problem 3.26.
   Ans. $11.76 \cong 11.8$

4.27. Considering the examination scores in Problem 4.25 to be a statistical population, determine the standard deviation by use of (*a*) the deviations formula and (*b*) the alternative computational formula.
   Ans.   (*a*) $15.294 \cong 15.3$, (*b*) $15.294 \cong 15.3$

4.28. The number of accidents which occurred during a given month in the 13 manufacturing departments of an industrial plant was: 2, 0, 0, 3, 3, 12, 1, 0, 8, 1, 0, 5, 1. Determine the (*a*) range and (*b*) interquartile range for the number of accidents.
   Ans.   (*a*) 12.0, (*b*) 3.5

4.29. Compute the mean absolute deviation for the data in Problem 4.28. The mean number of accidents was determined to be 2.8 in Problem 3.28.
   Ans. $2.646 \cong 2.6$

4.30. Considering the accident data in Problem 4.28 to be a statistical population, compute the standard deviation by using the alternative computational formula.
   Ans. $3.465 \cong 3.5$

USE OF THE STANDARD DEVIATION

4.31. Packages of a certain brand of cereal are known to be normally distributed, with a mean weight of 13.0 oz and a standard deviation of 0.1 oz, with the weights being normally distributed. Determine the approximate percentage of packages that would have weights between (*a*) 12.9 and 13.1 oz and (*b*) 12.9 and 13.2 oz.
   Ans.   (*a*) 68%, (*b*) 81.5%

4.32. Refer to the distribution of cereal weights in Problem 4.31. What percentile values correspond to weights of (*a*) 13.0, (*b*) 13.1, and (*c*) 13,2 oz?
   Ans.   (*a*) 50, (*b*) 84, (*c*) 97.5

THE COEFFICIENT OF VARIATION

4.33. Determine the coefficient of variation for the car-sales data analyzed in Problems 4.19 through 4.21.
   Ans. $CV = 41.7\%$

4.34. Refer to Problem 4.33. In another (larger) dealership, the mean number of cars sold per salesperson during a particular month was $\mu = 17.6$, with a standard deviation of $\sigma = 6.5$. Compare the variability of car sales per salesperson (*a*) on an absolute basis and (*b*) relative to the mean level of car sales at the two dealerships.

Ans.   (*a*) The standard deviation in the first dealership (4.0) is smaller than the standard deviation in the second dealership (6.5). (*b*) The coefficient of variation in the first dealership (41.7%) is larger than the coefficient of variation in the second dealership (36.9%).

PEARSON'S COEFFICIENT OF SKEWNESS

4.35.   Compute the coefficient of skewness for the car-sales data analyzed in Problems 4.19 through 4.21. The median for these data was determined to be 10.0 in Problem 3.19.
    Ans.   Skewness $= -0.30$ (Thus, the distribution of car sales is slightly negatively skewed, or skewed to the left.)

4.36.   Compute the coefficient of skewness for the accident data analyzed in Problems 4.28 through 4.30. The median for these data was determined to be 1.0 in Problem 3.28.
    Ans.   Skewness $= 1.54$ (Thus, the distribution of accidents is positively skewed.)

COMPUTER OUTPUT

4.37.   Use computer software to determine the (*a*) mean, (*b*) median, (*c*) range, (*d*) interquartile range, and (*e*) standard deviation for the sample of 40 loan amounts in Table 2.19 (page 41).
    Ans.   (*a*) $1,097; (*b*) $945; (*c*) $2,700; (*d*) $897; (*e*) $642

Probability

CHAPTER 5

5.1 BASIC DEFINITIONS OF PROBABILITY

Historically, three different conceptual approaches have been developed for defining probability and for determining probability values: the classical, relative frequency, and subjective approaches.

By the *classical approach* to probability, if $N(A)$ possible elementary outcomes are favorable to event A, $N(S)$ possible outcomes are included in the sample space, and all the elementary outcomes are equally likely and mutually exclusive, then the probability that event A will occur is

$$P(A) = \frac{N(A)}{N(S)} \tag{5.1}$$

Note that the classical approach to probability is based on the assumption that each outcome is equally likely. Because this approach (when it is applicable) permits determination of probability values before any sample events are observed, it has also been called *a priori approach*.

EXAMPLE 1. In a well-shuffled deck of cards which contains 4 aces and 48 other cards, the probability of an ace (A) being obtained on a single draw is

$$P(A) = \frac{N(A)}{N(S)} = \frac{4}{52} = \frac{1}{13}$$

By the *relative frequency approach*, the probability is determined on the basis of the proportion of times that a favorable outcome occurs in a number of observations or experiments. No prior assumption of equal likelihood is involved. Because determination of the probability values is based on observation and collection of data, this approach has also been called the *empirical approach*. The probability that event A will occur by the relative frequency approach is

$$P(A) = \frac{\text{no. of observations of } A}{\text{sample size}} = \frac{n(A)}{n} \tag{5.2}$$

EXAMPLE 2. Before including coverage for certain types of dental problems in health insurance policies for employed adults, an insurance company wishes to determine the probability of occurrence of such problems, so that the insurance rate can be set accordingly. Therefore, the statistician collects data for 10,000 adults in the appropriate age categories and finds that 100 people have experienced the particular dental problem during the past year. The probability of occurrence is thus

$$P(A) = \frac{n(A)}{n} = \frac{100}{10,000} = 0.01, \text{ or } 1\%$$

Both the classical and relative frequency approaches yield *objective* probability values, in the sense that the probability values indicate the relative rate of occurrence of the event in the long run. In contrast, the *subjective approach* to probability is particularly appropriate when there is only one opportunity for the event to occur, and it will either occur or not occur that one time. By the subjective approach, the probability of an event is the *degree of belief* by an individual that the event will occur, based on all evidence available to the individual. Because the probability value is a personal judgment, the subjective approach has also been called the *personalistic approach*. This approach to probability has been developed relatively recently, and is related to *decision analysis* (see Chapter 18).

EXAMPLE 3. Because of taxes and alternative uses for the funds, an investor has determined that the purchase of land parcels is worthwhile only if there is at least a probability of 0.90 that the land will appreciate in value by 50 percent or more during the next four years. In evaluating a certain parcel of land, the investor studies price changes in the area during recent years, considers present price levels, studies the current and likely future status of land development projects, and reviews the statistics concerned with the economic development of the overall geographic area. On the basis of this review the investor concludes that there is a probability of about 0.75 that the required appreciation in value will in fact occur. Because this probability value is less than the required minimum probability of 0.90, the investment should not be made.

5.2 EXPRESSING PROBABILITY

The symbol P is used to designate the probability of an event. Thus $P(A)$ denotes the probability that event A will occur in a single observation or experiment.

The smallest value that a probability statement can have is 0 (indicating the event is impossible) and the largest value it can have is 1 (indicating the event is certain to occur). Thus, in general:

$$0 \leq P(A) \leq 1 \tag{5.3}$$

In a given observation or experiment, an event must either occur or not occur. Therefore, the sum of the probability of occurrence plus the probability of nonoccurrence always equals 1. Thus, where A' indicates the nonoccurrence of event A, we have

$$P(A) + P(A') = 1 \tag{5.4}$$

A *Venn diagram* is a diagram related to set theory in mathematics by which the events that can occur in a particular observation or experiment can be portrayed. An enclosed figure represents a sample space, and portions of the area within the space are designated to represent particular elementary or composite events, or event spaces.

EXAMPLE 4. Figure 5-1 represents the probabilities of the two events, A and A' (read "not-A"). Because $P(A) + P(A') = 1$, all of the area within the diagram is accounted for.

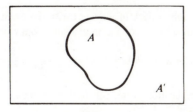

Fig. 5-1

As an alternative to probability values, probabilities can also be expressed in terms of *odds*. The odds ratio favoring the occurrence of an event is the ratio of the relative number of outcomes, designated by a, that are favorable to A, to the relative number of outcomes, designated by b, that are not favorable to A:

$$\text{Odds} = a : b \text{ (read "}a \text{ to } b\text{")} \tag{5.5}$$

Odds of $5:2$ (read "5 to 2") indicate that for every five elementary events constituting success there are two elementary events constituting failure. Note that by the classical approach to probability discussed in Section 5.1 the probability value equivalent to an odds ratio of $5:2$ is

$$P(A) = \frac{N(A)}{N(S)} = \frac{a}{a+b} = \frac{5}{5+2} = \frac{5}{7}$$

EXAMPLE 5. Suppose success is defined as drawing any face card *or* an ace from a well-shuffled deck of 52 cards. Because 16 cards out of 52 are either the jack, queen, king, or ace, the odds associated with success are $16:36$, or $4:9$. The probability of success is $16/(16+36) = 16/52 = 4/13$.

5.3   MUTUALLY EXCLUSIVE AND NONEXCLUSIVE EVENTS

Two or more events are *mutually exclusive*, or *disjoint*, if they cannot occur together. That is, the occurrence of one event automatically precludes the occurrence of the other event (or events). For instance, suppose we consider the two possible events "ace" and "king" with respect to a card being drawn from a deck of playing cards. These two events are mutually exclusive, because any given card cannot be both an ace and a king.

Two or more events are *nonexclusive* when it is possible for them to occur together. Note that this definition does *not* indicate that such events must necessarily always occur jointly. For instance, suppose we consider the two possible events "ace" and "spade." These events are not mutually exclusive, because a given card can be both an ace and a spade; however, it does not follow that every ace is a spade or every spade is an ace.

EXAMPLE 6. In a study of consumer behavior, an analyst classifies the people who enter a clothing store according to sex ("male" or "female") and according to age ("under 30" or "30 and over"). The two events, or classifications, "male" and "female" are mutually exclusive, since any given person would be classified in one category or the other. Similarly, the events "under 30" and "30 and over" are also mutually exclusive. However, the events "male" and "under 30" are not mutually exclusive, because a randomly chosen person could have both characteristics.

5.4   THE RULES OF ADDITION

The rules of addition are used when we wish to determine the probability of one event *or* another (or both) occurring in a single observation. Symbolically, we can represent the probability of event A or event B occurring by $P(A \text{ or } B)$. In the language of set theory this is called the *union* of A and B and the probability is designated by $P(A \cup B)$ (read "probability of A union B").

There are two variations of the rule of addition, depending on whether or not the two events are mutually exclusive. The rule of addition for mutually exclusive events is

$$P(A \text{ or } B) = P(A \cup B) = P(A) + P(B) \qquad (5.6)$$

EXAMPLE 7. When drawing a card from a deck of playing cards, the events "ace" (A) and "king" (K) are mutually exclusive. The probability of drawing either an ace or a king in a single draw is

$$P(A \text{ or } K) = P(A) + P(K) = \frac{4}{52} + \frac{4}{52} = \frac{8}{52} = \frac{2}{13}$$

(*Note*: Problem 5.4 extends the application of this rule to three events.)

For events that are *not* mutually exclusive, the probability of the joint occurrence of the two events is subtracted from the sum of the simple probabilities of the two events. We can represent the probability of joint occurrence by $P(A \text{ and } B)$. In the language of set theory this is called the *intersection* of A and B and the probability is designated by $P(A \cap B)$ (read "probability of A intersect B"). See Fig. 5-2(b) on the following page. Thus, the rule of addition for events that are not mutually exclusive is

$$P(A \text{ or } B) = P(A) + P(B) - P(A \text{ and } B) \qquad (5.7)$$

Formula (*5.7*) is also often called the *general rule of addition*, because for events that are mutually exclusive the last term would always be equal to zero, resulting in formula (*5.7*) then being equivalent to formula (*5.6*) for mutually exclusive events.

EXAMPLE 8.   When drawing a card from a deck of playing cards, the events "ace" and "spade" are not mutually exclusive. The probability of drawing an ace (*A*) or spade (*S*) (or both) in a single draw is

$$P(A \text{ or } S) = P(A) + P(S) - P(A \text{ and } S) = \frac{4}{52} + \frac{13}{52} - \frac{1}{52} = \frac{16}{52} = \frac{4}{13}$$

Venn diagrams can be used to portray the rationale underlying the two rules of addition. In Fig. 5-2(*a*), note that the probability of *A* or *B* occurring is conceptually equivalent to adding the proportion of area included in *A* and *B*. In Fig. 5-2(*b*), for events that are not mutually exclusive, some elementary events are included in *both A* and *B*; thus, there is overlap between these event sets. When the areas included in *A* and *B* are added together for events that are not mutually exclusive, the area of overlap is essentially added in twice. Thus, the rationale of subtracting *P(A and B)* in the rule of addition for nonexclusive events is to correct the sum for the duplicate addition of the intersect area.

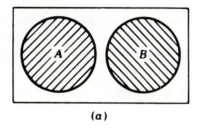
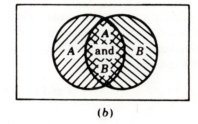

(*a*)   (*b*)

Fig. 5-2

5.5   INDEPENDENT EVENTS, DEPENDENT EVENTS, AND CONDITIONAL PROBABILITY

Two events are *independent* when the occurrence or nonoccurrence of one event has no effect on the probability of occurrence of the other event. Two events are *dependent* when the occurrence or nonoccurrence of one event *does* affect the probability of occurrence of the other event.

EXAMPLE 9.   The outcomes associated with tossing a fair coin twice in succession are considered to be independent events, because the outcome of the first toss has no effect on the respective probabilities of a head or tail occurring on the second toss. The drawing of two cards *without replacement* from a deck of playing cards are dependent events, because the probabilities associated with the second draw are dependent on the outcome of the first draw. Specifically, if an "ace" occurred on the first draw, then the probability of an "ace" occurring on the second draw is the ratio of the number of aces still remaining in the deck to the total number of cards remaining in the deck, or 3/51.

When two events are dependent, the concept of *conditional probability* is employed to designate the probability of occurrence of the related event. The expression *P(B|A)* indicates the probability of event *B* occurring *given* that event *A* has occurred. Note that *B|A* is *not* a fraction.

Conditional probability expressions are not required for independent events because by definition there is no relationship between the occurrence of such events. Therefore, if events *A* and *B* are independent, the conditional probability *P(B|A)* is always equal to the simple (unconditional) probability *P(B)*. Therefore, one approach by which the independence of two events *A* and *B* can be tested is by comparing

$$P(B|A) \stackrel{?}{=} P(B) \tag{5.8}$$

or
$$P(A|B) \stackrel{?}{=} P(A) \tag{5.9}$$

(See Problems 5.8 through 5.10.)

If the simple (unconditional) probability of a first event A and the joint probability of two events A and B are known, then the conditional probability $P(B|A)$ can be determined by

$$P(B|A) = \frac{P(A \text{ and } B)}{P(A)} \qquad\qquad (5.10)$$

(See Problems 5.8 through 5.10.)

There is often some confusion regarding the distinction between mutually exclusive and nonexclusive events on the one hand, and the concepts of independence and dependence on the other hand. Particularly, note the difference between events that are mutually exclusive and events that are independent. Mutual exclusiveness indicates that two events *cannot* both occur, whereas independence indicates that the probability of occurrence of one event is not affected by the occurrence of the other event. Therefore it follows that if two events are mutually exclusive, this is a particular example of highly *dependent* events, because the probability of one event given that the other has occurred would always be equal to zero. See Problem 5.10.

5.6   THE RULES OF MULTIPLICATION

The rules of multiplication are concerned with determining the probability of the joint occurrence of A and B. As explained in Section 5.4, this concerns the intersection of A and B: $P(A \cap B)$. There are two variations of the rule of multiplication, according to whether the two events are independent or dependent. The rule of multiplication for independent events is

$$P(A \text{ and } B) = P(A \cap B) = P(A)P(B) \qquad\qquad (5.11)$$

EXAMPLE 10.   By formula *(5.11)*, if a fair coin is tossed twice the probability that both outcomes will be "heads" is $(\frac{1}{2}) \times (\frac{1}{2}) = (\frac{1}{4})$.

(*Note*:   Problem 5.11 extends the application of this rule to three events.)

The tree diagram is particularly useful as a method of portraying the possible events associated with sequential observations, or sequential trials. Figure 5-3 is an example of such a diagram for the events associated with tossing a coin twice, and identifies the outcomes that are possible and the probability at each point in the sequence.

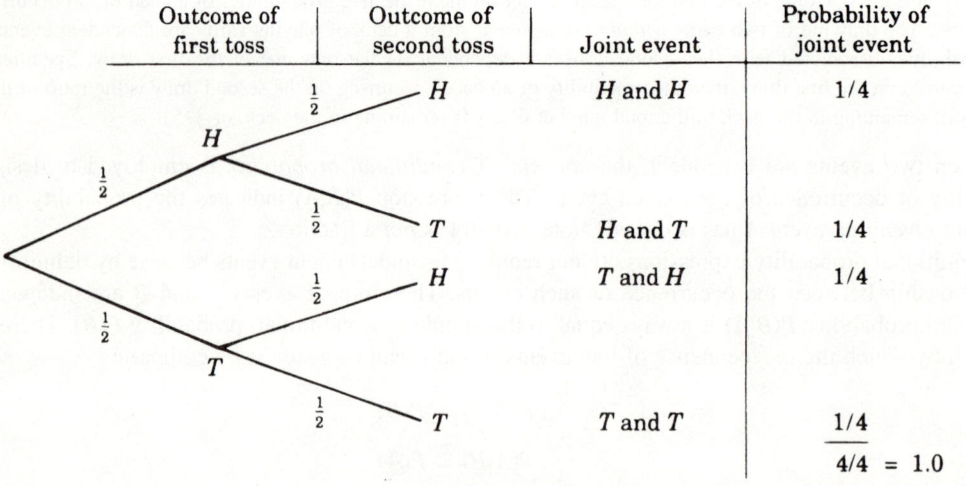

Outcome of first toss	Outcome of second toss	Joint event	Probability of joint event
H	H	H and H	1/4
	T	H and T	1/4
T	H	T and H	1/4
	T	T and T	1/4
			4/4 = 1.0

Fig. 5-3

EXAMPLE 11.   By reference to Fig. 5-3, we see that there are four types of sequences, or joint events, that are possible: H and H, H and T, T and H, and T and T. By the rule of multiplication for independent events, the probability of joint occurrences for any one of these sequences in this case is $1/4$, or 0.25. Since these are the only sequences which are possible, and since they are mutually exclusive sequences, by the rule of addition the sum of the four joint probabilities should be 1.0, which it is.

For dependent events the probability of the joint occurrence of A and B is the probability of A multiplied by the *conditional* probability of B given A. An equivalent value is obtained if the two events are reversed in position. Thus the rule of multiplication for dependent events is

$$P(A \text{ and } B) = P(A)P(B|A) \tag{5.12}$$

or
$$P(A \text{ and } B) = P(B \text{ and } A) = P(B)P(A|B) \tag{5.13}$$

Formula (*5.12*) [or (*5.13*)] is often called the *general rule of multiplication*, because for events that are independent the conditional probability $P(B|A)$ is always equal to the unconditional probability value $P(B)$, resulting in formula (*5.12*) then being equivalent to formula (*5.11*) for independent events.

EXAMPLE 12.   Suppose that a set of 10 spare parts is known to contain eight good parts (G) and two defective parts (D). Given that two parts are selected randomly without replacement, the sequence of possible outcomes and the probabilities are portrayed by the tree diagram in Fig. 5-4 (subscripts indicate sequential position of outcomes). Based on the multiplication rule for dependent events, the probability that the two parts selected are both good is

$$P(G_1 \text{ and } G_2) = P(G_1)P(G_2|G_1) = \left(\frac{8}{10}\right) \times \left(\frac{7}{9}\right) = \frac{56}{90} = \frac{28}{45}$$

[*Note*:   Problems 5.12(*b*) and 5.13 extend the application of this rule to three events.]

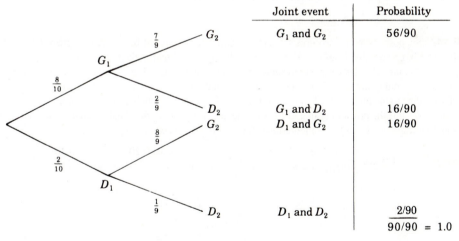

Fig. 5-4

If the probability of joint occurrence of two events is available directly without use of the multiplication rules as such, then as an alternative to formulas (*5.8*) and (*5.9*), the independence of two events A and B can be tested by comparing

$$P(A \text{ and } B) \stackrel{?}{=} P(A)P(B) \tag{5.14}$$

EXAMPLE 13. By our knowledge of a playing deck of 52 cards, we know that only one card is both an ace (A) and a spade (S), and thus that $P(A \text{ and } S) = 1/52$. We also know that the probability of drawing any ace is $4/52$ and the probability of drawing any spade is $13/52$. We thus can verify that the events "ace" and "spade" are independent events, as follows:

$$P(A \text{ and } S) \overset{?}{=} P(A)P(S)$$

$$\frac{1}{52} \overset{?}{=} \frac{4}{52} \times \frac{13}{52}$$

$$\frac{1}{52} = \frac{1}{52} \quad \text{(therefore the events } are \text{ independent)}$$

5.7 BAYES' THEOREM

In its simplest algebraic form, Bayes' theorem is concerned with determining the conditional probability of event A given that event B has occurred. The general form of Bayes' theorem is

$$P(A|B) = \frac{P(A \text{ and } B)}{P(B)} \tag{5.15}$$

Formula (5.15) is simply a particular application of the general formula for conditional probability presented in Section 5.5. However, the special importance of Bayes' theorem is that it is applied in the context of sequential events, and further, that the computational version of the formula provides the basis for determining the conditional probability of an event having occurred in the *first* sequential position given that a particular event has been observed in the *second* sequential position. The computational form of Bayes' theorem is

$$P(A|B) = \frac{P(A)P(B|A)}{P(A)P(B|A) + P(A')P(B|A')} \tag{5.16}$$

As illustrated in Problem 5.20(c), the denominator above is the overall (unconditional) probability of the event in the second sequential position; $P(B)$ for the formula above.

EXAMPLE 14. Suppose there are two urns U_1 and U_2. Urn 1 has eight red balls and two green balls, while urn 2 has four red balls and six green balls. If an urn is selected randomly, and a ball is then selected randomly from that urn, the sequential process and probabilities can be represented by the tree diagram in Fig. 5-5. The tree diagram indicates that the probability of choosing either urn is 0.50. and then the conditional probabilities of a red (R) or a green (G) ball being drawn are indicated according to the urn involved. Now, suppose we observe a green ball in Step 2 *without* knowing which urn was selected in Step 1. What is the probability that urn 1 was selected in Step 1? Symbolically, what is $P(U_1|G)$? Substituting U_1 and G for A and B, respectively, in the computational form of Bayes' theorem:

$$P(U_1|G) = \frac{P(U_1)P(G|U_1)}{P(U_1)P(G|U_1) + P(U_2)P(G|U_2)} = \frac{(0.50)(0.20)}{(0.50)(0.20) + (0.50)(0.60)} = \frac{0.10}{0.40} = 0.25$$

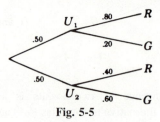

Fig. 5-5

In Example 14, note that Bayes' theorem presents the basis for obtaining what might be called a "backward conditional" probability value, since we can determine the probability that a particular urn was selected in Step 1 given the observation of a sampled item from that urn in Step 2.

5.8 JOINT PROBABILITY TABLES

A *joint probability table* is a table in which all possible events (or outcomes) for one variable are listed as row headings, all possible events for a second variable are listed as column headings, and the value entered in each cell of the table is the probability of each joint occurrence. Often, the probabilities in such a table are based on observed frequencies of occurrence for the various joint events, rather than being *a priori* in nature. The table of joint-occurrence frequencies which can serve as the basis for constructing a joint probability table is called a *contingency table*.

EXAMPLE 15.   Table 5.1(*a*) is a contingency table which describes 200 people who entered a clothing store according to sex and age, while Table 5.1(*b*) is the associated joint probability table. The frequency reported in each cell of the contingency table is converted into a probability value by dividing by the total number of observations, in this case, 200.

Table 5.1(a)   Contingency Table for Clothing Store Customers

	Sex		
Age	Male	Female	Total
Under 30	60	50	110
30 and over	80	10	90
Total	140	60	200

Table 5.1(b)   Joint Probability Table for Clothing Store Customers

	Sex		Marginal probability
Age	Male (*M*)	Female (*F*)	
Under 30 (*U*)	0.30	0.25	0.55
30 and over (*O*)	0.40	0.05	0.45
Marginal probability	0.70	0.30	1.00

In the context of joint probability tables, a *marginal probability* is so named because it is a marginal total of a row or a column. Whereas the probability values in the cells are probabilities of joint occurrence, the marginal probabilities are the unconditional, or simple, probabilities of particular events.

EXAMPLE 16.   The probability of 0.30 in row 1 and column 1 of Table 5.1(*b*) indicates that there is a probability of 0.30 that a randomly chosen person from this group of 200 people will be a male and under 30. The marginal probability of 0.70 for column 1 indicates that there is a probability of 0.70 that a randomly chosen person will be a male.

Recognizing that a joint probability table also includes all of the unconditional probability values as marginal totals, we can use formula (*5.10*) for determining any particular conditional probability value.

EXAMPLE 17.   Suppose we are interested in the probability that a randomly chosen person in Table 5.1(*b*) is "under 30" (*U*) given that he is a "male" (*M*). The probability, using formula (*5.10*), is

$$P(U|M) = \frac{P(M \text{ and } U)}{P(M)} = \frac{0.30}{0.70} = \frac{3}{7} \cong 0.43$$

5.9 PERMUTATIONS

By the classical approach to determining probabilities presented in Section 5.1, the probability value is based on the ratio of the number of equally likely elementary outcomes that are favorable to the total number of outcomes in the sample space. When the problems are simple, the number of elementary outcomes can be counted directly. However, for more complex problems the methods of permutations and combinations are required to determine the number of possible elementary outcomes.

The number of *permutations* of n objects is the number of ways in which the objects can be arranged in terms of order:

$$\text{Permutations of } n \text{ objects} = n! = (n) \times (n-1) \times \cdots \times (2) \times (1) \qquad (5.17)$$

The symbol $n!$ is read "n factorial." In permutations and combinations problems, n is always positive. Also, note that by definition $0! = 1$ in mathematics.

EXAMPLE 18. Three members of a social organization have volunteered to serve as officers for the following year, to take positions as President, Treasurer, and Secretary. The number of ways (permutations) in which the three can assume the positions is

$$n! = 3! = (3)(2)(1) = 6 \text{ ways}$$

This result can be portrayed by a sequential diagram. Suppose that the three people are designated as A, B, and C. The number of possible arrangements, or permutations, is presented in Fig. 5-6.

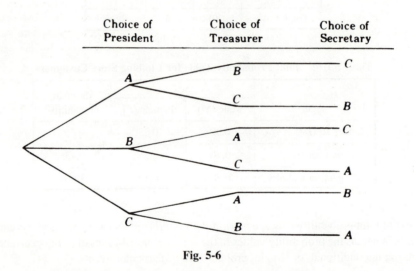

Fig. 5-6

Typically, we are concerned about the number of permutations of some *subgroup* of the n objects, rather than all n objects as such. That is, we are interested in the number of permutations of n objects taken r at a time, where r is less than n:

$$_nP_r = \frac{n!}{(n-r)!} \qquad (5.18)$$

EXAMPLE 19. In Example 18, suppose there are 10 members in the social organization and no nominations have yet been presented for the offices of President, Treasurer, and Secretary. The number of different arrangements of three officers elected from the 10 club members is

$$_nP_r = {_{10}P_3} = \frac{10!}{(10-3)!} = \frac{10!}{7!} = \frac{(10)(9)(8)(7!)}{7!} = (10)(9)(8) = 720$$

5.10 COMBINATIONS

In the case of permutations, the order in which the objects are arranged is important. In the case of *combinations*, we are concerned with the number of different groupings of objects that can occur *without* regard to their order. Therefore, an interest in combinations always concerns the number of different subgroups that can be taken from n objects. The number of combinations of n objects taken r at a time is

$$_nC_r = \frac{n!}{r!(n-r)!} \tag{5.19}$$

In many textbooks, the combination of n objects taken r at a time is represented by $\binom{n}{r}$. Note that this is *not* a fraction.

EXAMPLE 20. Suppose that three members from a small social organization containing a total of 10 members are to be chosen to form a committee. The number of different groups of three people which can be chosen, *without regard to the different orders in which each group might be chosen*, is

$$_nC_r = {_{10}C_3} = \frac{10!}{3!(10-3)!} = \frac{(10)(9)(8)(7!)}{3!(7!)} = \frac{(10)(9)(8)}{(3)(2)} = \frac{720}{6} = 120$$

As indicated in Section 5.9, the methods of permutations and combinations provide a basis for counting the possible outcomes in relatively complex situations. In terms of combinations, we can frequently determine the probability of an event by determining the number of combinations of outcomes which include that event as compared with the total number of combinations that are possible. Of course, this again represents the classical approach to probability and is based on the assumption that all combinations are equally likely.

EXAMPLE 21. Continuing with Example 20, if the group contains six women and four men, what is the probability that a random choice of the committee members will result in two women and one man being selected? The basic approach is to determine the number of combinations of outcomes that contain exactly two women (of the six women) and one man (of the four men) and then to take the ratio of this number to the total number of possible combinations:

Number of committees with $2W$ and $1M = {_6C_2} \times {_4C_1}$ (see explanatory note below)

$$= \frac{6!}{2!4!} \times \frac{4!}{1!3!} = 15 \times 4 = 60$$

Total number of possible combinations $= {_{10}C_3}$

$$= \frac{10!}{3!7!} = \frac{(10)(9)(8)}{(3)(2)(1)} = \frac{720}{6} = 120$$

$$P(2W \text{ and } 1M) = \frac{_6C_2 \times {_4C_1}}{_{10}C_3} = \frac{60}{120} = 0.50$$

Note: In Example 21, above, the so-called *method of multiplication* is used. In general, if one event can occur in n_1 ways and second event can occur in n_2 ways, then

Total number of ways two events can occur in combination $= n_1 \times n_2$ $\tag{5.20}$

The value of 60 in the solution in Example 21 is based on multiplying the number of ways that two women can be chosen from the six available women (15) by the number of ways that one man can be chosen from the four available men (4).

Solved Problems

DETERMINING PROBABILITY VALUES

5.1. For each of the following situations, indicate whether the classical, relative frequency, or subjective approach would be most useful for determining the required probability value.

(a) Probability that there will be a recession next year.

(b) Probability that a six-sided die will show either a 1 or 6 on a single toss.

(c) Probability that from a shipment of 20 parts known to contain one defective part, one randomly chosen part will turn out to be defective.

(d) Probability that a randomly chosen part taken from a large shipment of parts will turn out to be defective.

(e) Probability that a randomly chosen person who enters a large department store will make a purchase in that store.

(f) Probability that the Dow Jones Industrial Average will increase by at least 50 points during the next six months.

(a) Subjective, (b) classical, (c) classical, (d) relative frequency (Since there is no information about the overall proportion of the defective parts, the proportion of defective parts in a sample would be used as the basis for estimating the probability value.), (e) relative frequency, (f) subjective.

5.2. Determine the probability value applicable in each of the following situations.

(a) Probability of industrial injury in a particular industry on an annual basis. A random sample of 10 firms, employing a total of 8,000 people, reported that 400 industrial injuries occurred during a recent 12-month period.

(b) Probability of betting on a winning number in the game of roulette. The numbers on the wheel include a 0, 00, and 1 through 36.

(c) Probability that a fast-food franchise outlet will be financially successful. The prospective investor obtains data for other units in the franchise system, studies the development of the residential area in which the outlet is to be located, and considers the sales volume required for financial success based on the required capital investment and operational costs. Overall, it is the investor's judgment that there is an 80 percent chance that the outlet will be financially successful and a 20 percent chance that it will not.

(a) By the relative frequency approach, $P = 400/8,000 = 0.05$. Because this probability value is based on a sample, it is an estimate of the unknown true value. Also, the implicit assumption is made that safety standards have not changed since the 12-month sampled period.

(b) By the classical approach, $P = 1/38$. This value is based on the assumption that all numbers are equally likely, and therefore a well-balanced wheel is assumed.

(c) Based on the subjective approach, the value arrived at through the prospective investor's judgment is $P = 0.80$. Note that such a judgment should be based on knowledge of all available information within the scope of the time which is available to collect such information.

5.3. For each of the following reported odds ratios determine the equivalent probability value, and for each of the reported probability values determine the equivalent odds ratio.

(a) A puchasing agent estimates that the odds are $2:1$ that a shipment will arrive on schedule.

(b) The probability that a new component will not function properly when assembled is assessed as being $P = 1/5$.

(c) The odds that a new product will succeed are estimated as being $3:1$.

(d)   The probability that the home team will win the opening game of the season is assessed as being $1/3$.

(a)   The probability that the shipment will arrive on schedule is $P = 2/(2 + 1) = 2/3 \cong 0.67$.

(b)   The odds that it will not function properly are $1:4$.

(c)   The probability that the product will succeed is $P = 3/(3 + 1) = 3/4 = 0.75$.

(d)   The odds that the team will win are $1:2$.

APPLYING THE RULES OF ADDITION

5.4.   Determine the probability of obtaining an ace (A), king (K), or a deuce (D) when one card is drawn from a well-shuffled deck of 52 playing cards.

From formula (*5.6*),

$$P(A \text{ or } K \text{ or } D) = P(A) + P(K) + P(D) = \frac{4}{52} + \frac{4}{52} + \frac{4}{52} = \frac{12}{52} = \frac{3}{13}$$

(*Note*:   The events are mutually exclusive.)

5.5.   With reference to Table 5.2, what is the probability that a randomly chosen family will have household income (*a*) between \$20,000 and \$40,000, (*b*) less than \$40,000, (*c*) at one of the two extremes of being either less than \$20,000 or at least \$100,000?

Table 5.2   Annual Household Income for 500 Families

Category	Income range	Number of families
1	Less than \$20,000	60
2	\$20,000–\$40,000	100
3	\$40,000–\$60,000	160
4	\$60,000–\$100,000	140
5	\$100,000 and above	40
	Total	500

(a) $P(2) = \dfrac{100}{500} = \dfrac{1}{5} = 0.20$

(b) $P(1 \text{ or } 2) = \dfrac{60}{500} + \dfrac{100}{500} = \dfrac{160}{500} = \dfrac{8}{25} = 0.32$

(c) $P(1 \text{ or } 5) = \dfrac{60}{500} + \dfrac{40}{500} = \dfrac{100}{500} = \dfrac{1}{5} = 0.20$

(*Note*:   The events are mutually exclusive.)

5.6.   Of 300 business students, 100 are currently enrolled in accounting and 80 are currently enrolled in business statistics. These enrollment figures include 30 students who are in fact enrolled in both courses. What is the probability that a randomly chosen student will be enrolled in either accounting (A) or business statistics (B)?

From formula (*5.6*),

$$P(A \text{ or } B) = P(A) + P(B) - P(A \text{ and } B) = \frac{100}{300} + \frac{80}{300} - \frac{30}{300} = \frac{150}{300} = \frac{1}{2} = 0.50$$

(*Note*:   The events are not mutually exclusive.)

5.7. Of 100 individuals who applied for systems analyst positions with a large firm during the past year, 40 had some prior work experience (*W*), and 30 had a professional certificate (*C*). However, 20 of the applicants had both work experience and a certificate, and thus are included in both of the counts.

  (*a*) Construct a Venn diagram to portray these events.

  (*b*) What is the probability that a randomly chosen applicant had either work experience or a certificate (or both)?

  (*c*) What is the probability that a random chosen applicant had either work experience or a certificate *but not both*?

  (*a*) See Fig. 5-7.

  (*b*) $P(W \text{ or } C) = P(W) + P(C) - P(W \text{ and } C) = 0.40 + 0.30 - 0.20 = 0.50$
        (*Note*: The events are not mutually exclusive.)

  (*c*) $P(W \text{ or } C, \text{ but not both}) = P(W \text{ or } C) - P(W \text{ and } C) = 0.50 - 0.20 = 0.30$

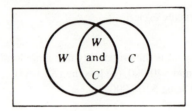

Fig. 5-7

INDEPENDENT EVENTS, DEPENDENT EVENTS, AND CONDITIONAL PROBABILITY

5.8. For Problem 5.7, (*a*) determine the conditional probability that a randomly chosen applicant has a certificate given that he has some previous work experience. (*b*) Apply an appropriate test to determine if work experience and certification are independent events.

  (*a*) $P(C|W) = \dfrac{P(C \text{ and } W)}{P(W)} = \dfrac{0.20}{0.40} = 0.50$

  (*b*) $P(C|W) \stackrel{?}{=} P(C)$. Since $0.50 \neq 0.30$, events *W* and *C* are dependent. Independence could also be tested by applying the multiplication rule for independent events—see Problem 5.14(*a*).

5.9. Two separate product divisions included in a large firm are Marine Products (*M*) and Office Equipment (*O*). The probability that the Marine Products division will have a profit margin of at least 10 percent this fiscal year is estimated to be 0.30, the probability that the Office Equipment division will have a profit margin of at least 10 percent is 0.20, and the probability that both divisions will have a profit margin of at least 10 percent is 0.06.

  (*a*) Determine the probability that the Office Equipment division will have at least a 10 percent profit margin given that the Marine Products division achieved this profit criterion.

  (*b*) Apply an appropriate test to determine if achievement of the profit goal in the two divisions is statistically independent.

  (*a*) $P(O|M) = \dfrac{P(O \text{ and } M)}{P(M)} = \dfrac{0.06}{0.30} = 0.20$

  (*b*) $P(O|M) \stackrel{?}{=} P(O)$. Since $0.20 = 0.20$, the two events are independent. [Independence could also be tested by applying the multiplication rule for independent events—see Problem 5.14(*b*).]

5.10. Suppose an optimist estimates that the probability of earning a final grade of A in the business statistics course is 0.60 and the probability of a B is 0.40. Of course, it is not possible to earn both grades as final grades, since they are mutually exclusive.

    (*a*)   Determine the conditional probability of earning a B given that, in fact, the final grade of A has been received, by use of the appropriate computational formula.

    (*b*)   Apply an appropriate test to demonstrate that such mutually exclusive events are dependent events.

    (*a*) $P(B|A) = \dfrac{P(B \text{ and } A)}{P(A)} = \dfrac{0}{0.60} = 0$

    (*b*) $P(B|A) \stackrel{?}{=} P(B)$. Since $0 \neq 0.40$, the events are dependent. See Section 5.5.

APPLYING THE RULES OF MULTIPLICATION

5.11. In general, the probability that a prospect will make a purchase after being contacted by a salesperson is $P = 0.40$. If a salesperson selects three prospects randomly from a file and makes contact with them, what is the probability that all three prospects will make a purchase?

    Since the actions of the prospects are assumed to be independent of one another, the rule of multiplication for independent events is applied.

$$P(\text{all three are purchasers}) = P(\text{first is a purchaser}) \times P(\text{second is a purchaser}) \times P(\text{third is a purchaser})$$
$$= (0.40) \times (0.40) \times (0.40) = 0.064$$

5.12. Of 12 accounts held in a file, four contain a procedural error in posting account balances.

    (*a*)   If an auditor randomly selects two of these accounts (without replacement), what is the probability that neither account will contain a procedural error? Construct a tree diagram to represent this sequential sampling process.

    (*b*)   If the auditor samples three accounts, what is the probability that none of the accounts includes the procedural error?

    (*a*)   In this example the events are dependent, because the outcome on the first sampled account affects the probabilities which apply to the second sampled account. Where E'_1 means no error in the first sampled account and E'_2 means no error in the second sampled account

$$P(E'_1 \text{ and } E'_2) = P(E'_1)P(E'_2|E'_1) = \frac{8}{12} \times \frac{7}{11} = \frac{56}{132} = \frac{14}{33} \cong 0.42$$

Note: In Fig. 5-8, E stands for an account with the procedural error, E' stands for an account with no procedural error, and the subscript indicates the sequential position of the sampled account.

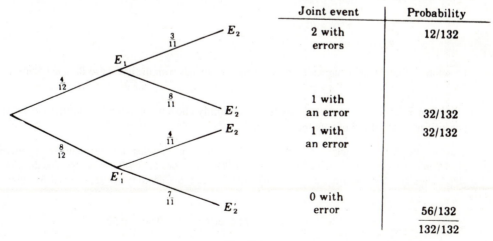

Joint event	Probability
2 with errors	12/132
1 with an error	32/132
1 with an error	32/132
0 with error	56/132
	132/132

Fig. 5-8

(b) $P(E_1' \text{ and } E_2' \text{ and } E_3') = P(E_1')P(E_2'|E_1')P(E_3'|P_1' \text{ and } E_2')$

$$= \frac{8}{12} \times \frac{7}{11} \times \frac{6}{10} = \frac{336}{1,320} = \frac{42}{165} \cong 0.25$$

5.13.   When sampling *without* replacement from a finite population, the probability values associated with various events are dependent on what events (sampled items) have already occurred. On the other hand, when sampling is done *with* replacement, the events are always independent.

(a)   Suppose that three cards are chosen randomly and without replacement from a playing deck of 52 cards. What is the probability that all three cards are aces?

(b)   Suppose that three cards are chosen randomly from a playing deck of 52 cards, but that after each selection the card is replaced and the deck is shuffled before the next selection of a card. What is the probability that all three cards are aces?

(a)   The rule of multiplication for dependent events applies in this case:

$$P(A_1 \text{ and } A_2 \text{ and } A_3) = P(A_1)P(A_2|A_1)P(A_3|A_1 \text{ and } A_2)$$

$$= \frac{4}{52} \times \frac{3}{51} \times \frac{2}{50} = \frac{24}{132,600} = \frac{1}{5,525} \cong 0.0002$$

(b)   The rule of multiplication for independent events applies in this case:

$$P(A_1 \text{ and } A_2 \text{ and } A_3) = P(A)P(A)P(A)$$

$$= \frac{4}{52} \times \frac{4}{52} \times \frac{4}{52} = \frac{64}{140,608} = \frac{1}{2,197} \cong 0.0005$$

5.14.   Test the independence (a) of the two events described in Problems 5.7 and 5.8, and (b) for the two events described in Problem 5.9, using the rule of multiplication for independent events.

(a) $P(W \text{ and } C) \overset{?}{=} P(W)P(C)$

$0.20 \overset{?}{=} (0.40) \times (0.30)$

$0.20 \neq 0.12$

Therefore, events W and C are dependent events. This corresponds with the answer to Problem 5.8(b).

(b) $P(M \text{ and } O) \overset{?}{=} P(M)P(O)$

$0.06 \overset{?}{=} (0.30) \times (0.20)$

$0.06 = 0.06$

Therefore, events M and O are independent. This corresponds with the answer to Problem 5.9(b).

5.15.   From Problem 5.7, what is the probability that a randomly chosen applicant has neither work experience nor a certificate? Are these events independent?

Symbolically, what is required is $P(W' \text{ and } C')$ for these events that are not mutually exclusive but are possibly dependent events. However, in this case neither $P(W'|C')$ nor $P(C'|W')$ is available, and therefore the rule of multiplication for dependent events cannot be used. Instead, the answer can be obtained by subtraction, as follows:

$$P(W' \text{ and } C') = 1 - P(W \text{ or } C) = 1 - 0.50 = 0.50$$

(The logic of this can most easily be understood by drawing a Venn diagram.)

We can now also demonstrate that the events are dependent rather than independent:

$$P(W' \text{ and } C') \overset{?}{=} P(W')P(C')$$

$$0.50 \overset{?}{=} [1 - P(W)][1 - P(C)]$$

$$0.50 \overset{?}{=} (0.60)(0.70)$$
$$0.50 \neq 0.42$$

The conclusion that the events are dependent coincides with the answer to Problem 5.14(*a*), which is directed to the complement of each of these two events.

5.16. Refer to Problem 5.11. (*a*) Construct a tree diagram to portray the sequence of three contacts, using *S* for sale and *S'* for no sale. (*b*) What is the probability that the salesperson will make *at least* two sales? (*c*) What is the probability that the salesperson will make *at least* one sale?

(*a*)   See Fig. 5-9.

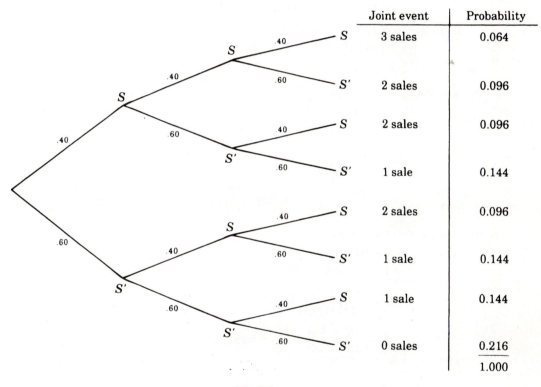

Fig. 5-9

(*b*)   "At least" two sales includes either two *or* three sales. Further, by reference to Fig. 5-9 we note that the two sales can occur in any of three different sequences. Therefore, we use the rule of multiplication for independent events to determine the probability of each sequence and the rule of addition to indicate that any of these sequences constitutes "success":

$$P(\text{at least 2 sales}) = P(S \text{ and } S \text{ and } S) + P(S \text{ and } S \text{ and } S')$$
$$+ P(S \text{ and } S' \text{ and } S) + P(S' \text{ and } S \text{ and } S)$$
$$= (0.064) + (0.096) + (0.096) + (0.096) = 0.352$$

(c)   Instead of following the approach in part (b), it is easier to obtain the answer to this question by subtraction:

$$P(\text{at least 1 sale}) = 1 - P(\text{no } S)$$
$$= 1 - P(S' \text{ and } S' \text{ and } S')$$
$$= 1 - 0.216 = 0.784$$

5.17.   In Problem 5.12 it was established that four of 12 accounts contain a procedural error.

(a)   If an auditor samples one account randomly, what is the probability that it will contain the error?

(b)   If an auditor samples two accounts randomly, what is the probability that at least one will contain the error?

(c)   If an auditor samples three accounts randomly, what is the probability that at least one will contain the error?

(a) $P(E) = \dfrac{\text{number of accts. with error}}{\text{total number of accts.}} = \dfrac{4}{12} = \dfrac{1}{3} \cong 0.33$

(b) $P(\text{at least one } E) = P(E_1 \text{ and } E_2) + P(E_1 \text{ and } E_2') + P(E_1' \text{ and } E_2)$
$$= P(E_1)P(E_2|E_1) + P(E_1)P(E_2'|E_1) + P(E_1')P(E2|E_1')$$
$$= \left(\frac{4}{12}\right)\left(\frac{3}{11}\right) + \left(\frac{4}{12}\right)\left(\frac{8}{11}\right) + \left(\frac{8}{12}\right)\left(\frac{4}{11}\right)$$
$$= \frac{12}{132} + \frac{32}{132} + \frac{32}{132} = \frac{76}{132} = \frac{19}{33} \cong 0.58$$

or

$$P(\text{at least one } E) = 1 - P(\text{no } E)$$
$$= 1 - P(E_1' \text{ and } E_2')$$
$$= 1 - P(E_1')P(E_2')P(E_2'|E_1')$$
$$= 1 - \left(\frac{8}{12}\right)\left(\frac{7}{11}\right)$$
$$= 1 - \frac{56}{132} = \frac{76}{132} = \frac{19}{33} \cong 0.58$$

(c) $P(\text{at least one } E) = 1 - P(\text{no } E)$
$$= 1 - P(E_1' \text{ and } E_2' \text{ and } E_3')$$
$$= 1 - P(E_1')P(E_2'|E_1')P(E_3'|E_1' \text{ and } E_2')$$
$$= 1 - \left(\frac{8}{12}\right)\left(\frac{7}{11}\right)\left(\frac{6}{10}\right)$$
$$= 1 - \frac{336}{1,320} = \frac{984}{1,320} = \frac{123}{165} \cong 0.75$$

BAYES' THEOREM

5.18.   Box A is known to contain one penny (P) and one dime (D), while box B contains two dimes. A box is chosen randomly and then a coin is randomly selected from the box. (a) Construct a tree diagram to portray this situation involving sequential events. (b) If box A is selected in the first step, what is the probability that a dime (D) will be selected in the second step? (c) If a dime (D) is selected in the second step, what is the probability that it came from box A? (d) If a penny (P) is selected in the second step, what is the probability that it came from box A?

(a)   See Fig. 5-10.

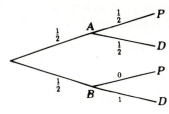

Fig. 5-10

(b) $P(D|A) = \frac{1}{2} = 0.50$

(c) $P(A|D) = \dfrac{P(A \text{ and } D)}{P(D)} = \dfrac{P(A)P(D|A)}{P(A)P(D|A) + P(B)P(D|B)}$

$$= \dfrac{(\frac{1}{2})(\frac{1}{2})}{(\frac{1}{2})(\frac{1}{2}) + (\frac{1}{2})(1)} = \dfrac{\frac{1}{4}}{\frac{1}{4} + \frac{1}{2}} = \dfrac{1}{3} \cong 0.33$$

(d) $P(A|P) = \dfrac{P(A \text{ and } P)}{P(P)} = \dfrac{P(A)P(P|A)}{P(A)P(P|A) + P(B)P(P|B)}$

$$= \dfrac{(\frac{1}{2})(\frac{1}{2})}{(\frac{1}{2})(\frac{1}{2}) + (\frac{1}{2})(0)} = \dfrac{\frac{1}{4}}{\frac{1}{4}} = 1$$

Thus, if a penny is obtained it must have come from box A.

5.19.   An analyst in a telecommunications firm estimates that the probability is 0.30 that a new company plans to offer competitive services within the next three years, and 0.70 that the firm does not. If the new firm has such plans, a new manufacturing facility would definitely be built. If the new firm does not have such plans, there is still a 60 percent chance that a new manufacturing facility would be built for other reasons.

(a)   Using T for the decision of the new firm to offer the telecommunications services and M for the addition of a new manufacturing facility, portray the possible events by means of a tree diagram.

(b)   Suppose we observe that the new firm has in fact begun work on a new manufacturing facility. Given this information, what is the probability that the firm has decided to offer competitive telecommunications services?

(a)   See Fig. 5-11.

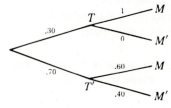

Fig. 5-11

(b) $P(T|M) = \dfrac{P(T \text{ and } M)}{P(M)} = \dfrac{P(T)P(M|T)}{P(T)P(M|T) + P(T')P(M|T')}$

$$= \dfrac{(0.30)(1)}{(0.30)(1) + (0.70)(0.60)} = \dfrac{0.30}{0.72} \cong 0.42$$

5.20. If there is an increase in capital investment next year, the probability that structural steel will increase in price is 0.90. If there is no increase in such investment, the probability of an increase is 0.40. Overall, we estimate that there is a 60 percent chance that capital investment will increase next year.

(*a*) Using *I* and *I'* for capital investment increasing and not increasing and using *R* and *R'* for a rise and nonrise in structural steel prices, construct a tree diagram for this situation involving dependent events.

(*b*) What is the probability that structural steel prices will not increase even though there is an increase in capital investment?

(*c*) What is the overall (unconditional) probability of an increase in structural steel prices next year?

(*d*) Suppose that during the next year structural steel prices in fact increase. What is the probability that there was an increase in capital investment?

(*a*) See Fig. 5-12.

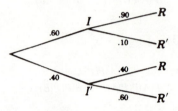

Fig. 5-12

(*b*) $P(R'|I) = 0.10$

(*c*) This is the denominator in Bayes' formula:

$$P(R) = P(I \text{ and } R) \quad \text{or} \quad P(I' \text{ and } R) = P(I)P(R|I) + P(I')P(R|I')$$
$$= (0.60)(0.90) + (0.40)(0.40) = 0.70$$

(*d*) By Bayes' formula:

$$P(I|R) = \frac{P(I \text{ and } R)}{P(R)} = \frac{P(I)P(R|I)}{P(I)P(R|I) + P(I')P(R|I')}$$

$$= \frac{(0.60)(0.90)}{(0.60)(0.90) + (0.40)(0.40)} = \frac{0.54}{0.70} \cong 0.77.$$

JOINT PROBABILITY TABLES

5.21. Table 5.3 is a contingency table which presents voter reactions to a new property tax plan according to party affiliation. (*a*) Prepare the joint probability table for these data. (*b*) Determine the marginal probabilities and indicate what they mean.

Table 5.3 Contingency Table for Voter Reactions to a New Property Tax Plan

Party affiliation	Reaction			Total
	In favor	Neutral	Opposed	
Democratic	120	20	20	160
Republican	50	30	60	140
Independent	50	10	40	100
Total	220	60	120	400

(*a*) See Table 5.4.

Table 5.4   Joint Probability Table for Voter Reactions to a New Property Tax Plan

Party affiliation	Reaction			Marginal probability
	In favor (F)	Neutral (N)	Opposed (O)	
Democratic (D)	0.30	0.05	0.05	0.40
Republican (R)	0.125	0.075	0.15	0.35
Independent (I)	0.125	0.025	0.10	0.25
Marginal probability	0.55	0.15	0.30	1.00

(*b*) Each marginal probability value indicates the unconditional probability of the event identified as the column or row heading. For example, if a person is chosen randomly from this group of 400 voters, the probability that the person will be in favor of the tax plan is $P(F) = 0.55$. If a voter is chosen randomly, the probability that the voter is a Republican is $P(R) = 0.35$.

5.22. Referring to Table 5.4, determine the following probabilities: (*a*) $P(O)$, (*b*) $P(R$ and $O)$, (*c*) $P(I)$, (*d*) $P(I$ and $F)$, (*e*) $P(O|R)$, (*f*) $P(R|O)$, (*g*) $P(R$ or $D)$, (*h*) $P(D$ or $F)$.

(*a*) $P(O) = 0.30$ (the marginal probability)

(*b*) $P(R$ and $O) = 0.15$ (the joint probability in the table)

(*c*) $P(I) = 0.25$ (the marginal probability)

(*d*) $P(I$ and $F) = 0.125$ (the joint probability in the table)

(*e*) $P(O|R) = \dfrac{P(O \text{ and } R)}{P(R)} = \dfrac{0.15}{0.35} = \dfrac{3}{7} \cong 0.43$ (the probability that the voter is opposed to the plan given that the voter is a Republican)

(*f*) $P(R|O) = \dfrac{P(R \text{ and } O)}{P(O)} = \dfrac{0.15}{0.30} = 0.50$ (the probability that the voter is a Republican given that the person is opposed to the plan)

(*g*) $P(R$ or $D) = P(R) + P(D) = 0.35 + 0.40 = 0.75$ (the probability that the voter is either a Democrat or a Republican, which are mutually exclusive events)

(*h*) $P(D$ or $F) = P(D) + P(F) - P(D \text{ and } F) = 0.40 + 0.55 - 0.30 = 0.65$ (the probability that the voter is either a Democrat or in favor of the proposal, which are not mutually exclusive events)

PERMUTATIONS AND COMBINATIONS

5.23. The five individuals constituting the top management of a small manufacturing firm are to be seated together at a banquet table. (*a*) Determine the number of different seating arrangements that are possible for the five individuals. (*b*) Suppose that only three of the five officers will be asked to represent the company at the banquet. How many different arrangements at the banquet table are possible, considering that any three of the five individuals may be chosen?

(*a*) $_nP_n = n! = (5)(4)(3)(2)(1) = 120$

(*b*) $_nP_r = \dfrac{n!}{(n-r)!} = \dfrac{5!}{(5-3)!} = \dfrac{(5)(4)(3)(2)(1)}{(2)(1)} = 60$

5.24. For Problem 5.23(*b*) suppose we are not concerned about the number of different possible seating arrangements but, rather, about the number of different groupings of three officers (out of the five) who might attend the banquet. How many different groupings are there?

Using formula (5.19),

$$_nC_r = \binom{n}{r} = \frac{n!}{r!(n-r)!} = \frac{5!}{3!(5-3)!} = \frac{(5)(4)(3)(2)(1)}{(3)(2)(1)(2)(1)} = 10$$

5.25. A sales representative must visit six cities during a trip.

    (a) If there are 10 cities in the geographic area to be visited, how many different groupings of six cities are there that the sales representative might visit?

    (b) Suppose that there are 10 cities in the geographic area the sales representative is to visit, and further that the sequence in which the visits to the six selected cities are scheduled is also of concern. How many different sequences are there of six cities chosen from the total of 10 cities?

    (c) Suppose that the six cities to be visited have been designated, but that the sequence of visiting the six cities has not been designated. How many sequences are possible for the six designated cities?

    (a) $\quad _nC_r = \binom{n}{r} = \frac{n!}{r!(n-r)!} = \frac{10!}{6!(10-6)!} = \frac{(10)(9)(8)(7)(6)(5)(4)(3)(2)(1)}{(6)(5)(4)(3)(2)(1)(4)(3)(2)(1)} = 210$

    (b) $\quad _nP_r = \frac{n!}{(n-r)!} = \frac{10!}{(10-6)!} = \frac{(10)(9)(8)(7)(6)(5)(4)(3)(2)(1)}{(4)(3)(2)(1)} = 151{,}200$

    (c) $\quad _nP_n = n! = 6! = (6)(5)(4)(3)(2)(1) = 720$

5.26. Of the cities described in Problem 5.25, suppose that six are in fact primary markets for the product in question while the other four are secondary markets. If the salesperson chooses the six cities to be visited on a random basis, what is the probability that (a) four of them will be primary market cities and two will be secondary market cities, (b) all six will turn out to be primary market cities?

    (a) $\quad P = \dfrac{\text{number of combinations which include four and two cities, respectively}}{\text{total number of different combinations of six cities}}$

$$= \frac{_6C_4 \times \,_4C_2}{_{10}C_6} = \frac{\dfrac{6!}{4!2!}\dfrac{4!}{2!2!}}{\dfrac{10!}{6!4!}} = \frac{(15)(6)}{210} = \frac{90}{210} = \frac{3}{7} \cong 0.43$$

    (b) $\quad P = \dfrac{_6C_6 \times \,_4C_0}{_{10}C_6} = \dfrac{\dfrac{6!}{6!0!}\dfrac{4!}{0!4!}}{\dfrac{10!}{6!4!}} = \dfrac{(1)(1)}{210} = \dfrac{1}{210} \cong 0.005$

For this problem, the answer can also be obtained by applying the multiplication rule for dependent events. The probability of selecting a primary market city on the first choice is $6/10$. Following this result, the probability on the next choice is $5/9$, and so forth. On this basis, the probability that all six will be primary market cities is

$$P = \left(\frac{6}{10}\right)\left(\frac{5}{9}\right)\left(\frac{4}{8}\right)\left(\frac{3}{7}\right)\left(\frac{2}{6}\right)\left(\frac{1}{5}\right) = \left(\frac{1}{210}\right) \cong 0.005$$

5.27. With respect to the banquet described in Problem 5.23, determine the probability that the group of three officers chosen from the five will include (a) one particular officer, (b) two particular officers, (c) three particular officers.

    (a) $\quad P = \dfrac{\text{number of combinations which include the particular offcer}}{\text{total number of different combinations of three offcers}}$

$$= \frac{_1C_1 \times \,_4C_2}{_5C_3} = \frac{\dfrac{1!}{1!0!}\dfrac{4!}{2!2!}}{\dfrac{5!}{3!2!}} = \frac{(1)(6)}{10} = \frac{6}{10} = 0.60$$

In this case, this probability value is equivalent simply to observing that $3/5$ of the officers will be chosen, and thus that the probability that any given individual will be chosen is $3/5$, or 0.60.

(b) $\quad P = \dfrac{{}_2C_2 \times {}_3C_1}{{}_5C_3} = \dfrac{\dfrac{2!}{2!0!} \dfrac{3!}{1!2!}}{\dfrac{5!}{3!2!}} = \dfrac{(1)(3)}{10} = \dfrac{3}{10} = 0.30$

(c) $\quad P = \dfrac{{}_3C_3 \times {}_2C_0}{{}_5C_3} = \dfrac{\dfrac{3!}{3!0!} \dfrac{2!}{0!2!}}{\dfrac{5!}{3!2!}} = \dfrac{(1)(1)}{10} = \dfrac{1}{10} = 0.10$

Supplementary Problems

DETERMINING PROBABILITY VALUES

5.28. Determine the probability value for each of the following events.

(a) Probability of randomly selecting one account receivable which is delinquent, given that 5 percent of the accounts are delinquent.

(b) Probability that a land investment will be successful. In the given area, only half of such investments are generally successful, but the particular investors' decision methods have resulted in their having a 30 percent better record than the average investor in the area.

(c) Probability that the sum of the dots showing on the face of two dice after they are tossed is seven.

Ans. (a) 0.05, (b) 0.65, (c) $1/6$

5.29. For each of the following reported odds ratios determine the equivalent probability value, and for each of the reported probability values determine the equivalent odds ratio.

(a) Probability of $P = 2/3$ that a target delivery date will be met.

(b) Probability of $P = 9/10$ that a new product will exceed the breakeven sales level.

(c) Odds of $1 : 2$ that a competitor will achieve the technological breakthrough.

(d) Odds of $5 : 1$ that a new product will be profitable.

Ans. (a) $2 : 1$, (b) $9 : 1$, (c) $P = 1/3$, (d) $P = 5/6$

APPLYING THE RULES OF ADDITION

5.30. During a given week the probability that a particular common stock issue will increase (I) in price, remain unchanged (U), or decline (D) in price is estimated to be 0.30, 0.20, and 0.50, respectively.

(a) What is the probability that the stock issue will increase in price or remain unchanged?

(b) What is the probability that the price of the issue will change during the week?

Ans. (a) 0.50, (b) 0.80

5.31. Of 500 employees, 200 participate in a company's profit-sharing plan (P), 400 have major-medical insurance coverage (M), and 200 employees participate in both programs. Construct a Venn diagram to portray the events designated P and M.

5.32. Refer to the Venn diagram prepared in Problem 5.31. What is the probability that a randomly selected employee (*a*) will be a participant in at least one of the two programs, (*b*) will not be a participant in either program?
Ans. 0.80, (*b*) 0.20

5.33. The probability that a new marketing approach will be successful (*S*) is assessed as being 0.60. The probability that the expenditure for developing the approach can be kept within the original budget (*B*) is 0.50. The probability that both of these objectives will be achieved is estimated at 0.30. What is the probability that at least one of these objectives will be achieved?
Ans. 0.80

INDEPENDENT EVENTS, DEPENDENT EVENTS, AND CONDITIONAL PROBABILITY

5.34. For the situation described in Problem 5.31, (*a*) determine the probability that an employee will be a participant in the profit-sharing plan (*P*) given that the employee has major-medical insurance coverage (*M*), and (*b*) determine if the two events are independent or dependent by reference to the conditional probability value.
Ans. (*a*) 0.50, (*b*) dependent

5.35. For Problem 5.33, determine (*a*) the probability that the new marketing approach will be successful (*S*) given that the development cost was kept within the original budget (*B*), and (*b*) if the two events are independent or dependent by reference to the conditional probability value.
Ans. (*a*) 0.60, (*b*) independent

5.36. The probability that automobile sales will increase next month (*A*) is estimated to be 0.40. The probability that the sale of replacement parts will increase (*R*) is estimated to be 0.50. The probability that both industries will experience an increase in sales is estimated to be 0.10. What is the probability that (*a*) automobile sales have increased during the month given that there is information that replacement parts sales have increased, (*b*) replacement parts sales have increased given information that automobile sales have increased during the month?
Ans. (*a*) 0.20, (*b*) 0.25

5.37. For Problem 5.36, determine if the two events are independent or dependent by reference to one of the conditional probability values.
Ans. Dependent

APPLYING THE RULES OF MULTIPLICATION

5.38. During a particular period, 80 percent of the common stock issues in an industry which includes just 10 companies have increased in market value. If an investor chose two of these issues randomly, what is the probability that both issues increased in market value during this period?
Ans. $56/90 \cong 0.62$

5.39. The overall proportion of defective items in a continuous production process is 0.10. What is the probability that (*a*) two randomly chosen items will both be nondefective (*D'*), (*b*) two randomly chosen items will both be defective (*D*), (*c*) at least one of two randomly chosen items will be nondefective (*D'*)?
Ans. (*a*) 0.81, (*b*) 0.01, (*c*) 0.99

5.40. Test the independence of the two events described in Problem 5.31 by using the rule of multiplication for independent events. Compare your answer with the result of the test in Problem 5.34(*b*).
Ans. Dependent

5.41. Test the independence of the two events described in Problem 5.33 by using the rule of multiplication for independent events. Compare your answer with the result of the test in Problem 5.35(*b*).
Ans. Independent

5.42. From Problem 5.38, suppose an investor chose three of these stock issues randomly. Construct a tree diagram to portray the various possible results for the sequence of three stock issues.

5.43. Referring to the tree diagram prepared in Problem 5.42, determine the probability that (*a*) only one of the three issues increased in market value, (*b*) two issues increased in market value, (*c*) *at least* two issues increased in market value.
Ans.   (*a*) $48/720 \cong 0.07$, (*b*) $336/720 \cong 0.47$, (*c*) $672/720 \cong 0.93$

5.44. Referring to Problem 5.39, suppose a sample of four items is chosen randomly. Construct a tree diagram to portray the various possible results in terms of individual items being defective (D) or nondefective (D').

5.45. Referring to the tree diagram prepared in Problem 5.44, determine the probability that (*a*) none of the four items is defective, (*b*) exactly one item is defective, (*c*) one or fewer items are defective.
Ans.   (*a*) $0.6561 \cong 0.66$, (*b*) $0.2916 \cong 0.29$, (*c*) $0.9477 \cong 0.95$

BAYES' THEOREM

5.46. Suppose there are two urns U_1 and U_2. U_1 contains two red balls and one green ball, while U_2 contains one red ball and two green balls.

(*a*)   An urn is randomly selected, and then one ball is randomly selected from the urn. The ball is red. What is the probability that the urn selected was U_1?

(*b*)   An urn is randomly selected, and then two balls are randomly selected (without replacement) from the urn. The first ball is red and the second ball is green. What is the probability that the urn selected was U_1?
Ans.   (*a*) $P(U_1) = 2/3$, (*b*) $P(U_1) = 1/2$

5.47. Refer to Problem 5.46.
(a)   Suppose an urn is randomly selected, and then two balls are randomly selected (without replacement) from the urn. Both balls are red. What is the probability that the urn selected was U_1?

(*b*)   Suppose an urn is randomly selected and then two balls are randomly selected, *but with the first selected ball being placed back in the urn before the second ball is drawn*. Both balls are red. What is the probability that the urn selected was U_1?
Ans.   (*a*) $P(U_1) = 1$, (*b*) $P(U_1) = 4/5$

5.48. Eighty percent of the vinyl material received from Vendor A is of exceptional quality while only 50 percent of the vinyl material received from Vendor B is of exceptional quality. However, the manufacturing capacity of Vendor A is limited, and for this reason only 40 percent of the vinyl material purchased by our firm comes from Vendor A. The other 60 percent comes from Vendor B. An incoming shipment of vinyl material is inspected, and found to be of exceptional quality. What is the probability that it came from Vendor A?
Ans. $P(A) = 0.52$

5.49. Gasoline is being produced at three refineries with daily production levels of 100,00, 200,000, and 300,000 gallons, respectively. The proportion of the output which is below the octane specifications for name-brand sale at the three refineries is 0.03, 0.05, and 0.44, respectively. A gasoline tank truck is found to be carrying gasoline which is below the octane specifications, and therefore the gasoline is to be marketed outside of the name-brand distribution system. Determine the probability that the tank truck came from each of the three refineries, respectively, (*a*) without reference to the information that the shipment is below the octane specifications and (*b*) given the additional information that the shipment is below the octane specifications.
Ans.   (*a*) $P(1) = \frac{1}{6} \cong 0.17$, $P(2) = \frac{2}{6} \cong 0.33$, $P(3) = \frac{3}{6} = 0.50$, (*b*) $P(1) = 0.02$, $P(2) = 0.07$, $P(3) = 0.91$

JOINT PROBABILITY TABLES

5.50. Table 5.5 is a contingency table which presents a classification of 150 sampled companies according to four industry groups and according to whether return on equity is above or below the average return in this sample of 150 firms. Prepare the joint probability table based on these sample data.

**Table 5.5   Contingency Table for Return on Equity
According to Industry Group**

Industry category	Return on equity		Total
	Above average (A)	Below average (B)	
I	20	40	60
II	10	10	20
III	20	10	30
IV	25	15	40
Total	75	75	150

5.51.   Referring to the joint probability table prepared in Problem 5.50, indicate the following probabilities: (*a*) $P(\text{I})$, (*b*) $P(\text{II})$, (*c*) $P(\text{III})$, (*d*) $P(\text{IV})$.
Ans.   (*a*) 0.40, (*b*) 0.13, (*c*) 0.20, (*d*) 0.27

5.52.   Referring to the joint probability table prepared in Problem 5.50, determine the following probabilities: (*a*) $P(\text{I and }A)$, (*b*) $P(\text{II or }B)$, (*c*) $P(A)$, (*d*) $P(\text{I or II})$, (*e*) $P(\text{I and II})$, (*f*) $P(A \text{ or } B)$, (*g*) $P(A|\text{I})$, (*h*) $P(\text{III}|A)$.
Ans.   (*a*) 0.13, (*b*) 0.57, (*c*) 0.50, (*d*) 0.53, (*e*) 0, (*f*) 1.0, (*g*) 0.33, (*h*) 0.27

PERMUTATIONS AND COMBINATIONS

5.53.   Suppose there are eight different management trainee positions to be assigned to eight employees in a company's junior management training program. In how many different ways can the eight individuals be assigned to the eight different positions?
Ans.   40,320

5.54.   Referring to the situation described in Problem 5.53, suppose only six different positions are available for the eight qualified individuals. In how many different ways can six individuals from the eight be assigned to the six different positions?
Ans.   20,160

5.55.   Referring to the situation described in Problem 5.54, suppose that the six available positions can all be considered comparable, and not really different for practical purposes. In how many ways can the six individuals be chosen from the eight qualified people to fill the six positions?
Ans.   28

5.56.   A project group of two engineers and three technicians is to be assigned from a departmental group which includes five engineers and nine technicians. How many different project groups can be assigned from the fourteen available personnel?
Ans.   840

5.57.   For the personnel assignment situation described in Problem 5.56, suppose the five individuals are assigned randomly from the fourteen personnel in the department, without reference to whether each person is an engineer or a technician. What is the probability that the project group will include (*a*) exactly two engineers, (*b*) no engineers. (*c*) no technicians?
Ans.   (*a*) $P \cong 0.42$, (*b*) $P \cong 0.06$, (*c*) $P \cong 0.0005$

CHAPTER 6

Probability Distributions for Discrete Random Variables: Binomial, Hypergeometric, and Poisson

6.1 WHAT IS A RANDOM VARIABLE?

In contrast to categorical events, such as that of drawing a particular card from a deck of cards, as discussed in Chapter 5, a *random variable* is defined as a *numerical* event whose value is determined by a chance process. When probability values are assigned to all possible numerical values of a random variable X, either by a listing or by a mathematical function, the result is a *probability distribution*. The sum of the probabilities for all the possible numerical outcomes must equal 1.0. Individual probability values may be denoted by the symbol $f(x)$, which indicates that a mathematical function is involved, by $P(x = X)$, which recognizes that the random variable can have various specific values, or simply by $P(X)$.

For a *discrete random variable* observed values can occur only at isolated points along a scale of values. Therefore, it is possible that all numerical values for the variable can be listed in a table with accompanying probabilities. There are several standard probability distributions that can serve as models for a wide variety of discrete random variables involved in business applications. The standard models described in this chapter are the binomial, hypergeometric, and Poisson probability distributions.

For a *continuous random variable* all possible fractional values of the variable cannot be listed, and therefore the probabilities that are determined by a mathematical function are portrayed graphically by a probability density function, or probability curve. Several standard probability distributions that can serve as models for continuous random variables are described in Chapter 7. See Section 1.4 for an explanation of the difference between discrete and continuous variables.

EXAMPLE 1. The number of vans that have been requested for rental at a car rental agency during a 50-day period is identified in Table 6.1. The observed frequencies have been converted into probabilities for this 50-day period in the last column of the table. Thus, we can observe that the probability of exactly seven vans being requested on a randomly chosen day in this period is 0.20, and the probability of six *or more* being requested is $0.28 + 0.20 + 0.08 = 0.56$.

Table 6.1 Daily Demand for Rental of Vans during a 50-Day Period

Possible demand X	Number of days	Probability $[P(X)]$
3	3	0.06
4	7	0.14
5	12	0.24
6	14	0.28
7	10	0.20
8	4	0.08
	50	1.00

6.2 DESCRIBING A DISCRETE RANDOM VARIABLE

Just as for collections of sample and population data, it is often useful to describe a random variable in terms of its *mean* (see Section 3.2) and its *variance*, or *standard deviation* (see Section 4.6). The (long-run) mean for a random variable X is called the *expected value* and is denoted by $E(X)$. For a discrete random variable, it is the weighted average of all possible numerical values of the variable with the respective probabilities used as weights. Because the sum of the weights (probabilities) is 1.0, formula (*3.3*) can be simplified, and the expected value for a discrete random variable is

$$E(X) = \sum XP(X) \qquad (6.1)$$

EXAMPLE 2. Based on the data in Table 6.1, the calculation of the expected value for the random variable is presented in Table 6.2. The expected value is 5.66 vans. Note that the expected value for a discrete variable can be a fractional value, because it represents the long-run average value, not the specific value for any given observation.

The variance of a random variable X is denoted by $V(X)$; it is computed with respect to $E(X)$ as the mean of the probability distribution. The general deviations form of the formula for the variance of a discrete random variable is

$$V(X) = \sum [X - E(X)]^2 P(X) \qquad (6.2)$$

**Table 6.2   Expected Value Calculation for the Demand
for Vans**

Possible demand X	Probability [P(X)]	Weighted value [XP(X)]
3	0.06	0.18
4	0.14	0.56
5	0.24	1.20
6	0.28	1.68
7	0.20	1.40
8	0.08	0.64
	$\overline{1.00}$	$E(X) = \overline{5.66}$

The computational form of the formula for the variance of a discrete random variable, which does not require the determination of deviations from the mean, is

$$V(X) = \sum X^2 P(X) - \left[\sum XP(X) \right]^2$$
$$= E(X^2) - [E(X)]^2 \qquad\qquad (6.3)$$

EXAMPLE 3. The worksheet for the calculation of the variance for the demand for van rentals is presented in Table 6.3, using the computational version of the formula. As indicated below, the variance has a value of 1.74.

$$V(X) = E(X^2) - [E(X)]^2 = 33.78 - (5.66)^2 = 33.78 - 32.04 = 1.74$$

Table 6.3   Worksheet for the Calculation of the Variance for the Demand for Vans

Possible demand X	Probability [P(X)]	Weighted value [XP(X)]	Squared demand (X²)	Weighted square [X²P(X)]
3	0.06	0.18	9	0.54
4	0.14	0.56	16	2.24
5	0.24	1.20	25	6.00
6	0.28	1.68	36	10.08
7	0.20	1.40	49	9.80
8	0.08	0.64	64	5.12
		$E(X) = \overline{5.66}$		$E(X^2) = \overline{33.78}$

As is true in Section 4.6 for populations and samples, the standard deviation for a random variable is simply the square root of the variance:

$$\sigma = \sqrt{V(X)} \qquad\qquad (6.4)$$

An advantage of the standard deviation is that it is expressed in the same units as the random variable, rather than being in squared units.

EXAMPLE 4. The standard deviation with respect to the demand for van rentals is

$$\sigma = \sqrt{V(X)} = \sqrt{1.74} = 1.32 \text{ vans}$$

6.3 THE BINOMIAL DISTRIBUTION

The binomial distribution is a discrete probability distribution that is applicable as a model for decision-making situations in which a sampling process can be assumed to conform to a Bernoulli process. A *Bernoulli process* is a sampling process in which

(1) Only two mutually exclusive possible outcomes are possible in each trial, or observation. For convenience these are called *success* and *failure*.

(2) The outcomes in the series of trials, or observations, constitute *independent events*.

(3) The probability of success in each trial, denoted by p, remains constant from trial to trial. That is, the process is stationary.

The binomial distribution can be used to determine the probability of obtaining a designated number of successes in a Bernoulli process. Three values are required: the designated number of successes (X); the number of trials, or observations (n); and the probability of success in each trial (p). Where $q = (1 - p)$, the formula for determining the probability of a specific number of successes X for a binomial distribution is

$$P(X|n, p) = {}_nC_X \, p^X q^{n-X}$$

$$= \frac{n!}{X!(n - X)!} p^X q^{n-X} \tag{6.5}$$

EXAMPLE 5. The probability that a randomly chosen sales prospect will make a purchase is 0.20. If a sales representative calls on six propects, the probability that exactly four sales will be made is determined as follows:

$$P(X = 4|n = 6, p = 0.20) = {}_6C_4(0.20)^4(0.80)^2 = \frac{6!}{4!2!}(0.20)^4(0.80)^2$$

$$= \frac{6 \times 5 \times 4 \times 3 \times 2}{(4 \times 3 \times 2)(2)}(0.0016)(0.64) = 0.01536 \cong 0.015$$

Often there is an interest in the cumulative probability of "X or more" successes or "X or fewer" successes occurring in n trials. In such a case, the probability of each outcome included within the designated interval must be determined, and then these probabilities are summed.

EXAMPLE 6. For Example 5, the probability that the salesperson will make four or more sales is determined as follows:

$$P(X \geq 4|n = 6, p = 0.20) = P(X = 4) + P(X = 5) + P(X = 6)$$
$$= 0.01536 + 0.001536 + 0.000064 = 0.016960 \cong 0.017$$

where $P(X = 4) = 0.01536$ (from Example 5)

$$P(X = 5) = {}_6C_5(0.20)^5(0.80)^1 = \frac{6!}{5!1!}(0.20)^5(0.80) = 6(0.00032)(0.80) = 0.001536$$

$$P(X = 6) = {}_6C_6(0.20)^6(0.80)^0 = \frac{6!}{6!0!}(0.000064)(1) = (1)(0.000064) = 0.000064$$

(*Note*: Recall that any value raised to the zero power is equal to 1.)

Because use of the binomial formula involves considerable arithmetic when the sample is relatively large, tables of binomial probabilities are often used. (See Appendix 2.)

EXAMPLE 7. If the probability that a randomly chosen sales prospect will make a purchase is 0.20, the probability that a salesperson who calls on 15 prospects will make fewer than three sales is

$$P(X < 3|n = 15, p = 0.20) = P(X \leq 2) = P(X = 0) + P(X = 1) + P(X = 2)$$
$$= 0.0352 + 0.1319 + 0.2309 \text{ (from Appendix 2)}$$
$$= 0.3980 \cong 0.40$$

The values of p referenced in Appendix 2 do not exceed $p = 0.50$. If the value of p in a particular application exceeds 0.50, the problem is restated so that the event is defined in terms of the number of failures rather than the number of successes (see Problem 6.9).

The expected value (long-run mean) and variance for a given binomial distribution could be determined by listing the probability distribution in a table and applying the formulas presented in Section 6.2. However, the expected number of successes can be computed directly:

$$E(X) = np \qquad (6.6)$$

Where $q = (1 - p)$, the variance of the number of successes can also be computed directly:

$$V(X) = npq \qquad (6.7)$$

EXAMPLE 8. For Example 7, the expected number of sales (as a long-run average), the variance, and the standard deviation associated with making calls on 15 prospects are

$$E(X) = np = 15(0.20) = 3.00 \text{ sales}$$
$$V(X) = np(q) = 15(0.20)(0.80) = 2.40$$

$$\sigma = \sqrt{V(X)} = \sqrt{2.4} = 1.55 \text{ sales}$$

6.4   THE BINOMIAL VARIABLE EXPRESSED BY PROPORTIONS

Instead of expressing the random binomial variable as the number of successes X, we can designate it in terms of the *proportion* of successes $\hat{p}$, which is the ratio of the number of successes to the number of trials:

$$\hat{p} = \frac{X}{n} \qquad (6.8)$$

In such cases, formula (6.5) is modified only with respect to defining the proportion. Thus, the probability of observing exactly $\hat{p}$ proportion of successes in n Bernoulli trials is

$$P\left(\hat{p} = \frac{X}{n} | n, p\right) = {}_nC_X p^X q^{n-X} \qquad (6.9)$$

or

$$P\left(\hat{p} = \frac{X}{n} | n, \pi\right) = {}_nC_X \pi^X (1 - \pi)^{n-X} \qquad (6.10)$$

In formula (6.10), π (Greek "pí") is the equivalent of p except that it specifically indicates that the probability of success in an individual trial is a population or process parameter.

EXAMPLE 9. The probability that a randomly selected salaried employee is a participant in an optional retirement program is 0.40. If five salaried employees are chosen randomly, the probability that the proportion of participants is exactly 0.60, or $3/5$ of the five sampled employees, is

$$P(\hat{p} = 0.60) = P\left(\hat{p} = \frac{3}{5} | n = 5, p = 0.40\right) = {}_5C_3(0.40)^3(0.60)^2 = \frac{5!}{3!2!}(0.064)(0.36) = 0.2304 \cong 0.23$$

When the binomial variable is expressed as a proportion, the distribution is still discrete and not continuous. Only the particular proportions for which the number of successes X is a whole number can occur. For instance, in Example 9 it is not possible for there to be a proportion of 0.50 participant out of a sample of five. The use of the binomial table with respect to proportions simply requires converting the designated proportion $\hat{p}$ to the number of successes X for the given sample size n.

EXAMPLE 10. The probability that a randomly selected employee is a participant in an optional retirement program is 0.40. If 10 employees are chosen randomly, the probability that the proportion of participants is at least 0.70 is

$$P(\hat{p} \geq 0.70) = P(X \geq 7 | n = 10, p = 0.10) = P(X = 7) + P(X = 8) + P(X = 9) + P(X = 10)$$
$$= 0.0425 + 0.0106 + 0.0016 + 0.0001 = 0.0548$$

The expected value for a binomial probability distribution expressed by proportions is equal to the population proportion, which may be designated by either p or π:

$$E(\hat{p}) = p \qquad (6.11)$$

or

$$E(\hat{p}) = \pi \qquad (6.12)$$

The variance of the proportion of successes for a binomial probability distribution, when $q = (1 - p)$, is

$$V(\hat{p}) = \frac{pq}{n} \qquad (6.13)$$

or

$$V(\hat{p}) = \frac{\pi(1 - \pi)}{n} \qquad (6.14)$$

6.5 THE HYPERGEOMETRIC DISTRIBUTION

When sampling is done *without replacement* of each sampled item taken from a finite population of items, the Bernoulli process does not apply because there is a systematic change in the probability of success as items are removed from the population. When sampling without replacement is used in a situation that would otherwise qualify as a Bernoulli process, the hypergeometric distribution is the appropriate discrete probability distribution.

Given that X is the designated number of successes, N is the total number of items in the population, T is the total number of successes included in the population, and n is the number of items in the sample, the formula for determining hypergeometric probabilities is

$$P(X|N, T, n) = \frac{\binom{N - T}{n - X}\binom{T}{X}}{\binom{N}{n}} \qquad (6.15)$$

EXAMPLE 11. Of six employees, three have been with the company five or more years. If four employees are chosen randomly from the group of six, the probability that exactly two will have five or more years seniority is

$$P(X = 2|N = 6, T = 3, n = 4) = \frac{\binom{6 - 3}{4 - 2}\binom{3}{2}}{\binom{6}{4}} = \frac{\binom{3}{2}\binom{3}{2}}{\binom{6}{4}} = \frac{\dfrac{3!}{2!1!}\dfrac{3!}{2!1!}}{\dfrac{6!}{4!2!}} = \frac{(3)(3)}{15} = 0.60$$

Note that in Example 11, the required probability value is computed by determining the number of different combinations that would include two high-seniority and two low-seniority employees as a ratio of the total number of combinations of four employees taken from the six. Thus, the hypergeometric formula is a direct application of the rules of combinatorial analysis described in Section 5.10.

When the population is large and the sample is relatively small, the fact that sampling is done without replacement has little effect on the probability of success in each trial. A convenient rule of thumb is that a binomial probability can be used as an approximation of a hypergeometric probability value when $n < 0.05N$. That is, the sample size should be less than 5 percent of the population size. Different texts use somewhat different rules for determining when such approximation is appropriate.

6.6 THE POISSON DISTRIBUTION

The *Poisson distribution* can be used to determine the probability of a designated number of events occurring when the events occur in a continuum of time or space. Such a process is called a *Poisson process*;

it is similar to the Bernoulli process (see Section 6.3) except that the events occur over a continuum (e.g., during a time interval) and there are no trials as such. An example of such a process is the arrival of incoming calls at a telephone switchboard. As was the case for the Bernoulli process, it is assumed that the events are independent and that the process is stationary.

Only one value is required to determine the probability of a designated number of events occurring in a Poisson process: the long-run mean number of events for the specific time or space dimension of interest. This mean generally is represented by λ (Greek lambda), or possibly by μ. The formula for determining the probability of a designated number of successes X in a Poisson distribution is

$$P(X|\lambda) = \frac{\lambda^X e^{-\lambda}}{X!} \qquad\qquad (6.16)$$

Here e is the constant 2.7183 that is the base of natural logarithms, and the values of $e^{-\lambda}$ may be obtained from Appendix 3.

EXAMPLE 12.   An average of five calls for service per hour are received by a machine repair department. The probability that exactly three calls for service will be received in a randomly selected hour is

$$P(X = 3|\lambda = 5.0) = \frac{(5)^3 e^{-5}}{3!} = \frac{(125)(0.00674)}{6} = 0.1404$$

Alternatively, a table of Poisson probabilities may be used. Appendix 4 identifies the probability of each designated number of successes for various values of λ.

EXAMPLE 13.   We can determine the answer to Example 12 by use of Appendix 4 for Poisson probabilities as follows:

$$P(X = 3|\lambda = 5.0) = 0.1404$$

When there is an interest in the probability of "X or more" or "X or fewer" successes, the rule of addition for mutually exclusive events is applied.

EXAMPLE 14.   If an average of five service calls per hour are received at a machine repair department, the probability that *fewer than* three calls will be received during a randomly chosen hour is determined as follows:

$$P(X < 3|\lambda = 5.0) = P(X \leq 2) = P(X = 0) + P(X = 1) + P(X = 2)$$
$$= 0.0067 + 0.0337 + 0.0842 = 0.1246$$

where
$$P(X = 0|\lambda = 5.0) = 0.0067 \quad \text{(from Appendix 4)}$$
$$P(X = 1|\lambda = 5.0) = 0.0337$$
$$P(X = 2|\lambda = 5.0) = 0.0842$$

Because a Poisson process is assumed to be stationary, it follows that the mean of the process is always proportional to the length of the time or space continuum. Therefore, if the mean is available for one length of time, the mean for any other required time period can be determined.

This is important, because the value of λ which is used must apply to the time period of interest.

EXAMPLE 15. On the average, 12 people per hour ask questions of a decorating consultant in a fabric store. The probability that three or more people will approach the consultant with questions during a 10-min period (1/6 of an hour) is determined as follows:

$$\text{Average per hour} = 0.12$$

$$\lambda = \text{average per 10 min} = \frac{12}{6} = 2.0$$

$$P(X \geq 3|\lambda = 2.0) = P(X = 3|\lambda = 2.0) + P(X = 4|\lambda = 2.0) + P(X = 5|\lambda = 2.0) + \cdots$$
$$= 0.1804 + 0.0902 + 0.0361 + 0.0120 + 0.0034 + 0.0009 + 0.0002 = 0.3232$$

where

$$P(X = 3|\lambda = 2.0) = 0.1804) \quad \text{(from Appendix 4)}$$
$$P(X = 4|\lambda = 2.0) = 0.0902$$
$$P(X = 5|\lambda = 2.0) = 0.0361$$
$$P(X = 6|\lambda = 2.0) = 0.0120$$
$$P(X = 7|\lambda = 2.0) = 0.0034$$
$$P(X = 8|\lambda = 2.0) = 0.0009$$
$$P(X = 9|\lambda = 2.0) = 0.0002$$

By definition, the expected value (long-run mean) for a Poisson probability distribution is equal to the mean of the distribution:

$$E(X) = \lambda \qquad\qquad (6.17)$$

As it happens, the variance of the number of events for a Poisson probability distribution is also equal to the mean of the distribution, λ. The standard deviation then is the square root of λ:

$$V(X) = \lambda \qquad\qquad (6.18)$$

$$\sigma = \sqrt{\lambda} \qquad\qquad (6.19)$$

6.7   POISSON APPROXIMATION OF BINOMIAL PROBABILITIES

When the number of observations or trials n in a Bernoulli process is large, computations are quite tedious. Further, tabled probabilities for very small values of p are not generally available. Fortunately, the Poisson distribution is suitable as an approximation of binomial probabilities when n is large and p or q is small. A convenient rule is that such approximation can be made when $n \geq 30$, and either $np < 5$ or $nq < 5$. Different texts use somewhat different rules for determining when such approximation is appropriate.

The mean for the Poisson probability distribution that is used to approximate binomial probabilities is

$$\lambda = np \qquad\qquad (6.20)$$

EXAMPLE 16. For a large shipment of transistors from a supplier, 1 percent of the items is known to be defective. If a sample of 30 transistors is randomly selected, the probability that two or more transistors will be defective can be determined by use of the binomial probabilities in Appendix 2:

$$P(X \geq 2|n = 30, p = 0.01) = P(X = 2) + P(X = 3) + \cdots = 0.0328 + 0.0031 + 0.0002 = 0.0361$$

Where $\lambda = np = 30(0.01) = 0.3$, Poisson approximation of the above probability value is

$$P(X \geq 2|\lambda = 0.3) = P(X = 2) + P(X = 3) + \cdots = 0.0333 + 0.0033 + 0.0002 = 0.0368$$

Thus, the difference between the Poisson approximation and the actual binomial probability value is just 0.0007.

When n is large but neither np nor nq is less than 5.0, binomial probabilities can be approximated by use of the normal probability distribution (see Section 7.4).

Overall, the availability of computers has made the approximation of probabilities for one model based on another probability model less important.

6.8 USING EXCEL AND MINITAB

Computer software for statistical analysis typically includes the capability of providing probability values for the standard discrete probability distributions that are used as models for decision-making situations. Such availability is particularly useful when the particular probabilities are not available in standard tables. Solved Problems 6.21 and 6.22 illustrate the use of Excel and Minitab, respectively, for the determination of binomial probabilities. Problems 6.23 and 6.24 illustrate the use of Excel and Minitab, respectively, for the determination of Poisson probabilities.

Solved Problems

DISCRETE RANDOM VARIABLES

6.1. The number of trucks arriving hourly at a warehouse facility has been found to follow the probability distribution in Table 6.4. Calculate (*a*) the expected number of arrivals X per hour, (*b*) the variance, and (*c*) the standard deviation for the discrete random variable.

Table 6.4   Hourly Arrival of Trucks at a Warehouse

Number of trucks (X)	0	1	2	3	4	5	6
Probability [$P(X)$]	0.05	0.10	0.15	0.25	0.30	0.10	0.05

From Table 6.5,

(*a*) $E(X) = 3.15$ trucks

(*b*) $V(X) = E(X^2) - [E(X)]^2 = 12.05 - (3.15)^2 = 12.05 - 9.9225 = 2.1275 \cong 2.13$

(*c*) $\sigma = \sqrt{V(X)} = \sqrt{2.1275} = 1.46$ trucks

Table 6.5   Worksheet for the Truck Arrival Calculations

Number of trucks (X)	Probability [$P(X)$]	Weighted value [$XP(X)$]	Squared number (X^2)	Weighted square [$X^2P(X)$]
0	0.05	0	0	0
1	0.10	0.10	1	0.10
2	0.15	0.30	4	0.60
3	0.25	0.75	9	2.25
4	0.30	1.20	16	4.80
5	0.10	0.50	25	2.50
6	0.05	0.30	36	1.80
		$E(X) = \overline{3.15}$		$E(X^2) = \overline{12.05}$

6.2. Table 6.6 identifies the probability that a computer network will be inoperative the indicated number of periods per week during the initial installation phase for the network. Calculate (*a*) the expected number of times per week that the network is inoperative and (*b*) the standard deviation for this variable.

Table 6.6   Number of Inoperative Periods per Week for a New Computer Network

Number of periods (*X*)	4	5	6	7	8	9
Probability [*P(X)*]	0.01	0.08	0.29	0.42	0.14	0.06

Using Table 6.7,

(*a*) $E(X) = 6.78$ periods

(*b*) $V(X) = E(X^2) - [E(X)]^2 = 47.00 - (6.78)^2 = 47.00 - 45.9684 = 1.0316$

(*c*) $\sigma = \sqrt{V(X)} = \sqrt{1.0316} = 1.0157 \cong 1.02$ periods

Table 6.7   Worksheet for the Computer Malfunction Calculations

Number of periods (*X*)	Probability [*P(X)*]	Weighted value [*XP(X)*]	Squared number (*X²*)	Weighted square [*X²P(X)*]
4	0.01	0.04	16	0.16
5	0.08	0.40	25	2.00
6	0.29	1.74	36	10.44
7	0.42	2.94	49	20.58
8	0.14	1.12	64	8.96
9	0.06	0.54	81	4.86
	1.00	$E(X) = 6.78$		$E(X^2) = 47.00$

6.3. Table 6.8 lists the possible outcomes associated with the toss of two 6-sided dice and the probability associated with each outcome. The probabilities were determined by use of the rules of addition and multiplication discussed in Sections 5.4 and 5.6. For example, a 3 can be obtained by a combination of a 1 and 2, or a combination of a 2 and 1. Each sequence has a probability of occurrence of $(1/6) \times (1/6) = 1/36$, and since the two sequences are mutually exclusive, $P(X = 3) = 1/36 + 1/36 = 2.36$. Determine (*a*) the expected number on the throw of two dice and (*b*) the standard deviation of this distribution.

Table 6.8   Possible Outcomes on the Toss of Two Dice

Number on two dice (*X*)	2	3	4	5	6	7	8	9	10	11	12
Probability [*P(X)*]	$\frac{1}{36}$	$\frac{2}{36}$	$\frac{3}{36}$	$\frac{4}{36}$	$\frac{5}{36}$	$\frac{6}{36}$	$\frac{5}{36}$	$\frac{4}{36}$	$\frac{3}{36}$	$\frac{2}{36}$	$\frac{1}{36}$

From Table 6.9,

(*a*) $E(X) = 7$

(*b*) $V(X) = E(X^2) - [E(X)]^2 = 54.83 - (7)^2 = 54.83 - 49 = 5.83$

(*c*) $\sigma = \sqrt{V(X)} = \sqrt{5.83} \cong 2.41$

Table 6.9   Worksheet for the Calculations Concerning the Toss of Two Dice

Number (X)	Probability [P(X)]	Weighted value [XP(X)]	Squared number (X^2)	Weighted square $[X^2 P(X)]$
2	1/36	2/36	4	4/36
3	2/36	6/36	9	18/36
4	3/36	12/36	16	48/36
5	4/36	20/36	25	100/36
6	5/36	30/36	36	180/36
7	6/36	42/36	49	294/36
8	5/36	40/36	64	320/36
9	4/36	36/36	81	324/36
10	3/36	30/36	100	300/36
11	2/36	22/36	121	242/36
12	1/36	12/36	144	144/36
	$\overline{36/36}$	$E(X) = \overline{252/36} = 7.0$		$E(X^2) = \overline{1{,}974/36} \cong 54.83$

THE BINOMIAL DISTRIBUTION

6.4. Because of economic conditions, a firm reports that 30 percent of its accounts receivable from other business firms are overdue. If an accountant takes a random sample of five such accounts, determine the probability of each of the following events by use of the formula for binomial probabilities: (*a*) none of the accounts is overdue, (*b*) exactly two accounts are overdue, (*c*) most of the accounts are overdue, (*d*) exactly 20 percent of the accounts are overdue.

(*a*) $P(X = 0 | n = 5, p = 0.30) = {}_5C_0(0.30)^0(0.70)^5 = \dfrac{5!}{0!5!}(0.30)^0(0.70)^5 = (1)(1)(0.16807) = 0.16807$

(*b*) $P(X = 2 | n = 5, p = 0.30) = {}_5C_2(0.30)^2(0.70)^3 = \dfrac{5!}{2!3!}(0.30)^2(0.70)^3 = (10)(0.09)(0.343) = 0.3087$

(*c*) $P(X \geq 3 | n = 5, p = 0.30) = P(X = 3) + P(X = 4) + P(X = 5) = 0.1323 + 0.02835 + 0.00243 = 0.16308$

where $P(X = 3) = \dfrac{5!}{3!2!}(0.30)^3(0.70)^2 = (10)(0.027)(0.49) = 0.1323$

$P(X = 4) = \dfrac{5!}{4!1!}(0.30)^4(0.70)^1 = (5)(0.0081)(0.70) = 0.02835$

$P(X = 5 = \dfrac{5!}{5!0!}(0.30)^5(0.70)^0 = (1)(0.00243)(1) = 0.00243$

(*d*) $P\left(\dfrac{X}{n} = 0.20 | n = 5, p = 0.30\right) = P(X = 1 | n = 5, p = 0.30) = {}_5C_1(0.30)^1(0.70)^4 = \dfrac{5!}{1!4!}(0.30)^1(0.70)^4$

$= (5)(0.30)(0.2401) = 0.36015$

6.5. A mail-order firm has a circular that elicits a 10 percent response rate. Suppose 20 of the circulars are mailed as a market test in a new geographic area. Assuming that the 10 percent response rate is applicable in the new area, determine the probabilities of the following events by use of Appendix 2: (*a*) no one responds, (*b*) exactly two people respond, (*c*) a majority of the people respond, (*d*) less than 20 percent of the people respond.

(*a*) $P(X = 0 | n = 20, p = 0.10) = 0.1216$

(*b*) $P(X = 2 | n = 20, p = 0.10) = 0.2852$

(c) $P(X = 11 | n = 20, p = 0.10) = P(X = 11) + P(X = 12) + \cdots = 0.0000 \cong 0$

(d) $P\left(\dfrac{X}{n} < 0.20 | n = 20, p = 0.10\right) = P(X \leq 3 | n = 20, p = 0.10)$

$$= P(X = 0) + P(X = 1) + P(X = 2) + P(X = 3)$$

$$= 0.1216 + 0.2702 + 0.2852 + 0.1901 = 0.8671$$

6.6. The binomial formula can be viewed as being composed of two parts: a combinations formula to determine the number of different ways in which the designated event can occur and the rule of multiplication to determine the probability of each sequence. Suppose that three items are selected randomly from a process known to produce 10 percent defectives. Construct a three-step tree diagram portraying the selection of the three items and using D for a defective item being selected and D' for a nondefective item being selected. Also, enter the appropriate probability values in the diagram and use the multiplication rule for independent events to determine the probability of each possible sequence of three events occurring.

See Fig. 6-1.

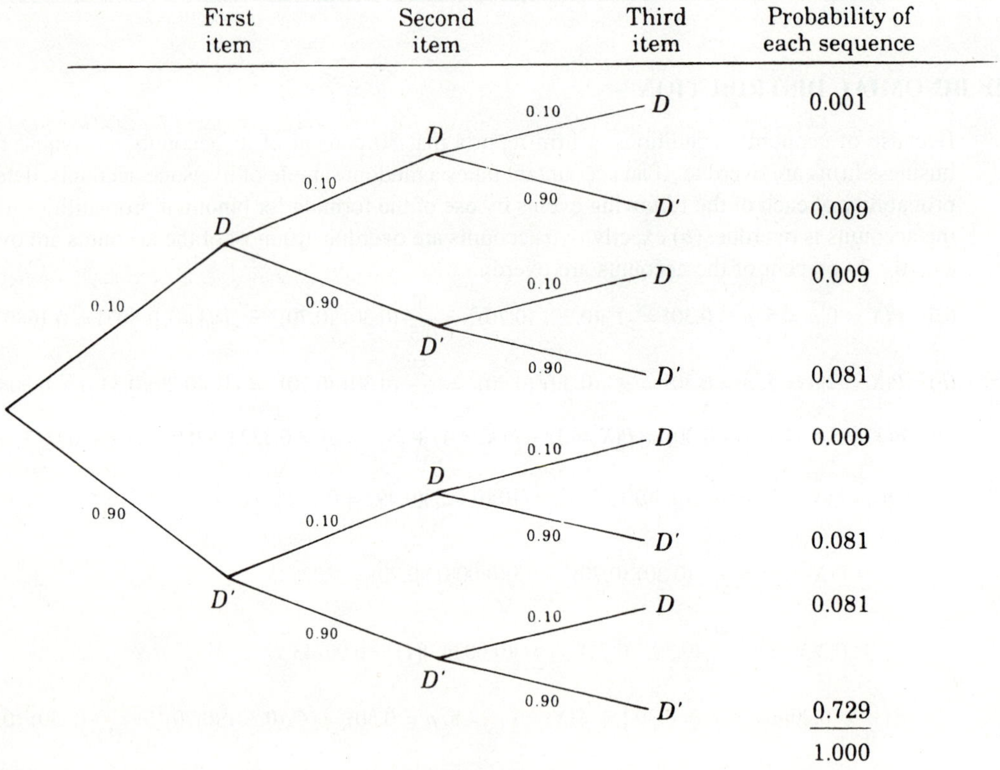

Fig. 6-1

6.7. From Problem 6.6, determine the probability that exactly one of the three sampled items is defective, referring to Fig. 6-1 and using the addition rule for mutually exclusive events.

Beginning from the top of the tree diagram, the fourth, sixth, and seventh sequences include exactly one defective item. Thus,

$$P(X = 1) = (D \text{ and } D' \text{ and } D') + (D' \text{ and } D \text{ and } D') + (D' \text{ and } D' \text{ and } D)$$

$$= 0.081 + 0.081 + 0.081 = 0.243$$

6.8. From Problems 6.6 and 6.7, determine the probability of obtaining exactly one defective item by use of the binomial formula, and note the correspondence between the values in the formula and the values obtained from the tree diagram.

Using formula (6.4),

$$P(X = 1|n = 3, p = 0.10) = {}_3C_1(0.10)^1(0.90)^2 = \frac{3!}{1!2!}(0.10)(0.81)$$

$$= 3(0.081) = 0.243$$

Thus, the first part of the binomial formula indicates the number of different sequences in the tree diagram that include the designated number of successes (in this case there are three ways in which one defective item can be included in the group of three items). The second part of the formula represents the rule of multiplication for the specified independent events.

6.9. During a particular year, 70 percent of the common stocks listed on the New York Stock Exchange increased in market value, while 30 percent were unchanged or declined in market value. At the beginning of the year a stock advisory service chose 10 stock issues as being "specially recommended." If the 10 issues represent a random selection, what is the probability that (*a*) all 10 issues and (*b*) at least eight issues increased in market value?

(*a*) $P(X = 10|n = 10, p = 0.70) = P(X' = 0|n = 10, q = 0.30) = 0.0282$
  (*Note*: When p is greater than 0.50, the problem has to be restated in terms of X' (read "not X") and it follows that $X' = n - X$. Thus, "all 10 increased" is the same event as "none decreased.")

(*b*) $P(X \geq 8|n = 10, p = 0.70) = P(X' \leq 2|n = 10, q = 0.30)$
  $$= P(X' = 0) + P(X' = 1) + P(X' = 2)$$
  $$= 0.0282 + 0.1211 + 0.2335 = 0.3828$$
  (*Note*: When a probability statement is restated in terms of X' instead of X and an inequality is involved, the inequality symbol in the original statement simply is reversed.)

6.10. Using Appendix 2, determine:

(*a*) $P(X = 5|n = 9, p = 0.50)$
(*b*) $P(X = 7|n = 15, p = 0.60)$
(*c*) $P(X \leq 3|n = 20, p = 0.05)$
(*d*) $P(X \geq 18|n = 20, p = 0.90)$
(*e*) $P(X > 8|n = 10, p = 0.70)$

(*a*) $P(X = 5|n = 9, p = 0.50) = 0.2461$
(*b*) $P(X = 7|n = 15, p = 0.60) = P(X' = 8|n = 15, q = 0.40) = 0.1181$
(*c*) $P(X \leq 3|n = 20, p = 0.05) = P(X = 0) + P(X = 1) + P(X = 2) + P(X = 3)$
  $$= 0.3585 + 0.3774 + 0.1887 + 0.0596 = 0.9842$$
(*d*) $P(X \geq 18|n = 20, p = 0.90) = P(X' \leq 2|n = 20, q = 0.10)$
  $$= P(X' = 0) + P(X' = 1) + P(X' = 2)$$
  $$= 0.1216 + 0.2702 + 0.2852 = 0.6770$$
(*e*) $P(X > 8|n = 10, p = 0.70) = P(X' < 2|n = 10, q = 0.30)$
  $$= P(X' = 0) + P(X' = 1) = 0.0282 + 0.1211 = 0.1493$$

6.11 If a fair coin is tossed five times, the probability distribution with respect to the number of heads observed is based on the binomial distribution, with $n = 5$ and $p = 0.50$ (see. Table 6.10). Determine (*a*) the expected number of heads and (*b*) the standard deviation for the number of heads by use of the *general* formulas for discrete random variables.

Table 6.10   Binomial Probability Distribution of the Number of Heads Occurring in Five Tosses of a Fair Coin

Number of heads (X)	0	1	2	3	4	5
Probability [$P(X)$]	0.0312	0.1562	0.3125	0.3125	0.1562	0.0312

Using Table 6.11.

(a) $E(X) = 2.4995 \cong 2.50$ heads

(b) $V(X) = E(X^2) - [E(X)]^2 = 7.4979 - (2.4995)^2 = 7.4979 - 6.2475 = 1.2504$

(c) $\sigma = \sqrt{V(X)} = \sqrt{1.2504} = 1.1182 \cong 1.12$ heads

Table 6.11   Worksheet for the Calculations for Problem 6.11

Number of heads (X)	Probability [$P(X)$]	Weighted value [$XP(X)$]	Squared number (X^2)	Weighted square [$X^2P(X)$]
0	0.0312	0	0	0
1	0.1562	0.1562	1	0.1562
2	0.3125	0.6250	4	1.2500
3	0.3125	0.9375	9	2.8125
4	0.1562	0.6248	16	2.4992
5	0.0312	0.1560	25	0.7800
		$E(X) = \overline{2.4995}$		$E(X^2) = \overline{7.4979}$

6.12. Referring to Problem 6.11, determine (a) the expected number of heads and (b) the standard deviation for the number of heads by use of the *special* formulas applicable for binomial probability distributions. (c) Compare your answers to those in Problem 6.11.

(a) $E(X) = np = 5(0.50) = 2.50$ heads

(b) $V(X) = npq = (5)(0.50)(0.50) = 1.2500$

$\sigma = \sqrt{V(X)} = \sqrt{1.2500} = 1.1180 \cong 1.12$ heads

(c)   Except for a slight difference due to rounding of values, the answers obtained with the special formulas that are applicable for binomial distributions correspond with the answers obtained by the lengthier general formulas applicable for any discrete random variable.

THE HYPERGEOMETRIC DISTRIBUTION

6.13. A manager randomly selects $n = 3$ individuals from a group of 10 employees in a department for assignment to a project team. Assuming that four of the employees were assigned to a similar project previously, construct a three-step tree diagram portraying the selection of the three individuals in terms of whether each individual chosen has had experience E or has no previous experience E' in such a project. Further, enter the appropriate probability values in the diagram and use the multiplication rule for dependent events to determine the probability of each possible sequence of three events occurring.

See Fig. 6-2.

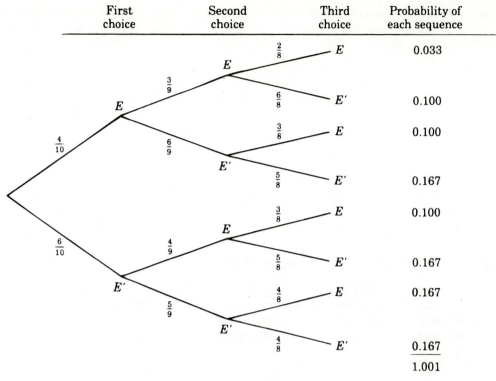

First choice	Second choice	Third choice	Probability of each sequence

Fig. 6-2

6.14. Referring to Problem 6.13, determine the probability that exactly two of the three employees selected have had previous experience in such a project by reference to Fig. 6-2 and use of the addition rule for mutually exclusive events.

Beginning from the top of the tree diagram, the second, third, and fifth sequences include exactly two employees with experience. Thus, by the rule of addition for these mutually exclusive sequences:

$$P(X = 2) = (E \text{ and } E \text{ and } E') + (E \text{ and } E' \text{ and } E) + (E' \text{ and } E \text{ and } E)$$
$$= 0.100 + 0.100 + 0.100 = 0.30$$

6.15. Referring to Problem 6.13, determine the probability that exactly two of the three employees have had the previous experience, using the formula for determining hypergeometric probabilities.

From formula (6.14),

$$P(X|N, T, n) = \frac{\binom{N-T}{n-X}\binom{T}{X}}{\binom{N}{n}}$$

$$P(X = 2|N = 10, T = 4, n = 3) = \frac{\binom{10-4}{3-2}\binom{4}{2}}{\binom{10}{3}} = \frac{\binom{6}{1}\binom{4}{2}}{\binom{10}{3}} = \frac{\left(\frac{6!}{1!5!}\right)\left(\frac{4!}{2!2!}\right)}{\left(\frac{10!}{3!7!}\right)} = \frac{(6)(6)}{120} = 0.30$$

6.16. Section 6.5 states that the hypergeometric formula is a direct application of the rules of combinatorial analysis described in Section 5.9. To demonstrate this, apply the hypergeometric formula to Problem 5.26(a).

$$P(X = 4 | N = 10, T = 6, n = 6) = \frac{\binom{10-6}{6-4}\binom{6}{6}}{\binom{10}{6}} = \frac{\left(\frac{4!}{2!2!}\right)\left(\frac{6!}{4!2!}\right)}{\left(\frac{10!}{6!4!}\right)}$$

$$= \frac{(6)(15)}{210} = \frac{90}{210} = \frac{3}{7} \cong 0.43$$

[*Note*: This result is equivalent to the use of the combinatorial analysis formula in the solution to Problem 5.26(a).]

THE POISSON PROBABILITY DISTRIBUTION

6.17. On average, five people per hour conduct transactions at a special services desk in a commercial bank. Assuming that the arrival of such people is independently distributed and equally likely throughout the period of concern, what is the probability that more than 10 people will wish to conduct transactions at the special services desk during a particular hour?

Using Appendix 4,

$$P(X > 10 | \lambda = 5.0) = P(X \geq 11 | \lambda = 5.0) = P(X = 11) + P(X = 12) + \cdots$$
$$= 0.0082 + 0.0034 + 0.0013 + 0.0005 + 0.0002 = 0.0136$$

6.18. On average, a ship arrives at a certain dock every second day. What is the probability that two or more ships will arrive on a randomly selected day?

Since the average per two days $= 1.0$, then $\lambda = $ average per day $= 1.0 \times (\frac{1}{2}) = 0.5$. Substituting from Appendix 4,

$$P(X \geq 2 | \lambda = 0.5) = P(X = 2) + P(X = 3) + \cdots$$
$$= 0.0758 + 0.0126 + 0.0016 + 0.0002 = 0.0902$$

6.19. Each 500-ft roll of sheet steel includes two flaws, on average. A flaw is a scratch or mar that would affect the use of that segment of sheet steel in the finished product. What is the probability that a particular 100-ft segment will include no flaws?

If the average per 500-ft roll $= 2.0$, then $\lambda = $ average per 100-ft roll $= 2.0 \times (100/500) = 0.40$. Thus, from Appendix 4,

$$P(X = 0 | \lambda = 0.40) = 0.6703$$

6.20. An insurance company is considering the addition of major-medical coverage for a relatively rare ailment. The probability that a randomly selected individual will have the ailment is 0.001, and 3,000 individuals are included in the group that is insured.

(a) What is the expected number of people who will have the ailment in the group?

(b) What is the probability that no one in this group of 3,000 people will have this ailment?

(a) The distribution of the number of people who will have the ailment would follow the binomial probability distribution with $n = 3,000$ and $p = 0.001$.

$$E(X) = np = (3,000)(0.001) = 3.0 \text{ people}$$

(b) Tabled binomial probabilities are not available for $n = 3{,}000$ and $p = 0.001$. Also, algebraic solution of the binomial formula is not appealing, because of the large numbers that are involved. However, we can use the Poisson distribution to approximate the binomial probability, because $n \geq 30$ and $np < 5$. Therefore:

$$\lambda = np = (3{,}000)(0.001) = 3.0$$
$$P_{\text{Binomial}}(X = 0 | n = 3{,}000,\, p = 0.001) \cong P_{\text{Poisson}}(X = 0 | \lambda = 3.0) = 0.0498$$

(from Appendix 4).

COMPUTER OUTPUT: BINOMIAL DISTRIBUTION

6.21. The probability that a salesperson will complete a sale with a prescreened prospect based on an established method of product presentation is 0.33.

(a) Use Excel to determine the probability of *exactly* 5 sales being completed, given that $n = 10$ calls are made.

(b) What is the probability that *5 or fewer* sales are completed?

(c) What is the probability that *more than 5* sales are completed?

(a) From the Excel output given in Fig. 6-3, the probability of exactly 5 sales is 0.133150945, or more simply, 0.1332. The output was obtained as follows:

(1) Open Excel.

(2) Click **Insert → Function**.

(3) For **Function category** click **Statistical**. For **Function name** click **BINOMDIST**. Click **OK**.

(4) For **Numbers_s** enter: 5. (Notice that the bottom of the dialog box indicates what is required in the selected box.)

(5) For **Trials** enter: 10. For **Probability_s** enter: 0.33. For **Cumulative** enter: FALSE (because we require $P(X = 5)$, *not* $P(X \leq 5)$). The probability value of 0.133150945 (or more simply, 0.1332) now appears at the bottom of the dialog box, as shown in Fig. 6-3.

(6) Click **OK**. The dialog box disappears, and the probability value appears in the initiating cell of the worksheet (usually A1).

(b) In **Step 5** of the Excel instructions for part (a), above, for **cumulative** enter: TRUE. The answer that then appears for $P(X \leq 5)$ is 0.926799543, or more simply, 0.9268.

(c) $P(X > 5) = 1 - P(X \leq 5) = 1 - 0.9268 = 0.0732$.

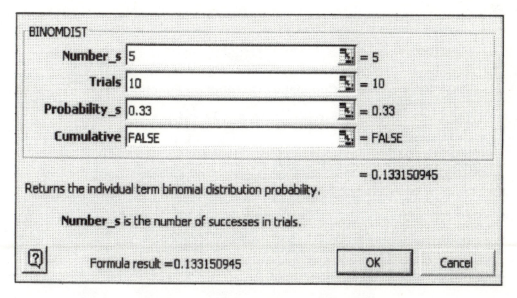

Fig. 6-3 Excel output of a binomial probability.

6.22. The probability that a salesperson will complete a sale with a prescreened prospect based on an established method of product presentation is 0.33.

(a) Use Minitab to determine the probability of *exactly* 5 sales being completed, given that $n = 10$ calls are made.

(b) What is the probability that *5 or fewer* sales are completed?

(c) What is the probability that *more than 5* sales are completed?

(a) Figure 6-4 presents the probability of each possible number of sales. From the printout, we see that the probability of exactly 5 sales being completed is 0.1332. The Minitab instructions that result in the output are

(1) Open Minitab.

(2) Name column C1 "Sales." Enter the numbers 0, 1, 2, ..., 10 in this column.

(3) Click **Calc** → **Probability Distributions** → **Binomial**.

(4) In the dialog box, select **Probability**.

(5) For **Number of trials** enter: 10. For **Probability of success** enter: 0.33. For **Input column** enter: Sales.

(6) Click **OK**.

Probability Density Function

Binomial with n = 10 and p = 0.330000

x	P(X = x)
0.00	0.0182
1.00	0.0898
2.00	0.1990
3.00	0.2614
4.00	0.2253
5.00	0.1332
6.00	0.0547
7.00	0.0154
8.00	0.0028
9.00	0.0003
10.00	0.0000

Fig. 6-4   Minitab output of binomial probabilities.

(b) Figure 6-5 presents the cumulative distribution function from Minitab. In **Step 4**, above, select **Cumulative probability** to obtain the output. From the table, we see that $P(X \leq 5) = 0.9268$.

(c) $P(X > 5) = 1 - P(X \leq 5) = 1 - 0.9268 = 0.0732$.

Cumulative Distribution Function

Binomial with n = 10 and p = 0.330000

x	P(X <= x)
0.00	0.0182
1.00	0.1080
2.00	0.3070
3.00	0.5684
4.00	0.7936
5.00	0.9268
6.00	0.9815
7.00	0.9968
8.00	0.9997
9.00	1.0000
10.00	1.0000

Fig. 6-5   Minitab output of cumulative binomial probabilities.

COMPUTER OUTPUT: POISSON DISTRIBUTION

6.23. Arrivals at a self-service gasoline station average 15 vehicles per hour. Suppose the attendant leaves the service booth for 5 minutes.

   (*a*)   Using Excel, what is the probability that *no one* arrives for service during the 5-minute period?

   (*b*)   What is the probability that *at least* one vehicle arrives?

   (*a*)   The Excel output given in Fig. 6-6 was obtained as follows:

   (1)   Open Excel.

   (2)   Click **Insert → Function**.

   (3)   For **Function category** click **Statistical**. For **Function name** click **POISSON**. Click **OK**.

   (4)   For **X** enter: 0. For **Mean** enter: 1.25.
         (*Note*: Since there are 15 arrivals *per hour*, the arrival rate *per minute* = 0.25, and the arrival rate per 5-minute periods = 5 × 0.25 = 1.25.)

   (5)   For **Cumulative** enter: FALSE (because we require the probability of one specific outcome, that there are 0 arrivals). The probability value of 0.286504797 (or more simply, 0.2865) now appears at the bottom of the dialog box, as shown in Figure 6-6.

   (6)   Click **OK**. The dialog box disappears, and the probability value appears in the initiating cell of the worksheet (usually A1).

   (*b*)   The probability that *at least* one vehicle arrives is 1 minus the probability that no vehicle arrives, obtained from part (*a*): $P(X \geq 1) = 1 - P(X = 0) = 1 - 0.2865 = 0.7135$.

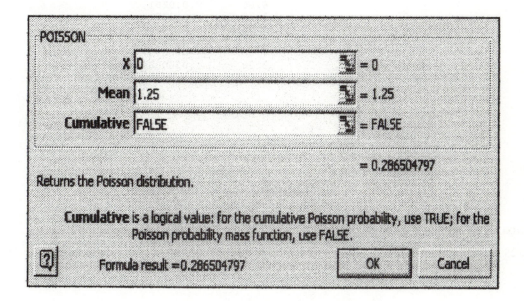

Fig. 6-6   Excel output of a Poisson probability.

6.24. Arrivals at a self-service gasoline station average 15 vehicles per hour. Suppose the attendant leaves the service booth for 5 minutes.

   (*a*)   Using Minitab, what is the probability that *no one* arrives for service during the 5-minute period?

   (*b*)   What is the probability that *at least* one vehicle arrives?

(a) Figure 6-7 presents the probability of each possible number of arrivals. From the printout, we see that the probability of 0 vehicles arriving is 0.2865. The Minitab instruction that result in the output are

(1) Open Minitab.

(2) Name column C1 "Arrivals." Enter the numbers 0, 1, 2,..., 10 in this column.

(3) Click **Calc** → **Probability Distributions** → **Poisson**.

(4) In the dialog box, select **Probability**.

(5) For **Mean** enter: 1.25.
    (*Note*:   Since there are 15 arrivals *per hour*, the arrival rate *per minute* = 0.25, and the arrival rate per 5-*minute periods* = $5 \times 0.25 = 1.25$.)

(6) For **Input column** enter: Arrivals.

(7) Click **OK**.

(b) The probability that *at least* one vehicle arrives is 1 minus the probability that no vehicle arrives, obtained from part (*a*): $P(X \geq 1) = 1 - P(X = 0) = 1 - 0.2865 = 0.7135$.

Probability Density Function

```
Poisson with mu = 1.25000

          x        P( X = x )
       0.00          0.2865
       1.00          0.3581
       2.00          0.2238
       3.00          0.0933
       4.00          0.0291
       5.00          0.0073
       6.00          0.0015
       7.00          0.0003
       8.00          0.0000
       9.00          0.0000
      10.00          0.0000
```

Fig. 6-7   Minitab output of Poisson probabilities.

Supplementary Problems

DISCRETE RANDOM VARIABLES

6.25. The arrival of customers during randomly chosen 10-min intervals at a drive-in facility specializing in photo development and film sales has been found to follow the probability distribution in Table 6.12. Calculate the expected number of arrivals for 10-min intervals and the standard deviation of the arrivals.

Table 6.12   Arrivals of Customers at a Photo-processing Facility during 10-min Intervals

Number of arrivals (X)	0	1	2	3	4	5
Probability [$P(X)$]	0.15	0.25	0.25	0.20	0.10	0.05

Ans. $E(X) = 2.00$, $\sigma = 1.38$ arrivals

6.26. The newsstand sales of a monthly magazine have been found to follow the probability distribution in Table 6.13. Calculate the expected value and the standard deviation for the magazine sales, in thousands.

Table 6.13 Newsstand Sales of a Monthly Magazine

Number of magazines (X), thousands	15	16	17	18	19	20
Probability [$P(X)$]	0.05	0.10	0.25	0.30	0.20	0.10

Ans. $E(X) = 17.80$, $\sigma = 1.29$

6.27. A salesperson has found that the probability of making various numbers of sales per day, given that calls on 10 sales prospects can be made, is presented in Table 6.14. Calculate the expected number of sales per day and the standard deviation of the number of sales.

Table 6.14 Sales per Day when 10 Prospects Are Contacted

Number of sales (X)	1	2	3	4	5	6	7	8
Probability [$P(X)$]	0.04	0.15	0.20	0.25	0.19	0.10	0.05	0.02

Ans. $E(X) = 4.00$, $\sigma = 1.59$ sales

6.28. Referring to Problem 6.27, suppose the sales representative earns a commission of \$25 per sale. Determine the expected daily commission earnings by (*a*) substituting the commission amount for each of the sales numbers in Table 6.14 and calculating the expected commission amount, and (*b*) multiplying the expected sales number calculated in Problem 6.27 by the commission rate.
Ans. (*a*) \$100.00, (*b*) \$100.00

THE BINOMIAL DISTRIBUTION

6.29. There is a 90 percent chance that a particular type of component will perform adequately under high temperature conditions. If the device involved has four such components, determine the probability of each of the following events by use of the formula for binomial probabilities.

(*a*) All of the components perform adequately and therefore the device is operative.

(*b*) The device is inoperative because exactly one of the four components fails.

(*c*) The device is inoperative because one *or more* of the components fail.

Ans. (*a*) 0.6561, (*b*) 0.2916, (*c*) 0.3439

6.30. Verify the answers to Problem 6.29 by constructing a tree diagram and determining the probabilities by the use of the appropriate rules of multiplication and of addition.

6.31. Verify the answers to Problem 6.29 by use of Appendix 2.

6.32. Using the table of binomial probabilities, determine:.

(*a*) $P(X = 8 | n = 20, p = 0.30)$ (*d*) $P(X = 5 | n = 10, p = 0.40)$

(*b*) $P(X \geq 10 | n = 20, p = 0.30)$ (*e*) $P(X > 5 | n = 10, p = 0.40)$

(*c*) $P(X \leq 5 | n = 20, p = 0.30)$ (*f*) $P(X < 5 | n = 10, p = 0.40)$

Ans. (*a*) 0.1144, (*b*) 0.0479, (*c*) 0.4165, (*d*) 0.2007, (*e*) 0.1663, (*f*) 0.6330

6.33. Using the table of binomial probabilities, determine:.

(a) $P(X = 4 | n = 12, p = 0.70)$ (d) $P(X < 3 | n = 8, p = 0.60)$

(b) $P(X \geq 9 | n = 12, p = 0.70)$ (e) $P(X = 5 | n = 10, p = 0.90)$

(c) $P(X \leq 3 | n = 8, p = 0.60)$ (f) $P(X > 7 | n = 10, p = 0.90)$

Ans. (a) 0.0078, (b) 0.4925, (c) 0.1738, (d) 0.0499, (e) 0.0015, (f) 0.9298

6.34. Suppose that 40 percent of the employees in a large firm are in favor of union representation, and a random sample of 10 employees are contacted and asked for an anonymous response. What is the probability that (a) a majority of the respondents and (b) fewer than half of the respondents will be in favor of union representation? *Ans.* (a) 0.1663, (b) 0.6330

6.35. Determine the probabilities in Problem 6.34, if 60 percent of the employees are in favor of union representation. *Ans.* (a) 0.6330, (b) 0.1663

6.36. Refer to the probability distribution in Problem 6.27. Does this probability distribution appear to follow a binomial probability distribution in its form? [*Hint*: Convert the $E(X)$ found in Problem 6.27 into a proportion and use this value as the value of p for comparison with the binomial distribution with $n = 10$.] *Ans.* The two probability distributions correspond quite closely.

THE HYPERGEOMETRIC DISTRIBUTION

6.37. In a class containing 20 students, 15 are dissatisfied with the text used. If a random sample of four students are asked about the text, determine the probability that (a) exactly three, and (b) at least three are dissatisfied with the text. *Ans.* (a) $P \cong 0.47$, (b) $P \cong 0.75$

6.38. Verify the answers to Problem 6.37 by constructing a tree diagram and determining the probabilities by use of the appropriate rules of multiplication and of addition.

6.39. In Section 6.5 it is suggested that the binomial distribution can generally be used to approximate hypergeometric probabilities when $n < 0.05 \ N$. Demonstrate that the binomial approximation of the probability values requested in Problem 6.35 is quite poor. (*Hint*: Use T/N as the p value for the binomial table, which does *not* conform to the sample size requirement, with $n = 4$ being much more than $0.05(20) = 1$.)

6.40 A department group includes five engineers and nine technicians. If five individuals are randomly chosen and assigned to a project, what is the probability that the project group will include exactly two engineers? (*Note*: This is a restatement of Problem 5.57(a), for which the answer was determined by combinational analysis.) *Ans.* $P \cong 0.42$

THE POISSON PROBABILITY DISTRIBUTION

6.41. On average, six people per hour use an electronic teller machine during the prime shopping hours in a department store. What is the probability that

(a) exactly six people will use the machine during a randomly selected hour?

(b) fewer than five people will use the machine during a randomly selected hour?

(c) no one will use the facility during a 10-min interval?

(d) no one will use the facility during a 5-min interval?

Ans. (a) 0.1606, (b) 0.2851, (c) 0.3679, (d) 0.6065

6.42. Suppose that the manuscript for a textbook has a total of 50 errors, or typos, included in the 500 pages of material, and that the errors are distributed randomly throughout the text. What is the probability that

(a) a 30-page chapter has two or more errors?

(b) a 50-page chapter has two or more errors?

(c)   a randomly selected page has no error?

Ans.   (a) 0.8008, (b) 0.9596, (c) 0.9048

6.43.   Only one personal computer per thousand is found to be defective after assembly in a manufacturing plant, and the defective PCs are distributed randomly throughout the production run.

(a)   What is the probability that a shipment of 500 PCs includes no defective computer?

(b)   What is the probability that a shipment of 100 PCs includes at least one defective computer?

Ans.   By the Poisson approximation of binomial probabilities, (a) 0.6065, (b) 0.0952

6.44.   Refer to the probability distribution in Problem 6.24. Does this probability distribution of arrivals appear to follow a Poisson probability distribution in its form? [*Hint*: Use the $E(X)$ calculated in Problem 6.25 as the mean (λ) for determining the Poisson distribution with which the probabilities are to be compared.]
Ans.   The two probability distributions correspond quite closely.

COMPUTER APPLICATIONS

6.45.   The probability that a particular electronic component will be defective is 0.005.

(a)   Using available computer software, determine the probability that exactly one component is defective.

(b)   Using available computer software, determine the probability that one or more components are defective.

Ans.   (a) 0.0386, (b) 0.0393

6.46.   The number of paint blisters that occur in an automated painting process is known to be Poisson-distributed with a mean of 0.005 blisters per square foot. The process is to be used to paint storage-shed panels measuring 10×15 ft.

(a)   Using available software, determine the probability that no blister occurs on a particular panel.

(b)   What is the probability that at least one blister occurs on the panel?

Ans.   (a) $P = 0.4724$ (based on $\lambda = 0.75$ per 10×15 ft panel), (b) $P = 0.5276$

CHAPTER 7

Probability Distributions for Continuous Random Variables: Normal and Exponential

7.1 CONTINUOUS RANDOM VARIABLES

As contrasted to a discrete random variable, a *continuous random variable* is one that can assume any fractional value within a defined range of values. (See Section 1.4.) Because there is an infinite number of possible fractional measurements, one cannot list every possible value with a corresponding probability. Instead, a *probability density function* is defined. This mathematical expression gives the function of X, represented by the symbol $f(X)$, for any designated value of the random variable X. The plot for such a function is called a *probability curve*, and the area between any two points under the curve indicates the probability of a value between these two points occurring by chance.

EXAMPLE 1. For the continuous probability distribution in Fig. 7-1, the probability that a randomly selected shipment will have a net weight between 6,000 and 8,000 lb is equal to the proportion of the total area under the curve that is included within the shaded area. That is, the total area under the probability density function is defined as being equal to 1, and the proportion of this area that is included between the two designated points can be determined by applying the method of integration (from calculus) in conjunction with the mathematical probability density function for this probability curve.

Several standard continuous probability distributions are applicable as models to a wide variety of continuous variables under designated circumstances. Probability tables have been prepared for these standard

122

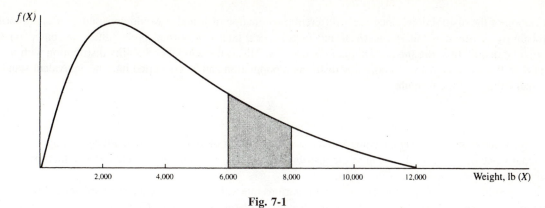

Fig. 7-1

distributions, making it unnecessary to use the method of integration in order to determine areas under the probability curve for these distributions. The standard continuous probability models described in this chapter are the normal and exponential probability distributions.

7.2 THE NORMAL PROBABILITY DISTRIBUTION

The *normal probability distribution* is a continuous probability distribution that is *both symmetrical* and *mesokurtic* (defined in Section 2.4). The probability curve representing the normal probability distribution is often described as being bell-shaped, as exemplified by the probability curve in Fig. 7-2.

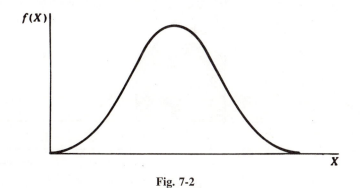

Fig. 7-2

The normal probability distribution is important in statistical inference for three distinct reasons:

(1) The measurements obtained in many random processes are known to follow this distribution.

(2) Normal probabilities can often be used to approximate other probability distributions, such as the binomial and Poisson distributions.

(3) Distributions of such statistics as the sample mean and sample proportion are normally distributed when the sample size is large, regardless of the distribution of the parent population (see Section 8.4).

As is true for any continuous probability distribution, a probability value for a continuous random variable can be determined only for an *interval* of values. The height of the density function, or probability curve, for a normally distributed variable is given by

$$f(X) = \frac{1}{\sqrt{2\pi\sigma^2}} e^{-[(X-\mu)^2/2\sigma^2]} \qquad (7.1)$$

where π is the constant 3.1416, e is the constant 2.7183, μ is the mean of the distribution, and σ is the standard deviation of the distribution. Since every different combination of μ and σ would generate a different normal probability distribution (all symmetrical and mesokurtic), tables of normal probabilities are based on one particular distribution: the *standard normal distribution*. This is the normal probability distribution with $\mu = 0$ and $\sigma = 1$. Any value X from a normally distributed population can be converted into the equivalent standard normal value z by the formula

$$z = \frac{X - \mu}{\sigma} \qquad (7.2)$$

A z value restates the original value X in terms of the number of units of the standard deviation by which the original value differs from the mean of the distribution. A negative value of z would indicate that the original value X was below the value of the mean.

Appendix 5 indicates proportions of area for various intervals of values for the standard normal probability distribution, with the lower boundary of the interval always being at the mean. Converting designated values of the variable X into standard normal values makes use of this table possible, and makes use of the method of integration with respect to the equation for the density function unnecessary.

EXAMPLE 2.   The lifetime of an electrical component is known to follow a normal distribution with a mean $\mu = 2,000$ hr and a standard deviation $\sigma = 200$ hr. The probability that a randomly selected component will last between 2,000 and 2,400 hr is determined as follows.

Figure 7-3 portrays the probability curve (density function) for this problem and also indicates the relationship between the hours X scale and the standard normal z scale. Further, the area under the curve corresponding to the interval "2,000 to 2,400" has been shaded.

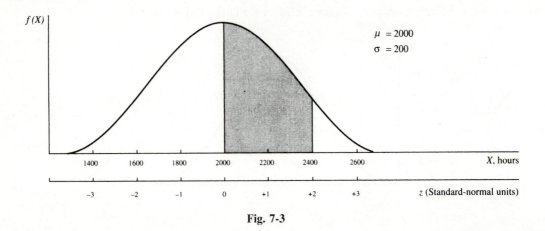

Fig. 7-3

The lower boundary of the interval is at the mean of the distribution, and therefore is at the value $z = 0$. The upper boundary of the designated interval in terms of a z value is

$$z = \frac{X - \mu}{\sigma} = \frac{2,400 - 2,000}{200} = \frac{400}{200} = +2.0$$

The value $z = +2.0$ indicates that 2,400 hr is two standard deviations above the mean of 2,000 hr.

By reference to Appendix 5, we find that

$$P(0 \leq z \leq +2.0) = 0.4772$$

Therefore, $P(2,000 \leq X \leq 2,400) = 0.4772$

Of course, not all problems involve an interval with the mean as the lower boundary. However, Appendix 5 can be used to determine the probability value associated with any designated interval, either by appropriate addition or subtraction of areas or by recognizing that the curve is symmetrical. Example 3 and Problems 7.1 through 7.6 include several varieties of such applications.

EXAMPLE 3. With respect to the electrical components described in Example 2, suppose we are interested in the probability that a randomly selected component will last *more* than 2,200 hr.

Note that by definition the total proportion of area to the right of the mean of 2,000 in Fig. 7-4 is 0.5000. Therefore, if we determine the proportion between the mean and 2,200, we can subtract this value from 0.5000 to obtain the probability of the hours X being greater than 2,200, which is shaded in Fig. 7-4.

$$z = \frac{2,200 - 2,000}{200} = +1.0$$

Thus, 2,200 hr is one standard deviation above the mean of 2,000 hr.

$$P(0 \leq z \leq +1.0) = 0.3413 \qquad \text{(from Appendix 5)}$$
$$P(z > +1.0) = 0.5000 - 0.3413 = 0.1587$$

Therefore, $\qquad\qquad P(X > 2,200) = 0.1587$

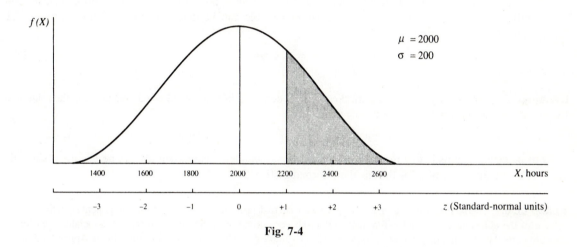

Fig. 7-4

Where the mean μ for a population can be calculated by the formulas presented in Section 3.2, the expected value of a normally distributed random variable is

$$E(X) = \mu \qquad\qquad\qquad (7.3)$$

Where the variance σ^2 for a population can be calculated by the formulas presented in Section 4.6 and 4.7, the variance of a normally distributed random variable is

$$V(X) = \sigma^2 \qquad\qquad\qquad (7.4)$$

7.3 PERCENTILE POINTS FOR NORMALLY DISTRIBUTED VARIABLES

Recall from Section 3.10 that the 90th percentile point, for example, is that point in a distribution such that 90 percent of the values are below this point and 10 percent of the values are above this point. For the standard normal distribution, it is the value of z such that the total proportion of area to the left of this value under the normal curve is 0.90.

EXAMPLE 4. Figure 7-5 illustrates the position of the 90th percentile point for the standard normal distribution. To determine the required value of z, we use Appendix 5 in the *reverse* of the usual direction, because in this case the area under the curve between the mean and the point of interest is known to be 0.40, and we wish to look up the associated value of z.

In Appendix 5 we look in the *body* of the table for the value closest to 0.4000. It is 0.3997. From the row and column headings, the value of z associated with this area is 1.28, and therefore $z_{0.90} = +1.28$. The sign is positive because the 90th percentile point is greater than the mean, and thus the value of z is above its mean of 0.

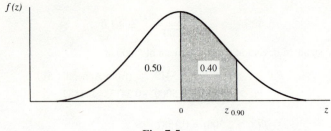

Fig. 7-5

Given the procedure in Example 4 for determining a percentile point for the standard normal distribution, a percentile point for a normally distributed random variable can be determined by solving Formula (7.2) for X (rather than z), resulting in:

$$X = \mu + z\sigma \tag{7.5}$$

EXAMPLE 5. For the lifetime of the electrical component described in Examples 2 and 3, and utilizing the solution in Example 4, the 90th percentile point for the life of the component is

$$X = \mu + z\sigma = 2{,}000 + (1.28)(200) = 2{,}256\,\text{hr}$$

For percentile points below the 50th percentile, the associated z value will always be negative, since the value is below the mean of 0 for the standard normal distribution.

EXAMPLE 6. Continuing from Example 5, suppose we wish to determine the lifetime of the component such that only 10 percent of the components will fail before that time (10th percentile point). See Fig. 7-6 for the associated area for the standard normal probability distribution. Just as we did in Example 4, we look in the body of the table in Appendix 5 for the area closest to 0.4000, but in this case the value of z is taken to be negative. The solution is

$$X = \mu + z\sigma = 2{,}000 + (-1.28)(200) = 1{,}744\,\text{hr}$$

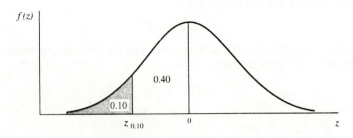

Fig. 7-6

7.4 NORMAL APPROXIMATION OF BINOMIAL PROBABILITIES

When the number of observations or trials n is relatively large, the normal probability distribution can be used to approximate binomial probabilities. A convenient rule is that such approximation is acceptable when $n \geq 30$, and both $np \geq 5$ and $nq \geq 5$. This rule, combined with the one given in Section 6.7 for the Poisson approximation of binomial probabilities, means that whenever $n \geq 30$, binomial probabilities can be approximated by either the normal or the Poisson distribution, depending on the values of np and nq. Different texts use somewhat different rules for determining when such approximations are appropriate.

When the normal probability distribution is used as the basis for approximating a binomial probability value, the mean and standard deviation are based on the expected value and variance of the number of successes for the binomial distribution, as given in Section 6.3. The mean number of successes is

$$\mu = np \tag{7.6}$$

The standard deviation of the number of successes is

$$\sigma = \sqrt{npq} \tag{7.7}$$

EXAMPLE 7.   For a large group of sales prospects, it has been observed that 20 percent of those contacted personally by a sales representative will make a purchase. If a sales representative contacts 30 prospects, we can determine the probability that 10 or more will make a purchase by reference to the binomial probabilities in Appendix 2:

$$P(X \geq 10|n = 30, p = 0.20) = P(X = 10) + P(X = 11) + \cdots$$
$$= 0.0355 + 0.0161 + 0.0064 + 0.0022 + 0.0007 + 0.0002$$
$$= 0.0611 \text{ (the exact binomial probability value)}$$

Now we check to determine if the criteria for normal approximation are satisfied:

Is $n \geq 30$?   Yes, $n = 30$

Is $np \geq 5$?   Yes, $np = 30(0.20) = 6$

Is $nq \geq 5$?   Yes, $nq = 30(0.80) = 24$

The normal approximation of the binomial probability value is

$$\mu = np = (30)(0.20) = 60$$
$$\sigma = \sqrt{npq} = \sqrt{(30)(0.20)(0.80)} = \sqrt{4.8} \cong 2.19$$
$$P_{\text{Binomial}}(X \geq 10|n = 30, p = 0.20) \cong P_{\text{Normal}}(X \geq 9.5|\mu = 6.0, \sigma = 2.19)$$

(*Note*:   This includes the correction for continuity discussed below.)

$$z = \frac{X - \mu}{\sigma} = \frac{9.5 - 6.0}{2.19} = \frac{3.5}{2.19} \cong + 1.60$$

$$P(X \geq 9.5|\mu = 6.0, \sigma = 2.19) = P(z \geq + 1.60)$$
$$= 0.5000 - P(0 \leq z \leq + 1.60) = 0.5000 - 0.4452$$
$$= 0.0548 \quad \text{(the normal approximation)}$$

In Example 7, the class of events "10 or more" is assumed to begin at 9.5 when the normal approximation is used. This adjustment by one-half unit is called the *correction for continuity*. It is required because all the area under the continuous normal distribution has to be assigned to some numeric event, even though no fractional number of successes is possible, for example, between "9 purchasers" and "10 purchasers." Put another way, in the process of normal approximation, a discrete event such as "10 purchasers" has to be considered as a continuous interval of values ranging from an exact lower limit of 9.5 to an exact upper limit of 10.5. Therefore, if Example 7 had asked for the probability of "more than 10 purchasers," the appropriate correction for continuity would involve adding 0.5 to the 10 and determining the area for the interval beginning at 10.5. By the above rationale, the 0.5 is either added or subtracted as a continuity correction according to the form of the probability statement:

(1)   Subtract 0.5 from X when $P(X \geq X_i)$ is required.

(2)   Subtract 0.5 from X when $P(X < X_i)$ is required.

(3)   Add 0.5 to X when $P(X \leq X_i)$ is required.

(4)   Add 0.5 to X when $P(X > X_i)$ is required.

7.5 NORMAL APPROXIMATION OF POISSON PROBABILITIES

When the mean λ of a Poisson distribution is relatively large, the normal probability distribution can be used to approximate Poisson probabilities. A convenient rule is that such approximation is acceptable when $\lambda \geq 10.0$.

The mean and standard deviation of the normal probability distribution are based on the expected value and the variance of the number of events in a Poisson process, as given in Section 6.6. This mean is

$$\mu = \lambda \tag{7.8}$$

The standard deviation is

$$\sigma = \sqrt{\lambda} \tag{7.9}$$

EXAMPLE 8. The average number of calls for service received by a machine repair department per 8-hr shift is 10.0. We can determine the probability that more than 15 calls will be received during a randomly selected 8-hr shift using Appendix 4:

$$P(X > 15 | \lambda = 10.0) = P(X = 16) + P(X = 17) + \cdots$$
$$= 0.0217 + 0.0128 + 0.0071 + 0.0037 + 0.0019 + 0.0009 + 0.0004 + 0.0002 + 0.0001$$
$$= 0.0488 \quad \text{(the exact Poisson probability)}$$

Because the value of λ is (at least) 10, the normal approximation of the Poisson probability value is acceptable. The normal approximation of the Poisson probability value is

$$\mu = \lambda = 10.0$$
$$\sigma = \sqrt{\lambda} = \sqrt{10.0} \cong 3.16$$
$$P_{\text{Poisson}}(X > 15 | \lambda = 10.0) \cong P_{\text{Normal}}(X \geq 15.5 | \mu = 10.0, \sigma = 3.16)$$

(*Note*: This includes the correction for continuity, discussed below.)

$$z = \frac{X - \mu}{\sigma} = \frac{15.5 - 10.0}{3.16} = \frac{5.5}{3.16} \cong +1.74$$

$$P(z \geq +1.74) = 0.5000 - P(0 \leq z \leq +1.74) = 0.5000 - 0.4591 = 0.0409 \quad \text{(the normal approximation)}$$

The correction for continuity applied in Example 8 is the same type of correction described for the normal approximation of binomial probabilities. The rules provided in Section 7.4 as to when 0.5 is added to and subtracted from X apply equally to the situation in which the normal probability distribution is used to approximate Poisson probabilities.

7.6 THE EXPONENTIAL PROBABILITY DISTRIBUTION

If events occur in the context of a Poisson process, as described in Section 6.6, then the length of time or space between successive events follows an *exponential probability distribution*. Because the time or space is a continuum, such a measurement is a continuous random variable. As is the case of any continuous random variable, it is not meaningful to ask, "What is the probability that the first request for service will arrive in *exactly* one minute?" Rather, we must designate an *interval* within which the event is to occur, such as by asking, "What is the probability that the first request for service will arrive *within* a minute?"

Since the Poisson process is stationary, with equal likelihood of the event occurring throughout the relevant period of time, the exponential distribution applies whether we are concerned with the time (or space) *until* the very first event, the time *between* two successive events, or the time until the first event occurs after any selected point in time.

Where λ is the mean number of occurrences for the *interval of interest* (see Section 6.6), the exponential probability that the first event will occur *within* the designated interval of time or space is

$$P(T \leq t) = 1 - e^{-\lambda} \tag{7.10}$$

Similarly, the exponential probability that the first event *will not* occur within the designated interval of time or space is

$$P(T > t) = e^{-\lambda} \qquad (7.11)$$

For both of the above formulas the value of $e^{-\lambda}$ may be obtained from Appendix 3.

EXAMPLE 9. An average of five calls per hour are received by a machine repair department. Beginning the observation at any point in time, the probability that the first call for service will arrive within a *half hour* is

$$\text{Average per hour} = 5.0$$

$$\lambda = \text{Average per half hour} = 2.5$$

$$P = 1 - e^{-\lambda} = 1 - e^{-2.5} = 1 - 0.08208 = 0.91792 \qquad \text{(from Appendix 3)}$$

The expected value and the variance of an exponential probability distribution, where the variable is designated as time T and λ is for *one* unit of time or space (such as one hour), are

$$E(T) = \frac{1}{\lambda} \qquad (7.12)$$

$$V(T) = \frac{1}{\lambda^2} \qquad (7.13)$$

7.7   USING EXCEL AND MINITAB

Computer software for statistical analysis frequently includes the capability of providing probabilities for intervals of values for normally distributed variables. Solved Problems 7.23 through 7.26 are concerned with determining normal probabilities and with determining percentile points for normally distributed variables, using both Excel and Minitab.

Solved Problems

THE NORMAL PROBABILITY DISTRIBUTION

7.1. The packaging process in a breakfast cereal company has been adjusted so that an average of $\mu = 13.0$ oz of cereal is placed in each package. Of course, not all packages have precisely 13.0 oz because of random sources of variability. The standard deviation of the actual net weight is $\sigma = 0.1$ oz, and the distribution of weights is known to follow the normal probability distribution. Determine the probability that a randomly chosen package will contain between 13.0 and 13.2 oz of cereal and illustrate the proportion of area under the normal curve which is associated with this probability value.

From Fig 7-7,

$$z = \frac{X - \mu}{\sigma} = \frac{13.2 - 13.0}{0.1} = +2.0$$

$$P(13.0 \leq X \leq 13.2) = P(0 \leq z \leq +2.0) = 0.4772 \qquad \text{(from Appendix 5)}$$

7.2. For the situation described in Problem 7.1, what is the probability that the weight of the cereal will exceed 13.25 oz? Illustrate the proportion of area under the normal curve which is relevant in this case.

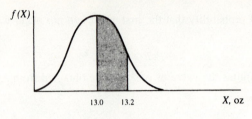

Fig. 7-7

With reference to Fig. 7-8,

$$z = \frac{X - \mu}{\sigma} = \frac{13.25 - 13.0}{0.1} = +2.5$$

$$P(X > 13.25) = P(z > +2.5) = 0.5000 - 0.4938 = 0.0062$$

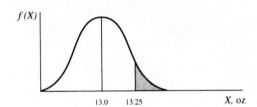

Fig. 7-8

7.3. From Problem 7.1, what is the probability that the weight of the cereal will be between 12.9 and 13.1 oz? Illustrate the proportion of area under the normal curve that is relevant in this case.

Referring to Fig. 7-9,

$$z_1 = \frac{X_1 - \mu}{\sigma} = \frac{12.9 - 13.0}{0.1} = -1.0$$

$$z_2 = \frac{X_2 - \mu}{\sigma} = \frac{13.1 - 13.0}{0.1} = +1.0$$

$$P(12.9 \le X \le 13.1) = P(-1.0 \le z \le +1.0) = 0.3413 + 0.3413 = 0.6826$$

(*Note*:   This is the proportion of area from $-1.0z$ to μ, plus the proportion from μ to $+1.0z$. Also note that because the normal probability distribution is symmetrical, areas to the left of the mean for negative z values are equivalent to areas to the right of the mean.)

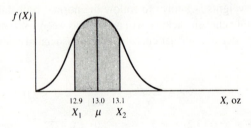

Fig. 7-9

7.4. What is the probability that the weight of the cereal in Problem 7.1 will be between 12.8 and 13.1 oz? Illustrate the proportion of area under the normal curve which is relevant in this case.

With reference to Fig. 7-10,

$$z_1 = \frac{X_1 - \mu}{\sigma} = \frac{12.8 - 13.0}{0.1} = \frac{-0.2}{0.1} = -2.0$$

$$z_2 = \frac{X_2 - \mu}{\sigma} = \frac{13.1 - 13.0}{0.1} = \frac{0.1}{0.1} = +1.0$$

$$P(12.8 \le X \le 13.1) = P(-2.0 \le z \le 1.0) = 0.4772 + 0.3413 = 0.8185$$

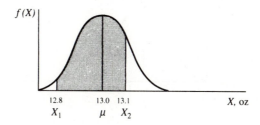

Fig. 7-10

7.5.   From Problem 7.1, what is the probability that the weight of the cereal will be between 13.1 and 13.2 oz? Illustrate the proportion of area under the normal curve which is relevant in this case.

Referring to Fig. 7-11,

$$z_1 = \frac{X_1 - \mu}{\sigma} = \frac{13.1 - 13.0}{0.1} = +1.0$$

$$z_2 = \frac{X_2 - \mu}{\sigma} = \frac{13.2 - 13.0}{0.1} = +2.0$$

$$P(13.1 \le X \le 13.2) = P(+1.0 \le z \le +2.0) = 0.4772 - 0.3413 = 0.1359$$

(*Note*:   The probability is equal to the proportion of area from 13.0 to 13.2, minus the proportion of area from 13.0 to 13.1.)

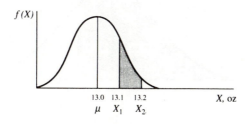

Fig. 7-11

7.6.   The amount of time required for routine automobile transmission service is normally distributed with the mean $\mu = 45$ min and the standard deviation $\sigma = 8.0$ min. The service manager plans to have work begin on the transmission of a customer's car 10 min after the car is dropped off, and the customer is told that the car will be ready within 1 hr total time. What is the probability that the service manager will be wrong? Illustrate the proportion of area under the normal curve which is relevant in this case.

From Fig. 7-12,

$$P(\text{Wrong}) = P(X > 50), \text{ since actual work is to begin in 10 min}$$

$$z = \frac{X - \mu}{\sigma} = \frac{50 - 45}{8.0} = \frac{5.0}{8.0} = +0.62$$

$$P(X > 50) = P(z > +0.62) = 0.5000 - 0.2324 = 0.2676$$

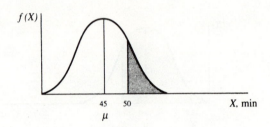

Fig. 7-12

PERCENTILE POINTS FOR NORMALLY DISTRIBUTED VARIABLES

7.7. Referring to Problem 7.6, what is. the required working time allotment such that there is a 75 percent chance that the transmission service will be completed within that time? Illustrate the proportion of area that is relevant.

As illustrated in Fig. 7-13, a proportion of area of 0.2500 is included between the mean and the 75th percentile point. Therefore, as the first step in the solution we determine the required z value by finding the area in the body of the table in Appendix 5 that is closest to 0.2500. The closest area is 0.2486, with $z_{0.75} = +0.67$. We then convert this value of z into the required value of X by:

$$X = \mu + z\sigma = 45 + (0.67)(8.0) = 50.36 \text{ min}$$

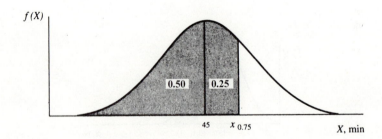

Fig. 7-13

7.8. With reference to Problem 7.6, what is the working time allotment such that there is a probability of just 30 percent that the transmission service can be completed within that time? Illustrate the proportion of area which is relevant.

Since a proportion of area of 0.30 is to the left of the unknown value of X in Fig. 7-14, it follows that a proportion of 0.20 is between that percentile point and the mean. By reference to Appendix 5, the proportion of area closest to this 0.1985, with $z_{0.30} = -0.52$. The z value is negative because the percentile point is to the left of the mean. Finally, the z value is converted to the required value of X:

$$X = \mu + z\sigma$$
$$X = 45 + (-0.52)(8.0) = 45 - 4.16 = 40.84 \text{ min}$$

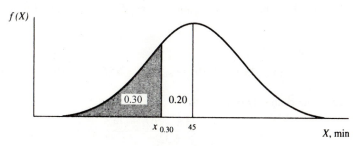

Fig. 7-14

NORMAL APPROXIMATION OF BINOMIAL AND POISSON PROBABILITIES

7.9. Of the people who enter a large shopping mall, it has been found that 70 percent will make at least one purchase. For a sample of $n = 50$ individuals, what is the probability that at least 40 people make one or more purchases each?

The normal approximation of the required binomial probability value can be used, because $n \geq 30$, $np \geq 5$, and $n(q) \geq 5$.

$$\mu = np = (50)(0.70) = 35.0$$
$$\sigma = \sqrt{npq} = \sqrt{(50)(0.70)(0.30)} = \sqrt{10.5} = 3.24$$
$$P_{\text{Binomial}}(X \geq 40 | n = 50, p = 0.70) \cong P_{\text{Normal}}(X \geq 39.5 | \mu = 35.0, \sigma = 3.24)$$

(*Note*: The correction for continuity is included, as described in Section 7.4.)

$$z = \frac{X - \mu}{\sigma} = \frac{39.5 - 35.0}{3.24} = \frac{4.5}{3.24} = +1.39$$
$$P(X \geq 39.5) = P(z \geq +1.39) = 0.5000 - 0.4177 = 0.0823$$

7.10. For the situation described in Problem 7.9, what is the probability that fewer than 30 of the 50 sampled individuals make at least one purchase?

Since, from Problem 7.9, $\mu = 35.0$ and $\sigma = 3.24$,

$$P_{\text{Binomial}}(X < 30 | n = 50, p = 0.70) \cong P_{\text{Normal}}(X \leq 29.5 | \mu = 35.0, \sigma = 3.24)$$

(*Note*: The correction for continuity is included.)

$$z = \frac{X - \mu}{\sigma} = \frac{29.5 - 35.0}{3.24} = \frac{-5.5}{3.24} = -1.70$$
$$P(X \leq 29.5) = P(z \leq -1.70) = 0.5000 - 0.4554 = 0.0446$$

7.11. Calls for service are known to arrive randomly and as a stationary process at an average of five calls per hour. What is the probability that more than 50 calls for service will be received during an 8-hr shift?

Because the mean for the 8-hr period for this Poisson process exceeds $\lambda = 10$ ($\lambda = 8 \times 5 = 40$), the normal probability distribution can be used to approximate the Poisson probability value. With $\mu = \lambda = 40.0$ and $\sigma = \sqrt{\lambda} = \sqrt{40.0} = 6.32$,

$$P_{\text{Poisson}}(X > 50 | \lambda = 40.0) \cong P_{\text{Normal}}(X \geq 50.5 | \mu = 40.0, \sigma = 6.32)$$

(*Note*: The correction for continuity is included.)

$$z = \frac{X - \mu}{\sigma} = \frac{50.5 - 40.0}{6.32} = \frac{10.5}{6.32} = +1.66$$

$$P(X \geq 50.5) = P(z \geq +1.66) = 0.5000 - 0.4515 = 0.0485$$

7.12. Referring to Problem 7.11, what is the probability that 35 or fewer calls for service will be received during an 8-hr shift?

Since $\mu = 40.0$ and $\sigma = 6.32$,

$$P_{\text{Poisson}}(X \leq 35 | \lambda = 40.0) \cong P_{\text{Normal}}(X \leq 35.5 | \mu = 40.0, \sigma = 6.32)$$

(*Note*: The correction for continuity is included.)

$$z = \frac{X - \mu}{\sigma} = \frac{35.5 - 40.0}{6.32} = \frac{-4.5}{6.32} = -0.71$$

$$P(X \leq 35.5) = P(z \leq -0.71) = 0.5000 - 0.2612 = 0.2388$$

THE EXPONENTIAL PROBABILITY DISTRIBUTION

7.13. On the average, a ship arrives at a certain dock every second day. What is the probability that after the departure of a ship four days will pass before the arrival of the next ship?

$$\text{Average per 2 days} = 1.0$$
$$\text{Average per day} = 0.5$$
$$\lambda = \text{average per 4-day period} = 4 \times 0.5 = 2.0$$
$$P(T > 4) = e^{-\lambda} = e^{-2.0} = 0.13534 \quad \text{(from Appendix 3)}$$

7.14. Each 500-ft roll of sheet steel includes two flaws on average. What is the probability that as the sheet steel is unrolled the first flaw occurs within the first 50-ft segment?

$$\text{Average per 500-ft roll} = 2.0$$

$$\lambda = \text{average per 50-ft segment} = \frac{2.0}{10} = 0.20$$

$$P(T \leq 50) = 1 - e^{-\lambda} = 1 - e^{-0.20} = 1 - 0.81873 = 0.18127 \quad \text{(from Appendix 3)}$$

7.15. An application that is concerned with use of the exponential distribution can be transformed into Poisson distribution form, and vice versa. To illustrate such transformation, suppose that an average of four aircraft per 8-hr day arrive for repairs at a repair facility. (*a*) What is the probability that the first arrival does *not* occur during the first hour of work? (*b*) Demonstrate that the equivalent Poisson-oriented problem is the probability that there will be *no* arrivals in the 1-hr period. (*c*) What is the probability that the first arrival occurs within the first hour? (*d*) Demonstrate that the equivalent Poisson-oriented problem is the probability that there will be one or more arrivals during the 1-hr period.

(*a*) $\lambda = 0.5$ (per hour)
    $P(T > 1) = e^{-\lambda} = e^{-0.5} = 0.60653$ (from Appendix 3)

(*b*) $P(X = 0 | \lambda = 0.5) = 0.6065$ (from Appendix 4)

(*c*) $\lambda = 0.5$ (per hour)
    $P(T \leq 1) = 1 - e^{-\lambda} = 1 - e^{-0.5} = 1 - 0.60653 = 0.39347$ (from Appendix 3)

(*d*) $P(X \geq 1 | \lambda = 0.5) = 1 - P(X = 0) = 1.0000 - 0.6065 = 0.3935$ (from Appendix 4)

Thus, in the case of both transformations the answers are identical, except for the number of digits which happen to be carried in the two tables.

MISCELLANEOUS PROBLEMS CONCERNING PROBABILITY DISTRIBUTIONS

(*Note*:   Problems 7.16 through 7.22 involve the use of all of the probability distributions covered in Chapters 6 and 7.)

7.16.   A shipment of 10 engines includes one that is defective. If seven engines arc chosen randomly from this shipment, what is the probability that none of the seven is defective?

Using the hypergeometric distribution (see Section 6.5),

$$P(X|N, T, n) = \frac{\binom{N-T}{n-X}\binom{T}{X}}{\binom{N}{n}}$$

$$P(X = 0|N = 10, T = 1, n = 7) = \frac{\binom{10-1}{7-0}\binom{1}{0}}{\binom{10}{7}} = \frac{\left(\frac{9!}{7!2!}\right)\left(\frac{1!}{0!1!}\right)}{\left(\frac{10!}{7!3!}\right)} = \frac{(36)(1)}{120} = 0.30$$

7.17.   Suppose that in Problem 7.16 the overall proportion of engines with some defect is 0.10, but that a very large number are being assembled in an engine-assembly plant. What is the probability that a random sample of seven engines will include no defective engines?

Using the binomial distribution (see Section 6.3),

$$P(X = 0|n = 7, p = 0.10) = 0.4783 \qquad \text{(from Appendix 2)}$$

7.18.   Suppose that the proportion of engines that contain a defect in an assembly operation is 0.10, and a sample of 200 engines is included in a particular shipment. What is the probability that at least 30 of the 200 engines contain a defect?

Use of the normal approximation of the binomial probability distribution as described in Section 7.4 is acceptable, because $n \geq 30$, $np \geq 5$, and $n(q) \geq 5$.

$$\mu = np = (200)(0.10) = 20.0$$
$$\sigma = \sqrt{np(q)} = \sqrt{(200)(0.10)(0.90)} = \sqrt{18.00} \cong 4.24$$
$$P_{\text{Binomial}}(X \geq 30|n = 200, p = 0.10) \cong P_{\text{Normal}}(X \geq 29.5|\mu = 20.0, \sigma = 4.24)$$

(*Note*:   The correction for continuity is included.)

$$z = \frac{X - \mu}{\sigma} = \frac{29.5 - 20.0}{4.24} = \frac{9.5}{4.24} = +2.24$$

$$P(X \geq 29.5) = P(z \geq +2.24) = 0.5000 - 0.4875 = 0.0125 \qquad \text{(from Appendix 5)}$$

7.19.   Suppose that the proportion of engines that contain a defect in an assembly operation is 0.01, and a sample of 200 engines are included in a particular shipment. What is the probability that three or fewer engines contain a defect?

Use of the Poisson approximation of the binomial probability distribution (see Section 6.7) is acceptable in this case because $n \geq 30$ and $np < 5$.

$$\lambda = np = (200)(0.01) = 2.0$$
$$P_{\text{Binomial}}(X \leq 3|n = 200, p = 0.01) \cong P_{\text{Poisson}}(X \leq 3|\lambda = 2.0)$$
$$= 0.1353 + 0.2707 + 0.2707 + 0.1804 = 0.8571$$

(from Appendix 4)

7.20.   An average of 0.5 customer per minute arrives at a checkout stand. After an attendant opens the stand, what is the probability that there will be a wait of at least 3 min before the first customer arrives?

Using the exponential probability distribution described in Section 7.6,

$$\text{Average per minute} = 0.5$$
$$\lambda = \text{average for 3 min} = 0.5 \times 3 = 1.5$$
$$P(T > 3) = e^{-\lambda} = e^{-1.5} = 0.22313 \qquad \text{(from Appendix 3)}$$

7.21. An average of 0.5 customer per minute arrives at a checkout stand. What is the probability that five or more customers will arrive in a given 5-min interval?

From Section 6.6 on the Poisson probability distribution,

$$\text{Average per minute} = 0.5$$
$$\lambda = \text{average for 5 min} = 0.5 \times 5 = 2.5$$
$$P(X \geq 5|\lambda = 2.5) = 0.0668 + 0.0278 + 0.0099 + 0.0031 + 0.0009 + 0.0002 = 0.1087$$

(from Appendix 4)

7.22. An average of 0.5 curomer per minute arrives at a checkout stand. What is the probability that more than 20 customers arrive at the stand during a particular interval of 0.5 hr?

Use of the normal approximation of the Poisson probability distribution described in Section 7.5 is acceptable because $\lambda \geq 10.0$.

$$\text{Average per minute} = 0.5$$
$$\lambda = \text{average for 30 min} = 0.5 \times 30 = 15.0$$
$$\mu = \lambda = 15.0$$
$$\sigma = \sqrt{\lambda} = \sqrt{15.0} \cong 3.87$$
$$P_{\text{Poisson}}(X > 20|\lambda = 15.0) \cong P_{\text{Normal}}(X \geq 20.5|\mu = 15.0, \sigma = 3.87)$$

(*Note*: The correction for continuity is included.)

$$z = \frac{X - \mu}{\sigma} = \frac{20.5 - 15.0}{3.87} = \frac{5.50}{3.87} = +1.42$$
$$P(X \geq 20.5) = P(z \geq +1.42) = 0.5000 - 0.4222 = 0.0778 \qquad \text{(from Appendix 5)}$$

COMPUTER APPLICATIONS: DETERMINING NORMAL PROBABILITIES

7.23. From Problem 7.1, the mean weight of cereal per package is $\mu = 13.0$ oz with a $\sigma = 0.1$ oz. The weights are normally distributed. Using Excel, determine probability that the weight of a randomly selected package exceeds 13.25 oz.

Refer to Fig. 7-15. The (rounded) probability reported at the bottom of the dialog box of 0.9938 is the cumulative probability of the weight being *less than or equal to* 13.25 oz. Therefore, the probability that the weight will *exceed* 13.25 oz is obtained by subtracting the reported value from 1.0:

$$P(X > 13.25) = 1.0 - P(X \leq 13.25)$$
$$= 1.0 - 0.9938 = 0.0062$$

The above result corresponds to the manually derived answer obtained in Problem 7.2. The Excel output given in Fig. 7-15 was obtained as follows:

(1) Open Excel.

(2) Click **Insert** → **Function**.

(3) For **Function category** choose **Statistical**. For **Function name** choose **NORMDIST**. Click **OK**.

(4)   In the dialog box, for **X** insert: 13.25. For **Mean** insert: 13.0. For **Standard dev** insert 0.1. For **Cumulative** insert: TRUE. The probability value of 0.99379032 (or more simply, 0.9938) now appears at the bottom of the dialog box, as shown in Fig. 7-15.

(5)   Click **OK**. The dialog box disappears and the probability value appears in the initiating cell of the worksheet (usually A1).

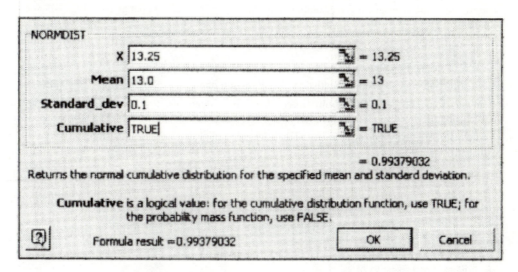

Fig. 7-15   Excel output of a normal probability.

7.24. From Problem 7.1, the mean weight of cereal per package is $\mu = 13.0$ oz with $\sigma = 0.1$ oz. The weights are normally distributed. Using Minitab, determine the probability that the weight of one randomly selected package exceeds 13.25 oz.

Refer to Fig. 7-16. The probability reported value of 0.9938 that is reported is the cumulative probability of the weight being *less than or equal to* 13.25 oz. Therefore, the probability that the weight will *exceed* 13.25 oz is obtained by subtracting the reported value from 1.0:

$$P(X > 13.25) = 1.0 - P(X \leq 13.25)$$
$$= 1.0 - 0.9938 = 0.0062$$

The above result corresponds to the manually derived answer in Problem 7.2. The Minitab output given in Fig. 7-16 was obtained as follows:

(1)   Open Minitab.

(2)   Click **Calc** → **Probability distributions** → **Normal**.

(3)   In the dialog box, select **Cumulative probability**. For **Mean** enter: 13.0. For **Standard deviation** enter: 0.1. For **Input constant** enter 13.25.

(4)   Click **OK**.

Cumulative Distribution Function

```
Normal with mean = 13.0000 and standard deviation = 0.100000

        x      P( X <= x )
  13.2500         0.9938
```

Fig. 7-16   Minitab output of a normal probability.

COMPUTER APPLICATIONS: DETERMINING PERCENTILES

7.25. From Problem 7.6, the amount of time required for transmission service is normally distributed, with $\mu = 45$ min and $\sigma = 8.0$ min. Using Excel, determine the time amount at the 75th percentile.

From Fig. 7-17 the answer given at the bottom of the dialog box is 50.4 min (rounded). This answer corresponds to the manually derived solution in Problem 7.7. The Excel output given in Fig. 7-17 was obtained as follows:

(1) Open Excel.

(2) Click **Insert** → **Function**.

(3) For **Function category** choose **Statistical**. For **Function name** choose **NORMINV**. Click **OK**.

(4) In the dialog box, for **Probability** insert: 0.75. For **Mean** insert: 45.0. For **Standard dev** insert 8.0. The value 50.39592293 (or more simply, 50.4) now appears at the bottom of the dialog box, as shown in Fig. 7-15.

(5) Click **OK**. The dialog box disappears and the 75th percentile value appears in the initiating cell of the worksheet (usually Al).

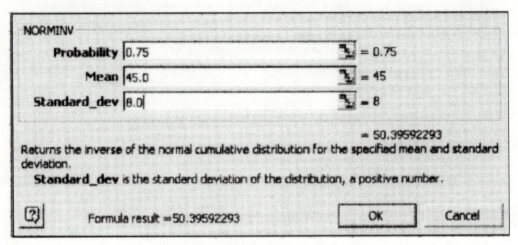

Fig. 7-17   Excel output of a percentile.

7.26. From Problem 7.6, the amount of time required for transmission service is normally distributed, with $\mu = 45$ min and $\sigma = 8.0$ min. Using Minitab, determine the time amount at the 75th percentile.

From Fig. 7-18 the answer given is 50.3959, or 50.4 min rounded. This answer corresponds to the manually derived solution in Problem 7.7. The Minitab output given in Fig. 7-18 was obtained as follows:

(1) Open Minitab.

(2) Click **Calc** → **Probability distributions** → **Normal**.

(3) In the dialog box, select **Inverse cumulative probability**. For **Mean** enter: 45.0. For **Standard deviation** enter: 8.0. For **Input constant** enter: 0.75.

(4) Click **OK**.

Inverse Cumulative Distribution Function

```
Normal with mean = 45.0000 and standard deviation = 8.00000

P( X <= x )          x
    0.7500      50.3959
```

Fig. 7-18   Minitab output of a percentile.

Supplementary Problems

THE NORMAL PROBABILITY DISTRIBUTION

7.27. The reported scores on a nationally standardized achievement test for high school graduates have a mean of $\mu = 500$ with the standard deviation $\sigma = 100$. The scores are approximately normally distributed. What is the probability that the score of a randomly chosen individual will be (*a*) between 500 and 650? (*b*) Between 450 and 600?
Ans. (*a*) 0.4332, (*b*) 0.5328

7.28. For a nationally standardized achievement test the mean is $\mu = 500$ with $\sigma = 100$. The scores are normally distributed. What is the probability that a randomly chosen individual will have a score (*a*) below 300? (*b*) Above 650?
Ans. (*a*) 0.0228, (*b*) 0.0668

7.29. The useful life of a certain brand of performance tires has been found to follow a normal distribution with $\mu = 38{,}000$ miles and $\sigma = 3{,}000$ miles. (*a*) What is the probability that a randomly selected tire will have a useful life of at least 35,000 miles? (*b*) What is the probability that it will last more than 45,000 miles?
Ans. (*a*) 0.8413, (*b*) 0.0099

7.30. A dealer orders 500 of the tires specified in Problem 7.29 for resale. Approximately what number of tires will last (*a*) between 40,000 and 45,000 miles? (*b*) 40,000 miles or more?
Ans. (*a*) 121, (*b*) 126

7.31. An individual buys four of the tires described in Problem 7.29. What is the probability that all four tires will last (*a*) at least 38,000 miles? (*b*) At least 35,000 miles? (*Hint*: After obtaining the probability for one tire, use the multiplication rule for independent events from Section 5.6 to determine the probability for all four tires.)
Ans. (*a*) 0.0625, (*b*) 0.5010

7.32. The amount of time required per individual at a bank teller's window has been found to be approximately normally distributed with $\mu = 130$ sec and $\sigma = 45$ sec. What is the probability that a randomly selected individual will (*a*) require less than 100 sec to complete a transaction? (*b*) Spend between 2.0 and 3.0 min at the teller's window?
Ans. (*a*) 0.2514, (*b*) 0.4536

PERCENTILE POINTS FOR NORMALLY DISTRIBUTED VARIABLES

7.33. For a nationally standardized achievement test the mean is $\mu = 500$ with $\sigma = 100$. The scores are normally distributed. What score is at the (*a*) 50th percentile point, (*b*) 30th percentile point, and (*c*) 90th percentile point?
Ans. (*a*) 500, (*b*) 448, (*c*) 628

7.34. Under the conditions specified in Problem 7.32, (*a*) within what length of time do the 20 percent of individuals with the simplest transactions complete their business at the window? (*b*) At least what length of time is required for the individuals in the top 5 percent of required time?
Ans. (*a*) 92 sec, (*b*) 204 sec

NORMAL APPROXIMATION OF BINOMIAL AND POISSON PROBABILITIES

7.35. For the several thousand items stocked by a mail-order firm, there is an overall probability of 0.08 that a particular item (including specific size and color, etc.) is out of stock. If a shipment covers orders for 120 different items, what is the probability that 15 or more items are out of stock?
Ans. 0.0495

7.36. For the shipment described in Problem 7.35, what is the probability that there are between 10 and 15 items out of stock?
Ans. 0.4887

7.37. During the 4 P.M. to 6 P.M. peak period in an automobile service station, one car enters the station every 3 min, on average. What is the probability that at least 25 cars enter the station for service between 4 P.M. and 5 P.M.?
Ans.   0.1562

7.38. For the service station arrivals in Problem 7.37, what is the probability that fewer than 30 cars enter the station between 4 P.M. and 6 P.M. on a randomly selected day?
Ans.   0.0485

THE EXPONENTIAL PROBABILITY DISTRIBUTION

7.39. On average, six people per hour use an electronic teller machine during the prime shopping hours in a department store.

(a)   What is the probability that at least 10 min will pass between the arrival of two customers?

(b)   What is the probability that after a customer leaves, another customer does not arrive for at least 20 min?

(c)   What is the probability that a second customer arrives within 1 min after a first customer begins a banking transaction?

Ans.   (a) 0.36788, (b) 0.13534, (c) 0.09516

7.40. Suppose that the manuscript for a textbook has a total of 50 errors, or typos, included in the 500 pages of material, and that the errors are distributed randomly throughout the text. As the technical proofreader begins reading a particular chapter, what is the probability that the first error in that chapter (a) is included within the first five pages? (b) Occurs beyond the first 15 pages?
Ans.   (a) 0.39347, (b) 0.22313

MISCELLANEOUS PROBLEMS CONCERNING PROBABILITY DISTRIBUTIONS

(*Note*:   Problems 7.41 through 7.48 involve the use of all of the probability distributions covered in Chapters 6 and 7.)

7.41. The frequency distribution of the length of stay of Medicare patients in a community hospital has been found to be approximately symmetrical and mesokurtic, with $\mu = 8.4$ days and $\sigma = 2.6$ days (with fractions of days measured). What is the probability that a randomly chosen individual will be in the hospital for (a) less than 5.0 days? (b) More than 8.0 days?
Ans.   (a) 0.0951, (b) 0.5596

7.42. A firm that manufactures and markets a wide variety of low-priced specialty toys (such as a ball that bounces in unexpected directions) has found that in the long run 40 percent of the toys which it develops have at least moderate market success. If six new toys have been developed for market introduction next summer, what is the probability that at least three of them will have moderate market success?
Ans.   0.4557

7.43. The firm in Problem 7.42 has 60 toy ideas in the process of development for introduction during the next few years. If all 60 of these are eventually marketed, what is the probability that at least 30 of them will have moderate market success?
Ans.   0.0735

7.44. From Problems 7.42 and 7.43, above, suppose 5 percent of the toys that are marketed turn out to be outstanding sales successes. If 60 new toys are introduced during the next few years, what is the probability that none of them will turn out to be an outstanding sales success?
Ans.   0.0498

7.45. Customers arrive at a refreshment stand located in a sports arena at an average rate of two per minute. What is the probability that five or more people will approach the stand for refreshments during a randomly chosen minute?
Ans.   0.0526

7.46. From Problem 7.45, what is the probability that after the refreshment stand opens, two full minutes pass before the first customer arrives?
Ans. 0.01832

7.47. For the situation described in Problem 7.45, what is the probability that more than 50 people will come to the stand during a half-hour period?
Ans. 0.8907

7.48. Of the eight hotels located in a resort area, three can be described as being mediocre in terms of customer services. A travel agent chooses two of the hotels randomly for each of two clients planning vacations in the resort area. What is the probabilty that at least one of the clients will end up in one of the mediocre hotels?
Ans. 0.6429

COMPUTER APPLICATIONS

7.49. From Problem 7.28, the scores on a nationally standardized achievement test are normally distributed, with $\mu = 500$ and $\sigma = 100$. Using an available computer program, determine the probability that a randomly chosen individual will have a score (*a*) below 300 and (*b*) above 650.
Ans. (*a*) 0.0228, (*b*) 0.0668 (which correspond to the manual solutions in Problem 7.28)

7.50. From Problem 7.33, the scores on a nationally standardized achievement test are normally distributed, with $\mu = 500$ and $\sigma = 100$. Using an available computer program, determine the value at the (*a*) 30th percentile point and (*b*) 90th percentile point.
Ans. (*a*) 448, (*b*) 628 (which correspond to the manual solutions in Problem 7.33)

CHAPTER 8

Sampling Distributions and Confidence Intervals for the Mean

8.1 POINT ESTIMATION OF A POPULATION OR PROCESS PARAMETER

Because of factors such as time and cost, the parameters of a population or process frequently are estimated on the basis of sample statistics. As defined in Section 1.2, a *parameter* is a summary value for a population or process, whereas a *sample statistic* is a summary value for a sample. In order to use a sample statistic as an estimator of a parameter, the sample must be a *random sample* from a population (see Section 1.6) or a *rational subgroup* from a process (see Section 1.7).

EXAMPLE 1. The mean μ and standard deviation σ of a population of measurements are population parameters. The mean $\bar{X}$ and standard deviation s of a sample of measurements are sample statistics.

A *point estimator* is the numeric value of a sample statistic that is used to estimate the value of a population or process parameter. One of the most important characteristics of an estimator is that it be unbiased. An *unbiased estimator* is a sample statistic whose expected value is equal to the parameter being estimated. As explained in Section 6.2, an *expected value* is the long-run mean average of the sample statistic. The elimination of any systematic bias is assured when the sample statistic is for a *random sample* taken from a population (see Section 1.6) or a *rational subgroup* taken from a process (see Section 1.7). Either sampling method assures that the sample is unbiased but does not eliminate sampling variability, or *sampling error*, as explained in the following section.

Table 8.1 presents some frequently used point estimators of population parameters. In every case, the appropriate estimator of a population parameter simply is the corresponding sample statistic. However, note that in Section 4.6, Formula (*4.6*) for the sample variance includes a correction factor. Without this correction, the sample variance would be a biased estimator of the population variance.

142

Table 8.1   Frequently Used Point Estimators

Population parameter	Estimator
Mean, μ	$\bar{X}$
Difference between the means of two populations, $\mu_1 - \mu_2$	$\bar{X}_1 - \bar{X}_2$
Proportion, π	$\hat{p}$
Difference between the proportions in two populations, $\pi_1 - \pi_2$	$\hat{p}_1 - \hat{p}_2$
Variance, σ^2	s^2
Standard deviation, σ	s

8.2   THE CONCEPT OF A SAMPLING DISTRIBUTION

Your understanding of the concept of a sampling distribution is fundamental to your understanding of statistical inference. As we have already established, a *population distribution* is the distribution of all the individual measurements in a population, and a *sample distribution* is the distribution of the individual values included in a sample. In contrast to such distributions for individual measurements, a *sampling distribution* refers to the distribution of different values that a sample statistic, or estimator, would have over many samples of the same size. Thus, even though we typically would have just one random sample or rational subgroup, we recognize that the particular sample statistic that we determine, such as the sample mean or median, is not exactly equal to the respective population parameter. Further, *a sample statistic will vary in value from sample to sample* because of random sampling variability, or *sampling error*. This is the idea underlying the concept that any sample statistic is in fact a type of variable whose distribution of values is represented by a sampling distribution.

EXAMPLE 2.   Table 8.2 presents the individual weights included in a sample of five rational subgroups of size $n = 4$ packages of potato chips. The five samples were taken from a process that was known to be stable, and with a normal distribution of weights being packaged for which the mean is $\mu = 15.0$ oz and the standard deviation is $\sigma = 0.10$ oz. The sample mean, median, and standard deviation are reported for each sample. Note that these three sample statistics all vary in their values from sample to sample. Also note that the values of the sample statistics cluster around the respective process parameter value. That is, the five sample means are clustered around the process mean of 15.0 oz, the five sample medians are clustered around the process median of 15.0 oz (because the process measurements are normally distributed and therefore symmetrical, the process median is the same as the process mean), and the five sample standard deviations are clustered around the process standard deviation of 0.10 oz.

Table 8.2   Five Samples Taken from the Same Process

	Sample 1	Sample 2	Sample 3	Sample 4	Sample 5
	14.95	14.99	15.09	14.71	14.96
	14.96	15.07	14.98	14.94	15.20
	14.95	15.08	15.05	14.88	15.31
	15.03	14.94	14.99	14.98	15.21
$\bar{X}$	14.97	15.02	15.03	14.88	15.17
Med	14.96	15.03	15.02	14.91	15.08
s	0.039	0.067	0.052	0.119	0.149

8.3   SAMPLING DISTRIBUTION OF THE MEAN

We now turn our attention specifically to the sampling distribution of the sample mean. In the next chapter we shall consider sampling distributions for other sample statistics.

When the mean of just one sample is used in statistical inference about a population mean, it would be useful to know the (long-run) expected value and the variability to be expected from sample to sample. Amazingly, we are able to determine both the expected value and the variability of the sample mean by knowing the mean and standard deviation of the population (or process). But what if the parameter values are not known, and we have data from only one sample? Even then, the variability of the sample statistic, such as the sample mean, from sample to sample can still be determined and used in statistical inference.

The sampling distribution of the mean is described by determining the mean of such a distribution, which is the expected value $E(\bar{X})$, and the standard deviation of the distribution of sample means, designated $\sigma_{\bar{x}}$. Because this standard deviation is indicative of the accuracy of the sample statistic as an estimator of a population mean, $\sigma_{\bar{x}}$ usually is called the *standard error of the mean*. When the population or process parameters are known, the expected value and standard error for the sampling distribution of the mean are

$$E(\bar{X}) = \mu \tag{8.1}$$

$$\sigma_{\bar{x}} = \frac{\sigma}{\sqrt{n}} \tag{8.2}$$

EXAMPLE 3.   Suppose the mean of a very large population is $\mu = 50.0$ and the standard deviation of the measurements is $\sigma = 12.0$. We determine the sampling distribution of the sample means for a sample size of $n = 36$, in terms of the expected value and the standard error of the distribution, as follows:

$$E(\bar{X}) = \mu = 50.0$$

$$\sigma_{\bar{x}} = \frac{\sigma}{\sqrt{n}} = \frac{12.0}{\sqrt{36}} = \frac{12.0}{6} = 2.0$$

When sampling from a population that is finite and of limited size, a *finite correction factor* is available for the correct determination of the standard error. The effect of this correction factor is always to reduce the value that otherwise would be calculated. As a general rule, the correction is negligible and can be omitted when $n < 0.05N$, that is, when the sample size is less than 5 percent of the population size. Because populations from which samples are taken are usually large, many texts and virtually all computer programs do not include this correction option. The formula for the standard error of the mean with the finite correction factor included is

$$\sigma_{\bar{x}} = \frac{\sigma}{\sqrt{n}} \sqrt{\frac{N-n}{N-1}} \tag{8.3}$$

The correction factor in the above formula is the factor under the square root that has been appended to the basic formula for the standard error of the mean. *This same correction factor can be appended to the formulas for any of the standard error formulas for the mean, difference between means, proportion, and difference between proportions that are described and used in this and the following chapters.* However, we omit any consideration of the finite correction factor after this chapter.

EXAMPLE 4.   To illustrate that the finite correction factor reduces the size of the standard error of the mean when its use is appropriate, suppose that in Example 3 the sample of $n = 36$ values was taken from a population of just 100 values. The sample thus constitutes 36 percent of the population. The expected value and standard error of the sampling distribution of the mean are

$$E(\bar{X}) = \mu = 50.0$$

$$\sigma_{\bar{x}} = \frac{\sigma}{\sqrt{n}} \sqrt{\frac{N-n}{N-1}} = \frac{12.0}{\sqrt{36}} \sqrt{\frac{100-36}{100-1}} = 2.00(0.80) = 1.60$$

If the standard deviation of the population or process is not known, the standard error of the mean can be estimated by using the sample standard deviation as an estimator of the population standard deviation. To differentiate this estimated standard error from the precise one based on a known σ, it is designated by the symbol $s_{\bar{x}}$ (or by $\hat{\sigma}_{\bar{x}}$ in some texts). A few textbooks do not differentiate the exact standard error from the estimated standard error, and instead use the simplified $SE(\bar{X})$ to represent the standard error of the mean. The formula for the estimated standard error of the mean is

$$s_{\bar{x}} = \frac{s}{\sqrt{n}} \tag{8.4}$$

EXAMPLE 5.   An auditor takes a random sample of size $n = 16$ from a set of $N = 1,500$ accounts receivable. The standard deviation of the amounts of the receivables for the entire group of 1,500 accounts is not known. However, the sample standard deviation is $s = \$57.00$. We determine the value of the standard error for the sampling distribution of the mean as follows:

$$s_{\bar{x}} = \frac{s}{\sqrt{n}} = \frac{57.00}{\sqrt{16}} = \$14.25$$

8.4   THE CENTRAL LIMIT THEOREM

If the population or process from which a sample is taken is normally distributed, then the sampling distribution of the mean also will be normally distributed, regardless of sample size. However, what if a population is *not* normally distributed? Remarkably, a theorem from mathematical statistics still permits application of the normal distribution with respect to such sampling distributions. The *central limit theorem* states that as sample size is increased, the sampling distribution of the mean (and for other sample statistics as well) approaches the normal distribution in form, *regardless of the form of the population distribution from which the sample was taken.* For practical purposes, the sampling distribution of the mean can be assumed to be approximately normally distributed, even for the most nonnormal populations or processes, whenever the sample size is $n \geq 30$. For populations that are only somewhat nonnormal, even a smaller sample size will suffice. But a sample size of at least 30 will take care of the most adverse population situation.

8.5   DETERMINING PROBABILITY VALUES FOR THE SAMPLE MEAN

If the sampling distribution of the mean is normally distributed, either because the population is normally distributed or because the central limit theorem is invoked, then we can determine probabilities regarding the possible values of the sample mean, given that the population mean and standard deviation are known. The process is analogous to determining probabilities for individual observations using the normal distribution, as described in Section 7.2. In the present application, however, it is the designated value of the *sample mean* that is converted into a value of z in order to use the table of normal probabilities. This conversion formula uses the *standard error of the mean* because this is the standard deviation for the $\bar{X}$ variable. Thus, the conversion formula is

$$z = \frac{\bar{X} - \mu}{\sigma_{\bar{x}}} \qquad\qquad (8.5)$$

EXAMPLE 6.   An auditor takes a random sample of size $n = 36$ from a population of 1,000 accounts receivable. The mean value of the accounts receivable for the population is $\mu = \$260.00$, with the population standard deviation $\sigma = \$45.00$. What is the probability that the sample mean will be less than $\$250.00$?

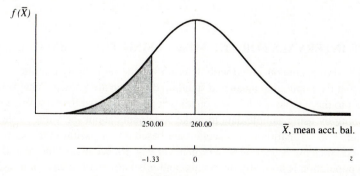

Fig. 8-1

Figure 8-1 portrays the probability curve. The sampling distribution is described by the mean and standard error:

$$E(\bar{X}) = \mu = 260.00 \quad \text{(as given)}$$

$$\sigma_{\bar{x}} = \frac{\sigma}{\sqrt{n}} = \frac{45.00}{\sqrt{36}} = \frac{45.00}{6} = 7.50$$

$$z = \frac{\bar{X} - \mu}{\sigma_{\bar{x}}} = \frac{250.00 - 260.00}{7.50} = \frac{-10.00}{7.50} = -1.33$$

Therefore,

$$P(\bar{X} < 250.00 | \mu = 260.00, \sigma_{\bar{x}} = 7.50) = P(z < -1.33)$$
$$P(z < -1.33) = 0.5000 - P(-1.33 \le z \le 0)$$
$$= 0.5000 - 0.4082 = 0.0918$$

EXAMPLE 7.   With reference to Example 6, what is the probability that the sample mean will be within \$15.00 of the population mean?

Figure 8-2 portrays the probability curve for the sampling distribution.

$$P(245.00 \le \bar{X} \le 275.00 | \mu = 260.00, \sigma_{\bar{x}} = 7.50)$$

where

$$z_1 = \frac{245.00 - 260.00}{7.50} = -2.00$$

$$z_2 = \frac{275.00 - 260.00}{7.50} = +2.00$$

$$P(-2.00 \le z \le +2.00) = 0.4772 + 0.4772 = 0.9544 \cong 95\%$$

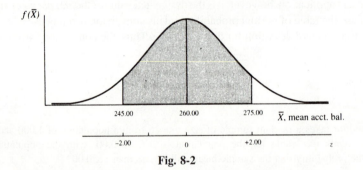

Fig. 8-2

8.6   CONFIDENCE INTERVALS FOR THE MEAN USING THE NORMAL DISTRIBUTION

Examples 6 and 7, above, are concerned with determining the probability that the sample mean will have various values given that the population mean and standard deviation are known. What is involved is *deductive reasoning* with respect to the sample result based on known population parameters. We now concern ourselves with *inductive reasoning* by using sample data to make statements about the value of the population mean.

The methods of interval estimation in this section are based on the assumption that the normal probability distribution can be used. Such use is warranted (1) whenever $n \ge 30$, because of the central limit theorem, or (2) when $n < 30$ but the population is normally distributed and σ is known. (The case of $n < 30$ with σ not known is considered in Section 8.8.)

Although the sample mean is useful as an unbiased estimator of the population mean, there is no way of expressing the degree of accuracy of a point estimator. In fact, mathematically speaking, the probability that the sample mean is *exactly* correct as an estimator of the population mean is $P = 0$. A *confidence interval* for the mean is an estimate interval constructed with respect to the sample mean by which the likelihood that the interval includes the value of the population mean can be specified. The *level of confidence* associated with a confidence interval indicates the long-run percentage of such intervals which would include the parameter being estimated.

Confidence intervals for the mean typically are constructed with the unbiased estimator $\bar{X}$ at the midpoint of the interval. However, Problems 8.14 and 8.15 demonstrate the construction of a so-called one-sided confidence interval, for which the sample mean is not at the midpoint of the interval. When use of the normal probability distribution is warranted, the confidence interval for the mean is determined by

$$\bar{X} \pm z\sigma_{\bar{x}} \tag{8.6}$$

or when the population σ is not known, by

$$\bar{X} \pm zs_{\bar{x}} \tag{8.7}$$

The $\pm z\sigma_{\bar{x}}$ or $\pm zs_{\bar{x}}$ frequently is called the *margin of error* for the confidence interval.

The most frequently used confidence intervals are the 90 percent, 95 percent, and 99 percent confidence intervals. The values of z required in conjuction with such intervals are given in Table 8.3.

Table 8.3   Selected Proportions of Area under the Normal Curve

z (the number of standard deviation units from the mean)	Proportion of area in the interval $\mu \pm z\sigma$
1.645	0.90
1.96	0.95
2.58	0.99

EXAMPLE 8.   For a given week, a random sample of 30 hourly employees selected from a very large number of employees in a manufacturing firm has a sample mean wage of $\bar{X} = \$180.00$, with a sample standard deviation of $s = \$14.00$. We estimate the mean wage for all hourly employees in the firm with an interval estimate such that we can be 95 percent confident that the interval includes the value of the population mean, as follows:

$$\bar{X} \pm 1.96s_{\bar{x}} = 180.000 \pm 1.96(2.56) = \$174.98 \text{ to } \$185.02$$

where $\bar{X} = \$180.00$ (as given)

$$s_{\bar{x}} = \frac{s}{\sqrt{n}} = \frac{14.00}{\sqrt{30}} = 2.56$$

(*Note*: s is used as an estimator of σ.)

Thus, we can state that the mean wage level for all employees is between $174.98 and $185.02, with a 95 percent level of confidence in this estimate.

In addition to estimating the value of the population mean as such, there is sometimes an interest in estimating the total quantity, or total amount, of something in the population. See Problem 8.11(*b*).

8.7   DETERMINING THE REQUIRED SAMPLE SIZE FOR ESTIMATING THE MEAN

Suppose the desired size of a confidence interval and the level of confidence to be associated with it are specified. If σ is known or can be estimated, such as from the results of similar studies, the required sample size based on use of the normal distribution is

$$n = \left(\frac{z\sigma}{E}\right)^2 \tag{8.8}$$

In Formula (8.8), z is the value used for the specified level of confidence, σ is the standard deviation of the population (or estimate thereof), and E is the plus and minus sampling error allowed in the interval (always one-half the total confidence interval).

(*Note*:   When solving for sample size, any fractional result is always rounded up. Further, unless σ is known *and* the population is normally distributed, any computed sample size below 30 should be increased to 30 because formula (8.8) is based on use of the normal distribution.)

EXAMPLE 9.   A personnel department analyst wishes to estimate the mean number of training hours annually for supervisors in a division of the company within 3.0 hr (plus or minus) and with 90 percent confidence. Based on data from other divisions, the analyst estimates the standard deviation of training hours to be $\sigma = 20.0$ hr. The minimum required sample size is

$$n = \left(\frac{z\sigma}{E}\right)^2 = \left[\frac{(1.645)(20.0)}{3.0}\right]^2 = \left(\frac{32.9}{3.0}\right)^2 = 120.27 \cong 121$$

8.8   THE t DISTRIBUTION AND CONFIDENCE INTERVALS FOR THE MEAN

In Section 8.4 we indicated that use of the normal distribution in estimating a population mean is warranted for any large sample ($n \geq 30$), and for a small sample ($n < 30$) only if the population is normally distributed *and* σ is known. In this section we handle the situation in which the sample is small and the population is normally distributed, but σ is not known.

If a population is normally distributed, the sampling distribution of the mean for any sample size will also be normally distributed; this is true whether σ is known or not. However, in the process of inference each value of the mean is converted to a standard normal value, *and herein lies the problem.* If σ is unknown, the conversion formula $(\bar{X} - \mu)/s_{\bar{x}}$ includes a variable in the denominator, because s, and therefore $s_{\bar{x}}$, will be somewhat different from sample to sample. The result is that use of the variable $s_{\bar{x}}$ rather than the constant $\sigma_{\bar{x}}$ in the denominator results in converted values that are *not* distributed as z values. Instead, the values are distributed according to the t distribution, which is platykurtic (flat) as compared with the distribution of z. Appendix 6 indicates proportions of area for the t distribution. The distribution is a family of distributions, with a somewhat different distribution associated with the *degrees of freedom* (df). For a confidence interval for the population mean based on a sample of size n, $df = n - 1$.

The degrees of freedom indicate the number of values that are in fact "free to vary" in the sample that serves as the basis for the confidence interval. Offhand, it would seem that all of the values in the sample are always free to vary in their measured values. However, what is different for the t distribution as compared to the z is that *both* the sample mean and the sample standard deviation are required as parameter estimators in order to define a confidence interval for the population mean. The need for the additional parameter estimate is a limitation on the sample. Without considering the mathematical abstractions, the bottom line is that, in general, one degree of freedom is lost with each additional parameter estimate that is required beyond the one parameter toward which the statistical inference is directed.

Use of the t distribution for inference concerning the population mean is appropriate whenever σ is not known and the sampling distribution of the mean is normal (either because the population is normally distributed or the central limit theorem is invoked). Just as is true for the z distribution, the t distribution has a mean of 0. However, it is flatter and wider than the z (and thus has a standard deviation > 1.0). With increasing sample size and df, the t distribution approaches the form of the standard normal z distribution. For hand calculations, a general rule is that required t values can be approximated by z values when $n > 30$ (or $df > 29$). For computer applications there is no need to use approximations, and therefore the t distribution is used for large as well as small samples whenever the standard error is estimated on the basis of the sample standard deviation.

Note that the values of t reported in Appendix 6 indicate the proportion in the upper tail of the distribution, rather than the proportion between the mean and a given point, as in Appendix 5 for the normal distribution. Where $df = n - 1$, the confidence interval for estimating the population mean when use of the t distribution is appropriate is

$$\bar{X} \pm t_{df} s_{\bar{x}} \qquad (8.9)$$

EXAMPLE 10.   The mean operating life for a random sample of $n = 10$ light bulbs is $\bar{X} = 4,000$ hr, with the sample standard deviation $s = 200$ hr. The operating life of bulbs in general is assumed to be approximately normally distributed. We estimate the mean operating life for the population of bulbs from which this sample was taken, using a 95 percent confidence interval, as follows:

$$
\begin{aligned}
95\% \text{ Int.} &= \bar{X} \pm t_{df} s_{\bar{x}} \\
&= 4,000 \pm (2.262)(63.3) \\
&= 3,856.8 \text{ to } 4,143.2 \cong 3,857 \text{ to } 4,143 \text{ hr}
\end{aligned}
$$

where $\bar{X} = 4,000$ (as given)

$$t_{df} = t_{n-1} = t_9 = 2.262$$

$$s_{\bar{x}} = \frac{s}{\sqrt{n}} = \frac{200}{\sqrt{10}} = \frac{200}{3.16} = 63.3$$

8.9   SUMMARY TABLE FOR INTERVAL ESTIMATION OF THE POPULATION MEAN

Table 8.4   Interval Estimation of the Population Mean

Population	Sample size	σ known	σ unknown
Normally distributed	Large ($n \geq 30$)	$\bar{X} \pm z\sigma_{\bar{x}}$	$\bar{X} \pm t s_{\bar{x}}$ or $\bar{X} \pm z s_{\bar{x}}^{**}$
	Small ($n < 30$)	$\bar{X} \pm z\sigma_{\bar{x}}$	$\bar{X} \pm t s_{\bar{x}}$
Not normally distributed	Large ($n \geq 30$)	$\bar{X} \pm z\sigma_{\bar{x}}^{*}$	$\bar{X} \pm t s_{\bar{x}}^{*}$ or $\bar{X} \pm z s_{\bar{x}}^{\dagger}$
	Small ($n < 30$)	Nonparametric procedures directed toward the median generally would be used. (See Chapter 17.)	

* Central limit theorem is invoked.
** z is used as an approximation of t.
† Central limit theorem is invoked, and z is used as an approximation of t.

8.10   USING EXCEL AND MINITAB

Computer software used for statistical analysis generally allows the user to specify the percent confidence interval for the mean that is desired based on random sample data. Solved Problems 8.18 and 8.19 illustrate the use of Excel and Minitab, respectively, for the determination of confidence intervals for the population mean.

Solved Problems

SAMPLING DISTRIBUTION OF THE MEAN

8.1. For a particular brand of TV picture tube, it is known that the mean operating life of the tubes is $\mu = 9{,}000$ hr with a standard deviation of $\sigma = 500$ hr. (*a*) Determine the expected value and standard error of the sampling distribution of the mean given a sample size of $n = 25$. (*b*) Interpret the meaning of the computed values.

(*a*)
$$E(\bar{X}) = \mu = 9{,}000$$

$$\sigma_{\bar{x}} = \frac{\sigma}{\sqrt{n}} = \frac{500}{\sqrt{25}} = \frac{500}{5} = 100$$

(*b*) These calculations indicate that in the long run the mean of a large group of sample means, each based on a sample size of $n = 25$, will be equal to 9,000 hr. Further, the variability of these sample means with respect to the expected value of 9,000 hr is expressed by a standard deviation of 100 hr.

8.2. For a large population of normally distributed account balances, the mean balance is $\mu = \$150.00$ with standard deviation $\sigma = \$35.00$. What is the probability that *one* randomly sampled account has a balance that exceeds $160.00?

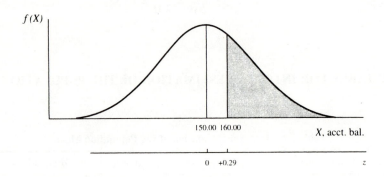

Fig. 8-3

Figure 8-3 portrays the probability curve for the variable.

$$z = \frac{X - \mu}{\sigma} = \frac{160.00 - 150.00}{35.00} = +0.29$$

$$P(X > 160.00 | \mu = 150.00, \sigma = 35.00) = P(z > +0.29)$$
$$= 0.5000 - P(0 \leq z \leq +0.29) = 0.5000 - 0.1141 = 0.3859$$

8.3. With reference to Problem 8.2 above, what is the probability that the *mean* for a random sample of $n = 40$ accounts will exceed $160.00?

Figure 8-4 portrays the probability curve for the sampling distribution $E(\bar{X}) = \mu = \$150.00$.

$$\sigma_{\bar{x}} = \frac{\sigma}{\sqrt{n}} = \frac{35.00}{40} = \$5.53$$

$$z = \frac{\bar{X} - \mu}{\sigma_{\bar{x}}} = \frac{160.00 - 150.00}{5.53} = \frac{10.00}{5.53} = +1.81$$

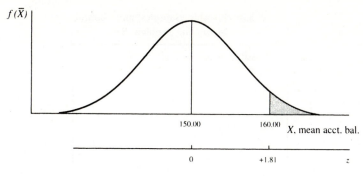

Fig. 8-4

Therefore,

$$P(\bar{X} > 160.00 | \mu = 150.00, \sigma_{\bar{x}} = 5.53) = P(z > +1.81)$$
$$= 0.5000 - P(0 \le z \le +1.81)$$
$$= 0.5000 - 0.4649 = 0.0351$$

8.4. This problem and the following two problems serve to illustrate the meaning of the sampling distribution of the mean by reference to a highly simplified population. Suppose a population consists of just the four values 3, 5, 7, and 8. Compute (*a*) the population mean μ and (*b*) the population standard deviation σ.

With reference to Table 8.5,

(*a*)
$$\mu = \frac{\Sigma X}{N} = \frac{23}{4} = 5.75$$

(*b*)
$$\sigma = \sqrt{\frac{\Sigma X^2}{N} - \left(\frac{\Sigma X}{N}\right)^2} = \sqrt{\frac{147}{4} - \left(\frac{23}{4}\right)^2}$$
$$= \sqrt{36.75 - (5.75)^2} = \sqrt{36.75 - 33.0625} = 1.92$$

Table 8.5   Worksheet for Problem 8.4

X	X^2
3	9
5	25
7	49
8	64
$\Sigma X = \overline{23}$	$\Sigma X^2 = \overline{147}$

8.5. For the population described in Problem 8.4, suppose that simple random samples of size $n = 2$ each are taken from this population. For each sample the first sampled item is *not* replaced in the population before the second item is sampled.

(*a*)   List all possible pairs of values which can constitute a sample.

(*b*)   For each of the pairs identified in (*a*), compute the sample mean $\bar{X}$ and demonstrate that the mean of all possible sample means $\mu_{\bar{x}}$ is equal to the mean of the population from which the samples were selected.

(*a*)   and (*b*) From Table 8.6,

$$\mu_{\bar{x}} = \frac{\Sigma \bar{X}}{N_{\text{samples}}} = \frac{34.5}{6} = 5.75$$

[which equals μ as computed in Problem 8.4(*a*)].

Table 8.6   Possible Samples and Sample Means for Problem 8.5

Possible samples	$\bar{X}$
3, 5	4.0
3, 7	5.0
3, 8	5.5
5, 7	6.0
5, 8	6.5
7, 8	7.5
	$\Sigma \bar{X} = \overline{34.5}$

8.6.   For the sampling situation described in Problems 8.4 and 8.5, (*a*) compute the standard error of the mean by determining the standard deviation of the six possible sample means identified in Problem 8.5 with respect to the population mean μ. (*b*) Then compute the standard error of the mean based on σ being known and sampling from a finite population, using the appropriate formula from this chapter. Verify that the two standard error values are the same.

With reference to Table 8.6, we get Table 8.7

Table 8.7   Worksheet for Problem 8.6

$\bar{X}$	$\bar{X}^2$
4.0	16.00
5.0	25.00
5.5	30.25
6.0	36.00
6.5	42.25
7.5	56.25
$\Sigma \bar{X} = \overline{34.5}$	$\Sigma \bar{X}^2 = \overline{205.75}$

(*a*)   First method:

$$\sigma_{\bar{x}} = \sqrt{\frac{\Sigma \bar{X}^2}{N_s} - \left(\frac{\Sigma \bar{X}}{N_s}\right)^2} = \sqrt{\frac{205.75}{6} - \left(\frac{34.5}{6}\right)^2}$$

$$= \sqrt{34.2917 - (5.75)^2} = \sqrt{34.2917 - 33.0625} = 1.11$$

(*b*)   Second method:

$$\sigma_{\bar{x}} = \frac{\sigma}{\sqrt{n}} \sqrt{\frac{N-n}{N-1}} = \frac{1.92}{\sqrt{2}} \sqrt{\frac{4-2}{4-1}}$$

$$= \frac{1.92}{1.414} \sqrt{0.6666} = 1.358(0.816) = 1.11$$

Of course, the second method is the one always used for determining the standard error of the mean in actual data situations. But conceptually, the first method illustrates more directly the meaning of the standard error of the mean.

CONFIDENCE INTERVALS FOR THE MEAN USING THE NORMAL DISTRIBUTION

8.7. Suppose that the standard deviation of the tube life for a particular brand of TV picture tube is known to be $\sigma = 500$, but that the mean operating life is not known. Overall, the operating life of the tubes is assumed to be approximately normally distributed. For a sample of $n = 15$, the mean operating life is $\bar{X} = 8,900$ hr. Determine (*a*) the 95 percent and (*b*) the 90 percent confidence intervals for estimating the population mean.

The normal probability distribution can be used in this case because the population is normally distributed and σ is known.

(*a*)
$$\bar{X} \pm z\sigma_{\bar{x}} = 8,900 \pm 1.96 \frac{\sigma}{\sqrt{n}}$$

$$= 8,900 \pm 1.96 \frac{500}{\sqrt{15}} = 8,900 \pm 1.96 \left(\frac{500}{3.87}\right)$$

$$= 8,900 \pm 1.96(129.10) = 8,900 \pm 253 = 8,647 \text{ to } 9,153$$

(*b*)
$$\bar{X} \pm z\sigma_{\bar{x}} = 8,900 \pm 1.645(129.20) = 8,900 \pm 213 = 8,687 \text{ to } 9,113 \text{ hr}$$

8.8. With respect to Problem 8.7, suppose that the population of tube life cannot be assumed to be normally distributed. However, the sample mean of $\bar{X} = 8,900$ is based on a sample of $n = 35$. Determine the 95 percent confidence interval for estimating the population mean.

The normal probability distribution can be used in this case by invoking the central limit theorem, which indicates that for $n \geq 30$ the sampling distribution can be assumed to be normally distributed even though the population is not normally distributed. Thus,

$$\bar{X} \pm z\sigma_{\bar{x}} = 8,900 \pm 1.96 \frac{\sigma}{\sqrt{n}} = 8,900 \pm 1.96 \frac{500}{\sqrt{35}}$$

$$= 8,900 \pm 1.96 \left(\frac{500}{5.92}\right) = 8,900 \pm 1.96(84.46) = 8,734 \text{ to } 9,066 \text{ hr}$$

8.9. With respect to Problem 8.8, suppose that the population can be assumed to be normally distributed, but that the population standard deviation is not known. Rather, the sample standard deviation $s = 500$ and $\bar{X} = 8,900$. Estimate the population mean using a 90 percent confidence interval.

Because $n \geq 30$ the normal distribution can be used as an approximation of the t distribution. However, because the population is normally distributed, the central limit theorem need not be invoked. Therefore,

$$\bar{X} \pm z s_{\bar{x}} = 8,900 \pm 1.645 \left(\frac{500}{\sqrt{35}}\right) = 8,900 \pm 1.645(84.46) = 8,761 \text{ to } 9,039 \text{ hr}$$

8.10. With respect to Problems 8.8 and 8.9, suppose that the population *cannot* be assumed to be normally distributed and, further, that the population σ is not known. As before, $n = 35$, $s = 500$, and $\bar{X} = 8,900$. Estimate the population mean using a 99 percent confidence interval.

In this case the central limit theorem is invoked, as in Problem 8.8, and z is used as an approximation of t, as in Problem 8.9.

$$\bar{X} \pm z s_{\bar{x}} = 8,900 \pm 2.58 \left(\frac{500}{\sqrt{35}}\right) = 8,900 \pm 2.58(84.46) = 8,682 \text{ to } 9,118 \text{ hr}$$

8.11. A marketing research analyst collects data for a random sample of 100 customers out of the 4,000 who purchased a particular "coupon special." The 100 people spent an average of $\bar{X} = \$24.57$ in the store with a standard deviation of $s = \$6.60$. Using a 95 percent confidence interval, estimate (*a*) the mean purchase amount for all 4,000 customers and (*b*) the total dollar amount of purchases by the 4,000 customers.

(*a*) $s_{\bar{x}} = \dfrac{s}{\sqrt{n}} = \dfrac{6.60}{\sqrt{100}} = 0.66$

$\bar{X} \pm z s_{\bar{x}} = 24.57 \pm 1.96(0.66) = \$24.57 \pm \$1.29 = \$23.28$ to $\$25.86$

(*b*) $N(\bar{X} \pm z s_{\bar{x}}) = 4{,}000(\$23.28$ to $\$25.86) = \$93{,}120$ to $\$103{,}440$

or

$N\bar{X} \pm N(z s_{\bar{x}}) = 4{,}000(24.57) \pm 4{,}000(1.29)$
$= 98{,}280 \pm 5{,}160 = \$93{,}120$ to $\$103{,}440$

(*Note*:   The confidence interval for the dollar amount of purchases is simply the total number of customers *in the population* multiplied by the confidence limits for the mean purchase amount per customer. Such a population value is referred to as the *total quantity* in some textbooks.)

DETERMINING THE REQUIRED SAMPLE SIZE FOR ESTIMATING THE MEAN

8.12.   A prospective purchaser wishes to estimate the mean dollar amount of sales per customer at a toy store located at an airlines terminal. Based on data from other similar airports, the standard deviation of such sales amounts is estimated to be about $\sigma = \$3.20$. What size of random sample should be collected, as a minimum, if the purchaser wants to estimate the mean sales amount within $\$1.00$ and with 99 percent confidence?

$$n = \left(\frac{z\sigma}{E}\right)^2 = \left[\frac{(2.58)(3.20)}{1.00}\right]^2 = (8.256)^2 = 68.16 \cong 69$$

8.13.   Referring to Problem 8.12, what is the minimum required sample size if the distribution of sales amounts is not assumed to be normal and the purchaser wishes to estimate the mean sales amount within $\$2.00$ with 99 percent confidence?

$$n = \left(\frac{z\sigma}{E}\right)^2 = \left[\frac{(2.58)(3.20)}{2.00}\right]^2 = (4.128)^2 = 17.04 \cong 18$$

However, because the population is not assumed to be normally distributed, the minimum sample size is $n = 30$, so that the central limit theorem can be invoked as the basis for using the normal probability distribution for constructing the confidence interval.

ONE-SIDED CONFIDENCE INTERVALS FOR THE POPULATION MEAN

8.14.   Occasionally, a *one-sided confidence interval* may be of greater interest than the usual two-sided interval. Such would be the case if we are interested only in the highest (or only in the lowest) value of the mean at the indicated level of confidence. An "upper 95 percent interval" extends from a computed lower limit to positive infinity, with a proportion of 0.05 of the area under the normal curve being to the left of the lower limit. Similarly, a "lower 95 percent confidence interval" extends from negative infinity to a computed upper limit, with a proportion of 0.05 of the area under the normal curve being to the right of the upper limit.

Suppose a prospective purchaser of a toy store at an airlines terminal observes a random sample of $n = 64$ sales and finds that the sample mean is $\bar{X} = \$14.63$, with the sample standard deviation

$s = \$2.40$. Determine the upper 95 percent confidence interval so that the *minimum* value of the population mean is identified with a 95 percent degree of confidence.

$$s_{\bar{x}} = \frac{s}{\sqrt{n}} = \frac{2.40}{\sqrt{64}} = \frac{2.40}{8} = 0.30$$

Upper 95% int. $= \bar{X} - zs_{\bar{x}} = 14.63 - 1.645(0.30) = \$14.14$ or higher

Thus, with a 95 percent degree of confidence we can state that the mean sales amount for the population of all customers is equal to or greater than \$14.14.

8.15. With 99 percent confidence, what is the estimate of the maximum value of the mean sales amount in Problem 8.14?

Since $\bar{X} = \$14.63$ and $s_{\bar{x}} = 0.30$,

Lower 99% int. $= \bar{X} + zs_{\bar{x}} = 14.63 + 2.33(0.30) = \$15.33$ or less

Thus, with a 99 percent degree of confidence, we can state that the mean sales amount is no larger than \$15.33.

USE OF THE *t* DISTRIBUTION

8.16. In Problem 8.7 we constructed confidence intervals for estimating the mean operating life of a particular brand of TV picture tube based on the assumption that the operating life of all tubes is approximately normally distributed and $\sigma = 500$, and given a sample of $n = 15$ with $\bar{X} = 8,900$ hr. Suppose that σ is *not* known, but rather, that the sample standard deviation is $s = 500$.

(a) Determine the 95 percent confidence interval for estimating the population mean and compare this interval with the answer to Problem 8.7(a).

(b) Determine the 90 percent confidence interval for estimating the population mean and compare this interval with the answer to Problem 8.7(b).

(*Note:* Use of a *t* distribution is required in this case because the population is assumed to be normally distributed, σ is not known, and the sample is small ($n < 30$).)

(a) $\bar{X} \pm t_{df}s_{\bar{x}} = 8,900 \pm 2.145\dfrac{s}{\sqrt{n}} = 8,900 \pm 2.145\dfrac{500}{\sqrt{15}}$

$= 8,900 \pm 2.145\left(\dfrac{500}{3.87}\right) = 8,900 \pm 2.145(129.199) = 8,900 \pm 277 = 8,623$ to $9,177$ hr

The confidence interval is wider than the one in Problem 8.7(a), reflecting the difference between the *t* distribution with $df = 15 - 1 = 14$, and the normal probability distribution.

(b) $\bar{X} \pm t_{df}s_{\bar{x}} = 8,900 \pm 1.761(129.199) = 8,900 \pm 228 = 8,672$ to $9,128$ hr

Again, the confidence interval is wider than the one in Problem 8.7(b).

8.17. As a commercial buyer for a private supermarket brand, suppose you take a random sample of 12 No. 303 cans of green beans at a canning plant. The net weight of the drained beans in each can is reported in Table 8.8. Determine (a) the mean net weight of string beans being packed in each can for this sample and (b) the sample standard deviation. (c) Assuming that the net weights per can are normally distributed, estimate the mean weight per can of beans being packed using a 95 percent confidence interval.

Table 8.8   Net Weight of Beans Packed in 12 No. 303 Cans

Ounces per can	15.7	15.8	15.9	16.0	16.1	16.2
Number of cans	1	2	2	3	3	1

Table 8.9   Worksheet for Problem 8.17

X per can	No. of cans	Total X	X^2 per can	Total X^2
15.7	1	15.7	246.49	246.49
15.8	2	31.6	249.64	499.28
15.9	2	31.8	252.81	505.62
16.0	3	48.0	256.00	768.00
16.1	3	48.3	259.21	777.63
16.2	1	16.2	262.44	262.44
	$n = \overline{12}$	$\Sigma X = \overline{191.6}$		$\Sigma X^2 = \overline{3{,}059.46}$

Referring to Table 8.9,

(a)
$$\bar{X} = \frac{\Sigma X}{n} = \frac{191.6}{12} = 15.97 \, \text{oz}$$

(b)
$$s = \sqrt{\frac{n\Sigma X^2 - (\Sigma X)^2}{n(n-1)}} = \sqrt{\frac{12(3{,}059.46) - (191.6)^2}{12(11)}} = \sqrt{0.0224} = 0.15$$

(c)
$$\bar{X} \pm t_{df}s_{\bar{x}} = 15.97 \pm t_{11}\frac{s}{\sqrt{n}} = 15.97 \pm 2.201\left(\frac{0.15}{\sqrt{12}}\right)$$

$$= 15.97 \pm 2.201\left(\frac{0.15}{3.46}\right) = 15.97 \pm 2.201(0.043)$$

$$= 15.97 \pm 0.10 = 15.87 \text{ to } 16.07 \, \text{oz}$$

COMPUTER OUTPUT: CONFIDENCE INTERVAL FOR THE MEAN

8.18. Refer to Problem 8.17, concerning the net weight of green beans packed in a random sample of $n = 12$ cans. Using Excel, determine the 95 percent confidence interval for the mean weight of all cans in the population of cans that was sampled.

Refer to Fig. 8-5. The last line of the output gives the plus-and-minus margin of error for the 95 percent confidence interval *based on use of the z-distribution*. Therefore, the margin of error that is reported will be an understated approximation of the correct value. However, unless the sample is *very* small, the approximation is generally close enough to the correct value to be acceptable. With reference to the hand-calculated solution in Problem 8.17, we see that whereas the correct margin of error to four decimal places is 0.0953, the margin of error reported in Fig. 8-5 is 0.0951, *a very small difference, indeed!* Although Excel does have the *t*-distribution function available, it is not easily used for determining confidence intervals for the population mean. Rounding the sample mean and the margin of error reported Fig. 8-5 to two places, the calculated 95 percent confidence interval is

$$\bar{X} \pm 0.10 = 15.97 \pm 0.10 = 15.87 \text{ to } 16.07 \, \text{oz.}$$

The Excel output given in Fig. 8-5 was obtained as follows:

(1) Open Excel. In cell A1 enter the column label: Weight. Enter the 12 weights in column A beginning at cell A2.

(2) Click **Tools** → **Data Analysis** → **Descriptive Statistics**. Click **OK**.

(3) Designate the **Input Range** as: $A$1:$A$13.

(4) Select **Labels in First Row**.

(5) Select **Confidence Level for Mean**: 95%.

(6) Click **OK**.

Weight	
Mean	15.96666667
Standard Error	0.043228311
Median	16
Mode	16
Standard Deviation	0.149747262
Sample Variance	0.022424242
Kurtosis	-0.725566107
Skewness	-0.288774851
Range	0.5
Minimum	15.7
Maximum	16.2
Sum	191.6
Count	12
Confidence Level(95.0%)	0.095144919

Fig. 8-5   Excel output.

8.19. Refer to Problem 8.17, concerning the net weight of green beans packed in a random sample of $n = 12$ cans. Using Minitab, determine the 95 percent confidence interval for the mean weight of all cans in the population of cans that was sampled.

Refer to Fig. 8-6.   As reported, the 95 percent confidence interval for the population of the cans of green beans from which the sample was taken, rounded to two decimal places, is 15.87 to 16.06 oz. Although this output is somewhat different from the hand-calculated result in Problem 8.17, the output is in fact the more accurate result because less rounding of values was done in the Minitab calculations using the *t*-distribution function.

The Minitab output given in Fig. 8-6 was obtained as follows:

(1)   Open Minitab. In the column-name cell for column C1 enter: Weight. Enter the 12 weights in column C1.

(2)   Click **Stat** → **Basic Statistics** → **1-Sample t**.

(3)   In the **Variable** box enter: Weight.

(4)   Click **Options** and designate **Confidence level** as: 95.0. For **Alternative** choose: **not equal** (so that a *two-sided* confidence interval is obtained). Click **OK**.

(5)   Back in the original dialog box, click **OK**.

One-Sample T: Weight

```
Variable      N      Mean     StDev    SE Mean        95.0% CI
Weight       12    15.9667    0.1497    0.0432    ( 15.8715, 16.0618)
```

Fig. 8-6   Minitab output.

Supplementary Problems

SAMPLING DISTRIBUTION OF THE MEAN

8.20. The mean dollar value of the sales amounts for a particular consumer product last year is known to be normally distributed with $\mu = \$3,400$ per retail outlet with a standard deviation of $\sigma = \$200$. If a large number of outlets handle the product, determine the standard error of the mean for a sample of size $n = 25$.
Ans.   \$40.00

8.21. Refer to Problem 8.20. What is the probability that the sales amount for *one* randomly sampled retail outlet will be (*a*) greater than \$3,500? (*b*) Between \$3,350 and \$3,450?
Ans. (*a*) 0.3085, (*b*) 0.1974

8.22. Refer to Problem 8.20. What is the probability that the *sample mean* for the sample of $n = 25$ will be (*a*) greater than \$3,500? (*b*) Between \$3,350 and \$3,450? Compare your answers with the answers to Problem 8.21.
Ans. (*a*) 0.0062, (*b*) 0.7888

CONFIDENCE INTERVALS FOR THE MEAN

8.23. Suppose that you wish to estimate the mean sales amount per retail outlet for a particular consumer product during the past year. The number of retail outlets is large. Determine the 95 percent confidence interval given that the sales amounts are assumed to be normally distributed, $\bar{X} = \$3,425$, $\sigma = \$200$, and $n = 25$.
Ans. \$3,346.60 to \$3,503.40

8.24. Referring to Problem 8.23, determine the 95 percent confidence interval given that the population is assumed to be normally distributed, $\bar{X} = \$3,425$, $s = \$200$, and $n = 25$.
Ans. \$3,342.44 to \$3,507.56

8.25. For Problem 8.23, determine the 95 percent confidence interval given that the population is *not* assumed to be normally distributed, $\bar{X} = \$3,425$, $s = \$200$, and $n = 50$.
Ans. \$3,369.55 to \$3,480.45

8.26. For a sample of 50 firms taken from a particular industry the mean number of employees per firm is 420.4 with a sample standard deviation of 55.7. *There is a total of just 380 firms in this industry*. Determine the standard error of the mean to be used in conjunction with estimating the population mean by a confidence interval.
Ans. 7.33

8.27. For Problem 8.26, determine the 90 percent confidence interval for estimating the average number of workers per firm in the industry.
Ans. 408.3 to 432.5

8.28. For the situations described in Problems 8.26 and 8.27, determine the 90 percent confidence interval for estimating the total number of workers employed in the industry.
Ans. 155,154 to 164,350

8.29. An analyst in a personnel department randomly selects the records of 16 hourly employees and finds that the mean wage rate per hour is \$9.50. The wage rates in the firm are assumed to be normally distributed. If the standard deviation of the wage rates is known to be \$1.00, estimate the mean wage rate in the firm using an 80 percent confidence interval.
Ans. \$9.18 to \$9.82

8.30. Referring to Problem 8.29, suppose that the standard deviation of the population is not known, but that the standard deviation of the sample is \$1.00. Estimate the mean wage rate in the firm using an 80 percent confidence interval.
Ans. \$9.16 to \$9.84

8.31. The mean diameter of a sample of $n = 12$ cylindrical rods included in a shipment is 2.350 mm with a sample standard deviation of 0.050 mm. The distribution of the diameters of all of the rods included in the shipment is assumed to be approximately normal. Determine the 99 percent confidence interval for estimating the mean diameter of all of the rods included in the shipment.
Ans. 2.307 to 2.393 mm

8.32. The mean diameter of a sample of $n = 100$ rods included in a shipment is 2.350 mm with a standard deviation of 0.050 mm. Estimate the mean diameter of all rods included in the shipment if the shipment contains 500 rods, using a 99 percent confidence interval.

Ans.   2.338 to 2.362 mm

8.33. The mean weight per rod for the sample of 100 rods in Problem 8.32 is 8.45 g with a standard deviation of 0.25 g. Estimate the total weight of the entire shipment (exclusive of packing materials), using a 99 percent confidence interval.

Ans.   4,195 to 4,255 g

DETERMINING THE REQUIRED SAMPLE SIZE FOR ESTIMATING THE MEAN

8.34. From historical records, the standard deviation of the sales level per retail outlet for a consumer product is known to be $\sigma = \$200$, and the population of sales amounts per outlet is assumed to be normally distributed. What is the minimum sample size required to estimate the mean sales per outlet within \$100 and with 95 percent confidence?

Ans. $15.37 \cong 16$

8.35. An analyst wishes to estimate the mean hourly wage of workers in a particular company within 25¢ and 90 percent confidence. The standard deviation of the wage rates is estimated as being no larger than \$1.00. What is the number of personnel records that should be sampled, as a minimum, to satisfy this research objective?

Ans. $43.56 \cong 44$

ONE-SIDED CONFIDENCE INTERVALS FOR THE POPULATION MEAN

8.36. Instead of the two-sided confidence interval constructed in Problem 8.23, suppose we wish to estimate the *minimum* value of the mean level of sales per retail outlet for a particular product during the past year. As before, the distribution of sales amounts per store is assumed to be approximately normal. Determine the minimum value of the mean using a 95 percent confidence interval given that $\bar{X} = \$3,425$, $\sigma = \$200$, and $n = 25$. Compare your confidence interval with the one constructed in Problem 8.23.

Ans.   Est. $\mu \geq \$3,359$

8.37. Using the data in Problem 8.31, determine the 99 percent lower confidence interval for estimating the mean diameter of all the rods included in the shipment. Compare the interval with the one constructed in Problem 8.31.

Ans.   Est. $\mu \leq 2.388$ mm

COMPUTER OUTPUT

8.38. Refer to Table 2.19 (page 41) for the amounts of 40 personal loans. Assuming that these are random sample data, use available computer software to determine the 99 percent confidence interval for the mean loan amount in the population.

Ans.   \$822 to \$1,372

CHAPTER 9

Other Confidence Intervals

9.1 CONFIDENCE INTERVALS FOR THE DIFFERENCE BETWEEN TWO MEANS USING THE NORMAL DISTRIBUTION

There is often a need to estimate the difference between two population means, such as the difference between the wage levels in two firms. As indicated in Section 8.1, the unbiased point estimate of $(\mu_1 - \mu_2)$ is $(\bar{X}_1 - \bar{X}_2)$. The confidence interval is constructed in a manner similar to that used for estimating the mean, except that the relevant standard error for the sampling distribution is the standard error of the *difference* between means. Use of the normal distribution is based on the same conditions as for the sampling distribution of the mean (see Section 8.4), except that two samples are involved. The formula used for estimating the difference between two population means with confidence intervals is

$$(\bar{X}_1 - \bar{X}_2) \pm z\sigma_{\bar{x}_1 - \bar{x}_2} \tag{9.1}$$

or

$$(\bar{X}_1 - \bar{X}_2) \pm zs_{\bar{x}_1 - \bar{x}_2} \tag{9.2}$$

When the standard deviations of the two populations are known, the standard error of the difference between means is

$$\sigma_{\bar{x}_1 - \bar{x}_2} = \sqrt{\sigma_{\bar{x}_1}^2 + \sigma_{\bar{x}_2}^2} \tag{9.3}$$

When the standard deviations of the populations are not known, the estimated standard error of the difference between means given that use of the normal distribution is appropriate is

$$s_{\bar{x}_1 - \bar{x}_2} = \sqrt{s_{\bar{x}_1}^2 + s_{\bar{x}_2}^2} \tag{9.4}$$

The values of the standard errors of the respective means included in these formulas are calculated by the formulas given in Section 8.3, including the possibility of using finite correction factors when appropriate.

EXAMPLE 1.   The mean weekly wage for a sample of $n = 30$ employees in a large manufacturing firm is $\bar{X} = \$280.00$ with a sample standard deviation of $s = \$14.00$. In another large firm a random sample of $n = 40$ hourly employees has

160

a mean weekly wage of $270.00 with a sample standard deviation of $s = \$10.00$. The 99 percent confidence interval for estimating the difference between the mean weekly wage levels in the two firms is

$$99\% \text{ Int.} = (\bar{X}_1 - \bar{X}_2) \pm zs_{\bar{x}_1 - \bar{x}_2}$$
$$= \$10.00 \pm 2.58(3.01)$$
$$= \$10.00 \pm 7.77$$
$$= \$2.23 \text{ to } \$17.77$$

where

$$\bar{X}_1 - \bar{X}_2 = \$280.00 - \$270.00 = \$10.00$$

$$z = 2.58$$

$$s_{\bar{x}_1} = \frac{s_1}{\sqrt{n_1}} = \frac{14.00}{\sqrt{30}} = \frac{14.00}{5.477} = 2.56$$

$$s_{\bar{x}_2} = \frac{s_2}{\sqrt{n_2}} = \frac{10.00}{\sqrt{40}} = \frac{10.00}{6.325} = 1.58$$

$$s_{\bar{x}_1 - \bar{x}_2} = \sqrt{s_{\bar{x}_1}^2 + s_{\bar{x}_2}^2} = \sqrt{(2.56)^2 + (1.58)^2} = \sqrt{6.5536 + 2.4964} \cong 3.01$$

Thus, we can state that the average weekly wage in the first firm is greater than the average in the second firm by an amount somewhere between $2.23 and $17.77, with 99 percent confidence in this interval estimate. Note that the sample sizes are large enough to permit the use of Z to approximate the t value (see Sec. 9.2, which follows).

In addition to the two-sided confidence interval, a one-sided confidence interval for the difference between means can also be constructed. (See Problems 9.4 and 9.5.)

9.2   THE t DISTRIBUTION AND CONFIDENCE INTERVALS FOR THE DIFFERENCE BETWEEN TWO MEANS

As explained in Section 8.8, use of the t distribution in conjunction with one sample is necessary when

(1) Population standard deviations σ are not known.

(2) Samples are small ($n < 30$). If samples are large, then t values can be approximated by the standard normal z.

(3) Populations are assumed to be approximately normally distributed (note that the central limit theorem cannot be invoked for small samples).

In addition to the above, when the t distribution is used to define confidence intervals for the difference between two means, rather than for inference concerning only one population mean, an additional assumption usually required is

(4) The two (unknown) population variances are equal, $\sigma_1^2 = \sigma_2^2$.

Because of the above equality assumption, the first step in determining the standard error of the difference between means when the t distribution is to be used typically is to pool the two sample variances:

$$\hat{\sigma}^2 = \frac{(n_1 - 1)s_1^2 + (n_2 - 1)s_2^2}{n_1 + n_2 - 2} \tag{9.5}$$

The standard error of the difference between means based on using the pooled variance estimate $\hat{\sigma}^2$ is

$$\hat{\sigma}_{\bar{x}_1 - \bar{x}_2} = \sqrt{\frac{\hat{\sigma}^2}{n_1} + \frac{\hat{\sigma}^2}{n_2}} \tag{9.6}$$

Where $df = n_1 + n_2 - 2$, the confidence interval is

$$(\bar{X}_1 - \bar{X}_2) \pm t_{df}\hat{\sigma}_{\bar{x}_1 - \bar{x}_2} \tag{9.7}$$

Note: Some computer software does not require that the two population variances be assumed to be equal. Instead, a corrected value for the degrees of freedom is determined that results in reduced *df*, and thus in a somewhat larger value of *t* and somewhat wider confidence interval.

EXAMPLE 2. For a random sample of $n_1 = 10$ bulbs, the mean bulb life is $\bar{X}_1 = 4.600$ hr with $s_1 = 250$ hr. For another brand of bulbs the mean bulb life and standard deviation for a sample of $n_2 = 8$ bulbs are $\bar{X}_2 = 4,000$ hr and $s_2 = 200$ hr. The bulb life for both brands is assumed to be normally distributed. The 90 percent confidence interval for estimating the difference between the mean operating life of the two brands of bulbs is

$$90\% \text{ Int.} = (\bar{X}_1 - \bar{X}_2) \pm t_{16}\hat{\sigma}_{\bar{x}_1 - \bar{x}_2}$$
$$= 600 \pm 1.746(108.847) = 600 \pm 190 = 410 \text{ to } 790 \text{ hr}$$

where

$$\bar{X}_1 - \bar{X}_2 = 4,600 - 4,000 = 600$$

$$t_{df} = t_{n_1+n_2-2} = t_{16} = 1.746$$

$$\hat{\sigma}^2 = \frac{(n_1 - 1)s_1^2 + (n_2 - 1)s_2^2}{n_1 + n_2 - 2} = \frac{9(250)^2 + 7(200)^2}{10 + 8 - 2} = 52,656.25$$

$$\hat{\sigma}_{\bar{x}_1 - \bar{x}_2} = \sqrt{\frac{\hat{\sigma}^2}{n_1} + \frac{\hat{\sigma}^2}{n_2}} = \sqrt{\frac{52,656.25}{10} + \frac{52,656.25}{8}} = 108.847$$

Thus, we can state with 90 percent confidence that the first brand of bulbs has a mean life that is greater than that of the second brand by an amount between 410 and 790 hr.

Note that in the two-sample case it is possible for each sample to be small ($n < 30$), and yet the normal distribution could be used to approximate the *t* because $df \geq 29$. However, in such use the two populations must be assumed to be approximately normally distributed, because the central limit theorem cannot be invoked with respect to a small sample.

9.3   CONFIDENCE INTERVALS FOR THE POPULATION PROPORTION

As explained in Section 6.4, the probability distribution that is applicable to proportions is the binomial probability distribution. However, the mathematics associated with determining a confidence interval for an unknown population proportion on the basis of the Bernoulli process described in Section 6.3 are complex. Therefore, all applications-oriented textbooks utilize the normal distribution as an approximation of the exact solution for confidence intervals for proportions. As explained in Section 7.4, such approximation is appropriate when $n \geq 30$ and both $np \geq 5$ and $nq \geq 5$ (where $q = 1 - p$). *However, when the population proportion p (or π) is not known, most statisticians suggest that a sample of $n \geq 100$ should be taken.* Note that in the context of statistical estimation π is not known, but is estimated by $\hat{p}$.

The variance of the distribution of proportions (see Section 6.4) serves as the basis for the standard error. Given an observed sample proportion, $\hat{p}$, the estimated standard error of the proportion is

$$s_{\hat{p}} = \sqrt{\frac{\hat{p}(1 - \hat{p})}{n}} \tag{9.8}$$

In the context of statistical estimation, the population p (or π) would not be known because that is the value being estimated. If the population is finite, then use of the finite correction factor is appropriate (see Section 8.3). As was the case for the standard error of the mean, use of this correction is generally not considered necessary if $n < 0.05N$, that is, when the sample size is less than 5 percent of the population size.

The approximate confidence interval for a population proportion is

$$\hat{p} \pm zs_{\hat{p}} \tag{9.9}$$

In addition to the two-sided confidence interval, a one-sided confidence interval for the population proportion can also be determined. (See Problem 9.11.)

EXAMPLE 3. A marketing research firm contacts a random sample of 100 men in a large community and finds that a sample proportion of 0.40 prefer the razor blades manufactured by the client firm to all other brands. The 95 percent confidence interval for the proportion of all men in the community who prefer the client firm's razor blades is determined as follows:

$$s_{\hat{p}} = \sqrt{\frac{\hat{p}(1-\hat{p})}{n}} = \sqrt{\frac{(0.40)(0.60)}{100}} = \sqrt{\frac{0.24}{100}} = \sqrt{0.0024} \cong 0.05$$

$$\hat{p} \pm z s_{\hat{p}} = 0.40 \pm 1.96(0.05)$$
$$= 0.40 \pm 0.098 \cong 0.40 \pm 0.10 = 0.30 \text{ to } 0.50$$

Therefore, with 95 percent confidence we estimate the proportion of all men in the community who prefer the client firm's blades to be somewhere between 0.30 and 0.50.

9.4 DETERMINING THE REQUIRED SAMPLE SIZE FOR ESTIMATING THE PROPORTION

Before a sample is actually collected, the minimum required sample size can be determined by specifying the level of confidence required, the sampling error that is acceptable, and by making an initial (subjective) estimate of π, the unknown population proportion:

$$n = \frac{z^2 \pi(1-\pi)}{E^2} \qquad (9.10)$$

In (9.10), z is the value used for the specified confidence interval, π is the initial estimate of the population proportion, and E is the "plus and minus" sampling error allowed in the interval (always one-half the total confidence interval).

If an initial estimate of π is not possible, then it should be estimated as being 0.50. Such an estimate is conservative in that it is the value for which the largest sample size would be required. Under such an assumption, the general formula for sample size is simplified as follows:

$$n = \left(\frac{z}{2E}\right)^2 \qquad (9.11)$$

(*Note*: When solving for sample size, any fractional result is always rounded up. Further, any computed sample size below 100 should be increased to 100 because Formulas (9.10) and (9.11) are based on use of the normal distribution.)

EXAMPLE 4. For the study in Example 3, suppose that before data were collected it was specified that the 95 percent interval estimate should be within ± 0.05 and no prior judgment was made about the likely value of π. The minimum sample size which should be collected is

$$n = \left(\frac{z}{2E}\right)^2 = \left[\frac{1.96}{2(0.05)}\right]^2 = \left(\frac{1.96}{0.10}\right)^2 = (19.6)^2 = 384.16 = 385$$

In addition to estimating the population proportion, the *total number* in a category of the population can also be estimated. [See Problem 9.7(*b*).]

9.5 CONFIDENCE INTERVALS FOR THE DIFFERENCE BETWEEN TWO PROPORTIONS

In order to estimate the difference between the proportions in two populations, the unbiased point estimate of $(\pi_1 - \pi_2)$ is $(\hat{p}_1 - \hat{p}_2)$. See Section 8.1. The confidence interval involves use of the standard error of the *difference* between proportions. Use of the normal distribution is based on the same conditions as for the sampling distribution of the proportion in Section 9.3, except that two samples are involved and the requirements apply to each of the two samples. The confidence interval for estimating the difference between two population proportions is

$$(\hat{p}_1 - \hat{p}_2) \pm z s_{\hat{p}_1 - \hat{p}_2} \tag{9.12}$$

The standard error of the difference between proportions is determined by (*9.13*), wherein the value of each respective standard error of the proportion is calculated as described in Section 9.3:

$$s_{\hat{p}_1 - \hat{p}_2} = \sqrt{s_{\hat{p}_1}^2 + s_{\hat{p}_2}^2} \tag{9.13}$$

EXAMPLE 5. In Example 3 it was reported that a proportion of 0.40 men out of a random sample of 100 in a large community preferred the client firm's razor blades to all others. In another large community, 60 men out of a random sample of 200 men prefer the client firm's blades. The 90 percent confidence interval for the difference in the proportion of men in the two communities preferring the client firm's blades is

$$\begin{aligned}
90\% \text{ Int.} &= (\hat{p}_1 - \hat{p}_2) \pm z s_{\hat{p}_1 - \hat{p}_2} \\
&= 0.100 \pm 1.645(0.059) \\
&= 0.100 \pm 0.097 \\
&= 0.003 \text{ to } 0.197
\end{aligned}$$

where

$$\bar{p}_1 - \bar{p}_2 = 0.40 - 0.30 = 0.10$$

$$z = 1.645$$

$$s_{\hat{p}_1}^2 = \frac{\hat{p}_1(1 - \hat{p}_1)}{n_1} = \frac{(0.40)(0.60)}{100} = 0.0024$$

$$s_{\hat{p}_2}^2 = \frac{\hat{p}_2(1 - \hat{p}_2)}{n_2} = \frac{(0.30)(0.70)}{200} = 0.00105$$

$$s_{\hat{p}_1 - \hat{p}_2} = \sqrt{s_{\hat{p}_1}^2 + s_{\hat{p}_2}^2} = \sqrt{0.0024 + 0.00105} = \sqrt{0.00345} \cong 0.059$$

9.6   THE CHI-SQUARE DISTRIBUTION AND CONFIDENCE INTERVALS FOR THE VARIANCE AND STANDARD DEVIATION

Given a normally distributed population of values, the χ^2 (chi-square) distributions can be shown to be the appropriate probability distributions for the ratio $(n - 1)s^2/\sigma^2$. There is a different chi-square distribution according to the value of $n - 1$, which represents the degrees of freedom (*df*). Thus,

$$\chi_{df}^2 = \frac{(n - 1)s^2}{\sigma^2} \tag{9.14}$$

Because the sample variance is the unbiased estimator of the population variance, the long-run expected value of the above ratio is equal to the degrees of freedom, or $n - 1$. However, in any given sample the sample variance generally is *not* identical in value to the population variance. Since the ratio above is known to follow a chi-square distribution, this probability distribution can be used for statistical inference concerning an unknown variance or standard deviation.

Chi-square distributions are not symmetrical. Therefore, a two-sided confidence interval for a variance or standard deviation involves the use of two different χ^2 values, rather than the plus-and-minus approach used with the confidence intervals based on the normal and t distributions. The formula for constructing a confidence interval for the population variance is

$$\frac{(n-1)s^2}{\chi^2_{df,\,\text{upper}}} \le \sigma^2 \le \frac{(n-1)s^2}{\chi^2_{df,\,\text{lower}}} \qquad\qquad (9.15)$$

The confidence interval for the population standard deviation is

$$\sqrt{\frac{(n-1)s^2}{\chi^2_{df,\,\text{upper}}}} \le \sigma \le \sqrt{\frac{(n-1)s^2}{\chi^2_{df,\,\text{lower}}}} \qquad\qquad (9.16)$$

Appendix 7 indicates the proportions of area under the chi-square distributions according to various degrees of freedom, or df. In the general formula above, the subscripts upper and lower identify the percentile points on the particular χ^2 distribution to be used for constructing the confidence interval. For example, for a 90 percent confidence interval the upper point is $\chi^2_{0.95}$ and the lower point is $\chi^2_{0.05}$. By excluding the highest 5 percent and lowest 5 percent of the chi-square distribution, what remains is the "middle" 90 percent.

EXAMPLE 6. The mean weekly wage for a sample of 30 hourly employees in a large firm is $\bar{X} = \$280.00$ with a sample standard deviation of $s = \$14.00$. The weekly wage amounts in the firm are assumed to be approximately normally distributed. The 95 percent confidence interval for estimating the standard deviation of weekly wages in the population is

$$\sqrt{\frac{(n-1)s^2}{\chi^2_{df,\,\text{upper}}}} \le \sigma \le \sqrt{\frac{(n-1)s^2}{\chi^2_{df,\,\text{lower}}}}$$

$$\sqrt{\frac{(29)(196.00)}{\chi^2_{29,0.975}}} \le \sigma \le \sqrt{\frac{(29)(196.00)}{\chi^2_{29,0.025}}}$$

$$\sqrt{\frac{5,684.00}{45.72}} \le \sigma \le \sqrt{\frac{5,684.00}{16.05}}$$

$$\sqrt{124.3220} \le \sigma \le \sqrt{354.1433}$$

$$11.15 \le \sigma \le 18.82$$

In the above example, note that because the column headings in Appendix 7 are right-tail probabilities, rather than percentile values, the column headings that are used in the table are the complementary values of the required upper and lower percentile values.

As an alternative to a two-sided confidence interval, a one-sided confidence interval for the variance or standard deviation can also be determined. (See Problem 9.14.)

9.7   USING EXCEL AND MINITAB

Computer software for statistical analysis generally includes the capability to determine a number of types of confidence intervals, in addition to confidence intervals for the population mean. Solved Problems 9.15 and 9.16 illustrate the use of Excel and Minitab, respectively, to obtain confidence intervals for the difference between two population means.

Solved Problems

CONFIDENCE INTERVALS FOR THE DIFFERENCE BETWEEN TWO MEANS USING THE NORMAL DISTRIBUTION

9.1. For the study reported in Problem 8.11, suppose that there were 9,000 customers who did not purchase the "coupon special" but who did make other purchases in the store during the period of the study. For a sample of 200 of these customers, the mean purchase amount was $\bar{X} = \$19.60$ with a sample standard deviation of $s = \$8.40$.

   (a) Estimate the mean purchase amount for the noncoupon customers, using a 95 percent confidence interval.

   (b) Estimate the difference between the mean purchase amount of coupon and noncoupon customers, using a 90 percent confidence interval.

   (a)
$$s_{\bar{x}} = \frac{s}{\sqrt{n}} = \frac{8.40}{\sqrt{200}} = \frac{8.40}{14.142}\sqrt{0.7786} = 0.59$$

$$\bar{X} \pm zs_{\bar{x}} = 19.60 \pm 1.96(0.59) = \$19.60 \pm 1.16 = \$18.44 \text{ to } \$20.76$$

   (b)
$$s_{\bar{x}_1 - \bar{x}_2} = \sqrt{s_{\bar{x}_1}^2 + s_{\bar{x}_2}^2} = \sqrt{(0.66)^2 + (0.59)^2} = \sqrt{0.4356 + 0.3481} = 0.885$$

$$(\bar{X}_1 - \bar{X}_2) \pm zs_{\bar{x}_1 - \bar{x}_2} = (24.57 - 19.60) \pm 1.645(0.885) = \$4.97 \pm 1.46 = \$3.51 \text{ to } \$6.43$$

   Thus, we can state with 90 percent confidence that the mean level of sales for coupon customers exceeds that for noncoupon customers by an amount somewhere between $3.51 and $6.43.

9.2. A random sample of 50 households in community A has a mean household income of $\bar{X} = \$44,600$ with a standard deviation $s = \$2,200$. A random sample of 50 households in community B has a mean of $\bar{X} = \$43,800$ with a standard deviation of $s = \$2,800$. Estimate the difference in the average household income in the two communities using a 95 percent confidence interval.

$$s_{\bar{x}_1} = \frac{s_1}{\sqrt{n_1}} = \frac{2,200}{\sqrt{50}} = \frac{2,200}{7.07} = \$311.17$$

$$s_{\bar{x}_2} = \frac{s_2}{\sqrt{n_2}} = \frac{2,800}{\sqrt{50}} = \frac{2,800}{7.07} = \$396.04$$

$$s_{\bar{x}_1 - \bar{x}_2} = \sqrt{s_{\bar{x}_1}^2 + s_{\bar{x}_2}^2} = \sqrt{(311.17)^2 + (396.04)^2} = \sqrt{96,826.77 + 156,847.68} = \$503.66$$

$$(\bar{X}_1 - \bar{X}_2) \pm zs_{\bar{x}_1 - \bar{x}_2} = (44,600 - 43,800) \pm 1.96(503.66)$$

$$= 800 \pm 987.17 = -\$187.17 \text{ to } \$1,787.17$$

   With a 95 percent level of confidence, the limits of the confidence interval indicate that the mean in the first community might be less than the mean in the second community by $187.17, while at the other limit the mean of the first community might exceed that in the second by as much as $1,787.17. Note that the possibility that there is no actual difference between the two population means is included within this 95 percent confidence interval.

USE OF THE t DISTRIBUTION

9.3. In one canning plant the average net weight of string beans being packed in No. 303 cans for a sample of $n = 12$ cans is $\bar{X}_1 = 15.97$ oz, with $s_1 = 0.15$ oz. At another canning plant the average net weight of string beans being packed in No. 303 cans for a sample of $n_2 = 15$ cans is $\bar{X}_2 = 16.14$ oz with a standard deviation of $s_2 = 0.09$ oz. The distributions of the amounts packed are assumed to be approximately normal. Estimate the difference between the average net weight of beans being packed in No. 303 cans at the two plants, using a 90 percent confidence interval.

$$\hat{\sigma}^2 = \frac{(n_1 - 1)s_1^2 + (n_2 - 1)s_2^2}{n_1 + n_2 - 2} = \frac{11(0.15)^2 + 14(0.09)^2}{12 + 15 - 2} = 0.014436$$

$$\hat{\sigma}_{\bar{x}_1 - \bar{x}_2} = \sqrt{\frac{\hat{\sigma}^2}{n_1} + \frac{\hat{\sigma}^2}{n_2}} = \sqrt{\frac{0.014436}{12} + \frac{0.014436}{15}} = 0.047$$

$$(\bar{x}_1 - \bar{x}_2) \pm t_{df}\hat{\sigma}_{\bar{x}_1 - \bar{x}_2} = (15.97 - 16.14) \pm t_{25}(0.047)$$

$$= (-0.17) \pm 1.708(0.047) = (-0.17) \pm 0.08 = -0.25 \text{ to } -0.09$$

In other words, with 90 percent confidence we can state the average net weight being packed at the *second* plant is somewhere between 0.09 and 0.25 oz more than at the first plant.

ONE-SIDED CONFIDENCE INTERVALS FOR THE DIFFERENCE BETWEEN TWO MEANS

9.4. Just as for the mean, as explained in Problem 8.14, a difference between means can be estimated by the use of a one-sided confidence interval. Referring to the data in Problem 9.1(*b*), estimate the minimum difference between the mean purchase amounts of "coupon" and "noncoupon" customers by constructing a 90 percent upper confidence interval.

Since, from Problem 9.1(*b*), $\bar{X}_1 - \bar{X}_2 = \$4.97$ and $s_{\bar{x}_1 - \bar{x}_2} = 0.772$,

$$\text{Est. } (\mu_1 - \mu_2) \geq (\bar{X}_1 - \bar{X}_2) - zs_{\bar{x}_1 - \bar{x}_2}$$
$$\geq \$4.97 - (1.28)(0.772)$$
$$\geq \$3.98$$

9.5. For the income data reported in Problem 9.2, estimate the maximum difference between the mean income levels in the first and second community by constructing a 95 percent lower confidence interval.

Since, from Problem 9.2, $\bar{X}_1 - \bar{X}_2 = \$800$ and $s_{\bar{x}_1 - \bar{x}_2} = \$503.66$,

$$\text{Est. } (\mu_1 - \mu_2) \leq (\bar{X}_1 - \bar{X}_2) + zs_{\bar{x}_1 - \bar{x}_2}$$
$$\leq \$800 + 1.645(503.66)$$
$$\leq \$1,628.52$$

CONFIDENCE INTERVALS FOR ESTIMATING THE POPULATION PROPORTION

9.6. A college administrator collects data on a nationwide random sample of 230 students enrolled in M.B.A. programs and finds that 54 of these students have undergraduate degrees in business. Estimate the proportion of such students in the nationwide population who have undergraduate degrees in business, using a 90 percent confidence interval.

$$\hat{p} = \frac{54}{230} = 0.235$$

$$s_{\hat{p}} = \sqrt{\frac{\hat{p}(1 - \hat{p})}{n}} = \sqrt{\frac{(0.235)(0.765)}{230}} = \sqrt{\frac{0.179775}{230}} = \sqrt{0.0007816} = 0.028$$

$$\hat{p} \pm zs_{\hat{p}} = 0.235 \pm 1.645(0.028)$$
$$= 0.235 \pm 0.046 \cong 0.19 \text{ to } 0.28$$

9.7. In a large metropolitan area in which a total of 800 gasoline service stations are located, for a random sample of $n = 36$ stations, 20 of them carry a particular nationally advertised brand of oil. Using a

95 percent confidence interval estimate (*a*) the proportion of all stations in the area that carry the oil and (*b*) the total number of service stations in the area that carry the oil.

(*a*)
$$\hat{p} = \frac{20}{36} = 0.5555 \cong 0.56$$

$$s_{\hat{p}} = \sqrt{\frac{\hat{p}(1-\hat{p})}{n}} = \sqrt{\frac{(0.56)(0.44)}{36}} = \sqrt{\frac{0.2464}{36}} = \sqrt{0.006844} = 0.083$$

$$\hat{p} \pm zs_{\hat{p}} = 0.56 \pm 1.96(0.083) = 0.40 \text{ to } 0.72$$

(*b*) [*Note*:   As was the case in the solution to Problem 8.11(*b*) for the mean and the total quantity, the total *number* in a category of the population is determined by multiplying the confidence limits for the proportion by the total number of all elements in the population.]

$$N(\hat{p} \pm zs_{\hat{p}}) = 800(0.40 \text{ to } 0.72) = 320 \text{ to } 576 \text{ stations}$$

(or) $$N(\hat{p}) \pm N(zs_{\hat{p}}) = 800(0.56) \pm 800(0.16) = 320 \text{ to } 576 \text{ stations}$$

DETERMINING THE REQUIRED SAMPLE SIZE FOR ESTIMATING THE PROPORTION

9.8.   A university administrator wishes to estimate within ± 0.05 and with 90 percent confidence the proportion of students enrolled in M.B.A. programs who also have undergraduate degrees in business. What sample size should be collected, as a minimum, if there is no basis for estimating the approximate value of the proportion before the sample is taken?

Using formula (*9.11*),

$$n = \left(\frac{z}{2E}\right)^2 = \left(\frac{1.645}{2(0.05)}\right)^2 = (16.45)^2 = 270.60 \cong 271$$

9.9.   With respect to Problem 9.8, what is the minimum sample size required if prior data and information indicate that the proportion will be no larger than 0.30?

From formula (*9.10*),

$$n = \frac{z^2 \pi(1-\pi)}{E^2} = \frac{(1.645)^2(0.30)(0.70)}{(0.05)^2} = 227.31 \cong 228$$

CONFIDENCE INTERVALS FOR THE DIFFERENCE BETWEEN TWO PROPORTIONS

9.10.   In attempting to gauge voter sentiment regarding a school-bond proposal, a superintendent of schools collects random samples of $n = 100$ in each of the two major residential areas included within the school district. In the first area 70 of the 100 sampled voters indicate that they intend to vote for the proposal, while in the second area 50 of 100 sampled voters indicate this intention. Estimate the difference between the actual proportions of voters in the two areas who intend to vote for the proposal, using 95 percent confidence limits.

$$s_{\hat{p}_1}^2 = \frac{\hat{p}_1(1-\hat{p}_1)}{n_1} = \frac{(0.70)(0.30)}{100} = \frac{0.21}{100} = 0.0021$$

$$s_{\hat{p}_2}^2 = \frac{\hat{p}_2(1-\hat{p}_2)}{n_2} = \frac{(0.50)(0.50)}{100} = \frac{0.25}{100} = 0.0025$$

Therefore,

$$s_{\hat{p}_1-\hat{p}_2} = \sqrt{s_{\hat{p}_1}^2 + s_{\hat{p}_2}^2} = \sqrt{0.0021 + 0.0025} = \sqrt{0.0046} = 0.068$$

$$(\hat{p}_1 - \hat{p}_2) \pm zs_{\hat{p}_1-\hat{p}_2} = (0.70 - 0.50) \pm 1.96(0.068) = 0.20 \pm 0.13 = 0.07 \text{ to } 0.33$$

Thus, the difference in the population proportions is somewhere between 0.07 and 0.33 (or 7 to 33 percent).

ONE-SIDED CONFIDENCE INTERVALS FOR PROPORTIONS

9.11. Just as for the mean and difference between means (see Problems 8.14, 9.4, and 9.5), a proportion or difference between proportions can be estimated by the use of a one-sided confidence interval. For the data of Problem 9.6, find the *minimum* proportion of the graduate students who have an undergraduate degree in business, using a 90 percent confidence interval.

Since, from Problem 9.6, $\hat{p} = 0.235$ and $s_{\hat{p}} = 0.028$,

$$\hat{p} - zs_{\hat{p}} = 0.235 - 1.28(0.028) = 0.199 \text{ or higher}$$

9.12. For the data of Problem 9.10, what is the upper 95 percent confidence interval for the difference in the proportions of people in the first and second neighborhoods who intend to vote for the bonding proposal?

$$(\hat{p}_1 - \hat{p}_2) - zs_{\hat{p}_1 - \hat{p}_2} = (0.70 - 0.50) - 1.645(0.068) = 0.088 \text{ or higher}$$

Thus, with a 95 percent degree of confidence we can state that the *minimum* difference between the proportions of voters in the two neighborhoods who intend to vote in favor of the school bonding proposal is 0.088, or 8.8 percent.

CONFIDENCE INTERVALS FOR THE VARIANCE AND STANDARD DEVIATION

9.13. For the random sample of $n = 12$ cans of string beans in Problem 8.17, the mean was $\bar{X} = 15.97$ oz, the variance was $s^2 = 0.0224$, and the standard deviation was $s = 0.15$. Estimate the (*a*) variance and (*b*) standard deviation for all No. 303 cans of beans being packed in the plant, using 90 percent confidence intervals.

(*a*)
$$\frac{(n-1)s^2}{\chi^2_{df,\,upper}} \leq \sigma^2 \leq \frac{(n-1)s^2}{\chi^2_{df,\,lower}}$$

$$\frac{(11)(0.0224)}{\chi^2_{11,0.95}} \leq \sigma^2 \leq \frac{(11)(0.0224)}{\chi^2_{11,0.05}}$$

$$\frac{0.2464}{19.68} \leq \sigma^2 \leq \frac{0.2464}{4.57}$$

$$0.0125 \leq \sigma^2 \leq 0.0539$$

(*b*)
$$\sqrt{0.0125} \leq \sigma \leq \sqrt{0.0539}$$

$$0.11 \leq \sigma \leq 0.23$$

9.14. Just as is the case for the mean and proportion (see Problems 8.14 and 9.11), a population variance or standard deviation can be estimated by the use of a one-sided confidence interval. The usual concern is with respect to the upper limit of the variance or standard deviation, and thus the lower confidence interval is the most frequent type of one-sided interval. For the data of Problem 9.13, what is the lower 90 percent confidence interval for estimating the population standard deviation?

$$\text{Est. } \sigma \leq \sqrt{\frac{(n-1)s^2}{\chi^2_{df,\,lower}}} \leq \sqrt{\frac{(11)(0.0224)}{\chi^2_{11,\,0.90}}}$$

$$\leq \sqrt{\frac{0.2464}{5.58}} \leq \sqrt{0.04416} \leq 0.21$$

Thus, with a 90 percent level of confidence we can state that the standard deviation of the population is no larger than 0.21.

COMPUTER OUTPUT: DIFFERENCE BETWEEN MEANS

9.15. Table 9.1 presents the amounts of 10 randomly sampled automobile claims for each of two geographic areas for a large insurance company. The claims are assumed to be approximately normally distributed and the variance of the claims is assumed to be about the same in the two areas. Using Excel, obtain the 95 percent confidence interval for the difference between the overall mean dollar amounts of claims in the two areas.

Table 9.1   Automobile Damage Claims in Two Geographic Areas

Area 1		Area 2	
$1,033	$1,069	$1,177	$1,146
1,274	1,121	258	1,096
1,114	1,269	715	742
924	1,150	1,027	796
1,421	921	871	905

The standard output from Excel does not include the confidence interval. Instead, the output focuses on hypothesis testing, and we will revisit this example problem again from that perspective in Solved Problem 11.17. For now, we can use the output for the sample means and the pooled variance as given in Fig. 9-1 to do the remaining hand calculations that are required, as follows:

$$95\% \text{ Int.} = (\bar{X}_1 - \bar{X}_2) + t_{18}\hat{\sigma}_{\bar{x}_1 - \bar{x}_2}$$

$$= (1129.6 - 873.3) \pm 2.101\sqrt{\frac{49579}{10} + \frac{49579}{10}}$$

$$= 256.3 \pm 2.101(99.578)$$

$$= 256.3 \pm 209.2$$

$$= \$47.10 \text{ to } \$465.50$$

Based on the result of the calculations above, we can conclude the mean claim in Area 1 is greater than that in Area 2 by an amount somewhere between $47.10 and $465.50, with 95 percent confidence. The wide confidence interval is associated with the large amount of variability in the dollar amounts of the claims in each area as well as the small sample sizes.

The Excel output given in Fig. 9-1 was obtained as follows:

(1) Open Excel. In cell Al enter the column label: Area 1. Enter the 10 claim amounts for Area 1 in column A beginning at cell A2. In cell B1 enter the column label: Area 2. Enter the 10 claim amounts for Area 2 in column B, beginning at cell B2.

(2) Click **Tools** → **Data Analysis** → **t-Test: Two-Sample Assuming Equal Variances**. Click **OK**.

(3) In the dialog box designate **Variable 1 Range** as: $A$1:$A$11. Designate **Variable 2 Range** as: $B$1:$B$11.

(4) Set the **Hypothesized Mean Difference** as: 0. Select the **Labels** box. Select **Alpha** as 0.05 (because alpha = 1− confidence level).

(5) Designate the **Output Range** as: $C$1.

(6) Click **OK**.

Area 1	Area 2	t-Test: Two-Sample Assuming Equal Variances		
1033	1177			
1274	258		Area 1	Area 2
1114	715	Mean	1129.6	873.3
924	1027	Variance	24968.933	74188.45556
1421	871	Observations	10	10
1069	1146	Pooled Variance	49578.694	
1121	1096	Hypothesized Mean [	0	
1269	742	df	18	
1150	796	t Stat	2.5738668	
921	905	P(T<=t) one-tail	0.0095601	
		t Critical one-tail	1.7340631	
		P(T<=t) two-tail	0.0191201	
		t Critical two-tail	2.1009237	

Fig. 9-1 Excel output.

9.16. Table 9.1 presents the amounts of 10 randomly sampled automobile claims for each of two geographic areas for a large insurance company. The claims are assumed to be approximately normally distributed and the variance of the claims is assumed to be about the same in the two areas. Using Minitab, obtain the 95 percent confidence interval for the difference between the overall mean dollar amounts of claims in the two areas.

As can be observed in the relevant portion of the output in Fig. 9-2, we can conclude that the mean claim amount in Area 1 is greater than that in Area 2 by an amount somewhere between \$47.10 and \$465.50, with 95 percent confidence. The wide confidence interval is associated with the large amount of variability in the dollar amounts of the claims in each area as well as the small sample sizes. (The part of the output in Fig. 9-2 that follows the confidence interval output will be discussed in Solved Problem 11.18, which is concerned with hypothesis testing.)

The Minitab output given in Fig. 9-2 was obtained as follows:

(1) Open Minitab. In the column-name cell for C1 enter: Area 1. Enter the 10 claim amounts for Area 1 in column C1. In the column-name cell for C2 enter: Area 2. Enter the 10 claim amounts for Area 2 in column C2.

(2) Click **Stat** → **Basic Statistics** → **2-Sample t**.

(3) Select **Samples in different columns**. In **First** enter: C1. In **Second** enter: C2. Select **Assume Equal Variances**.

(4) Click **Options**. Designate **Confidence level** as: 95.0. Designate **Test Mean** as: 0.0 (for the hypothesized difference between the two population means before any samples were collected). For **Alternative** choose **not equal** (for a *two-sided* confidence interval). Click **OK**.

(5) Back in the original dialog box, click **OK**.

```
Two-Sample T-Test and CI: Area 1, Area 2


Two-sample T for Area 1 vs Area 2

          N     Mean    StDev   SE Mean
Area 1   10     1130      158        50
Area 2   10      873      272        86

Difference = mu Area 1 - mu Area 2
Estimate for difference:  256.3
95% CI for difference: (47.1, 465.5)
T-Test of difference = 0 (vs not =): T-Value = 2.57  P-Value = 0.019  DF = 18
Both use Pooled StDev =  223
```

Fig. 9-2 Minitab output.

Supplementary Problems

CONFIDENCE INTERVALS FOR THE DIFFERENCE BETWEEN TWO MEANS

9.17. For a particular consumer product, the mean dollar sales per retail outlet last year in a sample of $n_1 = 10$ stores was $\bar{X}_1 = \$3,425$ with $s_1 = \$200$. For a second product the mean dollar sales per outlet in a sample of $n_2 = 12$ stores was $\bar{X}_2 = \$3,250$ with $s_2 = \$175$. The sales amounts per outlet are assumed to be normally distributed for both products. Estimate the difference between the mean level of sales per outlet last year using a 95 percent confidence interval.
Ans. \$8.28 to \$341.72

9.18. From the data in Problem 9.17, suppose the two sample sizes were $n_1 = 20$ and $n_2 = 24$. Determine the 95 percent confidence interval for the difference between the two means based on normal approximation of the t distribution.
Ans. \$62.83 to \$287.17

9.19. Using the data in Problem 9.17, suppose that we are interested in only the *minimum* difference between the sales levels of the first and second product. Determine the lower limit of such an estimation interval at the 95 percent level of confidence.
Ans. \$37.13 or more

9.20. For a sample of 50 firms taken from a particular industry, the mean number of employees per firm is $\bar{X}_1 = 420.4$ with $s_1 = 55.7$. In a second industry the mean number of employees in a sample of 50 firms is $\bar{X}_2 = 392.5$ employees with $s_2 = 87.9$. Estimate the difference in the mean number of employees per firm in the two industries, using a 90 percent confidence interval.
Ans. 3.7 to 52.1 employees

9.21. Construct the 95 percent confidence interval for the difference between means for Problem 9.20.
Ans. -1.0 to 56.8 employees

9.22. For a sample of 30 employees in one large firm, the mean hourly wage is $\bar{X}_1 = \$9.50$ with $s_1 = \$1.00$. In a second large firm, the mean hourly wage for a sample of 40 employees is $\hat{X}_2 = \$9.05$ with $s_2 = \$1.20$. Estimate the difference between the mean hourly wage at the two firms, using a 90 percent confidence interval.
Ans. \$0.02 to \$0.88 per hour

9.23. For the data in Problem 9.22, suppose we are concerned with determining the maximum difference between the mean wage rates, using a 90 percent confidence interval. Construct such a lower confidence interval.
Ans. Est. $(\mu_1 - \mu_2) \leq \$0.78$ per hour

CONFIDENCE INTERVALS FOR ESTIMATING THE POPULATION PROPORTION

9.24. For a random sample of 100 households in a large metropolitan area, the number of households in which at least one adult is currently unemployed and seeking a full-time job is 12. Estimate the percentage of households in the area in which at least one adult is unemployed, using a 95 percent confidence interval.
(*Note*: Percentage limits can be obtained by first determining the confidence interval for the proportion, and then multiplying these limits by 100.)
Ans. 5.7% to 18.3%

9.25. Suppose the confidence interval obtained in Problem 9.24 is considered to be too wide for practical purposes (i.e., it is lacking in precision). Instead, we desire that the 95 percent confidence interval be within two percentage points of the true percentage of households with at least one adult unemployed. What is the minimum sample size required to satisfy this specification (*a*) if we make no assumption about the true percentage before collecting a larger sample and (*b*) if, on the basis of the sample collected in Problem 9.23, we assume that the true percentage is no larger than 18 percent?
Ans. (*a*) 2,401, (*b*) 1,418

9.26. A manufacturer has purchased a batch of 2,000 small electronic parts from the excess inventory of a large firm. For a random sample of 50 of the parts, five are found to be defective. Estimate the proportion of all the parts in the shipment that are defective, using a 90 percent confidence interval.
Ans. 0.03 to 0.17

9.27. For Problem 9.26, estimate the total number of the 2,000 parts in the shipment that are defective, using a 90 percent confidence interval.
    Ans.   60 to 340

9.28. For the situation in Problem 9.26, suppose the price of the electronics parts was such that the purchaser would be satisfied with the purchase as long as the true proportion of defective parts does not exceed 0.20. Construct a one-sided 95 percent confidence interval and observe whether the upper limit of this interval exceeds the proportion 0.20.
    Ans.   Est. $\pi \leq 0.17$

CONFIDENCE INTERVALS FOR THE DIFFERENCE BETWEEN TWO PROPORTIONS

9.29. In contrast to the data in Problem 9.24, in a second metropolitan area a random sample of 100 households yields only six households in which at least one adult is unemployed and seeking a full-time job. Estimate the difference in the percentage of households in the two areas that include an unemployed adult, using a 90 percent confidence interval.
    Ans. -0.6% to $+12.6\%$

9.30. Referring to Problem 9.29, what is the maximum percentage by which the household unemployment in the first metropolitan area exceeds the percentage unemployment in the second area, using a 90 percent one-sided confidence interval?
    Ans.   Est. Dif. $\leq 11.1\%$

CONFIDENCE INTERVALS FOR THE VARIANCE AND STANDARD DEVIATION

9.31. For a particular consumer product, the mean dollar sales per retail outlet last year in a sample of $n = 10$ stores was $\bar{X} = \$3,425$ with $s = \$200$. The sales amounts per outlet are assumed to be normally distributed. Estimate the (*a*) variance and (*b*) standard deviation of dollar sales of this product in all stores last year, using a 90 percent confidence interval.
    Ans.   (*a*) $21.278 \leq \sigma^2 \leq 108{,}271$, (*b*) $145.9 \leq \sigma \leq 329.0$

9.32. With reference to Problem 9.31, there is particular concern about how *large* the standard deviation of dollar sales might be. Construct the 90 percent one-sided confidence interval that identifies this value.
    Ans. $\sigma \leq 293.9$

COMPUTER OUTPUT

9.33. A business firm that processes many of its orders by telephone has two types of customers: general and commercial. Table 9.2 reports the required per item telephone order times for a random sample of 12 general-customer calls and 10 commercial-customer calls. The amounts of time required for each type of call are assumed to be approximately normally distributed. Using available computer software, obtain the 95 percent confidence interval for the difference in the mean amount of per item time required for each type of call.
    Ans. -23 to 52 sec

Table 9.2   Time (in Seconds) Required per Item Order

General customers	Commercial customers
48	81
66	137
106	107
84	110
146	107
139	40
154	154
150	142
177	34
156	165
122	
121	

CHAPTER 10

Testing Hypotheses Concerning the Value of the Population Mean

10.1 INTRODUCTON

The purpose of hypothesis testing is to determine whether a claimed (hypothesized) value for a population parameter, such as a population mean, should be accepted as being plausible based on sample evidence. Recall from Section 8.2 on sampling distributions that a sample mean generally will differ in value from the population mean. If the observed value of a sample statistic, such as the sample mean, is close to the claimed parameter value and differs only by an amount that would be expected because of random sampling, then the hypothesized value is not rejected. If the sample statistic differs from the claim by an amount that cannot be ascribed to chance, then the hypothesis is rejected as not being plausible.

Three different procedures have been developed for testing hypotheses, with all of them leading to the same decision when the same probability (and risk) standards are used. In this chapter we first describe the *critical value approach* to hypothesis testing. By this approach, the so-called critical values of the test statistic that would dictate rejection of a hypothesis are determined, and then the observed test statistic is compared to the critical values. This is the first approach that was developed, and thus much of the language of hypothesis testing stems from it. More recently, the *P-value approach* has become popular because it is the one most easily applied with computer software. This approach is based on determining the conditional probability that the observed value of a sample statistic could occur by chance, given that a particular claim for the value of the associated population parameter is in fact true. The *P*-value approach is described in Section 10.7. Finally, the *confidence interval approach* is based on observing whether the claimed value of a population parameter is included within the range of values that define a confidence interval for that parameter. This approach to hypothesis testing is described in Section 10.8.

No matter which approach to hypothesis testing is used, note that if a hypothesized value is not rejected, and therefore is accepted, this does not constitute a "proof" that the hypothesized value is correct. Acceptance of a claimed value for the parameter simply indicates that it is a plausible value, based on the observed value of the sample statistic.

10.2   BASIC STEPS IN HYPOTHESIS TESTING BY THE CRITICAL VALUE APPROACH

Step 1.   Formulate the null hypothesis and the alternative hypothesis. The *null hypothesis* (H_0) is the hypothesized parameter value which is compared with the sample result. It is rejected *only if* the sample result is unlikely to have occurred given the correctness of the hypothesis. The *alternative hypothesis* (H_1) is accepted only if the null hypothesis is rejected. The alternative hypothesis is also designated by H_a in many texts.

EXAMPLE 1.   An auditor wishes to test the assumption that the mean value of all accounts receivable in a given firm is $260.00 by taking a sample of $n = 36$ and computing the sample mean. The auditor wishes to reject the assumed value of $260.00 only if it is clearly contradicted by the sample mean, and thus the hypothesized value should be given the benefit of the doubt in the testing procedure. The null and alternative hypotheses for this test are H_0: $\mu = \$260.00$ and H_1: $\mu \neq \$260.00$.

Step 2.   Specify the level of significance to be used. The level of significance is the statistical standard which is specified for rejecting the null hypothesis. If a 5 percent level of significance is specified, then the null hypothesis is rejected only if the sample result is so different from the hypothesized value that a difference of that amount or larger would occur by chance with a probability of 0.05 or less.

Note that if the 5 percent level of significance is used, there is a probability of 0.05 of rejecting the null hypothesis when it is in fact true. This is called *Type I error*. The probability of Type I error is always equal to the level of significance that is used as the standard for rejecting the null hypothesis; it is designated by the lowercase Greek α (alpha), and thus α also designates the level of significance. The most frequently used levels of significance in hypothesis testing are the 5 percent and 1 percent levels.

A *Type II error* occurs if the null hypothesis is not rejected, and therefore accepted, when it is in fact false. Determining the probability of Type II error is explained in Section 10.4. Table 10.1 summarizes the types of decisions and the possible consequences of the decisions which are made in hypothesis testing.

Table 10.1   Consequences of Decisions in Hypothesis Testing

	Possible states	
Possible decision	Null hypothesis true	Null hypothesis false
Accept null hypothesis	Correctly accepted	Type II error
Reject null hypothesis	Type I error	Correctly rejected

Step 3.   Select the test statistic. The test statistic will either be the sample statistic (the unbiased estimator of the parameter being tested), or a standardized version of the sample statistic. For example, in order to test a hypothesized value of the population mean, the mean of a random sample taken from that population could serve as the test statistic. However, if the sampling distribution of the mean is normally distributed, then the value of the sample mean typically is converted into a z value, which then serves as the test statistic.

Step 4.   Establish the critical value or values of the test statistic. Having specified the null hypothesis, the level of significance, and the test statistic to be used, we now establish the critical value(s) of the test statistic. There may be one or two such values, depending on whether a so-called one-sided or two-sided test is involved (see Section 10.3). In either case, a *critical value* identifies the value of the test statistic that is required to reject the null hypothesis.

Step 5.   *Determine the actual value of the test statistic.* For example, in testing a hypothesized value of the population mean, a random sample is collected and the value of sample mean is determined. If the critical value was established as a z value, then the sample mean is converted into a z value.

Step 6.   *Make the decision.* The observed value of the sample statistic is compared with the critical value (or values) of the test statistic. The null hypothesis is then either rejected or not rejected. If the null hypothesis is rejected, the alternative hypothesis is accepted. In turn, this decision will have relevance to other decisions to be made by operating managers, such as whether a standard of performance is being maintained or which of two marketing strategies should be used.

10.3   TESTING A HYPOTHESIS CONCERNING THE MEAN BY USE OF THE NORMAL DISTRIBUTION

The normal probability distribution can be used for testing a hypothesized value of the population mean (1) whenever $n \geq 30$, because of the central limit theorem, or (2) when $n < 30$ but the population is normally distributed and σ is known. (See Sections 8.3 and 8.4.)

A *two-sided test* is used when we are concerned about a possible deviation in *either* direction from the hypothesized value of the mean. The formula used to establish the critical values of the sample mean is similar to the formula for determining confidence limits for estimating the population mean (see Section 8.6), except that the hypothesized value of the population mean μ_0 is the reference point rather than the sample mean. The critical values of the sample mean for a two-sided test, according to whether or not σ is known, are

$$\bar{X}_{CR} = \mu_0 \pm z\sigma_{\bar{x}} \tag{10.1}$$

or

$$\bar{X}_{CR} = \mu_0 \pm zs_{\bar{x}} \tag{10.2}$$

EXAMPLE 2.   For the null hypothesis formulated in Example 1, determine the critical values of the sample mean for testing the hypothesis at the 5 percent level of significance. Given that the standard deviation of the accounts receivable amounts is known to be $\sigma = \$43.00$, the critical values are

Hypotheses: H_0: $\mu = \$260.00$; H_1: $\mu \neq \$260.00$

Level of significance: $\alpha = 0.05$

Test statistic: $\bar{X}$ based on a sample of $n = 36$ and with $\sigma = 43.00$

$\bar{X}_{CR}$ = critical values of the sample mean

$$\bar{X}_{CR} = \mu_0 \pm z\sigma_{\bar{x}} = 260.00 \pm 1.96 \frac{\sigma}{\sqrt{n}} = 260 \pm 1.96 \frac{43.00}{\sqrt{36}}$$

$$= 260.00 \pm 1.96(7.17) = 260.00 \pm 14.05 = \$245.95 \text{ and } \$274.05$$

Therefore, in order to reject the null hypothesis the sample mean must have a value that is less than $245.95 *or* greater than $274.05. Thus, there are two regions of rejection in the case of a two-sided test (see Fig. 10-1). The z values of ± 1.96 are used to establish the critical limits, because for the standard normal distribution a proportion of 0.05 of the area remains in the two tails, which corresponds to the specified $\alpha = 0.05$.

Instead of establishing critical values in terms of the sample mean, the critical values in hypothesis testing typically are specified in terms of z values. For the 5 percent level of significance the critical values z for a two-sided test are -1.96 and $+1.96$, for example. When the value of the sample mean is determined, it is converted

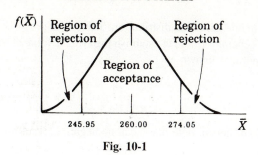

Fig. 10-1

to a z value so that it can be compared with the critical values of z. The conversion formula, according to whether or not σ is known, is

$$z = \frac{\bar{X} - \mu_0}{\sigma_{\bar{x}}} \qquad (10.3)$$

or

$$z = \frac{\bar{X} - \mu_0}{s_{\bar{x}}} \qquad (10.4)$$

EXAMPLE 3. For the hypothesis testing problem in Examples 1 and 2, suppose the sample mean is $\bar{X} = \$240.00$. We determine whether the null hypothesis should be rejected by converting this mean to a z value and comparing it to the critical values of ± 1.96 as follows:

$$\sigma_{\bar{x}} = 7.17 \quad \text{(from Example 2)}$$

$$z = \frac{\bar{X} - \mu_0}{\sigma_{\bar{x}}} = \frac{240.00 - 260.00}{7.17} = \frac{-20.00}{7.17} = -2.79$$

This value of z is in the left-tail region of rejection of the hypothesis testing model portrayed in Fig. 10-2. Thus, the null hypothesis is rejected and the alternative, that $\mu \neq \$260.00$, is accepted. Note that the same conclusion would be reached in Example 2 by comparing the sample mean of $\bar{X} = \$240.00$ with the critical limits for the mean identified in Fig. 10-1.

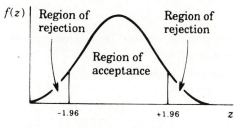

Fig. 10-2

A *one-sided test* is appropriate when we are concerned about possible deviations in only one direction from the hypothesized value of the mean. The auditor in Example 1 may not be concerned that the true average of all accounts receivable exceeds \$260.00, but only that it might be less than \$260.00. Thus, if the auditor gives the benefit of the doubt to the stated claim that the true mean is *at least* \$260.00, the null and alternative hypotheses are

$$H_0: \mu = \$260.00 \qquad \text{and} \qquad H_1: \mu < \$260.00$$

Note: In some texts the above null hypothesis would be stated as $H_0: \mu \geq \$260.00$. We include only the equal sign because, even for a one-sided test, the procedure is carried out with respect to this particular value. Put another way, it is the *alternative* hypothesis that is one-sided.

There is only one region of rejection for a one-sided test, and for the above example the test is thus a lower-tail test. The region of rejection for a one-sided test is always in the tail that represents support of the *alternative* hypothesis. As is the case for a two-sided test, the critical value can be determined for the mean, as such, or in terms of a z value. However, critical values for one-sided tests differ from those for two-sided tests because the given proportion of area is all in one tail of the distribution. Table 10.2 presents the values of z needed for one-sided and two-sided tests. The general formula to establish the critical value of the sample mean for a one-sided test, according to whether or not σ is known, is

$$\bar{X}_{CR} = \mu_0 + z\sigma_{\bar{x}} \tag{10.5}$$

or

$$\bar{X}_{CR} = \mu_0 + zs_{\bar{x}} \tag{10.6}$$

In formulas (10.5) and (10.6) above, note that z can be negative, resulting in a subtraction of the second term in each formula.

Table 10.2   Critical Values of z in Hypothesis Testing

Level of significance	Type of test	
	One-sided	Two-sided
5%	+1.645 (or −1.645)	± 1.96
1%	+2.33 (or −2.33)	± 2.58

EXAMPLE 4.   Assume that the auditor in Examples 1 through 3 began with the alternative hypothesis that the mean value of all accounts receivable is less than $260.00. Given that the sample mean is $240.00, we test this hypothesis at the 5 percent level of significance by the following two separate procedures.

(1)   Determining the critical value of the sample mean, where H_0: $\mu = \$260.00$ and H_1:$\mu < \$260.00$.

$$\bar{X}_{CR} = \mu_0 + z\sigma_{\bar{x}} = 260 + (-1.645)(7.17) = \$248.21$$

Since $\bar{X} = \$240.00$, it is in the region of rejection. The null hypothesis is therefore rejected and the alternative hypothesis, that $\mu < \$260.00$, is accepted.

(2)   Specifying the critical value in terms of z, where critical $z(\alpha = 0.05) = -1.645$:

$$z = \frac{\bar{X} - \mu_0}{\sigma_{\bar{x}}} = \frac{240.00 - 260.00}{7.17} = -2.79$$

Since $z = -2.79$ is in the region of rejection (to the left of the critical value of -1.645), the null hypothesis is rejected. Figure 10-3 portrays the critical value for this one-sided test in terms of $\bar{X}$ and z.

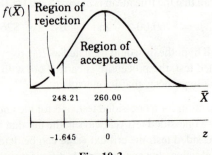

Fig. 10-3

10.4 TYPE I AND TYPE II ERRORS IN HYPOTHESIS TESTING

In this section Type I and Type II errors (defined in Section 10.2) are considered entirely with respect to one-sided tests of a hypothesized mean. However, the basic concepts illustrated here apply to other hypothesis testing models as well.

The maximum probability of Type I error is designated by the Greek α (alpha). It is always equal to the level of significance used in testing the null hypothesis. This is so because by definition the proportion of area in the region of rejection is equal to the proportion of sample results that would occur in that region given that the null hypothesis is true.

The probability of Type II error is generally designated by the Greek β (beta). The only way it can be determined is with respect to a *specific* value included within the range of the *alternative* hypothesis.

EXAMPLE 5.   As in Example 4, the null hypothesis is that the mean of all accounts receivable is \$260.00 with the alternative hypothesis being that it is less than this amount, and this test is to be carried out at the 5 percent level of significance. Further, the auditor indicates that an actual mean of \$240.00 (or less) would be considered to be an important and material difference from the hypothesized value of \$260.00. As before, $\sigma = \$43.00$ and the sample size is $n = 36$ accounts. The determination of the probability of Type II error requires that we

(1)   formulate the null and alternative hypotheses for this testing situation,

(2)   determine the critical value of the sample mean to be used in testing the null hypothesis at the 5 percent level of significance,

(3)   identify the probability of Type I error associated with using the critical value computed above as the basis for the decision rule,

(4)   determine the probability of Type II error associated with the decision rule given the specific alternative mean value of \$240.00.

The complete solution is

(1) H_0: $\mu = \$260.00$ H_1: $\mu < \$260.00$

(2) $\bar{X}_{CR} = \mu_0 + z\sigma_{\bar{x}} = 260.00 + (-1.645)(7.17) = \$248.21$

where $\sigma_{\bar{x}} = \dfrac{\sigma}{\sqrt{n}} = \dfrac{43.00}{\sqrt{36}} = \dfrac{43.00}{6} = 7.17$

(3)   The maximum probability of Type I error equals 0.05 (the level of significance used in testing the null hypothesis).

(4)   The probability of Type II error is the probability that the mean of the random sample will equal or exceed \$248.21, given that the mean of all accounts is actually at \$240.00.

$$z = \frac{\bar{X}_{CR} - \mu_1}{\sigma_{\bar{x}}} = \frac{248.21 - 240.00}{7.17} = \frac{8.21}{7.17} = +1.15$$

$$P(\text{Type II error}) = P(z \geq +1.15) = 0.5000 - 0.3749 = 0.1251 \cong 0.13$$

Figure 10-4 illustrates the approach followed in Example 5. In general, the critical value of the mean determined with respect to the null hypothesis is "brought down" and used as the critical value with respect to the specific alternative hypothesis. Problem 10.13 illustrates the determination of the probability of Type II error for a two-sided test.

With the level of significance and sample size held constant, the probability of Type II error decreases as the specific alternative value of the mean is set farther from the value in the null hypothesis. It increases as the alternative value is set closer to the value in the null hypothesis. *An operating characteristic (OC) curve* portrays the probability of accepting the null hypothesis given various alternative values of the population mean. Figure 10-5 is the *OC* curve applicable to any *lower-tail test* for a hypothesized mean carried out at the 5 percent level of significance and based on the use of the normal probability distribution. Note that it is applicable to *any* such test, because the values on the horizontal axis are stated in units of the standard error of the mean. For any values to the left of μ_0, the probability of acceptance indicates the probability of Type II error. To the right of μ_0,

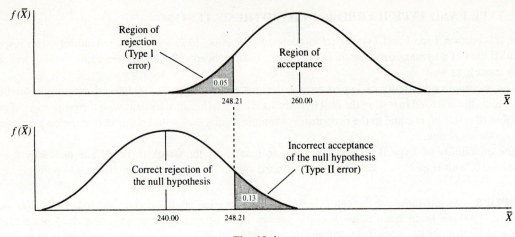

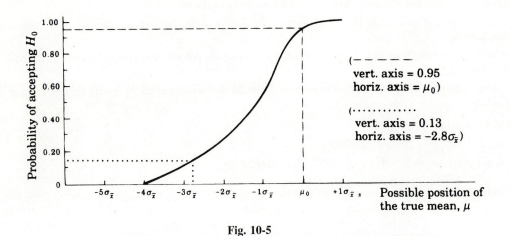

Fig. 10-4

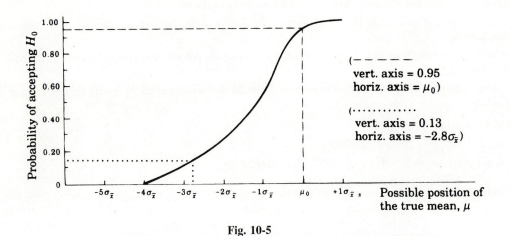

Fig. 10-5

the probabilities indicate correct acceptance of the null hypothesis. As indicated by the dashed lines, when $\mu = \mu_0$, the probability of accepting the null hypothesis is $1 - \alpha$, or in this case, $1 - 0.05 = 0.95$.

EXAMPLE 6. We can verify the probability of Type II error determined in Example 5 by reference to Fig. 10-5, as follows:

As identified in Example 5, $\mu_0 = \$260.00$, $\mu_1 = \$240.00$, and $\sigma_{\bar{x}} = 7.17$. Therefore, the difference between the two designated values of the mean *in units of the standard error* is

$$z = \frac{\mu_1 - \mu_0}{\sigma_{\bar{x}}} = \frac{240 - 260}{7.17} = -2.8$$

By reference to Fig. 10-5, the height of the curve at a horizontal axis value of $\mu_0 - 2.8\sigma_{\bar{x}}$ can be seen to be just above 0.10, as indicated by the dotted lines. The actual computed value in Example 5 is 0.13.

In hypothesis testing, the concept of *power* refers to the probability of rejecting a null hypothesis that is false, given a specific alternative value of the parameter (in our examples, the population mean). Where the probability of Type II error is designated β, it follows that the power of the test is always $1 - \beta$. Referring to

Fig. 10-5, note that the power for alternative values of the mean is the difference between the value indicated by the *OC* curve and 1.0, and thus a *power curve* can be obtained by subtraction, with reference to the *OC* curve.

EXAMPLE 7.   Referring to Example 5, we determine the power of the test, given the specific alternative value of the mean of $240.00, as follows:

Since $\beta = P(\text{Type II error}) = 0.13$ (from Example 5),

$$\text{Power} = 1 - \beta = 1.00 - 0.13 = 0.87$$

(*Note*:   This is the probability of correctly rejecting the null hypothesis when $\mu = \$240.00$.)

10.5   DETERMINING THE REQUIRED SAMPLE SIZE FOR TESTING THE MEAN

Before a sample is actually collected, the required sample size can be determined by specifying (1) the hypothesized value of the mean, (2) a specific alternative value of the mean such that the difference from the null hypothesized value is considered important, (3) the level of significance to be used in the test, (4) the probability of Type II error which is to be permitted, and (5) the value of the population standard deviation σ. The formula for determining the minimum sample size required in conjunction with testing a hypothesized value of the mean, based on use of the normal distribution, is

$$n = \frac{(z_0 - z_1)^2 \sigma^2}{(\mu_1 - \mu_0)^2} \tag{10.7}$$

In (*10.7*), z_0 is the critical value of z used in conjunction with the specified level of significance (α level), while z_1 is the value of z with respect to the designated probability of Type II error (β level). The value of σ either must be known or be estimated. Formula (*10.7*) can be used for either one-sided or two-sided tests. The only value that differs for the two types of tests is the value of z_0 which is used (see Examples 8 and 9).

[*Note*:   When solving for minimum sample size, any fractional result is always rounded up. Further, unless σ is known *and* the population is normally distributed, any computed sample size below 30 should be increased to 30 because (*10.7*) is based on the use of the normal distribution.]

EXAMPLE 8.   An auditor wishes to test the null hypothesis that the mean value of all accounts receivable is $260.00 against the alternative that it is less than this amount. The auditor considers that the difference would be material and important if the true mean is at the specific alternative of $240.00 (or less). The acceptable levels of Type I error (α) and Type II error (β) are set at 0.05 and 0.10, respectively. The standard deviation of the accounts receivable amounts is known to be $\sigma = \$43.00$. The size of the sample which should be collected, as a minimum, to carry out this test is

$$n = \frac{(z_0 - z_1)^2 \sigma^2}{(\mu_1 - \mu_0)^2} = \frac{(-1.645 - 1.28)^2 (43.00)^2}{(240.00 - 260.00)^2} = \frac{(8.5556)(1,849)}{400} = 39.55 \cong 40$$

(*Note*:   Because z_0 and z_1 would always have opposite algebraic signs, the result is that the two z values are always accumulated in the numerator above. If the accumulated value is a negative value, the process of squaring results in a positive value.)

EXAMPLE 9.   Suppose the auditor in Example 8 is concerned about a discrepancy in *either* direction from the null hypothesized value of $260.00, and that a discrepancy of $20 in either direction would be considered important. Given the other information and specifications in Example 8, the minimum size of the sample that should be collected is

$$n = \frac{(z_0 - z_1)^2 \sigma^2}{(\mu_1 - \mu_0)^2} = \frac{(-1.96 - 1.28)^2 \sigma^2}{(240.00 - 260.00)^2} \quad \text{or} \quad \frac{[1.96 - (-1.28)]^2 \sigma^2}{(280.00 - 260.00)^2}$$

$$= \frac{(-3.24)^2 (43.00)^2}{(-20)^2} \quad \text{or} \quad \frac{(3.24)^2 (43.00)^2}{(20)^2}$$

$$= \frac{(10.4976)(1,849)}{400} = 48.53 \cong 49$$

(*Note*:   Because any deviation from the hypothesized value can be only in one direction or the other, we use either $+1.96$ or -1.96 as the value of z_0 in conjunction with the then relevant value of z_1. As in Example 8, the two z values will, in effect, always be accumulated before being squared.)

10.6   TESTING A HYPOTHESIS CONCERNING THE MEAN BY USE OF THE *t* DISTRIBUTION

The t distribution (see Section 8.8) is the appropriate basis for determining the standardized test statistic when the sampling distribution of the mean is normally distributed but σ is not known. The sampling distribution can be assumed to be normal either because the population is normal or because the sample is large enough to invoke the central limit theorem. (See Section 8.4.) As in Section 8.8, the t distribution is required when the sample is small ($n < 30$). For larger samples, normal approximation can be used. For the critical value approach, the procedure is identical to that described in Section 10.3 for the normal distribution, except for the use of t instead of z as the test statistic. The test statistic is

$$t = \frac{\bar{X} - \mu_0}{s_{\bar{x}}} \qquad\qquad (10.8)$$

EXAMPLE 10.   The null hypothesis that the mean operating life of light bulbs of a particular brand is 4,200 hr has been formulated against the alternative that it is less. The mean operating life for a random sample of $n = 10$ light bulbs is $\bar{X} = 4,000$ hr with a sample standard deviation of $s = 200$ hr. The operating life of bulbs in general is assumed to be normally distributed. We test the null hypothesis at the 5 percent level of significance as follows:

$$H_0: \mu = 4,200 \qquad H_1: \mu < 4,200$$
$$\text{Critical } t(df = 9, \, \alpha = 0.05) = -1.833$$
$$s_{\bar{x}} = \frac{s}{\sqrt{n}} = \frac{200}{\sqrt{10}} = \frac{200}{3.16} = 63.3 \text{ hr}$$
$$t = \frac{\bar{X} - \mu_0}{s_{\bar{x}}} = \frac{4,000 - 4,200}{63.3} = \frac{-200}{63.3} = -3.16$$

Because -3.16 is in the left-tail region of rejection (to the left of the critical value -1.833), the null hypothesis is rejected and the alternative hypothesis; that the true mean operating life is less than 4,200 hours, is accepted.

10.7   THE *P*-VALUE APPROACH TO TESTING HYPOTHESES CONCERNING THE POPULATION MEAN

The probability of the observed sample result occurring, given that the null hypothesis is true, is determined by the P-value approach, and this probability is then compared to the designated level of significance α. Consistent with the critical value approach we described in the preceding sections, the idea is that a low P value indicates that the sample would be unlikely to occur when the null hypothesis is true; therefore, obtaining a low P value leads to rejection of the null hypothesis. Note that the P value is *not* the probability that the null hypothesis is true given the sample result. Rather, it is the probability of the sample result given that the null hypothesis is true.

EXAMPLE 11.   Refer to Example 4, in which $H_0: \mu = \$260.00$, $H_1: \mu < \$260.00$, $\alpha = 0.05$, and $\bar{X} = \$240.00$. Because the sample mean is in the direction of the alternative hypothesis for this one-sided test, we determine the probability of a sample mean having a value this small or smaller:

$$P(\bar{X} \leq 240.00) \qquad \text{where} \qquad z = \frac{\bar{X} - \mu_0}{\sigma_{\bar{x}}} = \frac{240.00 - 260.00}{7.17} = -2.79$$

$$= P(z \leq -2.79) = 0.5000 - 0.4974 = 0.0026$$

Figure 10-6 portrays the left-tail area for which the probability has been determined. Because the P value of 0.0026 is less than the designated level of significance of $\alpha = 0.05$, the null hypothesis is rejected.

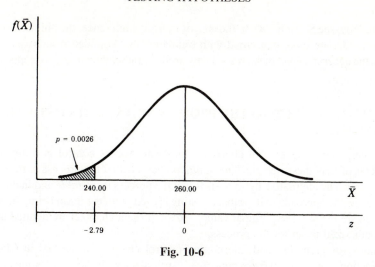

Fig. 10-6

For two-sided tests, the P value for the smaller tail of the distribution is determined, and then *doubled*. The resulting value indicates the probability of the observed amount of difference in *either* direction between the values of the sample mean and the hypothesized population mean.

The P-value approach has become popular because the standard format of computer output for hypothesis testing includes P values. The reader of the output determines whether a null hypothesis is rejected by comparing the reported P value with the desired level of significance. (See Problems 10.25 and 10.26.)

When hand calculation of probabilities based on the use of the t distribution is required, an exact P value cannot be determined because of the limitations of the standard table. (See Problem 10.21.) However, no such limitation exists when using computer software.

10.8   THE CONFIDENCE INTERVAL APPROACH TO TESTING HYPOTHESES CONCERNING THE MEAN

By this approach, a confidence interval for the population mean is constructed based on the sample results, and then we observe whether the hypothesized value of the population mean is included within the confidence interval. If the hypothesized value is included within the interval, then the null hypothesis cannot be rejected. If the hypothesized value is not included in the interval, then the null hypothesis is rejected. Where α is the level of significance to be used for the test, the $1 - \alpha$ confidence interval is constructed.

EXAMPLE 12.   Refer to Example 3, in which H_0: $\mu = \$260.00, H_1$: $\mu \neq \$260.00, \alpha = 0.05, \bar{X} = \$240.00$, and $\sigma_{\bar{x}} = 7.17$. We can test the null hypothesis at the 5 percent level of significance by constructing the 95 percent confidence interval:

$$\bar{X} \pm z\sigma_{\bar{x}} = 240.00 \pm 1.96(7.17) = 240 \pm 14.05$$
$$= \$225.95 \text{ to } \$254.05$$

Because the hypothesized value of $\$260.00$ is not included within the 95 percent confidence interval, the null hypothesis is rejected at the 5 percent level of significance.

For a one-tail test, a one-sided confidence interval is appropriate. (See Problem 10.23.) However, a simpler approach is to determine a two-sided interval, but at the level of confidence that would include the desired area in the one tail of interest. Specifically, for a one-sided test at $\alpha = 0.05$, the 90 percent, two-sided confidence interval is appropriate because this interval includes the area of 0.05 in the one tail of interest. (See Problem 10.24.)

The confidence interval approach is favored in texts that emphasize the so-called *data-analysis* approach to business statistics. In the area of statistical description, the data-analysis approach gives special attention to *exploratory data analysis* (see Section 2.8). In the area of statistical inference, the philosophy of the data-analysis approach is that managers are more concerned with estimation and confidence intervals concerning unknown parameters, such as the uncertain level of sales for a new product, rather than in the concepts of hypothesis testing.

10.9 TESTING WITH RESPECT TO THE PROCESS MEAN IN STATISTICAL PROCESS CONTROL

The use and interpretation of control charts in statistical process control is a direct application of the methods and concepts of hypothesis testing. The null hypothesis is that the process is *stable* and only common causes of variation exist. The alternative hypothesis is that the process is *unstable* and includes assignable-cause variation. The critical value approach to hypothesis testing is used, with the norm being that the lower and upper control limits (which are the same as "critical values" in the present chapter) are defined at ± 3 standard error units from the hypothesized mean for the process.

The methodology for preparing and interpreting control charts is described in Chapter 19, Statistical Process Control. Sections 19.5 and 19.6 are concerned particulary with the process mean.

EXAMPLE 13. Example 16 in Chapter 2 (page 19) presents a sequence of mean weights for samples of $n = 4$ packages of potato chips taken in a packaging process. The run chart for the sequence of weights is portrayed in Fig. 2-11. Suppose that the process specifications call for a mean weight of $\mu = 15.0$ oz. An overview of Fig. 2-11 might lead one to question whether this standard is being maintained throughout the process, and particularly at samples #8 and #9. In Problems 19.12 and 19.15 we shall observe that these two sample means are beyond the lower control limit and not likely to have occurred simply because of common-cause variation. Therefore, we shall reject the null hypothesis that the process mean throughout the time period has been 15.0, and conclude that there is strong evidence of assignable-cause variation with respect to the process mean.

10.10 SUMMARY TABLE FOR TESTING A HYPOTHESIZED VALUE OF THE MEAN

Table 10.3 Testing a Hypothesized Value of the Mean

Population	Sample size	σ known	σ unknown
Normally distributed	Large ($n \geq 30$)	$z = \dfrac{\bar{X} - \mu_0}{\sigma_{\bar{x}}}$	$t = \dfrac{\bar{X} - \mu_0}{s_{\bar{x}}}$ or $z = \dfrac{\bar{X} - \mu_0}{s_{\bar{x}}}^{**}$
	Small ($n < 30$)	$z = \dfrac{\bar{X} - \mu_0}{\sigma_{\bar{x}}}$	$t = \dfrac{\bar{X} - \mu_0}{s_{\bar{x}}}$
Not normally distributed	Large ($n \geq 30$)	$z = \dfrac{\bar{X} - \mu_0}{\sigma_{\bar{x}}}^{*}$	$t = \dfrac{\bar{X} - \mu_0}{s_{\bar{x}}}^{*}$ or $z = \dfrac{\bar{X} - \mu_0}{s_{\bar{x}}}^{\dagger}$
	Small ($n < 30$)	Nonparametric tests directed toward the median generally would be used. (See Chapter 17).	

* Central limit theorem is invoked.
** z is used as an approximation of t.
† Central limit theorem is invoked and z is used as an approximation of t.

10.11   USING EXCEL AND MINITAB

Computer software for statistical analysis generally includes the capability of testing hypotheses concerning the value of the population mean. Solved Problems 10.25 and 10.26 illustrate the use of Excel and Minitab, respectively, for such a purpose.

Solved Problems

TESTING A HYPOTHESIS CONCERNING THE MEAN BY USE OF THE NORMAL DISTRIBUTION

10.1.   A representative of a community group informs the prospective developer of a shopping center that the average income per household in the area is \$45,000. Suppose that for the type of area involved household income can be assumed to be approximately normally distributed, and that the standard deviation can be accepted as being equal to $\sigma = \$2,000$, based on an earlier study. For a random sample of $n = 15$ households, the mean household income is found to be $\bar{X} = \$44,000$. Test the null hypothesis that $\mu = \$45,000$ by establishing critical limits of the sample mean in terms of dollars, using the 5 percent level of significance.

(*Note:*   The normal probability distribution can be used even though the sample is small, because the population is assumed to be normally distributed *and* σ is known.)

Since H_0: $\mu = \$45,000$ and H_1: $\mu \neq \$45,000$, the critical limits of $\bar{X}(\alpha = 0.05)$ are

$$\bar{X}_{CR} = \mu_0 \pm z\sigma_{\bar{x}} = \mu_0 z\left(\frac{\sigma}{\sqrt{n}}\right) = 45,000 \pm 1.96\left(\frac{2,000}{\sqrt{15}}\right)$$

$$= 45,000 \pm 1.96\left(\frac{2,000}{3.87}\right) = 45,000 \pm 1.96(516.80) = \$43,987 \text{ and } \$46,013$$

Since the sample mean of $\bar{X} = \$44,000$ is between the two critical limits and in the region of acceptance of the null hypothesis, the community representative's claim cannot be rejected at the 5 percent level of significance.

10.2.   Test the hypothesis in Problem 10.1, by using the standard normal variable z as the test statistic.

$$H_0: \mu = \$45,000 \qquad H_1: \mu \neq \$45,000$$
$$\text{Critical } z \ (\alpha = 0.05) = \pm 1.96$$

Thus,

$$\sigma_{\bar{x}} = \frac{\sigma}{\sqrt{n}} = \frac{2,000}{\sqrt{15}} = \frac{2,000}{3.87} = \$516.80$$

$$z = \frac{\bar{x} - \mu_0}{\sigma_{\bar{x}}} = \frac{44,000 - 45,000}{516.80} = \frac{-1,000}{516.80} = -1.93$$

Since the computed z of -1.93 is in the region of acceptance of the null hypothesis, the community representative's claim cannot be rejected at the 5 percent level of significance.

10.3.   With reference to Problems 10.1 and 10.2, the prospective developer is not really concerned about the possibility that the average household income is higher than the claimed \$45,000, but only that it might be lower. Accordingly, reformulate the null and alternate hypotheses and carry out the appropriate statistical test, still giving the benefit of the doubt to the community representative's claim.

$$H_0: \mu = \$45,000 \qquad H_1: \mu < \$45,000$$
$$\text{Critical } z \, (\alpha = 0.05) = -1.645$$
$$z = -1.93 \quad \text{(from Problem 10.2)}$$

The computed z of -1.93 is less than the critical z of -1.645 for this lower-tail test. Therefore, null hypothesis is rejected at the 5 percent level of significance, and the alternative hypothesis, that the mean household income is less than \$45,000, is accepted. The reason for the change in the decision from Problem 10.2 is that the 5 percent region of rejection is located entirely in one tail of the distribution.

10.4. For Problem 10.3, suppose that the population standard deviation is not known, which typically would be the case, and the population of income figures is not assumed to be normally distributed. For a sample of $n = 30$ households, the sample standard deviation is $s = \$2,000$ and the sample mean remains $\bar{X} = \$44,000$. Test the null hypothesis that the mean household income in the population is at least \$45,000, using the 5 percent level of significance.

(*Note*:   The normal probability distribution can be used both because of the central limit theorem and because z can be used as an approximation of t when $n \geq 30$.)

$$H_0: \mu = \$45,000 \qquad H_1: \mu < \$45,000$$
$$\text{Critical } z \, (\alpha = 0.05) = -1.645$$
$$s_{\bar{x}} = \frac{s}{\sqrt{n}} = \frac{2,000}{\sqrt{30}} = \frac{2,000}{5.48} = \$364.96$$
$$z = \frac{\bar{X} - \mu_0}{s_{\bar{x}}} = \frac{44,000 - 45,000}{364.96} = \frac{-1,000}{364.96} = -2.74$$

The computed value of z of -2.74 is less than the critical z of -1.645 for this lower-tail test. Therefore, the null hypothesis is rejected at the 5 percent level of significance. Notice that the computed value of z in this case is arithmetically smaller in value and more clearly in the region of rejection as compared with Problem 10.3. This is due entirely to the increase in sample size from $n = 15$ to $n = 30$, which results in a smaller value for the standard error of the mean.

10.5. A manufacturer contemplating the purchase of new toolmaking equipment has specified that, on average, the equipment should not require more than 10 min of setup time per hour of operation. The purchasing agent visits a company where the equipment being considered is installed; from records there the agent notes that 40 randomly selected hours of operation included a total of 7 hr and 30 min of setup time, and the standard deviation of setup time per hour was 3.0 min. Based on this sample result, can the assumption that the equipment meets setup time specifications be rejected at the 1 percent level of significance?

$$H_0: \mu = 10.0 \text{ min (per hour)} \qquad H_1: \mu > 10.0 \text{ min (per hour)}$$
$$\text{Critical } z \, (\alpha = 0.01) = +2.33$$
$$\bar{X} = \frac{\Sigma X}{n} = \frac{450 \text{ min}}{40} = 11.25 \text{ min}$$
$$s_{\bar{x}} = \frac{s}{\sqrt{n}} = \frac{3.0}{\sqrt{40}} = \frac{3.0}{6.32} = 0.47 \text{ min}$$
$$z = \frac{\bar{X} - \mu_0}{s_{\bar{x}}} = \frac{11.25 - 10.0}{0.47} = \frac{1.25}{0.47} = +2.66$$

The calculated z of $+2.66$ is greater than the critical value of $+2.33$ for this upper-tail test. Therefore, the null hypothesis is rejected at the 1 percent level of significance, and the alternative hypothesis, that the average setup time for this equipment is greater than 10 min per hour of operation, is accepted.

10.6. The standard deviation of the life for a particular brand of ultraviolet tube is known to be $\sigma = 500$ hr, and the operating life of the tubes is normally distributed. The manufacturer claims that average tube life is at least 9,000 hr. Test this claim at the 5 percent level of significance against the alternative hypothesis that the mean life is less than 9,000 hr, and given that for a sample of $n = 15$ tubes the mean operating life was $\bar{X} = 8,800$ hr.

$$H_0: \mu = 9,000 \qquad H_1: \mu < 9,000$$
$$\text{Critical } z \, (\alpha = 0.05) = -1.645$$
$$\sigma_{\bar{x}} = \frac{\sigma}{\sqrt{n}} = \frac{500}{\sqrt{15}} = \frac{500}{3.87} = 129.20$$
$$z = \frac{\bar{X} - \mu_0}{\sigma_{\bar{x}}} = \frac{8,000 - 9,000}{129.20} = \frac{-200}{129.20} = -1.55$$

The calculated z of -1.55 is *not* less than the critical z of -1.645 for this lower-tail test. Therefore, the null hypothesis cannot be rejected at the 5 percent level of significance.

10.7. With respect to Problem 10.6, suppose the sample data were obtained for a sample of $n = 35$ sets. Test the claim at the 5 percent level of significance.

$$H_0: \mu = 9,000 \qquad H_1: \mu < 9,000$$
$$\text{Critical } z \, (\alpha = 0.05) = -1.645$$
$$\sigma_{\bar{x}} = \frac{\sigma}{\sqrt{n}} = \frac{500}{\sqrt{35}} = \frac{500}{5.92} = 84.46$$
$$z = \frac{\bar{X} - \mu_0}{\sigma_{\bar{x}}} = \frac{8,800 - 9,000}{84.46} = \frac{-200}{84.46} = -2.37$$

The calculated z of -2.37 is less than the critical z of -1.645 for this lower-tail test. Therefore, the null hypothesis is rejected at the 5 percent level of significance.

10.8. A marketing research analyst collects data for a random sample of 100 customers out of the 4,000 who purchased a particular "coupon special." The 100 people spent an average of $\bar{X} = \$24.57$ in the store with a standard deviation of $s = \$6.60$. Before seeing these sample results, the marketing manager had claimed that the average purchase by those responding to the coupon offer would be at least \$25.00. Can this claim be rejected, using the 5 percent level of significance?

$$H_0: \mu = \$25.00 \qquad H_1: \mu < \$25.00$$
$$\text{Critical } z \, (\alpha = 0.05) = -1.645$$
$$s_{\bar{x}} = \frac{s}{\sqrt{n}} = \frac{6.60}{\sqrt{100}} = \frac{6.60}{10} = 0.66$$
$$z = \frac{\bar{X} - \mu_0}{s_{\bar{x}}} = \frac{24.57 - 25.00}{0.66} = \frac{-0.43}{0.66} = -0.65$$

The calculated z of -0.65 is *not* less than the critical z of -1.645 for this lower-tail test. Therefore, the claim cannot be rejected at the 5 percent level of significance. Note that z is used as an approximation of t in this solution.

TYPE I AND TYPE II ERRORS IN HYPOTHESIS TESTING

10.9. For Problem 10.3, suppose the prospective developer would consider it an important discrepancy if the average household income were at or below \$43,500, as contrasted to the \$45,000 claimed income level.

Identify (a) the probability of Type I error, (b) the probability of Type II error, (c) the power associated with this lower-tail test.

(a) $P(\text{Type I error}) = 0.05$ (the α-level, or level of significance)

(b) $P(\text{Type II error}) = P(\text{critical limit of } \bar{X} \text{ will be exceeded given } \mu = \$43,500)$

Lower critical limit of $\bar{X} = \mu_0 + z\sigma_{\bar{x}} = 45,000 + (-1.645)(516.80) = \$44,149.86$
where $\mu_0 = \$45,000$
$z = -1.645$

$$\sigma_{\bar{x}} = \frac{\sigma}{\sqrt{n}} = \frac{2,000}{\sqrt{15}} = \frac{2,000}{3.87} = \$516.80$$

$$P(\text{Type II error}) = P(\bar{X} \geq 44,149.86 \mid \mu_1 = 43,500, \sigma_{\bar{x}} = 516.80)$$

$$z_1 = \frac{\bar{X}_{CR} - \mu_1}{\sigma_{\bar{x}}} = \frac{44,149.86 - 43,500}{516.80} = \frac{649.86}{516.80} = 1.26$$

$$P(\text{Type II error}) = P(z_1 \geq +1.26) = 0.5000 - 0.3962 = 0.1038 \cong 0.10$$

(c) $\text{Power} = 1 - P(\text{Type II error}) = 1.00 - 0.10 = 0.90$

10.10. With respect to Problems 10.3 and 10.9, the specific null hypothesized value of the mean is $\mu_0 = \$45,000$ and the specific alternative value is $\mu_1 = \$43,500$. Based on the sample of $n = 15$, $\sigma_{\bar{x}} = 516.80$ and the critical value of the sample mean is $\bar{X}_{CR} = \$44,149.86$. (a) Explain what is meant by calling the last value above a "critical" value. (b) If the true value of the population mean is $\mu = \$43,000$, what is the power of the statistical test?

(a)   The \$44,149.86 value is the "critical" value of the sample mean in that if the sample mean equals or exceeds this value, the null hypothesis (H_0: $\mu = \$45,000$) will be accepted, whereas if the sample mean is less than this value, the null hypothesis will be rejected and the alternative hypothesis (H_1: $\mu < \$45,000$) will be accepted.

(b)   Power $= P(\text{rejecting a false null hypothesis given a specific value of } \mu)$. In this case, Power $= P(\bar{X} < 44,149.86 \mid \mu_1 = 43,000, \sigma_{\bar{x}} = 516.80)$

$$z = \frac{\bar{X}_{CR} - \mu_1}{\sigma_{\bar{x}}} = \frac{44,149.86 - 43,000}{516.80} = \frac{1,149.86}{516.80} = +2.22$$

$$\text{Power} = P(z < +2.22) = 0.5000 + 0.4868 = 0.9868 \cong 0.99$$

In other words, given a population mean of $\mu = \$43,000$, there is about a 99 percent chance that the null hypothesis will be (correctly) rejected, and about a 1 percent chance that it will be (incorrectly) accepted (Type II error).

10.11. Referring to Problem 10.10,

(a)   What is the power of the statistical test if the population mean is $\mu = 44,000$? Compare this answer with the value obtained for $\mu = \$43,000$ in the answer to Problem 10.10(b).

(b)   What is the power of the statistical test if the population mean is $\mu = \$44,500$? Compare this answer with the values obtained for $\mu = \$43,000$ in Problem 10.10(b) and for $\mu = \$44,000$ in (a) above.

(a) $\text{Power} = P(\bar{X} < 44,149.86 \mid \mu = 44,000, \sigma_{\bar{x}} = 516.80) = P(z < 0.29)$
$$= 0.5000 + 0.1141 = 0.6141 \cong 0.61$$

where $$z = \frac{\bar{X}_{CR} - \mu_1}{\sigma_{\bar{x}}} = \frac{44,149.86 - 44,000}{516.80} = \frac{149.86}{516.80} = +0.29$$

The power of the test in this case is substantially lower than the power of 0.99 in Problem 10.10(b). This would be expected, since the present mean of $\mu = \$44,000$ is closer in value to the null-hypothesized $\mu = \$45,000$.

(b) $\text{Power} = P(\bar{X} < 44{,}149.86 \mid \mu = 44{,}500, \sigma_{\bar{x}} = 516.80) = P(z < -0.68)$

$= 0.5000 - 0.2518 = 0.2482 \cong 0.25$

where $z = \dfrac{\bar{X}_{CR} - \mu_1}{\sigma_{\bar{x}}} = \dfrac{44{,}149.86 - 44{,}500}{516.80} = \dfrac{-350.14}{516.80} = -0.68$

The power of the test is substantially lower than the previous values of 0.99 and 0.61.

10.12. In Problems 10.9, 10.10, and 10.11, the power of the one-sided statistical test associated with alternative values of the population mean of \$44,500, \$44,000, \$43,500, and \$43,000 was determined to be 0.25, 0.61, 0.89, and 0.99, respectively. Determine the *OC* values associated with these alternative values of the population mean, and also for the case where $\mu = \$45{,}000$ (with $H_0: \mu = \$45{,}000$).

Since *OC* value $= P$ (accepting the null hypothesis given a specific value of μ), *OC* value $= 1 - $ power (for each specific value of μ), as reported in Table 10.4.

Table 10.4   Power and *OC* Values

Value of μ	Power	*OC* Value
\$45,000	0.05	0.95
44,500	0.25	0.75
44,000	0.61	0.39
43,500	0.90	0.10
43,000	0.99	0.01

In Table 10.4, since \$45,000 is the null-hypothesized value, the power is in fact the probability of incorrect rejection of the null hypothesis and is also therefore equal to the level of significance and the probability of Type I error. When μ is less than \$45,000 in the table, the *OC* value is the probability of incorrectly accepting the null hypothesis and is thus the probability of Type II error.

10.13. For Problems 10.1 and 10.2, suppose that the prospective developer would consider it important if the average household income per year differed from the claimed \$45,000 by \$1,500 or more in *either* direction. Given that the null hypothesis is being tested at the 5 percent level of significance, identify the probability of Type I and Type II error.

(*Note*:   This solution is an extension of the explanation given in Section 10.3 except that a two-tail test rather than a one-tail test is involved.)

$P(\text{Type I error}) = 0.05$ (the α-level, or level of significance)

$P(\text{Type II error}) = P(\text{lower critical limit of } \bar{X} \text{ will be exceeded given } \mu = \$43{,}500)$ or

$= P(\bar{X} \text{ will be below the upper critical limit given } \mu = \$46{,}500)$

(*Note*:   Either calculation will yield the solution for the probability of Type II error. These two values are not accumulated, because the specific alternative value can be at only one point in a given situation. The calculation below is by the first of the two alternative approaches.)

Since, from Problem 10.1, the lower critical limit of $\bar{X} = \$43{,}987$ and $\sigma_{\bar{x}} = \$516.80$,

$P(\text{Type II error}) = P(\bar{X} \geq 43{,}987 \mid \mu_1 = 43{,}500, \sigma_{\bar{x}} = 516.80) = P(z \geq +0.94)$

$= 0.5000 - 0.3264 = 0.1736 \cong 0.17$

where $z_1 = \dfrac{\bar{X}_{CR} - \mu_1}{\sigma_{\bar{x}}} = \dfrac{43{,}987 - 43{,}500}{516.80} = \dfrac{487}{516.80} = +0.94$

DETERMINING THE REQUIRED SAMPLE SIZE FOR TESTING THE MEAN

10.14. Suppose the prospective developer of the shopping center in Problem 10.3 wishes to test the null hypothesis at the 5 percent level of significance and considers it an important difference if the average household income level is at (or below) \$43,500. Because the developer is particularly concerned about the error of developing a shopping center in an area where it cannot be supported, the desired level of Type II error is set at $\beta = 0.01$. If the standard deviation for such income data is assumed to be $\sigma = \$2,000$, determine the size of the sample required to achieve the developer's objectives in regard to Type I and Type II error if no assumption is made about the normality of the population.

$$n = \frac{(z_0 - z_1)^2 \sigma^2}{(\mu_1 - \mu_0)^2} = \frac{[-1.645 - (+2.33)]^2 (2,000)^2}{(43,500 - 45,000)^2} = \frac{(-3.975)^2 (4,000,000)}{(-1,500)^2}$$

$$= \frac{63,202,500}{2,250,000} = 28.09 = 29 \text{ households}$$

However, because the population is not assumed to be normally distributed, the required sample size is increased to $n = 30$, so that the central limit theorem can be invoked as the basis for using the normal probability distribution.

10.15. Refer to Problem 10.5. Suppose the manufacturer would be particularly concerned if the average set-up time per hour were 12.0 min or more. The standard deviation is estimated at about $\sigma = 3.0$ min, and a variable such as setup time is assumed to be normally distributed. Because of the long-run cost implications of this decision, the manufacturer designates that the probability of both Type I error and Type II error should be held to 0.01. How many randomly selected hours of equipment operation should be sampled, as a minimum, to satisfy the testing objectives?

$$n = \frac{(z_0 - z_1)^2 \sigma^2}{(\mu_1 - \mu_0)^2} = \frac{[2.33 - (-2.33)]^2 (3.0)^2}{(12.0 - 10.0)^2}$$

$$= \frac{(4.66)^2 (9)}{(2.0)^2} = \frac{21.7156(9)}{4.0} = \frac{195.4404}{4.0} = 48.86 = 49 \text{ hr}$$

USE OF THE *t* DISTRIBUTION

10.16. As a modification of Problem 10.3, a representative of a community group informs the prospective developer of a shopping center that the average household income in the community is *at least* $\mu = \$45,000$, and this claim is given the benefit of doubt in the hypothesis testing procedure. As before, the population of income figures in the community is assumed to be normally distributed. For a random sample of $n = 15$ households taken in the community, the sample mean is $\bar{X} = \$44,000$ and the sample standard deviation is $s = \$2,000$. Test the null hypothesis at the 5 percent level of significance.

(*Note*: The *t* distribution is appropriate because the sample is small ($n < 30$), σ is not known, and the population is assumed to be normally distributed.)

$$H_0: \mu = \$45,000 \qquad H_1: \mu < \$45,000$$

$$\text{Critical } t \ (df = 14, \ \alpha = 0.05) = -1.761$$

$$s_{\bar{x}} = \frac{s}{\sqrt{n}} = \frac{2,000}{\sqrt{15}} = \frac{2,000}{3.87} = 516.80$$

$$t = \frac{\bar{X} - \mu_0}{s_{\bar{x}}} = \frac{44,000 - 45,000}{516.80} = \frac{-1,000}{516.80} = -1.935$$

The calculated t of -1.935 is less than the critical t of -1.761 for this lower-tail test. Therefore the null hypothesis is rejected at the 5 percent level of significance. The decision is the same as in Problem 10.3 in which σ was known, except that in the former case z was the test statistic, and the critical value was $z = -1.645$.

10.17. For a large group of juniors and seniors majoring in accounting, a random sample of $n = 12$ students has a mean grade-point average of 2.70 (where $A = 4.00$) with a sample standard deviation of $s = 0.40$. Grade-point averages for juniors and seniors are assumed to be normally distributed. Test the hypothesis that the overall grade-point average for all students majoring in accounting is at least 3.00, using the 1 percent level of significance.

$$H_0: \mu = 3.00 \qquad H_1: \mu < 3.00$$
$$\text{Critical } t \ (df = 11, \ \alpha = 0.01) = -2.718$$
$$s_{\bar{x}} = \frac{s}{\sqrt{n}} = \frac{0.40}{\sqrt{12}} = \frac{0.40}{3.46} = 0.116$$
$$t = \frac{\bar{X} - \mu_0}{s_{\bar{x}}} = \frac{2.70 - 3.00}{0.116} = \frac{-0.30}{0.116} = -2.586$$

The calculated t of -2.586 is *not* less than the critical value of -2.718 for this lower-tail test. Therefore, the null hypothesis cannot be rejected and is accepted as being plausible.

10.18. As a commercial buyer for a private supermarket brand, suppose you take a random sample of 12 No. 303 cans of string beans at a canning plant. The average weight of the drained beans in each can is found to be $\bar{X} = 15.97$ oz, with $s = 0.15$. The claimed minimum average net weight of the drained beans per can is 16.0 oz. Can this claim be rejected at the 10 percent level of significance?

$$H_0: \mu = 16.0 \qquad H_1: \mu < 16.0$$
$$\text{Critical } t \ (df = 11, \ \alpha = 0.10) = -1.363$$
$$s_{\bar{x}} = \frac{s}{\sqrt{n}} = \frac{0.15}{\sqrt{12}} = \frac{0.15}{3.46} = 0.043 \text{ oz}$$
$$t = \frac{\bar{X} - \mu_0}{s_{\bar{x}}} = \frac{15.97 - 16.00}{0.043} = \frac{-0.03}{0.043} = -0.698$$

The calculated t of -0.698 is *not* less than the critical value of -1.363 for this lower-tail test. Therefore the claim cannot be rejected at the 10 percent level of significance.

THE *P*-VALUE APPROACH TO TESTING HYPOTHESES CONCERNING THE POPULATION MEAN

10.19. Using the *P*-value approach, test the null hypothesis in Problem 10.2 at the 5 percent level of significance.

$$H_0: \mu = \$45,000 \qquad H_1: \mu \neq \$45,000$$
$$z = -1.93 \qquad \text{(from Problem 10.2)}$$
$$P(z \leq -1.93) = 0.5000 - 0.4732 = 0.0268$$

Finally, because this is a two-tail test:

$$P = 2(0.0268) = 0.0536$$

Because the P value of 0.0536 is larger than the level of significance of 0.05, the null hypothesis *cannot* be rejected at this level. Therefore, we cannot reject the claim that the mean household income in the population is $45,000 and we accept this value as being plausible.

10.20. Using the *P*-value approach, test the null hypothesis in Problem 10.3 at the 5 percent level of significance.

$$H_0: \mu = \$45,000 \qquad H_1: \mu < \$45,000$$
$$z = -1.93 \qquad \text{(from Problem 10.3)}$$

(Note that the *z* statistic is in the direction of the region of rejection for this left-tail test.)

$$P(z \leq -1.93) = 0.5000 - 0.4732 = 0.0268$$

Because the *P* value of 0.0268 is smaller than the level of significance of 0.05, we reject the null hypothesis. Therefore the alternative hypothesis, that the mean household income in the population is less than \$45,000, is accepted.

10.21. Using the *P*-value approach, test the null hypothesis in Problem 10.16 at the 5 percent level of significance.

$$H_0: \mu = \$45,000 \qquad H_1: \mu < \$45,000$$
$$t = -19.3 \qquad \text{(from Problem 10.16)}$$

For this left-tail test, and with $df = 14$:

$$P(t \leq -1.93) = (0.025 < P < 0.05)$$

The probability of the *t* statistic of -1.93 occurring by chance when the null hypothesis is true is somewhere between 0.025 and 0.05, because a *t* value of -2.145 is required for a left-tail probability of 0.025 while a *t* value of -1.761 is required for a left-tail probability of 0.05. Therefore, the null hypothesis is rejected at the 5 percent level of significance, and we conclude that the mean household income in the population is less than \$45,000. With the use of computer software an exact probability could be determined (see Problems 10.25 and 10.26).

THE CONFIDENCE INTERVAL APPROACH TO TESTING HYPOTHESES CONCERNING THE MEAN

10.22. Apply the confidence interval approach to testing the null hypothesis in Problem 10.2, using the 5 percent level of significance.

$$H_0: \mu = \$45,000 \qquad H_1: \mu \neq \$45,000$$
$$\bar{X} = \$44,000$$
$$\sigma_{\bar{x}} = \$516.80 \qquad \text{(from Problem 10.2)}$$
$$95\% \text{ Conf. Int.} = \bar{X} \pm z\sigma_{\bar{x}} = 44,000 \pm 1.96(516.80)$$
$$= 44,000 \pm 1,012.93 = \$42,987.07 \text{ to } \$45,012.93$$

Because the 95 percent confidence interval includes the hypothesized value of \$45,000, the null hypothesis cannot be rejected at the 5 percent level of significance.

10.23. Apply the confidence interval approach to test the null hypothesis in Problem 10.3, by defining a one-sided confidence interval and using the 5 percent level of significance.

$$H_0: \mu = 45,000 \qquad H_1: \mu < \$45,000$$
$$\bar{X} = \$44,000$$
$$\sigma_{\bar{x}} = \$516.80 \qquad \text{(from Problem 10.3)}$$
$$\text{Upper Conf. Limit} = \bar{X} + z\sigma_{\bar{x}} = 44,000 + 1.645(516.80)$$
$$= 44,000 + 850.14 = \$44,850.14$$

With 95 percent confidence, we conclude that the population mean can be as large as $44,850.14. Because this one-sided confidence interval does not include the hypothesized value of $45,000, the null hypothesis is rejected at the 5 percent level of significance.

10.24. Determine the solution for Problem 10.23, above, by defining the two-sided confidence interval that can be used with respect to this one-sided test.

We define the 90 percent confidence interval, and then for this one-sided test, we consider only the *largest* plausible value of the population mean. That is, we focus only on the upper limit of the interval:

$$90\% \text{ confidence interval} = \bar{X} \pm z\sigma_{\bar{x}} = 44,000 + 1.645(516.80)$$
$$= 44,000 \pm 850.14 = \$43,149.86 \text{ to } \$44,850.14$$

The upper limit of $44,850.14 corresponds exactly to the limit for the one-sided interval in Problem 10.23. Again, the null hypothesis that the mean household income is (at least) $45,000 is rejected as being plausible.

COMPUTER OUTPUT: HYPOTHESIS TESTING FOR THE MEAN

10.25. Table 10.5 presents the dollar amounts of automobile damage claims filed by a random sample of 10 insured drivers involved in minor automobile collisions in a particular geographic area. Use Excel to test the null hypothesis that the mean amount of the claims in the sampled population is $1,000 against the alternative that it is different from this amount.

Table 10.5   Automobile Damage Claims

$1,033	$1,069
1,274	1,121
1,114	1,269
924	1,150
1,421	921

The standard Excel output does not provide *P*-values with respect to one-sample statistical tests. From Fig. 10-7, we utilize the margin of error reported in the last line of the output to test the null hypothesis at the 5 percent level by use of the confidence interval approach. The 95 percent confidence interval is

$$\bar{X} \pm 113.04 = 1129.60 \pm 113.04 = \$1,016.56 \text{ to } \$1,242.64$$

Because the 95 percent confidence interval above does *not* include the hypothesized value of $1,000, the null hypothesis is rejected at the associated 5 percent level of significance. We conclude that the mean claim amount in the sampled population is not equal to $1,000, but rather, it is different.

$$H_0: \mu = \$1,000 \qquad H_1: \mu \neq \$1,000 \qquad \alpha = 0.05$$

The Excel output given in Fig. 10-7 was obtained as follows:

(1) Open Excel. In cell A1 enter the column label: Claims. Enter the 10 claim amounts in column A beginning at cell A2.
(2) Click **Tools → Data Analysis → Descriptive Statistics**. Click **OK**.
(3) Designate **Input Range** as: $A$1:$A$11.
(4) Select **Labels in First Row**.
(5) Select **Confidence Level for Mean**: 95%
(6) Click **OK**.

Claims	
Mean	1129.6
Standard Error	49.96892
Median	1117.5
Mode	#N/A
Standard Deviation	158.0156
Sample Variance	24968.93
Kurtosis	-0.20702
Skewness	0.407492
Range	500
Minimum	921
Maximum	1421
Sum	11296
Count	10
Confidence Level(95.0%)	113.0376

Fig. 10-7   Excel output.

10.26. Table 10.5 presents the dollar amounts of automobile damage claims filed by a random sample of 10 insured drivers involved in minor automobile collisions in a particular geographic area. Use Minitab to test the null hypothesis that the mean amount of the claims in the sampled population is $1,000 against the alternative that it is different from this amount.

Refer to Fig. 10-8. Note that in the first line of output the test is correctly identified as being a two-tail test ("... vs mu not = 1000"). In the last line of output the P value is reported as being 0.029. Because this probability is less than the designated level of significance of 0.05, the null hypothesis is rejected. We conclude that the mean claim amount in the population is not equal to $1,000, but is different.

$$H_0: \mu = \$1,000 \qquad H_1: \mu \neq \$1,000 \qquad \alpha = 0.05$$

The Minitab output given in Fig. 10-8 was obtained as follows:

(1)   Open Minitab. In the column-name cell for column C1 enter: Claims. Enter the 10 claim amounts in C1.
(2)   Click **Stat** → **Basic Statistics** → **1-Sample t**.
(3)   In the **Variable** box enter: Claims.
(4)   For **Test mean** enter: 1000.
(5)   Click **Options** and designate **Confidence level** as: 95.0 (because this is the confidence level that is equivalent to a test at the 5 percent level). Designate **Alternative** as: not equal (because a *two-sided* test is required—a test for a difference in *either* direction from the null-hypothesized value).
(6)   Click **OK**.
(7)   Back in the original dialog box, click **OK**.

One-Sample T: Claims

Test of mu = 1000 vs mu not = 1000

Variable	N	Mean	StDev	SE Mean
Claims	10	1129.6	158.0	50.0

Variable	95.0% CI		T	P
Claims	(1016.6,	1242.6)	2.59	0.029

Fig. 10-8   Minitab output.

Supplementary Problems

TESTING A HYPOTHESIZED VALUE OF THE MEAN

10.27. A fast-food chain will build a new outlet in a proposed location only if more than 200 cars per hour pass the location during certain hours. For 20 randomly sampled hours during the designated hours, the average number of cars passing the location is $\bar{X} = 208.5$ with $s = 30.0$. The statistical population is assumed to be approximately normal. The management of the chain conservatively adopted the alternative hypothesis $H_1: \mu > 200.0$. Can the null hypothesis be rejected at the 5 percent level of significance?
Ans. No.

10.28. Suppose the sample results in Problem 10.27 are based on a sample of $n = 50$ hr. Can the null hypothesis be rejected at the 5 percent level of significance?
Ans. Yes.

10.29. The mean sales amount per retail outlet for a particular consumer product during the past year is found to be $\bar{X} = \$3,425$ in a sample of $n = 25$ outlets. Based on sales data for other similar products, the distribution of sales is assumed to be normal and the standard deviation of the population is assumed to be $\sigma = \$200$. Suppose it was claimed that the true sales amount per outlet is at least $3,500. Test this claim at the (*a*) 5 percent and (*b*) 1 percent level of significance.
Ans. (*a*) Reject H_0, (*b*) accept H_0.

10.30. In Problem 10.29, suppose that no assumption was made about the population standard deviation, but that $s = \$200$. Test the claim at the (*a*) 5 percent and (*b*) 1 percent level of significance.
Ans. (*a*) Reject H_0, (*b*) accept H_0.

10.31. The manufacturer of a new compact car claims that the car will average at least 35 miles per gallon in general highway driving. For 40 test runs, the car averaged 34.5 miles per gallon, with a standard deviation of 2.3 miles per gallon. Can the manufacturer's claim be rejected at the 5 percent level of significance?
Ans. No.

10.32. Referring to Problem 10.31, before the highway tests were carried out, a consumer advocate claimed that the compact car would *not* exceed 35 miles per gallon in general highway driving. Can this claim be rejected at the 5 percent level of significance? Consider the implications of your answer to this question and in Problem 10.31 regarding the importance of which hypothesis is designated as the alternative hypothesis.
Ans. No.

10.33. An analyst in a personnel department randomly selects the records of 16 hourly employees and finds that the mean wage rate is $\bar{X} = \$9.50$ with a standard deviation of $s = \$1.00$. The wage rates in the firm are assumed to be normally distributed. Test the null hypothesis $H_0: \mu = \$10.00$, using the 10 percent level of significance.
Ans. Reject H_0.

10.34. A random sample of 30 employees at the Secretary II level in a large organization take a standardized word processing test. The sample results are $\bar{X} = 63.0$ wpm (words per minute) with $s = 5.0$ wpm. Test the null hypothesis that the word-processing operators in general do *not* exceed a keyboarding speed of 60 wpm, using the 1 percent level of significance.
Ans. Reject H_0.

10.35. An automatic soft ice cream dispenser has been set to dispense 4.00 oz per serving. For a sample of $n = 10$ servings, the average amount of ice cream is $\bar{X} = 4.05$ oz with $s = 0.10$ oz. The amounts being dispensed are assumed to be normally distributed. Basing the null hypothesis on the assumption that the process is "in control," should the dispenser be reset as a result of applying a test at the 5 percent level of significance?
Ans. No.

TYPE I AND TYPE II ERRORS IN HYPOTHESIS TESTING

10.36. With reference to Problem 10.34, suppose it is considered an important difference from the hypothesized value of the mean if the average typing speed is at least 64.0 wpm. Determine the probability of (*a*) Type I error and (*b*) Type II error.
Ans. (*a*) $\alpha = 0.01$, (*b*) $\beta = 0.0192 \cong 0.02$.

10.37. For Problem 10.36, determine the probability of Type II error (*a*) if the level of significance is changed to the 5 percent level and (*b*) if the level of significance is kept at the 1 percent level, but the sample size is $n = 60$ instead of $n = 30$.
   Ans.   (*a*) $\beta = 0.003$, (*b*) $\beta < 0.001$.

10.38. For the testing procedure described in Problem 10.31, suppose it is considered an important discrepancy from the claim if the average mileage is 34.0 miles per gallon or less. Given this additional information, determine (*a*) the minimum *OC* value if the null hypothesis is true, and (*b*) the minimum power associated with the, statistical test if the discrepancy from the claim is an important one.
   Ans.   (*a*) $OC = 0.95$, (*b*) power $= 0.8729 \cong 0.87$.

10.39. Determine the minimum power of the test in Problem 10.38, given that it is considered an important discrepancy if the true mileage is (*a*) 0.5 mile per gallon and (*b*) 0.1 mile per gallon less than the claim. Comparing the several power values, consider the implication of the standard used to define an "important discrepancy."
   Ans.   (*a*) Power $= 0.4013 \cong 0.40$, (*b*) power $= 0.0869 \cong 0.09$.

DETERMINING THE REQUIRED SAMPLE SIZE FOR TESTING THE MEAN

10.40. Before collecting any sample data, the fast-food chain in Problem 10.27 stipulates that the level of Type I error should be no larger than $\alpha = 0.01$, and that if the number of cars passing the site is at or above $\mu = 210$ per hour, then the level of Type II error also should not exceed $\beta = 0.01$. The population standard deviation is estimated as being no larger than $\sigma = 40$. What sample size is required to achieve these objectives?
   Ans. $n = 347.45 = 348$.

10.41. For the testing situation described in Problem 10.29, it is considered an important discrepancy if the mean sales amount per outlet is $100 less than the claimed amount. What sample size is required if the test is to be carried out at the 1 percent level of significance, allowing a maximum probability of Type II error of $\beta = 0.05$?
   Ans. $n = 63.20 = 64$.

THE *P*-VALUE APPROACH TO TESTING HYPOTHESES CONCERNING THE POPULATION MEAN

10.42. Using the *P*-value approach, test the null hypothesis in Problem 10.28 at the 5 percent level of significance.
   Ans.   Reject H_0 ($P = 0.0228$).

10.43. Using the *P*-value approach, test the null hypothesis in Problem 10.29 at the 5 percent level of significance.
   Ans.   Reject H_0 ($P = 0.0307$).

THE CONFIDENCE INTERVAL APPROACH TO TESTING HYPOTHESES CONCERNING THE MEAN

10.44. Apply the confidence interval approach to testing the null hypothesis in Problem 10.28 using the 5 percent level of significance.
   Ans.   Reject H_0.

10.45. Apply the confidence interval approach to testing the null hypothesis in Problem 10.33, using the 10 percent level of significance.
   Ans.   Reject H_0.

COMPUTER OUTPUT

10.46. Refer to Table 2.19 (page 41) for the amounts of 40 personal loans. Assuming that these are random sample data, use available computer software to test the null hypothesis that the mean loan amount in the population is $1,000.00 against the alternative that it is different, using the 1 percent level of significance.
   Ans.   Accept H_0 ($P = 0.34$).

CHAPTER 11

Testing Other Hypotheses

11.1 TESTING THE DIFFERENCE BETWEEN TWO MEANS USING THE NORMAL DISTRIBUTION

The procedure associated with testing a hypothesis concerning the difference between two population means is similar to that for testing a hypothesis concerning the value of one population mean (see Sections 10.2 and 10.3). The procedure differs only in that the standard error of the *difference* between the means is used to determine the z (or t) value associated with the sample result. Use of the normal distribution is based on the same conditions as in the one-sample case, except that *two* independent random samples are involved. The general formula for determining the z value for testing a hypothesis concerning the difference between two means, according to whether the σ values for the two populations are known, is

$$z = \frac{(\bar{X}_1 - \bar{X}_2) - (\mu_1 - \mu_2)_0}{\sigma_{\bar{x}_1 - \bar{x}_2}} \qquad (11.1)$$

or
$$z = \frac{(\bar{X}_1 - \bar{X}_2) - (\mu_1 - \mu_2)_0}{s_{\bar{x}_1 - \bar{x}_2}} \qquad (11.2)$$

As implied by (11.1) and (11.2), we may begin with any particular hypothesized difference, $(\mu_1 - \mu_2)_0$, that is to be tested. However, the usual null hypothesis is that the two samples have been obtained from populations with means that are equal. In this case $(\mu_1 - \mu_2)_0 = 0$, and the above formulas are simplified as follows:

$$z = \frac{\bar{X}_1 - \bar{X}_2}{\sigma_{\bar{x}_1 - \bar{x}_2}} \qquad (11.3)$$

or
$$z = \frac{\bar{X}_1 - \bar{X}_2}{s_{\bar{x}_1 - \bar{x}_2}} \qquad (11.4)$$

In general, the standard error of the difference between means is computed as described in Section 9.1 [see Formulas (9.3) and (9.4)]. However, in testing the difference between two means, the null hypothesis of interest is generally not only that the sample means were obtained from populations with equal means, but that the two samples were in fact obtained from the *same* population of values. This means that $\sigma_1 = \sigma_2$, which we can

197

simply designate σ. The assumed common variance is often estimated by pooling the two sample variances, and the estimated value of σ^2 is then used as the basis for the standard error of the difference. The pooled estimate of the population variance is

$$\hat{\sigma}^2 = \frac{(n_1 - 1)s_1^2 + (n_2 - 1)s_2^2}{n_1 + n_2 - 2} \qquad (11.5)$$

The estimated standard error of the difference based on the assumption that the population standard deviations (and variances) are equal is

$$\hat{\sigma}_{\bar{x}_1 - \bar{x}_2} = \sqrt{\frac{\hat{\sigma}^2}{n_1} + \frac{\hat{\sigma}^2}{n_2}} \qquad (11.6)$$

The assumption that the two sample variances were obtained from populations with equal variances can itself be tested as the null hypothesis (see Section 11.10).

Tests concerned with the difference between means can be either two-sided or one-sided, as illustrated in the following examples.

EXAMPLE 1.   The mean weekly wage for a sample of $n_1 = 30$ employees in a large manufacturing firm is $\bar{X}_1 = \$280.00$ with a sample standard deviation of $s_1 = \$14.00$. In another large firm a random sample of $n_2 = 40$ employees has a mean wage of $\bar{X}_2 = \$270.00$ with a standard deviation of $s_2 = \$10.00$. The standard deviations of the two populations of wage amounts are not assumed to be equal. We test the hypothesis that there is no difference between the mean weekly wage amounts in the two firms, using the 5 percent level of significance, as follows:

$H_0: (\mu_1 - \mu_2) = 0$ or, equivalently, $\mu_1 = \mu_2$ $\bar{X}_1 = \$280.00$ $\bar{X}_2 = \$270.00$

$H_1: (\mu_1 - \mu_2) \neq 0$ or, equivalently, $\mu_1 \neq \mu_2$ $s_1 = \$14.00$ $s_2 = \$10.00$

$\qquad\qquad\qquad\qquad\qquad\qquad\qquad\qquad\qquad\qquad\qquad n_1 = 30 \qquad\qquad n_2 = 40$

Critical $z\,(\alpha = 0.05) = \pm 1.96$

$$z = \frac{\bar{X}_1 - \bar{X}_1}{s_{\bar{x}_1 - \bar{x}_2}}$$

$$= \frac{280 - 270}{3.01} = \frac{10.0}{3.01} = +3.32$$

where

$$s_{\bar{x}_1} = \frac{s_1}{\sqrt{n_1}} = \frac{14.00}{\sqrt{30}} = \frac{14.00}{5.477} = 2.56$$

$$s_{\bar{x}_2} = \frac{s_2}{\sqrt{n_2}} = \frac{10.00}{\sqrt{40}} = \frac{10.00}{6.325} = 1.58$$

$$s_{\bar{x}_1 - \bar{x}_2} = \sqrt{s_{\bar{x}_1}^2 + s_{\bar{x}_2}^2} = \sqrt{(2.56)^2 + (1.58)^2} = \sqrt{6.5536 + 2.4964} = 3.01$$

The computed z of $+3.32$ is in the region of rejection of the hypothesis testing model portrayed in Fig. 11-1. Therefore, the null hypothesis is rejected, and the alternative hypothesis, that the average weekly wage in the two firms is different, is accepted.

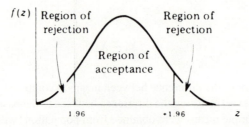

Fig. 11-1

EXAMPLE 2. Before seeing the sample results in Example 1, a wage analyst believed that the average wage in the first firm was greater than the wage in the second firm. In order to subject this belief to a critical test, the analyst gives the benefit of the doubt to the opposite possibility, and formulates the null hypothesis that the average wage in the first firm is equal to or less than the average in the second firm. We test this hypothesis at the 1 percent level of significance, again without assuming that the standard deviations of the two populations are equal, as follows:

$$H_0: (\mu_1 - \mu_2) \leq 0 \qquad \text{or, equivalently,} \qquad \mu_1 \leq \mu_2$$
$$H_1: (\mu_1 - \mu_2) > 0 \qquad \text{or, equivalently,} \qquad \mu_1 > \mu_2$$
$$\text{Critical } z \,(\alpha = 0.01) = +2.33$$
$$\text{Computed } z = +3.32 \quad \text{(from Example 1)}$$

The computed z of $+3.32$ is greater than the critical value of $+2.33$ for this upper-tail test, as portrayed in Fig. 11-2. Therefore, the null hypothesis is rejected and the alternative hypothesis, that the average wage in the first firm is *greater than* the average wage in the second firm, is accepted.

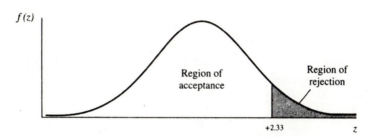

Fig. 11-2

11.2 TESTING THE DIFFERENCE BETWEEN MEANS USING THE t DISTRIBUTION

When the difference between two means is tested by the use of the t distribution, a necessary assumption in the standard procedure used in most texts is that the variances of the two populations are equal. Therefore, in such a test the estimated standard error of the mean is calculated from (11.5) and (11.6). The several requirements associated with the appropriate use of the t distribution are described in Sections 8.8 and 10.6.

EXAMPLE 3. For a random sample of $n_1 = 10$ light bulbs, the mean bulb life is $\bar{X}_1 = 4{,}000$ hr with $s_1 = 200$. For another brand of bulbs whose useful life is also assumed to be normally distributed, a random sample of $n_2 = 8$ has a sample mean of $\bar{X}_2 = 4{,}300$ hr and a sample standard deviation of $s = 250$. We test the hypothesis that there is no difference between the mean operating life of the two brands of bulbs, using the 1 percent level of significance, as follows:

$$H_0: (\mu_1 - \mu_2) = 0 \qquad \bar{X}_1 = 4{,}000 \,\text{hr} \qquad \bar{X}_2 = 4{,}300 \,\text{hr}$$
$$H_1: (\mu_1 - \mu_2) \neq 0 \qquad s_1 = 200 \,\text{hr} \qquad s_2 = 250 \,\text{hr}$$
$$n_1 = 10 \qquad n_2 = 8$$
$$df = n_1 + n_2 - 2 = 10 + 8 - 2 = 16$$
$$\text{Critical } t \,(df = 16, \, \alpha = 0.01) = \pm 2.921$$

$$\hat{\sigma}^2 = \frac{(n_1 - 1)s_1^2 + (n_2 - 1)s_2^2}{n_1 + n_2 - 2} = \frac{(9)(200)^2 + (7)(250)^2}{10 + 8 - 2} = \frac{360{,}000 + 437{,}500}{16} = 49{,}843.75$$

$$\hat{\sigma}_{\bar{x}_1 - \bar{x}_2} = \sqrt{\frac{\hat{\sigma}^2}{n_1} + \frac{\hat{\sigma}^2}{n_2}} = \sqrt{\frac{49{,}843.75}{10} + \frac{49{,}843.75}{8}} = \sqrt{11{,}214.843} = 105.9$$

$$t = \frac{\bar{X}_1 - \bar{X}_2}{\hat{\sigma}_{\bar{x}_1 - \bar{x}_2}} = \frac{4{,}000 - 4{,}300}{105.9} = \frac{-300}{105.9} = -2.833$$

The computed t of -2.833 is in the region of acceptance of the null hypothesis. Therefore, the null hypothesis cannot be rejected at the 1 percent level of significance.

11.3 TESTING THE DIFFERENCE BETWEEN MEANS BASED ON PAIRED OBSERVATIONS

The procedures in Sections 11.1 and 11.2 are based on the assumption that the two samples were collected as two independent random samples. However, in many situations the samples are collected as pairs of values, such as when determining the productivity level of each worker before and after a training program. These are referred to as *paired observations*, or *matched pairs*. Also, as contrasted to independent samples, two samples that contain paired observations often are called *dependent samples*.

For paired observations the appropriate approach for testing the difference between the means of the two samples is to first determine the difference d between each pair of values, and then test the null hypothesis that the mean population *difference* is zero. Thus, from the computational standpoint the test is applied to the *one* sample of d values, with H_0: $\mu_d = 0$.

The mean and standard deviation of the sample d values are obtained by use of the basic formulas in Chapters 3 and 4, except that d is substituted for X. The mean difference for a set of differences between paired observations is

$$\bar{d} = \frac{\Sigma d}{n} \qquad (11.7)$$

The deviations formula and the computational formula for the standard deviation of the differences between paired observations are, respectively,

$$s_d = \sqrt{\frac{\Sigma(d - \bar{d})^2}{n - 1}} \qquad (11.8)$$

$$s_d = \sqrt{\frac{\Sigma d^2 - n\bar{d}^2}{n - 1}} \qquad (11.9)$$

The standard error of the mean difference between paired observations is obtained by Formula (8.4) for the standard error of the mean, except that d is again substituted for X:

$$s_{\bar{d}} = \frac{s_d}{\sqrt{n}} \qquad (11.0)$$

Because the standard error of the mean difference is computed on the basis of the standard deviation of the sample of differences (that is, the population value σ_d is unknown) and because values of d generally can be assumed to be normally distributed, the t distribution is appropriate for testing the null hypothesis that $\mu_d = 0$.

The degrees of freedom is the number of differences minus one, or $n - 1$. As discussed in Section 8.8, the standard normal z distribution can be used as an approximation of the t distributions when $n \geq 30$. Example 4 illustrates a two-sided test, whereas Problem 11.5 illustrates a one-sided test. The test statistic used to test the hypothesis that there is no difference between the means of a set of paired observations is

$$t = \frac{\bar{d}}{s_{\bar{d}}} \qquad (11.11)$$

EXAMPLE 4. An automobile manufacturer collects mileage data for a sample of $n = 10$ cars in various weight categories using a standard grade of gasoline with and without a particular additive. Of course, the engines were tuned to the same specifications before each run, and the same drivers were used for the two gasoline conditions (with the driver in fact being unaware of which gasoline was being used on a particular run). Given the mileage data in Table 11.1, we test the hypothesis that there is no difference between the mean mileage obtained with and without the additive, using the 5 percent level of significance, as follows:

$$\text{Average with additive} = \frac{276.8}{10} = 27.68 \text{ mpg}$$

$$\text{Average without additive} = \frac{275.1}{10} = 27.51 \text{ mpg}$$

$$H_0: \mu_d = 0$$

$$H_1: \mu_d \neq 0$$

Critical $t \, (df = 9, \, \alpha = 0.05) = \pm 2.262$

$$\bar{d} = \frac{\Sigma d}{n} = \frac{1.7}{10} = 0.17$$

$$s_d = \sqrt{\frac{\Sigma d^2 - n\bar{d}^2}{n-1}} = \sqrt{\frac{1.31 - 10(0.17)^2}{10-1}} = \sqrt{\frac{1.31 - 10(0.0289)}{9}} = \sqrt{0.1134} = 0.337$$

$$s_{\bar{d}} = \frac{s_d}{\sqrt{n}} = \frac{0.337}{\sqrt{10}} = \frac{0.337}{3.16} = 0.107$$

$$t = \frac{\bar{d}}{s_{\bar{d}}} = \frac{0.17}{0.107} = +1.59$$

Table 11.1 Automobile Mileage Data and Worksheet for Computing the Mean Difference and the Standard Deviation of the Difference

Automobile	Mileage with additive	Mileage without additive	d	d^2
1	36.7	36.2	0.5	0.25
2	35.8	35.7	0.1	0.01
3	31.9	32.3	-0.4	0.16
4	29.3	29.6	-0.3	0.09
5	28.4	28.1	0.3	0.09
6	25.7	25.8	-0.1	0.01
7	24.2	23.9	0.3	0.09
8	22.6	22.0	0.6	0.36
9	21.9	21.5	0.4	0.16
10	20.3	20.0	0.3	0.09
Total	276.8	275.1	$+1.7$	1.31

The computed t of $+1.59$ is not in the region of rejection of the null hypothesis. Therefore, the null hypothesis that there is no difference in the miles per gallon obtained with as compared to without the additive is accepted as being plausible.

11.4 TESTING A HYPOTHESIS CONCERNING THE VALUE OF THE POPULATION PROPORTION

As explained in Section 7.4, the normal distribution can be used as an approximation of a binomial distribution when $n \geq 30$ and both $np \geq 5$ and $n(q) \geq 5$, where $q = 1 - p$. This is the basis upon which confidence intervals for the proportion are determined in Section 9.3, where the standard error of the proportion is also discussed. However, in the case of confidence intervals, a sample size of at least $n = 100$ is generally required, as explained in Section 9.3.

In determining confidence intervals in Section 9.3 the sample proportion $\hat{p}$ serves as the basis for the standard error. In hypothesis testing, the value of the standard error of the proportion generally is based on using the hypothesized value π_0:

$$\sigma_{\hat{p}} = \sqrt{\frac{\pi_0(1 - \pi_0)}{n}} \qquad (11.12)$$

The procedure associated with testing a hypothesized value of the population proportion is identical to that described in Section 10.3, except that the null hypothesis is concerned with a value of the population proportion rather than the population mean. Thus, the formula for the z statistic for testing a hypothesis concerning the value of the population proportion is

$$z = \frac{\hat{p} - \pi_0}{\sigma_{\hat{p}}} \qquad (11.13)$$

EXAMPLE 5.   The director of a university placement office claimed that at least 50 percent of the graduating seniors had finalized job arrangements by March 1. Suppose a random sample of $n = 30$ seniors was polled, and only 10 of the students indicated that they had concluded their job arrangements by March 1. Can the placement director's claim be rejected at the 5 percent level of significance? We utilize z as the test statistic, as follows:

$$H_0: \pi = 0.50 \qquad H_1: \pi < 0.50$$

$$\text{Critical } z \ (\alpha = 0.05) = -1.645$$

[Use of the normal distribution is warranted because $n \geq 30$, $n\pi_0 \geq 5$, and $n(1 - \pi_0) \geq 5$.]

$$\sigma_{\hat{p}} = \sqrt{\frac{\pi_0(1 - \pi_0)}{n}} = \sqrt{\frac{(0.50)(0.50)}{30}} = \sqrt{\frac{0.25}{30}} = \sqrt{0.0083} = 0.09$$

$$z = \frac{\hat{p} - \pi_0}{\sigma_{\hat{p}}} = \frac{0.33 - 0.50}{0.09} = \frac{-0.17}{0.09} = -1.88$$

The computed z of -1.88 is less than the critical value of -1.645 for this lower-tail test. Therefore, the director's claim is rejected at the 5 percent level of significance.

11.5   DETERMINING REQUIRED SAMPLE SIZE FOR TESTING THE PROPORTION

Before a sample is actually collected, the required sample size for testing a hypothesis concerning the population proportion can be determined by specifying (1) the hypothesized value of the proportion, (2) a specific alternative value of the proportion such that the difference from the null-hypothesized value is considered important, (3) the level of significance to be used in the test, and (4) the probability of Type II error that is to be permitted. The formula for determining the minimum sample size required for testing a hypothesized value of the proportion is

$$n = \left[\frac{z_0\sqrt{\pi_0(1 - \pi_0)} - z_1\sqrt{\pi_1(1 - \pi_1)}}{\pi_1 - \pi_0} \right]^2 \qquad (11.14)$$

In (11.14), z_0 is the critical value of z used in conjunction with the specified level of significance (α level), while z_1 is the value of z with respect to the designated probability of Type II error (β level). As was true in Section 10.5 on determining sample size for testing the mean, z_0 and z_1 always have opposite algebraic signs. The result is that the two products in the numerator will always be accumulated. Also, Formula (11.14) can be used in conjunction with either one-tail or two-tail tests and any fractional sample size is rounded up. Finally, the sample size should be large enough to warrant use of the normal ability probability distribution in conjunction with π_0 and π_1, as reviewed in Section 11.4.

EXAMPLE 6.   A member of Congress wishes to test the hypothesis that at least 60 percent of constituents are in favor of labor legislation being introduced in Congress, using the 5 percent level of significance. The discrepancy from this hypothesis is considered to be important if only 50 percent (or fewer) favor the legislation, and the risk of a Type II error of $\beta = 0.05$ is acceptable. The sample size which should be collected, as a minimum, to satisfy these decision-making specifications is

$$n = \left[\frac{z_0\sqrt{\pi_0(1 - \pi_0)} - z_1\sqrt{\pi_1(1 - \pi_1)}}{\pi_1 - \pi_0} \right]^2 = \left[\frac{-1.645\sqrt{(0.60)(0.40)} - (+1.645)\sqrt{(0.50)(0.50)}}{0.50 - 0.60} \right]^2$$

$$= \left[\frac{-1.645(0.49) - 1.645(0.50)}{-0.10} \right]^2 = \left(\frac{-0.806 - 0.822}{-0.10} \right)^2 = (16.28)^2 = 265.04 = 266$$

11.6   TESTING WITH RESPECT TO THE PROCESS PROPORTION IN STATISTICAL PROCESS CONTROL

As described in Section 10.9, the use and interpretation of control charts in statistical process control is a direct application of the methods and concepts of hypothesis testing. Just as is true for the process mean in Section 10.9, the control limits for a process proportion are defined at ± 3 standard error units for the hypothesized (acceptable) value. The methodology for preparing and interpreting control charts is described in Chapter 19, Statistical Process Control. Section 19.9 is concerned particularly with the process proportion.

EXAMPLE 7.   When a coupon redemption process is in control, a maximum of 3 percent of the rebates are done incorrectly, for a maximum acceptable proportion of errors of 0.03. For 20 sequential samples of 100 coupon redemptions each, an audit reveals that the number of errors found in the rational subgroup samples is: 2, 2, 3, 6, 1, 3, 6, 4, 7, 2, 5, 0, 3, 2, 4, 5, 3, 8, 1, and 4. The run chart for the sequence of the sample proportions of error for the 20 samples is portrayed in Fig. 2-31 (page 35). An overview of this figure might lead one to question whether the standard of allowing a maximum proportion of errors of 0.03 in the process is being maintained, particularly at samples #9 and #18. In Problems 19.22 through 19.25 we shall observe that these two sample proportions are *not* beyond the upper control limits, and thus could have occurred simply because of common-cause variation. Therefore, we will not reject the null hypothesis that the process proportion of defectives is being maintained at 0.03.and that the process is stable.

11.7   TESTING THE DIFFERENCE BETWEEN TWO POPULATION PROPORTIONS

When we wish to test the hypothesis that the proportions in two populations are not different, the two sample proportions are pooled as a basis for determining the standard error of the difference between proportions. Note that this differs from the procedure used in Section 9.5 on statistical estimation, in which the assumption of no difference was *not* made. Further, the present procedure is conceptually similar to that presented in Section 11.1, in which the two sample variances are pooled as the basis for computing the standard error of the difference between means. The pooled estimate of the population proportion, based on the proportions obtained in two independent samples, is

$$\hat{\pi} = \frac{n_1 \hat{p}_1 + n_2 \hat{p}_2}{n_1 - n_2} \tag{11.15}$$

The standard error of the difference between proportions used in conjunction with testing the assumption of no difference is

$$\hat{\sigma}_{\hat{p}_1 - \hat{p}_2} = \sqrt{\frac{\hat{\pi}(1 - \hat{\pi})}{n_1} + \frac{\hat{\pi}(1 - \hat{\pi})}{n_2}} \tag{11.16}$$

The formula for the z statistic for testing the null hypothesis that there is no difference between two population proportions is

$$z = \frac{\hat{p}_1 - \hat{p}_2}{\hat{\sigma}_{\hat{p}_1 - \hat{p}_2}} \tag{11.17}$$

A test of the difference between proportions can be carried out as either a one-sided test (see Problem 11.8) or a two-sided test (see Example 8).

EXAMPLE 8.   A sample of 50 households in one community shows that 10 of them are watching a TV special on the national economy. In a second community, 15 of a random sample of 50 households are watching the TV special. We test the hypothesis that the overall proportion of viewers in the two communities does not differ, using the 1 percent level of significance, as follows:

$$H_0: (\pi_2 - \pi_2) = 0 \quad \text{or, equivalently,} \quad \pi_1 = \pi_2$$
$$H_1: (\pi_1 - \pi_2) \neq 0 \quad \text{or, equivalently,} \quad \pi_1 \neq \pi_2$$

$$\text{Critical } z \ (\alpha = 0.01) = \pm 2.58$$

$$\hat{\pi} = \frac{n_1 \hat{p}_1 + n_2 \hat{p}_2}{n_1 + n_2} = \frac{50(0.20) + 50(0.30)}{50 + 50} = \frac{10 + 15}{100} = 0.25$$

$$\hat{\sigma}_{\hat{p}_1 - \hat{p}_2} = \sqrt{\frac{\hat{\pi}(1 - \hat{\pi})}{n_1} + \frac{\hat{\pi}(1 - \hat{\pi})}{n_2}} = \sqrt{\frac{(0.25)(0.75)}{50} + \frac{(0.25)(0.75)}{50}} = \sqrt{0.00375 + 0.00375} = 0.087$$

$$z = \frac{\hat{p}_1 - \hat{p}_2}{\hat{\sigma}_{\hat{p}_1 - \hat{p}_2}} = \frac{0.20 - 0.30}{0.087} = \frac{-0.10}{0.087} = -1.15$$

The computed z of -1.15 is in the region of acceptance of the null hypothesis. Therefore, the hypothesis that there is no difference in the proportion of viewers in the two areas cannot be rejected.

11.8 TESTING A HYPOTHESIZED VALUE OF THE VARIANCE USING THE CHI-SQUARE DISTRIBUTION

As explained in Section 9.6, for a normally distributed population the ratio $(n-1)s^2/\sigma^2$ follows a χ^2 probability distribution, with there being a different chi-square distribution according to degrees of freedom $(n-1)$. Therefore, the statistic which is used to test a hypothesis concerning the value of the population variance is

$$\chi^2 = \frac{(n-1)s^2}{\sigma_0^2} \qquad\qquad (11.18)$$

The test based on (11.18) can be either a one-sided test or a two-sided test, although most often hypotheses about a population variance relate to one-sided tests. Appendix 7 can be used to determine the critical value(s) of the chi-square statistic for various levels of significance.

EXAMPLE 9. The mean operating life for a random sample of $n = 10$ light bulbs is $\bar{X} = 4,000$ hr with a standard deviation of $s = 200$ hr. The operating life of bulbs in general is assumed to be normally distributed. Suppose that before the sample was collected, it was hypothesized that the population standard deviation is no larger than $\sigma = 150$. Based on the sample results, this hypothesis is tested at the 1 percent level of significance as follows:

$$H_0: \sigma^2 = 22,500 \ [\text{because } \sigma_0^2 = (150)^2 = 22,500] \qquad H_1: \sigma^2 > 22,500$$

$$\text{Critical } \chi^2 \ (df = 0, \ \alpha = 0.01) = 21.67$$

$$\chi^2 = \frac{(n-1)s^2}{\sigma_0^2} = \frac{(9)(40,000)}{22,500} = \frac{360,000}{22,500} = 16.0$$

Because the calculated test statistic of 16.0 does *not* exceed the critical value of 21.67 for this upper-tail test, the null hypothesis that $\sigma \leq 150$ cannot be rejected at the 1 percent level of significance.

11.9 TESTING WITH RESPECT TO PROCESS VARIABILITY IN STATISTICAL PROCESS CONTROL

As described in Section 10.9 on testing the process mean and in Section 11.6 on testing the process proportion, the use and interpretation of control charts in statistical process control is a direct application of the methods and concepts of hypothesis testing. Process variability is monitored and controlled either with respect to the process *standard deviation* or the process *range*. As is the case with control charts for the process mean and process proportion, the control limits are defined at ± 3 standard error units with respect to the expected centerline value on the chart when the null hypothesis that there is no assignable-cause variation is true. The methodology for preparing and interpreting control charts is described in Chapter 19, Statistical Process

Control. Section 19.7 is concerned with the process standard deviation and Section 19.8 is concerned with the process range.

EXAMPLE 10. Rational-subgroup samples of $n = 4$ packages of potato chips are taken in a packaging process. In Example 13 of Chapter 10 (page 184) we considered whether the process appears to be stable with respect to the process mean. For the sequence of 15 samples, the sample standard deviations are (in oz): 0.148, 0.045, 0.088, 0.057, 0.042, 0.071, 0.083, 0.116, 0.127, 0.066, 0.141, 0.056, 0.047, 0.068, and 0.125. Figure 11-3 is the run chart for this sequence of standard deviations. Viewing the run chart, it is unclear whether there are any unusual sample standard deviations, since the apparent large amount of variability throughout the chart could just be a matter of how the vertical axis was scaled. In Solved Problems 19.16 through 19.19 we shall in fact observe that all the sample standard deviations are within the lower and upper control limits. Thus, the null hypothesis that there is no assignable-cause variation will not be rejected, and we will conclude that the process is stable with respect to the standard deviation of package contents. Incidentally, just because there is no assignable-cause variation does not in itself make the variability in the process acceptable. If there is too much continuing variability due to common causes, then the process needs to be redesigned and improved.

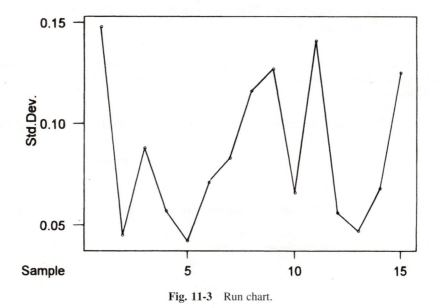

Fig. 11-3   Run chart.

11.10   THE *F* DISTRIBUTION AND TESTING THE EQUALITY OF TWO POPULATION VARIANCES

The *F* distribution can be shown to be the appropriate probability model for the ratio of the variances of two samples taken independently from the same normally distributed population, with there being a different *F* distribution for every combination of the degrees of freedom *df* associated with each sample. For each sample, $df = n - 1$. The statistic that is used to test the null hypothesis that two population variances are equal is

$$F_{df_1, df_2} = \frac{s_1^2}{s_2^2} \tag{11.19}$$

Since each sample variance is an unbiased estimator of the same population variance, the long-run expected value of the above ratio is about 1.0. (*Note*: The expected value is not exactly 1.0, but rather is $df_2/(df_2 - 2)$, for mathematical reasons that are outside of the scope of this outline.) However, for any given pair of samples the sample variances are not likely to be identical in value, even though the null hypothesis is true. Since this ratio is known to follow an *F* distribution, this probability distribution can be used in conjunction with testing the difference between two variances. Although a necessary mathematical assumption is that the two populations are normally distributed, the F test has been demonstrated to be relatively robust, and insensitive to departures from normality when each population is unimodal and the sample sizes are about equal.

Appendix 8 indicates the values of F exceeded by proportions of 0.05 and 0.01 of the distribution of F values. The degrees of freedom df associated with the numerator of the calculated F ratio are the column headings of this table and the degrees of freedom for the denominator are the row headings. The table does not identify any critical values of F for the lower tail of the distribution, partly because the F distribution typically is used in conjunction with tests that require only upper-tail probabilities. This is particularly true for the use of the F distribution in the analysis of variance (see Chapter 13). Another reason for providing only upper-tail F values is that required lower-tail values of F can be calculated by the so-called *reciprocal property* of the F distribution, as follows:

$$F_{df_1, df_2, \text{lower}} = \frac{1}{F_{df_2, df_1, \text{upper}}} \tag{11.20}$$

In applying Formula (*11.20*), an F value at the lower 5 percent point is determined by entering an upper-tail value at the 5 percent point in the denominator. Note, however, that the two df values in the denominator are the *reverse* of the order in the required F value.

EXAMPLE 11.   For the data in Example 3, bulb life is assumed to be normally distributed. We test the null hypothesis that the samples were obtained from populations with equal variances, using the 10 percent level of significance for the test, by use of the F distribution:

$$H_0: \sigma_1^2 = \sigma_2^2 \qquad \text{or equivalently,} \qquad \frac{\sigma_1^2}{\sigma_2^2} = 1.0 \qquad s_1 = 200 \, \text{hr} \qquad s_2 = 250 \, \text{hr}$$

$$H_1: \sigma_1^2 \neq \sigma_2^2 \qquad \text{or equivalently,} \qquad \frac{\sigma_1^2}{\sigma_2^2} \neq 1.0 \qquad s_1^2 = 40{,}000 \qquad s_2^2 = 62{,}500$$

$$n_1 = 10 \qquad n_2 = 8$$

For the test at the 10 percent level of significance, the upper 5 percent point for F and the lower 5 percent point for F are the critical values:

$$\text{Critical } F_{9,7} \text{ (upper 5\%)} = 3.68$$

$$\text{Critical } F_{9,7} \text{ (lower 5\%)} = \frac{1}{F_{7,9}(\text{upper 5\%})} = \frac{1}{3.29} = 0.304$$

$$F_{df_1, df_2} = \frac{s_1^2}{s_2^2}$$

$$F_{9,7} = \frac{40{,}000}{62{,}500} = 0.64$$

Since the computed F ratio is neither smaller than 0.304 nor larger than 3.68, it is in the region of acceptance of the null hypothesis. Thus, the assumption that the variances of the two populations are equal cannot be rejected at the 10 percent level of significance.

11.11   ALTERNATIVE APPROACHES TO TESTING NULL HYPOTHESES

As described in Sections 10.7 and 10.8, the P-value approach and the confidence interval approach are alternatives to the critical value approach to hypothesis testing used in the preceding sections of this chapter.

By the P-value approach, instead of comparing the observed value of a test statistic with a critical value, the probability of the occurrence of the test statistic, given that the null hypothesis is true, is determined and compared to the level of significance α. The null hypothesis is rejected if the P value is *less* than the designated α. Problems 11.13 and 11.14 illustrate the application of the P-value approach to two-tail and one-tail tests, respectively, concerning the difference between means.

By the confidence interval approach, the $1 - \alpha$ confidence interval is constructed for the parameter value of concern. If the hypothesized value of the parameter is not included in the interval, then the null hypothesis is rejected. Problems 11.15 and 11.16 illustrate the application of the confidence interval approach to two-tail and one-tail tests, respectively, concerning the difference between means.

11.12 USING EXCEL AND MINITAB

Computer software is available for most of the hypothesis-testing applications described in this chapter. The P-value approach to hypothesis testing generally is used, as described in Section 11.11. The use of Excel and Minitab for testing the difference between the means of two independent samples is illustrated in Solved Problems 11.17 and 11.18, respectively, while the use of Excel and Minitab with the paired-observations design for testing the difference between means is illustrated in Problems 11.19 and 11.20.

Solved Problems

TESTING THE DIFFERENCE BETWEEN TWO MEANS USING THE NORMAL DISTRIBUTION

11.1. A developer is considering two alternative sites for a regional shopping center. Since household income in the community is one important consideration in such site selection, the developer wishes to test the null hypothesis that there is no difference between the mean household income amounts in the two communities. Consistent with this hypothesis, it is assumed that the standard deviation of household income is also the same in the two communities. For a sample of $n_1 = 30$ households in the first community, the average annual income is $\bar{X}_1 = \$45,500$ with the sample standard deviation $s_1 = \$1,800$. For a sample of $n_2 = 40$ households in the second community, $\bar{X}_2 = \$44,600$ and $s_2 = \$2,400$. Test the null hypothesis at the 5 percent level of significance.

$$H_0: (\mu_1 = \mu_2) = 0 \qquad\qquad H_1: (\mu_1 - \mu_2) \neq 0$$

$$\bar{X}_1 = \$45,500 \qquad\qquad \bar{X}_2 = \$44,600$$

$$s_1 = \$1,800 \qquad\qquad s_2 = \$2,400$$

$$n_1 = 30 \qquad\qquad n_2 = \$40$$

$$\text{Critical } z \,(\alpha = 0.05) = \pm 1.96$$

$$\hat{\sigma}^2 = \frac{(n_1 - 1)s_1^2 + (n_2 - 1)s_2^2}{n_1 + n_2 - 2} = \frac{29(1,800)^2 + 39(2,400)^2}{30 + 40 - 2} = \frac{318,600,000}{68} = \$4,685,294$$

(The variances are pooled because of the assumption that the standard deviation values in the two populations are equal.)

$$\hat{\sigma}_{\bar{x}_1 - \bar{x}_2} = \sqrt{\frac{\hat{\sigma}^2}{n_1} + \frac{\hat{\sigma}^2}{n_2}} = \sqrt{\frac{4,685,294}{30} + \frac{4,685,294}{40}} = \sqrt{156,176.46 + 117,132.35} = \$522.79$$

$$z = \frac{\bar{X}_1 - \bar{X}_2}{\hat{\sigma}_{\bar{x}_1 - \bar{x}_2}} = \frac{35,500 - 34,600}{522.79} = \frac{900}{522.79} = +1.72$$

The computed z value of $+1.72$ is in the region of acceptance of the null hypothesis. Therefore the null hypothesis cannot be rejected at the 5 percent level of significance, and the hypothesis that the average income per household in the two communities does not differ is accepted as being plausible.

11.2. With reference to Problem 11.1, before any data were collected it was the developer's judgment that income in the first community might be higher. In order to subject this judgment to a critical test, the developer gave the benefit of doubt to the other possibility and formulated the null hypothesis

H_0: $(\mu_1 - \mu_2) \leq 0$. Test this hypothesis at the 5 percent level of significance with the further assumption that the standard deviation values for the two populations are *not* necessarily equal.

$$H_0: (\mu_1 - \mu_2) = 0 \qquad H_1: (\mu_1 - \mu_2) > 0$$

$$\text{Critical } z \, (\alpha = 0.05) = +1.645$$

$$s_{\bar{x}_1} = \frac{s_1}{\sqrt{n_1}} = \frac{1,800}{\sqrt{30}} = \frac{1,800}{5.48} = \$328.47$$

$$s_{\bar{x}_2} = \frac{s_2}{\sqrt{n_2}} = \frac{2,400}{\sqrt{40}} = \frac{2,400}{6.32} = \$379.75$$

$$s_{\bar{x}_1 - \bar{x}_2} = \sqrt{s_{\bar{x}_1}^2 + s_{\bar{x}_2}^2} = \sqrt{(328.47)^2 + (379.75)^2} = \sqrt{252,102.60} = \$502.10$$

$$z = \frac{\bar{X}_1 - \bar{X}_2}{s_{\bar{x}_1 - \bar{x}_2}} = \frac{45,500 - 44,600}{502.10} = \frac{900}{502.10} = +1.79$$

The computed z value of $+1.79$ is larger than the critical value of $+1.645$ for this upper-tail test. Therefore, the null hypothesis is rejected at the 5 percent level of significance, and the alternative hypothesis that average household income is larger in the first community as compared with the second is accepted.

11.3. With respect to Problems 11.1 and 11.2, before any data were collected it was the developer's judgment that the average income in the first community exceeded the average in the second community by at least $1,500 per year. In this case, give this judgment the benefit of the doubt and test the assumption as the null hypothesis using the 5 percent level of significance. The population standard deviations are not assumed to be equal.

$$H_0: (\mu_1 - \mu_2) - 1,500 \qquad H_1: (\mu_1 - \mu_2) < 1,500$$
$$\text{Critical } z \, (\alpha = 0.05) = -1.645$$
$$s_{\bar{x}_1 - \bar{x}_2} = \$502.10 \quad \text{(from Problem 11.2)}$$

$$z = \frac{(\bar{X}_1 - \bar{X}_2) - (\mu_1 - \mu_2)_0}{s_{\bar{x}_1 - \bar{x}_2}} = \frac{(45,500 - 44,600) - 1,500}{502.10} = \frac{-600}{502.10} = -1.19$$

The calculated z value of -1.19 is *not* less than the critical value of -1.645 for this lower-tail test. Therefore, the null hypothesis cannot be rejected at the 5 percent level of significance. Although the sample difference of $900 does not meet the $1,500 difference hypothesized by the developer, it is not different enough when the assumption is given the benefit of the doubt by being designated as the null hypothesis.

TESTING THE DIFFERENCE BETWEEN MEANS USING THE t DISTRIBUTION

11.4. A random sample of $n_1 = 12$ students majoring in accounting in a college of business has a mean grade-point average of 2.70 (where $A = 4.00$) with a sample standard deviation of 0.40. For the students majoring in computer information systems, a random sample of $n_2 = 10$ students has a mean grade-point average of $\bar{X}_2 = 2.90$ with a standard deviation of 0.30. The grade-point values are assumed to be normally distributed. Test the null hypothesis that the mean grade-point average for the two categories of students is not different, using the 5 percent level of significance.

$$H_0: (\mu_1 = \mu_2) = 0 \qquad H_1: (\mu_1 - \mu_2) \neq 0$$

$$\bar{X}_1 = 2.70 \qquad\qquad \bar{X}_2 = 2.90$$

$$s_1 = 0.40 \qquad\qquad s_2 = 0.30$$

$$n_1 = 12 \qquad\qquad n_2 = 10$$

$$\text{Critical } t \, (df = 20, \, \alpha = 0.05) = \pm 2.086$$

(*Note*:   Section 11.2 specifies that the usual assumption when using a t distribution for testing a difference between means is that the variances are equal.) Therefore, the two sample variances are pooled:

$$\hat{\sigma}^2 = \frac{(n_1 - 1)s_1^2 + (n_2 - 1)s_2^2}{n_1 + n_2 - 2} = \frac{(11)(0.40)^2 + (9)(0.30)^2}{12 + 10 - 2} = \frac{1.76 + 0.81}{20} = \frac{2.57}{20} = 0.128$$

$$\hat{\sigma}_{\bar{x}_1 - \bar{x}_2} = \sqrt{\frac{\hat{\sigma}^2}{n_1} + \frac{\hat{\sigma}^2}{n_2}} = \sqrt{\frac{0.128}{12} + \frac{0.128}{10}}$$

$$= \sqrt{0.011 + 0.013} = \sqrt{0.024} = 0.155$$

$$t = \frac{\bar{X}_1 - \bar{X}_2}{\hat{\sigma}_{\bar{x}_1 - \bar{x}_2}} = \frac{2.70 - 2.90}{0.155} = \frac{-0.20}{0.155} = -1.290$$

The calculated value of $t = -1.290$ is in the region of acceptance of the null hypothesis. Therefore, the null hypothesis that there is no difference between the grade-point averages for the two populations of students cannot be rejected at the 5 percent level of significance.

TESTING THE DIFFERENCE BETWEEN MEANS BASED ON PAIRED OBSERVATIONS

11.5.   A company training director wishes to compare a new approach to technical training, involving a combination of tutorial computer disks and laboratory problem solving, with the traditional lecture-discussion approach. Twelve pairs of trainees are matched according to prior background and academic performance, and one member of each pair is assigned to the traditional class and the other to the new approach. At the end of the course, the level of learning is determined by an examination covering basic information as well as the ability to apply the information. Because the training director wishes to give the benefit of the doubt to the established instructional system, the null hypothesis is formulated that the mean performance scores for the established system is equal to or greater than the mean level of performance for the new system. Test this hypothesis at the 5 percent level of significance. The sample performance data are presented in the first three columns of Table 11.2.

Table 11.2   Training Program Data and Worksheet for Computing the Mean Difference and the Standard Deviation of the Difference

Trainee pair	Old method (X_1)	New method (X_2)	d ($X_1 - X_2$)	d^2
1	89	94	−5	25
2	87	91	−4	16
3	70	68	2	4
4	83	88	−5	25
5	67	75	−8	64
6	71	66	5	25
7	92	94	−2	4
8	81	88	−7	49
9	97	96	1	1
10	78	88	−10	100
11	94	95	−1	1
12	79	87	−8	64
Total	988	1,030	−42	378

$$\text{Mean performance (traditional method)} = \frac{988}{12} = 82.33$$

$$\text{Mean performance (new approach)} = \frac{1,030}{12} = 85.83$$

$$H_0: \mu_d = 0 \qquad H_1: \mu_d < 0$$

$$\text{Critical } t(df = 11, \alpha = 0.05) = -1.796$$

$$\bar{d} = \frac{\Sigma d}{n} = \frac{-42}{12} = -3.5$$

$$s_d = \sqrt{\frac{\Sigma d^2 - n\bar{d}^2}{n-1}} = \sqrt{\frac{378 - 12(-3.5)^2}{11}} = \sqrt{\frac{378 - 147}{11}} = \sqrt{\frac{231}{11}} = \sqrt{21} = 4.58$$

$$s_{\bar{d}} = \frac{s_d}{\sqrt{n}} = \frac{4.58}{\sqrt{12}} = \frac{4.58}{3.46} = 1.32$$

$$t = \frac{\bar{d}}{s_{\bar{d}}} = \frac{-3.5}{1.32} = -2.652$$

The computed value of t of -2.652 is less than the critical value of -1.796 for this lower-tail test. Therefore, the null hypothesis is rejected at the 5 percent level of significance, and we conclude that the mean level of performance for those trained by the new approach is superior to those trained by the traditional method.

TESTING A HYPOTHESIS CONCERNING THE POPULATION PROPORTION

11.6. It is hypothesized that no more than 5 percent of the parts being produced in a manufacturing process are defective. For a random sample of $n = 100$ parts, 10 are found to be defective. Test the null hypothesis at the 5 percent level of significance.

$$H_0: \pi = 0.05 \qquad H_1: \pi > 0.05$$

$$\text{Critical } z(\alpha = 0.05) = +1.645$$

(Use of the normal distribution is warranted because $n \geq 30$, $n\pi_0 \geq 5$, and $n(1 - \pi_0) \geq 5$.)

$$\sigma_{\hat{p}} = \sqrt{\frac{\pi_0(1 - \pi_0)}{n}} = \sqrt{\frac{(0.05)(0.95)}{100}} = \sqrt{\frac{0.0475}{100}} = \sqrt{0.000475} = 0.022$$

$$z = \frac{\hat{p} - \pi_0}{\sigma_{\hat{p}}} = \frac{0.10 - 0.05}{0.022} = \frac{0.05}{0.022} = +2.27$$

The calculated value of z of $+2.27$ is greater than the critical value of $+1.645$ for this upper-tail test. Therefore, with 10 parts out of 100 found to be defective, the hypothesis that the proportion defective in the population is at or below 0.05 is rejected, using the 5 percent level of significance in the test.

11.7. For Problem 11.6, the manager stipulates that the probability of stopping the process for adjustment when it is in fact not necessary should be at only a 1 percent level, while the probability of *not* stopping the process when the true proportion defective is at $\pi = 0.10$ can be set at 5 percent. What sample size should be obtained, as a minimum, to satisfy these test objectives?

$$n = \left[\frac{z_0\sqrt{\pi_0(1 - \pi_0)} - z_1\sqrt{\pi_1(1 - \pi_1)}}{\pi_1 - \pi_0} \right]^2 = \left[\frac{2.33\sqrt{(0.05)(0.95)} - (-1.645)\sqrt{(0.10)(0.90)}}{0.10 - 0.05} \right]^2$$

$$= \left[\frac{2.33(0.218) + 1.645(0.300)}{0.05} \right]^2 = \left(\frac{1.0014}{0.05} \right)^2 = (20.03)^2 = 401.2 = 402 \text{ parts}$$

For industrial sampling purposes this is a rather large sample, so the manager might well want to reconsider the test objectives in regard to the designated P (Type I error) of 0.01 and P (Type II error) of 0.05. Further, instead of relying on just one sample, a sequence of smaller rational-group samples would be taken. This procedure is illustrated in Chapter 19, Statistical Process Control.

TESTING THE DIFFERENCE BETWEEN TWO POPULATION PROPORTIONS

11.8. A manufacturer is evaluating two types of equipment for the fabrication of a component. A random sample of $n_1 = 50$ is collected for the first brand of equipment, and five items are found to be defective. A random sample of $n_2 = 80$ is collected for the second brand and six items are found to be defective. The fabrication rate is the same for the two brands. However, because the first brand costs substantially less, the manufacturer gives this brand the benefit of the doubt and formulates the hypothesis H_0: $\pi_1 \leq \pi_2$. Test this hypothesis at the 5 percent level of significance.

$$H_0: (\pi_1 - \pi_2) = 0 \qquad H_1: (\pi_1 - \pi_2) > 0$$
$$\text{Critical } z \ (\alpha = 0.05) = +1.645$$

$$\hat{\pi} = \frac{n_1 \hat{p}_1 + n_2 \hat{p}_2}{n_1 + n_2} = \frac{50(0.10) + 80(0.075)}{50 + 80} = \frac{5 + 6}{130} = 0.085$$

$$\hat{\sigma}_{\hat{p}_1 - \hat{p}_2} = \sqrt{\frac{\hat{\pi}(1 - \hat{\pi})}{n_1} + \frac{\hat{\pi}(1 - \hat{\pi})}{n_2}} = \sqrt{\frac{(0.085)(0.915)}{50} + \frac{(0.085)(0.915)}{80}}$$

$$= \sqrt{\frac{0.0778}{50} + \frac{0.0778}{80}} = \sqrt{0.0016 + 0.0010} = 0.051$$

$$z = \frac{\hat{p}_1 - \hat{p}_2}{\hat{\sigma}_{\hat{p}_1 - \hat{p}_2}} = \frac{0.10 - 0.075}{0.051} = \frac{0.025}{0.051} = +0.49$$

The calculated value of z of $+0.49$ is not greater than $+1.645$ for this upper-tail test. Therefore, the null hypothesis cannot be rejected at the 5 percent level of significance.

TESTING A HYPOTHESIZED VALUE OF THE VARIANCE USING THE CHI-SQUARE DISTRIBUTION

11.9. Suppose it is hypothesized that the standard deviation of household income per year in a particular community is \$3,000. For a sample of $n = 15$ randomly selected households, the standard deviation is $s = \$2,000$. The household income figures for the population are assumed to be normally distributed. On the basis of this sample result, can the null hypothesis be rejected using the 5 percent level of significance?

$$H_0: \sigma^2 = (3,000)^2 = 9,000,000 \qquad H_1: \sigma^2 \neq 9,000,000$$
$$\text{Critical } \chi^2(df = 14, \alpha = 0.05) = 5.63 \text{ and } 26.12 \text{ (respectively, for the two-tail test)}$$

$$\chi^2 = \frac{(n-1)s^2}{\sigma_0^2} = \frac{(14)(2,000)^2}{(3,000)^2} = \frac{14(4,000,000)}{9,000,000} = \frac{56,000,000}{9,000,000} = 6.22$$

The computed value of 6.22 is neither less than the lower critical value of 5.63 nor larger than the upper critical value of 26.12 for this two-tail test. Therefore the hypothesis that $\sigma = \$3,000$ is not rejected at the 5 percent level of significance. It is plausible that the population standard deviation is \$3,000.

11.10. For Problem 11.9, suppose the null hypothesis was that the population standard deviation is *at least* \$3,000. Test this hypothesis at the 5 percent level of significance.

$$H_0: \sigma^2 = 9,000,000 \qquad H_1: \sigma^2 < 9,000,000$$
$$\text{Critical } \chi^2(df = 14, \alpha = 0.05) = 6.57 \text{ (lower-tail critical value)}$$
$$\chi^2 = 6.22 \qquad \text{(from Problem 11.9)}$$

The calculated test statistic of 6.22 is just less than the critical value of 6.57 for this lower-tail test. Therefore the null hypothesis is rejected at the 5 percent level of significance, and the alternative hypothesis, that $\sigma^2 < 9,000,000$ (that $\sigma < \$3,000$), is accepted.

TESTING THE EQUALITY OF TWO POPULATION VARIANCES

11.11. In Problem 11.4, concerned with testing the difference between two means using a t distribution, a necessary assumption was that the two population variances are equal. The two sample variances were $s_1^2 = 0.40^2 = 0.16$, and $s_2^2 = 0.30^2 = 0.09$, with $n_1 = 12$ and $n_2 = 10$, respectively. Test the null hypothesis that the two population variances are indeed equal, using a 10 percent level of significance.

$$H_0: \sigma_1^2 = \sigma_2^2 \qquad s_1^2 = 0.16 \qquad s_2^2 = 0.09$$
$$H_1: \sigma_1^2 \neq \sigma_2^2 \qquad n_1 = 12 \qquad n_2 = 10$$

$$\text{Critical } F_{11,9}(\text{upper } 5\%) = 3.10 \qquad (\text{from Appendix 8})$$

$$\text{Critical } F_{11,9} (\text{lower } 5\%) = \frac{1}{F_{9,11}(\text{upper } 5\%)} = \frac{1}{2.90} = 0.345$$

$$F_{df_1, df_2} = \frac{s_1^2}{s_2^2} = \frac{0.16}{0.09} = 1.78$$

The calculated F statistic of 1.78 is neither less than the lower critical value of 0.345 nor greater than the upper critical value of 3.10. Therefore, the hypothesis of no difference between the variances cannot be rejected, and the assumption of equal variances is warranted.

11.12. In Problem 11.1, the assumption was made that the variance of household income was not different in the two communities. Test the null hypothesis that the two variances are equal, using the 10 percent level of significance.

$$H_0: \sigma_1^2 = \sigma_2^2 \qquad s_1^2 = (1,800)^2 = 3,240,000 \qquad s_2^2 = (2,400)^2 = 5,760,000$$
$$H_1: \sigma_1^2 \neq \sigma_2^2 \qquad n_1 = 30 \qquad n_2 = 40$$

(*Note*: Because of limitations in Appendix 8, the specific F values for 29 and 39 degrees of freedom cannot be determined exactly. Therefore, the approximate F values are determined by using the nearest degrees of freedom of 30 and 40, respectively.)

$$\text{Critical } F_{30, 40} (\text{upper } 5\%) = 1.74$$

$$\text{Critical } F_{30, 40} (\text{lower } 5\%) = \frac{1}{F_{40, 30}(\text{upper } 5\%)} = \frac{1}{1.79} = 0.599$$

$$F_{df_1, df_2} = \frac{s_1^2}{s_2^2} = \frac{3,240,000}{5,760,000} = 0.562$$

The computed F statistic is neither less than the lower critical value of 0.559 nor greater than the upper critical value of 1.74. Therefore, the F statistic is just within the region of acceptance of the null hypothesis at the 10 percent level of significance, and the assumption of equal variances is warranted.

ALTERNATIVE APPROACHES TO TESTING NULL HYPOTHESES

11.13. Using the P-value approach, test the null hypothesis in Problem 11.1 at the 5 percent level of significance.

$$H_0: (\mu_1 - \mu_2) = 0 \qquad H_1: (\mu_1 - \mu_2) \neq 0$$
$$z = +1.72 \qquad (\text{from Problem 11.1})$$
$$P(z \geq +1.72) = 0.5000 - 0.4573 = 0.0427$$

Finally, because this is a two-tail test,

$$P = 2(0.0427) = 0.0854$$

Because the P value of 0.0854 is larger than the level of significance of 0.05, the null hypothesis *cannot* be rejected at this level. Therefore, we conclude that there is no difference between the mean household income amounts in the two communities.

11.14. Using the P-value approach, test the null hypothesis in Problem 11.2 at the 5 percent level of significance.

$$H_0: (\mu_1 - \mu_2) = 0 \qquad H_1: (\mu_1 - \mu_2) > 0$$
$$z = +1.79 \qquad \text{(from Problem 11.2)}$$

(Note that the z statistic is in the direction of the region of rejection for this upper-tail test.)

$$P(z \geq +1.79) = 0.5000 - 0.4633 = 0.0367$$

Because the P value of 0.0367 is smaller than the level of significance of 0.05, we reject the null hypothesis and conclude that the mean level of income in the first community is greater than the mean income in the second community.

11.15. Apply the confidence interval approach to testing the null hypothesis in Problem 11.1, using the 5 percent level, of significance.

$$H_0: (\mu_1 - \mu_2) = 0 \qquad H_1: (\mu_1 - \mu_2) \neq 0$$
$$\bar{X}_1 = \$45,500 \qquad \bar{X}_2 = \$44,600$$
$$\hat{\sigma}_{\bar{x}_1 - \bar{x}_2} = \$522.79 \qquad \text{(from Problem 11.1)}$$
$$95\% \text{ Confidence interval} = (\bar{X}_1 - \bar{X}_2) \pm z \hat{\sigma}_{\bar{x}_1 - \bar{x}_2}$$
$$= (45,500 - 44,600) \pm 1.96(522.79)$$
$$= 900 \pm 1,024.67 = -\$124.67 \text{ to } \$1,924.67$$

Because the 95 percent confidence interval includes the hypothesized difference of \$0, the null hypothesis cannot be rejected at the 5 percent level of significance.

11.16. Apply the confidence interval approach to testing the null hypothesis in Problem 11.2.

$$H_0: (\mu_1 - \mu_2) = 0 \qquad H_1: (\mu_1 - \mu_2) > 0$$
$$\bar{X}_1 = \$45,500 \qquad \bar{X}_2 = \$44,600$$
$$s_{\bar{x}_1 - \bar{x}_2} = \$502.10 \qquad \text{(from Problem 11.2)}$$
$$\text{Lower confidence limit} = (\bar{X}_1 - \bar{X}_2) - z \, s_{\bar{x}_1 - \bar{x}_2}$$
$$= (45,500 - 44,600) - 1.645(502.10)$$
$$= 900 - 825.95 = \$74.05$$

With 95 percent confidence, we conclude that the difference between the population means can be as small as \$74.05. Because this one-sided confidence interval does not include the hypothesized value of \$0 (or less), the null hypothesis is rejected at the 5 percent level of significance, and we conclude that the average household income in the first community is greater than the average household income in the second community.

COMPUTER OUTPUT: DIFFERENCE BETWEEN MEANS (INDEPENDENT SAMPLES)

11.17. Refer to the Excel output for Problem 9.15 (Fig. 9-1, page 171). The data are for two random samples of automobile damage claims, each sample taken from a different geographic area. In Problem 9.15 the output was used for determining the 95 percent confidence interval for the difference between the two population means. For our purpose now, test the null hypothesis that there is no difference between the means of the two populations, using the 5 percent level of significance for the test.

$$H_0: (\mu_1 - \mu_2) = 0 \qquad H_1: (\mu_1 - \mu_2) \neq 0 \qquad \alpha = 0.05$$

The lower portion of the output in Fig. 9-1 reports that $P = 0.019$ (rounded) for the two-tail test. Because this reported probability is less that the designated level of significance of 0.05, the null hypothesis that there is no difference between the population means is rejected. We conclude that there *is* a difference in the mean-average level of dollar claims in the two areas.

11.18. Refer to the Minitab output for Problem 9.16 (Fig. 9-2, page 171). The data are for two random samples of automobile damage claims, each sample taken from a different geographic area. In Problem 9.16 the output was used for determining the 95 percent confidence interval for the difference between the two population means. For our purpose now, test the null hypothesis that there is no difference between the means of the two populations, using the 5 percent level of significance for the test.

$$H_0: (\mu_1 - \mu_2) = 0 \qquad H_1: (\mu_1 - \mu_2) \neq 0 \qquad \alpha = 0.05$$

The lower portion of the output in Fig. 9-2 reports that the P value $= 0.019$ (rounded) for the two-tail test. Because this reported probability is less that the designated level of significance of 0.05, the null hypothesis that there is no difference between the population means is rejected. We conclude that there *is* a difference in the mean-average level of dollar claims in the two areas.

COMPUTER OUTPUT: DIFFERENCE BETWEEN MEANS (PAIRED OBSERVATIONS)

11.19. Refer to the data in Table 11.2 in Problem 11.5, associated with testing the difference between means of paired samples, using hand calculations. Use Excel to test the null hypothesis presented in that problem at the 5 percent level of significance.

$$H_0: \mu_d = 0 \qquad H_1: \mu_d < 0 \qquad \alpha = 0.05$$

Refer to the Excel output in Fig. 11-4. The reported P value for the one-tail test is 0.011 (rounded). Because this probability of the sample paired difference occurring by chance is less than the designated level of significance of 0.05, the null hypothesis is rejected and we conclude that the mean performance score of those trained by the new method is superior to the mean score of those trained by the old method. This conclusion coincides with the result of the hand calculation that used the critical value approach to hypothesis testing.

Old	New	t-Test: Paired Two Sample for Means		
89	94			
87	91		Old	New
70	68	Mean	82.33333	85.83333
83	88	Variance	96.24242	108.3333
67	75	Observations	12	12
71	66	Pearson Correlation	0.89892	
92	94	Hypothesized Mean Difference	0	
81	88	df	11	
97	96	t Stat	-2.64575	
78	88	P(T<=t) one-tail	0.011379	
94	95	t Critical one-tail	1.795884	
79	87	P(T<=t) two-tail	0.022758	
		t Critical two-tail	2.200986	

Fig. 11-4 Excel output for paired observations.

The Excel output given in Fig. 11-4 was obtained as follows:

(1) Open Excel. In cell A1 enter the column label: Old. Enter the 12 scores for the Old method in column A beginning at cell A2. In cell B1 enter the column label: New. Enter the 12 claim amounts for the New method in column B, beginning at cell B2.

(2) Click **Tools → Data Analysis → t-Test: Paired Two-Sample for Means**. Click **OK**.

(3) In the dialog box designate **Variable 1 Range** as: $A$1:$A$13. Designate **Variable 2 Range** as: $B$1:$B$13.

(4) Set the **Hypothesized Mean Difference** as: 0. Select the **Labels** box. Select **Alpha** as 0.05.

(5) Designate the **Output Range** as: $C$1.

(6) Click **OK**.

11.20. Refer to the data in Table 11.2 in Problem 11.5, associated with testing the difference between means of paired samples, using hand calculations. Use Minitab to test the null hypothesis presented in that problem at the 5 percent level of significance.

$$H_0: \mu_d = 0 \qquad H_1: \mu_d < 0 \qquad \alpha = 0.05$$

Refer to the Minitab output in Fig. 11-5. The reported P value for the one-tail test is 0.011. Because this probability of the sample paired difference occurring by chance is less than the designated level of significance of 0.05, the null hypothesis is rejected and we conclude that the mean performance score of those trained by the new method is superior to the mean score of those trained by the old method. This conclusion coincides with the result of the hand calculation that used the critical value approach to hypothesis testing.

The Minitab output given in Fig. 11-5 was obtained as follows:

(1) Open Minitab. In the column name cell for C1 enter: Old. Enter the 12 scores for the Old method in column C1. In the column name cell for C2 enter: New. Enter the 12 claim amounts for the New method in column C2.

(2) Click **Stat → Basic Statistics → Paired t**.

(3) For **First sample** enter: Old. For **Second sample** enter: New.

(4) Click **Options**. Designate **Confidence level** as: 95.0. Designate **Test Mean** as: 0.0. For **Alternative** choose **less than** (for a *one-tail* test). Click **OK**.

(5) Back in the original dialog box, click **OK**.

Paired T-Test and CI: Old, New

```
Paired T for Old - New

                N       Mean     StDev    SE Mean
Old            12      82.33      9.81       2.83
New            12      85.83     10.41       3.00
Difference     12      -3.50      4.58       1.32

95% upper bound for mean difference: -1.12
T-Test of mean difference = 0 (vs < 0): T-Value = -2.65  P-Value = 0.011
```

Fig. 11-5 Minitab output for paired observations.

Supplementary Problems

TESTING THE DIFFERENCE BETWEEN TWO MEANS

11.21. As reported in Problem 9.17, for one consumer product the mean dollar sales per retail outlet last year in a sample of $n_1 = 10$ stores was $\bar{X}_1 = \$3,425$ with $s_1 = \$200$. For a second product the mean dollar sales per outlet in a sample of $n_2 = 12$ stores was $\bar{X}_2 = \$3,250$ with $s_2 = \$175$. The sales amounts per outlet are assumed to be normally distributed for both products. Test the null hypothesis that there is no difference between the mean dollar sales for the two products using the 1 percent level of significance.
Ans. Accept H_0.

11.22. For the data in Problem 11.21, suppose the two sample sizes were $n_1 = 20$ and $n_2 = 24$. Test the difference between the two means at the 1 percent level of significance.
Ans. Reject H_0.

11.23. For a sample of 30 employees in one large firm, the mean hourly wage is $\bar{X}_1 = \$9.50$ with $s_1 = \$1.00$. In a second large firm, the mean hourly wage for a sample of 40 employees is $\bar{X}_2 = \$9.05$ with $s_2 = \$1.20$. Test the hypothesis that there is no difference between the average wage rate being earned in the two firms, using the 5 percent level of significance and assuming that the variances of the two populations are not necessarily equal.
Ans. Accept H_0.

11.24. In Problem 11.23, suppose the alternative hypothesis is that the average wage in the second firm is less than the average wage rate in the first firm. Can the null hypothesis be rejected at the 5 percent level of significance?
Ans. Yes.

11.25. A random sample of $n_1 = 10$ salespeople are placed on one incentive system while a random sample of $n_2 = 10$ other salespeople are placed under a second incentive system. During the comparison period, those under the first system have average weekly sales of $\bar{X}_1 = \$5,000$ with a standard deviation of $s_1 = \$1,200$ while those under the second system have sales of $\bar{X}_2 = \$4,600$ with a standard deviation of $\$1,000$. Test the null hypothesis that there is no difference between the mean sales per week for the two incentive systems, using the 5 percent level of significance.
Ans. Accept H_0.

11.26. In order to compare two computer software packages, a manager has 10 individuals use each software package to perform a standard set of tasks typical of those encountered in the office. Of course, in carrying out the comparison the manager was careful to use individuals who did not have an established preference or skill with either type of software, and five individuals were randomly selected to use Software A first while the other five used Software B first. The time required to perform the standard set of tasks, to the nearest minute, is reported in Table 11.3. Test the null hypothesis that there is no difference between the mean time required to perform the standard tasks by the two software packages, using the 5 percent level of significance.
Ans. Reject H_0.

Table 11.3   Time Required to Perform a Standard Set of Tasks Using Two Software Packages (Nearest Minute)

Individual	1	2	3	4	5	6	7	8	9	10
Software A	12	16	15	13	16	10	15	17	14	12
Software B	10	17	18	16	19	12	17	15	17	14

TESTING A HYPOTHESIS CONCERNING THE POPULATION PROPORTION

11.27. A sales consultant claims to have obtained orders from at least 30 percent of the prospects contacted. Suppose that for a sample of 100 prospects orders are received from 20 of them. Giving the Consultant the benefit of the doubt, can the claim be rejected at the (*a*) 5 percent and (*b*) 1 percent level of significance?
Ans. (*a*) Yes, (*b*) no.

11.28. The sponsor of a television special expected that at least 40 percent of the viewing audience would watch the show in a particular metropolitan area. For a random sample of 100 households with television sets turned on, 30 of them are found to be watching the special. Designating the sponsor's assumption the benefit of doubt, can it be rejected as being true for all viewers in the metropolitan area at the (*a*) 10 percent and (*b*) 5 percent level of significance?
Ans. (*a*) Yes, (*b*) yes.

11.29. For Problem 11.28, suppose the sponsor specifies that as the result of the study the probability of rejecting a true claim should be no larger than $P = 0.02$, and the probability of accepting the claim given that the percentage viewing the program is actually 30 percent or less should be no larger than $P = 0.05$. What sample size is required in the study, as a minimum, to satisfy this requirement?
Ans. 311 households.

11.30. For Problem 11.28, it was suggested that the program might appeal differently to urban versus suburban residents, but there was a difference of opinion among the production staff regarding the direction of the difference. For a random sample of 50 urban households, 20 reported watching the program. For a random sample of 50 suburban households, 30 reported watching the program. Can the difference be considered significant at the (*a*) 10 percent and (*b*) 5 percent level?
Ans. (*a*) Yes, (*b*) yes.

TESTING A HYPOTHESIZED VALUE OF THE VARIANCE AND THE EQUALITY OF TWO VARIANCES

11.31. Based on the specifications provided by the process designer, the standard deviation of casting diameters is hypothesized to be no larger than 3.0 mm. For a sample of $n = 12$ castings, the sample standard deviation is $s = 4.2$ mm. The distribution of the diameters is assumed to be approximately normal. Can the null hypothesis that the true standard deviation is no larger than 3.0 mm be rejected at the (*a*) 5 percent and (*b*) 1 percent level of significance?
Ans. (*a*) Yes, (*b*) no.

11.32. In Problem 11.21, under the necessary assumption that the variances of the two populations are equal, the null hypothesis that the means are equal could not be rejected using the *t* test at the 1 percent level of significance. At the 10 percent level of significance, is the assumption that the two variances are not different warranted?
Ans. Yes.

11.33. A new molding process is designed to reduce the variability of casting diameters. To test the new process, we conservatively formulate the alternative hypothesis that the variance of casting diameters under the new process is less than the variance for the old process. Rejection of the null hypothesis would then permit us to accept the alternative hypothesis that the variance associated with the new process is smaller than that associated with the old process. For a sample of $n_1 = 8$ castings produced by the new process $s_1 = 4.2$ mm. For a sample of $n_2 = 10$ castings produced by the old process $s_2 = 5.8$ mm. Can the null hypothesis be rejected at the 5 percent level of significance?
Ans. No.

ALTERNATIVE APPROACHES TO TESTING NULL HYPOTHESES

11.34. Using the *P*-value approach, test the null hypothesis in Problem 11.23 at the 5 percent level of significance.
Ans. Accept H_0 $(P = 0.0836)$.

11.35. Using the *P*-value approach, test the null hypothesis in Problem 11.24 at the 5 percent level of significance.
Ans. Reject H_0 $(P = 0.0418)$.

11.36. Apply the confidence interval approach to testing the null hypothesis in Problem 11.23, using the 5 percent level of significance.
Ans. Accept H_0.

11.37. Apply the confidence interval approach to testing the null hypothesis in Problem 11.24, using the 5 percent level of significance.
Ans. Reject H_0.

COMPUTER OUTPUT

11.38. Refer to the data in Table 9.2, which was used to obtain the 95 percent confidence interval for the difference between means in Problem 9.33. Using available computer software, test the null hypothesis that the mean amount of per-item time does not differ for the two types of calls, using the 5 percent level of significance.
Ans.   Accept H_0 ($P = 0.42$).

11.39. Refer to the data in Table 11.3, concerned with the time required to perform a standard set of tasks using two different software packages. The null hypothesis that there is no difference between the average time required for the two packages was tested in Problem 11.26. Using available computer software, again test this hypothesis at the 5 percent level of significance.
Ans.   Reject H_0 ($P = 0.038$).

CHAPTER 12

The Chi-Square Test for the Analysis of Qualitative Data

12.1 GENERAL PURPOSE OF THE CHI-SQUARE TEST

The procedures that are described in this chapter all involve the comparison of the observed pattern of the frequencies of observations for sample data that have been entered into defined data catagories, with the expected pattern of frequencies based on a particular null hypothesis.

Use of the χ^2 (chi-square) probability distribution with respect to statistical inference concerning the population variance is described in Sections 9.6 and 11.8. The test statistic presented in the following sections also is distributed as the chi-square probability model, and since hypothesis testing is involved, the basic steps in hypothesis testing described in Section 10.2 apply in this chapter as well.

This chapter covers the use of the chi-square test for testing the *goodness of fit*, testing the *independence of two variables*, and testing *hypotheses concerning proportions*. One of the tests of proportions is that of testing the *differences among several population proportions*, which is an extension of testing the difference between two population proportions, as described in Section 11.7.

12.2 GOODNESS OF FIT TESTS

The null hypothesis in a goodness of fit test is a stipulation concerning the expected pattern of frequencies in a set of categories. The expected pattern may conform to the assumption of equal likelihood and may therefore be uniform, or the expected pattern may conform to such patterns as the binomial, Poisson, or normal.

EXAMPLE 1. A regional distributor of air-conditioning systems has subdivided the region into four territories. A prospective purchaser of the distributionship is told that installations of the equipment are about equally distributed among the four territories. The prospective purchaser takes a random sample of 40 installations performed during the past year from

219

the company's files, and finds that the number installed in each of the four territories is as listed in the first row of Table 12.1 (where f_o means "observed frequency"). On the basis of the hypothesis that installations are equally distributed, the expected uniform distribution of the installations is given in the second row of Table 12.1 (where f_e means "expected frequency").

Table 12.1   Number of Installations of Air-Conditioning Systems According to Territory

	Territory				
	A	B	C	D	Total
Number installed in sample, f_o	6	12	14	8	40
Expected number of installations, f_e	10	10	10	10	40

For the null hypothesis to be accepted, the differences between observed and expected frequencies must be attributable to sampling variability at the designated level of significance. Thus, the chi-square test statistic is based on the magnitude of this difference for each category in the frequency distribution.

The chi-square value for testing the difference between an obtained and expected pattern of frequencies is

$$\chi^2 = \sum \frac{(f_o - f_e)^2}{f_e} \qquad (12.1)$$

By Formula (12.1) above, note that if the observed frequencies are very close to the expected frequencies, then the calculated value of the chi-square statistic will be close to zero. As the observed frequencies become increasingly different from the expected frequencies, the value of chi-square becomes larger. Therefore it follows that the chi-square test involves the use of just the *upper tail* of the chi-square distribution to determine whether an observed pattern of frequencies is different from an expected pattern.

EXAMPLE 2.   The calculation of the chi-square test statistic for the pattern of observed and expected frequencies in Table 12.1 is as follows:

$$\chi^2 = \sum \frac{(f_o - f_e)^2}{f_e} = \frac{(6 - 10)^2}{10} + \frac{(12 - 10)^2}{10} + \frac{(14 - 10)^2}{10} + \frac{(8 - 10)^2}{10} = \frac{40}{10} = 4.00$$

The required value of the chi-square test statistic to reject the null hypothesis depends on the level of significance that is specified and the degrees of freedom. In goodness of fit tests, the degrees of freedom df are equal to the number of categories minus the number of parameter estimators based on the sample and minus 1. Where k = number of categories of data and m = number of parameter values estimated on the basis of the sample, the degrees of freedom in a chi-square goodness of fit test are

$$df = k - m - 1 \qquad (12.2)$$

When the null hypothesis is that the frequencies are equally distributed, no parameter estimation is ever involved and $m = 0$. (Examples in which m is greater than zero are provided in Problems 12.6 and 12.8.) The subtraction of 1 is always included, because given a total number of observations, once observed frequencies have been entered in $k - 1$ categories of a table of frequencies, the last cell is in fact not free to vary. For instance, given that the first three categories in Table 12.1 have observed frequencies of 6, 12, and 14, respectively, it follows that the fourth category must have a frequency of 8 in order to cumulate to the designated sample size of $n = 40$.

EXAMPLE 3. Following is a complete presentation of the hypothesis testing procedure associated with the data in Table 12.1, with the null hypothesis being tested at the 5 percent level of significance.

H_0: The number of installations is uniformly distributed among the four territories.

H_1: The number of installations is not uniformly distributed among the four territories.

$$df = k - m - 1 = 4 - 0 - 1 = 3$$

Critical $\chi^2(df = 3, \alpha = 0.05) = 7.81$ (from Appendix 7)

Computed $\chi^2 = 4.00$ (from Example 2)

Because the calculated value of chi-square of 4.00 is not greater than the critical value of 7.81, the null hypothesis that the installations are equally distributed among the four territories cannot be rejected at the 5 percent level of significance.

Computed values of the chi-square test statistic are based on discrete counts, whereas the chi-square distribution is a continuous distribution. When the expected frequencies f_e for the cells are not small, this factor is not important in terms of the extent to which the distribution of the test statistic is approximated by the chi-square distribution. A *frequently used rule is that the expected frequency f_e for each cell, or category, should be at least 5*. Cells that do not meet this criterion should be combined with adjacent categories, when possible, so that this requirement is satisfied. The reduced number of categories then becomes the basis for determining the degrees of freedom *df* applicable in the test situation. See Problems 12.6 and 12.8. The expected frequencies for all cells of a data table also can be increased by increasing the overall sample size. Compare the expected frequencies in Problems 12.1 and 12.3.

The expected frequencies may be based on any hypothesis regarding the form of the population frequency distribution. If the hypothesis is based on the observed historical pattern of frequencies, then, as in the case of the equally likely hypothesis, no parameter estimation is involved, and $df = k - m - 1 = k - 0 - 1 = k - 1$.

EXAMPLE 4. Historically, a manufacturer of TV sets has had 40 percent of sales in small-screen sets (under 20 in), 40 percent in the mid-range sizes (20 in to 27 in), and 20 percent in the large-screen category (above 27 in). In order to ascertain appropriate production schedules for the next month, a random sample of 100 purchases during the current period is taken and it is found that 55 of the sets purchased were small, 35 were middle-sized, and 10 were large. Below we test the null hypothesis that the historical pattern of sales still prevails, using the 1 percent level of significance.

H_0: The percentages of all purchases in the small-, medium-, and large-screen categories of TV sets are 40 percent, 40 percent, and 20 percent, respectively.

H_1: The present pattern of TV set purchases is different from the historical pattern in H_0.

$$df = k - m - 1 = 3 - 0 - 1 = 2$$

Critical $\chi^2(df = 2, \alpha = 0.01) = 9.21$

Computed χ^2 (see Table 12.2 for observed and expected frequencies):

$$\chi^2 = \sum \frac{(f_o - f_e)^2}{f_e} = \frac{(55 - 40)^2}{40} + \frac{(35 - 40)^2}{40} + \frac{(10 - 20)^2}{20} = 11.25$$

The calculated chi-square statistic of 11.25 is greater than the critical value of 9.21. Therefore, the null hypothesis is rejected at the 1 percent level of significance. Comparing the obtained and expected frequencies in Table 12.2, we find that the principal change involves more small sets and fewer large sets being sold, with some reduction in middle-sized sets also possibly occurring.

Table 12.2   Observed and Expected Purchases of TV Sets by Screen Size

	Screen size			
	Small	Medium	Large	Total
Observed frequency, f_o	55	35	10	100
Historical pattern, f_e	40	40	20	100

12.3 TESTS FOR THE INDEPENDENCE OF TWO CATEGORICAL VARIABLES (CONTINGENCY TABLE TESTS)

In the case of goodness of fit tests, there is only one categorical variable, such as the screen size of TV sets that have been sold, and what is tested is a hypothesis concerning the pattern of frequencies, or the distribution, of the variable. The observed frequencies can be listed as a single row, or as a single column, of categories. *Tests for independence* involve (at least) two categorical variables, and what is tested is the assumption that the variables are statistically independent. Independence implies that knowledge of the category in which an observation is classified with respect to one variable has no affect on the probability of the other variable being in one of the several categories. When two variables are involved, the observed frequencies are entered in a two-way classification table, or *contingency table* (see Section 5.8). The dimensions of such tables are defined by $r \times k$, in which r indicates the number of rows and k indicates the number of columns.

EXAMPLE 5. Table 12.3 is repeated from Section 5.8 and is an example of the simplest possible format for a contingency table, in that each of the two variables (sex and age) has only two classification levels, or categories. Thus, this is a 2×2 contingency table.

Table 12.3   Contingency Table for Stereo Shop Customers

Age	Sex		Total
	Male	Female	
Under 30	60	50	110
30 and over	80	10	90
Total	140	60	200

If the null hypothesis of independence is rejected for classified data such as in Table 12.3, this indicates that the two variables are *dependent* and that there is a *relationship* between them. For Table 12.3, for instance, this would indicate that there is a relationship between age and the sex of stereo shop customers.

Given the hypothesis of independence of the two variables, the expected frequency associated with each cell of a contingency table should be proportionate to the total observed frequencies included in the column and in the row in which the cell is located as related to the total sample size. Where f_r is the total frequency in a given row and f_k is the total frequency in a given column, a convenient formula for determining the expected frequency for the cell of the contingency table that is located in that row and column is

$$f_e = \frac{f_r f_k}{n} \qquad (12.3)$$

The general formula for the degrees of freedom associated with a test for independence is

$$df = (r-1)(k-1) \qquad (12.4)$$

EXAMPLE 6. The expected frequencies for the data of Table 12.3 are reported in Table 12.4. For row 1, column 1, for instance, the calculation of the expected frequency is

$$f_e = \frac{f_r f_k}{n} = \frac{(110)(140)}{200} = \frac{15,400}{200} = 77$$

Note that in this case the three remaining expected frequencies can be obtained by subtraction from row and column totals, as an alternative to using (12.3). This is a direct indication that there is one degree of freedom for a 2×2 contingency table, and that only one cell frequency is free to vary.

**Table 12.4	Table of Expected Frequencies for
the Observed Frequencies Reported
in Table 12.3**

Age	Sex		Total
	Male	Female	
Under 30	77	33	110
30 and over	63	27	90
Total	140	60	200

The chi-square test statistic for contingency tables is computed exactly as for the goodness of fit tests (see Section 12.2).

EXAMPLE 7.	Following is the test of the null hypothesis of independence for the data of Table 12.3, using the 1 percent level of significance.

H_0: Sex and age of stereo shop customers are independent.

H_1: Sex and age are dependent variables (there is a relationship between the variables).

$$df = (r - 1)(k - 1) = (2 - 1)(2 - 1) = 1$$

$$\text{Critical } \chi^2(df = 1, \alpha = 0.01) = 6.63$$

$$\chi^2 = \sum \frac{(f_o - f_e)^2}{f_e} = \frac{(60 - 77)^2}{77} + \frac{(50 - 33)^2}{33} + \frac{(80 - 63)^2}{63} + \frac{(10 - 27)^2}{27} = 27.80$$

The calculated test statistic of 27.80 exceeds the required critical value of 6.63. Therefore, the null hypothesis of independence is rejected at the 1 percent level of significance. Referring to Table 12.3, we see that male customers are more likely to be over 30 years of age while female customers are more likely to be under 30. The result of the chi-square test indicates that this observed relationship in the sample cannot be ascribed to chance at the 1 percent level of significance.

## 12.4	TESTING HYPOTHESES CONCERNING PROPORTIONS

Testing a Hypothesized Value of the Proportion.	Given a hypothesized population proportion and an observed proportion for a random sample taken from the population, in Section 11.4 we used the normal probability distribution as an approximation for the binomial process in order to test the null hypothesis. Mathematically it can be shown that such a two-sided test is equivalent to a chi-square goodness of fit test involving one row of frequencies and two categories (a 1×2 table). Since the chi-square test involves an analysis of differences between obtained and expected frequencies regardless of the direction of the differences, there is no chi-square test procedure that is the equivalent of a one-sided test concerning the value of a population proportion.

EXAMPLE 8.	A personnel department manager estimates that a proportion of $\pi = 0.40$ of the employees in a large firm will participate in a new stock investment program. A random sample of $n = 50$ employees is contacted, and 10 indicate their intention to participate. The hypothesized value of the population proportion could be tested using the normal probability distribution, as described in Section 11.4. Following is the use of the chi-square test to accomplish the same objective, using the 5 percent level of significance.

$$H_0: \pi = 0.40 \qquad H_1: \pi \neq 0.40$$

$$df = k - m - 1 = 2 - 0 - 1 = 1$$

(There are two categories of observed frequencies, as indicated in Table 12.5.)

Table 12.5   Observed and Expected Frequencies for Example 8

	Participation in program		
	Yes	No	Total
Number observed in sample, f_o	10	40	50
Number expected in sample, f_e	20	30	50

Critical $\chi^2(df = 1, v = 0.05) = 3.84$

Computed χ^2 (Table 12.5 indicates the observed and expected frequencies):

$$\chi^2 = \sum \frac{(f_o - f_e)^2}{f_e} = \frac{(10 - 20)^2}{20} + \frac{(40 - 30)^2}{30} = 8.33$$

The calculated test statistic of 8.33 exceeds the critical value of 3.84. Therefore, the null hypothesis is rejected at the 5 percent level of significance, and we conclude that the proportion of program participants in the entire firm is not 0.40.

Testing the Difference between Two Population Proportions.   A procedure for testing the null hypothesis that there is no difference between two proportions based on use of the normal probability distribution is presented in Section 11.7. Mathematically, it can be shown that such a two-tail test is equivalent to a chi-square contingency table test in which the observed frequencies are entered in a 2×2 table. Again, there is no chi-square test equivalent to a one-sided test based on use of the normal probability distribution.

The sampling procedure used in conjunction with testing the difference between two proportions is that *two* random samples are collected, one for each of the two (k) categories. This contrasts with use of a 2×2 table for testing the independence of two variables in Section 12.3, in which *one* random sample is collected for the overall analysis.

EXAMPLE 9.   Example 8 in Section 11.7 reports that 10 out of 50 households in one community watched a TV special on the national economy and 15 out of 50 households in a second community watched the TV special. In that example the null hypothesis H_0: $(\pi_1 - \pi_2) = 0$ or, equivalently, H_0: $\pi_1 = \pi_2$ is tested at the 1 percent level of significance. Below is the equivalent test using the chi-square test statistic.

$$H_0: \pi_1 = \pi_2 \qquad H_1: \pi_1 \neq \pi_1$$
$$df = (r - 1)(k - 1) = (2 - 1)(2 - 1) = 1$$

(The observed frequencies are entered in a 2×2 table, as indicated in Table 12.6.)

Table 12.6   Extent of TV Program Viewing in Two Communities

	Communities		
	Community 1	Community 2	Total
Number watching	10	15	25
Number not watching	40	35	75
Total	50	50	100

Critical $\chi^2(df = 1, \alpha = 0.01) = 6.63$

Computed χ^2 (The observed frequencies are presented in Table 12.6 while the expected frequencies, calculated by formula (*12.3*), are presented in Table 12.7):

$$\chi^2 = \sum \frac{(f_o - f_e)^2}{f_e} = \frac{(10 - 12.5)^2}{12.5} + \frac{(15 - 12.5)^2}{12.5} + \frac{(40 - 37.5)^2}{37.5} + \frac{(35 - 37.5)^2}{37.5} = 1.34$$

Table 12.7   Expected Frequencies for the Data of Table 12.6

	Communities		
	Community 1	Community 2	Total
Number watching	12.5	12.5	25
Number not watching	37.5	37.5	75
Total	50	50	100

The calculated test statistic of 1.34 is *not* greater than the critical value of 6.63. Therefore, the null hypothesis cannot be rejected at the 1 percent level of significance, and we conclude that the proportion of viewers in the two communities may not differ. This is the same conclusion as in Section 11.7, using the z statistic.

Testing the Differences among Several Population Proportions.   Given the basic approach in Example 9, the chi-square test can be used to test the differences among several (k) population proportions by using a $2 \times k$ tabular design for the analysis of the frequencies. In this case, there is no mathematically equivalent procedure based on use of the z statistic. The null hypothesis is that the several population proportions are all mutually equal (or, that the several different sample proportions could have been obtained by chance from the same population). The sampling procedure is that several independent random samples are collected, one for each of the k data categories.

EXAMPLE 10.   From Example 9, suppose households in four communities are sampled in regard to the number viewing a TV special on the national economy. Table 12.8 presents the observed sample data while Table 12.9 presents the expected frequencies, based on Formula (*12.3*). The test of the null hypothesis that there are no differences among the population proportions, using the 1 percent level of significance, follows.

$$H_0\colon \pi_1 = \pi_2 = \pi_3 = \pi_4 \qquad H_1\colon \text{Not all } \pi_1 = \pi_2 = \pi_3 = \pi_4.$$

(*Note*:   Rejection of the null hypothesis does not indicate that *all* of the equalities are untrue, but only that *at least one* equality is untrue.)

$$df = (r - 1)(k - 1) = (2 - 1)(4 - 1) = 3$$

$$\text{Critical } \chi^2(df = 3, \alpha = 0.01) = 11.35$$

$$\chi^2 = \sum \frac{(f_o - f_e)^2}{f_e} = \frac{(10 - 12)^2}{12} + \frac{(15 - 12)^2}{12} + \frac{(5 - 12)^2}{12} + \frac{(18 - 12)^2}{12}$$

$$+ \frac{(40 - 38)^2}{38} + \frac{(35 - 38)^2}{38} + \frac{(45 - 38)^2}{38} + \frac{(32 - 38)^2}{38}$$

$$= 0.33 + 0.75 + 4.08 + 3.0 + 0.11 + 0.24 + 1.29 + 0.95 = 10.75$$

Table 12.8   Extent of TV Program Viewing in Four Communities

	Communities				
	1	2	3	4	Total
Number watching	10	15	5	18	48
Number not watching	40	35	45	32	152
Total	50	50	50	50	200

Table 12.9   Expected Frequencies for the Data of Table 12.8

	Communities				
	1	2	3	4	Total
Number watching	12.0	12.0	12.0	12.0	48
Number not watching	38.0	38.0	38.0	38.0	152
Total	50	50	50	50	200

The calculated chi-square statistic of 10.75 is *not* greater than the critical value of 11.35. Therefore the differences in the proportion of viewers among the four sampled communities are not large enough to reject the null hypothesis at the 1 percent level of significance. It is plausible that the proportions of the viewers in the several communities are the same, and do not differ.

12.5   USING COMPUTER SOFTWARE

Computer software for statistical analysis generally includes the capability of carrying out both goodness of fit tests and contingency table tests. For goodness of fit tests, both the observed frequencies and the expected frequencies usually have to be input for the analysis. The expected frequencies have to be input because they are based on the particular null hypothesis to be tested. For contingency table tests the expected frequencies are determined directly from the sample data. Therefore, such tests require input only of the observed frequencies in order to carry out the test. As explained in Sections 12.3 and 12.4, contingency table tests can be used for testing the independence of two categorical variables or for testing hypotheses concerning the equality of two or more population proportions. Excel requires a rather complex combination of procedures to carry out chi-square tests. Therefore, Solved Problem 12.15 illustrates only the use of Minitab.

Solved Problems

GOODNESS OF FIT TESTS

12.1.   It is claimed that an equal number of men and women patronize a retail outlet specializing in the sale of jeans. A random sample of 40 customers is observed, with 25 being men and 15 being women. Test the null hypothesis that the overall number of men and women customers is equal by applying the chi-square test and using the 5 percent level of significance.

From Table 12.10,

H_0: The number of men and women customers is equal (the pattern of frequencies is uniform).

H_1: The number of men and women customers is not equal.

$$df = k - m - 1 = 2 - 0 - 1 = 1$$

Critical $\chi^2(df = 1, \alpha = 0.05) = 3.84$

$$\chi^2 = \sum \frac{(f_o - f_e)^2}{f_e} = \frac{(25 - 20)^2}{20} + \frac{(15 - 20)^2}{20}$$

$$= \frac{(5)^2}{20} + \frac{(-5)^2}{20} = 2.50$$

The calculated test statistic of 2.50 is *not* greater than the critical value of 3.84. Therefore, the null hypothesis cannot be rejected at the 5 percent level of significance.

Table 12.10   Obtained and Expected Frequencies for Problem 12.1

	Customers		
	Men	Women	Total
Number in sample (f_o)	25	15	40
Number expected (f_e)	20	20	40

12.2.   With reference to Problem 12.1, suppose it had instead been claimed that twice as many men as compared with women were store customers. Using the observed data in Table 12.11, test this hypothesis using the 5 percent level of significance.

Table 12.11   Obtained and Expected Frequencies for Problem 12.2

	Customers		
	Men	Women	Total
Number in sample (f_o)	25	15	40
Number expected (f_e)	26.67	13.33	40

From Table 12.11

H_0: There are twice as many men as there are women customers.

H_1: There are not twice as many men as women customers.

$$df = k - m - 1 = 2 - 0 - 1 = 1$$

$$\text{Critical } \chi^2(df = 1, \alpha = 0.05) = 3.84$$

$$\chi^2 = \sum \frac{(f_o - f_e)^2}{f_e} = \frac{(25 - 26.67)^2}{26.67} + \frac{(15 - 13.33)^2}{13.33}$$

$$= \frac{(-1.67)^2}{26.67} + \frac{(1.67)^2}{13.33} = 0.10 + 0.21 = 0.31$$

The calculated chi-square statistic of 0.31 clearly does not exceed the critical value of 3.84. Therefore, the null hypothesis cannot be rejected at the 5 percent level of significance. The fact that neither of the null hypotheses in Problems 12.1 and 12.2 could be rejected demonstrates the benefit of the doubt given to the null hypothesis in each case. However, the size of the sample also affects the probability of sample results (see Problem 12.3).

12.3.   For the situation described in Problem 12.1, suppose the same null hypothesis is tested, but that the sample frequencies in each category are exactly doubled. That is, of 80 randomly selected customers 50 are men and 30 are women. Test the null hypothesis at the 5 percent level of significance and compare your decision with the one in Problem 12.1.

From Table 12.12,

H_0: The number of men and women customers is equal.

H_1: The number of men and women customers is not equal.

$$df = k - m - 1 = 2 - 0 - 1 = 1$$

$$\text{Critical } \chi^2(df = 1, \alpha = 0.05) = 3.84$$

$$\chi^2 = \sum \frac{(f_o - f_e)^2}{f_e} = \frac{(50 - 40)^2}{40} + \frac{(30 - 40)^2}{40} = 5.00$$

The calculated chi-square value of 5.00 is greater than the critical value of 3.84. Therefore, the null hypothesis is rejected at the 5 percent level of significance. Even though the sample data are proportionally the same as in Problem 12.1, the decision now is reject H_0 instead of accept H_0. This demonstrates the greater sensitivity of a statistical test associated with a larger sample size.

Table 12.12   Obtained and Expected Frequencies for Problem 12.3

	Customers		
	Men	Women	Total
Number in sample (f_o)	50	30	80
Number expected (f_e)	40	40	80

12.4. A manufacturer of refrigerators offers three basic product lines, which can be described as being low, intermediate, and high in terms of comparative price. Before a sales promotion aimed at highlighting the virtues of the high-priced refrigerators, the percentage of sales in the three categories was 45, 30, and 25, respectively. Of a random sample of 50 refrigerators sold after the promotion, the number sold in the low-, intermediate-, and high-priced categories is 15, 15, and 20, respectively. Test the null hypothesis that the current pattern of sales does not differ from the historical pattern, using the 5 percent level of significance.

With reference to Table 12.13,

H_0: The present pattern of sales frequencies follows the historical pattern.

H_1: The present pattern of sales frequencies is different from the historical pattern.

$$df = k - m - 1 = 3 - 0 - 1 = 2$$

$$\text{Critical } \chi^2(df = 2, \alpha = 0.05) = 5.99$$

$$\chi^2 = \sum \frac{(f_o - f_e)^2}{f_e} = \frac{(15 - 22.5)^2}{22.5} + \frac{(15 - 15)^2}{15} + \frac{(20 - 12.5)^2}{12.5}$$

$$= \frac{(-7.5)^2}{22.5} + \frac{(0)^2}{15} + \frac{(7.5)^2}{12.5} = 7.00$$

Table 12.13   Obtained and Expected Frequencies for Problem 12.4

	Price category of refrigerator			
	Low	Intermediate	High	Total
Number sold (f_o)	15	15	20	50
Number expected to be sold (f_e)	22.5	15	12.5	50

The calculated value of the test statistic of 7.00 is greater than the critical value of 5.99. Therefore, the null hypothesis is rejected at the 5 percent level of significance. Although such rejection does not itself indicate in what respect the present pattern of sales differs from the historical pattern, a review of Table 12.13 indicates that more high-priced and fewer low-priced refrigerators were sold than would be expected in terms of the historical pattern of sales.

12.5. Any probability model can serve as the basis for determining the expected frequencies associated with a goodness of fit test (see Section 12.2). Suppose it is hypothesized that the distribution of machine breakdowns per hour in any assembly plant conforms to a Poisson probability distribution, as described in Section 6.6. However, the particular Poisson distribution as determined by the mean of the distribution, λ, is not specified. Table 12.14 presents the observed number of breakdowns during 40 sampled hours.

Table 12.14   Observed Number of Machine Breakdowns during 40 Sampled Hours and Worksheet for the Calculation of the Average Number of Breakdowns per Hour

Number of breakdowns (X)	Observed frequency (f_o)	$f_o(X)$
0	0	0
1	6	6
2	8	16
3	11	33
4	7	28
5	4	20
6	3	18
7	1	7
	$\Sigma f_o = \overline{40}$	$\Sigma[f_o(X)] = \overline{128}$

(*a*)   Determine the value of λ to be used to test the hypothesis that the number of machine breakdowns conforms to a Poisson probability distribution.

(*b*)   Construct the table of expected frequencies based on use of the Poisson distribution identified in (*a*) for a sample of $n = 40$ hr.

(*a*) $\bar{X} = \dfrac{\Sigma[f_o(X)]}{\Sigma f_o} = \dfrac{128}{40} = 3.2$ breakdowns per hour

Therefore, we set the mean of the Poisson distribution at $\lambda = 3.2$.

(*b*)   The expected frequencies are determined by reference to Appendix 4 for the Poisson probability distribution. See Table 12.15

Table 12.15   Determination of Expected Frequencies for the Machine-Breakdown Problem According to the Poisson Distribution, with $\lambda = 3.2$ and $n = 40$

Number of breakdowns (X)	Probability (P)	Expected frequency $f_e(=nP)$
0	0.0408	1.6
1	0.1304	5.2
2	0.2087	8.3
3	0.2226	8.9
4	0.1781	7.1
5	0.1140	4.6
6	0.0608	2.4
7	0.0278	1.1
8	0.0111	0.4
9	0.0040	0.2
10	0.0013	0.1
11	0.0004	0.0
12	0.0001	0.0
13	0.0000	0.0
Total	1.0001	39.9

12.6. Given the information in Tables 12.14 and 12.15, test the null hypothesis that the distribution of machine breakdowns per hour conforms to a Poisson pattern at the 5 percent level of significance.

H_0: The observed distribution of machine breakdowns per hour conforms to a Poisson-distributed variable.

H_1: The distribution of machine breakdowns does not conform to a Poisson-distributed variable.

Critical χ^2: Table 12.16 indicates the observed and expected frequencies to be compared. Note that in order to satisfy the requirement that each f_e be at least 5, a number of categories at each end of the frequency distribution had to be combined. Further, one parameter, λ, was estimated on the basis of the sample. Therefore, $df = k - m - 1 = 5 - 1 - 1 = 3$, and the critical $\chi^2(df = 3, \alpha = 0.05) = 7.81$.

Computed χ^2: As indicated in Table 12.16, the computed $\chi^2 = 0.675$.

Table 12.16   Observed and Expected Frequencies for the Machine-Breakdown Problem and the Calculation of the Chi-Square Value

Number of breakdowns	Observed frequency (f_o)	Expected frequency (f_e)	$\dfrac{(f_o - f_e)^2}{f_e}$
0	0 ⎫ 6	1.6 ⎫ 6.8	0.094
1	6 ⎭	5.2 ⎭	
2	8	8.3	0.011
3	11	8.9	0.496
4	7	7.1	0.001
5	4 ⎫	4.6 ⎫	
6	3 ⎪	2.4 ⎪	
7	1 ⎬ 8	1.1 ⎬ 8.8	0.073
8	0 ⎪	0.4 ⎪	
9	0 ⎪	0.2 ⎪	
10	0 ⎭	0.1 ⎭	$\chi^2 = \overline{0.675}$

Because the calculated test statistic of 0.675 clearly does not exceed the critical value of 7.81, the null hypothesis that the number of machine breakdowns per hour is a Poisson-distributed variable cannot be rejected at the 5 percent level of significance.

12.7. With respect to the sample data presented in Problem 12.5, suppose that in an established similar assembly plant machine breakdowns per hour follow a Poisson distribution with $\lambda = 2.5$. Determine if the breakdowns in the present plant differ significantly from a Poisson pattern based on $\lambda = 2.5$, using the 5 percent level of significance.

In this case, no parameter is estimated on the basis of the sample, and the expected frequencies are determined on the basis of the Poisson distribution with the mean $\lambda = 2.5$.

H_0: The observed distribution of machine breakdowns per hour conforms to a Poisson-distributed variable with $\lambda = 2.5$.

H_1: The observed distribution of machine breakdowns per hour does not conform to a Poisson-distributed variable with $\lambda = 2.5$.

Table 12.17 illustrates the determination of the expected frequencies.

Table 12.17   Determination of Expected Frequencies for the Machine-Breakdown Problem According to the Poisson Distribution, with $\lambda = 2.5$ and with $n = 40$

Number of breakdowns (X)	Probability (P)	Expected frequency $f_e(=nP)$
0	0.0821	3.3
1	0.2052	8.2
2	0.2565	10.3
3	0.2138	8.6
4	0.1336	5.3
5	0.0668	2.7
6	0.0278	1.1
7	0.0099	0.4
8	0.0031	0.1
9	0.0009	0.0
10	0.0002	0.0
Total	0.9999	40.0

Critical χ^2: Table 12.18 indicates the observed and expected frequencies to be compared. With the reduced number of categories being $k = 4$, and with no parameter estimated on the basis of the sample, $df = k - m - 1 = 4 - 0 - 1 = 3$, and critical $\chi^2(df = 3, \alpha = 0.05) = 7.81$.

Computed χ^2: As indicated in Table 12.18, the computed $\chi^2 = 6.85$.

The calculated chi-square statistic of 6.85 does not exceed the critical value of 7.81. Therefore, the null hypothesis that the number of machine breakdowns per hour is distributed as a Poisson variable with $\lambda = 2.5$ cannot be rejected at the 5 percent level of significance. As would be expected, the χ^2 test statistic is larger in this problem than in Problem 12.6, where λ was based on the sample mean itself. However, the test statistic is still in the region of acceptance of the null hypothesis.

Table 12.18   Observed and Expected Frequencies for the Machine-Breakdown Problem and the Calculation of the Chi-Square Value

Number of breakdowns (X)	Observed frequency (f_o)	Expected frequency (f_e)	$\dfrac{(f_o - f_e)^2}{f_e}$
0	0 } 6	3.3 } 11.5	2.63
1	6	8.2	
2	8	10.3	0.51
3	11	8.6	0.67
4	7	5.3	
5	4	2.7	
6	3 } 15	1.1 } 9.6	3.04
7	1	0.4	
8	0	0.1	
			$\chi^2 = \overline{6.85}$

Table 12.19   Industrial Injuries in 50 Firms

Average number of injuries per thousand worker-hours	Number of firms
1.5–1.7	3
1.8–2.0	12
2.1–2.3	14
2.4–2.6	9
2.7–2.9	7
3.0–3.2	5
	$\overline{50}$

12.8.   Table 12.19, taken from Problem 2.16, indicates the average number of injuries per thousand worker-hours in a sample of 50 firms taken from a particular industry. The mean for this variable is $\bar{X} = 2.32$ and the sample standard deviation is $s = 0.42$. Test the null hypothesis that the population pattern of frequencies is distributed as a normal distribution, using the 5 percent level of significance.

H_0: The frequency distribution follows a normal distribution.

H_1: The frequency distribution does not follow a normal distribution.

The expected frequencies are determined in Table 12.20, based on use of Appendix 5 for the standard normal distribution and using the sample mean and sample standard deviation as estimators for the respective population parameters. Table 12.21 indicates the observed and expected frequencies to be compared.

$$df = k - m - 1 = 4 - 2 - 1 = 1$$
$$\text{Critical } \chi^2(df = 1, \alpha = 0.05) = 3.84$$
$$\text{Computed } \chi^2 = 1.65 \quad \text{(as indicated in Table 12.21)}$$

The calculated chi-square statistic of 1.65 is not greater than the critical value of 3.84. Therefore, the null hypothesis that the frequency distribution of accident rates is normally distributed cannot be rejected at the 5 percent level of significance, and the hypothesis is therefore accepted as being plausible.

Table 12.20   Determination of Expected Frequencies for the Industrial Injuries in 50 Firms

Average number of injuries per thousand worker-hours (class boundaries)	Class boundaries in standard-normal units (z)*	Probability of being in each category $(P)^{\dagger}$	Expected frequency $(= 50 \times P)$
1.45–1.75	-2.07 to -1.36	0.09	4.5
1.75–2.05	-1.36 to -0.64	0.17	8.5
2.05–2.35	-0.64 to 0.07	0.27	13.5
2.35–2.65	0.07 to 0.79	0.26	13.0
2.65–2.95	0.79 to 1.50	0.15	7.5
2.95–3.25	1.50 to 2.21	0.07	3.5
		$\overline{1.01}$	$\overline{50.5}$

* Based on $\hat{\mu} = \bar{X} = 2.32$ and $\hat{\sigma} = s = 0.42$; for example, for $X = 1.45$, $z = (X - \hat{\mu})/\hat{\sigma} = (1.45 - 2.32)/0.42 = -2.07$.

$\dagger$ The first probability value of 0.09 is the proportion of area in the entire tail to the left of $z = -1.36$ and the last probability value of 0.07 is the proportion of area in the entire tail to the right of $z = 1.50$. This procedure is necessary for the end classes so that the entire area under the normal curve is allocated in the frequency distribution.

Table 12.21   Observed and Expected Frequencies for the Industrial Injuries Data and the Determinations of the χ^2 Value

Average number of injuries per thousand worker-hours	Observed frequency (f_o)	Expected frequency (f_e)	$\dfrac{(f_o - f_e)^2}{f_e}$
1.5–1.7	3 ⎫ 15	4.5 ⎫ 13.0	0.31
1.8–2.0	12 ⎭	8.5 ⎭	
2.1–2.3	14	13.5	0.02
2.4–2.6	9	13.0	1.23
2.7–2.9	7 ⎫ 12	7.5 ⎫ 11.0	0.09
3.0–3.2	5 ⎭	3.5 ⎭	
			$\chi^2 = \overline{1.65}$

TESTS FOR THE INDEPENDENCE OF TWO CATEGORICAL VARIABLES (CONTINGENCY TABLE TESTS)

12.9.   Table 12.22 (a contingency table taken from Problem 5.21) presents voter reactions to a new property tax plan according to party affiliation. From these data, construct a table of the expected frequencies based on the assumption that there is no relationship between party affiliation and reaction to the tax plan.

Table 12.22   Contingency Table for Voter Reactions to a New Property Tax Plan

Party affiliation	Reaction			Total
	In favor	Neutral	Opposed	
Democratic	120	20	20	160
Republican	50	30	60	140
Independent	50	10	40	100
Total	220	60	120	400

The expected cell frequencies presented in Table 12.23 are determined by the formula $f_e = (f_r f_k)/n$ (see Section 12.3).

Table 12.23   Table of Expected Frequencies for the Observed Frequencies Reported in Table 12.22

Party affiliation	Reaction			Total
	In favor	Neutral	Opposed	
Democratic	88	24	48	160
Republican	77	21	42	140
Independent	55	15	30	100
Total	220	60	120	400

12.10. Referring to Table 12.22 and 12.23, test the null hypothesis that there is no relationship between party affiliation and voter reaction, using the 1 percent level of significance.

H_0: Party affiliation and voter reaction are independent (there is no relationship).

H_1: Party affiliation and voter reaction are not independent.

$$df = (r - 1)(k - 1) = (3 - 1)(3 - 1) = 4$$

$$\text{Critical } \chi^2(df = 4, \alpha = 0.01) = 13.28$$

$$\chi^2 = \sum \frac{(f_o - f_e)^2}{f_e} = \frac{(120 - 88)^2}{88} + \frac{(20 - 24)^2}{24} + \frac{(20 - 48)^2}{48} + \frac{(50 - 77)^2}{77}$$

$$+ \frac{(30 - 21)^2}{21} + \frac{(60 - 42)^2}{42} + \frac{(50 - 55)^2}{55} + \frac{(10 - 15)^2}{15} + \frac{(40 - 30)^2}{30}$$

$$= 11.64 + 0.67 + 16.33 + 9.47 + 3.86 + 7.71 + 0.45 + 1.67 + 3.33 = 55.13$$

The calculated test statistic of 55.13 clearly exceeds the critical value of 13.28. Therefore, the null hypothesis is rejected at the 1 percent level of significance, and we conclude that there is a relationship between party affiliation and reaction to the new tax plan.

12.11. Table 12.24 indicates student reaction to expansion of a college athletic program according to class standing where "lower division" indicates freshman or sophomore class standing and "upper division" indicates junior or senior class standing. Test the null hypothesis that class standing and reaction to expanding the athletic program are independent variables, using the 5 percent level of significance.

H_0: Class standing and reaction to expanding the athletic program are independent.

H_1: Class standing and reaction to expanding the athletic program are not independent.

$$df = (r - 1)(k - 1) = (2 - 1)(2 - 1) = 1$$

$$\text{Critical } \chi^2(df = 1, \alpha = 0.05) = 3.84$$

Table 12.24   Student Reaction to Expanding the Athletic Program According to Class Standing

Reaction	Class standing		Total
	Lower division	Upper division	
In favor	20	19	39
Against	10	16	26
Total	30	35	65

Computed χ^2 (The expected cell frequencies are presented in Table 12.25):

$$\chi^2 = \sum \frac{(f_o - f_e)^2}{f_e} = \frac{(20 - 18)^2}{18} + \frac{(19 - 21)^2}{21} + \frac{(10 - 12)^2}{12} + \frac{(16 - 14)^2}{14} = 1.03$$

The calculated test statistic of 1.03 is *not* greater than the critical value of 3.84. Therefore, the null hypothesis cannot be rejected at the 5 percent level of significance, and the hypothesis that the two variables are independent is accepted as being plausible.

TESTING HYPOTHESES CONCERNING PROPORTIONS

12.12. Since Problem 12.1 involves a 1×2 table of observed frequencies, the procedure is equivalent to testing a hypothesis concerning the value of the population proportion, as explained in Section 12.4.

Table 12.25   Table of Expected Frequencies for the Observed Frequencies Reported in Table 12.24

Reaction	Class standing		Total
	Lower division	Upper division	
In favor	18	21	39
Against	12	14	26
Total	30	35	65

(a)   Formulate the null hypothesis as a hypothesized proportion and interpret the result of the test carried out in Problem 12.1 from this standpoint.

(b)   Test the hypothesized proportion by using the normal probability distribution as the basis of the test and demonstrate that the result is equivalent to using the chi-square test.

(a) H_0: The proportion of mean customers $\pi = 0.50$; H_1: $\pi \neq 0.50$

$$\text{Critical } \chi^1(df = 1, \alpha = 0.05) = 3.84$$
$$\chi^2 = 2.50 \qquad \text{(from Problem 12.1)}$$

The calculated chi-square value of 2.50 is not greater than the critical value of 3.84. Therefore, we cannot reject the hypothesis that $\pi = 0.50$ at the 5 percent level of significance.

(b) H_0: $\pi = 0.50$ H_1: $\pi \neq 0.50$

$$\text{Critical } z(\alpha = 0.05) = \pm 1.96$$

Using formula (*11.12*),

$$\sigma_{\hat{p}} = \sqrt{\frac{\pi_0(1 - \pi_0)}{n}} = \sqrt{\frac{(0.50)(0.50)}{40}} = \sqrt{\frac{0.25}{40}} = \sqrt{0.00625} = 0.079$$

From formula (*11.14*),

$$z = \frac{\hat{p} - \pi_0}{\sigma_{\hat{p}}} = \frac{0.375 - 0.50}{0.079} = \frac{-0.125}{0.079} = -1.58$$

The calculated z value of -1.58 is not in a region of rejection of the null hypothesis. Therefore, the null hypothesis cannot be rejected at the 5 percent level of significance, and we conclude that $\pi = 0.50$.

12.13. Because Problem 12.11 involves a 2×2 table of observed frequencies, the procedure is equivalent to testing the null hypothesis that there is no difference between two population proportions. State the null and alternative hypothesis from this point of view and interpret the test carried out in Problem 12.11. In this case we assume that two independent random samples, one for each student class standing, were collected.

$$H_0: \pi_1 = \pi_2 \qquad H_1: \pi_1 \neq \pi_2$$

where π_1 = proportion of lower-division students in favor of expanding the athletic program
     π_2 = proportion of upper-division students in favor of expanding the athletic program

$$\text{Critical } \chi^2(df = 1, \alpha = 0.05) = 3.84$$
$$\chi^2 = 1.03 \qquad \text{(from Problem 12.11)}$$

The calculated test statistic of 1.03 is not greater than the critical value of 3.84. Therefore, the null hypothesis cannot be rejected at the 5 percent level of significance, and the hypothesis that the proportion of lower-division students in favor of expanding the athletic program is equal to the proportion of upper-division students with this view is accepted as being plausible.

12.14. Table 12.26 represents an extension of the study discussed in Problems 12.11 and 12.13. Formulate the null hypothesis from the viewpoint that a $2 \times k$ table of frequencies can be used to test the equality of several population proportions, and carry out the test using the 5 percent level of significance. In this case we assume that three independent random samples were collected, one for each student class standing.

$$H_0: \pi_1 = \pi_2 = \pi_3 \qquad H_1: \text{Not all } \pi_1 = \pi_2 = \pi_3$$

where π_1 = proportion of lower-division students in favor of expanding the athletic program
π_2 = proportion of upper-division students in favor of expanding the athletic program
π_3 = proportion of graduate students in favor of expanding the athletic program

$$df = (r-1)(k-1) = (2-1)(3-1) = 2$$
$$\text{Critical } \chi^2(df = 2, \alpha = 0.05) = 5.99$$

Table 12.26   Student Reaction to Expanding the Athletic Program According to Class Standing

Reaction	Class standing			Total
	Lower division	Upper division	Graduate	
In favor	20	19	15	54
Against	10	16	35	61
Total	30	35	50	115

Computed χ^2 (The expected cell frequencies are presented in Table 12.27):

$$\chi^2 = \sum \frac{(f_o - f_e)^2}{f_e} = \frac{(20 - 14.1)^2}{14.1} + \frac{(19 - 16.4)^2}{16.4} + \frac{(15 - 23.5)^2}{23.5}$$
$$+ \frac{(10 - 15.9)^2}{15.9} + \frac{(16 - 18.6)^2}{18.6} + \frac{(35 - 26.5)^2}{26.5} = 11.23$$

Table 12.27   Table of Expected Frequencies for the Observed Frequencies in Table 12.26

Reaction	Class standing			Total
	Lower division	Upper division	Graduate	
In favor	14.1	16.4	23.5	54
Against	15.9	18.6	26.5	61
Total	30	35	50	115

The calculated chi-square test statistic of 11.23 exceeds the critical value of 5.99. Therefore, the null hypothesis is rejected at the 5 percent level of significance and we conclude that all three population proportions are not equal. Thus, there is a difference in student reaction according to class standing.

USING MINITAB

12.15. Refer to the contingency table data in Table 12.22. Using Minitab, test the null hypothesis that there is no relationship between party affiliation and voter reaction, using the 1 percent level of significance.

H_0: Party affiliation and voter reaction are independent (there is no relationship).
H_1: Party affiliation and voter reaction are not independent.

From the computer output in Fig. 12-1:

$$df = 4$$
$$\text{Computed } \chi^2 = 55.130$$
$$\text{Critical } \chi^2(df = 4, \alpha = 0.01) = 13.28 \quad \text{(from Appendix 7)}$$

Refer to Fig. 12-1. The Minitab output includes the expected frequencies, as well as the observed frequencies, the calculated chi-square test statistic, the degrees of freedom for the test, and the calculated P value. The reported chi-square value corresponds to the hand-calculated value in Problem 12.10. The P value is 0.000 (to the third decimal place). Therefore, the null hypothesis is rejected, and we conclude that there is a relationship between party affiliation and reaction to the new tax plan in the sampled population.

The Minitab output given in Fig. 12-1 was obtained as follows:

Chi-Square Test: In favor, Neutral, Opposed

```
Expected counts are printed below observed counts

        In favor  Neutral  Opposed    Total
   1        120       20       20       160
          88.00    24.00    48.00

   2         50       30       60       140
          77.00    21.00    42.00

   3         50       10       40       100
          55.00    15.00    30.00

Total       220       60      120       400

Chi-Sq = 11.636 +  0.667 + 16.333 +
          9.468 +  3.857 +  7.714 +
          0.455 +  1.667 +  3.333 = 55.130
DF = 4, P-Value = 0.000
```

Fig. 12-1 Minitab output.

(1) Open Minitab. In the column name cell for C1, enter: In Favor. Enter the three observed frequencies for this category in column C1. In the column name cell for C2 enter: Neutral. Enter the three associated frequencies in column C2. In the column name cell for C3 enter: Opposed. Enter the three associated frequencies in column C3.

(2) Click **Stat** → **Tables** → **Chi-Square Test**.

(3) In the resulting dialog box, for **Columns containing the table** enter: C1-C3. Click **OK**.

Supplementary Problems

GOODNESS OF FIT TESTS

12.16. Refer to Table 12.28 and test the null hypothesis that the consumer preferences for the four brands of wine are equal, using the 1 percent level of significance.
Ans. Reject H_0.

12.17. Using Table 12.28, test the hypothesis that Brand C is preferred by as many as the other three brands combined at the 1 percent level of significance.
Ans. Accept H_0.

Table 12.28   Consumer Panel Preferences for Four Brands of Rhine Wine

Brand				
A	B	C	D	Total
30	20	40	10	100

12.18. Table 12.29 reports the single most important safety feature desired by a random sample of car purchasers. Test the null hypothesis that the general population of car buyers is equally distributed in terms of primary preference for these safety features, using the (*a*) 5 percent and (*b*) 1 percent level of significance.
   Ans.   (*a*) Reject H_0, (*b*) accept H_0.

Table 12.29   Identification of Most Important Safety Feature Desired by Car Buyers

Safety feature					
ABS brakes	Modified suspension	Air bags	Automatic door locks	Cruise control	Total
20	10	30	25	15	100

12.19. In a college course in business statistics, the historical distribution of the A, B, C, D, and E grades has been 10, 30, 40, 10, and 10 percent, respectively. A particular class taught by a new instructor completes the semester with 8 students earning a grade of A, 17 with B, 20 with C, 3 with D, and 2 with E. Test the null hypothesis that this sample does not differ significantly from the historical pattern, using the 5 percent level of significance.
   Ans.   Accept H_0.

12.20. Table 12.30 reports the number of computer chips that do not meet a stringent quality requirement in 20 samples of $n = 10$ each. Test the null hypothesis that this distribution is not significantly different from the binomial distribution with $n = 10$ and $p = 0.30$, using the 5 percent level of significance.
   Ans.   Reject H_0.

Table 12.30   Number of Defective Computer Chips in 20 Samples of Size $n = 10$ Each

Number defective per sample	0	1	2	3	4	5	6	7	8	9	10
Number of samples	0	1	2	4	5	5	2	1	0	0	0

12.21. Refer to Table 2.18 (page 40). For these data, $\bar{X} = 28.95$ and $s = 2.52$. Test the null hypothesis that this distribution of frequencies conforms to a normal distribution pattern at the 5 percent level of significance.
   Ans.   Cannot be tested, because $df = 0$.

12.22. Refer to Table 2.21 (page 42). For this sample data, $\bar{X} = 23.3$ years and $s = 3.4$ years. Test the null hypothesis that this distribution of frequencies follows a normal distribution pattern, using the 1 percent level of significance.
   Ans.   Reject H_0.

TESTS FOR THE INDEPENDENCE OF TWO CATEGORICAL VARIABLES (CONTINGENCY TABLE TESTS)

12.23. As an extension of Problem 12.18, the opinions of men and women were tallied separately (see Table 12.31). Test the hypothesis that there is no relationship between sex and which safety feature is preferred, using the 1 percent level of significance.

Ans.   Reject H_0.

Table 12.31   Identification of Most Important Safety Feature Desired by Car Buyers, According to Sex

Respondents	ABS brakes	Modified suspension	Air bags	Automatic door locks	Cruise control	Total
Men	15	5	20	5	5	50
Women	5	5	10	20	10	50
Total	20	10	30	25	15	100

12.24. In order to investigate the relationship between employment status at the time a loan was arranged and whether or not the loan is now in default, a loan company manager randomly chooses 100 accounts, with the results indicated in Table 12.32. Test the null hypothesis that employment status and status of the loan are independent variables, using the 5 percent level of significance for the test.

Ans.   Accept H_0.

Table 12.32   Employment Status and Loan Status for a Sample of 100 Accounts

Present status of loan	Employment status at time of loan		Total
	Employed	Unemployed	
In default	10	8	18
Not in default	60	22	82
Total	70	30	100

12.25. An elementary school principal categorizes parents into three income categories according to residential area, and into three levels of participation in school programs. From Table 12.33, test the hypothesis that there is no relationship between income level and school program participation, using the 5 percent level of significance. Consider the meaning of the test results.

Ans.   Reject H_0.

TESTING HYPOTHESES CONCERNING PROPORTIONS

12.26. Refer to Problems 12.16 to 12.25 and identify those applications of the chi-square test that are equivalent to testing a hypothesis concerning the value of the population proportion. For each problem you identify, formulate such a null hypothesis.

Ans.   Problem 12.17

$$H_0: \pi \text{ (for Brand C)} = 0.50; \qquad H_1: \pi \neq 0.50$$

Table 12.33   Income Level and Participation in School Programs by Parents of Elementary School Students

Program participation	Income level			Total
	Low	Middle	High	
Never	28	48	16	92
Occasional	22	65	14	101
Regular	17	74	3	94
Total	67	187	33	287

12.27. Refer to Problems 12.16 to 12.25 and identify those applications which are equivalent to testing the null hypothesis that there is no difference between two population proportions, recognizing that two separate random samples are required. For each problem you identify, formulate such a null hypothesis.
Ans. Problem 12.24.

$$H_0: \pi_1 = \pi_2;$$
$$H_1: \pi_1 \neq \pi_2 \text{ (where } \pi_1 = \text{proportion of employed in default and}$$
$$\pi_2 = \text{proportion of unemployed in default)}$$

COMPUTER OUTPUT

12.28. Refer to the contingency table data in Table 12.33. Use available computer software to test the null hypothesis that there is no relationship between income level and program participation, using the 5 percent level of significance.
Ans. Reject H_0.

CHAPTER 13

Analysis of Variance

13.1 BASIC RATIONALE ASSOCIATED WITH TESTING THE DIFFERENCES AMONG SEVERAL POPULATION MEANS

Whereas the chi-square test can be used to test the differences among several population proportions (see Section 12.4), the analysis of variance can be used to test the differences among several population means. The null hypothesis is that the several population means are mutually equal. The sampling procedure used is that several independent random samples are collected, one for each of the data categories (treatment levels).

The assumption underlying the use of the analysis of variance is that the several sample means were obtained from normally distributed populations having the same variance σ^2. However, the test procedure has been found to be relatively unaffected by violations of the normality assumption when the populations are unimodal and the sample sizes are approximately equal. Because the null hypothesis is that the population means are equal, the assumption of equal variance (*homogeneity of variance*) also implies that for practical purposes the test is concerned with the hypothesis that the means came from the same population. This is so because any normally distributed population is defined by the mean and variance (or standard deviation) as the two parameters. (See Section 7.2 for a general description of the normal probability distribution.) All of the computational procedures presented in this chapter are for fixed-effects models as contrasted to random-effects models. This distinction is explained in Section 13.6.

The basic rationale underlying the analysis of variance was first developed by the British statistician Ronald A. Fisher for the purpose of designing experiments and interpreting experimental data. The F distribution described below was named in his honor. The conceptual rationale is as follows:

(1) Compute the mean for each sample group and then determine the standard error of the mean $s_{\bar{x}}$ *based only on the several sample means*. Computationally, this is the standard deviation of these several mean values.

(2) Now, given the formula $s_{\bar{x}} = s/\sqrt{n}$, it follows that $s = \sqrt{n}s_{\bar{x}}$ and that $s^2 = ns_{\bar{x}}^2$. Therefore, the standard error of the mean computed in (1) can be used to estimate the variance of the (common) population from which the several samples were obtained. This estimate of the population variance is called the *mean square among treatment groups* (*MSTR*). Fisher called any variance estimate a mean square because computationally a variance is the mean of the squared deviations from the group mean (see Section 4.6).

(3) Compute the variance separately for each sample group and with respect to each group mean. Then pool these variance values by weighting them according to $n - 1$ for each sample. This weighting procedure for the variance is an extension of the procedure for combining and weighting two sample

241

variances (see Section 11.1). The resulting estimate of the population variance is called the *mean square error (MSE)* and is based on *within* group differences only. Again, it is called a mean square because it is a variance estimate. It is due to "error" because the deviations within each of the sample groups can be due only to random sampling error, and they cannot be due to any differences among the means of the population groups.

(4)   If the null hypothesis that $\mu_1 = \mu_2 = \mu_3 = \cdots = \mu_k$ is true, then it follows that each of the two mean squares obtained in (2) and (3) is an unbiased and independent estimator of the same population variance σ^2. However, if the null hypothesis is false, then the expected value of *MSTR* is larger than *MSE*. Essentially, any differences among the population means will inflate *MSTR* while having no effect on *MSE*, which is based on *within* group differences only.

(5)   Based on the observation in (4), the *F* distribution can be used to test the difference between the two variances, as described in Section 11.9. A one-sided test is involved, and the general form of the *F* test in the analysis of variance is

$$F_{df_1, df_2} = \frac{MSTR}{MSE} \tag{13.1}$$

If the *F* ratio is in the region of rejection for the specified level of significance, then the null hypothesis that the several population means are mutually equal is rejected.

Problem 13.1 illustrates the application of these five steps to a hypothesis testing problem involving three data categories, or treatments.

Although the above steps are useful for describing the conceptual approach underlying the analysis of variance (ANOVA), extension of this procedure for designs that are more complex than the simple comparison of *k* sample means is cumbersome. Therefore, in the following sections of this chapter each design is described in terms of the linear model that identifies the components influencing the random variable. Also, a standard analysis of variance table that includes the formulas that are needed for the calculation of the required mean square values is presented for each type of experimental design.

13.2   ONE-FACTOR COMPLETELY RANDOMIZED DESIGN (ONE-WAY ANOVA)

The one-way analysis of variance procedure is concerned with testing the difference among *k* sample means when the subjects are assigned randomly to each of the several treatment groups. Therefore, the general explanation in Section 13.1 concerns this one-way classification model.

The linear equation, or model, that represents the one-factor completely randomized design is

$$X_{ik} = \mu + \alpha_k + \varepsilon_{ik} \tag{13.2}$$

where $\mu =$ the overall mean of all *k* treatment populations
$\alpha_k =$ effect of the treatment in the particular group *k* from which the value was sampled
$\varepsilon_{ik} =$ the random error associated with the process of sampling (ε is the Greek epsilon)

Table 13.1 is the summary table for the one-factor completely randomized design of the analysis of variance, including all computational formulas. The application of these formulas to sample data is illustrated in Problems 13.2 to 13.4. The symbol system used in this table is somewhat different from that used in Section 13.1 because of the need to use a system which can be extended logically to two-way analysis of variance. Thus, *MSTR* becomes the *mean square among the A treatment groups (MSA)*. Further, note that the definition of symbols in the context of analysis of variance is not necessarily consistent with the use of these symbols in general statistical analysis. For example, α_k in *(13.2)* is concerned with the effect on a randomly sampled value originating from the treatment group in which the value is located; it has nothing to do with the concept of α in general hypothesis testing procedures as described in Section 10.2. Similarly, *N* in Table 13.1 designates the total size of the sample for all treatment groups combined, rather than a population size. New symbols included in Table 13.1 are T_k, which represents the sum (total) of the values in a particular treatment group, and *T*, which represents the sum of the sampled values in all groups combined.

Table 13.1   Summary Table for One-Way Analysis of Variance (Treatment Groups Need Not Be Equal)

Source of variation	Degrees of freedom (df)	Sum of squares (SS)	Mean square (MS)	F ratio
Among treatment groups (A)	$K - 1$	$SSA = \sum_{k=1}^{K} \dfrac{T_k^2}{n_k} - \dfrac{T^2}{N}$	$MSA = \dfrac{SSA}{K - 1}$	$F = \dfrac{MSA}{MSE}$
Sampling error (E)	$N - K$	$SSE = SST - SSA$	$MSE = \dfrac{SSE}{N - K}$	
Total (T)	$N - 1$	$SST = \sum_{i=1}^{n} \sum_{k=1}^{K} X^2 - \dfrac{T^2}{N}$		

Instead of the form of the null hypothesis described in paragraph (4) of Section 13.1, the general form of the null hypothesis in the analysis of variance makes reference to the relevant component of the linear model. Thus, for the one-way analysis of variance the null and alternative hypotheses can be stated as

H_0: $\mu_1 = \mu_2 = \cdots = \mu_k$ $\qquad$ or, equivalently, $\qquad$ H_0: $\alpha_k = 0$ $\quad$ for all treatments (factor levels)

H_1: not all $\mu_1 = \mu_2 = \cdots = \mu_k$ $\qquad\qquad\qquad\qquad\qquad$ H_1: $\alpha_k \neq 0$ $\quad$ for some treatments

13.3   TWO-WAY ANALYSIS OF VARIANCE (TWO-WAY ANOVA)

Two-way analysis of variance is based on two dimensions of classifications, or treatments. For example, in analyzing the level of achievement in a training program we could consider both the effect of the method of instruction and the effect of prior school achievement. Similarly, we could investigate gasoline mileage according to the weight category of the car and according to the grade of gasoline. In data tables, the treatments identified in the column headings are typically called the A treatments; those in the row headings are called the B treatments.

Interaction in a two-factor experiment means that the two treatments are not independent, and that the effect of a particular treatment in one factor differs according to levels of the other factor. For example, in studying automobile mileage a higher-octane gasoline may improve mileage for certain types of cars but not for others. Similarly, the effectiveness of various methods of instruction may differ according to the ability levels of the students. In order to test for interaction, more than one observation or sampled measurement (i.e., *replication*) has to be included in each cell of the two-way data table. Section 13.4 presents the analytical procedure that is appropriate when there is only one observation per cell, and in which interaction between the two factors cannot be tested. The analytical procedure is extended to include replication and the analysis of interaction effects in Section 13.5.

13.4   THE RANDOMIZED BLOCK DESIGN (TWO-WAY ANOVA, ONE OBSERVATION PER CELL)

The two-way analysis of variance model in which there is only one observation per cell is generally referred to as the *randomized block design*, because of the principal use for this model. What if we extend the idea of using paired observations to compare two sample means (see Section 11.3) to the basic one-way analysis of variance model, and have groups of k *matched* individuals assigned randomly to each treatment level? In analysis of variance, such matched groups are called *blocks*, and because the individuals (or items) are randomly assigned based on the identified block membership, the design is referred to as the randomized block design. In such a design the blocks dimension is not a treatment dimension as such. The objective of using this design is not for the specific purpose of testing for a blocks effect. Rather, by being able to assign some of the variability among subjects to prior achievement, for example, the *MSE* can be reduced and the resulting test of the A treatments effect is more sensitive.

The linear model for the two-way analysis of variance model with one observation per cell (with no replication) is

$$X_{jk} = \mu + \beta_j + \alpha_k + \varepsilon_{jk} \tag{13.3}$$

where
μ = the overall mean regardless of any treatment
β_j = effect of the treatment j or block j in the B dimension of classification
α_k = effect of the treatment k in the A dimension of classification
ε_{jk} = the random error associated with the process of sampling

Table 13.2 is the summary table for the two-way analysis of variance without replication. As compared with Table 13.1 for the one-way analysis of variance, the only new symbol in this table is T_j^2, which indicates that the total of each j group (for the B treatments, or blocks) is squared. See Problems 13.5 and 13.6 for application of these formulas.

Table 13.2 Summary Table for Two-Way Analysis of Variance with One Observation per Cell (Randomized Block Design)

Source of variation	Degrees of freedom (df)	Sum of squares (SS)	Mean square (MS)	F ratio
Among treatment groups (A)	$K-1$	$SSA = \sum_{k=1}^{K} \dfrac{T_k^2}{n_k} - \dfrac{T^2}{N}$	$MSA = \dfrac{SSA}{K-1}$	$F = \dfrac{MSA}{MSE}$
Among treatment groups, or blocks (B)	$J-1$	$SSB = \dfrac{1}{K}\sum_{j=1}^{J} T_j^2 - \dfrac{T^2}{N}$	$MSB = \dfrac{SSB}{J-1}$	$F = \dfrac{MSB}{MSE}$
Sampling error (E)	$(J-1)(K-1)$	$SSE = SST - SSA - SSB$	$MSE = \dfrac{SSE}{(J-1)(K-1)}$	
Total (T)	$N-1$	$SST = \sum_{j=1}^{J}\sum_{k=1}^{K} X^2 - \dfrac{T^2}{N}$		

13.5 TWO-FACTOR COMPLETELY RANDOMIZED DESIGN (TWO-WAY ANOVA, n OBSERVATIONS PER CELL)

As explained in Section 13.3, when replication is included within a two-way design, the interaction between the two factors can be tested. Thus, when such a design is used, three different null hypotheses can be tested by the analysis of variance: that there are no column effects (the column means are not significantly different), that there are no row effects (the row means are not significantly different), and that there is no interaction between the two factors (the two factors are independent). A significant interaction effect indicates that the effect of treatments for one factor varies according to levels of the other factor. In such a case, the existence of column and/or row effects may not be meaningful from the standpoint of the application of research results.

The linear model for the two-way analysis of variance when replication is included is

$$X_{ijk} = \mu + \beta_j + \alpha_k + \iota_{jk} + \varepsilon_{ijk} \tag{13.4}$$

where μ = the overall mean regardless of any treatment
β_j = effect of the treatment j in the B (row) dimension
α_k = effect of the treatment k in the A (column) dimension
ι_{jk} = effect of interaction between treatment j (of factor B) and treatment k (of factor A)
(where ι is the Greek iota)
ε_{ijk} = the random error associated with the process of sampling

Table 13.3 is the summary table for the two-way analysis of variance with replication. The formulas included in this table are based on the assumption that there are an equal number of observations in all of the cells. See Problem 13.7 for application of these formulas.

Table 13.3 Summary Table for Two-Way Analysis of Variance with More than One Observation per Cell

Source of variation	Degrees of freedom (df)	Sum of squares (SS)	Mean square (MS)	F ratio
Among treatment groups (A)	$K-1$	$SSA = \sum_{k=1}^{K} \dfrac{T_k^2}{nJ} - \dfrac{T^2}{N}$	$MSA = \dfrac{SSA}{K-1}$	$F = \dfrac{MSA}{MSE}$
Among treatment groups (B)	$J-1$	$SSB = \sum_{j=1}^{J} \dfrac{T_j^2}{nK} - \dfrac{T^2}{N}$	$MSB = \dfrac{SSB}{J-1}$	$F = \dfrac{MSB}{MSE}$
Interaction (between) factors (A and B) (I)	$(J-1)(K-1)$	$SSI = \dfrac{1}{n}\sum_{j=1}^{J}\sum_{k=1}^{K}\left(\sum_{i=1}^{n} X\right)^2$ $- SSA - SSB - \dfrac{T^2}{N}$	$MSI = \dfrac{SSI}{(J-1)(K-1)}$	$F = \dfrac{MSI}{MSE}$
Sampling error (E)	$JK(n-1)$	$SSE = SST - SSA$ $- SSB - SSI$	$MSE = \dfrac{SSE}{JK(n-1)}$	
Total (T)	$N-1$	$SST = \sum_{i=1}^{n}\sum_{j=1}^{J}\sum_{k=1}^{K} X^2 - \dfrac{T^2}{N}$		

13.6 ADDITIONAL CONSIDERATIONS

All of the computational procedures presented in this chapter are for fixed-effects models of the analysis of variance. In a *fixed-effects* model, all of the treatments of concern for a given factor are included in the experiment. For instance, in Problem 13.1 it is assumed that the only instructional methods of concern are the three methods included in the design. A *random-effects model*, however, includes only a random sample from all the possible treatments for the factor in the experiment. For instance, out of ten different instructional methods, three might have been randomly chosen. A different computational method is required in the latter case because the null hypothesis is that there are no differences among the various instructional methods in general, and not just among the particular instructional methods that were included in the experiment. In most experiments the fixed-effects model is appropriate, and therefore the presentation in this chapter has been limited to such models.

The concepts presented in this chapter can be extended to more than two factors, or dimensions. Designs involving three or more factors are called *factorial designs*, and in fact most statisticians include the two-way analysis of variance with replication in this category. Although a number of different null hypotheses can be tested with the same body of data by the use of factorial designs, the extension of such designs can lead to an extremely large number of categories (cells) in the data table, with related sampling problems. Because of such difficulties, designs have been developed that do not require every possible combination of the treatment levels of every factor being included in the analysis. Such designs as the *Latin Square design* and *incomplete block designs* are examples of such developments and are described in specialized textbooks in the analysis of variance.

Whatever experimental design is used, rejection of a null hypothesis in the analysis of variance typically does not present the analyst with the basis for final decisions, because such rejection does not serve to pinpoint the exact differences among the treatments, or factor levels. For example, given that there is a significant difference in student achievement among three instructional methods, we would next want to determine which of the pairs of methods are different from one another. Various procedures have been developed for such pairwise comparisons carried out in conjunction with the analysis of variance.

13.7   USING EXCEL AND MINITAB

Computer software is available for all the designs of the analysis of variance described in this chapter, as well as for more complex designs that are outside the scope of this book. Application of Excel and Minitab for the one-factor completely randomized design, for the randomized block design, and for the two-factor completely randomized design are illustrated in Solved Problems 13.8 through 13.13.

Solved Problems

ONE-FACTOR COMPLETELY RANDOMIZED DESIGN

13.1. Fifteen trainees in a technical program are randomly assigned to three different types of instructional approaches, all of which are concerned with developing a specified level of skill in computer-assisted design. The achievement test scores at the conclusion of the instructional unit are reported in Table 13.4, along with the mean performance score associated with each instructional approach. Use the analysis of variance procedure in Section 13.1 to test the null hypothesis that the three sample means were obtained from the same population, using the 5 percent level of significance for the test.

Table 13.4   Achievement Test Scores of Trainees under Three Methods of Instruction

Instructional method	Test scores					Total scores	Mean test scores
A_1	86	79	81	70	84	400	80
A_2	90	76	88	82	89	425	85
A_3	82	68	73	71	81	375	75

$$H_0: \mu_1 = \mu_2 = \mu_3 \qquad \text{or, equivalently,} \qquad H_0: \alpha_k = 0 \text{ for all treatments}$$
$$H_1: \text{ not all } \mu_1 = \mu_2 = \mu_3 \qquad\qquad\qquad\qquad H_1: \alpha_k \neq 0 \text{ for some treatments}$$

(1)   The overall mean of all 15 test scores is

$$\bar{X}_T = \frac{\Sigma X}{n} = \frac{1{,}200}{15} = 80.0$$

The standard error of the mean, based on the three sample means reported, is

$$s_{\bar{x}} = \sqrt{\frac{\Sigma(\bar{X} - \bar{X}_T)^2}{\text{No. means} - 1}} = \sqrt{\frac{(80 - 80)^2 + (85 - 80)^2 + (75 - 80)^2}{3 - 1}} = \sqrt{\frac{50}{2}} = 5.0$$

(2) $MSTR = ns_{\bar{x}}^2 = 5(5.0)^2 = 5(25.0) = 125.0$

(3)   From the general formula:

$$s^2 = \frac{\Sigma(X - \bar{X})^2}{n - 1}$$

the variance for each of the three samples is

$$s_1^2 = \frac{(86-80)^2 + (79-80)^2 + (81-80)^2 + (70-80)^2 + (84-80)^2}{5-1} = \frac{154}{4} = 38.5$$

$$s_2^2 = \frac{(90-85)^2 + (76-85)^2 + (88-85)^2 + (82-85)^2 + (89-85)^2}{5-1} = \frac{140}{4} = 35.0$$

$$s_3^2 = \frac{(82-75)^2 + (68-75)^2 + (73-75)^2 + (71-75)^2 + (81-75)^2}{5-1} = \frac{154}{4} = 38.5$$

Then,

$$\hat{\sigma}^2 \ (\text{pooled}) = \frac{(n_1-1)s_1^2 + (n_2-1)s_2^2 + (n_3-1)s_3^2}{n_1 + n_2 + n_3 - 3} = \frac{(4)(38.5) + 4(35.0) + 4(38.5)}{5+5+5-3} = \frac{448.0}{12} = 37.3$$

Thus, $MSE = 37.3$,

(4)   Since $MSTR$ is larger than MSE, a test of the null hypothesis is appropriate.

$$\text{Critical } F \ (df = k-1, kn-k; \ \alpha = 0.05) = F \ (2, 12; \ \alpha = 0.05) = 3.88$$

(5) $F = MSTR/MSE = 125/37.3 = 3.35$

Because the calculated F statistic of 3.35 is not greater than the critical F value of 3.88, the null hypothesis that the mean test scores for the three instructional methods in the population are all mutually equal cannot be rejected at the 5 percent level of significance.

13.2.   Repeat the analysis of variance in Problem 13.1 (data in Table 13.4) by using the general procedure described in Section 13.2 with the accompanying formulas in Table 13.1.

The various quantities required for substitution in the formulas in Table 13.1 are

$n_1 = 5$	$n_2 = 5$	$n_3 = 5$	$N = 15$
$T_1 = 400$	$T_2 = 425$	$T_3 = 375$	$T = 1,200$
$T_1^2 = 160,000$	$T_2^2 = 180,625$	$T_3^2 = 140,625$	$T^2 = 1,440,000$

$$\frac{T^2}{N} = \frac{1,440,000}{15} = 96,000$$

$$\sum_{i=1}^{n}\sum_{k=1}^{K} X^2 = 86^2 + 79^2 + \cdots + 81^2 = 96,698$$

$$SST = \sum_{i=1}^{n}\sum_{k=1}^{K} X^2 - \frac{T^2}{N} = 96,698 - 96,000 = 698$$

$$SSA = \sum_{k=1}^{K} \frac{T_k^2}{n_k} - \frac{T^2}{N} = \frac{160,000}{5} + \frac{180,625}{5} + \frac{140,625}{5} - 96,000 = 250$$

$$SSE = SST - SSA = 698 - 250 = 448$$

Table 13.5 presents the analysis of variance for the data in Table 13.4. As expected, the F ratio is identical to the one computed in Problem 13.1, and based on the 2 and 12 degrees of freedom, it is less than the critical F of 3.88 required for significance at the 5 percent level. Thus, we conclude that there is no effect associated with the treatment levels (methods of instruction) and thereby also conclude that the null hypothesis that there are no differences among the means cannot be rejected at the 5 percent level of significance.

Table 13.5   ANOVA Table for Analysis of Three Methods of Instruction (Data in Table 13.4)

Source of variation	Degrees of freedom (df)	Sum of squares (SS)	Mean square (MS)	F ratio
Among treatment groups (A)	$3 - 1 = 2$	250	$\dfrac{250}{2} = 125$	$\dfrac{125}{37.33} = 3.35$
Sampling error (E)	$15 - 3 = 12$	448	$\dfrac{448}{12} = 37.33$	
Total (T)	$15 - 1 = 14$	698		

ONE-WAY ANALYSIS OF VARIANCE WITH UNEQUAL GROUPS

13.3. Sometimes the data that are analyzed do not have equal sample sizes for the several treatment levels. Table 13.6 reports the words per minute entered in a word processor using three different keyboard positions, with the data being obtained after the individuals in each sample had an equal amount of time to familiarize themselves with the keyboard position to be used. Test the null hypothesis that the mean words per minute achieved for the three keyboard positions is not different, using the 5 percent level of significance.

Table 13.6   Average Words per Minute for Three Keyboard Positions Based on a 15-min Test Period

Typewriter brand	number of words per minute					Total WPM	Mean WPM
A_1	79	83	62	51	77	352	70.4
A_2	74	85	72	—	—	231	77.0
A_3	81	65	79	55	—	280	70.0

H_0: $\mu_1 = \mu_2 = \mu_3$ or, equivalently, H_0: $\alpha_k = 0$ for all treatments (typewriter brands)
H_1: not all $\mu_1 = \mu_2 = \mu_3$ H_1: $\alpha_k \neq 0$ for some treatments

The various quantities required for substitution in the standard formulas for the one-way analysis of variance are

$$n_1 = 5 \qquad n_2 = 3 \qquad n_3 = 4 \qquad N = 12$$
$$T_1 = 352 \qquad T_2 = 231 \qquad T_3 = 280 \qquad T = 863$$
$$T_1^2 = 123{,}904 \qquad T_2^2 = 53{,}361 \qquad T_3^2 = 78{,}400 \qquad T^2 = 744{,}769$$

$$\frac{T^2}{N} = \frac{744{,}769}{12} = 62{,}064.1$$

$$\sum_{i=1}^{n} \sum_{k=1}^{K} X^2 = 79^2 + 83^2 + \cdots + 55^2 = 63{,}441$$

$$SST = \sum_{i=1}^{n} \sum_{k=1}^{K} X^2 - \frac{T^2}{N} = 63{,}441 - 62{,}064.1 = 1{,}376.9$$

$$SSA = \sum_{k=1}^{K} \frac{T_k^2}{n_k} - \frac{T^2}{N} = \frac{123{,}904}{5} + \frac{53{,}361}{3} + \frac{78{,}400}{4} - 62{,}064.1 = 103.7$$

$$SSE = SST - SSA = 1{,}376.9 - 103.7 = 1{,}273.2$$

Table 13.7 presents the analysis of variance for this test. At the 5 percent level of significance, the critical value of F ($df = 2, 9$) is 4.26. The computed F ratio of 0.37 is thus in the region of acceptance of the null hypothesis, and we conclude that based on these sample results there are no differences among the three keyboard positions in terms of word-entry speed. In fact, because $MSTR$ is smaller than MSE we can observe that the variability among the three keyboard positions is less than the expected variability given that there are no differences among the positions.

Table 13.7   ANOVA Table for the Analysis of Keyboard Position and Word Processing Speed

Source of variation	Degrees of freedom (df)	Sum of squares (SS)	Mean square (MS)	F ratio
Among treatment groups (A) (position of keyboard)	$3 - 1 = 2$	103.7	$\dfrac{103.7}{2} = 51.8$	$\dfrac{51.8}{141.5} = 0.37$
Sampling error (E)	$12 - 3 = 9$	1,273.2	$\dfrac{1,273.2}{9} = 141.5$	
Total (T)	$12 - 1 = 11$	1,376.9		

RELATIONSHIP OF THE ONE-FACTOR COMPLETELY RANDOMIZED DESIGN TO THE t TEST FOR TESTING THE DIFFERENCE BETWEEN THE MEANS OF TWO INDEPENDENT SAMPLES

13.4. The one-factor completely randomized design can be considered an extension to k groups of testing the difference between the means of two independent samples by use of the t distribution. In both types of applications a necessary assumption is that the samples have been obtained from the same normally distributed population for which the population variance σ^2 is unknown (see Section 11.2). Therefore, it follows that when one-way analysis of variance is applied to a design in which $k = 2$, the result is directly equivalent to using the t distribution to test the difference. In fact, for the analysis in which $k = 2$, $F = t^2$ both in terms of the respective critical values required for significance and the respective computed test-statistic values for the sample data. To demonstrate these observations, carry out (a) a t test and (b) the one-way analysis of variance for the difference between the means of the first two keyboard positions reported in Table 13.6. Use the 5 percent level of significance to test the null hypothesis that there is no difference between the two population means.

(a)   Using the t test for independent groups:

$$H_0: \mu_0 - \mu_2 = 0 \qquad (\text{or } \mu_1 = \mu_2) \qquad \bar{X}_1 = 70.4 \qquad \bar{X}_2 = 77.0$$
$$H_1: (\mu_1 - \mu_2 \neq 0) \qquad (\text{or } \mu_1 \neq \mu_2) \qquad n_1 = 5 \qquad n_2 = 3$$
$$\text{Critical } t \ (df = 6, \alpha = 0.05) = \pm 2.447$$

$$s_1^2 = \frac{\Sigma(X - \bar{X}_1)^2}{n_1 - 1} = \frac{(79 - 70.4)^2 + (83 - 70.4)^2 + (62 - 70.4)^2 + (51 - 70.4)^2 + (77 - 70.4)^2}{5 - 1}$$
$$= \frac{723.20}{4} = 180.8$$

$$s_2^2 = \frac{\Sigma(X - \bar{X}_2)^2}{n_2 - 1} = \frac{(74 - 77.0)^2 + (85 - 77.0)^2 + (72 - 77.0)^2}{3 - 1} = \frac{98.0}{2} = 49.0$$

$$\hat{\sigma}^2 = \frac{(n_1 - 1)s_1^2 + (n_2 - 1)s_2^2}{n_1 + n_2 - 2} = \frac{(4)180.8 + (2)49.0}{5 + 3 - 2} = \frac{821.2}{6} = 136.8667$$

$$\hat{\sigma}_{\bar{x}_1 - \bar{x}_2} = \sqrt{\frac{\hat{\sigma}^2}{n_1} + \frac{\hat{\sigma}^2}{n_2}} = \sqrt{\frac{136.8667}{5} + \frac{136.8667}{3}} = \sqrt{72.9955} = 8.54$$

$$t = \frac{\bar{X}_1 - \bar{X}_2}{\hat{\sigma}_{\bar{x}_1 - \bar{x}_2}} = \frac{70.4 - 77.0}{8.54} = \frac{-6.6}{8.54} = -0.77$$

The computed t statistic of -0.77 is in the region of acceptance of the null hypothesis, and therefore the null hypothesis cannot be rejected at the 5 percent level of significance.

(b)   For the two treatment levels (keyboard positions), based on the one-way analysis of variance:

$$H_0: \mu_1 = \mu_2 \quad (\text{or } \alpha_k = 0) \qquad n_1 = 5 \qquad\qquad n_2 = 3 \qquad\qquad N = 8$$
$$H_1: \mu_1 \neq \mu_2 \quad (\text{or } \alpha_k \neq 0) \qquad T_1 = 352 \qquad\qquad T_2 = 231 \qquad\qquad T = 583$$
$$T_1^2 = 123{,}904 \qquad\qquad T_2^2 = 53{,}361 \qquad T^2 = 339{,}889$$

$$\frac{T^2}{N} = \frac{339{,}889}{8} = 42{,}486.1$$

$$\sum_{i=1}^{n}\sum_{k=1}^{K} X^2 = 79^2 + 83^2 + \cdots + 72^2 = 43{,}389$$

$$SST = \sum_{i=1}^{n}\sum_{k=1}^{K} X^2 = \frac{T^2}{N} = 43{,}389 - 42{,}468.1 = 902.9$$

$$SSA = \sum_{k=1}^{K} \frac{T_k^2}{n_k} - \frac{T^2}{N} = \frac{123{,}904}{5} + \frac{53{,}361}{3} - 42{,}486.1 = 81.7$$

$$SSE = SST - SSA = 902.9 - 81.7 = 821.2$$

Table 13.8 presents the analysis of variance for this test. At the 5 percent level of significance, the critical value of F ($df = 1$, 6) is 5.99. Since the computed F statistic of 0.60 is the region of acceptance of the null hypothesis, the hypothesis that there is no treatment effect cannot be rejected.

Table 13.8   ANOVA Table for the Analysis of Keyboard Position and Word Processing Speed

Source of variation	Degrees of freedom (df)	Sum of squares (SS)	Mean square (MS)	F ratio
Among treatment (A) (position of keyboard)	$2 - 1 = 1$	81.7	$\dfrac{81.7}{1} = 81.7$	$\dfrac{81.7}{136.9} = 0.60$
Sampling error (E)	$8 - 2 = 6$	821.2	$\dfrac{821.2}{6} = 136.96$	
Total (T)	$8 - 1 = 7$	902.9		

Thus, the observation about the comparability of the two testing procedures is supported. In terms of the critical values, critical $F = 5.99$ and critical $t = \pm 2.447$. Thus, $(\pm 2.447)^2 = 5.99$. As for the computed test-statistic values of F and t, $F = 0.60$ and $t = -0.77$; $(-0.77)^2 = 0.59 \cong 0.60$, with the slight difference being due solely to rounding error.

THE RANDOMIZED BLOCK DESIGN (TWO-WAY ANALYSIS WITHOUT INTERACTION)

13.5.   For the data in Table 13.4, suppose a randomized block design was in fact used and trainees were matched before the experiment, with a trainee from each ability group (based on prior course achievement) assigned to each method of instruction. Table 13.9 is a revision of Table 13.4 in that the values reported are reorganized to reflect the randomized block design. Note, however, that the same values are included in each A treatment group as in Table 13.4, except that they are reported according to the B ability groups and therefore are arranged in a different order. Test the null hypothesis that there is no difference in the mean performance among the three methods of instruction, using the 5 percent level of significance.

Table 13.9   Achievement Test Scores of Trainees under Methods of Instruction, According to Ability Level

Level of ability (Block)	Method of instruction			Total (T_j)	Mean ($\bar{X}_j$)
	A_1	A_2	A_3		
B_1	86	90	82	258	86.0
B_2	84	89	81	254	84.7
B_3	81	88	73	242	80.7
B_4	79	76	68	223	74.3
B_5	70	82	71	223	74.3
Total (T_k)	400	425	375	Grand total $T = 1,200$	
Mean ($\bar{X}_k$)	80.0	85.0	75.0		Grand mean $\bar{X}_T = 80.0$

The various quantities required for the analysis of variance table are

For j:

$$T_1 = 258 \qquad T_2 = 254 \qquad T_3 = 242 \qquad T_4 = 223 \qquad T_5 = 223$$
$$T_1^2 = 66{,}564 \qquad T_2^2 = 64{,}516 \qquad T_3^2 = 58{,}564 \qquad T_4^2 = 49{,}729 \qquad T_5^2 = 49{,}729$$

For k:

$$T_1 = 400 \qquad T_2 = 425 \qquad T_3 = 375$$
$$T_1^2 = 160{,}000 \qquad T_2^2 = 180{,}625 \qquad T_3^2 = 140{,}625$$
$$n_1 = 5 \qquad n_2 = 5 \qquad n_3 = 5$$

Overall:

$$T = 1{,}200 \qquad T^2 = 1{,}440{,}000 \qquad N = 15$$

$$\frac{T^2}{N} = \frac{1{,}440{,}000}{15} = 96{,}000$$

$$\sum_{j=1}^{J}\sum_{k=1}^{K} X^2 + 86^2 + 84^2 + \cdots + 71^2 = 96{,}698$$

$$SST = \sum_{j=1}^{J}\sum_{k=1}^{K} X^2 - \frac{T^2}{N} = 96{,}698 - 96{,}000 = 698$$

$$SSA = \sum_{k=1}^{K} \frac{T_k^2}{n_k} - \frac{T^2}{N} = \frac{160{,}000}{5} + \frac{180{,}625}{5} + \frac{140{,}625}{5} - 96{,}000 = 250$$

$$SSB = \frac{1}{K}\sum_{j=1}^{J} T_j^2 - \frac{T^2}{N} = \frac{1}{3}(66{,}564 + 64{,}516 + 58{,}564 + 49{,}729 + 49{,}729) - 96{,}000 = 367.3$$

$$SSE = SST - SSA - SSB = 698 - 250 - 367.3 = 80.7$$

Table 13.10 presents the analysis of variance for these data. With respect to the linear equation representing this model, the two F ratios in Table 13.10 are concerned with the tests of the following null and alternative hypotheses:

$$H_0: \alpha_k = 0 \text{ for all columns} \qquad H_0: \beta_j = 0 \text{ for all rows}$$
$$H_1: \alpha_k \neq 0 \text{ for some columns} \qquad H_1: \beta_j \neq 0 \text{ for some rows}$$

In terms of practical implications, the first null hypothesis is concerned with testing the difference among the column means, which is the basic purpose of the analysis. The second null hypothesis is concerned with testing the difference among the row means, which reflect the blocking that was done according to level of ability.

Table 13.10   ANOVA Table for Analysis of Three Methods of Instruction According to Ability Level

Source variation	Sum of squares (SS)	Degrees of freedom (df)	Mean square (MS)	F ratio
Among treatment groups (A) (method)	250.0	$3 - 1 = 2$	$\dfrac{250.0}{2} = 125.0$	$\dfrac{125}{10.1} = 12.4$
Among blocks (B) (ability level)	367.3	$5 - 1 = 4$	$\dfrac{367.3}{4} = 91.8$	$\dfrac{91.8}{10.1} = 9.1$
Sampling error (E)	80.7	$(5 - 1)(3 - 1) = 8$	$\dfrac{80.7}{8} = 10.1$	
Total (T)	698.0	$15 - 1 = 14$		

Using the 5 percent level of significance, the required F ratio for the rejection of the first null hypothesis $(df = 2, 8) = 4.46$ while the required F for the second null hypothesis $(df = 4, 8) = 3.84$. Thus, both of the calculated F ratios in Table 13.10 are in the region of rejection of the null hypothesis. We conclude that there is a significant difference in achievement test scores for the different methods of instruction, and also that there is a significant difference in achievement test scores for the different levels of ability. Note that this is in contrast to the result in Problem 13.2, where the data were treated as three independent samples. The MSE in the present analysis is substantially lower than that determined in Problem 13.2 because much of that variability could be identified as being due to differences in ability level.

RELATIONSHIP OF THE RANDOMIZED BLOCK DESIGN TO THE t TEST FOR TESTING THE DIFFERENCE BETWEEN TWO MEANS USING PAIRED OBSERVATIONS

13.6. When $k = 2$, the randomized block design is equivalent to the t test for the difference between the means of paired observations and $F = t^2$. This is similar to the case in Problem 13.4 for two independent samples. To demonstrate these points, apply the analysis of variance to the data in Table 13.11, taken

Table 13.11   Automobile Mileage Obtained with and without a Gasoline Additive for 10 Sampled Cars

Automobile	Mileage with additive (per gal)	Mileage without additive (per gal)	Total (T_j)	Mean ($\bar{X}_j$)
1	36.7	36.2	72.9	36.45
2	35.8	35.7	71.5	35.75
3	31.9	32.3	64.2	32.10
4	29.3	29.6	58.9	29.45
5	28.4	28.1	56.5	18.25
6	25.7	25.8	51.5	25.75
7	24.2	23.9	48.1	24.05
8	22.6	22.0	44.6	22.30
9	21.9	21.5	43.4	21.70
10	20.3	20.0	40.3	20.15
Total (T_k)	276.8	275.1	Grand total $T = 551.9$	
Mean ($\bar{X}_k$)	27.68	27.51		Grand mean $\bar{X}_T = 27.60$

from Example 4 in Chapter 11. In Example 4 the critical t $(df = 9, \alpha = 0.05)$ is ± 2.262 and the computed t statistic is $+1.59$; thus, the null hypothesis of no difference could not be rejected. Carry out the test at the 5 percent level of significance using the analysis of variance.

The various quantities required for the analysis of variance table are
For j:

$T_1 = 72.9$	$T_2 = 71.5$	$T_3 = 64.2$	$T_4 = 58.9$	$T_5 = 56.5$
$T_1^2 = 5,314.41$	$T_2^2 = 5,112.25$	$T_3^2 = 4,121.64$	$T_4^2 = 3,469.21$	$T_5^2 = 3,192.25$
$T_6 = 51.5$	$T_7 = 48.1$	$T_8 = 44.6$	$T_9 = 43.4$	$T_{10} = 40.3$
$T_6^2 = 2,652.25$	$T_7^2 = 2,313.61$	$T_8^2 = 1,989.56$	$T_9^2 = 1,883.56$	$T_{10}^2 = 1,624.09$

For k:

$$T_1 = 276.8 \qquad T_2 = 275.1$$
$$T_1^2 = 76,618.24 \qquad T_2^2 = 75,680.01$$
$$n_1 = 10 \qquad n_2 = 10$$

Overall:

$$T = 551.9 \qquad T^2 = 304,593.61 \qquad N = 20$$
$$\frac{T^2}{N} = \frac{304,593.61}{20} = 15,229.68$$

$$\sum_{j=1}^{J}\sum_{k=1}^{K} X^2 = 36.7^2 + 35.8^2 + \cdots + 20.0^2 = 6,798.87$$

$$SST = \sum_{j=1}^{J}\sum_{k=1}^{K} X^2 - \frac{T^2}{N} = 15,836.87 - 15,229.68 = 607.19$$

$$SSA = \sum_{k=1}^{K} \frac{T_k^2}{n_k} - \frac{T^2}{N} = \frac{76,618.24}{10} + \frac{75,680.01}{10} - 15,229.68 = 0.145$$

$$SSB = \frac{1}{K}\sum_{j=1}^{J} T_j^2 - \frac{T^2}{N} = \frac{1}{2}(5,314.41 + \cdots + 1,624.09) - 15,229.68 = 606.535$$

$$SSE = SST - SSA - SSB = 607.19 - 0.145 - 606.535 = 0.510$$

Table 13.12 presents the analysis of variance for the data of Table 13.11. The null hypothesis of interest, which is conceptually the same one tested in Example 4 of Chapter 11, is, for the treatment groups, H_0: $\alpha_k = 0$ and H_1: $\alpha_k \neq 0$. Critical F $(df = 1, 1; \alpha = 0.05) = 5.12$.

Table 13.12   ANOVA Table for Analysis of Automobile Mileage with and without a Gasoline Additive

Source of variation	Degrees of freedom (df)	Sum of squares (SS)	Mean square (MS)	F ratio
Among treatment groups (A)	$2 - 1 = 1$	0.145	$\dfrac{0.145}{1} = 0.145$	$\dfrac{0.145}{0.057} = 2.54$
Among blocks (B) (different automobiles)	$10 - 1 = 9$	606.535	$\dfrac{606.535}{9} = 67.39$	$\dfrac{67.39}{0.057} = 1,182.28$
Sampling error (E)	$(2 - 1)(10 - 1) = 9$	0.510	$\dfrac{0.510}{9} = 0.057$	
Total (T)	$20 - 1 = 19$	607.190		

Since the computed value of F statistic of 2.54 is not greater than the critical value of 5.12, the hypothesis of no treatment effect (of no difference between the means) cannot be rejected at the 5 percent level of significance. Thus we conclude that the additive does *not* increase automobile mileage.

Note the very large value of the computed F for the blocks dimension. Referring to the data in Table 13.11, this result is not surprising, since the 10 automobiles were apparently in different weight categories and differed substantially in mileage achieved according to category.

As expected, the critical value of F in this problem is equal to the square of the critical value used in the t test: $5.12 = (\pm 2.262)^2$. Also, except for the rounding error, the computed t^2 value in Example 4 of Chapter 11 is equal to the computed F of 2.54 here, with $t^2 = (1.59)^2 = 2.53$.

TWO-FACTOR COMPLETELY RANDOMIZED DESIGN

13.7. Nine trainees in each of four different subject areas were randomly assigned to three different methods of instruction. Three students were assigned to each instructional method. With reference to Table 13.13, test the various null hypotheses that are of interest with respect to such a design at the 5 percent level of significance.

The various quantities required for the analysis of variance table are

For J:

$$T_1 = 717 \qquad T_2 = 709 \qquad T_3 = 722 \qquad T_4 = 732$$
$$T_1^2 = 514{,}089 \qquad T_2^2 = 502{,}681 \qquad T_3^2 = 521{,}284 \qquad T_4^2 = 535{,}824$$

For k:

$$T_1 = 960 \qquad T_2 = 1{,}020 \qquad T_3 = 900$$
$$T_1^2 = 921{,}600 \qquad T_2^2 = 1{,}040{,}000 \qquad T_3^2 = 810{,}000$$

Overall:

$$T = 2{,}880 \qquad T^2 = 8{,}294{,}400 \qquad N = 36$$
$$\frac{T^2}{N} = \frac{8{,}294{,}400}{36} = 230{,}400$$

$$\sum_{j=1}^{J} \sum_{k=1}^{K} \left(\sum_{i=1}^{n} X \right)^2 = (70 + 79 + 72)^2 + (77 + 81 + 79)^2 + \cdots + (68 + 71 + 69)^2 = 694{,}694$$

$$\sum_{i=1}^{n} \sum_{j=1}^{J} \sum_{k=1}^{K} X^2 = 70^2 + 79^2 + 72^2 + 77^2 + \cdots + 69^2 = 232{,}000$$

$$SST = \sum_{i=1}^{n} \sum_{j=1}^{J} \sum_{k=1}^{K} X^2 - \frac{T^2}{N} = 232{,}000 - 230{,}400 = 1{,}600$$

$$SSA = \sum_{k=1}^{K} \frac{T_k^2}{nJ} - \frac{T^2}{N} = \frac{921{,}600}{(3)(4)} + \frac{1{,}040{,}400}{(3)(4)} + \frac{810{,}000}{(3)(4)} - 230{,}400 = 600$$

$$SSB = \sum_{j=1}^{J} \frac{T_j^2}{nK} - \frac{T^2}{N} = \frac{514{,}089}{(3)(3)} + \frac{502{,}681}{(3)(3)} + \frac{521{,}284}{(3)(3)} + \frac{535{,}824}{(3)(3)} = 230{,}400 = 30.8$$

$$SSI = \frac{1}{n} \sum_{j=1}^{J} \sum_{k=1}^{K} \left(\sum_{i=1}^{n} X \right)^2 + SSA - SSB - \frac{T^2}{N} = \frac{1}{3}(694{,}694) - 600 - 30.8 - 230{,}400 = 533.9$$

$$SSE = SST - SSA - SSB - SSI = 1{,}600.0 - 600.0 - 30.8 - 533.9 = 435.3$$

**Table 13.13   Achievement Test Scores of Trainees under Three Methods
of Instruction and for Four Subject Areas**

Subject area	Method of instruction			Total (T_j)	Mean $(\bar{X}_j)$
	A_1	A_2	A_3		
B_1	70	83	81	717	79.7
	79	89	86		
	72	78	79		
B_2	77	77	74	709	78.8
	81	87	69		
	79	88	77		
B_3	82	94	72	722	80.2
	78	83	79		
	80	79	75		
B_4	85	84	68	732	81.3
	90	90	71		
	87	88	69		
Total (T_k)	960	1,020	900	Grand total $T = 2,880$	
Mean $(\bar{X}_k)$	80	85	75		Grand mean $\bar{X}_T = 80$

Table 13.14 presents the analysis of variance for the data of Table 13.13. With respect to the linear model for two-way analysis of variance with replication, the three F ratios reported in Table 13.14 are concerned with the following null and alternative hypotheses:

$$H_0: \alpha_k = 0 \text{ for all columns ;} \qquad H_1: \alpha_k \neq 0 \text{ for some columns}$$
$$H_0: \beta_j = 0 \text{ for all rows;} \qquad H_1: \beta_j \neq 0 \text{ for some rows}$$
$$H_0: \iota_{jk} = 0 \text{ for all cells;} \qquad H_1: \iota_{jk} \neq 0 \text{ for some cells}$$

Using the 5 percent level of significance, the required F ratio for the rejection of the first null hypothesis $(df = 2, 24)$ is 3.40, for the second the required F $(df = 3, 24)$ is 3.01, and for the third the required F $(df = 6, 24)$

Table 13.14   ANOVA Table for Analysis of Three Methods of Instruction Applied in Four Subject Areas

Source of variation	Degrees of freedom (df)	Sum of squares (SS)	Mean square (MS)	F ratio
Between treatment groups (A) (method)	$3 - 1 = 2$	600.0	$\dfrac{600.0}{2} = 300.0$	$\dfrac{300.0}{18.1} = 16.57$
Between treatment groups (B) (subject)	$4 - 1 = 3$	30.8	$\dfrac{30.8}{3} = 10.3$	$\dfrac{10.3}{18.1} = 0.57$
Interaction between method and subject (I)	$(4 - 1)(3 - 1) = 6$	533.9	$\dfrac{533.9}{6} = 89.0$	$\dfrac{89.0}{18.1} = 4.92$
Sampling error (E)	$(4)(3)(3 - 1) = 24$	435.3	$\dfrac{435.3}{24} = 18.1$	
Total (T)	$36 - 1 = 35$	1,600.0		

is 2.51. Thus, we conclude that there is a significant difference in test scores for the different methods of instruction, that there is no significant difference among the different subject areas, and that there is significant interaction between the two factors. The last conclusion indicates that the effectiveness of the three methods of instruction varies for the different subject areas. For example, in Table 13.13 notice that for subject area B_1 method A_1 was the least effective method, while for subject are a B_4, method A_3 was the least effective method. In reviewing this table, however, method A_2 is observed to be at least equal to the other methods for every subject area. Thus, the possibility of using different methods of instruction as being best for different subject areas does not appear to be the appropriate decision in this case, even though there was a significant interaction effect.

COMPUTER OUTPUT: ONE-FACTOR COMPLETELY RANDOMIZED DESIGN

13.8. Use Excel to carry out the analysis in Problem 13.2 (data is Table 13.4).

The output given in Fig. 13-1 corresponds to the results obtained by manual calculation in Table 13.5. Whereas the critical-value approach to hypothesis testing had to be used in the hand calculation, the printout provides the *P* value, which is 0.069909, or 0.070 rounded. Since this value is *not* less than 0.05, the null hypothesis that there are no differences among the population means cannot be rejected at the 5 percent level of significance.

The Excel output given in Fig. 13-1 was obtained as follows:

(1)   Open Excel. In cell A1 enter: A1 (the label for the first instructional method). In cell B1 enter: A2. In cell C1 enter: A3. Then enter the 5 scores for each method in the respective column. (Note that the data are entered by *column*, even though they are listed by row in Table 13.4.)

(2)   Click **Tools** → **Data Analysis** → **Anova: Single Factor**. Click **OK**.

(3)   In the dialog box, for **Input Range** enter: $A$1:$C$6. Select **Columns**. Check **Labels in First Row**. For **Output Range** enter: $D$1. Click **OK**.

A1	A2	A3	Anova: Single Factor				
86	90	82					
79	76	68	SUMMARY				
81	88	73	*Groups*	*Count*	*Sum*	*Average*	*Variance*
70	82	71	A1	5	400	80	38.5
84	89	81	A2	5	425	85	35
			A3	5	375	75	38.5

ANOVA						
Source of Variation	*SS*	*df*	*MS*	*F*	*P-value*	*F crit*
Between Groups	250	2	125	3.348214	0.069909	3.88529
Within Groups	448	12	37.33333			
Total	698	14				

Fig. 13-1 Excel output for one-factor design.

13.9. Use Minitab to carry out the analysis in Problem 13.2 (data is Table 13.4).

The output given in Fig. 13-2 corresponds to the results obtained by manual calculation in Table 13.5. Whereas the critical-value approach to hypothesis testing had to be used in the hand calculation, the printout provides the *P* value, which is 0.070. Since this value is *not* less than 0.05, the null hypothesis that there are no differences among the population means cannot be rejected at the 5 percent level of significance.

The Minitab output given in Fig. 13-2 was obtained as follows:

(1)   Open Minitab. In the column-name for C1 enter: Method. In the column name for C2 enter: Score. Since there are 5 scores for each method, in C1 enter five 1s, five 2s and five 3s, which are the method labels. In C2 enter the 15 test scores, each associated (in groups of 5) with one of the three methods of instruction in C1.

(2)   Click **Stat** → **ANOVA** → **One-way**. For **Response** enter: Score. For **Factor** enter: Method. Click **OK**.

One-way ANOVA: Score versus Method

```
Analysis of Variance for Score
Source      DF        SS        MS        F        P
Method       2     250.0     125.0     3.35     0.070
Error       12     448.0      37.3
Total       14     698.0
                                  Individual 95% CIs For Mean
                                  Based on Pooled StDev
Level        N      Mean     StDev   -----+---------+---------+---------+-
1            5    80.000     6.205           (---------*---------)
2            5    85.000     5.916                   (---------*---------)
3            5    75.000     6.205   (---------*---------)
                                     -----+---------+---------+---------+-
Pooled StDev =     6.110            72.0      78.0      84.0      90.0
```

Fig. 13-2   Minitab output for one-factor design.

COMPUTER OUTPUT: RANDOMIZED BLOCK DESIGN

13.10.   Use Excel to carry out the analysis in Problem 13.5 (data in Table 13.9).

The output given in Fig. 13-3 corresponds to the results obtained by manual calculation in Table 13.10. In the printout, "Columns" designates the Method dimension. The reported P value is 0.003542, or 0.004 rounded. Because this P value is less than 0.05, we reject the null hypothesis at the 5 percent level of significance and

Level	A1	A2	A3	Anova: Two-Factor Without Replication
B1	86	90	82	
B2	84	89	81	
B3	81	88	73	
B4	79	76	68	
B5	70	82	71	

SUMMARY	Count	Sum	Average	Variance
B1	3	258	86	16
B2	3	254	84.66667	16.33333
B3	3	242	80.66667	56.33333
B4	3	223	74.33333	32.33333
B5	3	223	74.33333	44.33333
A1	5	400	80	38.5
A2	5	425	85	35
A3	5	375	75	38.5

ANOVA

Source of Variation	SS	df	MS	F	P-value	F crit
Rows	367.3333	4	91.83333	9.107438	0.004499	3.837854
Columns	250	2	125	12.39669	0.003542	4.458968
Error	80.66667	8	10.08333			
Total	698	14				

Fig. 13-3   Excel output for randomized block design.

conclude that there is a difference among the means in the sampled population for the different methods of instruction. Note that there is also a difference among the means with respect to the blocking factor of level of ability (with $P = 0.004499$). But this is not the focus of our interest, and indeed, we would expect that trainees at different levels of ability would perform differently.

The Excel output given in Fig. 13-3 was obtained as follows:

(1) Open Excel. In cell A1 enter: Level. Enter the labels for the 5 levels of ability in column A, beginning at cell A2: B1, B2, B3, B4, and B5. In cells B1 to D1 enter the labels A1, A2, and A3, respectively. Enter the data in each column as given in Table 13.9.

(2) Click **Tools** → **Data Analysis** → **Anova: Two-Factor Without Replication**. Click **OK**.

(3) In the dialog box, for **Input Range** enter: $A$1:$D$6. Check **Labels**. For **Output Range** enter: $E$1. Click **OK**.

13.11. Use Minitab to carry out the analysis in Problem 13.5 (data in Table 13.9).

The output given in Fig. 13-4 corresponds to the results obtained by manual calculation in Table 13.10. The reported P value for the Method dimension is 0.004. Because this P value is less than 0.05, we reject the null hypothesis at the 5 percent level of significance and conclude that there is a difference among the means in the sampled population for the different methods of instruction. Note that there is also a difference among the means with respect to the blocking factor of level of ability (with $P = 0.004$). But this is not the focus of our interest, and indeed, we would expect that trainees at different levels of ability would perform differently.

The Minitab output given in Fig. 13-4 was obtained as follows:

(1) Open Minitab. In the column name for C1 enter: Method. In the column name for C2 enter: Block. In the column name for C3 enter: Score. Since there are five scores for each method, in C1 enter five 1s, five 2s, and five 3s, which are the method labels. In C2 the blocking is identified by entering the labels sequence 1, 2, 3, 4, and 5 three times, once for each method of instruction. In C3 enter the 15 test scores in the column order as listed in Table 13.9.

(2) Click **Stat** → **ANOVA** → **Two-way**. For **Response** enter: Score. For **Row factor** enter: Method, and check **Display means**. For **Column factor** enter: Block. Click **OK**.

Two-way ANOVA: Score versus Method, Block

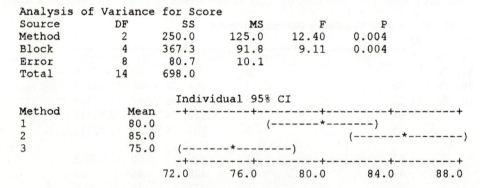

```
Analysis of Variance for Score
Source          DF        SS        MS        F         P
Method          2       250.0     125.0     12.40     0.004
Block           4       367.3      91.8      9.11     0.004
Error           8        80.7      10.1
Total          14       698.0

                            Individual 95% CI
Method          Mean    -+---------+---------+---------+---------+
1               80.0                      (-------*-------)
2               85.0                                  (-------*--------)
3               75.0      (-------*--------)
                        -+---------+---------+---------+---------+
                        72.0      76.0      80.0      84.0      88.0
```

Fig. 13-4   Minitab output for randomized block design.

COMPUTER OUTPUT: TWO-FACTOR COMPLETELY RANDOMIZED DESIGN

13.12. Use Excel to carry out the analysis in Problem 13.7 (data in Table 13.13).

The output given in Fig. 13-5 corresponds to the results obtained by manual calculation in Table 13.14. Three P values are reported. The $P = 0.641678$ for "Sample" is for the differences among the means for the subject areas; the result indicates that there is no difference in mean scores according to subject area of instruction. The $P = 3.05E - 05$, or less than 0.000, is for the mean differences among the methods of instruction; at the designated

5 percent level of significance, the null hypothesis is rejected, and there *is* a difference among the mean scores according to the method of instruction in the population. The $P = 0.002111$ is for the interaction effect between method of instruction and subject area; consequently, at the 5 percent level of significance, we reject the null hypothesis that there is no interaction effect in the population. This means that in the population the effectiveness of the three methods of instruction varies according to subject area.

The Excel output given in Fig. 13-5 was obtained as follows:

(1) Open Excel. In cell A1 enter: Subject. In cells B1-D1 enter A1, A2, and A3, respectively. Then in column A, in cell A2 enter: B1. In cell A5 enter: B2. In cell A8 enter: B3. In cell A11 enter: B4. Enter the date in columns B to D as given in Table 13.13.

(2) Click **Tools → Data Analysis → Anova: Two-Factor With Replication**. Click **OK**.

(3) In the dialog box, for **Input Range** enter: $A\$1:\$D\$13. For **Rows per sample** enter: 3. For **Output Range** enter: $E\$1. Click **OK**.

Subject	A1	A2	A3	Anova: Two-Factor With Replication
B1	70	83	81	
	79	89	86	
	72	78	79	
B2	77	77	74	
	81	87	69	
	79	88	77	
B3	82	94	72	
	78	83	79	
	80	79	75	
B4	85	84	68	
	90	90	71	
	87	88	69	

SUMMARY	A1	A2	A3	Total
B1				
Count	3	3	3	9
Sum	221	250	246	717
Average	73.66667	83.33333	82	79.66667
Variance	22.33333	30.33333	13	37
B2				
Count	3	3	3	9
Sum	237	252	220	709
Average	79	84	73.33333	78.77778
Variance	4	37	16.33333	35.69444
B3				
Count	3	3	3	9
Sum	240	256	226	722
Average	80	85.33333	75.33333	80.22222
Variance	4	60.33333	12.33333	37.94444
B4				
Count	3	3	3	9
Sum	262	262	208	732
Average	87.33333	87.33333	69.33333	81.33333
Variance	6.333333	9.333333	2.333333	85.5
Total				
Count	12	12	12	
Sum	960	1020	900	
Average	80	85	75	
Variance	32.54545	27.45455	30.90909	

ANOVA

Source of Variation	SS	df	MS	F	P-value	F crit
Sample	30.88889	3	10.2963	0.567637	0.641678	3.008786
Columns	600	2	300	16.53905	3.05E-05	3.402832
Interaction	533.7778	6	88.96296	4.904543	0.002111	2.508187
Within	435.3333	24	18.13889			
Total	1600	35				

Fig. 13-5 Excel output for two-factor design.

13.13. Use Minitab to carry out the analysis in Problem 13.7 (data in Table 13.13).

The output given in Fig. 13-6 corresponds to the results obtained by manual calculation in Table 13.14. Three P values are reported. The $P = 0.0000$ is for the differences among the means for the methods of instruction; at the designated 5 percent level of significance the null hypothesis is rejected, and there *is* a difference according to the methods of instruction. The $P = 0.642$ is for the differences among the means for the subject areas; the result indicates that there is no difference in mean scores according to subject area of instruction. The $P = 0.002$ is for the interaction effect between method of instruction and subject area; consequently, at the 5 percent level we reject the null hypothesis that there is no interaction effect in the population. This means that in the population the effectiveness of the three methods of instruction varies according to subject area.

The Minitab output given in Fig. 13-6 was obtained as follows:

(1) Open Minitab. In the column-name for C1 enter: Method. In the column name for C2 enter: Subject. In the column name for C3 enter: Score. In C1 enter twelve 1s, twelve 2s, and twelve 3s. In C2 enter the sequence of coded subject areas (1, 1, 1; 2, 2, 2; 3, 3, 3; and 4, 4, 4) three times, so that each such sequence is associated with each method in C1. In C3 enter the 36 test scores in the column order as listed in Table 13.13.

(2) Click **Stat** → **ANOVA** → **Two-way**. For **Response** enter: Score. For **Row factor** enter: Method, and check **Display means**. For **Column factor** enter: Subject. Click **OK**.

Two-way ANOVA: Score versus Method, Subject

```
Analysis of Variance for Score
Source          DF          SS          MS          F          P
Method           2       600.0       300.0      16.54      0.000
Subject          3        30.9        10.3       0.57      0.642
Interaction      6       533.8        89.0       4.90      0.002
Error           24       435.3        18.1
Total           35      1600.0

                           Individual 95% CI
Method           Mean     ---------+---------+---------+---------+--
1                80.0                   (-----*-----)
2                85.0                                  (-----*------)
3                75.0       (-----*------)
                           ---------+---------+---------+---------+--
                              76.0      80.0      84.0      88.0
```

Fig. 13-6 Minitab output for two-factor design.

Supplementary Problems

ONE-FACTOR COMPLETELY RANDOMIZED DESIGN

13.14. Four types of advertising displays were set up in 12 retail outlets, with three outlets randomly assigned to each of the displays, for the purpose of studying the point-of-sale impact of the displays. With reference to Table 13.15, test the null hypothesis that there are no differences among the mean sales values for the four types of displays, using the 5 percent level of significance.

Ans. Critical F ($df = 3, 8$) = 4.07. Computed $F = 4.53$. Therefore, reject the null hypothesis that $\alpha_k = 0$ for all treatment levels.

Table 13.15   Product Sales According to Advertising Display Used

Type display	Sales			Total sales	Mean sales
A_1	40	44	43	127	42.3
A_2	53	54	59	166	55.3
A_3	48	38	46	132	44.0
A_4	48	61	47	156	52.0

13.15. Use available computer software to carry out the analysis in Problem 13.14 (data in Table 13.15) for the one-factor completely randomized design.

Ans. Same as for Problem 13.14.

THE RANDOMIZED BLOCK DESIGN (TWO-WAY ANALYSIS WITHOUT INTERACTION)

13.16. The designs produced by four automobile designers are evaluated by three product managers, as reported in Table 13.16. Test the null hypothesis that the average ratings of the designs do not differ, using the 1 percent level of significance.

Ans. Critical F ($df = 3, 6$) = 9.78. Computed $F = 12.29$. Therefore, reject the null hypothesis that $\alpha_k = 0$ for all treatment (column) effects.

Table 13.16   Ratings of Automobile Designs

Evaluator	Designer				Total (T_j)	Mean ($\bar{X}_j$)
	1	2	3	4		
A	87	79	83	92	341	85.25
B	83	73	85	89	330	82.50
C	91	85	90	92	358	89.50
Total (T_k)	261	237	258	273	Grand Total $T = 1,029$	
Mean rating ($\bar{X}_k$)	87.0	79.0	86.0	91.0		Grand mean $\bar{X}_T = 85.75$

13.17. Use available computer software to carry out the analysis in Problem 13.16 (data in Table 13.16) for the randomized block design.

Ans. Same as for Problem 13.16.

TWO-FACTOR COMPLETELY RANDOMIZED DESIGN

13.18. The smallest data table for which two-way analysis of variance with interaction can be carried out is a 2×2 table with two observations per cell. Table 13.17, which presents sales data for a consumer product in eight randomly assigned regions, is such a table. Test the effect of the two factors and of the interaction between the two factors on the weekly sales levels, using the 1 percent level of significance. Consider the meaning of your test results.

Ans. At the 1 percent level of significance the critical values of F associated with the column, row, and interaction effects are, respectively, F ($df = 1, 4$) = 21.20; F ($df = 1, 4$) = 21.20; and F ($df = 1, 4$) = 21.20. The computed F ratios are, respectively, $F = 96.00$, $F = 49.52$, and $F = 7.66$. Therefore, there are significant column and row effects, but no significant interaction effects. Both advertising and discounting influence the level of sales, and they do so independently of each other.

Table 13.17   Weekly Sales in Thousands of Dollars with and without Advertising, and with and without Discount Pricing

Discount pricing	With advertising	Without advertising	Total (T_j)	Mean ($\bar{X}_j$)
With discounting	9.8 10.6	6.0 5.3	31.7	7.925
Without discounting	6.2 7.1	4.3 3.9	21.5	5.375
Total (T_k)	33.7	19.5	Grand total $T = 53.2$	
Mean ($\bar{X}_k$)	8.425	4.875		Grand mean $\bar{X}_T = 6.650$

13.19. Use available computer software to carry out the analysis in Problem 13.18 (data in Table 13.17) for the two-factor completely randomized design.

Ans.   Same as for Problem 13.18 except for slight rounding differences.

CHAPTER 14

Linear Regression and Correlation Analysis

14.1 OBJECTIVES AND ASSUMPTIONS OF REGRESSION ANALYSIS

The primary objective of regression analysis is to estimate the value of a random variable (the *dependent variable*) given that the value of an associated variable (the *independent variable*) is known. The dependent variable is also called the *response variable*, while the independent variable is also called the *predictor variable*. The *regression equation* is the algebraic formula by which the estimated value of the dependent, or response, variable is determined (see Section 14.3).

The term *simple regression analysis* indicates that the value of a dependent variable is estimated on the basis of one independent, or predictor, variable. *Multiple regression analysis* (covered in Chapter 15) is concerned with estimating the value of a dependent variable on the basis of two or more independent variables.

The general assumptions underlying the regression analysis model presented in this chapter are that (1) the dependent variable is a random variable, and (2) the independent and dependent variables are linearly associated. Assumption (1) indicates that although the values of the independent variable may be controlled, the values of the dependent variable must be obtained through the process of random sampling.

If interval estimation or hypothesis testing is done in the regression analysis, three additional required assumptions are that (3) the variances of the conditional distributions of the dependent variable, given different values for the independent variable, are all equal, (4) the conditional distributions of the dependent variable, given different values for the independent variable, are all normally distributed in the population of values, and (5) the observed values of the dependent variable are independent of each other.

EXAMPLE 1. An analyst wishes to estimate delivery time as the dependent variable, based on distance as the independent variable for industrial parts shipped by truck. Suppose 10 recent shipments are chosen from the company's records such that the highway distances involved are about equally dispersed between 100 miles distance and 1,000 miles distance, and the delivery times for each shipment are recorded. Since the highway distance is to be used as the independent variable, this selection of trips of specific distances is acceptable. On the other hand, the dependent variable of delivery time is a random variable in this study, which conforms to the assumption underlying regression analysis. Whether or not the two variables have a linear relationship would generally be investigated by constructing a scatter plot (see Section 14.2) or a residual plot (see Section 14.4). Such diagrams also are used to observe whether the vertical scatter (variance) is about equal along the regression line.

14.2 THE SCATTER PLOT

A *scatter plot* is a graph in which each plotted point represents an observed pair of values for the independent and dependent variables. The value of the independent variable X is plotted with respect to the horizontal axis, and the value of the dependent variable Y is plotted with respect to the vertical axis. (See Problem 14.1.)

The form of the relationship represented by the scatter plot can be *curvilinear* rather than linear. While regression analysis for curvilinear relationships is outside the scope of this book, there is a limited discussion of curvilinear trend analysis in Section 16.2. For relationships that are not linear, a frequent approach is to determine a method of transforming values of one or both variables so that the relationship of the transformed values is linear. Then linear regression analysis can be applied to the transformed values, and estimated values of the dependent variable can be transformed back to the original measurement scale.

EXAMPLE 2. An example of a curvilinear relationship would be the relationship between years since incorporation for a company and sales level, given that each year the sales level has increased by the same percentage over the preceding year. The resulting curve with an increasing slope would be indicative of a so-called exponential relationship.

If the scatter plot indicates a relationship that is generally linear, then a straight line is fitted to the data. The precise location of this line is determined by the method of least squares (see Section 14.3). As illustrated in Example 3, a regression line with a positive slope indicates a direct relationship between the variables, a negative slope indicates an inverse relationship between the variables, and a slope of zero indicates that the variables are unrelated. Further, the extent of vertical scatter of the plotted points with respect to the regression line indicates the degree of relationship between the two variables.

EXAMPLE 3. Figure 14-1 includes several scatter plots and associated regression lines demonstrating several types of relationships between the variables.

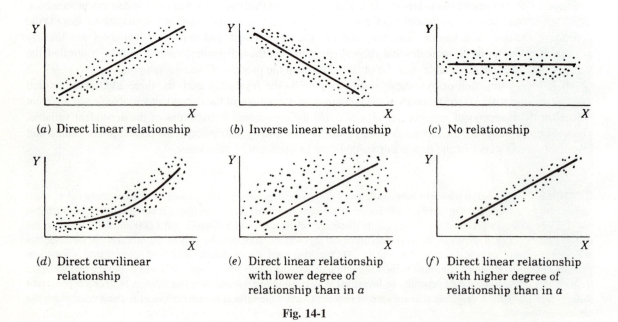

(*a*) Direct linear relationship

(*b*) Inverse linear relationship

(*c*) No relationship

(*d*) Direct curvilinear relationship

(*e*) Direct linear relationship with lower degree of relationship than in *a*

(*f*) Direct linear relationship with higher degree of relationship than in *a*

Fig. 14-1

14.3   THE METHOD OF LEAST SQUARES FOR FITTING A REGRESSION LINE

The linear equation that represents the simple linear regression model is

$$Y_i = \beta_0 + \beta_1 X_i + \varepsilon_i \qquad (14.1)$$

where Y_i = value of the dependent variable in the ith trial, or observation

$\quad\quad \beta_0$ = first parameter of the regression equation, which indicates the value of Y when $X = 0$

$\quad\quad \beta_1$ = second parameter of the regression equation, called the regression coefficients, which indicates the slope of the regression line

$\quad\quad X_i$ = the specified value of the independent variable in the ith trial, or observation

$\quad\quad \varepsilon_i$ = random-sampling error in the ith trial, or observation (ε is the Greek epsilon)

The parameters β_0 and β_1 in the linear regression model are estimated by the values b_0 and b_1 that are based on sample data. Thus, the linear regression equation based on sample data that is used to estimate a single (conditional) value of the dependent variable, where the "hat" over the Y indicates that it is an estimated value, is

$$\hat{Y} = b_0 + b_1 X \qquad (14.2)$$

Depending on the mathematical criterion used, a number of different linear equations can be developed for a given scatter plot. By the *least-squares criterion* the best-fitting regression line (and the best equation) is that for which the sum of the squared deviations between the estimated and actual values of the dependent variable for the sample data is minimized. The computational formulas by which the values of b_0 and b_1 in the regression equation can be determined for the equation which satisfies the least-squares criterion are

$$b_1 = \frac{\Sigma XY - n\bar{X}\bar{Y}}{\Sigma X^2 - n\bar{X}^2} \qquad (14.3)$$

$$b_0 = \bar{Y} - b_1\bar{X} \qquad (14.4)$$

Once the regression equation is formulated, then this equation can be used to estimate the value of the dependent variable given the value of the independent variable. However, such estimation should be done only within the range of the values of the independent variable originally sampled, since there is no statistical basis to assume that the regression line is appropriate outside these limits. Further, it should be determined whether the relationship expressed by the regression equation is real or could have occurred in the sample data purely by chance (see Section 14.6). Problem 14.2 illustrates the determination of a regression equation based on sample data.

14.4   RESIDUALS AND RESIDUAL PLOTS

For a given value X of the independent variable, the regression line value $\hat{Y}$ often is called the *fitted value* of the dependent variable. The difference between the observed value Y and the fitted value $\hat{Y}$ is called the *residual* for that observation and is denoted by e:

$$e = Y - \hat{Y} \qquad (14.5)$$

Problem 14.3 reports the full set of residuals for particular sample data. A *residual plot* is obtained by plotting the residuals e with respect to the independent variable X or, alternatively with respect to the fitted regression line values $\hat{Y}$. Such a plot can be used as an alternative to the use of the scatter plot to investigate whether the assumptions concerning linearity and equality of conditional variances appear to be satisfied.

Problem 14.3 includes a residual plot for the data. Residual plots are particularly important in multiple regression analysis, as described in Chapter 15.

The set of residuals for the sample data also serve as the basis for calculating the standard error of estimate, as described in the following section.

14.5   THE STANDARD ERROR OF ESTIMATE

The *standard error of estimate* is the conditional standard deviation of the dependent variable Y given a value of the independent variable X. For population data, the standard error of estimate is represented by the symbol $\sigma_{Y.X}$. The deviations formula by which this value is estimated on the basis of sample data is

$$s_{Y.X} = \sqrt{\frac{\Sigma(Y - \hat{Y})^2}{n - 2}} = \sqrt{\frac{\Sigma e^2}{n - 2}} \qquad (14.6)$$

Note that the numerator in Formula (*14.6*) is the sum of the squares of the residuals described in the preceding section. Although Formula (*14.6*) clearly reflects the idea that the standard error of estimate is the standard deviation with respect to the regression line (that is, it is the standard deviation of the vertical "scatter" about the line), computationally the formula requires that every fitted value $\hat{Y}$ be calculated for the sample data. The alternative computational formula, which does not require determination of each fitted value and is therefore generally easier to use, is

$$s_{Y.X} = \sqrt{\frac{\Sigma Y^2 - b_0 \Sigma Y - b_1 \Sigma XY}{n - 2}} \qquad (14.7)$$

As will be seen in the following sections, the standard error of estimate serves as the cornerstone for the various standard errors used in the hypothesis testing and interval-estimation procedures in regression analysis. Problems 14.5 and 14.6 illustrate the calculation of the standard error of estimate by the computational formula and deviations formula, respectively.

14.6   INFERENCES CONCERNING THE SLOPE

Before a regression equation is used for the purpose of estimation or prediction, we should first determine if a relationship appears to exist between the two variables in the population, or whether the observed relationship in the sample could have occurred by chance. In the absence of any relationship in the population, the slope of the population regression line would, by definition, be zero: $\beta_1 = 0$. Therefore the usual null hypothesis tested is H_0: $\beta_1 = 0$. The null hypothesis can also be formulated as a one-tail test, in which case the alternative hypothesis is not simply that the two variables are related, but that the relationship is of a specific type (direct or inverse).

A hypothesized value of the slope is tested by computing a t statistic and using $n - 2$ degrees of freedom. Two degrees of freedom are lost in the process of inference because *two* parameter estimates, b_0 and b_1, are included in the regression equation. The standard formula is

$$t = \frac{b_1 - (\beta_1)_0}{s_{b_1}} \qquad (14.8)$$

where

$$s_{b_1} = \frac{s_{Y.X}}{\sqrt{\Sigma X^2 - n\bar{X}^2}} \qquad (14.9)$$

However, when the null hypothesis is that the slope is zero, which generally is the hypothesis, then formula (14.8) is simplified and is stated as

$$t = \frac{b_1}{s_{b_1}} \tag{14.10}$$

Problems 14.7 and 14.8 illustrate a two-tail test and a one-tail test for the slope, respectively.

The confidence interval for the population slope β_1, in which the degrees of freedom associated with the t are once again $n - 2$, is constructed as follows:

$$b_1 \pm t s_{b_1} \tag{14.11}$$

Problem 14.9 illustrates the construction of a confidence interval for the population slope.

14.7 CONFIDENCE INTERVALS FOR THE CONDITIONAL MEAN

The point estimate for the conditional *mean* of the dependent variable, given a specific value of X, is the regression line value $\hat{Y}$. When we use the regression equation to estimate the conditional *mean*, the appropriate symbol for the conditional mean of Y that is estimated is $\hat{\mu}_Y$:

$$\hat{\mu}_Y = b_0 + b_1 X \tag{14.12}$$

Based on sample data, the standard error of the conditional mean varies in value according to the designated value of X and is

$$s_{\bar{Y}.X} = s_{Y.X} \sqrt{\frac{1}{n} + \frac{(X - \bar{X})^2}{\Sigma X^2 - [(\Sigma X)^2 / n]}} \tag{14.13}$$

Given the point estimate of the conditional mean and the standard error of the conditional mean, the confidence interval for the conditional mean, using $n - 2$ degrees of freedom, is

$$\hat{\mu}_Y \pm t s_{\bar{Y}.X} \tag{14.14}$$

Again, it is $n - 2$ degrees of freedom because the two parameter estimates b_0 and b_1 are required in the regression equation. Problem 14.10 illustrates the construction of a confidence interval for the conditional mean.

14.8 PREDICTION INTERVALS FOR INDIVIDUAL VALUES OF THE DEPENDENT VARIABLE

As contrasted to a confidence interval, which is concerned with estimating a population parameter, a *prediction interval* is concerned with estimating an *individual* value and is therefore a probability interval. It might seem that a prediction interval could be constructed by using the standard error of estimate defined in Formulas (14.6) and (14.7). However, such an interval would be incomplete, because the standard error of estimate does not include the uncertainty associated with the fact that the position of the regression line based on sample data includes sampling error and generally is not identical to the population regression line. The complete standard error for a prediction interval is called the *standard error of forecast*, and it includes the uncertainty associated with the vertical "scatter" about the regression line *plus* the uncertainty associated with the position of the regression line value itself. The basic formula for the standard error of forecast is

$$s_{Y(\text{next})} = \sqrt{s_{Y.X}^2 + s_{\bar{Y}.X}^2} \tag{14.15}$$

The computational version of the formula for the standard error of forecast is

$$s_{Y(\text{next})} = s_{Y.X}\sqrt{1 + \frac{1}{n} + \frac{(X - \bar{X})^2}{\Sigma X^2 - [(\Sigma X)^2/n]}} \qquad (14.16)$$

Finally, the prediction interval for an individual value of the dependent, variable, using $n - 2$ degrees of freedom, is

$$\hat{Y} \pm ts_{Y(\text{next})} \qquad (14.17)$$

The determination of the standard error of forecast and the construction of a prediction interval is illustrated in Problem 14.11.

14.9   OBJECTIVES AND ASSUMPTIONS OF CORRELATION ANALYSIS

In contrast to regression analysis, correlation analysis measures the degree of relationship between the variables. As was true in our coverage of regression analysis, in this chapter we restrict our coverage to *simple correlation analysis*, which is concerned with measuring the relationship between only one independent variable and the dependent variable. In Chapter 15, we describe multiple correlation analysis.

The population assumptions underlying simple correlation analysis are that (1) the relationship between the two variables is linear, (2) both of the variables are random variables, (3) for each variable the conditional variances, given different values of the other variable, are equal, (4) for each variable, observed values are independent of other observed values for that variable, and (5) for each variable the conditional distributions, given different values of the other variable, are all normal distributions. The last assumption is that of a *bivariate normal distribution*. Note that these assumptions are similar to the assumptions underlying statistical inference in regression analysis, except that in correlation analysis the assumptions apply to *both* variables, whereas in regression analysis the independent variable can be set at various specific values and need not be a random variable.

EXAMPLE 4.   Refer to the data collection procedure in Example 1, which concerns the variables of highway distance and delivery time for a sample of 10 recent shipments of industrial parts shipped by truck. Instead of the analyst choosing the 10 shipments so that they are about equally dispersed from 100 miles distance to 1,000 miles distance, the 10 shipments are chosen entirely randomly, without regard to either the highway distance or the delivery time included in each observation, Unlike Example 1, in which only the delivery time is a random variable, in the revised sampling plan both variables are random variables and therefore clearly qualify for correlation analysis.

14.10   THE COEFFICIENT OF DETERMINATION

Consider that if an individual value of the dependent variable Y were estimated without knowledge of the value of any other variable, then the variance associated with this estimate, and the basis for constructing a prediction interval, would be the variance σ_Y^2. Given a value of X, however, the variance associated with the estimate is reduced and is represented by $\sigma_{Y.X}^2$ (or $s_{Y.X}^2$ for sample data), as described in Section 14.5. If there is a relationship between the two variables, then $\sigma_{Y.X}^2$ will always be smaller than σ_Y^2. For a perfect relationship, in which all values of the dependent variable are equal to the respective fitted regression line values, $\sigma_{Y.X}^2 = 0$. Therefore, in the absence of a perfect relationship, the value of $\sigma_{Y.X}^2$ indicates the uncertainty remaining *after* consideration of the value of the independent variable. Or, we can say that the ratio of $\sigma_{Y.X}^2$ to σ_Y^2 indicates the proportion of variance (uncertainty) in the dependent variable that remains unexplained after a specific value of the independent variable has been given:

$$\left(\begin{array}{c} \text{proportion of variance} \\ \text{remaining unexplained} \end{array} \right) = \frac{\sigma^2_{Y.X}}{\sigma_Y 2} = \frac{\text{unexplained variance remaining in } Y}{\text{total variance in } Y} \qquad (14.18)$$

In (14.18) $\sigma^2_{Y.X}$ is determined by the procedure described in Section 14.5 (except that population data are assumed) and σ^2_Y is calculated by the general formulas presented in Sections 4.6 and 4.7.

Given the proportion of unexplained variance, a useful measure of relationship is the *coefficient of determination*—the complement of the above ratio, indicating the proportion of variance in the dependent variable that is statistically *explained* by the regression equation (i.e., by knowledge of the associated independent variable X). For population data the coefficient of determination is represented by the Greek ρ^2 (rho squared) and is determined by

$$\rho^2 = 1 - \frac{\sigma^2_{Y.X}}{\sigma^2_Y} \qquad (14.19)$$

proportion of explained variance $= 1 - $ (proportion of unexplained variance)

For sample data, the estimated value of the coefficient of determination can be obtained by the corresponding formula:

$$r^2 = 1 - \frac{s^2_{Y.X}}{s^2_Y} \qquad (14.20)$$

For computational purposes, the following formula for the sample coefficient of determination is convenient:

$$r^2 = \frac{b_0 \Sigma Y + b_1 \Sigma XY - n\bar{Y}^2}{\Sigma Y^2 - n\bar{Y}^2} \qquad (14.21)$$

Application of (14.21) is illustrated in Problem 14.12. Although this is a frequently used formula for computing the coefficient of determination for sample data, it does not incorporate any correction for biasedness and includes a slight positive bias. See the following section for the correction factor that can be used.

14.11   THE COEFFICIENT OF CORRELATION

Although the coefficient of determination r^2 is relatively easy to interpret, it does not lend itself to statistical testing. However, the square root of the coefficient of determination, which is called the *coefficient of correlation r*, does lend itself to statistical testing because it can be used to define a test statistic that is distributed as the t distribution when the population correlation ρ equals 0. The value of the correlation coefficient can range from -1.00 to $+1.00$. The arithmetic sign associated with the correlation coefficient, which is always the same as the sign associated with β_1 in the regression equation, indicates the direction of the relationship between X and Y (positive $=$ direct; negative $=$ inverse). The coefficient of correlation for population data, with the arithmetic sign being the same as that for the slope β_1 in the regression equation, is

$$\rho = \sqrt{\rho^2} \qquad (14.22)$$

The coefficient of correlation for sample data, with the arithmetic sign being the same as that for the sample slope b_1, is

$$r = \sqrt{r^2} \qquad (14.23)$$

In summary, the sign of the correlation coefficient indicates the direction of the relationship between the X and Y variables, while the absolute value of the coefficient indicates the extent of relationship. The squared value of the correlation coefficient is the coefficient of determination and indicates the proportion of the variance in Y explained by knowledge of X (and vice versa).

EXAMPLE 5. Figure 14-2 illustrates the general appearance of the scatter diagrams associated with several correlation values.

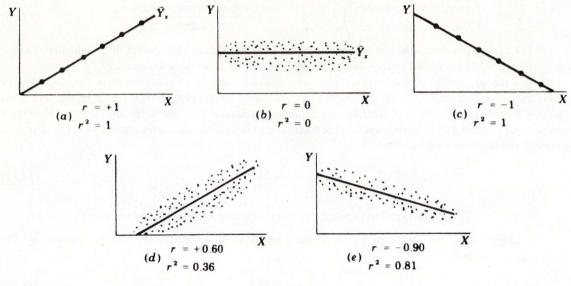

Fig. 14-2

As an alternative to (*14.21*), the following formula does not require prior determination of the regression value of b_0 and b_1. This formula would be used when the purpose of the analysis is to determine the extent and type of relationship between two variables, but without an accompanying interest in estimating Y given X. When this formula is used, the sign of the correlation coefficient is determined automatically, without the necessity of observing or calculating the slope of the regression line. The formula is

$$r = \frac{n\Sigma XY - \Sigma X \Sigma Y}{\sqrt{n\Sigma X^2 - (\Sigma X)^2}\sqrt{n\Sigma Y^2 - (\Sigma Y)^2}} \tag{14.24}$$

Application of (*14.24*) is illustrated in Problem 14.13.

The sample coefficient of correlation r is somewhat biased as an estimator of ρ, with an absolute value that is too large. This factor is not mentioned in many textbooks because the amount of bias is slight, except for very small samples. An unbiased estimator for the coefficient of determination for the population can be obtained as follows:

$$\hat{\rho}^2 = 1 - (1 - r^2)\left(\frac{n-1}{n-2}\right) \tag{14.25}$$

14.12 THE COVARIANCE APPROACH TO UNDERSTANDING THE CORRELATION COEFFICIENT

Another measure that can be used to express the relationship between two random variables is the sample *covariance*. The covariance measures the extent to which two variables "vary together" and is used by financial analysts for determining the total risk associated with interrelated investments. Just as for the correlation coefficient, a positive sign indicates a *direct* relationship while a negative sign indicates an *inverse* relationship. The formula for the sample covariances is

$$\text{cov}(X, Y) = \frac{\Sigma[(X - \bar{X})(Y - \bar{Y})]}{n - 1} \tag{14.26}$$

By studying Formula (*14.26*) we can conclude, for example, that when the observed value of Y tends to vary in the same direction from its mean as does the observed value of X from its mean, then the products of those deviations will tend to be positive values. The sum of such products will then be positive, indicating the direct, rather than inverse, relationship. Whereas the coefficient of correlation is a standardized measure of relationship that can range in value between only -1.00 and $+1.00$, the covariance has no such limits in value and is not a standardized measure. The formula by which the covariance can be converted into the coefficient of correlation is

$$r = \frac{\text{cov}(X, Y)}{s_X s_Y} \qquad (14.27)$$

Problem 14.14 illustrates the determination of a sample covariance and its conversion into the associated correlation coefficient.

14.13 SIGNIFICANCE TESTING WITH RESPECT TO THE CORRELATION COEFFICIENT

Typically, the null hypothesis of interest is that the population correlation $\rho = 0$, for if this hypothesis is rejected at a specified α level, we would conclude that there is a relationship between the two variables in the population. The hypothesis can also be formulated as a one-tail test. Given that the assumptions in Section 14.9 are satisfied, the following sampling statistic involving r is distributed as the t distribution with $df = n - 2$ when $\rho = 0$:

$$t = \frac{r}{\sqrt{\dfrac{1 - r^2}{n - 2}}} \qquad (14.28)$$

Testing the null hypothesis that $\rho = 0$ is equivalent to testing the null hypothesis that $\beta = 0$ in the regression equation. (See Problem 14.15.)

14.14 PITFALLS AND LIMITATIONS ASSOCIATED WITH REGRESSION AND CORRELATION ANALYSIS

(1) In regression analysis a value of Y cannot be legitimately estimated if the value of X is outside the range of values that served as the basis for the regression equation.

(2) If the estimate of Y involves the prediction of a result that has not yet occurred, the historical data that served as the basis for the regression equation may not be relevant for future events.

(3) The use of a prediction or a confidence interval is based on the assumption that the conditional distributions of Y, and thus of the residuals, are normal and have equal variances.

(4) A significant correlation coefficient does not necessarily indicate causation, but rather may indicate a common linkage to other events.

(5) A significant correlation is not necessarily an important correlation. Given a large sample, a correlation of, say, $r = +0.10$ can be significantly different from 0 at $\alpha = 0.05$. Yet the coefficient of determination of $r^2 = 0.01$ for this example indicates that only 1 percent of the variance in Y is statistically explained by knowing X.

(6) The interpretation of the coefficients of correlation and determination is based on the assumption of a bivariate normal distribution for the population and, for each variable, equal conditional variances.

(7) For both regression and correlation analysis, a linear model is assumed. For a relationship that is curvilinear, a transformation to achieve linearity may be available. Another possibility is to restrict the analysis to the range of values within which the relationship is essentially linear.

14.15 USING EXCEL AND MINITAB

Computer software is available to carry out the various procedures of simple regression and correlation analysis that are covered in this chapter. Solved Problem 14.17 illustrates the use of Excel and compares the output to the results obtained by manual calculation in the preceding end-of-chapter problems. Problem 14.18 illustrates the use of Minitab and compares the output to the results obtained by manual calculation in the preceding end-of-chapter problems.

Solved Problems

LINEAR REGRESSION ANALYSIS

14.1. Suppose an analyst takes a random sample of 10 recent truck shipments made by a company and records the distance in miles and delivery time to the nearest half-day from the time that the shipment was made available for pick-up. Construct the scatter plot for the data in Table 14.1 and consider whether linear regression analysis appears appropriate.

Table 14.1   Sample Observations of Trucking Distance and Delivery Time for 10 Randomly Selected Shipments

Sampled shipment	1	2	3	4	5	6	7	8	9	10
Distance (X), miles	825	215	1,070	550	480	920	1,350	325	670	1,215
Delivery time (Y), days	3.5	1.0	4.0	2.0	1.0	3.0	4.5	1.5	3.0	5.0

The scatter plot for these data is portrayed in Fig. 14-3. The first reported pair of values in the table is represented by the dot entered above 825 on the X axis and aligned with 3.5 with respect to the Y axis. The other nine points in the scatter plot were similarly entered. From the diagram, it appears that the plotted points generally follow a linear relationship and the vertical scatter at the line is about the same for low values and high values of X. Thus linear regression analysis appears appropriate.

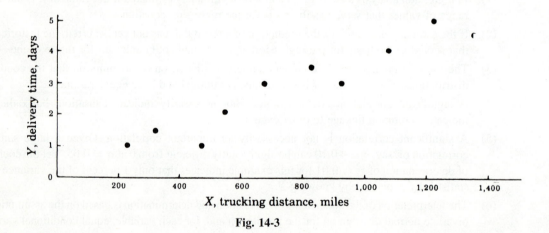

Fig. 14-3

14.2. Determine the least-squares regression equation for the data in Problem 14.1, and enter the regression line on the scatter plot for these data.

Referring to Table 14.2,

$$b_1 = \frac{\Sigma XY - n\bar{X}\bar{Y}}{\Sigma X^2 - n\bar{X}^2} = \frac{(26,370) - (10)(762)(2.85)}{7,104,300 - (10)(762)^2} = \frac{4,653}{1,297,860} = 0.0035851 \cong 0.0036$$

$$b_0 = \bar{Y} - b\bar{X} = 2.85 - (0.0036)(762) = 0.1068 \cong 0.11$$

Therefore, $$\bar{Y} = b_0 + b_1X = 0.11 + 0.0036X$$

Table 14.2   Calculations Associated with Determining the Linear Regression Equation for Estimating Delivery Time on the Basis of Trucking Distance

Sampled shipment	Distance (X), miles	Delivery time (Y), days	XY	X^2	Y^2
1	825	3.5	2,887.5	680,625	12.25
2	215	1.0	215.0	46,225	1.00
3	1,070	4.0	4,280.0	1,144,900	16.00
4	550	2.0	1,100.0	302,500	4.00
5	480	1.0	480.0	230,400	1.00
6	920	3.0	2,760.0	846,400	9.00
7	1,350	4.5	6,075.0	1,822,500	20.25
8	325	1.5	487.5	105,625	2.25
9	670	3.0	2,010.0	448,900	9.00
10	1,215	5.0	6,075.0	1,476,225	25.00
Totals	7,620	2.85	26,370.0	7,104,300	99.75
Mean	$\bar{X} = \dfrac{\Sigma X}{n} = \dfrac{7,620}{10}$ $= 762$	$\bar{Y} = \dfrac{\Sigma Y}{n} = \dfrac{28.5}{10}$ $= 2.85$			

This estimated regression line based on sample data is entered in the scatter plot for these data in Fig. 14-4. Note the dashed lines indicating the amount of deviation between each sampled value of Y and the corresponding estimated value, $\hat{Y}$. It is the sum of these squared deviations that is minimized by the linear regression line determined by the above procedure.

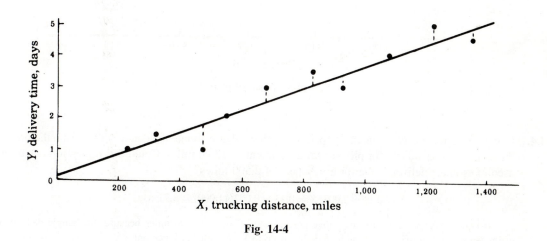

Fig. 14-4

14.3. Determine the residuals and construct a residual plot with respect to the fitted values for the data in Table 14.2, using the regression equation developed in Problem 14.2. Compare the residual plot to the scatter plot in Fig. 14-4.

Table 14.3 presents the calculation of the residuals, while Fig. 14-5 portrays the residual plot. Note that the general form of the scatter of the dependent-variable values Y with respect to the regression line in the scatter plot and the scatter of the residuals e with respect to the "0" line of deviation in the residual plot are similar, except for the "stretched" vertical scale in the residual plot.

Table 14.3   Calculation of Residuals for the Delivery Time Problem

Sampled shipment	Distance (X), miles	Delivery time (Y), days	Fitted value $(\hat{Y})$	Residual $(e = Y - \hat{Y})$
1	825	3.50	3.08	0.42
2	215	1.00	0.88	0.12
3	1,070	4.00	3.96	0.04
4	550	2.00	2.09	−0.09
5	480	1.00	1.84	−0.84
6	920	3.00	3.42	−0.42
7	1,350	4.50	4.97	−0.47
8	325	1.50	1.28	0.22
9	670	3.00	2.52	0.48
10	1,215	5.00	4.48	0.52

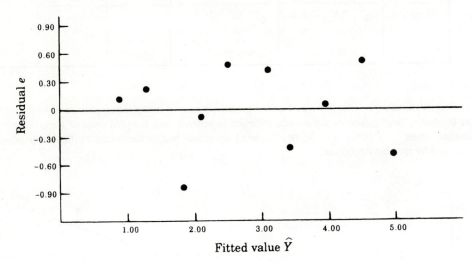

Fig. 14-5   Residual plot.

14.4.   Using the regression equation developed in Problem 14.2, estimate the delivery time from the time that the shipment is available for pick-up for a shipment of 1,000 miles. Could this regression equation be used to estimate delivery time for a shipment of 2,500 miles?

$$\hat{Y} = 0.11 + 0.0036X = 0.11 + 0.0036(1,000) = 3.71 \text{ days}$$

It is not appropriate to use the above equation for a trip of 2,500 miles because the sample data for this estimated linear regression equation included trips up to 1,350 miles distance only.

14.5.   Compute the standard error of estimate for the delivery-time analysis problem, referring to values determined in the solution to Problem 14.2.

$$s_{Y.X} = \sqrt{\frac{\Sigma Y^2 - b_0 \Sigma Y - b_1 \Sigma XY}{n-2}} = \sqrt{\frac{99.75 - (0.11)(28.5) - (0.0036)(26,370)}{10-2}}$$

$$= \sqrt{\frac{1.683}{8}} = \sqrt{0.2104} = 0.4587 \cong 0.46$$

14.6. Compute the standard error of estimate by the basic formula that utilizes the residuals determined in Problem 14.3. Compare your answer to that obtained by the computational formula in Problem 14.5 above.

$$s_{Y.X} = \sqrt{\frac{\Sigma e^2}{n-2}} = \sqrt{\frac{1.8526}{10-2}} = 0.4812 \cong 0.48$$

Except for a slight rounding difference, this answer corresponds to the one obtained in Problem 14.5.

14.7. Using the standard error of estimate from Problem 14.5, test the null hypothesis H_0: $\beta_1 = 0$ for the trucking distance and delivery-time data in Table 14.2, using the 5 percent level of significance.

Given $s_{Y.X} = 0.46$ and the values in Table 14.2,

$$s_{b_1} = \frac{s_{Y.X}}{\sqrt{\Sigma X^2 - n\bar{X}^2}} = \frac{0.46}{\sqrt{7,104,300 - 10(762)^2}} = \frac{0.46}{1,139.24} = 0.0004$$

$$H_0: \beta_1 = 0 \qquad H_1: \beta_1 \neq 0$$
$$\text{Critical } t(df = 8, \alpha = 0.05) = \pm 2.306$$
$$t = \frac{b_1}{s_{b_1}} = \frac{0.0036}{0.0004} = +9.00$$

Because the calculated t of $+9.00$ is in a region of rejection for this two-sided test, we conclude that there is a significant relationship between trucking distance and delivery time.

14.8. Referring to Problem 14.7, above, test the null hypothesis H_0: $\beta_1 \leq 0$ at the 5 percent level of significance.

$$H_0: \beta_1 = 0 \qquad H_1: \beta_1 > 0$$
$$\text{Critical } t(df = 8, \alpha = 0.05) = +1.860$$
$$t = +9.00 \qquad \text{(from Problem 14.7)}$$

Because the calculated t statistic of $+9.00$ exceeds the critical value of $+1.860$, the null hypothesis is rejected. For this one-tail test, we conclude that the slope of the population regression line is positive, and thus that there is a direct (rather than inverse) relationship between shipment distance and delivery time.

14.9. Determine the 95 percent confidence interval for β_1 for the trucking distance and delivery-time data discussed in the preceding problems.

Since $b_1 = 0.0036$ (from Problem 14.2) and $df = n - 2 = 10 - 2 = 8$, the 95 percent confidence interval for β_1 is

$$b_1 \pm ts_{b_1} = 0.0036 \pm (2.306)(0.0004) = 0.0036 \pm 0.0009 = 0.0027 \text{ to } 0.0045$$

Thus, with each additional mile of distance, the number of additional days required for delivery is somewhere between 0.0027 and 0.0045 with 95 percent confidence. Assuming a 24-hour day at receiving docks, this is equivalent to the additional delivery time per mile being somewhere between 3.9 and 6.5 min, with 95 percent confidence.

14.10. Using the values determined in the preceding problems, construct the 95 percent confidence interval for the *mean* delivery time for a trucking distance of 1,000 miles.

Given $\hat{\mu}_{\bar{Y}}$ (for $X = 1,000$) = 3.71 days, $s_{Y.X} = 0.46$, and the values in Table 14.2,

$$s_{\hat{Y}.X} = s_{Y.X}\sqrt{\frac{1}{n} + \frac{(X - \bar{X})^2}{\Sigma X^2 - (\Sigma X)^2/n}} = 0.46\sqrt{\frac{1}{10} + \frac{(1000 - 762)^2}{7,104,300 - (7,620)^2/10}} = 0.1748 \cong 0.17$$

The 95 percent confidence interval for the conditional mean (where $df = 10 - 2 = 8$) is

$$\hat{\mu}_Y \pm ts_{\hat{Y}.X} = 3.71 \pm (2.306)(0.17) = 3.71 \pm 0.39 = 3.32 \text{ to } 4.10 \text{ days}$$

Thus, for truck shipments of 1,000 miles, we estimate that the mean delivery time from the time that the shipment is available is between 3.32 and 4.10 days, with 95 percent confidence in this estimation interval.

14.11. Using the values determined in the preceding problems, determine the 95 percent prediction interval for the delivery time of a single shipment given that a distance of 1,000 miles is involved. Compare this interval with the one constructed in Problem 14.10.

Since $\hat{Y}$ (for $X = 1,000$) = 3.71 days, $s_{Y.X} = 0.46$, and $s_{\hat{Y}.X} = 0.17$,

$$s_{Y\text{next}} = \sqrt{s_{Y.X}^2 + s_{\hat{Y}.X}^2} = \sqrt{(0.46)^2 + (0.17)^2} = \sqrt{0.2405} = 0.4904 \cong 0.49$$

Where $df = 10 - 2 = 8$, the 95 percent prediction interval is

$$\hat{Y} \pm ts_{Y\text{next}} = 3.71 \pm 2.306(0.49) = 3.71 \pm 1.13 = 2.58 \text{ to } 4.84 \text{ days}$$

As expected, this prediction interval is somewhat wider than the confidence interval for the conditional mean in Problem 14.10, since in the present application the interval concerns an *individual* value for one particular shipment rather than a mean.

CORRELATION ANALYSIS

14.12. For the trucking distance and delivery-time data, the sampling procedure described in Problem 14.1 indicates that both variables are in fact random variables. If we further assume a bivariate normal distribution for the population and, for each variable, equal conditional variances, then correlation analysis can be applied to the sample data. Using values calculated in Problem 14.2, calculate the coefficient of determination for the sample data (ignore the slight biasedness associated with this coefficient).

$$r^2 = \frac{b_0 \Sigma Y + b_1 \Sigma XY - n\bar{Y}^2}{\Sigma Y^2 - n\bar{Y}^2}$$

$$= \frac{(0.11)(28.5) + (0.0036)(26,370) - (10)(2.85)^2}{99.75 - (10)(2.85)^2}$$

$$= \frac{16.842}{18.525} = 0.9091 \cong 0.91$$

Thus, as a point estimate we can conclude that about 91 percent of the variance in delivery time is statistically explained by the trucking distance involved. Further, given the trucking distance involved, we can also conclude that only about 9 percent of the variance remains unexplained.

14.13. For the trucking distance and delivery-time data, (*a*) calculate the coefficient of correlation by reference to the coefficient of determination in Problem 14.12, and (*b*) determine the coefficient of correlation by using the alternative computational formula for r.

(*a*) $$r = \sqrt{r^2} = \sqrt{0.9091} = +0.9535 \cong +0.95$$

The positive value for the correlation value is based on the observation that the slope b_1 of the regression line is positive, as determined in Problem 14.2.

(b)
$$r = \frac{n\Sigma XY - \Sigma X\Sigma Y}{\sqrt{n\Sigma X^2 - (\Sigma X)^2}\sqrt{n\Sigma Y^2 - (\Sigma Y)^2}} = \frac{(10)(26,370) - (7,620)(28.5)}{\sqrt{(10)(7,104,300) - (7,620)^2}\sqrt{(10)(99.75) - (28.5)^2}}$$

$$= \frac{46,530}{(3,602.5824)(13.6107)} = \frac{46,530}{49,033.668} = +0.9489 \cong +0.95$$

Except for a slight difference due to rounding, the two values are the same.

14.14. For the trucking distance and delivery-time data, (a) calculate the sample covariance, and (b) convert the covariance value into the coefficient of correlation. Compare your answer in (b) to the answers for the coefficient of correlation obtained in Problem 14.13 above.

(a)
$$\text{cov}(X, Y) = \frac{\Sigma[(X - \bar{X})(Y - \bar{Y})]}{n - 1}$$

$$= \frac{4,653}{9} = 517.00 \qquad \text{(from Table 14.4)}$$

(b)
$$r = \frac{\text{cov}(X, Y)}{s_X, s_Y}$$

where
$$s_X = \sqrt{\frac{\Sigma X^2 - n\bar{X}^2}{n - 1}} \qquad \text{[from formula (4.11)]}$$

$$= \sqrt{\frac{7,104,300 - 10(762)^2}{10 - 1}} \qquad \text{(from Table 14.2)}$$

$$= \sqrt{144,206.66} = 379.7455$$

$$s_Y = \sqrt{\frac{\Sigma Y^2 - n\bar{Y}^2}{n - 1}} \qquad \text{[from formula (4.11)]}$$

$$= \sqrt{\frac{99.75 - 10(2.85)^2}{10 - 1}} \qquad \text{(from Table 14.2)}$$

$$= \sqrt{2.058333} = 1.4347$$

$$r = \frac{517.00}{(379.7455)(1.4347)} = +0.9489 \cong +0.95$$

The correlation coefficient matches those calculated in Problem 14.13 above.

14.15. Determine whether the correlation value computed in Problem 14.14(b) is significantly different from zero at the 5 percent level of significance.

$$H_0: \rho = 0 \qquad H_1: \rho \neq 0$$

Critical $t(df = 8, \alpha = 0.05) = \pm 2.306$

$$t = \frac{r}{\sqrt{\frac{(1 - r^2)}{(n - 2)}}} = \frac{0.9489}{\sqrt{\frac{(1 - 0.9004)}{(10 - 2)}}} = \frac{0.9489}{0.1116} = +8.50$$

Because the test statistic of $t = +8.50$ is in a region of rejection, the null hypothesis that there is no relationship between the two variables is rejected, and we conclude that there is a significant relationship between trucking distance and delivery time. Note that this conclusion coincides with the test of the null hypothesis that $\beta_1 = 0$ in Problem 14.7. The difference in the calculated values of t in these two tests is due to rounding of values in the calculations.

Table 14.4   Calculation of the Covariance

Sampled shipment	Distance (X), miles	Delivery time (Y), days	$X - \bar{X}$	$Y - \bar{Y}$	$(X - \bar{X})(Y - \bar{Y})$
1	825	3.5	63	0.65	40.95
2	215	1.0	-547	-1.85	1,011.95
3	1,070	4.0	308	1.15	354.20
4	550	2.0	-212	-0.85	180.20
5	480	1.0	-282	-1.85	521.70
6	920	3.0	158	0.15	23.70
7	1,350	4.5	588	1.65	970.20
8	325	1.5	-437	-1.35	589.95
9	670	3.0	-92	0.15	-13.80
10	1,215	5.0	453	2.15	973.95
	$\bar{X} = 762$	$\bar{Y} = 2.85$			$\Sigma = 4,653.00$

14.16. For a sample of $n = 10$ loan recipients at a finance company, the correlation coefficient between household income and amount of outstanding short-term debt is found to be $r = +0.50$.

(a)   Test the hypothesis that there is no correlation between these two variables for the entire population of loan recipients, using the 5 percent level of significance.

(b)   Interpret the meaning of the correlation coefficient which was computed.

(a)

$$H_0: \rho = 0 \qquad H_1: \rho \neq 0$$

$$\text{Critical } t \,(df = 10 - 2 = 8, \alpha = 0.05) = \pm 2.306$$

$$t = \frac{r}{\sqrt{\dfrac{(1 - r^2)}{(n - 2)}}} = \frac{0.50}{\sqrt{\dfrac{(1 - 0.50)^2}{8}}} = \frac{0.50}{0.306} = +1.634$$

Because the computed t statistic of $+1.634$ is not in a region of rejection, the null hypothesis cannot be rejected, and we continue to accept the assumption that there is no relationship between the two variables. The observed sample relationship can be ascribed to chance at the 5 percent level of significance.

(b)   Based on the correlation coefficient of $r = +0.50$, we might be tempted to conclude that because $r^2 = 0.25$, approximately 25 percent of the variance in short-term debt is explained statistically by the amount of household income. This is true for the *sample* data. However, because the null hypothesis in part (a) above was not rejected, a more appropriate interpretation for the *population* is that none of the variance in Y can be assumed to be associated with changes in X.

COMPUTER OUTPUT

14.17. Use Excel to carry out the regression analysis for the data on distance and delivery time in Table 14.2. Compare the output with the results of some of the manual calculations in the preceding exercises.

Fig. 14-6 gives the standard regression output from Excel. Some of the output corresponds to the manual calculations done in the preceding Solved Problems. The numbered labels below identify such correspondence and refer to labels that have been inserted in Fig. 14-6.

(1)   The regression coefficients for the intercept and the slope correspond to the solution in Problem 14.2, except for the rounding of values in the manual calculations.

(2)   The t test for the null hypothesis, H_0: $\rho = 0$, corresponds to the solution in Problem 14.7, except that P value is also determined. Because a very small P of 2.79E-05 is less than the designated level of significance of 0.05, the null hypothesis is rejected, and we conclude that there is a relationship between distance and delivery time in the sampled population.

(3)   The coefficient of determination between distance and delivery time corresponds to the solution in Problem 14.12.

The Excel output given in Fig. 14-6 was obtained as follows:

(1)   Open Excel. In cell A1 enter: Distance. In cell B1 enter: Time. Enter the distance and time data in the respective columns.

(2)   Click **Tools** $\rightarrow$ **Data Analysis** $\rightarrow$ **Regression**. Click **OK**.

(3)   For **Input Y Range** enter: $B$1:$B$11. For **Input X Range** enter: $A$1:$A$11. Check **Labels**. Click **OK**.

SUMMARY OUTPUT

Regression Statistics	
Multiple R	0.948942768
R Square	0.900492377
Adjusted R Square	0.888053924
Standard Error	0.48002327
Observations	10

③

ANOVA

	df	SS	MS	F	Significance F
Regression	1	16.68162128	16.68162	72.39585	2.79477E-05
Residual	8	1.843378716	0.230422		
Total	9	18.525			

	Coefficients	Standard Error	t Stat	P-value	Lower 95%	Upper 95%
Intercept	0.118129074	0.355147706	0.33262	0.74797	-0.700843533	0.937101681
Distance	0.003585132	0.000421355	8.508575	2.79E-05	0.002613485	0.00455678

①   ②

Fig. 14-6   Regression output from Excel.

14.18. Use Minitab to carry out the regression analysis for the data on distance and delivery time in Table 14.2. Compare the output with the results of some of the manual calculations in the preceding exercises.

Fig. 14-7 gives the standard regression output from Minitab. The output corresponds to the manual calculations done in some of the preceding Solved Problems. The numbered labels below identify such correspondence and refer to labels that have been inserted in Fig. 14-7.

①   The regression equation in Fig. 14-7 corresponds to the solution in Problem 14.2, except for the rounding of values in the manual calculations.

②   The standard error of estimate corresponds to the solution in Problem 14.6.

③   The t test for the null hypothesis, H_0: $\rho = 0$, corresponds to the solution in Problem 14.7, except that the P value is also determined. Because the reported P of 0.000 is less than the designated level of significance of 0.05, the null hypothesis is rejected and we conclude that there is a relationship between distance and delivery time in the sampled population.

④   The coefficient of determination between distance and delivery time corresponds to the solution in Problem 14.12.

⑤   The estimated delivery time for a shipment of 1,000 miles in Fig. 14-7 corresponds to the solution in Problem 14.4.

⑥ The 95 percent confidence interval for the mean delivery time for all shipments of 1,000 miles in distance corresponds to the solution in Problem 14.10.

⑦ The 95 percent prediction interval for the delivery time for one particular shipment of 1,000 miles corresponds to the solution in Problem 14.11.

Regression Analysis: Time versus Distance

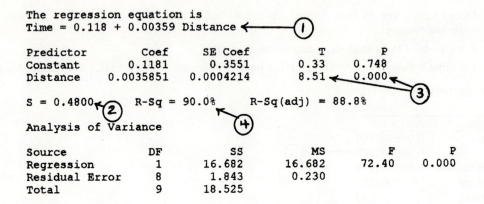

```
The regression equation is
Time = 0.118 + 0.00359 Distance  ←——  ①

Predictor         Coef      SE Coef        T        P
Constant        0.1181      0.3551     0.33    0.748
Distance     0.0035851   0.0004214     8.51 ← 0.000 ←
                                                        ③
S = 0.4800 ←   R-Sq = 90.0%    R-Sq(adj) = 88.8%
           ②
Analysis of Variance
                                        ④
Source           DF          SS         MS        F        P
Regression        1      16.682     16.682    72.40    0.000
Residual Error    8       1.843      0.230
Total             9      18.525
```

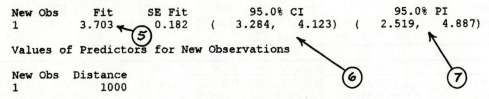

```
Predicted Values for New Observations

New Obs    Fit     SE Fit       95.0% CI            95.0% PI
1        3.703 ←   0.182  (  3.284,   4.123)  (  2.519,   4.887)
               ⑤
Values of Predictors for New Observations

New Obs  Distance
1            1000
```

Fig. 14-7 Regression output from Minitab.

The Minitab output in Fig. 14-7 was obtained as follows:

(1) Open Minitab. In the column name cell for C1 enter: Distance. In the column name cell for C2 enter: Time. Enter the distance and time data in the respective columns.

(2) Click **Stat → Regression → Regression**.

(3) In the dialog box, for **Response** enter: C2. For **Predictors** enter: C1. Click **Options**.

(4) In the dialog box, for **Prediction intervals for new observations** enter 1000. Click **OK**.

(5) Black in the original dialog box, click **OK**.

Supplementary Problems

LINEAR REGRESSION ANALYSIS

14.19. Table 14.5 presents sample data relating the number of study hours spent by students outside of class during a three-week period for a course in business statistics and their scores in an examination given at the end of that period. Prepare a scatter plot for these data and observe if the assumptions of linearity and equality of the variances seem to be satisfied.

Ans. Based on the scatter plot, the assumptions of linearity and equality of conditional variances seem to be reasonably satisfied.

**Table 14.5   Hours Spent on a Statistics Course and Examination Grades for a Sample
of $n = 8$ Students**

Sampled student	1	2	3	4	5	6	7	8
Study hours (X)	20	16	34	23	27	32	18	22
Examination grade (Y)	64	61	84	70	88	92	72	77

14.20. Determine the least-squares regression line for the data in Table 14.5 and enter the line on the plot constructed in Problem 14.19.

Ans. $\hat{Y} = 40 + 1.5X$

14.21. Determine the residuals and construct a residual plot with respect to the fitted values for the data in Table 14.5, using the regression equation developed in Problem 14.19. Compare the residual plot to the scatter plot prepared in Problem 14.19.

14.22. Calculate the standard error of estimate for the data in Table 14.5 by using the residuals determined in Problem 14.21.

Ans. $s_{Y.X} = 6.16$

14.23. For the sample information presented in Problem 14.19, (*a*) test the null hypothesis that the slope of the regression line is zero, using the 1 percent level of significance, and interpret the result of your test. (*b*) Repeat the test for the null hypothesis that the true regression coefficient is equal to *or less than* zero, using the 1 percent level of significance.

Ans.   (*a*) Reject H_0 and conclude that there is a significant relationship. (*b*) Reject H_0 and conclude that there is a significant positive relationship.

14.24. Use the regression equation determined in Problem 14.20 to estimate the examination grade of a student who devoted 30 hr of study to the course material.

Ans. $Y = 85$

14.25. Refer to Problems 14.22 and 14.24. Construct the 90 percent confidence interval for estimating the mean exam grade for students who devote 30 hr to course preparation.

Ans.   79.02 to 90.98

14.26. Referring to the preceding problems construct the 90 percent prediction interval for the examination grade of an individual student who devoted 30 hr to course preparation.

Ans.   71.59 to 98.41

14.27. Table 14.6 presents data relating the number of weeks of experience in a job involving the wiring of miniature electronic components and the number of components which were rejected during the past week for 12 randomly selected workers. Plot these sample data on a scatter plot.

**Table 14.6   Weeks of Experience and Number of Components Rejected During a Sampled Week for 12
Assembly Workers**

Sampled worker	1	2	3	4	5	6	7	8	9	10	11	12
Weeks of experience (X)	7	9	6	14	8	12	10	4	2	11	1	8
Number of rejects (Y)	26	20	28	16	23	18	24	26	38	22	32	25

14.28. From Table 14.6 determine the regression equation for predicting the number of components rejected given the number of weeks experience, and enter the regression line on the scatter plot. Comment on the nature of the relationship as indicated by the regression equation.

Ans. $\hat{Y} = 35.57 - 1.40X$

14.29. Test the null hypothesis that there is no relationship between the variables in Table 14.6, and that the slope of the population regression line is zero, using the 5 percent level of significance for the test.

Ans. Reject H_0 and conclude that there is a relationship.

14.30. For the sample information in Problems 14.27 and 14.28, construct the 95 percent confidence interval for estimating the value of the population regression coefficient β_1, and interpret the value of this coefficient.

Ans. -1.85 to -0.95

14.31. Using the regression equation developed in Problem 14.28, estimate the number of components rejected for an employee with three weeks of experience in the job.

Ans. $\hat{Y} = 31.37$

14.32. Continuing with Problem 14.31, construct the 95 percent confidence interval for estimating the mean number of rejects for employees with three weeks experience in the operation.

Ans. 28.74 to 34.00

14.33. Refer to Problems 14.31 and 14.32. Construct the 95 percent prediction interval for the number of components rejected for an employee with three weeks experience in the job.

Ans. 25.09 to 37.65

CORRELATION ANALYSIS

14.34. Compute the coefficient of determination and the coefficient of correlation for the data in Table 14.5 and analyzed in Problems 14.19 to 14.26, taking advantage of the fact that the values of b_0 and b_1 for the regression equation were calculated in Problem 14.20. Interpret the computed coefficients.

Ans. $r^2 = 0.7449 \cong 0.74$, $r = +0.863 \cong +0.86$

14.35. For the sample correlation value determined in Problem 14.34, test the null hypotheses that (a) $\rho = 0$ and (b) $p \leq 0$, using the 1 percent level of significance with respect to each test. Interpret your results.

Ans. (a) Reject H_0 and conclude that there is a significant relationship. (b) Reject H_0 and conclude that there is a significant positive relationship.

14.36. For the data in Table 14.5, (a) calculate the sample covariance and (b) convert the covariance value into the coefficient of correlation. Compare your answer in (b) to the correlation coefficient obtained in Problem 14.34.

Ans. (a) $\text{cov}(X, Y) = +62.86$, (b) $r = +08622 \cong +0.86$

14.37. For the sample data reported in Table 14.6 and analyzed in Problems 14.27 to 14.33, determine the value of the correlation coefficient by the formula which is not based on the use of the estimated regression line values of b_0 and b_1. Interpret the meaning of this value by computing the coefficient of determination.

Ans. $r = -0.908 \cong -0.91$, $r^2 = 0.8245 \cong 0.82$

COMPUTER OUTPUT

14.38. Use available computer software to carry out the regression and correlation analysis for the data in Table 14.6. As part of the output, determine the regression equation and the coefficient of determination. Compare the computer output to the results of the manual calculations in the preceding exercises.

Ans. Except for minor differences due to rounding, the results are the same as for the manual calculations.

CHAPTER 15

Multiple Regression and Correlation

15.1 OBJECTIVES AND ASSUMPTIONS OF MULTIPLE REGRESSION ANALYSIS

Multiple regression analysis is an extension of simple regression analysis, as described in Chapter 14, to applications involving the use of two or more independent variables (predictors) to estimate the value of the dependent variable (response variable). In the case of two independent variables, denoted by X_1 and X_2, the linear algebraic model is

$$Y_i = \beta_0 + \beta_1 X_{i,1} + \beta_2 X_{i,2} + \varepsilon_i \qquad (15.1)$$

The definitions of the above terms are equivalent to the definitions in Section 14.3 for simple regression analysis, except that more than one independent variable is involved in the present case. Based on sample data, the linear regression equation for the case of two independent variables is

$$\hat{Y} = b_0 + b_1 X_1 + b_2 X_2 \qquad (15.2)$$

(*Note*: In some textbooks and computer software the dependent variable is designated X_1, with the several independent variables then identified sequentially beginning with X_2.)

The multiple regression equation identifies the best-fitting line based on the method of least squares, as described in Section 14.3. In the case of multiple regression analysis, the best-fitting line is a line through n-dimensional space (3-dimensional in the case of two independent variables). The calculations required for determining the values of the parameter estimates in a multiple regression equation and the associated standard error values are quite complex and generally involve matrix algebra. However, computer software is widely available for carrying out such calculations, and the solved problems at the end of this chapter are referenced to the use of such software. Specialized textbooks in regression and correlation analysis include complete descriptions of the mathematical analyses involved.

The assumptions of multiple linear regression analysis are similar to those of the simple case involving only one independent variable. For point estimation, the principal assumptions are that (1) the dependent variable is a random variable, and (2) the relationship between the several independent variables and the one dependent variable is linear. Additional assumptions for statistical inference (estimation or hypothesis testing) are that (3) the variances of the conditional distributions of the dependent variable, given various combinations of values of the independent variables, are all equal, (4) the conditional distributions of the dependent variable are normally distributed, and (5) the observed values of the dependent variable are independent of each other. Violation of assumption (5), above, is called *autocorrelation*, as discussed in Section 15.8.

15.2   ADDITIONAL CONCEPTS IN MULTIPLE REGRESSION ANALYSIS

Constant (in the regression equation).   Although the b_0 and the several b_i values are all estimates of parameters in the regression equation, in most computer output the term constant refers to the value of the b_0 intercept. In multiple regression analysis, this is the regression equation value of the dependent variable Y given that all of the independent variables are equal to zero.

Partial regression coefficient (or *net regression coefficient*).   Each of the b_i regression coefficients is in fact a partial regression coefficient. A partial regression coefficient is the conditional coefficient given that one or more other independent variables (and their coefficients) are also included in the regression equation. Conceptually, a partial regression coefficient represents the slope of the regression line between the independent variable of interest and the dependent variable *given* that the other independent variables are included in the model and are thereby statistically "held constant." The symbol $b_{Y1.2}$ (or $b_{12.3}$ when the dependent variable is designated by X_1) is the partial regression coefficient for the first independent variable given that a second independent variable is also included in the regression equation. For simplicity, when the entire regression equation is presented, this coefficient usually is designated by b_1.

Use of the F test.   As described in Section 15.5, the analysis of variance is used in regression analysis to test for the significance of the overall model, as contrasted to considering the significance of the individual independent variables by use of t tests, below.

Use of t tests.   As illustrated in the Solved Problems at the end of the chapter, t tests are used to determine if the partial regression coefficient for each independent variable represents a significant contribution to the overall model.

Confidence interval for the conditional mean.   The determination of such a confidence interval is illustrated in Problem 15.9. Where the standard error of the conditional mean in the case of two independent variables is designated by $s_{\bar{Y}.12}$, the formula for the confidence interval is

$$\hat{\mu}_Y \pm ts_{\bar{Y}.12} \qquad\qquad (15.3)$$

Prediction intervals.   The prediction interval for estimating the value of an individual observation of the dependent variable, given the values of the several independent variables, is similar to the prediction interval in simple regression analysis as described in Section 14.8. Determination of such an interval is illustrated in Problem 15.10. The general formula for the prediction interval is

$$\hat{Y} \pm ts_{Y(\text{next})} \qquad\qquad (15.4)$$

Stepwise regression analysis.   In *forward* stepwise regression analysis, one independent variable is added to the model in each step of selecting such variables for inclusion in the final model. In *backward* stepwise regression analysis, we begin with all the variables under consideration being included in the model, and then (possibly) we remove one variable in each step. These are two of several available approaches to choosing the "best" set of independent variables for the model, as discussed in specialized books in linear algebraic models and multiple regression analysis, Computer software is available to do either forward or backward stepwise regression analysis.

15.3   THE USE OF INDICATOR (DUMMY) VARIABLES

Although the linear regression model is based upon the independent variables being on a quantitative measurement scale, it is possible to include a qualitative (categorical) variable in a multiple regression model.

Examples of such variables are the sex of an employee in a study of salary levels and the location codes in a real estate appraisal model.

The indicator variable utilizes a binary 0, 1 code. Where k designates the number of categories that exist for the qualitative variable, $k - 1$ indicator variables are required to code the qualitative variable. Thus, the sex of an employee can be coded by one indicator variable, because $k = 2$ in this case, and $2 - 1 = 1$. The code system then can be $0 =$ female and $1 =$ male (or vice versa). For a real estate appraisal model in which there are three types of locations, labeled A, B, and C, $k = 3$ and therefore $3 - 1 = 2$ indicator variables are required. These could be coded as follows, assuming that two other independent variables, X_1 and X_2, are already in the model:

Location	X_3	X_4
A	0	0
B	1	0
C	0	1

(*Note*:   In the binary code scheme illustrated above, there can be no more than one "1" in each row, and there must be exactly one "1" in each column.)

The difficulty associated with having a qualitative variable that has more than two categories is that more than one indicator is required to represent the variable in the regression equation. Specifically, indicator variables X_3 and X_4 above, taken *together*, represent the one variable of location. It then follows that such indicator variables must be considered together rather than individually, in stepwise regression. This issue is considered in advanced textbooks in regression analysis. The end-of-chapter Solved Problems include consideration only of a two-category qualitative variable, which requires only one indicator variable.

15.4   RESIDUALS AND RESIDUAL PLOTS

As originally defined in Section 14.4, a residual in regression analysis is

$$e = Y - \hat{Y} \tag{15.5}$$

In Section 14.4 the *residual plot* was defined as a plot of the residuals e with respect to the independent variable X or with respect to the fitted value $\hat{Y}$. In simple regression analysis, either a scatter plot or a residual plot can be used to observe if the assumptions of linearity and equality of conditional variances appear to be satisfied. In multiple regression analysis, however, the only type of plot that addresses these issues for the *overall* model is the residual plot with respect to the fitted value $\hat{Y}$, because this is the only two-dimensional plot that can incorporate the use of *several* independent variables. If a problem with respect to linearity or equality of conditional variances is observed to exist on such a plot, then individual scatter plots or residual plots can be prepared with respect to each independent variable in the model in order to trace the source of the problem. The computer output associated with the Solved Problems includes the residual plot for the overall model as well as residual plots for the individual independent variables.

15.5   ANALYSIS OF VARIANCE IN LINEAR REGRESSION ANALYSIS

As indicated in Section 15.2, an F test is used to test for the significance of the overall model. That is, it is used to test the null hypothesis that there is no relationship in the population between the (several) independent variables taken as a group and the one dependent variable. Specifically, the null hypothesis states that *all* of the net regression coefficients in the regression equation for the population are equal to zero. Therefore, for the case of two independent variables, or predictors, the null hypothesis with respect to the F test is H_0: $\beta_1 = \beta_2 = 0$.

If there is only one independent variable in the regression model, then the F test is equivalent to a two-tail t test directed at the slope b_1 ($H_0: \beta_1 = 0$). Therefore, use of the F test is not required in simple regression analysis. For clarity, however, we focus on the simple regression model to explain the rationale of using the analysis of variance. The explanation applies similarly to the case of multiple regression, except that the estimated $\hat{Y}$ values are based on several independent variables rather than only one.

Consider the scatter plot in Fig. 15-1. If there is *no* regression effect in the population, then the $\hat{Y}$ line differs from the $\bar{Y}$ line purely by chance. It follows that the variance estimate based on the differences $(\hat{Y} - \bar{Y})$, called *mean square regression (MSR)*, would be different only by chance from the variance estimate based on the residuals $(Y - \hat{Y})$, called *mean square error (MSE)*. On the other hand, if there *is* a regression effect, then the mean square regression is inflated in value as compared with the mean square error. Table 15.1 presents the standard format for the analysis of variance table that is used to test for the significance of an overall regression effect. The degrees of freedom k associated with MSR in the table is the number of independent variables in the multiple regression equation. As indicated in the table, the test statistic is

$$F = \frac{MSR}{MSE} \qquad\qquad (15.6)$$

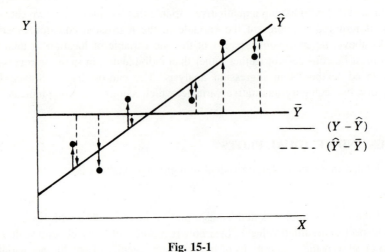

Fig. 15-1

Problems 15.8 and 15.14 illustrate the use of the F test in multiple regression analysis using Excel and Minitab, respectively.

Table 15.1   Analysis of Variance Table for Testing the Significance of the Regression Effect

Source of variation	Degrees of freedom (*df*)	Sum of squares (*SS*)	Mean square (*MS*)	*F* ratio
Regression (*R*)	k	SSR	$MSR = \dfrac{SSR}{k}$	$F = \dfrac{MSR}{MSE}$
Sampling error (*E*)	$n - k - 1$	SSE	$MSE = \dfrac{SSE}{n - k - 1}$	
Total (*T*)	$n - 1$	SST		

15.6   OBJECTIVES AND ASSUMPTIONS OF MULTIPLE CORRELATION ANALYSIS

Multiple correlation analysis is an extension of simple correlation analysis, as described in Chapter 14, to situations involving two or more independent variables and their degree of association with the dependent variable. As is the case for multiple regression analysis described in Section 15.1, the dependent variable is designated by Y, while the several independent variables are designated sequentially beginning with X_1. (*Note*: In some textbooks and computer software the dependent variable is designated by X_1, in which case the independent variables are designated sequentially beginning with X_2.)

The coefficient of multiple correlation, which is designated by the uppercase $R_{Y.12}$ for the case of two independent variables, is indicative of the extent of the relationship between two independent variables taken as a group and the dependent variable. It is possible that one of the independent variables alone could have a positive relationship with the dependent variable while the other independent variable could have a negative relationship with the dependent variable. All R values are reported as absolute values, without an arithmetic sign. Problem 15.12 includes determination of a coefficient of multiple correlation and consideration of how this coefficient is tested for significance.

The *coefficient of multiple determination* is designated by $R_{Y.12}^2$ for the case of two independent variables. Similar to the interpretation of the simple coefficient of determination (see Section 14.10), this coefficient indicates the proportion of variance in the dependent variable which is statistically accounted for by knowledge of the two (or more) independent variables. The sample coefficient of multiple determination for the case of two independent variables is

$$R_{Y.12}^2 = 1 - \frac{s_{Y.12}^2}{s_Y^2} \tag{15.7}$$

Formula (*15.7*) is equivalent to formula (*14.20*) in simple regression analysis and is presented for conceptual purposes, rather than for computational application. Because it is the orientation in this chapter that computer software should be used for multiple regression and correlation analysis, computational procedures are not included. Problem 15.12 includes consideration of a coefficient of multiple determination included in computer output and the interpretation of this coefficient.

The assumptions of multiple correlation analysis are similar to those of the simple case involving only one independent variable. These are that (1) all variables involved in the analysis are random variables, (2) the relationships are all linear, (3) the conditional variances are all equal (homoscedasticity), (4) for each variable, observed values are independent of other observed values for that variable, and (5) the conditional distributions are all normal. These requirements are quite stringent and are seldom completely satisfied in real data situations. However, multiple correlation analysis is quite robust in the sense that some of these assumptions, and particularly the assumption about all the conditional distributions being normally distributed, can be violated without serious consequences in terms of the validity of the results.

15.7   ADDITIONAL CONCEPTS IN MULTIPLE CORRELATION ANALYSIS

In addition to the coefficient of multiple correlation and the coefficient of multiple determination described in the preceding section, the following concepts or procedures are unique to multiple correlation analysis.

Coefficient of partial correlation.   Indicates the correlation between one of the independent variables in the multiple correlation analysis and the dependent variable, with the other independent variable(s) held constant statistically. The partial correlation with the first of two independent variables would be designated by $r_{Y1.2}$, while the partial correlation with the second of two independent variables would be designated by $r_{Y2.1}$. (If the dependent variable is designated by X_1, then these two coefficients would be designated by $r_{12.3}$ and $r_{13.2}$, respectively.) The partial correlation value is different from a simple correlation value because, for the latter case, other independent variables are not statistically controlled.

Coefficient of partial determination. This is the squared value of the coefficient of partial correlation described above. The coefficient indicates the proportion of variance statistically accounted for by one particular independent variable, with the other independent variable(s) held constant statistically.

15.8   PITFALLS AND LIMITATIONS ASSOCIATED WITH MULTIPLE REGRESSION AND MULTIPLE CORRELATION ANALYSIS

Two principal areas of difficulty are those associated with colinearity and autocorrelation. These are described briefly below. Detailed discussions of these problems and what can be done about them are included in specialized textbooks in regression and correlation analysis.

Colinearity. When the independent variables in a multiple regression analysis are highly correlated with each other, the partial (or net) regression coefficients are unreliable in terms of meaning. Similarly, the practical meaning of the coefficients of partial correlation may be questionable. It is possible, for example, that the partial correlation for a given independent variable will be highly negative even though the respective simple correlation is highly positive. In general, therefore, care should be taken in interpreting partial regression coefficients and partial correlation coefficients when the independent variables have a high positive or negative correlation with one another.

Autocorrelation (Serial Correlation). Refers to the absence of independence in the sequence of values of the dependent variable Y, and thus also in the sequence of the residuals $(Y - \hat{Y})$ with respect to the regression line. That is, in the case of positive autocorrelation, a value of Y that is above (or below) the regression line is likely to be followed sequentially by a Y value that is also so positioned. A negative autocorrelation would describe the situation in which an observed value of Y is likely to be followed sequentially by a Y value that is positioned on the *opposite* side (vertically) of the regression line. Autocorrelation is often associated with the dependent variable being a sequence of time-series values, rather than being randomly sampled observations. For time series values, such as a series of monthly dollar sales amounts or monthly closing stock prices, there is frequently a period-to-period relationship in the sequence of values and in the sequence of the residuals for those values. The effect of autocorrelation statistically is that the standard error values associated with each partial regression coefficient and the standard error of estimate are understated. The result is that null hypotheses concerning the absence of relationships are too often rejected, and the prediction intervals and confidence intervals are narrower (more precise) than they should be.

A statistical test for autocorrelation that is frequently reported in computer output is the *Durbin-Watson test*. The value of the test statistic can range from 0 to 4.0, and is approximately 2.0 when there is no autocorrelation (serial correlation) present with respect to the residuals. Advanced texts in statistics include tables of significant values for the test statistic. In general, a value of the statistic below 1.4 indicates the existence of strong positive serial correlation, while a value greater than 2.6 indicates the existence of strong negative serial correlation.

15.9   USING EXCEL AND MINITAB

Solved Problems 15.6 to 15.11 illustrate the use of Excel for multiple regression and correlation analysis. Problems 15.12 to 15.18 illustrate the use of Minitab for multiple regression and correlation analysis.

Solved Problems

15.1. Suppose that the regression equation has been determined for estimating home prices in a subdivision based on the square footage of the home. If the square footage of the land is added as a second predictor, would the regression coefficient for home size from the simple regression model be the same value in the model with two predictors?

The value of the coefficient for the original predictor will be different after a second predictor is added to the equation. The *partial*, or *net*, regression coefficient in multiple regression indicates the effect of that predictor on the value of the dependent variable *given that the other variables in the model are statistically held at constant values.* This is a different meaning from simple regression, in which any other potential predictors are uncontrolled, and are random variables. Thus, multiple regression is a powerful statistical tool by which values that cannot be controlled and held constant in the "real world" can nevertheless be statistically controlled.

15.2. What is the purpose of the analysis of variance, and the associated *F* test, in multiple regression analysis. Why is the use of this test not necessary in simple regression analysis?

The analysis of variance is required in order to test for the significance of the overall model, with several predictors. Specifically, the null hypothesis is that there is no relationship between the several predictors *taken as a group* and the response variable. Although the *F* test also is routinely included in computer output for simple regression analysis, it is not needed because the *t* test is used to test for the significance for the one predictor, and the result associated with either test is always the same.

15.3. In simple regression analysis, the linearity of the relationship between the two variables and other issues can be investigated by constructing a scatter plot. If there are three predictors, for example, one cannot possibly construct such a plot, which would require "4-dimensional space." How, then, can linearity and other associated issues be investigated in multiple regression?

A residual plot is used in multiple regression. A residual value is the difference between the observed value of the response variable and the estimated value based on the regression equation. There are several versions of residual plots, but they all have the purpose of investigating the linearity of the fit and the variability of the scatter with respect to the plot. A residual plot is described in Solved Problem 15.18.

15.4. What is "colinearity," and how can its existence be determined in multiple regression analysis?

The term colinearity refers to the situation in which some of the predictors are highly correlated with one another, in addition to being correlated with the response variable. This issue is not a serious one with respect to the usefulness of the overall model, but it does affect any attempt to interpret the meaning of the partial regression coefficients in the model. The existence of colinearity can be determined by determining the pairwise correlation coefficients for all of the predictors in the regression model.

15.5. How does "autocorrelation" in regression analysis differ from "colinearity"?

As contrasted to colinearity, as described in Solved Problem 15.4, above, autocorrelation refers to an association *among the sequence of values of the dependent*, or *response*, *variable.* Such association is typical in time series values. A series of such values as, for example, unemployment rates, certainly are not statistically independent from period to period. The result is understatement of standard error values, too often leading to the conclusion that a relationship exists where it does not exist.

MULTIPLE REGRESSION ANALYSIS WITH EXCEL

15.6. Use Excel to carry out multiple regression analysis for the data presented in Table 5.2. The data are for a random sample of electronic technicians employed in a telecommunications firm.

Table 15.2   Annual Salaries for a Sample of Technicians

Sampled individual	Annual salary (Y)	Years of experience (X_1)	Years of postsecondary education (X_2)	Sex (X_3)
1	$54,900	5.5	4.0	F
2	60,500	9.0	4.0	M
3	58,900	4.0	5.0	F
4	59,000	8.0	4.0	M
5	57,500	9.5	5.0	M
6	55,500	3.0	4.0	F
7	56,000	7.0	3.0	F
8	52,700	1.5	4.5	F
9	65,000	8.5	5.0	M
10	60,000	7.5	6.0	F
11	56,000	9.5	2.0	M
12	53,600	6.0	2.0	F
13	55,000	2.5	4.0	M
14	52,500	1.5	4.5	M

Fig. 15-2 presents the standard output for multiple regression analysis from Excel. We shall consider some of the major elements of this output in the Solved Problems that follow. The regression output given in Fig. 15-2 was obtained as follows:

(1)   Open Excel. In cell A1 enter: Salary. In cell B1 enter: Experience. In cell C1 enter: Education. In D1 enter: Sex. Enter the data in the respective columns. (*Note: For Sex use the numeric codes F = 0 and M = 1.*)

(2)   Click **Tools** → **DataAnalysis** → **Regression**. Click **OK**.

(3)   For **Input Y Range** enter: $A$1:$A$15. For **Input X Range** enter: $B$1:$D$15. Check **Labels**. Click **OK**.

15.7.   Based on the Excel output in Fig. 15-2, what is the multiple regression equation for estimating Salary based on Experience, Education, and Sex?

SUMMARY OUTPUT

Regression Statistics	
Multiple R	0.821590487
R Square	0.675010928
Adjusted R Square	0.577514206
Standard Error	2251.715826
Observations	14

ANOVA

	df	SS	MS	F	Significance F
Regression	3	105309901.3	35103300	6.9234218	0.008376182
Residual	10	50702241.6	5070224		
Total	13	156012142.9			

	Coefficients	Standard Error	t Stat	P-value	Lower 95%	Upper 95%
Intercept	45495.32938	2809.771399	16.19183	1.673E-08	39234.76747	51755.891
Experience	801.5711025	228.4684282	3.508455	0.0056462	292.511633	1310.6306
Education	1595.736538	560.6439792	2.846256	0.0173612	346.5436898	2844.9294
Sex	382.5720808	1287.410877	0.297164	0.7724225	-2485.95861	3251.1028

Fig. 15-2   Multiple regression output from Excel.

From the lower portion of the output, the equation with values rounded to the first decimal place is

$$Y = 45495.3 + 801.6X_1 + 1595.7X_2 + 382.6X_3$$

where $X_1 =$ Yrs. Experience; $X_2 =$ Yrs. Education; $X_3 =$ Sex (coded)

The above equation indicates, for example, that for each additional year of experience, and with the other predictors held constant in value, a person is paid about \$802 more per year of experience, on the average.

15.8. Based on Fig. 15-2, test the null hypothesis that there is no relationship in the population between the three predictors taken as a group and the annual salary of the technicians, using the 1 percent level of significance.

From the ANOVA table, we observe that the P value for the calculated F statistic is 0.008, rounded to three decimal places. Therefore, the hypothesis of no relationship is rejected, and we conclude that there is a relationship in the population between the three predictors as a group and annual salary.

15.9. Suppose that backward stepwise regression is to be used to remove any predictors that do not contribute to the regression model, using the 1 percent level of significance. What predictor would be removed from the present model? Why?

The variable Sex would clearly be removed. In the lower portion of the output in Fig. 15-2, the P value associated with this predictor *when used with the other two predictors* is 0.772 (rounded). Given the use of the other two predictors, this predictor does not contribute to the regression model for the sampled population. This result is "good news" for the company, since it indicates that the sex of the person does not affect annual salary, given that years of experience and education are taken into consideration.

15.10. Based on the Excel output, what is the coefficient of multiple correlation between the three predictors taken as a group and annual salary?

The coefficient of multiple correlation is 0.82 (rounded), as reported on the first line of output.

15.11. Interpret the coefficient of multiple correlation from the standpoint of the proportion of variance in the salary amounts that is statistically accounted for by the three predictors.

The proportion of variance in salary that is eliminated by use of the three predictors is 0.68 (rounded). This is the coefficient of multiple determination, which is labeled "R square" in Fig. 15-2.

MULTIPLE REGRESSION ANALYSIS WITH MINITAB

15.12. Use Minitab to carry out multiple regression analysis for the data presented in Table 5.2, including a plot of the residuals vs. the fitted values. The data are for a random sample of electronic technicians employed in a telecommunications firm.

Fig. 15-3 presents the standard output for multiple regression analysis from Minitab, while Fig. 15-4 is the required plot. The output given in these two figures was obtained as follows:

(1) Open Minitab. In the column name cell for C1 enter: Salary. In the column name cell for C2 enter: Experience. In the column name cell for C3 enter: Education. In the column name cell for C4 enter: Sex. Enter the data in the respective columns.

   (*Note:* For Sex use the numeric codes $F = 0$ and $M = 1$.)

(2) Click **Stat** $\rightarrow$ **Regression** $\rightarrow$ **Regression**.

(3) In the dialog box, for **Response** enter: C1. For **Predictors** enter: C2-C4. Click **Graphs**.

(4) In the dialog box for Graphs, check **Residuals versus fits**. Click **OK**.

(5) Back in the original dialog box, click **OK**.

15.13. Based on the Minitab output in Fig. 15-3, what is the multiple regression equation for estimating Salary based on Experience, Education, and Sex?

Regression Analysis: Salary versus Experience, Education, Sex

```
The regression equation is
Salary = 45495 + 802 Experience + 1596 Education + 383 Sex

Predictor        Coef      SE Coef          T          P
Constant         45495        2810      16.19      0.000
Experien         801.6       228.5       3.51      0.006
Educatio        1595.7       560.6       2.85      0.017
Sex                383        1287       0.30      0.772

S = 2252        R-Sq = 67.5%      R-Sq(adj) = 57.8%

Analysis of Variance

Source           DF          SS          MS          F          P
Regression        3   105309901    35103300       6.92      0.008
Residual Error   10    50702242     5070224
Total            13   156012143

Source           DF     Seq SS
Experien          1   63281479
Educatio          1   41580689
Sex               1     447733

Unusual Observations
Obs    Experien     Salary       Fit     SE Fit    Residual    St Resid
 5         9.50      57500     61472       1193       -3972      -2.08R
 9         8.50      65000     60670       1084        4330       2.19R

R denotes an observation with a large standardized residual
```

Fig. 15-3 Multiple regression output from Minitab.

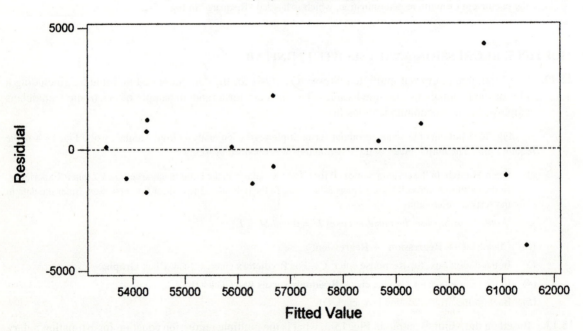

Fig. 15-4 Residual plot from Minitab.

From the top portion of the output, the equation is

$$\text{Salary} = 45495 + 802(\text{Experience}) + 1596(\text{Education}) + 383(\text{Sex})$$

The above equation indicates, for example, that with each additional year of experience, and with the other predictors held constant, a person is paid $802 more per year, on the average.

15.14. Based on Fig. 15-3, test the null hypothesis that there is no relationship in the population between the three predictors taken as a group and the annual salary of the technicians, using the 1 percent level of significance.

From the Analysis of Variance table included in Fig. 15-3, we observe that the P value for the calculated F statistic is 0.008. Therefore, the hypothesis of no relationship is rejected, and we conclude that there is a relationship in the population between the three predictors as a group and annual salary.

15.15. Suppose that backward stepwise regression is to be used to remove any predictors that do not contribute to the regression model, using the 1 percent level of significance. What predictor would be removed from the present model? Why?

The variable Sex would clearly be removed. In the portion of the output just below the regression equation in Fig. 15-2, the P value associated with this predictor *when used with the other two predictors* is 0.772. Given the use of the other two predictors, this predictor does not contribute to the regression model for the sampled population. This result is "good news" for the company, since it indicates that the sex of the person does not affect annual salary, given that years of experience and education are taken into consideration.

15.16. Based on the Minitab output, what is the coefficient of multiple correlation between the three predictors taken as a group and annual salary?

The coefficient of multiple correlation, R, is the square-root of the reported R-Sq value, which is 67.5 percent, or more properly, 0.675. Thus:

$$R = \sqrt{0.675} = 0.82 \text{ (rounded)}$$

15.17. Interpret the coefficient of multiple correlation from the standpoint of the proportion of variance in the salary amounts that is statistically accounted for by the three predictors.

The proportion of variance in salary that is eliminated by use of the three predictors is the coefficient of multiple determination, which is R-Sq in the output in Fig. 15-3, $= 67.5$ percent. Minitab expresses the result as a percentage, rather than as a proportion.

15.18. Interpret the residual plot in Fig. 15-4 that was obtained from Minitab.

The pattern of the scatter of the residuals with respect to the fitted values indicates that the linearity assumption is satisfied. However, notice that there appears to be greater variability in the residuals as the fitted values of the estimated annual salary amounts become larger for this limited sample. That people at the higher end of salaries tend to have greater differences among themselves comes as no surprise. However, the absence of uniform scatter in the residual plot means that any confidence and prediction intervals for salary will be unreliable.

Supplementary Problems

Table 15.3 reports single-family house prices, with a random sample of 10 houses taken from each of three housing subdivisions. As indicated, in addition to the subdivision and the price, the square footage of each house and each lot have been collected. With price being the dependent variable, carry out multiple regression analysis using computer software to serve as the basis for the solutions to the supplementary problems that follow. Use the binary coding scheme described in Section 15.3 for the two indicator variables that are required for coding the housing subdivision.

Table 15.3   Single-Family House Prices in Three Subdivisions

Sampled house	Price	Living area, sq. ft	Lot size, sq. ft	Subdivision
1	102,200	1,500	12,000	A
2	103,950	1,200	10,000	A
3	87,900	1,200	10,000	A
4	110,000	1,600	15,000	A
5	97,000	1,400	12,000	A
6	95,700	1,200	10,000	A
7	113,600	1,600	15,000	A
8	109,600	1,500	12,000	A
9	110,800	1,500	12,000	A
10	90,600	1,300	12,000	A
11	109,000	1,600	13,000	B
12	133,000	1,900	15,000	B
13	134,000	1,800	15,000	B
14	120,300	2,000	17,000	B
15	137,000	2,000	17,000	B
16	122,400	1,700	15,000	B
17	121,700	1,800	15,000	B
18	126,000	1,900	16,000	B
19	128,000	2,000	16,000	B
20	117,500	1,600	13,000	B
21	158,700	2,400	18,000	C
22	186,800	2,600	18,000	C
23	172,400	2,300	16,000	C
24	151,200	2,200	16,000	C
25	179,100	2,800	20,000	C
26	182,300	2,700	20,000	C
27	195,850	3,000	22,000	C
28	168,000	2,400	18,000	C
29	199,400	2,500	20,000	C
30	163,000	2,400	18,000	C

15.19. Obtain the multiple regression equation for estimating house price based on all three variables of house size, lot size, and location. Test the multiple regression model for significance at the 5 percent level.

Ans. $\hat{Y} = 40{,}462 + 36.0X_1 + 0.94X_2 + 4{,}267X_3 + 26{,}648X_4$. The regression model is significant at the 5 percent level ($F = 109.08$; $P = 0.000$).

15.20. Observe which variable has the partial regression coefficient with the lowest reported t statistic (and highest P value), and determine whether the contribution of that variable is significant at the 5 percent level. (*Note*: For our solution we take the view that given that the two indicator variables represent the *one* qualitative variable of location, either both should be removed or neither should be removed from the model. Therefore, we will consider only the *higher* of the two t ratios associated with the indicator variables.)

Ans. Lot size has the smallest test-statistic value ($t = 0.44$) and the highest P value ($P = 0.666$), and should be removed from the model.

15.21. Continuing from Problem 15.20, obtain the multiple regression equation for the reduced model and test the model for significance at the 5 percent level.

Ans. $\hat{Y} = 41{,}153 + 43.6X_1 + 4{,}025X_3 + 24{,}319X_4$. The regression model is significant at the 5 percent level ($F = 150.04$; $P = 0.000$).

15.22. As in Problem 15.14, observe which variable has the partial regression coefficient with the lowest reported t statistic (and highest P value), and determine whether the contribution of that variable to the multiple regression model is significant at the 5 percent level.

Ans. The lowest test statistic is for the first indicator variable ($t = 0.79$ with $P = 0.436$), which we ignore based on the approach to the indicator variables described in Problem 15.20. The next-lowest test statistic is for the second indicator variable ($t = 2.44$ with $P = 0.022$), and it is significant at the 5 percent level. Therefore, no variable should be removed from the model.

15.23. Use the regression model in Problem 15.21 and estimate the price of a house with (*a*) 1,200 sq. ft. and in subdivision A, (*b*) 1,800 sq. ft. and in subdivision B, (*c*) 2,400 sq. ft. and in subdivision C.

Ans. (*a*) $93,423, (*b*) $123,583, (*c*) $170,012

15.24. Use the regression model in Problem 15.21 to determine the 95 percent confidence interval for the conditional mean price of all houses with (*a*) 1,200 sq. ft. in subdivision A, (*b*) 1,800 sq. ft. in subdivision B, (*c*) 2,400 sq. ft. and in subdivision C (given that your software can provide such output).

Ans. (*a*) $87,118 to $99,728, (*b*) $118,229 to $128,937, (*c*) $164,250 to $175,774

15.25. Continuing with Problem 15.24, determine the 95 percent prediction interval for the price of an individual house in each of the three categories identified above (given that your software can provide such output).

Ans. (*a*) $75,428 to $111,419, (*b*) $105,898 to $141,268, (*c*) $152,200 to $187,825

15.26. Determine (*a*) the coefficient of multiple determination (uncorrected for degrees of freedom) and (*b*) the coefficient of multiple correlation for the final multiple regression model, from Problem 15.21.

Ans. (*a*) $R^2 = 0.945$, (*b*) $R = \sqrt{0.945} = 0.972$

CHAPTER 16

Time Series Analysis and Business Forecasting

16.1 THE CLASSICAL TIME SERIES MODEL

A *time series* is a set of observed values, such as production or sales data, for a sequentially ordered series of time periods. Examples of such data are sales of a particular product for a series of months and the number of workers employed in a particular industry for a series of years. A time series is portrayed graphically by a line graph (see Section 2.11), with the time periods represented on the horizontal axis and time series values represented on the vertical axis.

EXAMPLE 1. Figure 16-1 is a line graph that portrays the annual dollar sales for a graphics software company (fictional) that was incorporated in 1990. As can be observed, a *peak* in annual sales was achieved in 1995, followed by two years of declining sales that culminated in the *trough* (trŏf) in 1997, which was then followed by increasing levels of sales during the final three years of the reported time series values.

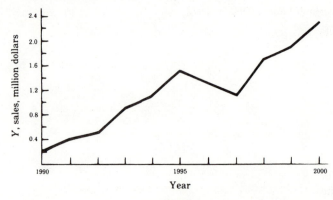

Fig. 16-1

296

Time series analysis is the procedure by which the time-related factors that influence the values observed in the time series are identified and segregated. Once identified, they can be used to aid in the interpretation of historical time series values and to forecast future time series values. The classical approach to time series analysis identifies four such influences, or, *components*:

(1) *Trend* (T): The general long-term movement in the time series values (Y) over an extended period of years.

(2) *Cyclical fluctuations* (C): Recurring up and down movements with respect to trend that have a duration of several years.

(3) *Seasonal variations* (S): Up and down movements with respect to trend that are completed within a year and recur annually. Such variations typically are identified on the basis of monthly or quarterly data.

(4) *Irregular variations* (I): The erratic variations from trend that cannot be ascribed to the cyclical or seasonal influences.

The model underlying classical time series analysis is based on the assumption that for any designated period in the time series the value of the variable is determined by the four components defined above, and, furthermore, that the components have a multiplicative relationship. Thus, where Y represents the observed time series value,

$$Y = T \times C \times S \times I \qquad (16.1)$$

The model represented by (16.1) is used as the basis for separating the influences of the various components that affect time series values, as described in the following sections of this chapter.

16.2   TREND ANALYSIS

Because trend analysis is concerned with the long-term direction of movement in the time series, such analysis generally is performed using annual data. Typically, at least 15 or 20 years of data should be used, so that cyclical movements, involving several years duration are not taken to be indicative of the overall trend of the time series values.

The method of least squares (see Section 14.3) is the most frequent basis used for identifying the trend component of the time series by determining the equation for the best-fitting trend line. Note that statistically speaking, a trend line is not a regression line, since the dependent variable Y is not a random variable, but, rather, a series of historical values. Further, there can be only one historical value for any given time period (not a distribution of values) and the values associated with adjoining time periods are likely to be dependent, rather than independent. Nevertheless, the least-squares method is a convenient basis for determining the trend component of a time series. When the long-term increase or decrease appears to follow a linear trend, the equation for the trend line values, with X representing the year, is

$$Y_T = b_0 + b_1 X \qquad (16.2)$$

As explained in Section 14.3, the b_0 in (16.2) represents the point of intersection of the trend line with the Y axis, whereas the b_1 represents the slope of the trend line. Where X is the year and Y is the observed time series value, the formulas for determining the values of b_0 and b_1 for the linear trend equation are

$$b_1 = \frac{\Sigma XY - n\bar{X}\bar{Y}}{\Sigma X^2 - n\bar{X}^2} \qquad (16.3)$$

$$b_0 = \bar{Y} - b_1\bar{X} \qquad (16.4)$$

See Problem 16.1 for the determination of a linear trend equation.

In the case of nonlinear trend, a type of trend curve often found to be useful is the exponential trend curve. A typical *exponential trend curve* is one that reflects a constant rate of growth during a period of years, as might

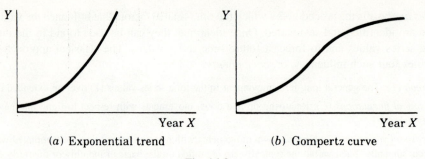

(a) Exponential trend   (b) Gompertz curve

Fig. 16-2

apply to the sales of personal computers during the 1980s. See Fig. 16-2(a). An exponential curve is so named because the independent variable X is the exponent of b_1 in the general equation:

$$Y_T = b_0 \, b_1^X \tag{16.5}$$

where b_0 = value of Y_T in Year 0
   b_1 = rate of growth (e.g., 1.10 = 10% rate of growth)

Taking the logarithm of both sides of (16.5) results in a linear logarithmic trend equation,

$$\log Y_T = \log b_0 + X \log b_1 \tag{16.6}$$

The advantage of the transformation into logarithms is that the linear equation for trend analysis can be applied to the logs of the values when the time series follows an exponential curve. The forecasted log values for Y_T can then be reconverted to the original measurement units by taking the antilog of the values. We do not demonstrate such analysis in this book.

Many time series for the sales of a particular product can be observed to include three stages: an *introductory stage* of slow growth in sales, a *middle stage* of rapid sales increases, and a *final stage* of slow growth as market saturation is reached. For some products, such as structural steel, the complete set of three stages may encompass many years. For other products, such as citizen band radios, the stage of saturation may be reached relatively quickly. One particular trend curve that includes the three stages just described is the S-shaped *Gompertz curve*, as portrayed in Fig. 16-2(b). An equation that can be used to fit the Gompertz trend curve is

$$Y_T = b_0 \, b_1^{(b_2)X} \tag{16.7}$$

The values of b_0, b_1, and b_2 are determined by first taking the logarithm of both sides of the equation, as follows:

$$\log Y_T = \log b_0 + (\log b_1) b_2^X \tag{16.8}$$

Finally, the values to form the trend curve are calculated by taking the antilog of the values calculated by Formula (16.8). The details of such calculations are included in specialized books on time series analysis.

16.3   ANALYSIS OF CYCLICAL VARIATIONS

Annual time series values represent the effects of only the trend and cyclical components, because the seasonal and irregular components are defined as short-run influences. Therefore, for annual data the cyclical component can be identified as being the component that would remain in the data after the influence of the trend component is removed. This removal is accomplished by dividing each of the observed values by the associated trend value, as follows:

$$\frac{Y}{Y_T} = \frac{T \times C}{T} = C \qquad\qquad (16.9)$$

The ratio in (16.9) is multiplied by 100 so that the mean cyclical relative will be 100.0. A cyclical relative of 100 would indicate the absence of any cyclical influence on the annual time series value. See Problem 16.2.

In order to aid in the interpretation of cyclical relatives, a *cycle chart* which portrays the cyclical relatives according to year is often prepared. The peaks and troughs associated with the cyclical component of the time series can be made more apparent by the construction of such a chart. See Problem 16.3.

16.4   MEASUREMENT OF SEASONAL VARIATIONS

The influence of the seasonal component on time series values is identified by determining the seasonal index number associated with each month (or quarter) of the year. The arithmetic mean of all 12 monthly index numbers (or four quarterly index numbers) is 100. The identification of positive and negative seasonal influences is important for production and inventory planning.

EXAMPLE 2.   An index number of 110 associated with a given month indicates that the time series values for that month have averaged 10 percent higher than for other months because of some positive seasonal factor. For instance, the unit sales of men's shavers might be 10 percent higher in June as compared with other months because of Father's Day.

The procedure most frequently used to determine seasonal index numbers is the *ratio-to-moving-average method*. By this method, the ratio of each monthly value to the moving average centered at that month is first determined. Because a moving average based on monthly (or quarterly) data for an entire year would average out the seasonal and irregular fluctuations, but not the longer-term trend and cyclical influences, the ratio of a monthly (or quarterly) value to a moving average can be represented symbolically by

$$\frac{Y}{\text{Moving average}} = \frac{T \times C \times S \times I}{T \times C} = S \times I \qquad\qquad (16.10)$$

The second step in the ratio-to-moving-average method is to average out the irregular component. This is typically done by listing the several ratios applicable to the same month (or quarter) for the several years, eliminating the highest and lowest values, and computing the mean of the remaining ratios. The resulting mean is called a *modified mean*, because of the elimination of the two extreme values.

The final step in the ratio-to-moving-average method is to adjust the modified mean ratios by a correction factor so that the sum of the 12 monthly ratios is 1,200 (or 400 for four quarterly ratios). See Problem 16.4.

16.5   APPLYING SEASONAL ADJUSTMENTS

One frequent application of seasonal indexes is that of adjusting observed time series data by removing the influence of the seasonal component from the data. Such adjusted data are called *seasonally adjusted data*, or *deseasonalized data*. Seasonal adjustments are particularly relevant if we wish to compare data for different months to determine if an increase (or decrease) relative to seasonal expectations has taken place.

EXAMPLE 3.   An increase in lawn fertilizer sales of 10 percent from April to May of a given year represents a relative *decrease* if the seasonal index number for May is 20 percent above the index number for April. In other words, if an increase occurs but is not as large as expected based on historical data, then relative to these expectations a relative decline in demand has occurred.

The observed monthly (or quarterly) time series values are adjusted for seasonal influence by dividing each value by the monthly (or quarterly) index for that month. The result is then multiplied by 100 to maintain the decimal position of the original data. The process of adjusting data for the influence of seasonal variations can be represented by

$$\frac{Y}{S} = \frac{T \times C \times S \times I}{S} = T \times C \times I \qquad (16.11)$$

Although the resulting values after the application of (16.11) are in the same measurement units as the original data, they do not represent actual data. Rather, they are relative values and are meaningful for comparative purposes only. See Problem 16.5.

16.6   FORECASTING BASED ON TREND AND SEASONAL FACTORS

A beginning point for long-term forecasting of annual values is provided by use of the trend line (16.2) equation. However, a particularly important consideration in long-term forecasting is the cyclical component of the time series. There is no standard method by which the cyclical component can be forecast based on historical time series values alone, but certain economic indicators (see Section 16.7) are useful for anticipating cyclical turning points.

For short-term forecasting, one possible approach is to deseasonalize the most-recent observed value and then to multiply this deseasonalized value by the seasonal index for the forecast period. This approach assumes that the only difference between the two periods will be the difference that is attributable to the seasonal influence. An alternative approach is to use the projected trend value as the basis for the forecast and then adjust it for the seasonal component. When the equation for the trend line is based on annual values, one must first "step down" the equation so that is expressed in terms of months (or quarters). A trend equation based on annual data is modified to obtain projected monthly values as follows:

$$Y_T = \frac{b_0}{12} + \left(\frac{b_1}{12}\right)\left(\frac{X}{12}\right) = \frac{b_0}{12} + \frac{b_1}{144} X \qquad (16.12)$$

A trend equation based on annual data is modified to obtain projected quarterly values as follows:

$$Y_T = \frac{b_0}{4} + \left(\frac{b_1}{4}\right)\left(\frac{X}{4}\right) = \frac{b_0}{4} + \frac{b_1}{16} X \qquad (16.13)$$

The basis for the above modifications is not obvious if one overlooks the fact that trend values are not associated with points in time, but rather, with periods of time. Because of this consideration, all *three* elements in the equation for annual trend (b_0, b_1, and X) have to be stepped down.

By the transformation for monthly data in (16.12), the base point in the year that was formerly coded $X = 0$ would be at the middle of the year, or July 1. Because it is necessary that the base point be at the middle of the first month of the base year, or January 15, the intercept $b_0/12$ in the modified equation is then reduced by 5.5 times the modified slope. A similar adjustment is made for quarterly data. Thus, a trend equation which is modified to obtain projected monthly values *and* with $X = 0$ placed at January 15 of the base year is

$$Y_T = \frac{b_0}{12} - (5.5)\left(\frac{b_1}{144}\right) + \frac{b_1}{144} X \qquad (16.14)$$

Similarly, a trend equation that is modified to obtain projected quarterly values *and* with $X = 0$ placed at the middle of the first quarter of the base year is

$$Y_T = \frac{b_0}{4} - (1.5)\left(\frac{b_i}{16}\right) + \frac{b_1}{16} X \qquad (16.15)$$

Problem 16.6 illustrates the process of stepping down a trend equation. After monthly (or quarterly) trend values have been determined, each value can be multiplied by the appropriate seasonal index (and divided by 100 to preserve the decimal location in the values) to establish a beginning point for short-term forecasting. See Problem 16.7.

16.7   CYCLICAL FORECASTING AND BUSINESS INDICATORS

As indicated in Section 16.6, forecasting based on the trend and seasonal components of a time series is considered only a beginning point in economic forecasting. One reason is the necessity to consider the likely effect of the cyclical component during the forecast period, while the second is the importance of identifying the specific causative factors that have influenced the time series variables.

For short-term forecasting, the effect of the cyclical component is often assumed to be the same as included in recent time series values. However, for longer periods, or even for short periods during economic instability, the identification of the *cyclical turning points* for the national economy is important. Of course, the cyclical variations associated with a particular product may or may not coincide with the general business cycle.

EXAMPLE 4.   Historically, factory sales of passenger cars have coincided closely with the general business cycle for the national economy. On the other hand, sales of automobile repair parts have often been countercyclic with respect to the general business cycle.

The National Bureau of Economic Research (NBER) has identified a number of published time series that historically have been indicators of cyclic revivals and recessions with respect to the general business cycle. One group, called *leading indicators*, has usually reached cyclical turning points prior to the corresponding change in general economic activity. The leading indicators include such measures as average weekly hours worked in manufacturing, value of new orders for consumer goods and materials, and a common stock price index. A second group, called *coincident indicators*, are time series which have generally had turning points coinciding with the general business cycle. Coincident indicators include such measures as the employment rate and the index of industrial production. The third group, called *lagging indicators*, are those time series for which the peaks and troughs usually lag behind those of the general business cycle. Lagging indicators include such measures as manufacturing and trade inventories and the average prime rate charged by banks.

In addition to considering the effect of cyclical fluctuations and forecasting such fluctuations, specific causative variables that have influenced the time series values historically should also be studied. Regression and correlation analysis (see Chapters 14 and 15) are particularly applicable for such studies as the relationship between pricing strategy and sales volume. Beyond the historical analyses, the possible implications of new products and of changes in the marketing environment are also areas of required attention.

16.8   FORECASTING BASED ON MOVING AVERAGES

A *moving average* is the average of the most recent n data values in a time series. This procedure can be represented by

$$MA = \frac{\Sigma \text{ (most recent } n \text{ values)}}{n} \qquad (16.16)$$

As each new data value becomes available in a time series, the newest observation replaces the oldest observation in the set of n values as the basis for determining the new average, and this is why it is called a *moving* average.

The moving average can be used to forecast the data value for the next (forthcoming) period in the time series, but not for periods that are farther in the future. It is an appropriate method of forecasting when there is no trend, cyclical or seasonal influence on the data, which of course is an unlikely situation. The procedure serves simply to average out the irregular component in the recent time series data. See Problem 16.8.

16.9   EXPONENTIAL SMOOTHING AS A FORECASTING METHOD

Exponential smoothing is a method of forecasting that is also based on using a moving average, but it is a *weighted* moving average rather than one in which the preceding data values are equally weighted. The basis for the weights is exponential because the greatest weight is given to the data value for the period immediately preceding the forecast period and the weights decrease exponentially for the data values of earlier periods. There are, in fact, several types of exponential smoothing models, as described in specialized books in business forecasting. The method presented here is called *simple exponential smoothing*.

The following algebraic model serves to represent how the exponentially decreasing weights are determined. Specifically, where α is a smoothing constant discussed below, the most recent value of the time series is weighted by α, the next most recent value is weighted by $\alpha(1 - \alpha)$, the next value by $\alpha(1 - \alpha)^2$, and so forth, and all the weighted values are then summed to determine the forecast:

$$\hat{Y}_{t-1} = \alpha Y_t + \alpha(1 - \alpha)Y_{t-1} + \alpha(1 - \alpha)^2 Y_{t-2} + \cdots + \alpha(1 - \alpha)^k Y_{t-k} \qquad (16.17)$$

where $\hat{Y}_{t+1}$ = forecast for the next period
$\qquad \alpha$ = smoothing constant $(0 \leq \alpha \leq 1)$
$\qquad Y_t$ = actual value for the most recent period
$\qquad Y_{t-1}$ = actual value for the period preceding the most recent period
$\qquad Y_{t-k}$ = actual value for k periods preceding the most recent period

Although the above formula serves to present the rationale of exponential smoothing, its use is quite cumbersome. A simplified procedure that requires an initial "seed" forecast but does not require the determination of weights is generally used instead. The formula for determining the forecast by the simplified method of exponential smoothing is

$$\hat{Y}_{t+1} = \hat{Y}_t + \alpha(Y_t - \hat{Y}_t) \qquad (16.18)$$

where $\hat{Y}_{t+1}$ = forecast for the next period
$\qquad \hat{Y}_t$ = forecast for the most recent period
$\qquad \alpha$ = smoothing constant $(0 \leq \alpha \leq 1)$
$\qquad Y_t$ = actual value for the most recent period

Because the most recent time series value must be available to determine a forecast for the following period, simple exponential smoothing can be used only to forecast the value for the *next* period in the time series, not for several periods into the future. The closer the value of the smoothing constant is set to 1.0, the more heavily is the forecast weighted by the most recent results. See Problem 16.9

16.10   OTHER FORECASTING METHODS THAT INCORPORATE SMOOTHING

Whereas the moving average is appropriate as the basis for forecasting only when the irregular influence causes the time series values to vary, simple exponential smoothing is most appropriate only when the cyclical and irregular influences comprise the main effects on the observed values. In both methods, a forecast can be obtained only for the next period in the time series, and not for periods farther into the future. Other more complex methods of smoothing incorporate more influences and permit forecasting for several periods into the future. These methods are briefly described below. Full explanations and descriptions of these methods are included in specialized textbooks on forecasting.

Linear exponential smoothing utilizes a linear trend equation based on the time series data. However, unlike the simple trend equation presented in Section 16.2, the values in the series are exponentially weighted based on the use of a smoothing constant. As in simple exponential smoothing, the constant can vary from 0 to 1.0.

Holt's exponential smoothing utilizes a linear trend equation based on using two smoothing constants: one to estimate the current level of the time series values and the other to estimate the slope.

Winter's exponential smoothing incorporates seasonal influences in the forecast. Three smoothing constants are used: one to estimate the current level of the time series values, the second to estimate the slope of the trend line, and the third to estimate the seasonal factor to be used as a multiplier.

Autoregressive integrated moving average (ARIMA) models are a category of forecasting methods in which previously observed values in the time series are used as independent variables in regression models. The most widely used method in this category was developed by Box and Jenkins, and is generally called the *Box-Jenkins method*. These methods make explicit use of the existence of *autocorrelation* in the time series, which is the correlation between a variable, lagged one or more periods, with itself. As described in Section 15.8, the *Durbin-Watson test* serves to detect the existence of autocorrelated residuals (*serial correlation*) in time series values. A value of the test statistic close to 2.0 supports the null hypothesis that no autocorrelation exists in the time series. A value below 1.4 generally is indicative of strong positive serial correlation, while a value greater than 2.6 indicates the existence of strong negative serial correlation.

16.11   USING COMPUTER SOFTWARE

Specialized software is available in time series analysis and business forecasting, with much of it incorporating the more sophisticated techniques that are described in the preceding section of this chapter. Problems 16.10 through 16.13 illustrate the use of Execustat for determining a linear trend equation, doing seasonal analysis, using the method of moving averages for the purpose of forecasting, and using simple exponential smoothing for the purpose of forecasting.

Solved Problems

TREND ANALYSIS

16.1 Table 16.1 presents sales data for an 11-year period for a graphics software company (fictional) incorporated in 1990, as described in Example 1, and for which the time series data are portrayed by the line graph in Fig. 16-1. Included also are worktable calculations needed to determine the equation for the trend line. (*a*) Determine the linear trend equation for these data by the least-square method, coding 1990 as 0 and carrying all values to two places beyond the decimal point. Using this equation determine the forecast of sales for the year 2001. (*b*) Enter the trend line on the line graph in Fig. 16.1.

(*a*) $Y_T = b_0 + b_1 X$

where $\bar{X} = \dfrac{\Sigma X}{n} = \dfrac{55}{11} = 5.00$

$\bar{Y} = \dfrac{\Sigma Y}{n} = \dfrac{12.9}{11} = 1.17$

$b_1 = \dfrac{\Sigma XY - n\bar{X}\bar{Y}}{\Sigma X^2 - n\bar{X}^2} = \dfrac{85.2 - 11(5.00)(1.17)}{385 - 11(5.00)^2}$

$= \dfrac{20.85}{110} = 0.19$

$b_0 = \bar{Y} - b_1\bar{X} = 1.17 - 0.19(5.00) = 0.22$

$Y_T = 0.22 + 0.19X(\text{with } X = 0 \text{ at } 1990)$

$Y_T(2001) = 0.22 + 0.19(11) = 2.31 \text{ (in millions)}$

Table 16.1 Historical Sales for a Graphics Software Firm, with Worktable to Determine the Equation for the Trend Line

Year	Coded year (X)	Sales, in $millions (Y)	X Y	X^2
1990	0	$0.2	0	0
1991	1	0.4	0.4	1
1992	2	0.5	1.0	4
1993	3	0.9	2.7	9
1994	4	1.1	4.4	16
1995	5	1.5	7.5	25
1996	6	1.3	7.8	36
1997	7	1.1	7.7	49
1998	8	1.7	13.6	64
1999	9	1.9	17.1	81
2000	10	2.3	23.0	100
Total	55	$12.9	85.2	385

This equation can be used as a beginning point for forecasting, as described in Section 16.6. The slope of 0.19 indicates that during the 11-year existence of the company there has been an average increase in sales of 0.19 million dollars ($190,000) annually.

(b) Figure 16-3 repeats the line graph in Fig. 16-1, but with the trend line entered in the graph. The peak and trough in the time series that were briefly discussed in Example 1 are now more clearly visible.

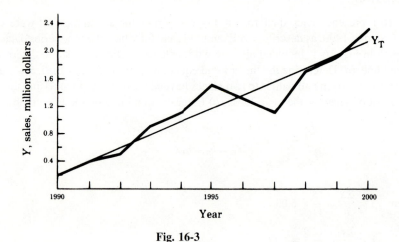

Fig. 16-3

ANALYSIS OF CYCLICAL VARIATIONS

16.2 Determine the cyclical component for each of the time series values reported in Table 16.1, utilizing the trend equation determined in Problem 16.1.

Table 16.2 presents the determination of the cyclic relatives. As indicated in the last column of the table, each cyclical relative is determined by multiplying the observed time series value by 100 and dividing by the trend value. Thus, the cyclical relative of 90.0 for 1990 was determined by calculating 100(0.20)/0.22.

Table 16.2   Determination of Cyclical Relatives

Year	Coded year (X)	Sales, in $millions		Cyclical relative 100 Y/Y
		Actual (Y)	Expected (Y)	
1990	0	0.20	0.22	90.9
1991	1	0.40	0.41	97.6
1992	2	0.50	0.60	83.3
1993	3	0.90	0.79	113.9
1994	4	1.10	0.98	112.2
1995	5	1.50	1.17	128.2
1996	6	1.30	1.36	95.6
1997	7	1.10	1.55	71.0
1998	8	1.70	1.74	97.7
1999	9	1.90	1.93	98.4
2000	10	2.30	2.12	108.5

16.3   Construct a cycle chart for the sales data reported in Table 16.1, based on the cyclical relatives determined in Table 16.2.

The cycle chart is presented in Fig. 16-4, and includes the peak and trough observed previously in Fig. 16-3.

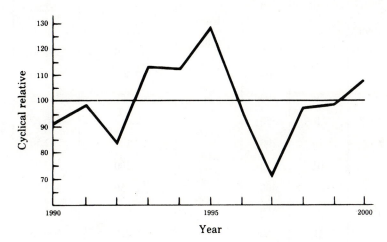

Fig. 16-4

MEASUREMENT OF SEASONAL VARIATIONS

16.4   Table 16.3 presents quarterly sales data for the graphics software company for which annual data are reported in Table 16.1. Determine the seasonal indexes by the ratio-to-moving-average method.

Table 16.4 is concerned with the first step in the ratio-to-moving-average method, that of computing the ratio of each quarterly value to the 4-quarter moving average centered at that quarter.

The 4-quarter moving totals are centered between the quarters in the table because as a moving total of an even number of quarters, the total would always fall between two quarters. For example, the first listed total of 1,500 (in $1,000s) is the total sales amount for the first through the fourth quarters of 1995. Since four quarters are involved, the total is centered vertically in the table between the second and third quarter.

Table 16.3   Quarterly Sales for the Graphics Software Firm

Quarter	Quarterly sales, in $1,000s					
	1995	1996	1997	1998	1999	2000
1	500	450	350	550	550	750
2	350	350	200	350	400	500
3	250	200	150	250	350	400
4	400	300	400	550	600	650

Table 16.4   Worktable for Determining the Ratio-to-Moving-Average for the Quarterly Sales Data (sales in $1,000s)

Year	Quarter	Sales	4-quarter moving total	2-year centered moving total	4-quarter centered moving average	Ratio-to-moving-average (percent)
1995	I	500				
	II	350				
			1,500			
	III	250		2,950	368.75	67.8
			1,450			
	IV	400		2,900	362.50	110.3
			1,450			
1996	I	450		2,850	356.25	126.3
			1,400			
	II	350		2,700	337.50	103.7
			1,300			
	III	200		2,500	312.50	64.0
			1,200			
	IV	300		2,250	281.25	106.7
			1,050			
1997	I	350		2,050	256.25	136.6
			1,000			
	II	200		2,100	262.50	76.2
			1,100			
	III	150		2,400	300.00	50.0
			1,300			
	IV	400		2,750	343.75	116.4
			1,450			
1998	I	550		3,000	375.00	146.7
			1,550			
	II	350		3,250	406.25	86.2
			1,700			
	III	250		3,400	425.00	58.8
			1,700			
	IV	550		3,450	431.25	127.5
			1,750			
1999	I	550		3,600	450.00	122.2
			1,850			
	II	400		3,750	468.75	85.3
			1,900			
	III	350		4,000	500.00	70.0
			2,100			
	IV	600		4,300	537.50	111.6
			2,200			
2000	I	750		4,450	556.25	134.8
			2,250			
	II	500		4,550	568.75	87.9
			2,300			
	III	400				
	IV	650				

Because it is desired that the moving average be centered at each quarter, instead of between quarters, adjoining 4-quarter moving totals are combined to form the 2-year centered moving totals. Note that this type of total does *not* include two years of data as such. Rather, two overlapping 4-quarter periods are included in the total. For example, the first centered moving total of 2,950 (in $1,000s) includes the 4-quarter total of 1,500 for the four quarters of 1995, plus the 4-quarter total of 1,450 for the second quarter of 1995 through the first quarter of 1996.

The 4-quarter centered moving average simply is the 2-year centered moving total divided by 8.

Finally, the ratio-to-moving-average in the last column of Table 16.4 is the ratio of each quarterly sales value to the centered moving average for that quarter. This ratio is multiplied by 100 and in effect is reported as a percentage.

Table 16.5 incorporates the second and third steps in determining the seasonal indexes. The modified mean for each quarter is the mean of the three remaining ratios for each quarter *after* elimination of the highest and lowest ratios. For example, for Quarter 1 the two extreme ratios 122.2 and 146.7, are eliminated from consideration, with the mean of the remaining three ratios being 132.6.

Table 16.5   Calculation of the Seasonal Indexes for the Quarterly Data

Quarter	1995	1996	1997	1998	1999	2000	Modified mean	Seasonal index: mean × 1.0116*
1		126.3	136.6	146.7	122.2	134.8	132.6	134.1
2		103.7	76.2	86.2	85.3	87.9	86.5	87.5
3	67.8	64.0	50.0	58.8	70.0		63.5	64.2
4	110.3	106.7	116.4	127.5	111.6		112.8	114.1
							395.4	399.9

*Adjustment factor = 400/395.4 = 1.0116.

Finally, the modified means are multiplied by an adjustment factor so that the sum of the index is approximately 400 (1,200 for monthly indexes). The adjustment factor used with modified mean quarterly indexes to obtain the quarterly indexes is

$$\text{Quarterly adjustment factor} = \frac{400}{\text{sum of quarterly means}} \qquad (16.19)$$

The adjustment factor used with modified mean monthly indexes to obtain the monthly indexes is

$$\text{Monthly adjustment factor} = \frac{1,200}{\text{sum of monthly means}} \qquad (16.20)$$

For the ratios in Table 16.5, the adjustment factor is 400/395.4, or 1.0116. Each modified mean is multiplied by this adjustment factor to obtain the quarterly indexes. Overall, we can observe that the quarter with the greatest positive seasonal effect is Quarter 1, with sales generally being about 34.1 percent higher than the typical quarter. On the other hand, sales in Quarter 3 generally are just 64.2 percent of the sales in the typical quarter. By being aware of such seasonal variations, a firm can take them into consideration when planning work schedules and in making forecasts of sales.

APPLYING SEASONAL ADJUSTMENTS

16.5   Refer to the seasonal indexes determined in Table 16.5.

(a)   Compute the seasonally adjusted value for each quarter, rounding the values to whole thousand dollar amounts.

(b)   Compare the results for the third and fourth quarters of 2000 based on (1) the reported level of actual sales, and (2) the seasonally adjusted values.

(a)   The seasonally adjusted values are reported in Table 16.6. Each deseasonalized value was determined by dividing the quarterly value in Table 16.3 by the seasonal index for that quarter (from Table 16.5), and multiplying by 100 to preserve the location of the decimal point. For example, the seasonally adjusted value of 373 (in $1,000s) for Quarter 1 of 1995 was obtained by dividing 500 (from Table 16.3) by 134.1 (from Table 16.5) and multiplying by 100.

Table 16.6   Seasonally Adjusted Values for the Quarterly Data

Quarter	1995	1996	1997	1998	1999	2000
1	$373	$336	$261	$410	$410	$559
2	400	400	229	400	457	571
3	389	312	234	389	545	623
4	351	263	351	482	526	570

(b)   The reported levels of sales for the third and fourth quarters indicate a substantial increase in sales between the two quarters—from $400,000 to $650,000. However, on a seasonally adjusted basis there is a decline of 8.5 percent, from $623,000 to $570,000. Thus, although sales increased in the fourth quarter, the increase was not as large as it should have been, based on the different historical seasonal influences for these two quarters

FORECASTING BASED ON TREND AND SEASONAL FACTORS

16.6   Step down the trend equation developed in Problem 16.1 so that it is expressed in terms of quarters rather than years. Also, adjust the equation so that the trend values are in thousands of dollars instead of millions of dollars. Carry the final values to the first place beyond the decimal point.

$$Y_T \text{ (quarterly)} = \frac{b_0}{4} - 1.5\left(\frac{b_1}{16}\right) + \left(\frac{b_1}{16}\right)X$$

$$= \frac{0.22}{4} - 15\left(\frac{0.19}{16}\right) + \left(\frac{0.19}{16}\right)X$$

$$= 0.0550 - 0.0178 + 0.0119X$$

$$= 0.0372 + 0.0119X$$

The quarterly trend equation in units of thousands of dollars is:

$$Y_T \text{ (quarterly)} = 1,000\,(0.0372 + 0.0119X) = 37.2 + 11.9X$$

For the above equation, $X = 0$ at the first quarter of 1990.

16.7   Forecast the level of quarterly sales for each quarter of 2001 based on the quarterly trend equation determined in Problem 16.6 and the seasonal indexes determined in Table 16.5.

The forecasted values based on the quarterly trend equation, and then adjusted for the quarterly seasonal indexes, are

$$\text{First quarter, } 2001 = [37.2 + 11.9(44)] \times \frac{134.1}{100} = 752.0$$

$$\text{Second quarter, } 2001 = [37.2 + 11.9(45)] \times \frac{87.5}{100} = 501.1$$

$$\text{Third quarter, } 2001 = [37.2 + 11.9(46)] \times \frac{64.2}{100} = 375.3$$

$$\text{Fourth quarter, } 2001 = [37.2 + 11.9(47)] \times \frac{114.1}{100} = 680.6$$

FORECASTING BASED ON MOVING AVERAGES

16.8 Refer to the annual time series data in Table 16.1. Begin with 1994 and determine the 3-year moving averages that would have been used to forecast the sales (in $millions) for the years subsequent to each group of three years. Determine the forecast error associated with each forecast.

Table 16.7 is the worktable that reports the forecasts and the forecast errors. For example, the forecast for the year 2000 is based on the 3-year average sales for 1997–99. The amounts of forecast error will be compared with those for the method of exponential smoothing in the next Solved Problem, 16.9.

Table 16.7   Year-by-Year Forecasts by the Method of Moving Averages

Year (t)	Sales in millions (Y_t)	Forecast $(\hat{Y}_t)$	Forecast error $(Y_t - \hat{Y}_t)$
1994	$1.1		
1995	1.5		
1996	1.3		
1997	1.1	$1.3	$-0.2
1998	1.7	1.3	0.4
1999	1.9	1.4	0.5
2000	2.3	1.6	0.7
2001		2.0	

EXPONENTIAL SMOOTHING AS A FORECASTING METHOD

16.9 Refer to the annual time series data in Table 16.1. Using the actual level of sales for 1994 of 1.1 million dollars as the "seed" forecast for 1995, determine the forecast for each annual sales amount by the method of simple exponential smoothing. First use a smoothing constant of $\alpha = 0.80$, then use a smoothing constant of $\alpha = 0.20$, and compare the two sets of forecasts.

Table 16.8 is the worktable that reports the two sets of forecasts. For example, the forecast amount for 1996 based on $\alpha = 0.20$ was determined as follows:

$$\hat{Y}_{t+1} = \hat{Y}_t + \alpha(Y_t - \hat{Y}_t)$$

$$\hat{Y}_{1996} = \hat{Y}_{1995} + \alpha(Y_{1995} - \hat{Y}_{1995})$$
$$= \$1.1 + 0.20(0.4) = 1.1 + 0.08 = 1.18 \cong \$1.2$$

Table 16.8 Year-by-Year Forecasts by the Method of Exponential Smoothing

Year (t)	Sales in millions (Y_t)	$\alpha = 0.20$ Forecast ($\hat{Y}_t$)	$\alpha = 0.20$ Forecast error ($Y_t - \hat{Y}_t$)	$\alpha = 0.80$ Forecast ($\hat{Y}_t$)	$\alpha = 0.80$ Forecast error ($Y_t - \hat{Y}_t$)
1995	$ 1.5	$ 1.1	$ 0.4	$1.1	$ 0.4
1996	1.3	1.2	0.1	1.4	−0.1
1997	1.1	1.2	−0.1	1.3	−0.2
1998	1.7	1.2	0.5	1.1	0.6
1999	1.9	1.3	0.6	1.6	0.3
2000	2.3	1.4	0.9	1.8	0.5
2001		1.6		2.2	

The forecast errors are generally lower for $\alpha = 0.80$. Thus, the greater weight given to the forecast errors leads to better forecasts for these data. Note also that the forecast errors for $\alpha = 0.80$ for 1997–2000 are somewhat lower than the forecast errors for the unweighted moving averages in Problem 16.8.

COMPUTER OUTPUT

16.10 Use computer software to obtain the linear trend equation for the annual sales in Table 16.1. Based on the trend equation, determine the forecasts for the years 2001–2003. Plot the time series data, the trend line, and the forecasts.

Figure 16-5 is Execustat output that reports the linear trend equation based on using the same coded years as in Table 16.1. Except for rounding, this equation corresponds to that determined manually in Problem 16.1. The additional output in the figure is concerned with the goodness of fit of the linear function, and is outside of our intended coverage.

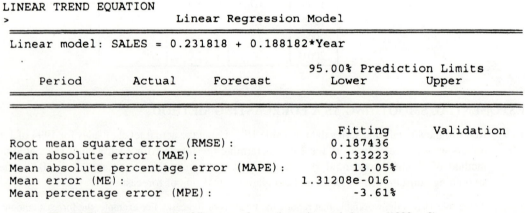

```
LINEAR TREND EQUATION
>                          Linear Regression Model
═══════════════════════════════════════════════════════════════════════
 Linear model: SALES = 0.231818 + 0.188182*Year

                                            95.00% Prediction Limits
       Period        Actual      Forecast     Lower        Upper
═══════════════════════════════════════════════════════════════════════



                                            Fitting        Validation
 Root mean squared error (RMSE):            0.187436
 Mean absolute error (MAE):                 0.133223
 Mean absolute percentage error (MAPE):       13.05%
 Mean error (ME):                          1.31208e-016
 Mean percentage error (MPE):                 -3.61%
```

Fig. 16-5 Execustat output of linear trend equation using coded years (1990 = 0).

Figure 16-6 reports the linear trend equation based on using the actual years, rather than the coded years, and also includes the forecasts for the years 2001–2003. Note that although the intercept for this trend line is different from that in Fig. 16-5, the slope of the trend lines is the same. For both equations, there is an annual increase in sales

```
LINEAR TREND FORECAST
>                          Linear Regression Model
```

Linear model: SALES = -374.25 + 0.188182*Year

| Period | Actual | Forecast | 95.00% Prediction Limits | |
			Lower	Upper
2001		2.3	1.74	2.86
2002		2.49	1.91	3.07
2003		2.68	2.07	3.28

	Fitting	Validation
Root mean squared error (RMSE):	0.187436	
Mean absolute error (MAE):	0.133223	
Mean absolute percentage error (MAPE):	13.05%	
Mean error (ME):	1.89343e-014	
Mean percentage error (MPE):	-3.61%	

Fig. 16-6 Execustat output of linear trend equation and forecasts using uncoded years.

of about $0.188 million (or $188,000). Figure 16-6 also reports the forecasts for the years 2001–2003 based on the trend equation, including 95 percent prediction limits. Note that the forecast for the year 2001 corresponds to the one we determined manually in Problem 16.1.

Figure 16-7 is the plot that includes the time series values, the trend line, and the forecasts for the years 2001–2003.

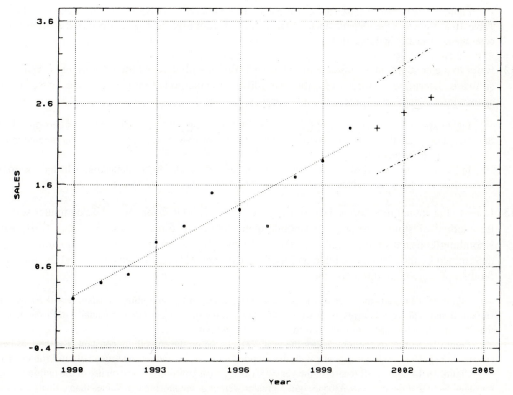

Fig. 16-7 Execustat plot for Problem 16.10.

16.11 Use computer software to determine the seasonal indexes based on the quarterly data in Table 16.3, and seasonally adjust the original data.

Figure 16-8 reports the quarterly indexes. Except for slight differences due to rounding, the indexes correspond to those determined manually in Problem 16.4.

```
QUARTERLY INDEXES
                          Time Series Analysis

Time series variable: SALES
Type : quarterly
Start: 1995-1
Seasonality: 4
Analysis quarters:    1995-1 to 2000-4
Validation quarters: <none>
Forecast quarters:   <none>


                Seasonal Decomposition (multiplicative)

Season      Index

1st         134.057
2nd          88.3413
3rd          62.4653
4th         115.137
```

Fig. 16-8   Quarterly indexes for Problem 16.11 (from Execustat).

Figure 16-9 reports the seasonally adjusted data. This output corresponds to the values determined manually in Table 16.6. Note that the column labeled "Trend" in Fig. 16-9 lists the 4-quarter centered moving averages, as determined manually in Table 16.4.

16.12 Refer to the annual time series data in Table 16.1. Begin with the data for 1994 as input. With computer software, determine the forecast for the year 2001 by the method of moving averages, based on a 3-year span. Plot the data, the 3-year moving averages, and the forecast.

Figure 16-10 reports the forecast for the year 2001 as being 1.97 (in $millions). This corresponds with the rounded value of 2.0 that was determined manually in Problem 16.8. Note that the 95 percent prediction limits are also determined for this forecast.

In Fig. 16-11 the historical 3-year moving averages are represented by the dotted line. The forecast for the year 2001, which is the 3-year average for the years 1998–2000, is represented by the " + ".

16.13 Refer to the annual time series data for the years 1994–2000 in Table 16.1. Use computer software and the method of simple exponential smoothing to determine forecasts for the year 2001 based on a smoothing constant of $\alpha = 0.20$, $\alpha = 0.80$, and then by use of the optimum smoothing constant as determined by the software. Obtain a plot of the exponentially smoothed values and the forecast based on the optimum smoothing constant.

Figure 16-12 reports the forecast for the year 2001, based on the smoothing constant $\alpha = 0.20$, as being 1.66 (in $millions). This result corresponds with the rounded value of 1.6 determined manually in Problem 16.9. Note that 95 percent prediction limits are also included in the output.

Figure 16-13 reports the forecast for the year 2001, based on the smoothing constant $\alpha = 0.80$, as being 2.21 (in $millions). This result corresponds with the rounded value of 2.2 determined manually in Problem 16.9.

Figure 16-14 reports a forecast for the year 2001 of 2.25 (in $millions) based on use of the optimum smoothing constant. Note that the $\alpha = 0.893365$ assigns a greater weight to the most recent values than either of the other two smoothing constants, above.

SEASONALLY ADJUSTED DATA
                        Time Series Analysis
═══

Time series variable: SALES
Type : quarterly
Start: 1995-1
Seasonality: 4
Analysis quarters: 1995-1 to 2000-4
Validation quarters: <none>
Forecast quarters: <none>
═══

                 Seasonal Decomposition (multiplicative)
───

Period	actual	trend	residual	adjusted
1	500			372.977
2	350			396.191
3	250	368.75	108.535	400.222
4	400	362.5	95.838	347.413
5	450	356.25	94.2257	335.679
6	350	337.5	117.39	396.191
7	200	312.5	102.457	320.178
8	300	281.25	92.6434	260.56
9	350	256.25	101.886	261.084
10	200	262.5	86.2456	226.395
11	150	300	80.0445	240.133
12	400	343.75	101.066	347.413
13	550	375	109.407	410.274
14	350	406.25	97.5239	396.191
15	250	425	94.17	400.222
16	550	431.25	110.769	477.693
17	550	450	91.1721	410.274
18	400	468.75	96.5951	452.789
19	350	500	112.062	560.311
20	600	537.5	96.9524	521.119
21	750	556.25	100.578	559.465
22	500	568.75	99.5142	565.987
23	400			640.356
24	650			564.546

Fig. 16-9   Seasonally adjusted data for Problem 16.11 (from Execustat).

MOVING AVERAGE FORECAST
>   Forecast Moving Averages
═══

| | | | 95.00% Prediction Limits | |
Period	Actual	Forecast	Lower	Upper
2001		1.97	1.22	2.72

	Fitting	Validation
Root mean squared error (RMSE):	0.505525	
Mean absolute error (MAE):	0.466667	
Mean absolute percentage error (MAPE):	25.42%	
Mean error (ME):	0.366667	
Mean percentage error (MPE):	16.33%	

Fig. 16-10   Execustat output for Problem 16.12.

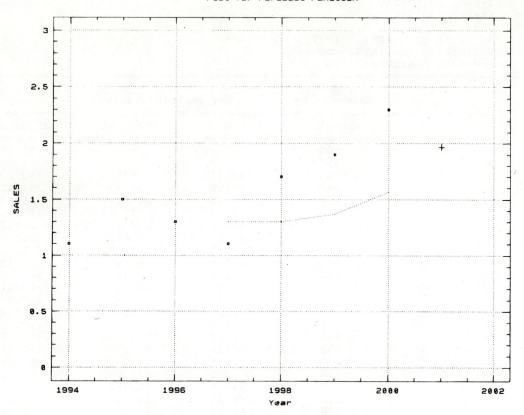

Fig. 16-11 Execustat plot of moving averages.

Figure 16-15 is the plot that includes the time series data the exponentially smoothed values based on the optimum smoothing constant, and the forecast for the year 2001. Because the most recent value is heavily weighted, note that the forecast for the year 2001 is close to the sales figure for the year 2000.

EXPONENTIAL SMOOTHING FORECAST (ALPHA = 0.20)
>   Simple Exponential Smoothing - alpha = 0.2

| | | | 95.00% Prediction Limits | |
Period	Actual	Forecast	Lower	Upper
2001		1.66	0.827	2.49

	Fitting	Validation
Root mean squared error (RMSE):	0.423806	
Mean absolute error (MAE):	0.36036	
Mean absolute percentage error (MAPE):	22.17%	
Mean error (ME):	0.159979	
Mean percentage error (MPE):	4.32%	

Fig. 16-12 Execustat output for Problem 16.13 ($\alpha = 0.20$).

```
EXPONENTIAL SMOOTHING FORECAST (ALPHA = 0.80)
>              Simple Exponential Smoothing - alpha = 0.8
```

| | | | 95.00% Prediction Limits | |
Period	Actual	Forecast	Lower	Upper
2001		2.21	1.5	2.91

	Fitting	Validation
Root mean squared error (RMSE):	0.360422	
Mean absolute error (MAE):	0.33635	
Mean absolute percentage error (MAPE):	21.78%	
Mean error (ME):	0.138255	
Mean percentage error (MPE):	4.31%	

Fig. 16-13   Execustat output for Problem 16.13 ($\alpha = 0.80$).

```
EXPONENTIAL SMOOTHING FORECAST (ALPHA OPTIMIZED)
>              Simple Exponential Smoothing - alpha = 0.893365
```

| | | | 95.00% Prediction Limits | |
Period	Actual	Forecast	Lower	Upper
2001		2.25	1.55	2.96

	Fitting	Validation
Root mean squared error (RMSE):	0.358826	
Mean absolute error (MAE):	0.334621	
Mean absolute percentage error (MAPE):	21.86%	
Mean error (ME):	0.131292	
Mean percentage error (MPE):	4.02%	

Fig. 16-14   Execustat output for Problem 16.13 (optimum α).

Supplementary Problems

TREND ANALYSIS

16.14   Given the data in Table 16.9, determine the linear trend equation for construction contracts for commercial and industrial buildings for a geographic area (data fictional), designating 1995 as the base year for the purpose of coding the years.

Ans. $Y_T = 269.401 + 4.274X$ (in thous. sq. ft)

6.15   Construct the line graph for the data in Table 16.9 and enter the trend line on this graph.

ANALYSIS OF CYCLICAL VARIATIONS

16.16   Determine the cyclical relatives for the annual time series data reported in Table 16.9.

16.17   Prepare a cycle chart to portray the cyclical relatives determined in Problem 16.16 above.

Ans.   The cyclical relatives would reflect peaks (e.g., 1999) and troughs (e.g., 2002) in the regional economy.

MEASUREMENT OF SEASONAL VARIATIONS

16.18   Table 16.10 presents quarterly data for the number of customer orders received in a mail-order firm (fictional). Determine the seasonal indexes based on these data, carrying three places beyond the decimal point during calculations and rounding the indexes to two places.

Ans.   I = 68.19, II = 93.76, III = 113.42, IV = 124.64

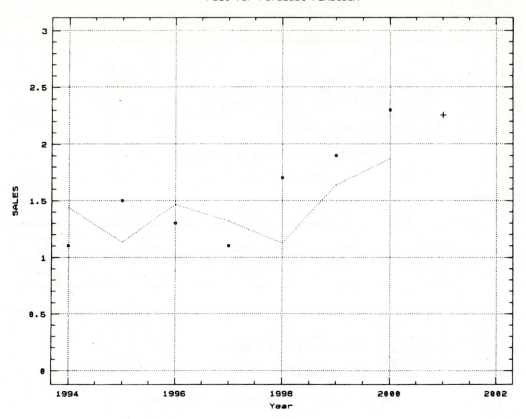

Fig. 16-15 Execustat plot for Problem 16.13.

Table 16.9 Construction Contracts for Commercial and Industrial Buildings, thous. sq. ft.

Year	Construction contracts
1995	291.60
1996	205.72
1997	251.84
1998	322.92
1999	361.36
2000	311.24
2001	310.88
2002	229.52
2003	255.44
2004	312.28
2005	345.68

**Table 16.10   Number of Customer Orders in a
Mail-Order Firm (in 1,000s)**

Quarter	Year				
	1996	1997	1998	1999	2000
I	9	10	13	11	14
II	16	15	22	17	18
III	18	18	17	25	25
IV	21	20	24	21	26

APPLYING SEASONAL ADJUSTMENTS

16.19 Continuing with Problem 16.18, seasonally adjust the data and comment on the comparison of the resulting values for the third and fourth quarters of 2000.

   Ans.   Although there was an increase in orders from the third to the fourth quarters in the original data, on a seasonally adjusted basis there was a decline in orders.

FORECASTING BASED ON TREND AND SEASONAL FACTORS

16.20 Suppose that the trend equation for quarterly sales orders (in thousands) is $Y_T = 13.91 + 0.43X$, with $X = 0$ at the first quarter of 1996. Forecast the number of orders for each of the four quarters of 2001 based on the trend and seasonal components of the time series.

   Ans.   I = 15.34, II = 21.51, III = 26.51, IV = 29.66

EXPONENTIAL SMOOTHING AS A FORECASTING METHOD

16.21 Refer to the construction data in Table 16.9. Using the year 2002 construction amount of 229.52 (thous. sq. ft.) as the "seed" forecast for 2003, use the method of simple exponential smoothing with a smoothing constant of $\alpha = 0.70$ to determine year-by-year forecasts for 2003 through 2006.

   Ans.   229.52, 273.58, 339.37, 350.10

COMPUTER OUTPUT

16.22 Use available computer software to determine the linear trend equation for the construction data in Table 16.9, designating 1995 as the coded year $X = 0$, Determine the forecast for 2006 based on the linear trend equations.

16.23 Use available computer software to (*a*) determine the quarterly seasonal indexes and (*b*) deseasonalize the data on the number of customer orders in Table 16.10.

16.24 Use available computer software to determine the forecast for the year 2006 for the construction data in Table 16.9 by use of simple exponential smoothing. Compare the output using smoothing constants of $\alpha = 0.30$ and $\alpha = 0.60$, and then using the optimum smoothing constant as determined by the software.

CHAPTER 17

Nonparametric Statistics

17.1 SCALES OF MEASUREMENT

Before considering how nonparametric methods of statistics differ from the parametric procedures that constitute most of this book, it is useful to define four types of measurement scales in terms of the precision represented by reported values.

In the *nominal scale*, numbers are used only to identify categories. They do not represent any amount or quantity as such.

EXAMPLE 1. If four sales regions are numbered 1 through 4 as general identification numbers only, then the nominal scale is involved, since the numbers simply serve as category names.

In the *ordinal scale*, the numbers represent ranks. The numbers indicate relative magnitude, but the differences between the ranks are not assumed to be equal.

EXAMPLE 2. An investment analyst ranks five stocks from 1 to 5 in terms of appreciation potential. The difference in the appreciation potential between the stocks ranked 1 and 2 generally would not be the same as, say, the difference between the stocks ranked 3 and 4.

In the *interval scale*, measured differences between values are represented. However, the zero point is arbitrary, and is not an "absolute" zero. Therefore, the numbers cannot be compared by ratios.

EXAMPLE 3. In either the Fahrenheit or the Celsius temperature scales, a 5° difference, from, say, 70°F, to 75°F is the same amount of difference in temperature as from 80°F to 85°F. However, we cannot say that 60°F is twice as warm as 30°F, because the 0°F point is *not* an absolute zero point (the complete absence of all heat).

In the *ratio scale*, there is a true zero point, and therefore measurements can be compared in the form of ratios.

318

EXAMPLE 4.   Not only is it true that a difference in inventory value of $5,000 is the same amount of difference whether between, say, $50,000 and $55,000 or between $60,000 and $65,000, it is also true that an inventory value of $100,000 is twice as great as an inventory value of $50,000.

17.2   PARAMETRIC VS. NONPARAMETRIC STATISTICAL METHODS

Most of the statistical methods described in this book are called *parametric methods*. The focal point of parametric analysis is some population *parameter* for which the sampling statistic follows a *known distribution*, with measurements being made at the *interval* or *ratio scale*. When one or more of these requirements or assumptions are not satisfied, then the so-called *nonparametric* methods can be used. An alternative term is *distribution-free methods*, which focuses particularly on the fact that the distribution of the sampling statistic is not known.

If use of a parametric test, such as the *t* test, is warranted, then we would always prefer its use to the nonparametric equivalent. This is so because if we use the same level of significance for both tests, then the power associated with the nonparametric test is always less than the parametric equivalent. (Recall from Section 10.4 that the power of a statistical test is the probability of rejecting a false null hypothesis.) Nonparametric tests often are used in conjunction with small samples, because for such samples the central limit theorem cannot be invoked (see Section 8.4).

Nonparametric tests can be directed toward hypotheses concerning the *form*, *dispersion*, or *location* (median) of the population. In the majority of the applications, the hypotheses are concerned with the value of a median, the difference between medians, or the differences among several medians. This contrasts with the parametric procedures that are focused principally on population means.

Of the statistical tests already described in this book, the chi-square test covered in Chapter 12 is a nonparametric test. Recall, for example, that the data that are analyzed are at the nominal scale (categorical data). A separate chapter was devoted to the chi-square test because of the extent of its use and the variety of its applications.

17.3   THE RUNS TEST FOR RANDOMNESS

Where a *run* is a series of like observations, the *runs test* is used to test the randomness of a series of observations when each observation can be assigned to one of two categories.

EXAMPLE 5.   For a random sample of $n = 10$ individuals, suppose that when they are categorized by sex, the sequence of observations is: M, M, M, M, F, F, F, F, M, M. For these data there are *three* runs, or series of like items.

For numeric data, one way by which the required two-category scheme can be achieved is to classify each observation as being either above or below the median of the group. In general, either too *few* runs or too *many* runs than would be expected by chance would result in rejecting the null hypothesis that the sequence of observations is a random sequence.

The number of runs of like items is determined for the sample data, with the symbol R used to designate the number of observed runs. Where n_1 equals the number of sampled items of one type and n_2 equals the number of sampled items of the second type, the mean and the standard error associated with the sampling distribution of the R test statistic when the sequence is random are

$$\mu_R = \frac{2n_1n_2}{n_1 + n_2} + 1 \qquad\qquad (17.1)$$

$$\sigma_R = \sqrt{\frac{2n_1n_2(2n_1n_2 - n_1 - n_2)}{(n_1 + n_2)^2(n_1 + n_2 - 1)}} \qquad\qquad (17.2)$$

If either $n_1 > 20$ or $n_2 > 20$, the sampling distribution of r approximates the normal distribution. Therefore under such circumstances the R statistic can be converted to the z test statistic as follows:

$$z = \frac{R - \mu_R}{\sigma_R} \qquad (17.3)$$

Where both $n_1 \leq 20$ and $n_2 \leq 20$, tables of critical values for the R test statistic are available in specialized textbooks in nonparametric statistics.

See Problem 17.1 for an application of the runs test for randomness.

17.4   ONE SAMPLE: THE SIGN TEST

The *sign test* can be used to test a null hypothesis concerning the value of the population median. Therefore, it is the nonparametric equivalent to testing a hypothesis concerning the value of the population mean. The values in the random sample are required to be at least at the ordinal scale, with no assumptions required about the form of the population distribution.

The null and alternative hypotheses can designate either a two-sided or a one-sided test. Where Med denotes the population median and Med_0 designates the hypothesized value, the null and alternative hypotheses for a two-sided test are

$$H_0\colon \text{Med} = \text{Med}_0$$
$$H_1\colon \text{Med} \neq \text{Med}_0$$

A plus sign is assigned for each observed sample value that is larger than the hypothesized value of the median, and a minus sign is assigned for each value that is smaller than the hypothesized value of the median. If a sample value is exactly equal to the hypothesized median, no sign is recorded and the effective sample size is thereby reduced. If the null hypothesis regarding the value of the median is true, the number of plus signs should approximately equal the number of minus signs. Or put another way, the proportion of plus signs (or minus signs) should be about 0.50. Therefore, the null hypothesis tested for a two-sided test is $H_0\colon \pi = 0.50$, where π is the population proportion of the plus (or the minus) signs. Thus, a hypothesis concerning the value of the median in fact is tested as a hypothesis concerning π. If the sample is large, the normal distribution can be used, as described in Section 11.4.

See Problem 17.2 for the use of the sign test to test a null hypothesis concerning the population median.

17.5   ONE SAMPLE: THE WILCOXON TEST

Just as is the case for the sign test, the *Wilcoxon test* can be used to test a null hypothesis concerning the value of the population median. Because the Wilcoxon test considers the magnitude of the difference between each sample value and the hypothesized value of the median, it is a more sensitive test than the sign test. On the other hand, because differences are determined, the values must be at least at the interval scale. No assumptions are required about the form of the population distribution.

The null and alternative hypotheses are formulated with respect to the population median as either a one-sided or two-sided test. The difference between each observed value and the hypothesized value of the median is determined, and this difference, with arithmetic sign, is designated $d\colon d = (X - \text{Med}_0)$. If any difference is equal to zero, the associated observation is dropped from the analysis and the effective sample size is thereby reduced. The absolute values of the differences are then ranked from lowest to highest, with the rank of 1 assigned to the smallest absolute difference. When absolute differences are equal, the mean rank is assigned to the tied values. Finally, the sum of the ranks is obtained separately for the positive and negative differences. The smaller of these two sums is the Wilcoxon T statistic for a two-sided test. In the case of a one-sided test, the smaller sum must be associated with the directionality of the null hypothesis. Appendix 10 identifies the critical values of T according to sample size and level of significance. For rejection of the null hypothesis, the obtained value of T must be *smaller* than the critical value given in the table.

When $n \geq 25$ and the null hypothesis is true, the T statistic is approximately normally distributed. The mean and standard error associated with this sampling distribution are, respectively,

$$\mu_T = \frac{n(n+1)}{4} \tag{17.4}$$

$$\sigma_T = \sqrt{\frac{n(n+1)(2n+1)}{24}} \tag{17.5}$$

Therefore, for a relatively large sample the test can be carried out by using the normal probability distribution and computing the z test statistic as follows:

$$z = \frac{T - \mu_T}{\sigma_T} \tag{17.6}$$

See Problem 17.3 for an application of the Wilcoxon test to test a null hypothesis concerning the population median.

17.6   TWO INDEPENDENT SAMPLES: THE MANN–WHITNEY TEST

The *Mann–Whitney test* can be used to test the null hypothesis that the medians of two populations are equal. It is assumed that the two populations have the same form and dispersion, because such differences also would lead to rejection of the null hypothesis. It is required that the values in the two independent random samples be at least at the ordinal scale.

Two samples are combined into one ordered array, with each sample value identified according to the original sample group. The values are then ranked from lowest to highest, with the rank of 1 assigned to the lowest observed sample value. For equal values the mean rank is assigned to the tied, or equal, values. If the null hypothesis is true, the average of the ranks for each sample group should be approximately equal. The statistic calculated to carry out this test is designated U, and it can be based on the sum of the ranks in either of the two random samples, as follows:

$$U_1 = n_1 n_2 + \frac{n_1(n_1+1)}{2} - R_1 \tag{17.7}$$

or

$$U_2 + n_1 n_2 + \frac{n_2(n_2+1)}{2} - R_2 \tag{17.8}$$

where n_1 = size of the first sample

n_2 = size of the second sample

R_1 = sum of the ranks in the first sample

R_2 = sum of the ranks in the second sample

Given that $n_1 > 10, n_2 > 10$, and the null hypothesis is true, the sampling distribution of U is approximately normal, with the following parameters:

$$\mu_U = \frac{n_1 n_2}{2} \tag{17.9}$$

$$\sigma_U = \sqrt{\frac{n_1 n_2 (n_1 + n_2 + 1)}{12}} \tag{17.10}$$

Therefore, the test statistic for testing the null hypothesis that the medians of two populations are equal is

$$z = \frac{U - \mu_U}{\sigma_U} \tag{17.11}$$

where U equals U_1 or U_2.

For data situations in which $n_1 < 10$, $n_2 < 10$, or both n_1 and $n_2 < 10$, the normal probability distribution cannot be used for this test. However, special tables for the U statistic are available for such small samples in specialized textbooks on nonparametric statistics.

Problem 17.4 illustrates the use of the Mann–Whitney test.

17.7   PAIRED OBSERVATIONS: THE SIGN TEST

For two samples collected as *paired observations* (see Section 11.3), the *sign test* described in Section 17.4 can be used to test the null hypothesis that the two population medians are equal. The sample values must be at least at the ordinal scale, and no assumptions are required about the forms of the two population distributions.

A plus sign is assigned for each pair of values for which the measurement in the first sample is greater than the measurement in the second sample, and a minus sign is assigned when the opposite condition is true. If a pair of measurements have the same value, these tied values are dropped from the analysis, with the effective sample size thereby being reduced. If the hypothesis that the two populations are at the same level of magnitude is true, the number of plus signs should approximately equal the number of minus signs. Therefore, the null hypothesis tested is H_0: $\pi = 0.50$, where π is the population proportion of the plus (or the minus) signs. If the sample is large ($n > 30$), the normal distribution can be used, as described in Section 11.5. Note that although two samples have been collected, the test is applied to the one set of plus and minus signs that results from the comparison of the pairs of measurements.

Problem 17.5 illustrates use of the sign test for testing the difference between two medians for data that have been collected as paired observations.

17.8   PAIRED OBSERVATIONS: THE WILCOXON TEST

For two samples collected as paired observations, the *Wilcoxon test* described in Section 17.5 can be used to test the null hypothesis that the two population medians are equal. Because the Wilcoxon test considers the magnitude of the difference between the values in each matched pair, and not just the direction or sign of the difference, it is a more sensitive test than the sign test. However, the sample values must be at the interval scale. No assumptions are required about the forms of the two distributions.

The difference between each pair of values is determined, and this difference, with the associated arithmetic sign, is designated by d. If any difference is equal to zero, this pair of observations is dropped from the analysis, thus reducing the effective sample size. Then the absolute values of the differences are ranked from lowest to highest, with the rank of 1 assigned to the smallest absolute difference. When absolute differences are equal, the mean rank is assigned to the tied values. Finally, the sum of the ranks is obtained separately for the positive and negative differences. The smaller of these two sums is the Wilcoxon T statistic for a two-sided test. For a one-sided test the smaller sum must be associated with the directionality of the null hypothesis, as illustrated in the one-sample application of the Wilcoxon test in Problem 17.3. Appendix 10 identifies the critical value of T according to sample size and level of significance. For rejection of the null hypothesis, the T statistic must be *smaller* than the critical value given in the table.

When $n \geq 25$ and the null hypothesis is true, the T statistic is approximately normally distributed. The formulas for the mean and standard error of the sampling distribution of T and the formula for the z test statistic are given in Section 17.5, on the one-sample application of the Wilcoxon test.

Problem 17.6 illustrates the use of the Wilcoxon test for testing the difference between two medians data that have been collected as paired observations.

17.9   SEVERAL INDEPENDENT SAMPLES: THE KRUSKAL–WALLIS TEST

The *Kruskal–Wallis test* is used to test the null hypothesis that several populations have the same medians. As such, it is the nonparametric equivalent of the one-factor completely randomized design of the analysis of variance. It is assumed that the several populations have the same form and dispersion for the above hypothesis to be applicable, because differences in form or dispersion would also lead to rejection of the null hypothesis. The values for the several independent random samples are required to be at least at the ordinal scale.

The several samples are first viewed as one array of values, and each value in this combined group is ranked from lowest to highest. For equal values the mean rank is assigned to the tied values. If the null hypothesis is true, the average of the ranks for each sample group should be about equal. The test statistic calculated is designated H and is based on the sum of the ranks in each of the several random samples, as follows:

$$H = \left\{ \left[\frac{12}{N(N+1)} \right] \left[\sum \frac{R_j^2}{n_j} \right] \right\} - 3(N+1) \qquad (17.12)$$

where N = combined sample size of the several samples

(note that N does not designate population size in this case)

R_j = sum of the ranks for the jth sample or treatment group

n_j = number of observations in the jth sample

Given that the size of each sample group is at least $n_j \geq 5$ and the null hypothesis is true, the sampling distribution of H is approximately distributed as the χ^2 distribution with $df = K - 1$, where K is the number of treatment or sample groups. The χ^2 value that approximates the critical value of the test statistic is always the upper-tail value. This test procedure is analogous to the upper tail of the F distribution being used in the analysis of variance.

For tied ranks the test statistic H should be corrected. The corrected value of the test statistic is designated H_c and is computed as follows:

$$H_c = \frac{H}{1 - [\sum (t_j^3 - t_j)/(N^3 - N)]} \qquad (17.13)$$

where t_j represents the number of tied scores in the jth sample.

The effect of this correction is to increase the value of the calculated H statistic. Therefore, if the uncorrected value of H leads to the rejection of the null hypothesis, there is no need to correct this value for the effect of tied ranks.

Problem 17.7 illustrates use of the Kruskal–Wallis test for testing the null hypothesis that several populations have the same median.

17.10   USING MINITAB

Whereas Excel has no direct method for nonparametric procedures, Minitab includes a variety of such techniques. Solved Problems 17.8 through 17.10 illustrate the use of Minitab for the one-sample Wilcoxon test, the two-sample Mann–Whitney test for independence, and the Kruskal–Wallis test for several independent samples.

Solved Problems

THE RUNS TEST FOR RANDOMNESS

17.1. A sample of 36 individuals were interviewed in a market-research survey, with 22 women (W) and 14 men (M) included in the sample. The sampled individuals were obtained in the following order: M̲, W̲, W, W, W, M̲, M, M, W̲, M̲, W̲, W, W, M̲, M, W̲, W, W, W, M̲, W̲, W, W, M̲, M, W̲, W, W, M̲, W̲, M̲, M, W̲, W, W, M̲. Use the runs test to test the randomness of this set of observations, using the 5 percent level of significance.

The number of runs in this sample is $R = 17$, as indicated by the underscores above. Where $n_1 =$ the number of women and $n_2 =$ the number of men, we can use the normal distribution to test the null hypothesis that the sampling process was random, because $n_1 > 20$. We compute the mean and the standard error of the sampling distribution of R as follows:

$$\mu_R = \frac{2n_1 n_2}{n_1 + n_2} + 1 = \frac{2(22)(14)}{22 + 14} + 1 = \frac{616}{36} + 1 = 18.1$$

$$\sigma_R = \sqrt{\frac{2n_1 n_2 (2n_1 n_2 - n_1 - n_2)}{(n_1 + n_2)^2 (n_1 + n_2 - 1)}} = \sqrt{\frac{2(22)(14)[2(22)(14) - 22 - 14]}{(22 + 14)^2 (22 + 14 - 1)}}$$

$$= \sqrt{\frac{616(616 - 36)}{36^2(35)}} = \sqrt{\frac{357,280}{45,360}} = \sqrt{7.8765} = 2.81$$

When the 5 percent level of significance is used, the critical values of the z statistic are $z = \pm 1.96$. The value of the z test statistic for these data is

$$z = \frac{R - \mu_R}{\sigma_R} = \frac{17 - 18.1}{2.81} = \frac{-1.1}{2.81} = -0.39$$

Therefore, using the 5 percent level of significance, we cannot reject the null hypothesis that the sequence of women and men occurred randomly.

ONE SAMPLE: THE SIGN TEST

17.2. It is claimed that the units assembled with a redesigned product assembly system will be greater than with the old system, for which the population median is 80 units per workshift. *Not* giving the benefit of the doubt to the redesigned system, formulate the null hypothesis and test it at the 5 percent level of significance. The sample data are reported in the first part of Table 17.1.

The null and alternative hypotheses are

$$H_0: \text{Med} = 80$$
$$H_1: \text{Med} > 80$$

Because no assumption is made about the form of the population distribution, a nonparametric test is appropriate. Using the sign test, the null and alternative hypotheses in terms of the proportion of plus signs of the differences, where $d = (X - 80)$, are

$$H_0: \pi = 0.50$$
$$H_1: \pi > 0.50$$

Table 17.1   Number of Units Assembled with the Redesigned Sampled

Sampled workshift	Units assembled (X)	Sign of difference ($X - 80$)
1	75	−
2	85	+
3	92	+
4	80	0
5	94	+
6	90	+
7	91	+
8	76	−
9	88	+
10	82	+
11	96	+
12	83	+

Referring to Table 17.1, we see that for the fourth sampled workshift the number of units assembled happened to be exactly equal to the hypothesized value of the population median. Therefore, this observation is omitted from the following analysis, resulting in an effective sample size of $n = 11$. Of the 11 signs of the differences reported in Table 17.1, 9 are plus signs. The test is to be carried out using the 5 percent level of significance.

Because the sample size is $n < 30$, the binomial distribution is the appropriate basis for this test. Using the P-value approach to hypothesis testing, as described in Section 10.7, we determine the probability of observing 9 or more plus signs in 11 observations, given that the population of plus signs is 0.50, by reference to Appendix 2 for binomial probabilities:

$$P(X \geq 9 \mid n = 11, \pi = 0.50) = 0.0269 + 0.0054 + 0.0005 = 0.0328$$

Since the P value associated with the sample result is less than 0.05, the null hypothesis is rejected at the 5 percent level of significance for this one-sided test. That is, the probability of observing such a large number (or more) of plus signs when the null hypothesis is true is less than 0.05; specifically, the probability is 0.0328. Therefore, we accept the alternative hypothesis and conclude that the median output per workshift for the new assembly system is greater than 80 units.

A two-sided sign test is illustrated in Problem 17.5, where the sign test is used in conjunction with paired observations.

ONE SAMPLE: THE WILCOXON TEST

17.3. Use the Wilcoxon test with respect to the null hypothesis and the data in Problem 17.2, above, and compare your solution to the one obtained in Problem 17.2.

$$H_0: \text{Med} = 80$$
$$H_1: \text{Med} > 80$$

The sample data are repeated in Table 17.2, which is the worktable for the Wilcoxon test. In this table note that for the fourth sampled workshift the number of units assembled happened to be exactly equal to the hypothesized value of the population median. Therefore, this observation was dropped from the analysis, resulting in an effective sample size of $n = 11$. Also note that the absolute value of d for the first and second sampled workshifts is the same, and therefore the mean rank of 4.5 was assigned to each of these sampled workshifts (in lieu of ranks 4 and 5). The next rank assigned is then rank 6.

Table 17.2 Number of Units Assembled with the Redesigned System and the Determination of Signed Ranks

Sampled workshift	Units assembled (X)	Difference $[d = (X - 80)]$	Rank of $\|d\|$	Signed rank	
				(+)	(−)
1	75	−5	4.5		4.5
2	85	5	4.5	4.5	
3	92	12	9	9	
4	80	0			
5	94	14	10	10	
6	90	10	7	7	
7	91	11	8	8	
8	76	−4	3		3
9	88	8	6	6	
10	82	2	1	1	
11	96	16	11	11	
12	83	3	2	2	
Total				58.5	$T = 7.5$

In order to reject the null hypothesis H_0: Med $= 80$ for this upper-tail test, it follows that the differences $d = (X - \text{Med}_0)$ must be predominantly positive, for negative differences would represent positive support for the null hypothesis. Therefore, for this upper-tail test the sum of the ranks for the negative differences must be the smaller sum. Referring to Table 17.2, we see that such is in fact the case, and the value of the Wilcoxon test statistic is $T = 7.5$.

The null hypothesis is to be tested at the 5 percent level of significance. Appendix 10 indicates that for $n = 11$ (the effective sample size) the critical value of T for a one-tail test at the 5 percent level of significance is $T = 14$. Because the obtained, value of T is smaller than the critical value, the null hypothesis is rejected at the 5 percent level of significance, and we conclude that the median units assembled with the new system is greater than 80 units. This is the same conclusion as with the use of the sign test in the preceding section, in which the P value for the test was $P = 0.0328$. However, reference to Appendix 10 for the Wilcoxon test indicates that for $n = 11$ and $\alpha = 0.025$ the critical value is $T = 11$. Therefore, the null hypothesis could be rejected at the 2.5 percent level of significance with the Wilcoxon test, but not with the sign test. This observation is consistent with our earlier observations that the Wilcoxon test is the more sensitive of the two tests.

TWO INDEPENDENT SAMPLES: THE MANN–WHITNEY TEST

17.4. To evaluate and compare two methods of instruction for industrial apprentices, a training director assigns 15 randomly selected trainees to each of the two methods. Because of normal attrition, 14 apprentices complete the course taught by method 1 and 12 apprentices complete the course taught by method 2. The same achievement test is then given to both trainee groups, as reported in Table 17.3. Test the null hypothesis that the median level of test performance does not differ for the two methods of instruction, using the 5 percent level of significance.

$$H_0: \text{Med}_1 = \text{Med}_2 \qquad H_1: \text{Med}_1 \neq \text{Med}_2$$

Table 17.3   Achievement Test Scores of Apprentice Trainees Taught by Two Methods of Instruction

Method 1	Method 2
70	86
90	78
82	90
64	82
86	65
77	87
84	80
79	88
82	95
89	85
73	76
81	94
83	
66	

Table 17.4 lists the achievement test scores in one array, ranked from lowest to highest score. The ranks are presented in the second column of Table 17.4. Notice the way the rankings are assigned to the tied scores: For the three test scores of 82, for example, the scores are at the rank positions 12, 13, and 14 in the second column of the table. Therefore, the mean of these three ranks, 13, is assigned to these three test scores. Then note that the next rank assigned is 15, and 14, because the assignment of the mean rank of 13 to the three scores of 82 has brought the score of 83 to the 15th position in the array. Similarly, there are two scores of 86; the ranks for these two positions are 18 and 19, and therefore the mean rank of 18.5 is assigned to each of these scores. The next score in the array, 87, is assigned the rank 20. The last two columns in Table 17.4 list the ranks according to the sample, which represents the teaching method used, and the sums of these two columns of ranks are the two values R_1 and R_2, respectively.

Applying Formula (17.7), we determine the value of U_1 as follows:

$$U_1 = n_1 n_2 + \frac{n_1(n_1 + 1)}{2} - R_1 = 14(12) + \frac{14(14 + 1)}{2} - 161$$

$$= 168 + \frac{210}{2} - 161 = 112$$

Because $n_1 > 10$ and $n_2 > 10$, the normal probability distribution can be used to test the null hypothesis that the value of μ_U is the same for both samples. The test is to be carried out at the 5 percent level of significance. Based on Formula (17.9), the value of μ_U is

$$\mu_U = \frac{n_1 n_2}{2} = \frac{14(12)}{2} = 84$$

Thus the hypotheses are

$$H_0: \mu_U = 84$$
$$H_1: \mu_U \neq 84$$

Table 17.4   Combined Array of the Achievement Test Scores with Associated Ranks

Score*	Rank	Method 1 ranks	Method 2 ranks
<u>64</u>	1	1	
65	2		2
<u>66</u>	3	3	
<u>70</u>	4	4	
<u>73</u>	5	5	
76	6		6
<u>77</u>	7	7	
78	8		8
<u>79</u>	9	9	
80	10		10
<u>81</u>	11	11	
<u>82</u>	13	13	
<u>82</u>	13	13	
82	13		13
<u>83</u>	15	15	
<u>84</u>	16	16	
85	17		17
<u>86</u>	18.5	18.5	
86	18.5		18.5
87	20		20
88	21		21
<u>89</u>	22	22	
<u>90</u>	23.5	23.5	
90	23.5		23.5
94	25		25
95	26		26
Totals		$R_1 = \overline{161.0}$	$R_2 = \overline{190.0}$

*Scores for method 1 are underscored.

Based on Formula (*17.10*), the standard error of U is

$$\sigma_U = \sqrt{\frac{n_1 n_2(n_1 + n_2 + 1)}{12}} = \sqrt{\frac{14(12)(14 + 12 + 1)}{12}} = \sqrt{\frac{4{,}536}{12}} = 19.4$$

Applying Formula (*17.11*), we determine the value of the z test statistic as follows:

$$z = \frac{U_1 - \mu_U}{\sigma_U} = \frac{112 - 84}{19.4} = 1.44$$

Because the critical values of z for a test at the 5 percent level of significance are $z = \pm 1.96$, the null hypothesis that there is no difference between the medians of the two distributions of achievement test scores cannot be rejected.

PAIRED OBSERVATIONS: THE SIGN TEST

17.5.   A consumer panel that includes 14 individuals is asked to rate two brands of cola according to a point evaluation system based on several criteria. Table 17.5 reports the points assigned and also indicates the sign of the difference for each pair of ratings. Test the null hypothesis that there is no difference in the level of ratings for the two brands of cola at the 5 percent level of significance by use of the sign test, formulating the null and alternative hypotheses in terms of the proportion of plus signs.

Table 17.5   Ratings Assigned to Two Brands of Cola by a Consumer Panel

Panel member	Point rating assigned to each brand		Sign of difference
	Brand 1	Brand 2	
1	20	16	+
2	24	26	−
3	28	18	+
4	24	17	+
5	20	20	0
6	29	21	+
7	19	23	−
8	27	22	+
9	20	23	−
10	30	20	+
11	18	18	0
12	28	21	+
13	26	17	+
14	24	26	−

$$H_0: \pi = 0.50$$
$$H_1: \pi \neq 0.50$$

Referring to Table 17.5, we see that two of the consumers rated the two brands of cola as equal, and therefore these two panel members are omitted from the following analysis, resulting in an effective sample size of $n = 12$. Of the 12 signs, 8 are plus signs.

Because the number of pairs of values is $n < 30$, the binomial distribution is the appropriate basis for this test. As in Problem 17.2, on the one-sample sign test, we use the P-value approach to hypothesis testing. The probability of observing 8 or more plus signs in 12 observations given that the population proportion of plus signs is 0.50 is determined by reference to Appendix 2 for binomial probabilities:

$$P(X \geq 8 \mid n = 12,\ \pi = 0.50) = 0.1208 + 0.0537 + 0.0161 + 0.0029 + 0.0002$$
$$= 0.1937$$

The probability calculated above is for the one-tail $P(X \geq 8)$. Because a two-sided test is involved in the present application, *this probability must be doubled* to obtain the P value: $P = 2 \times 0.1937 = 0.3874$. That is, the probability is 0.3874 that the observed deviation in *either* direction from the expected number of plus signs of $n\pi_0 = 12(0.50) = 6$. This P value is well above the 0.05 probability level, and therefore the null hypothesis that the two brands of cola have equal consumer preference clearly cannot be rejected.

PAIRED OBSERVATIONS: THE WILCOXON TEST

17.6. Apply the Wilcoxon test to the data in Problem 17.5, above, using the 5 percent level of significance.

We repeat the ratings in Table 17.6, determine the values of d, rank the absolute values of d, and finally, we determine the sum of the plus and minus rankings.

Referring to Table 17.6, note that the two panel members who rated the two brands of cola equally are dropped from the analysis, because the difference $d = 0$ is not assigned a rank. Therefore, the effective sample size is

$n = 12$. Of the 12 absolute values of d, several tied pairs result in the assignment of the mean ranks. For instance, there are two absolute differences tied for the positions of rank 1 and rank 2; therefore, each of these absolute differences is assigned the mean rank 1.5. The next rank assigned is then rank 3. Because the sum of the ranks for the negative differences is smaller than the sum for the positive differences, this smaller sum is labelled T in Table 17.6.

Table 17.6 Ratings Assigned to Two Brands of Cola by a Consumer Panel and the Determination of Signed Ranks

Panel member	Brand 1 (X_1)	Brand 2 (X_2)	Difference ($d = X_1 - X_2$)	Rank of $|d|$	Signed rank (+)	Signed rank (−)
1	20	16	4	4.5	4.5	
2	24	26	−2	1.5		1.5
3	28	18	10	11.5	11.5	
4	24	17	7	7.5	7.5	
5	20	20	0			
6	29	21	8	9	9	
7	19	23	−4	4.5		4.5
8	27	22	5	6	6	
9	20	23	−3	3		3
10	30	20	10	11.5	11.5	
11	18	18	0			
12	28	21	7	7.5	7.5	
13	26	17	9	10	10	
14	24	26	−2	1.5		1.5
Total					67.5	$T = 10.5$

Appendix 10 indicates that for $n = 12$ (the effective sample size) the critical value of the Wilcoxon T statistic for a two-sided test at the 5 percent level of significance is $T = 14$. Since T is the smaller sum of the signed ranks for a two-sided test, the obtained value of the test statistic as calculated in Table 17.6 is $T = 10.5$. Because this value is less than the critical value, the null hypothesis that there is no difference in the ratings for the two brands of cola is rejected.

Note that the null hypothesis of no difference could not be rejected at the 5 percent level when the sign test was applied to these same data in Problem 17.5. Because the Wilcoxon test considers the magnitude of the difference between each matched pair and not just the sign of the difference, the Wilcoxon test for paired observations is a more sensitive test than the sign test.

SEVERAL INDEPENDENT SAMPLES: THE KRUSKAL–WALLIS TEST

17.7. In Problem 13.1 on the one-factor completely randomized design of the analysis of variance, we presented achievement test scores for a random sample of $n = 5$ trainees randomly assigned to each of three instructional methods. In those sections the null hypothesis was that the mean levels of achievement for the three different levels of instruction did not differ, and because of the small samples it was necessary to assume that the three populations were normally distributed. Suppose we cannot make this assumption. Apply the Kruskal–Wallis test to test the null hypothesis that the several populations have the same median, using the 5 percent level of significance.

Table 17.7 repeats the data from Table 13.4 and also includes the ranks from lowest to highest when the achievement scores are viewed as one combined group. With reference to the table, we compute the value of the test statistic as follows:

$$H = \left\{ \left[\frac{12}{N(N+1)} \right] \left[\sum \frac{R_j^2}{n_j} \right] \right\} - 3(N+1)$$

$$= \left\{ \left[\frac{12}{15(15+1)} \right] \left[\frac{(38.5)^2}{5} + \frac{(56.5)^2}{5} + \frac{(25.0)^2}{5} \right] \right\} - 3(15+1)$$

$$= \frac{12}{240} \left(\frac{5{,}299.5}{5} \right) - 48 = \frac{63{,}594}{1{,}200} - 48 = 52.995 - 48 = 4.995$$

Table 17.7 Achievement Test Scores of Trainees under Three Methods of Instruction

Method A_1		Method A_2		Method A_3	
Score	Rank	Score	Rank	Score	Rank
86	12	90	15	82	9.5
79	6	76	5	68	1
81	7.5	88	13	73	4
70	2	82	9.5	71	3
84	11	89	14	81	7.5
Total	$R_1 = \overline{38.5}$		$R_2 = \overline{56.5}$		$R_3 = \overline{25.0}$

Because there were some ties in the achievement test scores, it is appropriate to correct the value of the test statistic:

$$H_c = \frac{H}{1 - [\sum (t_j^3 - t_j)/(N^3 - N)]}$$

$$= \frac{4.995}{1 - \{[(1^3 - 1) + (1^3 - 1) + (2^3 - 2)]/(15^3 - 15)\}}$$

$$= \frac{4.995}{1 - [(0 + 0 + 6)/(3{,}375 - 15)]} = \frac{4.995}{1 - (6/3{,}360)}$$

$$= \frac{4.995}{1 - 0.00179} = \frac{4.995}{0.99821} = 5.004$$

Thus, the corrected value $H_c = 5.004$ is only slightly larger than the uncorrected value of $H = 4.995$, and the ties have a negligible effect on the value of the test statistic. With $df = K - 1 = 3 - 1 = 2$, Appendix 7 indicates that the critical value of the test statistic is $\chi^2 = 5.99$. Because the observed value of the test statistic is less than this critical value, the null hypothesis that the three sample groups were obtained from populations that have the same median cannot be rejected at the 5 percent level of significance. This conclusion is consistent with the conclusion in Problems 13.1 and 13.2 in which the analysis of variance was applied to these data.

COMPUTER OUTPUT

17.8. Use Minitab to apply the one-sample Wilcoxon test to the situation described in Problem 17.3. Compare the output to the result of the manual procedure in Problem 17.3.

Fig. 17-1 gives the Minitab output for the application of the test. As compared with the manual solution in Problem 17.3, the program focuses on the sum of the ranks for the positive differences instead of the negative differences. The reported P value for the upper-tail test is given as $P = 0.013$. Therefore, the null hypothesis that the population median is equal to 80 is rejected at the 5 percent level, in favor of the alternative, that Med > 80. This conclusion corresponds to the result in Problem 17.3.

The Minitab output given in Fig. 17-1 was obtained as follows:

(1) Open Minitab. In the column name cell for C1 enter: Units Assembled. Enter the data for units assembled in column C1.
(2) Click **Stat** $\rightarrow$ **Nonparametrics** $\rightarrow$ **1-Sample Wilcoxon**.
(3) In the dialog box, for **Variables** enter: C1. For **Test median** enter: 80.0. For **Alternatives** choose **greater than**. Click **OK**.

Wilcoxon Signed Rank Test: Units Assembled

```
Test of median = 80.00 versus median  >  80.00

                   N for   Wilcoxon            Estimated
            N     Test    Statistic       P     Median
Units As   12      11        58.5     0.013     86.00
```

Fig. 17-1 Minitab output for Problem 17.8.

17.9. Use Minitab to apply the Mann–Whitney test for independent samples as presented in Problem 17.4. Compare the output to the result of the manual calculation in Problem 17.4

Whereas the standard-normal z distribution is used as an approximation method in the manual calculation, the computer output in Fig. 17-2 gives the exact result, including the determination of the P value for the null hypothesis that there is no difference between the two population medians. Because $P = 0.1572$, the null hypothesis *cannot* be rejected at the 5 percent level of significance. This conclusion corresponds to the result in Problem 17.4.

The Minitab output given in Fig. 17-2 Was obtained as follows:

(1) Open Minitab. In the column name cell for C1 enter: Method 1. In the column name cell for C2 enter: Method 2. Enter the data in the appropriate columns.
(2) Click **Stat** $\rightarrow$ **Nonparametrics** $\rightarrow$ **Mann–Whitney**.
(3) In the dialog box, for **First Sample** enter: C1. For **Second Sample** enter: C2. For **Alternative** choose **not equal**. Click **OK**.

Mann-Whitney Test and CI: Method 1, Method 2

```
Method 1   N =  14      Median =        81.50
Method 2   N =  12      Median =        85.50
Point estimate for ETA1-ETA2 is         -5.00
95.2 Percent CI for ETA1-ETA2 is (-12.00,2.00)
W = 161.0
Test of ETA1 = ETA2  vs  ETA1 not = ETA2 is significant at 0.1572
The test is significant at 0.1568 (adjusted for ties)

Cannot reject at alpha = 0.05
```

Fig. 17-2 Minitab output for Problem 17.9.

17.10. Use Minitab to apply the Kruskal–Wallis test to the situation described in Problem 17.7. Compare the computer output to the result of the manual calculation in that problem.

Figure 17-3 is the Minitab output with respect to the null hypothesis that the three population medians are not different against the alternative that there is a difference. In Problem 17.7 we could not reject the null hypothesis based on use of the critical value approach to hypothesis testing. The output in Fig. 17-3 gives the same values for H and H_c as calculated in Problem 17.7 and also provides the P value for the test, which is $P = 0.082$. Since $P > 0.05$, the null hypothesis cannot be rejected at the 5 percent level of significance.

The Minitab output in Fig. 17-3 was obtained as follows:

1. Open Minitab. In the column name cell for C1 enter: Method. In the column name cell for C2 enter: Score. Since there are 5 scores for each method, in C1 enter five 1s, five 2s, and five 3s, which are the method labels. In C2 enter the 15 test scores, each associated (in groups of 5) with one of the three methods of instruction in C1.
2. Click **Stat** → **Nonparametrics** → **Kruskal–Wallis**.
3. In the dialog box, for **Response** enter: C2. For **Factor** enter: C1. Click **OK**.

Kruskal-Wallis Test: Score versus Method

```
Kruskal-Wallis Test on Score

Method      N      Median    Ave Rank          Z
1           5       81.00         7.7      -0.18
2           5       88.00        11.3       2.02
3           5       73.00         5.0      -1.84
Overall    15                     8.0

H = 5.00   DF = 2   P = 0.082
H = 5.01   DF = 2   P = 0.082  (adjusted for ties)
```

Fig. 17-3   Minitab output for Problem 17.10.

Supplementary Problems

THE RUNS TEST FOR RANDOMNESS

17.11. Refer to Table 2.19 on page 41 in which 40 randomly sampled personal loan amounts are reported. The sequence of data collection was according to row in the table (that is, the sequence of observed amounts was \$932, \$1,000, \$356, etc.). The median loan amount for the data in the table is \$944.50. Test the randomness of this sequence of loan amounts by classifying each amount as being above or below the median, using the 5 percent level of significance.

Ans.   Critical $z = \pm 1.96$, $R = 28$, and $z = 2.56$. The null hypothesis that the sequence is random is rejected. There is an unusually large number of runs.

ONE SAMPLE: THE SIGN TEST

17.12. The following table reports the unit sales of a new tool in a sample of 12 outlets in a given month. The form of the distribution is unknown, and thus a parametric statistical test is not appropriate given the small sample size. Use the sign test with respect to the null hypothesis that the median sales amount in the population is no greater than 10.0 units per outlet, using the 5 percent level of significance.

Tools/outlet	8	18	9	12	10	14	16	7	14	11	10	20

Ans. $P = 0.1719$; the null hypothesis cannot be rejected.

ONE SAMPLE: THE WILCOXON TEST

17.13. Apply the Wilcoxon test with respect to the null hypothesis and the data in Problem 17.9, using the 5 percent level of significance.
Ans. Critical $T = 11$, $T = 10$; the null hypothesis is rejected.

TWO INDEPENDENT SAMPLES: THE MANN–WHITNEY TEST

17.14. A process control department wishes to compare the time required for two alternative systems to diagnose equipment failure. A sample of 30 equipment failures are randomly assigned for diagnosis to the two systems with 14 failures assigned for diagnosis to the first system and 16 assigned for diagnosis to the second system. Table 17.8 reports total time, in minutes, required to diagnose each failure. No assumption can be made concerning the distribution of the total time required to diagnose such failures. Using the 10 percent level of significance, test the null hypothesis that the two samples have been obtained from populations that have the same median.
Ans. $R_1 = 173.5$, $R_2 = 291.5$, critical $z = \pm 1.645$, $z = 1.87$; the null hypothesis is rejected at $\alpha = 0.10$.

Table 17.8 Time Required to Diagnose Equipment Failures (in Minutes)

System 1	System 2
25	18
29	37
42	40
16	56
31	49
14	28
33	20
45	34
26	39
34	47
30	31
43	65
28	38
19	32
	24
	49

PAIRED OBSERVATIONS: THE SIGN TEST

17.15. Instead of the experimental design used in Problem 17.14, the same random sample of 10 equipment failures is diagnosed by the two systems. Thus, each of the 10 pieces of equipment is subjected to diagnosis twice, and the time required in minutes to diagnose the failure by each system is noted. Table 17.9 indicates the number of minutes required for each diagnosis. Using the 10 percent level of significance, test the null hypothesis that the two samples came from populations that are not different in level. That is, the null hypothesis is that there is no difference in the median amount of time required to diagnose equipment failure by the two methods. Use the sign test for this analysis.
Ans. $P = 0.3438$; the null hypothesis cannot be rejected.

Table 17.9   Time in Minutes Required to Diagnose Equipment Failures by the Period Observations Design

Sampled equipment	System 1	System 2
1	23	21
2	40	48
3	35	45
4	24	22
5	17	19
6	32	37
7	27	29
8	32	38
9	25	24
10	30	36

PAIRED OBSERVATIONS: THE WILCOXON TEST

17.16. At the 10 percent level of significance apply the Wilcoxon test for matched pairs to the data in Table 17.9, again testing the null hypothesis that there is no difference in the median amount of time required by the two methods. Compare your results with those obtained in Problem 17.15.

Ans.   Critical $T = 11$, $T = 8.0$; the null hypothesis is rejected at $\alpha = 0.10$.

SEVERAL INDEPENDENT SAMPLES: THE KRUSKAL–WALLIS TEST

17.17. In addition to the data reported in Table 17.8, suppose that a third system for diagnosing equipment failure is also evaluated by randomly assigning 12 failures to this system and observing the time required in minutes to diagnose each failure. The required time periods are 21, 36, 34, 19, 46, 25, 38, 31, 20, 26, 30, and 18. Using the 10 percent level of significance, test the null hypothesis that the three samples were obtained from populations with the same median.

Ans. $R_1 = 260.5$, $R_2 = 431.0$, $R_3 = 211.5$, critical $\chi^2 = 4.61$, $H = 5.12$; the null hypothesis is rejected at $\alpha = 0.10$.

CHAPTER 18

Decision Analysis: Payoff Tables and Decision Trees

18.1 THE STRUCTURE OF PAYOFF TABLES

From the standpoint of statistical decision theory, a decision situation under conditions of uncertainty can be represented by certain common ingredients that are included in the structure of the *payoff table* for the situation. Essentially, a payoff table identifies the conditional gain (or loss) associated with every possible combination of decision acts and events; it also typically indicates the probability of occurrence for each of the mutually exclusive events.

Table 18.1   General Structure of a Payoff Table

Events	Probability	Acts				
		A_1	A_2	A_3	$\ldots$	A_n
E_1	P_1	X_{11}	X_{12}	X_{13}	$\ldots$	X_{1n}
E_2	P_2	X_{21}	X_{22}	X_{23}	$\ldots$	X_{2n}
E_3	P_3	X_{31}	X_{32}	X_{33}	$\ldots$	X_{3n}
$\ldots$	$\ldots$	$\ldots$	$\ldots$	$\ldots$	$\ldots$	$\ldots$
E_m	P_m	X_{m1}	X_{m2}	X_{m3}	$\ldots$	X_{mn}

In Table 18.1, the *acts* are the alternative courses of action, or strategies, that are available to the decision maker. As the result of the analysis, one of these acts is chosen as being the best act. The basis for this choice is the subject matter of this chapter. As a minimum, there must be at least two possible acts available, so that the opportunity for choice in fact exists. An example of an act is the number of units of a particular item to be ordered for stock.

336

The *events* identify the occurrences that are outside of the decision maker's control and that determine the level of success for a given act. These events are often called "states of nature," "states," or "outcomes." We are concerned only with discrete events in this chapter. An example of an event is the level of marked demand for a particular item during a stipulated time period.

The *probability* of each event is included as part of the general format of a decision table when such probability values are in fact available. However, one characteristic of decision analysis is that such probabilities should always be available since they can be based on either objective data or be determined subjectively on the basis of judgment. Because the events in the payoff table are mutually exclusive and exhaustive, the sum of the probability values should be 1.0.

Finally, the cell entries are the conditional values, or conditional economic consequences. These values are usually called *payoffs* in the literature, and they are conditional in the sense that the economic result which is experienced depends on the decision act that is chosen and the event that occurs.

EXAMPLE 1.   A heating and air-conditioning contractor must commit to the purchase of central air-conditioning units as of April 1 for resale and installation during the following summer season. Based on demand during the previous summer, current economic conditions, and competitive factors in the market, the contractor estimates that there is a 0.10 probability of selling only 5 units, a 0.30 probability of selling 10 units, a 0.40 probability of selling 15 units, and a 0.20 probability of selling 20 units. The air-conditioning units can be ordered only in groups of five, with the cost per unit being $1,000 and the retail price being $1,300 (plus installation charges). Any unsold units at the end of the season are returned to the manufacturer for a net credit of $800, after deduction of shipping charges.

Table 18.2 is the payoff table for this situation. Note that because we estimate there will be a market demand for at least 5 units but not more than 20 units, these are logically also the limits for our possible acts (units ordered). Our stipulation that units can be ordered only in groups of five serves to simplify the problem and reduce the size of the payoff table. The payoffs in Table 18.2 are based on a markup of $300 per unit sold and a loss of $200 for each unsold unit. Thus, for example, if 15 units are ordered for stock and only 10 are sold, the economic result is a gain of $3,000 on the 10 units sold less a loss of $1,000 on the 5 units returned to the manufacturer, for a resulting payoff of $2,000 at A_3, E_2 in the table.

Table 18.2   Payoff Table for the Number of Air-Conditioning Units to Be Ordered

Market demand	Probability	Order quantity			
		A_1: 5	A_2: 10	A_3: 15	A_4: 20
E_1: 5	0.10	$1,500	$ 500	− $ 500	− $1,500
E_2: 10	0.30	1,500	3,000	2,000	1,000
E_3: 15	0.40	1,500	3,000	4,500	3,500
E_4: 20	0.20	1,500	3,000	4,500	6,000
	1.00				

In the following sections we refer to Example 1 in order to demonstrate the application of different decision criteria, or standards, that can be used to identify the decision act which is considered to be the best act. The methods in this chapter, which involve the use of the probability values associated with each event, are concerned only with the probabilities formulated during the initial structuring of the payoff table. Because these values are formulated before the collection of any additional information, they are called *prior probabilities* in decision analysis.

18.2   DECISION MAKING BASED UPON PROBABILITIES ALONE

A complete application of Bayesian decision analysis involves use of all of the information included in a payoff table. However, in this section we briefly consider the criteria that could be used if the economic consequences were ignored (or not determined) and if the decision were based entirely on the probabilities associated with the possible events.

In such cases, one decision criterion that might be used is to identify the event with the *maximum probability* of occurrence and to choose the decision act corresponding with that event. Another basis for choosing the best act would be to calculate the *expectation* of the event and to choose the act accordingly. However, because neither of these criteria make reference to the economic consequences associated with the various decision acts and events, they represent an incomplete basis for choosing the best decision.

EXAMPLE 2. Table 18.3 presents the probability distribution for the market demand of central air-conditioning units in Example 1. The event with the maximum probability is $E_3 = 15$, for which $P = 0.40$. On the basis of the criterion of highest probability, the number of units ordered would be 15.

The calculation of the expected demand $E(D)$ is included in Table 18.3 (also see Section 6.2). Since the air-conditioning units can be ordered only as whole units, and further, only in groups of five, the expected demand level of 13.5 units cannot be ordered. Either 10 units would be ordered with the expectation of being 3.5 units short (as a long-run average), or 15 units would be ordered with the expectation of having an excess of 1.5 units, on the average.

Table 18.3 Probability Distribution of Market Demand for Air-Conditioning Units and the Calculation of the Expected Demand

Market demand (D)	Probability $[P(D)]$	$(D)P(D)$
$E_1 : 5$	0.10	0.5
$E_2 : 10$	0.30	3.0
$E_3 : 15$	0.40	6.0
$E_4 : 20$	0.20	4.0
	1.00	$E(D) = 13.5$

One difficulty associated with the two criteria described in Example 2 is that their long-run success cannot really be evaluated without some reference to economic consequences. For example, suppose the contractor can order air conditioners for stock without any prepayment and with the opportunity to return unsold units at the manufacturer's expense. In such a circumstance there would be no risk associated with overstocking, and the best decision would be to order 20 units so that the inventory would be adequate for the highest possible demand level.

18.3   DECISION MAKING BASED UPON ECONOMIC CONSEQUENCES ALONE

The payoff matrix that is used in conjunction with decision making based only upon economic consequences is similar to Table 18.1, except for the absence of the probability distribution associated with the possible events. Three criteria that have been described and used in conjunction with such a decision matrix are the maximin, maximax, and minimax regret criteria.

The *maximin criterion* is the standard by which the best act is the one for which the minimum value is larger than the minimum for any other decision act. Use of this criterion leads to a highly conservative decision strategy, in that the decision maker is particularly concerned about the "worst that can happen" with respect to each act. Computationally, the minimum value in each column of the payoff table is determined, and the best act is the one for which the resulting value is largest.

EXAMPLE 3. Table 18.4 presents the economic consequences associated with the various acts and events for the problem described in Example 1. The minimum value associated with each decision act is listed along the bottom of this table. Of these values, the largest economic result (the maximum of the four minima) is $1,500. Since the act "$A_1$: Order 5 air-conditioning units" is associated with this outcome, this is the best decision act from the standpoint of the maximin criterion.

**Table 18.4	Number of Air-Conditioning Units to Be Ordered According to the Maximin Criterion**

Market demand	A_1 : 5	A_2 : 10	A_3 : 15	A_4 : 20
E_1 : 5	$1,500	$ 500	−$ 500	−$1,500
E_2 : 10	1,500	3,000	2,000	1,000
E_3 : 15	1,500	3,000	4,500	3,500
E_4 : 20	1,500	3,000	4,500	6,000
Minimum	$1,500	$ 500	−$ 500	−$1,500

The *maximax criterion* is the standard by which the best act is the one for which the maximum value is larger than the maximum for any other decision act. This criterion is philosophically the opposite of the maximin criterion, since the decision maker is particularly oriented toward the "best that can happen" with respect to each act. Computationally, the maximum value in each column of the payoff table is determined, and the best act is the one for which the resulting value is largest.

EXAMPLE 4.   In Table 18.5 the *maximum* value associated with each decision act is listed along the bottom. The largest of these maximum values (the maximum of the maxima) is $6,000, and thus the associated act "A_4: Order 20 air-conditioning units" would be chosen as the best act from the standpoint of the maximax criterion. Rather than going through the two-step procedure of identifying column maxima and then determining the maximum of these several values, a shortcut which can be used is simply to locate the largest value in the table.

**Table 18.5	Number of Air-Conditioning Units to Be Ordered According to the Maximax Criterion**

Market demand	A_1 : 5	A_2 : 10	A_3 : 15	A_4 : 20
E_1 : 5	$1,500	$ 500	−$ 500	−$1,500
E_2 : 10	1,500	3,000	2,000	1,000
E_3 : 15	1,500	3,000	4,500	3,500
E_4 : 20	1,500	3,000	4,500	6,000
Maximum	$1,500	$3,000	−$ 500	$6,000

Analysis by the *minimax regret* criterion is based on so-called regrets rather than on conditional values as such. A *regret*, or conditional *opportunity loss*, for each act is the difference between the economic outcome for the act and the economic outcome of the best act *given that a particular event has occurred*. Thus, the best or most desirable regret value is "0," which indicates that the act is perfectly matched with the given event. Also, note that even when there is an economic gain associated with a particular act and a given event, there could also be an opportunity loss, because some other act could result in a higher payoff with the given event.

The construction of a table of opportunity losses, or regrets, is illustrated in Example 5. The best act is identified as being the one for which the maximum possible regret is smallest. Philosophically, the minimax regret criterion is similar to the maximin criterion in terms of "assuming the worst." However, use of the concept of opportunity loss results in a broader criterion, in that the failure to improve a payoff is considered to be a type of loss.

Example 5.   Table 18.6 is the table of opportunity losses associated with the conditional values in Table 18.5. Computationally, the regret values are determined given each event in turn, that is, according to rows. For example, given

Table 18.6 Opportunity Loss Table for the Number of Air-Conditioning Units to Be Ordered and Application of the Minimax Regret Criterion

Market demand	$A_1: 5$	$A_2: 10$	$A_3: 15$	$A_4: 20$
$E_1: 5$	$ 0	$1,000 (=$1,500 − 500)	$2,000 [=$1,500 − (−500)]	$3,000 [=$1,500 − (−1,500)]
$E_2: 10$	1,500 (=3,000 − 1,500)	0	1,000 (=3,000 − 2,000)	2,000 (=3,000 − 1,000)
$E_3: 15$	3,000 (=4,500 − 1,500)	1,500 (=4,500 − 3,000)	0	1,000 (=4,500 − 3,500)
$E_4: 20$	4,500 (=6,000 − 1,500)	3,000 (=6,000 − 3,000)	1,500 (=6,000 − 3,000)	0
Maximum regret	$4,500	$3,000	$2,000	$3,000

that E_1 occurs, the best act (by reference to the payoff matrix in Table 18.2) is A_1, with a value of $1,500. If A_2 is chosen, the result is $500, which differs from the best act by $1,000, and which is then the regret value for A_2. If A_3 is chosen, regret = $1,500 − (−500) = $2,000. If A_4 is chosen, regret = $1,500 − (−1,500) = $3,000. The remaining opportunity loss values are similarly determined, with the best conditional value in each row serving as the basis for determining regret values in that row. For instance, in row 2, for $E_2: 10$, the best act is $A_2: 10$ with a payoff value of $3,000 in Table 18.5.

The maximum regret which can occur in conjunction with each decision act is listed along the bottom of Table 18.6. The smallest of these maxima (the minimum of the maximum regrets) is $2,000; "$A_3$: Order 15 units" would thus be chosen as the best act from the standpoint of the minimax regret criterion.

18.4 DECISION MAKING BASED UPON BOTH PROBABILITIES AND ECONOMIC CONSEQUENCES: THE EXPECTED PAYOFF CRITERION

The methods presented in this section utilize all the information contained in the basic payoff table (see Section 18.1). Thus, we consider both the probabilities associated with the possible events and the economic consequences for all combinations of the several acts and several events.

The *expected payoff (EP)* criterion is the standard by which the best act is the one for which the expected economic outcome is the highest, as a long-run average. Note that in the present case we are concerned about the long-run average economic result, and not simply the-long-run average event value (demand level) discussed in Section 18.2. Computationally, the expected payoff for each act is determined by multiplying the conditional payoff for each event/act combination by the probability of the event and summing these products for each act.

EXAMPLE 6. Table 18.7 repeats the information from Table 18.2, except that the expected payoffs have been identified along the bottom. Table 18.8 illustrates the procedure by which such expected payoffs are calculated. In Table 18.7, the largest expected payoff is $3,250, and thus the associated act "A_3: Order 15 units" is the best act from the standpoint of the expected payoff criterion.

The expected payoff criterion often is referred to as the *Bayesian criterion*. Use of the adjective Bayesian here is distinct from the use of Bayes' theorem for revising a prior probability value, determined before the selection of a sample, by considering the sample outcome (see Section 5.7). Thus, a reference to Bayesian procedures in decision analysis can involve use of the expected payoff criterion, revision of prior probability values, or both.

Table 18.7   Payoff Table for the Number of Air-Conditioning Units to Be Ordered and Determination of the Best Act According to the Expected Payoff Criterion

Market demand	Probability	Order quantity			
		$A_1: 5$	$A_2: 10$	$A_3: 15$	$A_4: 20$
$E_1: 5$	0.10	$1,500	$ 500	$-$ 500	$-$1,500
$E_2: 10$	0.30	1,500	3,000	2,000	1,000
$E_3: 15$	0.40	1,500	3,000	4,500	3,500
$E_4: 20$	0.20	1,500	3,000	4,500	6,000
Expected payoff (EP)		$1,500	$2,750	$3,250	$2,750

Table 18.8   Determination of the Expected Payoff for Decision A_4 in Table 18.7

Market demand	Payoff for $A_4: X$	$P(X)$	$XP(X)$
$E_1: 5$	$-$1,500	0.10	$-$ 150
$E_2: 10$	1,000	0.30	300
$E_3: 15$	3,500	0.40	1,400
$E_4: 20$	6,000	0.20	1,200
			$\Sigma XP(X) + \overline{\$2,750}$

The best act identified by the expected payoff criterion can also be determined by identifying the act with the minimum expected opportunity loss (*EOL*) or expected regret. This is so because the act with the largest expected gain logically would have the smallest expected regret. In textbooks that refer to opportunity losses simply as *losses, expected losses* are understood to mean expected opportunity losses.

EXAMPLE 7.   Table 18.9 repeats the opportunity loss values from Table 18.6. It also shows the probability of each event and the expected opportunity loss associated with each decision act. Table 18.10 illustrates the procedure by which each expected opportunity loss was calculated. As indicated in Table 18.9, the minimum expected opportunity loss is $800, and thus the associated act "Order 15 units" is the best act from the standpoint of minimizing the expected opportunity loss. Note that this is the same act as identified by use of the expected payoff criterion in Example 6.

Table 18.9   Opportunity Loss Table for the Number of Air-Conditioning Units to Be Ordered and Computation of Expected Opportunity Losses

Market demand	Probability	Order quantity			
		$A_1: 5$	$A_2: 10$	$A_3: 15$	$A_4: 20$
$E_1: 5$	0.10	$ 0	$1,000	$2,000	$3,000
$E_2: 10$	0.30	1,500	0	1,000	2,000
$E_3: 15$	0.40	3,000	1,500	0	1,000
$E_4: 20$	0.20	4,500	3,000	1,500	0
Expected opportunity loss (*EOL*)		$2,550	$1,300	$ 800	$1,300

Table 18.10   Determination of the Expected Opportunity Loss for Decision A_4 in Table 18.9

Market demand	Conditional opportunity loss for A_4: OL	$P(OL)$	$(OL)P(OL)$
E_1: 5	$3,000	0.10	$ 300
E_2: 10	2,000	0.30	600
E_3: 15	1,000	0.40	400
E_4: 20	0	0.20	0
			$EOL = \overline{\$1,300}$

18.5   DECISION TREE ANALYSIS

Frequently a decision problem is complicated by the fact that the payoffs are associated not only with an initial decision, but also with subsequent events that lead to the need for additional decisions at each step of a sequential process. The evaluation of the alternative decision acts in the first step of such a sequential process must of necessity be based on an evaluation of the events and decisions in the overall process. *Decision tree analysis* is the method which can be used to identify the best initial act, as well as the best subsequent acts. The decision criterion satisfied is the Bayesian expected payoff criterion (see Section 18.4).

The first step in decision tree analysis is to construct the decision tree that corresponds to a sequential decision situation. The tree is constructed from left to right with appropriate identification of *decision points* (sequential points at which a choice has to be made) and *chance events* (sequential points at which a probabilistic event will occur). The construction of a valid decision tree for a sequential decision situation is particularly dependent on appropriate analysis of the overall decision situation. See Problem 18.12.

After a decision tree is constructed, the probability values associated with the chance events and the payoffs that can occur are entered in the diagram. Many of the payoffs are several steps removed from the initial decision point. In order to determine the expected payoffs of the alternative acts at the initial decision point, expected payoffs are systematically calculated from right to left in the decision tree. This process is sometimes called "folding back" (see Problem 18.13). As the result of applying this analytical process, the best act at the initial decision point can be identified.

18.6   EXPECTED UTILITY AS THE DECISION CRITERION

The expected payoff criterion is typically used in conjunction with both payoff table analysis and decision tree analysis (see Section 18.4). However, when the decision maker perceives one or more of the economic consequences as being unusually large or small, the expected payoff criterion does not necessarily provide the basis for identifying the "best" decision. This is particularly likely for unique, rather than repetitive situations.

EXAMPLE 8.   Consider the decision acts in Table 18.11 and assume that the choice with respect to each pair will be made only once. Although it can easily be demonstrated that the expected value of A_2 is greater than that for A_1 in every case, most

Table 18.11   Three Pairs of Alternative Decision Acts with Associated Consequences

A_1: Receive $1,000,000 for certain.	A_2: Receive $2,000,000 with a probability of 0.50 or receive $100 with a probability of 0.50.
A_1: Pay $10.	A_2: Experience a loss of $8,000 with a probability of 0.001 or experience no loss with a probability of 0.999.
A_1: Receive $15,000 with a probability of 0.50 or receive $5,000 with a probability of 0.50.	A_2: Receive $50,000 with a probability of 0.50 or experience a loss of $25,000 with a probability of 0.50.

people would choose A_1 in preference to A_2 for each of these pairs. In the context of each choice being a one-time act, the choice of A_1 is rational even though the expected payoff is not maximized. The implication of such a conclusion is that monetary values may not adequately represent true values to the decision maker in decision situations that include the possibility of exceptional losses and/or exceptional gains.

Utility is a measure of value that expresses the true relative value of various outcomes, including economic consequences, for a decision maker. This book deals only with the utility of economic consequences. Any given utility scale can begin at an arbitrary minimum value and have an arbitrarily assigned maximum value. However, it is convenient to have utility values begin at a minimum of 0 and extend to a maximum of 1.00, and this is the scale most frequently used. With such a scale, an outcome with a utility of 0.60 is understood to be twice, as desirable as one with a utility of 0.30. On the other hand, note that an economic outcome of $60,000 is not necessarily twice as desirable as an outcome of $30,000 for a decision maker with limited resources.

Using a *reference contract*, you can determine an individual's utility values for different monetary values. By this approach, the individual is asked to designate an *amount certain* that would be accepted, or paid, as being equivalent to each of a series of uncertain situations involving risk. The first risk situation portrayed always includes the two extreme limits of the range of monetary values of interest, i.e., lower and upper limits having utilities of 0 and 1.0, respectively. See Problem 18.14.

Once a reference-contract procedure has been established, it can be continued by changing either the designated probabilities or one or more of the economic consequences in the risk situation. In this way, the set of utility values corresponding to a range of monetary values can be determined. See Problem 18.15.

After the utility values have been determined, the paired values may be plotted on a graph. A best-fitting smooth line can be drawn through the plotted points as an approximation of the decision maker's *utility function* for various payoffs. The standard convention is to plot the monetary values with respect to the horizontal axis and the utility values with respect to the vertical axis. This graph can be used as the basis for estimating the utility value of any monetary outcome between the designated limits of the function. In turn, this makes it possible to substitute utility values for monetary values in a payoff table, and to determine the best act by identifying that act for which the *expected utility (EU)* is maximized. See Problems 18.16 and 18.17.

The form of the utility function indicates whether a decision maker is a risk averter or a risk seeker (see Fig. 18-1). For the risk averter [Fig. 18-1(*a*)], each additional dollar along the horizontal axis is associated with a declining slope of the utility function. That is, one might say that each additional increment has positive value to the decision maker, but not as much as the preceding increments (the curve is concave). Conversely, Fig. 18-1(*c*) indicates that for the risk seeker each additional monetary increment has increasing value to the decision maker (the curve is convex). It can also be shown that the risk averter designates an amount certain that is consistently *less* than the expected payoff for the risk situation, while the risk seeker designates an amount certain that is consistently *greater* than the expected payoff for the risk situation. See Problem 18.16.

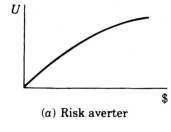 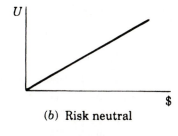 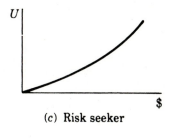

(*a*) **Risk averter**   (*b*) **Risk neutral**   (*c*) **Risk seeker**

Fig. 18-1

Overall, the form of the utility curve reflects a decision maker's attitude toward risk, and therefore is an important factor in determining which act is best *for the decision maker* at a particular time. For a firm in financial jeopardy, a particular contract opportunity that includes the possibility of a high loss and subsequent business failure may not represent a good opportunity even though the expected payoff associated with the contract is positive and represents a substantial return. The concept of utility provides the basis for demonstrating why both parties to a contract (such as insurer and insured) can experience a positive utility and why a risk situation which is "right" for one firm may not be right for another. However, if the utility function is linear or approximately so, as in Fig. 18-1(b), then the expected payoff criterion is equivalent to the expected utility criterion for that decision maker.

Solved Problems

PAYOFF TABLES

18.1 Based on a new technological approach, a manufacturer has developed a color TV set with a 45-in picture tube. The owner of a small retail store estimates that at the selling price of $2,800 the probability values associated with selling 2, 3, 4, or 5 sets during the three months of concern are 0.30, 0.40, 0.20, and 0.10, respectively. Based only on these probability values, how many sets should the retailer order for stock, assuming no reorders are possible during the period?

Based on the criterion of maximum probability, three sets would be ordered, since the probability 0.40 associated with three sets being sold is higher than the probability of any other event.

On the other hand, the expectation of the demand level is

$$2(0.30) + 3(0.40) + 4(0.20) + 5(0.10) = 3.1$$

Based on this expectation of the event, the act that comes closest to corresponding with it is also that of ordering three sets.

18.2 For the inventory decision situation in Problem 18.1, the profit margin for each set sold is $200. If any sets are not sold during the three months, the total loss per set to the retailer will be $300. Based on these economic consequences alone, and ignoring the probability values identified in Problem 18.1, determine the best decision act from the standpoint of the maximin and of the maximax criteria.

With reference to Table 18.12, for the maximin criterion the best act is A_1: Order two sets. For the maximax criterion, the best act is A_4: Order five sets.

Table 18.12   Number of TV Sets to Be Ordered According to the Maximin and Maximax Criteria

Market demand	Order quantity			
	$A_1 : 2$	$A_2 : 3$	$A_3 : 4$	$A_4 : 5$
$E_1 : 2$	$400	$100	$-$200$	$-\$ 500$
$E_2 : 3$	400	600	300	0
$E_3 : 4$	400	600	800	500
$E_4 : 5$	400	600	800	1,000
Minimum	$400	$100	$-$200$	$-\$ 500$
Maximum	$400	$600	$800	$1,000

18.3 Determine the best decision act from the standpoint of the minimax regret criterion for the decision situation described in Problems 18.1 and 18.2.

Table 18.13 indicates the opportunity losses (regrets) for this decision situation. From the standpoint of the minimax regret criterion, the best act is A_2: Order three sets.

Table 18.13   Opportunity Loss Table for the Number of TV Sets to Be Ordered and Application of the Minimax Regret Criterion

Market demand	Order quantity			
	$A_1 : 2$	$A_2 : 3$	$A_3 : 4$	$A_4 : 5$
$E_1 : 2$	$ 0	$300	$600	$900
$E_2 : 3$	200	0	300	600
$E_3 : 4$	400	200	0	300
$E_4 : 5$	600	400	200	0
Maximum regret	$600	$400	$600	$900

18.4   With reference to Problems 18.1 and 18.2, determine the best act from the standpoint of the expected payoff criterion.

Table 18.14 is the complete decision table for this problem and reports the expected payoffs associated with the possible decision acts. As indicated in the table, the best act from the standpoint of the expected payoff criterion is A_2: Order three sets.

Table 18.14   Payoff Table for the Number of TV Sets to Be Ordered and Application of the Expected Payoff Criterion

Market demand	Probability	Order quantity			
		$A_1 : 2$	$A_2 : 3$	$A_3 : 4$	$A_4 : 5$
$E_1 : 2$	0.30	$400	$100	− $200	$ 500
$E_2 : 3$	0.40	400	600	300	0
$E_3 : 4$	0.20	400	200	800	500
$E_4 : 5$	0.10	400	600	800	1,000
Expected payoff (EP)		$400	$450	$300	− $ 50

18.5   Using Table 18.14, determine the best act for the Bayesian criterion by identifying the act with the lowest expected opportunity loss.

Table 18.15 repeats the opportunity loss values from Table 18.13 and identifies the expected opportunity loss associated with each act. As indicated in the table, the best act from the standpoint of minimizing the expected opportunity loss is A_2 : Order three sets. This result was expected, since the act which satisfies the Bayesian criterion of maximizing the expected payoff will also be the act which has the minimum expected opportunity loss.

Table 18.15   Opportunity Loss Table for the Number of TV Sets to Be Ordered and Computation of Expected Opportunity Losses

Market demand	Probability	Order quantity			
		$A_1 : 2$	$A_2 : 3$	$A_3 : 4$	$A_4 : 5$
$E_1 : 2$	0.30	$ 0	$300	$600	$900
$E_2 : 3$	0.40	200	0	300	600
$E_3 : 4$	0.20	400	200	0	300
$E_4 : 5$	0.10	600	400	200	0
Expected opportunity loss (*EOL*)		$220	$170	$320	$570

18.6   Table 18.16 presents the payoffs (returns) associated with five alternative types of investment decisions for a 1-year period. Given that the probabilities associated with the possible states are not available, determine the best act from the standpoint of the maximin and of the maximax criteria.

Table 18.16   Monetary Returns Associated with Several Investment Alternatives for a $10,000 Fund

State of economy	Investment decision				
	A_1 Savings account	A_2 Corporate bonds	A_3 Blue chip stocks	A_4 Speculative stocks	A_5 Stock options
E_1 : Recession	$600	$500	− $2,500	− $ 5,000	− $10,000
E_2 : Stable	600	900	800	400	− 5,000
E_3 : Expansion	600	900	4,000	10,000	20,000

Table 18.17 identifies the minimum and maximum values for each act in Table 18.16. As would be expected, the maximin criterion leads to the selection of the very conservative decision A_1 : Invest in a savings account. The maximax criterion, on the other hand, leads to the selection of the decision act at the other extreme, A_5 : Invest in stock options.

Table 18.17   Investment Decision to Be Made According to the Maximin and Maximax Criteria

Economic consequence	Investment decision				
	A_1 Savings account	A_2 Corporate bonds	A_3 Blue chip stocks	A_4 Speculative stocks	A_5 Stock options
Minimum	$600	$500	− $2,500	− $5,000	− $10,000
Maximum	$600	$900	$4,000	$10,000	$20,000

18.7   Determine the best decision act from the standpoint of the minimax regret criterion for the situation described in Problem 18.6.

Table 18.18 indicates that the best act in this case is A_4: Invest in speculative stocks. Note the extent to which the maximum regret values for the first four acts are influenced by the possibility of the large gain with A_5, and that there is no consideration of probability values using the minimax regret criterion.

Table 18.18 Opportunity Loss Table for the Investment Decision Problem and Application of the Minimax Regret Criterion

State of economy	A_1 Savings account	A_2 Corporate bonds	A_3 Blue chip stocks	A_4 Speculative stocks	A_5 Stock options
			Investment decision		
E_1: Recession	$ 0	$ 100	$ 3,100	$ 5,600	$10,600
E_2: Stable Expansion	300	0	100	500	5,900
E_3: Expansion	19,400	19,100	16,000	10,000	0
Maximum regret	$19,400	$19,100	$16,000	$10,000	$10,600

18.8 For Problem 18.6, suppose the probabilities associated with recession, economic stability, and expansion are 0.30, 0.50, and 0.20, respectively. Determine the best act from the standpoint of the Bayesian criterion of maximizing the expected payoff.

Table 18.19 is the complete payoff table for this problem and also indicates the expected payoff associated with each decision act. The best act from the standpoint of the expected payoff criterion is A_2: Invest in corporate bonds.

Table 18.19 Payoff Table for the Investment Decision Problem and the Determination of the Best Act According to Expected Payoff Criterion

State of economy	Probability	A_1 Savings account	A_2 Corporate bonds	A_3 Blue Chip stocks	A_4 Speculative stocks	A_5 Stock options
E_1: Recession	0.30	$600	$500	−$2,500	−$ 5,000	−$10,000
E_2: Stable	0.50	600	900	800	400	−5,000
E_3: Expansion	0.20	600	900	4,000	10,000	20,000
Expected payoff (EP)		$600	$780	$ 450	$ 700	−$ 1,500

18.9 Thus far, we have been concerned with situations in which positive as well as negative economic consequences can occur. When the consequences are all *cost* values, the same techniques can be applied *provided that all cost figures are identified as being negative values* (payouts). However, although cost figures are frequently identified as "costs," they are reported as absolute values without the negative sign. In such a case, keep in mind that the minimum cost, rather than the maximum, is the "best" cost, and adjust the application of the various decision criteria accordingly. Using Table 18.20, determine the best act from the standpoint of the maximin and of the maximax criterions by modifying the application of these criteria appropriately.

Table 18.20 Cost Table Associated with Three Product Inspection Plans

Proportion defect in shipment	A_1 100% inspection	A_2 5% inspection	A_3 No inspection
E_1: 0.01	$100	$ 20	$ 0
E_2: 0.05	100	150	400

Since the lowest cost is the best cost and the highest cost is the worst cost, when the maximin criterion is applied, the objective is to choose the act with the smallest maximum cost. In this context, the maximin criterion could be called the "minimax cost" criterion. As indicated in Table 18.21, the decision act which satisfies this criterion is A_1: 100% inspection. By using this criterion, the maximum cost which can occur is minimized.

In the context of a table of costs, using the maximax criterion involves choosing the act with the smallest minimum value. Thus, the criterion could be called the "minimin cost" criterion in this case. As indicated in Table 18.21, the criterion which satisfies the optimistic orientation represented by the maximax criterion (i.e., which minimizes the minimum cost) is A_3: No inspection.

Table 18.21   Quality Inspection Plan to Be Chosen by the Maximin and Maximax Criteria

Proportion defective in shipment	Inspection plan		
	A_1 100% inspection	A_2 5% inspection	A_3 No inspection
E_1: 0.01 E_2: 0.05	$100 100	$ 20 150	$ 0 400
Maximum cost	$100	$150	$400
Minimum cost	$100	$ 20	$ 0

18.10 Determine the best decision act from the standpoint of the minimax regret criterion for the situation in Problem 18.9.

Refer to Table 18.22. Because the best act for a given state is the one which results in the *lowest* cost, that is the act which is assigned an opportunity loss of zero. Thus, given E_1, A_3 is the best act in terms of having the lowest cost, it thus has $0 regret. The act which minimizes the maximum regret which can occur is A_2: 5% inspection.

Table 18.22   Opportunity Loss Table for the Quality Inspection Plan Problem and Application of the Minimax Regret Criterion

Proportion defective in shipment	Inspection plan		
	A_1 100% inspection	A_2 5% inspection	A_3 No inspection
E_1: 0.01 E_2: 0.05	$100 0	$20 50	$ 0 300
Maximum regret	$100	$50	$300

18.11 From Problem 18.9, determine the best act from the standpoint of the general Bayesian criterion of maximizing the expected payoff, given that the probability is 0.80 that a shipment will contain a proportion of 0.01 defectives and the probability is 0.20 that a shipment will contain a proportion of 0.05 defectives.

Table 18.23   Cost Table for the Quality Inspection Plan Problem and Application of the Bayesian Criterion

Proportion defective in shipment	Probability	Inspection plan		
		A_1 100% inspection	A_2 5% inspection	A_3 No inspection
E_1: 0.01 E_2: 0.05	0.80 0.20	$100 100	$ 20 150	$ 0 400
Expected cost		$100	$ 46	$ 80

When dealing with cost figures, the Bayesian criterion is satisfied by choosing that act for which the expected cost is minimized. Table 18.23 is a complete decision table for this problem and indicates that the best act from this standpoint is A_2: 5% inspection. Note that in terms of expected (long-run) cost, the conservative strategy of 100% inspection is the least-preferred act.

DECISION TREE ANALYSIS

18.12 A manufacturer has been presented with a proposal for a new product and must decide whether or not to develop it. The cost of the development project is $200,000; the probability of success is 0.70. If development is unsuccessful, the project will be terminated. If it is successful, the manufacturer must then decide whether to begin manufacturing the product at a high level or at a low level. If demand is high, the incremental profit given a high level of manufacturing is $700,000; given a low level, it is $150,000. If demand is low, the incremental profit given a high level of manufacturing is $100,000; given a low level, it is $150,000. All of these incremental profit values are gross figures (i.e., *before* subtraction of the $200,000 development cost). The probability of high demand is estimated as $P = 0.40$, and of low demand as $P = 0.60$. Construct the decision tree for this situation.

Figure 18-2 is the decision tree for this problem. As is typical for such diagrams, each decision point is identified by a square and each chance event is identified by a circle.

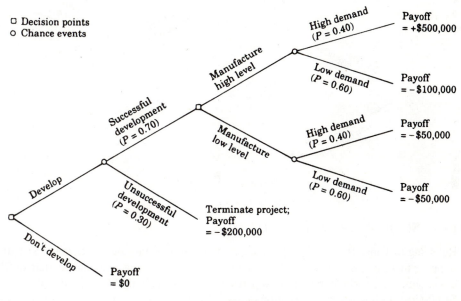

Fig. 18-2

18.13 Referring to Fig. 18-2, determine whether the manufacturer should proceed with the attempt to develop this product by determining the expected payoff associated with the alternative acts "develop" and "don't develop."

Figure 18-3 repeats the decision tree presented in Fig. 18-2, except that the expected payoffs associated with each possible decision in the sequential process have been entered, and the nonpreferred act at each decision point has been eliminated from further consideration in each case by superimposing a double bar (∥) at that branch. Working from right to left, the expected payoff of the act "high-level manufacturing" is $140,000, which is determined as follows:

$$EP(\text{high-level manufacturing}) = (0.40)(500,000) + (0.60)(-100,000) = \$140,000$$

Similarly,

$$EP(\text{low-level manufacturing}) = (0.40)(-50,000) + (0.60)(-50,000) = -\$50,000$$

Comparing the two expected payoffs, the best act is "high-level manufacturing"; the other act possibility is eliminated. Moving leftward to the next decision point (which is also the initial decision point in this case), the expected payoffs for the two possible decision acts are

$$EP(\text{develop}) = (0.70)(40,000) + (0.30)(-200,000) = \$38,000$$
$$EP(\text{don't develop}) = 0$$

Comparing the two expected payoffs, the best act at the initial decision point is "develop." In the calculation of the expected payoff for "develop," note that the probability of 0.70 (for "successful development") is multiplied by $140,000, with the $-50,000$ in the adjoining branch being ignored because it is associated with a decision act eliminated in the previous step of analysis.

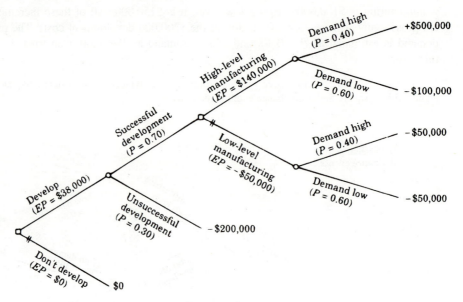

Fig. 18-3

UTILITY FUNCTIONS AND EXPECTED UTILITY

18.14 Referring to Table 18.2, we see that the two extreme monetary outcomes are $-\$1,500$ and $+\$6,000$. Suppose that a decision maker indicates indifference to receiving an amount certain of $1,200 in lieu of a risk situation in which there is a 50 percent chance of gaining $6,000 and a 50 percent chance of a $1,500 loss. Following the convention of assigning the extreme lower and upper monetary values with utility values of "0" and "1.0," respectively, determine the utility values associated with $-\$1,500$, $1,200, and $6,000.

We begin by assigning utility values to the two extreme monetary consequences:

$$U(-\$1,500) = 0 \qquad U(6,000) = 1.0$$

The utility associated with the amount certain of $1,200 is determined as follows:

$$U(\text{amount certain}) = P(U \text{ of high outcome}) + (1 - P)(U \text{ of low outcome})$$
$$U(\$1,200) = 0.50(1.0) + 0.50(0)$$
$$U(\$1,200) = 0.50$$

18.15 Continuing with Problem 18.14, suppose that four additional reference contracts are presented to the decision maker (see Table 18.24). Determine the utility values associated with each amount certain.

Table 18.24   Four Reference Contracts with Associated Amounts Certain

Contract number	Probability of $6,000 gain	Probability of $1,500 loss	Equivalent amount certain
1	0.10	0.90	$-$$1,000
2	0.30	0.70	0
3	0.70	0.30	3,000
4	0.90	0.10	5,000

Contract No. 1:

$$\text{Amount certain} = 0.10(+\$6,000) \text{ vs. } 0.90(-\$1,500)$$
$$-\$1,000 = 0.10(+\$6,000) \text{ vs. } 0.90(-\$1,500)$$
$$U(-\$1,000) = 0.10(1.0) + 0.90(0) = 0.10$$

Contract No. 2:

$$\text{Amount certain} = 0.30(+\$6,000) \text{ vs. } 0.70(-\$1,500)$$
$$\$0 = 0.30(+\$6,000) \text{ vs. } 0.70(-\$1,500)$$
$$U(\$0) = 0.30(1.0) + 0.70(0) = 0.30$$

Contract No. 3:

$$\text{Amount certain} = 0.70(+\$6,000) \text{ vs. } 0.30(-\$1,500)$$
$$\$3,000 = 0.70(+\$6,000) \text{ vs. } 0.30(-\$1,500)$$
$$U(\$3,000) = 0.70(1.0) + 0.30(0) = 0.70$$

Contract No. 4:

$$\text{Amount certain} = 0.90(+\$6,000) \text{ vs. } 0.10(-\$1,500)$$
$$\$5,000 = 0.90(+\$6,000) \text{ vs. } 0.10(-\$1,500)$$
$$U(\$5,000) = 0.90(1.0) + 0.10(0) = 0.90$$

Table 18.25 summarizes the utility values that are equivalent to the several monetary values determined above and in Problem 18.14. Note that when the risk situation in the reference contract involves the two extreme outcomes with the associated utility values of "1.0" and "0," the utility values of the amount certain which is designated by the decision maker is always equal to the probability of the outcome which has the assigned utility of 1 0.

Table 18.25   Utility Values and Equivalent Monetary Values

Monetary value, $	$-$1,500	$-$ 1,000	0	1,200	3,000	5,000	6,000
Utility value	0	0.10	0.30	0.50	0.70	0.90	1.0

18.16 Referring to Table 18.25, construct a graph to portray the utility function for this decision maker. Describe the attitude toward the risks inherent in the reference contracts that were presented to the decision maker.

Figure 18-4 shows that this decision maker is a risk averter in the range of monetary consequences included in this problem. See Fig. 18-1. Basically, this indicates that the *amount certain* which is designated as being equivalent to the designated risk situation in the reference contract is always less than the associated *expected payoff*, except for the two extreme end points of the utility curve. For instance, in Problem 18.14 the decision maker stated that a certain $1,200 was equivalent to a probability of 0.50 of gaining $6,000 and a probability of 0.50 of losing $1,500. However, the payoff of this risk situation is $0.50(\$6,000) + 0.50(-\$1,500) = \$3,000 + (-\$750) = \$2,250$.

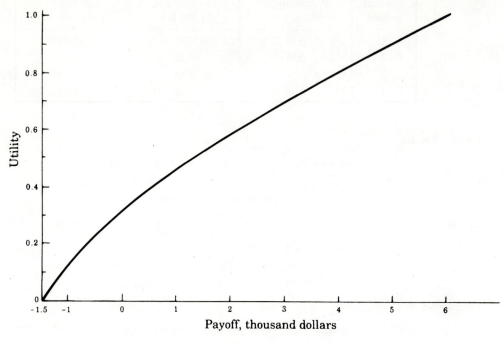

Payoff, thousand dollars

Fig. 18-4

18.17 Referring to the utility function in Fig. 18-4, determine the approximate utility values corresponding to each payoff in Table 18.2, and determine the best act from the standpoint of maximizing the expected utility.

Table 18.26 identifies the utility values that are equivalent to the payoffs in Table 18.2. Using the criterion of maximizing the expected utility, the best act is A_3, as it was for the expected payoff criterion (see Example 6). However, note that whereas the expected payoffs for acts A_2 and A_4 are equal in Table 18.7, the expected utility value of these two acts are not equal.

Table 18.26 Utility Table for the Number for Air-Conditioning Units to Be Ordered and Determination of the Best Act According to the Expected Utility Criterion

Market demand	Probability	Order quantity			
		$A_1 : 5$	$A_2 : 10$	$A_3 : 15$	$A_4 : 20$
$E_1 : 5$	0.10	0.55	0.38	0.21	0
$E_2 : 10$	0.30	0.55	0.70	0.61	0.47
$E_3 : 15$	0.40	0.55	0.70	0.86	0.78
$E_4 : 20$	0.20	0.55	0.70	0.86	1.00
Expected utility (*EU*)		0.550	0.668	0.720	0.653

Supplementary Problems

PAYOFF TABLES

18.18 An investment analyst estimates that there is about a 50 percent chance of an upturn in the chemical industry during the first quarter of the year, with the probabilities of no change and a downturn being about equal. A client is considering either the investment of $10,000 in a mutual fund specializing in chemical industry common stocks or investing in corporate AAA-rated bonds yielding 8.0 percent per year. If the chemical industry experiences an upturn during the first quarter, the value of the mutual fund shares (including dividends) will increase by 15.0 percent during the next 12 months. If there is no change, the value will increase by 3.0 percent. If there is a downturn, the value will *decrease* by 10.0 percent. Ignoring any commission costs, construct a payoff table for this investment problem.

18.19 For the investment decision described in Problem 18.18, determine the best decision act from the standpoint of the (*a*) maximin criterion and (*b*) maximax criterion.
   Ans.   (*a*) A_2: Invest in AAA bonds, (*b*) A_1: Invest in mutual fund

18.20 Determine the best act from the standpoint of the minimax regret criterion for Problem 18.18.
   Ans. A_2: Invest in AAA bonds

18.21 For Problem 18.18, determine the best act from the standpoint of the expected payoff criterion.
   Ans. A_2: Invest in AAA bonds

18.22 A retailer buys a certain product for $3 per case and sells it for $5 per case. The high markup is reflective of the perishability of the product, since it has no value after five days. Based on experience with similar products, the retailer is confident that the demand for the item will be somewhere between 9 and 12 cases, inclusive.
   Construct an appropriate payoff table. Determine the best act from the standpoint of (*a*) the maximin criterion and (*b*) the maximax criterion.
   Ans.   (*a*) A_1: Order 9 cases, (*b*) A_4: Order 12 cases

18.23 Construct the table of opportunity losses (regrets) for Problem 18.22, and determine the best act from the standpoint of the minimax regret criterion.
   Ans. A_2: Order 10 cases

18.24 Continuing with Problem 18.22, the retailer further estimates that the probability values associated with selling 9 to 12 cases of the item are 0.30, 0.40, 0.20, and 0.10, respectively. Determine the best decision acts from the standpoint of the (*a*) maximum probability criterion and (*b*) expectation of the event.
   Ans.   (*a*) A_2: Order 10 cases, (*b*) A_2: Order 10 cases

18.25 Referring to Problems 18.22 and 18.23, determine the best order quantity from the standpoint of the (*a*) expected payoff criterion and (*b*) the criterion of minimizing the expected opportunity loss. Demonstrate that these are equivalent criteria by also identifying the "second best" and "worst" acts with respect to each criterion.
   Ans.   (*a*) A_2: Order 10 cases, (*b*) A_2: Order 10 cases

18.26 In conjunction with the installation of a new marine engine, a charter vessel owner has the opportunity to buy spare propellers at $200 each for use during the coming cruise season. The propellers are custom fit for the vessel, and because the owner had already contracted to sell the boat after the cruise season, there is no value associated with having spare propellers left over after the season. If a spare propeller is not immediately available when needed, the cost of buying a needed spare propeller, including lost cruise time, is $400. Based on previous experience, the vessel owner estimates that the probability values associated with needing 0 to 3 propellers during the coming cruise season are 0.30, 0.30, 0.30, and 0.10, respectively. Construct a cost table for this problem and determine the number of propellers that should be ordered from the standpoint of (*a*) the maximin criterion and (*b*) the maximax criterion.
   Ans.   (*a*) A_4: Order three spare propellers, (*b*) A_1: Order no spare propellers

18.27 For the situation in Problem 18.26, determine the best act from the standpoint of the (a) maximum probability criterion and (b) the expectation of the event.

Ans. (a) Indifferent between 0, 1, and 2 propellers; (b) A_2: Order 1 propeller

18.28 For Problem 18.26, determine the best act from the standpoint of the expected payoff criterion (in this case, expected cost).

Ans. A_2: Order 1 propeller

18.29 Several weeks before an annual Water Carnival, a college social group must decide to order either blankets, beach umbrellas, or neither for resale at the event. The monetary success of the decision to sell one of the two items is dependent on the weather conditions, as indicated in Table 18.27. Determine the best act from the standpoint of the (a) maximin criterion and (b) maximax criterion.

Ans. (a) A_3: Neither, (b) A_2: Beach umbrellas

Table 18.27   Payoffs for the "Water Carnival" Decision Problem

Weather	A2: Blankets	A2: Beach umbrellas	A3: Neither
Cool	$100	− $ 80	$0
Hot	− 50	150	0

18.30 Determine the best act from the standpoint of the minimax regret criterion for Problem 18.29.

Ans. A_3: Neither

18.31 Continuing with Problem 18.29, one of the club members calls the weather bureau and learns that during the past 10 years the weather has been hot on 6 of the 10 days on the date when the Water Carnival is to be held. Use this information to estimate the probabilities associated with the two weather conditions. Then determine the best act from the standpoint of the (a) maximum probability and (b) expected payoff criterion.

Ans. (a) A_2: Beach umbrellas, (b) A_2: Beach umbrellas

DECISION TREE ANALYSIS

18.32 An investor is considering placing a $10,000 deposit to reserve a franchise opportunity in a new residential area for one year. There are two areas of uncertainty associated with this sequential decision situation: whether or not a prime franchise competitor will decide to locate an outlet in the same area and whether or not the residential area will develop to be a moderate or large market. The investor estimates that there is a 50–50 chance that the competing franchise system will develop an outlet. Thus, the investor must first decide whether to make the initial $10,000 down payment. After the decision of the competing system is known, the investor must then decide whether to proceed with constructing the franchise outlet. If there is competition and the market is large, the net gain during the relevant period is estimated as being $15,000; if the market is moderate, there will be a net loss of $10,000. If there is no competition and the market is large, the net gain will be $30,000; if the market is moderate, there will be a net gain of $10,000. The investor estimates that there is about a 40 percent chance that the market will be large. Using decision tree analysis, determine whether or not the initial deposit of $10,000 should be made.

Ans. Make the deposit (EP = $9,000)

UTILITY FUNCTIONS AND EXPECTED UTILITY

18.33 For Problems 18.6 to 18.8, the extreme points of the possible monetary consequences are − $10,000 and $20,000. Describe how you would go about developing a utility function for the individual who is involved in this investment decision.

18.34 Based on your answer to Problem 18.33, suppose the set of utility values reported in Table 18.28 has been developed. Construct the appropriate utility curve and use it to determine whether the investor can be described as a risk averter, a risk seeker, or neutral with respect to risk. Illustrate the meaning of your conclusion in the context of this decision problem.

Ans.   The decisions is a risk seeker.

Table 18.28   Utility Values Equivalent to Monetary Values for the Investment Decision Problem

Monetary value, $	−10,000	−2,500	2,000	10,000	14,000	18,000	20,000
Utility value	0	0.1	0.2	0.4	0.6	0.8	1.0

18.35 Determine the best act for the investment decision described in Problems 18.6 to 18.8, based on the expected utility criterion and using the utility function developed in Problem 18.34.

Ans. A_5: Invest in stock options ($EU \cong 0.230$)

CHAPTER 19

Statistical Process Control

19.1 TOTAL QUALITY MANAGEMENT

Total Quality Management (TQM) is an approach to management in which the quality of the organization's output is given first and foremost attention. The output can be in the form either of a *product* or a *service*. Further, the output may be one that is delivered to *external* customers, or it may be *internal* output to other units of the organization. How is quality determined? It is based on the judgment of the customer. Thus, customer satisfaction is the ultimate objective of TQM.

EXAMPLE 1. An example of an *external product* output is the production of video recorders. An example of an *external service* output is the services provided to patients and clients by a health maintenance organization (HMO). An example of an *internal product* output is the production of the gear department being sent to the transmission assembly department of a vehicle plant, while an example of an *internal service* output is the personnel training function carried out by a human resources department for other departments in the organization.

The TQM approach not only sets out to achieve high quality, but incorporates the philosophy by which this objective can be achieved. Traditional methods of quality assurance focused on finding and correcting product (and sometimes service) defects. The result was the use of a hierarchical command structure and an ever-increasing number of inspection steps. In an inspection-orientated manufacturing plant, half of the workers can be involved in finding and reworking rejects. The TQM philosophy is that quality should be *designed into the product or service*, and that sampling-based statistical quality control should be used, rather than attempting to inspect every unit of output. Further, quality should be monitored by those who are responsible for the output, rather than by staff personnel who represent higher management echelons. This approach results in elimination of traditional inspectors. Instead, employee teams have both the authority *and* responsibility for the quality of their output and its improvement. Thus, employee participation in setting unit goals and devising the strategies by which they are to be achieved is critical to the success of TQM.

EXAMPLE 2. In the traditional automobile manufacturing plant the inspectors in the various departments were employees of the industrial engineering department and not of the departments in which the inspection functions were performed. The theory was that inspection should be done by an outside objective party, thus setting the stage for so-called

356

line versus staff conflicts. In the TQM approach the employees of each group, with their supervisors, are responsible for and monitor product quality and are rewarded for their success as a team. For internal products, such as car parts, the ultimate judgment of the quality is made by the departments that use the parts for further processing.

19.2 STATISTICAL QUALITY CONTROL

Although there are several different ingredients that constitute Total Quality Management, the statistical contribution has its roots in statistical quality control. Sampling techniques for quality inspection date back to the 1930s. These include the development of statistically based sampling plans as an alternative to 100 percent inspection and the associated use of control charts. However, it was not until the 1970s, when U.S. industry began to react seriously to the high quality of products imported from Japan, that the application of statistical quality control became widespread. The continuing trade imbalance with Japan became a national issue during the 1980s and 1990s, and thus spurred further interest in quality improvement.

Ironically, the high quality of Japanese products was achieved largely because they adopted suggestions of U.S. consultants in the restructuring of their manufacturing processes after World War II. Preeminent among these consultants was the statistician W. Edwards Deming, after whom the Deming Award for Quality was named in Japan. Deming developed a philosophy of quality management that was the precursor of what is now called Total Quality Management, and which he summarized in his "14 Points."

EXAMPLE 3. Table 19-1 lists Deming's 14 points. Notice how closely many of the suggestions correspond to our description of TQM in the preceding section. For instance, there is a clear focus on quality in point #1, rejection of command-oriented mass inspection in point #3, the need for continual improvement in #5, and the call for action to establish the new participative environment in #14.

Table 19.1   Deming's 14 Points

1. Create consistency of purpose for improvement of products and services. That purpose should be quality, not short-term profits.
2. Adopt the new philosophy. Reject the focus on the inspection-rejection-rework viewpoint in favor of a preventive approach.
3. Cease dependence on mass inspection to achieve quality. Improve product design and institute sampling-based process control.
4. End the practice of awarding business on the basis of price tag alone. Consider quality and the development of supplier loyalty.
5. Improve constantly and forever the system of production and service.
6. Institute training.
7. Institute leadership. Autocratic management is not true leadership.
8. Drive out fear. People do their best work if they feel secure.
9. Break down barriers between departments. Different areas should not have conflicting goals.
10. Eliminate slogans, exhortations, and numerical targets for the work force. Simply telling people to improve does not work.
11. Eliminate numerical quotas. Such quotas do not take quality into consideration, and in centralized economies such quotas have often been achieved at the expense of other products or services.
12. Remove barriers to pride of workmanship. These include poor supervision, poor product design, defective materials, and defective machines.
13. Institute a vigorous program of education and self-improvement for everyone in the organization. This includes the need to know modern methods of statistical process control.
14. Take action to accomplish the transformation. This requires the leadership of top management to establish the new environment.

19.3 TYPES OF VARIATION IN PROCESSES

A *process* is a sequence of operations by which such inputs as labor, materials, and methods are transformed into outputs, in the form of products or services. In the first section of this chapter we differentiated internal and external outputs as well as product and service outputs. In any process, some *variation* in the quality measure from product to product or from service to service is unavoidable.

EXAMPLE 4.   One measure of output quality in an HMO is the waiting time before a patient with an appointment sees the medical practitioner. Even when all of the waiting times on a particular day are within a "reasonable" time limit, there will nevertheless be variation from patient to patient.

Statistical process control refers to the application of the methods of statistical quality control to the monitoring of processes (and not just, as in the earlier practice, to the inspection of the final outputs of the processes). The purpose is to control the quality of product or service outputs from a process by maintaining control of the process. When a process is described as being "in control," it means that the amount of variation in the output is relatively constant and within established limits that are deemed acceptable. There are two kinds of causes of variation in a process. *Common causes*, or *chance causes*, of variation are due to factors that are inherent in the design of the system, and reflect the usual amount of variation to be expected. *Assignable causes*, or *special causes*, of variation are due to unusual factors that are not part of the process design and not ordinarily part of the process.

A *stable process* is one in which only common causes of variation affect the output quality. Such a process can also be described as being in a state of *statistical control*. An unstable process is one in which both assignable causes and common causes affect the output quality. (Note that, by definition, the common causes are always present.) Such a process can also be described as being *out of control*, particularly when the assignable cause is controllable.

EXAMPLE 5.   If the waiting time for patients in an HMO on a particular day is deemed "reasonable," this would indicate that only common causes of variation in waiting time occurred on that day. Such common causes would include the variability in the amount of time spent with the patients who had appointments earlier in the day. If an "unreasonable" length of waiting time was experienced by some patients, this would indicate that one or more assignable causes of variation occurred. This could include such causes as a practitioner arriving late at the facility because of a medical emergency, an earlier patient who required more time than planned, or a delay in accessing medical records for patients because of a computer network problem.

The way we set out to improve the quality of output for a process depends on the source of process variation. *For a process that is stable*, improvement can take place only by improving the design of the process. A pervasive error in process management is *tampering*, which is to take actions (such as making machine adjustments) that presume that a process is not in control, when in fact it is stable. Such actions only increase variability, and are analogous to the over-correcting that new drivers do in learning to steer a car. *For a process that is unstable*, improvement can be achieved by identifying and correcting assignable causes.

EXAMPLE 6.   In our HMO example, *if the process is stable* we nevertheless have the opportunity to reduce the waiting time by improving the process. Suppose all patients are scheduled for 20-minute contact times with the physician. An alternative design would be to have variable contact times planned, based on the reason for the appointment. As indicated in Example 5, an unstable process could be due to a computer network problem on that day. *For an unstable process* such as this, correcting the computer network problem so that it does not recur would improve the process.

19.4 CONTROL CHARTS

As introduced in Section 2.12, a *run chart* is a *time series plot* that plots levels of output quality on the vertical axis, with respect to a sequence of time periods on the horizontal axis. In the context of statistical process control the measurements that are graphed are typically sample data that have been obtained by the *method of rational subgroups*, as described in Section 1.7. A *control chart* is a run chart that includes the *lower and upper control limits* that identify the range of variation that can be ascribed to common causes. Any outputs that are outside of the control limits suggest the existence of assignable-cause variation. The control limits are determined either by process parameters having been specified, or by observing sample outcomes during a period of time in which the process is deemed to be in a stable condition.

The statistical methods of process control are based on the concepts of hypothesis testing, as presented in Chapter 10. The rationale is presented in Table 19-2. The *null hypothesis* is that the process is stable and only common causes of variation exist. The *alternative hypothesis* is that the process is unstable and includes assignable-cause variation. Thus, the lower and upper control limits on a control chart are the critical values with respect to rejecting or not rejecting the null hypothesis that the process is stable and in control.

Table 19.2   Outcomes in Statistical Process Control

		Condition of Process	
		H_0 True: Stable	H_0 False: Unstable
Decision	Continue Process	Correct decision	Type II error: Allowing an unstable process to continue
	Adjust Process	Type I error: Adjusting a stable process	Correct decision

The standard practice is to place the control limits at three standard error units above and below the hypothesized value. This *3-sigma rule* is applied for all of the control chart examples in the Solved Problems included with this chapter. If a process is stable, not only should all sample statistics be within the control limits, but there also should be no discernable pattern in the sequence of the sample statistics.

In the following sections of this chapter we present the methods for determining control limits and we describe the interpretation of control charts for the *process mean*, *process standard deviation*, *process range*, and *process proportion*. Of these four, control charts for the mean, standard deviation, and range are designated as control charts for *variables*, because *measurements* are involved. Control charts for the proportion are designated as control charts for *attributes*, because *counts* (which are discrete rather than continuous variables) are involved.

19.5   CONTROL CHARTS FOR THE PROCESS MEAN: $\bar{X}$ CHARTS

Process Mean and Standard Deviation Known.   The process mean and standard deviation would be known either because they are process specifications or are based on historical observations of the process when it was deemed to be stable. The centerline for the $\bar{X}$ chart is set at the process mean. Using the 3-sigma rule, the control limits are defined by the same method as that used for determining critical values for hypothesis testing in Section 10.2:

$$\text{Control limits} = \mu \pm 3\frac{\sigma}{\sqrt{n}} \qquad (19.1)$$

Solved Problem 19.12 illustrates the determination of lower and upper control limits for an $\bar{X}$ chart when the process mean and standard deviation are known. Problem 19.13 presents the $\bar{X}$ chart that incorporates these control limits and that has the centerline at the designated process mean.

Process Mean and Standard Deviation Unknown. When the process mean and standard deviation are unknown, the required assumption is that the samples came from a stable process. Thus, recent sample results are used as the basis for determining the stability of the process as it continues. First the overall mean of the k sample means and the mean of the k sample standard deviations are determined:

$$\bar{\bar{X}} = \frac{\Sigma \bar{X}}{k} \tag{19.2}$$

$$\bar{s} = \frac{\Sigma s}{k} \tag{19.3}$$

Although $\bar{\bar{X}}$ (X double-bar) is an unbiased estimator of μ, $\bar{s}$ is a *biased* estimator of σ. This is true even though s^2 is an unbiased estimator of σ^2. Therefore, the formula for the control limits incorporates a correction for the biasedness in $\bar{s}$:

$$\text{Control limits} = \bar{\bar{X}} \pm 3 \frac{\bar{s}}{c_4 \sqrt{n}} \tag{19.4}$$

Values of c_4 are included in Appendix 9, Factors for Control Charts.

Solved Problem 19.15 illustrates the determination of lower and upper control limits for an $\bar{X}$ chart when the process mean and standard deviation are not known. Problem 19.16 then presents the $\bar{X}$ chart that incorporates these control limits, with the centerline for the chart being at $\bar{\bar{X}}$.

19.6 STANDARD TESTS USED FOR INTERPRETING $\bar{X}$ CHARTS

There are eight standard tests that are used to detect the presence of assignable-cause variation in $\bar{X}$ charts. Before considering these tests, it is useful to understand the logic of the zones that are identified on $\bar{X}$ charts, as illustrated in Fig. 19-1.

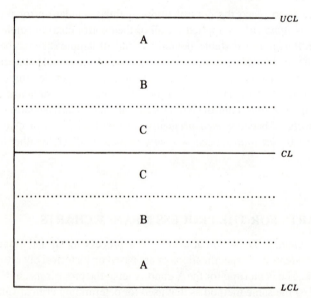

Fig. 19-1   Zones for an $\bar{X}$ chart (where CL = centerline, LCL = lower control limit, and UCL = upper control limit).

Because the sample means are approximately normally distributed if the process is stable, about 68 percent, 95 percent, and 99 percent of the sample means should be located within one, two, and three standard deviations (i.e., standard error units) of the centerline, respectively. In Fig. 19-1, observe that Zone C is the zone within one standard deviation of the centerline, Zone B is the zone between one and two standard deviations from the centerline, and Zone A, the outermost labeled zone, is between two and three standard deviations from the centerline.

The eight tests we now consider were developed by Lloyd S. Nelson, a process control expert. They are based on his determination that the identified patterns are very *unlikely* to occur in stable processes. Thus the existence of any of these patterns in an $\bar{X}$ chart indicates that the process may be unstable, and that one or more assignable causes may exist. Fig. 19-2 includes graphic examples of test failure for each of the eight tests, with a description for each graph as to what is required for the illustrated test failure.

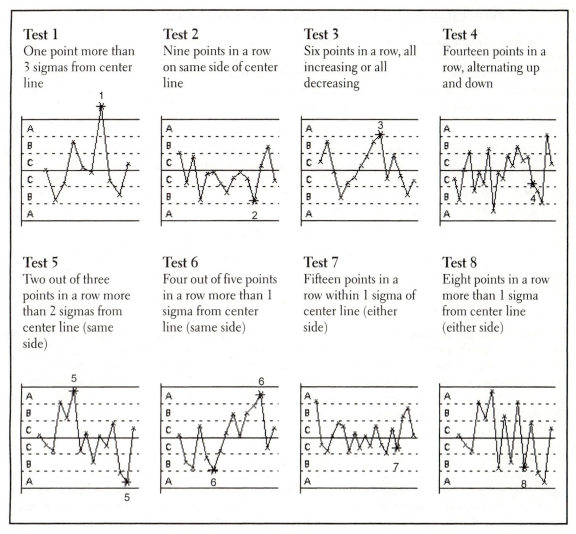

Fig. 19-2   Eight tests for assignable (special) cause variation. (Reprinted by permission from Exhibit 12.1, *User's Guide 2: Analysis and Quality Tools, Release 13*, © 2000 by Minitab Inc.)

The most obvious test in terms of its rationale is Test 1, which simply requires that at least one value of $\bar{X}$ be beyond Zone A. For a sample mean to be beyond three standard errors from the centerline is of course very unlikely in a stable process. The other seven patterns also are very unlikely. The one test whose rationale is not obvious is Test 7, which requires that 15 consecutive values of $\bar{X}$ be in Zone C, which is within one standard error of the centerline. Although this kind of pattern would seem to be very desirable, it is also very unlikely. It may, for example, indicate that the process standard deviation was overstated in the process specifications or that the sample measurements are in error. Whatever the cause, the results are too good to be true and therefore require investigation. Solved Problems 19.14 and 19.16 include interpretations of test results for $\bar{X}$ charts.

Although the eight tests were developed specifically for $\bar{X}$ charts, the first four tests also are applicable to p charts for sample proportions, as considered further in Section 19.9. The tests are *not* applicable to either s charts or R charts, both of which are concerned with the amount of sample-to-sample variation that exists in the variability of a process.

19.7   CONTROL CHARTS FOR THE PROCESS STANDARD DEVIATION: s CHARTS

Process Standard Deviation Known.   The centerline for the control chart is not set at the designated process standard deviation, as one might expect. The reason is that even though s^2 is an unbiased estimator of σ^2, the sample standard deviation s is a biased estimator of σ. Because it is required that the centerline be applicable for *sample* standard deviations, the value of the process σ must be adjusted so that the expected biasedness in the sample standard deviations is *included* :

$$E(s) = c_4\sigma \qquad\qquad (19.5)$$

The standard error of s has not been considered previously, and a full explanation is beyond the scope of this book. The constant c_5, included in Appendix 9, is used to determine the standard error of s:

$$\sigma_s = c_5\sigma \qquad\qquad (19.6)$$

The 3-sigma control limits for the s chart are

$$\text{Control limits} = c_4\sigma \pm 3c_5\sigma \qquad\qquad (19.7)$$

Solved Problem 19.17 illustrates the determination of the control limits for the standard deviation when the process standard deviation is known, while Problem 19.18 presents the s chart that incorporates these control limits.

Process Standard Deviation Unknown.   As explained for $\bar{X}$ charts, the required assumption is that the samples came from a stable process. Consistent with our discussion of biasedness in the paragraphs above, when σ is known, no correction in the biasedness of s is required in determining the centerline when σ is known. This is so because the individual sample standard deviations have this same biasedness expectation. However the c_4 correction for biasedness does need to be included in the formula for the estimated standard error of s. With the values for c_4 and c_5 taken from Appendix 9, the formula for the control limits then is

$$\text{Control limits} = \bar{s} \pm 3\frac{c_5\bar{s}}{c_4} \qquad\qquad (19.8)$$

Solved Problem 19.19 illustrates the determination of the control limits for an s chart when the process standard deviation is unknown, while Problem 19.20 presents the s chart that incorporates these control limits.

If the s chart indicates that the process is unstable in terms of process variability, then this issue should be addressed *before* there is any attempt to assess process stability with respect to the process mean.

19.8   CONTROL CHARTS FOR THE PROCESS RANGE: R CHARTS

The R chart is an alternative to the s chart for assessing the stability of a process with respect to variability. The s chart is preferred because this measure of variation considers the value of *every* sampled item, and thus leads to a more precise measure of variability. R charts were predominant for many years because of ease of computation, but this advantage is no longer relevant given the use of programmable devices in process control.

The centerline for the R chart is set at the unbiased estimator of the population range, R, which is the mean of the several sample ranges:

$$\bar{R} = \frac{\Sigma R}{k} \qquad (19.9)$$

The standard error of R has not been considered previously, and a full explanation is outside the scope of this book. The constants d_2 and d_3, included in Appendix 9, are required. The formula for the control limits then is

$$\text{Control limits} = \bar{R} \pm 3\bar{R}\frac{d_3}{d_2} = \bar{R}\left(1 \pm 3\frac{d_3}{d_2}\right) \qquad (19.10)$$

To achieve a simplified formula for practitioners, we first define the two factors:

$$D_3 = 1 - 3\frac{d_3}{d_2} \qquad (19.11)$$

$$D_4 = 1 + 3\frac{d_3}{d_2} \qquad (19.12)$$

Then using the values of D_3 and D_4 from Appendix 9, the simplified formulas for the control limits for R charts are

$$\text{Lower control limit} = \bar{R}D_3 \qquad (19.13)$$

$$\text{Upper control limit} = \bar{R}D_4 \qquad (19.14)$$

Solved Problem 19.21 illustrates the determination of lower and upper control limits for an R chart, while Problem 19.22 presents the R chart for the example.

If the R chart indicates that the process is unstable in terms of process variability, then this issue should be addressed *before* there is any attempt to assess process stability with respect to the process mean.

19.9   CONTROL CHARTS FOR THE PROCESS PROPORTION: p CHARTS

Process Proportion Known.   The process proportion would be known either because it is a process specification, such as the proportion defective that are acceptable, or it is based on historical observations of the process when it was deemed to be stable. The centerline for the p chart is set at the process proportion, π. Using the 3-sigma rule, the control limits are set by the same method used to determine critical values for hypothesis testing in Section 11.4:

$$\text{Control limits} = \pi \pm 3\sqrt{\frac{\pi(1-\pi)}{n}} \qquad (19.15)$$

Solved Problem 19.23 illustrates the determination of lower and upper control limits for a p chart when the process proportion is known, while Problem 19.24 presents the p chart that incorporates these control limits.

As indicated in Section 19.6, the first four of the eight standard tests that are used to detect assignable-cause variation in $\bar{X}$ charts also are used with respect to p charts. Solved Problem 19.24 includes interpretation of the test results for a p chart.

Process Proportion Unknown.   When the process proportion is unknown, the required assumption is that the recent samples come from a stable process. Thus the recent sample results are used as the basis for determining the stability of the process as it continues. Therefore, first the overall mean proportion for the k sample proportions is determined:

$$\bar{p} = \frac{\Sigma p}{k} \qquad (19.16)$$

Note: The *p* in the numerator of the above formula refers to the sample proportion for each individual sample, and thus is the same as *p*, as used in estimation and hypothesis testing in Sections 9.3 and 11.4. We use the symbol *p* in the present coverage to be consistent with the common practice in process control.

An alternative formula for $\bar{p}$ is to sum the number of items in each sample that have the identified characteristic, such as the number of defectives in each sample, and then divide by the total number of items in all *k* samples. Assuming equal sample sizes, the formula is

$$\bar{p} = \frac{\Sigma X}{k\,n} \qquad\qquad (19.17)$$

Because $\bar{p}$ is an unbiased estimator of π, the standard error of $\bar{p}$ is estimated by

$$s_{\bar{p}} = \sqrt{\frac{\bar{p}(1-\bar{p})}{n}} \qquad\qquad (19.18)$$

Therefore the formula for the control limits for the sample proportion is

$$\text{Control limits} = \bar{p} \pm 3\sqrt{\frac{\bar{p}(1-\bar{p})}{n}} \qquad\qquad (19.19)$$

Solved Problem 19.25 illustrates the determination of lower and upper control limits for a *p* chart when the process proportion is unknown. Problem 19.26 then presents the *p* chart that incorporates these control limits and includes interpretation of the four standard tests for assignable-cause variation as applied to the chart.

19.10   USING MINITAB

Whereas Excel has no direct method for obtaining control charts, Minitab provides a variety of such commands. Solved Problems 19.13, 19.15, 19.17, 19.19, 19.21, 19.23, and 19.25 illustrate the use of Minitab and include comparisons with hand-calculated solutions.

Solved Problems

TOTAL QUALITY MANAGEMENT

19.1   From the perspective of Total Quality Management (TQM), who ultimately determines the quality of a product or service?

> The customer of that product or service.

19.2   What is the difference between an *internal* versus an *external* product?

> An internal product is output in one unit of an organization that becomes the input for another unit in the same organization. An example is furniture casters produced in one department that are input into the furniture assembly process in another department. An external product is output intended for the final consumer; in our example, it would be the assembled furniture.

19.3   Who has responsibility for quality control in a traditional manufacturing plant, as contrasted to a plant that follows the TQM philosophy?

> By the traditional approach, inspectors are employees of a quality control staff that, in effect, represents upper management control of operations. In contrast, TQM places full authority *and* responsibility for quality on the employee groups and their supervisors who produce the output.

STATISTICAL QUALITY CONTROL

19.4   How does statistical quality control differ from the earlier approach to product inspection?

Statistical quality control is based on sampling, rather than 100 percent inspection, and the use of control charts for assessing the sample results. In contrast to correcting defective products, the focus of statistical quality control is on controlling the process itself, and thereby also controlling the quality of the output.

19.5   What was the contribution of W. Edwards Deming in the area of statistical quality control?

As described in Section 19.2, his work in post-World War II Japan had a dramatic impact on the quality of manufactured goods in that country. Further, he developed a philosophy in his "14 Points" for a quality orientation that was the forerunner of TQM.

TYPES OF VARIATION IN PROCSSES

19.6   Differentiate *common* (or *chance*) *causes* of variation in the quality of process output from *assignable* (or *special*) *causes*.

Common causes are inherent in the design of the system and reflect the typical variation to be expected. Assignable causes are special causes of variation that are ordinarily not part of the process, and should be corrected as warranted.

19.7   Differentiate a *stable* process from an *unstable* process.

A stable process is one that exhibits only common-cause variation. An unstable process exhibits variation due to both assignable and common causes.

19.8   Describe how the output of a stable process *can* be improved. What actions do *not* improve a stable process, but rather, make the output more variable?

A stable process can be improved only by changing the design of the process. Attempts to make adjustments to a stable process, which is called tampering, results in more variation in the quality of the output.

CONTROL CHARTS

19.9   What is the purpose of maintaining control charts?

Control charts are used to detect the occurrence of assignable causes affecting the quality of process output.

19.10   From what methodology of statistical inference are the techniques of statistical process control derived?

Hypothesis testing.

19.11   As contrasted to critical values being set according to levels of significance in hypothesis testing, what is the standard used for setting the control limits in process control?

The standard practice is to set the control limits at three standard errors from the centerline. Thus, they are called *3-sigma limits*.

CONTROL CHARTS FOR THE PROCESS MEAN: $\bar{X}$ CHARTS

19.12 Table 19.3 presents the weights, in ounces, for a sequence of 15 rational subgroup samples of potato chips, with $n = 4$ for each sample., The sample means, standard deviations, and ranges also are reported. Suppose that the packaging specifications call for a mean weight per package of $\mu = 15.0$ oz and a standard deviation of $\sigma = 0.1$ oz. Using these parameter values, determine the centerline and the lower and upper control limits for the $\bar{X}$ chart.

Centerline $= \mu = 15.0$ oz

$$\text{Control limits} = \mu \pm 3 \frac{\sigma}{\sqrt{n}}$$
$$= 15.0 \pm 3 \frac{0.1}{\sqrt{4}}$$
$$= 14.85 \text{ and } 15.15 \text{ oz}$$

Table 19.3   Weights of Packages of Potato Chips

Sample No.	Package weights (oz)				$\bar{X}$	s	R
1	15.01	14.98	15.16	14.80	14.99	0.148	0.36
2	15.09	15.14	15.08	15.03	15.08	0.045	0.11
3	15.04	15.10	14.93	15.13	15.05	0.088	0.20
4	14.90	15.03	14.94	14.92	14.95	0.057	0.13
5	15.04	15.05	15.08	14.98	15.04	0.042	0.10
6	14.96	14.81	14.96	14.91	14.91	0.071	0.15
7	15.01	15.10	14.90	15.03	15.01	0.083	0.20
8	14.71	14.92	14.77	14.95	14.84	0.116	0.24
9	14.81	14.80	14.64	14.95	14.80	0.127	0.31
10	15.03	14.89	14.99	15.03	14.98	0.066	0.14
11	15.16	14.91	14.95	14.83	14.96	0.141	0.33
12	14.92	15.05	15.01	15.02	15.00	0.056	0.13
13	15.06	15.03	14.95	15.02	15.02	0.047	0.11
14	14.99	15.14	15.04	15.11	15.07	0.068	0.15
15	14.94	15.08	14.90	15.17	15.02	0.125	0.27

19.13 Using Minitab, obtain the $\bar{X}$ chart for the data in Table 19.3 by use of the parameter values for the specified mean and standard deviation given in Problem 19.12, above. Compare the centerline and control limits with those calculated in Problem 19.12. Identity the test failures that occurred with respect to the eight standard tests for special causes, as described in Section 19.6.

Figure 19-3 presents the required chart. The centerline and control limits correspond to those calculated in Problem 19.12. As indicated in the output message given just below the chart, there were two sample means (for samples #8 and #9) that were beyond 3 sigmas from the centerline. From Table 19.3 we can observe that the two values were 14.84 oz and 14.80 oz, respectively. Thus, there is strong evidence of assignable-cause variation associated with these sample data.

The Minitab output given in Fig. 19-3 was obtained as follows:

(1) Open Minitab. In the column name cell for C1 enter: Weight. Enter the data *row by row* from Table 19.3 into column C1.

(2) Click **Stat** → **Control Charts** → **Xbar**.

(3) In the dialog box, for **Single column** enter: C1. For **Subgroup size** enter: 4. For **Historical mean** enter: 15.0. For **Historical sigma** enter: 0.1. Click **OK**.

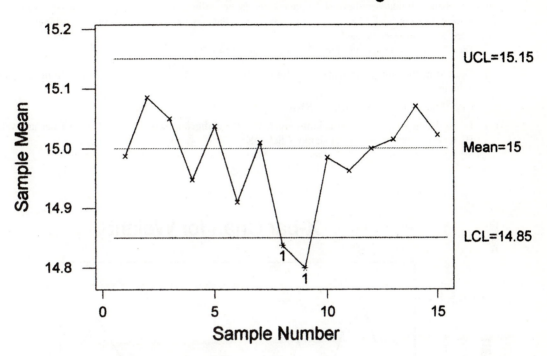

X-bar Chart: Weight

```
TEST 1. One point more than 3.00 sigmas from center line.
Test Failed at points: 8 9
```

Fig. 19-3 Minitab output for Problem 19.13.

19.14 For the package weights in Table 19.3, suppose that the process mean and standard deviation are *not* specified. Determine the centerline and control limits for the $\bar{X}$ chart.

$$\text{Centerline} = \bar{\bar{X}} = \frac{\Sigma \bar{X}}{k} = \frac{224.72}{15} = 14.98$$

$$\bar{s} = \frac{\Sigma s}{k} = \frac{1.280}{15} = 0.08551$$

$$\begin{aligned}
\text{Control limits} &= \bar{\bar{X}} \pm 3\frac{\bar{s}}{c_4\sqrt{n}} \\
&= 19.98 \pm 3\frac{0.08551}{0.9213\sqrt{4}} \\
&= 19.98 \pm 0.14 \\
&= 14.84 \text{ and } 15.12\,\text{oz}
\end{aligned}$$

19.15 Using Minitab, obtain the $\bar{X}$ chart for the data in Table 19.3 by use of the sample mean and sample standard deviation calculated in Problem 19.14, above. Compare the centerline and control limits with those calculated in Problem 19.14. Identify the test failures that occurred with respect to the eight standard tests for special causes, as described in Section 19.6.

Figure 19-4 presents the required chart. The centerline and control limits correspond to those calculated in Problem 19.14. As indicated in the output message given just below the chart, there were two sample means (for samples #8 and #9) that were beyond 3 sigmas from the centerline. From Table 19.3 we can observe that the two values were 14.84 oz and 14.80 oz, respectively. Thus, there is strong evidence of assignable-cause variation associated with these sample data.

The Minitab output given in Fig. 19-4 was obtained as follows:

(1) Open Minitab. In the column name cell for C1 enter: Weight. Enter the data *row by row* from Table 19.3 into column C1.

(2) Click **Stat → Control Charts → Xbar**.

(3) In the dialog box, for **Single column** enter: C1. For **Subgroup size** enter: 4. Do not enter any values for **Historical mean** or **Historical sigma**. Click **OK**.

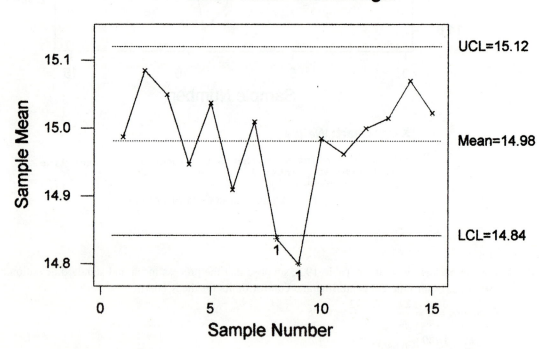

X-bar Chart: Weight

```
TEST 1. One point more than 3.00 sigmas from center line.
Test Failed at points: 8 9
```

Fig. 19-4 Minitab output for Problem 19.15.

CONTROL CHARTS FOR THE PROCESS STANDARD DEVIATION: s CHARTS

19.16 For the package weights in. Table 19.3, suppose that the process specifications require that $\sigma = 0.10$ oz. Determine the centerline and the lower and upper control limits for the s chart.

Centerline $= E(s) = c_4\sigma = 0.9213(0.10) = 0.09213$

Control limits $= c_4\sigma \pm 3c_5\sigma$

$\qquad\qquad = 0.09213 \pm 3(0.3889)(0.10)$

$\qquad\qquad = 0.09213 \pm 0.11667$

$\qquad\qquad = -0.02454$ and 0.2088

$\qquad\qquad = 0$ and 0.2088 (The lower control limit is set at zero because a negative standard deviation is not possible.)

19.17 Using Minitab, obtain the s chart for the data in Table 19.3 using the specified process standard deviation of 0.1. Compare the centerline and control limits with those calculated in Problem 19.16, above. Identify any test failures that occurred with respect to the first four standard tests for special causes, as described in Section 19.6, which are the only tests that are applied to s charts.

Figure 19-5 is the s chart given that the process standard deviation is specified. The centerline and control limits correspond to those calculated in Problem 19.16. As can be observed in the figure, only common-cause variation appears to exist. Therefore the associated $\bar{X}$ chart in Fig. 19-3 can be interpreted without concern that the observed variability in the sample means could be associated with a lack of control of process variability.

The Minitab output given in Fig. 19-5 was obtained as follows:

(1)   Open Minitab. In the column name cell for C1 enter: Weight. Enter the data *row by row* from Table 19.3 into column C1.

(2)   Click **Stat → Control Charts → s**.

(3)   In the dialog box, for **Single column** enter: C1. For **Subgroup size** enter: 4. For **Historical sigma** enter: 0.1. Click **OK**.

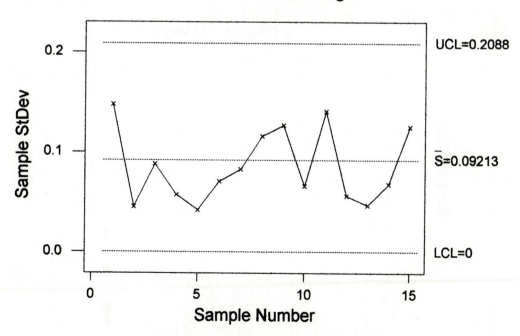

Fig. 19-5   Minitab output for Problem 19.17.

19.18 Suppose the process standard deviation was not specified for the package weights in Table 19.3. Determine the centerline and control limits for the s chart.

$$\text{Centerline} = \bar{s} = \frac{\Sigma s}{k} = \frac{1.280}{15} = 0.08551$$

$$\text{Control limits} = \bar{s} \pm 3 \frac{c_5 \bar{s}}{c_4}$$

$$= 0.08551 \pm 3 \frac{0.3889(0.08551)}{0.9213}$$

$$= 0.08551 \pm 0.1083$$

$$= -0.0228 \text{ and } 0.1938$$

$$= 0 \text{ and } 0.1938 \text{ (The lower control limit is set at zero because a negative}$$

standard deviation is not possible.)

19.19 Using Minitab, obtain the s chart for the data in Table 19.3 using the standard deviation based on the sample data. Compare the centerline and control limits with those calculated in Problem 19.18, above. Identify any test failures that occurred with respect to the first four standard tests for special causes, as described in Section 19.6, which are the only tests that are applied to s charts.

Figure 19-6 is the s chart given that the process standard deviation is not specified, but rather, is based on sample data. The centerline and control limits correspond to those calculated in Problem 19.18. As can be observed in the figure, only common-cause variation appears to exist. Therefore, the associated $\bar{X}$ chart in Fig. 19-4 can be interpreted without concern that the observed variability in the sample means could be associated with a lack of control of process variability.

The Minitab output given in Fig. 19-6 was obtained as follows:

(1) Open Minitab. In the column name cell for C1 enter: Weight. Enter the data *row by row* from Table 19.3 into column C1.

(2) Click **Stat → Control Charts → s**.

(3) In the dialog box, for **Single column** enter: C1. For **Subgroup size** enter: 4.

(4) In the **Estimate** dialog box choose **Pooled standard deviation**. Click **OK**.

(5) Back in the original dialog box, click **OK**.

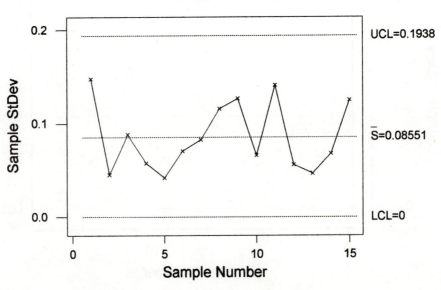

Fig. 19-6 Minitab output for Problem 19.19.

CONTROL CHARTS FOR THE PROCESS RANGE: *R* CHARTS

19.20 Determine the centerline and control limits with respect to the *R* chart for the package weights in Table 19.3.

$$\text{Centerline} = \bar{R} = \frac{\Sigma R}{k} = \frac{2.93}{15} = 0.19533$$

$$\text{Lower control limit} = \bar{R}D_3 = 0.19533(0) = 0$$

$$\text{Upper control limit} = \bar{R}D_4 = 0.19533(2.282) = 0.4458$$

19.21 Using Minitab, obtain the *R* chart for the weight data in Table 19.3 using the mean range that was determined in Problem 19.20, above. Compare the centerline and control limits in the chart with those calculated in Problem 19.20. Identify any test failures that occurred with respect to the first four standard tests for special causes, as described in Section 19.6, which are the only tests that are applied to *R* charts.

Figure 19-7 is the *R* chart obtained with Minitab. The centerline and control limits correspond to those calculated in Problem 19.20. As can be observed in the figure, only common-cause variation appears to exist. Therefore, the associated $\bar{X}$ chart in Fig. 19-4 can be interpreted without concern that the observed variability in the sample means could be associated with a lack of control of process variability.

The Minitab output given in Fig. 19-7 was obtained as follows:

(1) Open Minitab. In the column name cell for C1 enter: Weight. Enter the data *row by row* from Table 19.3 into column C1.

(2) Click **Stat → Control Charts → R**.

(3) In the dialog box, for **Single column** enter: C1. For **Subgroup size** enter: 4. Do not enter any value for **Historical sigma**. Click **OK**.

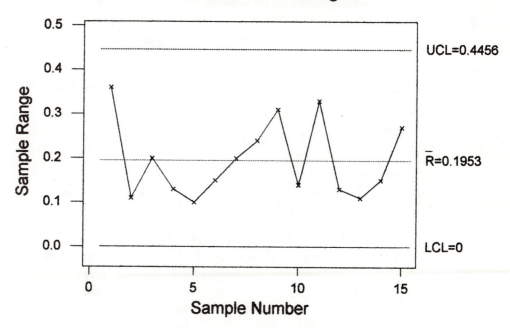

Fig. 19-7   Minitab output for Problem 19.21.

CONTROL CHARTS FOR THE PROCESS PROPORTION: p CHARTS

19.22 When a coupon redemption process is in control, then a maximum of 3 percent of the rebates are done incorrectly, for a maximum acceptable proportion of errors of 0.03. For 20 sequential samples of 100 coupon redemptions each, an audit reveals that the number of errors found in the rational subgroup samples is: 2, 2, 3, 6, 1, 3, 6, 4, 7, 2, 5, 0, 3, 2, 4, 5, 3, 8, 1, and 4. Determine the control limits for the proportion of errors per sample, given that the process proportion is specified as being $\pi = 0.03$.

$$\text{Control limits} = \pi \pm 3\sqrt{\frac{\pi(1-\pi)}{n}}$$

$$= 0.03 \pm 3\sqrt{\frac{0.0.3(0.97)}{100}}$$

$$= 0.03 \pm 3(0.0170587)$$

$$= 0.03 \pm 0.05118$$

$$= -0.02118 \text{ and } 0.08118$$

$$= 0 \text{ and } 0.08118 \text{ (The lower control limit is set at zero because a negative}$$

sample proportion is neither possible nor relevant for this one-sided test.)

19.23 Using Minitab, obtain the p chart for the data in Problem 19.22, above, given that the process proportion of errors is specified as 0.03. Compare the centerline and control limits in the chart with those calculated in Problem 19.22. Identify any test failures that occurred with respect to the first four standard tests for special causes, as described in Section 19.6, which are the only tests that are applied to p charts.

Figure 19-8 is the p chart obtained with Minitab. The centerline and control limits correspond to those calculated in Problem 19.22. As can be observed in the figure, only common-cause variation is included in the chart, and the process appears to be stable.

The Minitab output given in Fig. 19-8 was obtained as follows:

(1)   Open Minitab. In the column name cell for C1 enter: Errors. Enter the error data into C1.

(2)   Click **Stat** → **Control Charts** → **P**.

(3)   In the dialog box, for **Variable** enter: C1. For **Subgroup** size enter: 100. For **Historical** p **enter**: 0.03. Click **OK**.

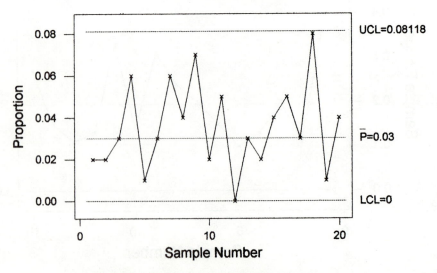

Fig. 19-8   Minitab output for Problem 19.23.

19.24 For the data in Problem 19.23, above, determine the centerline and the control limits for the p chart given that the process proportion was *not* specified.

$$\text{Centerline} = \bar{p} = \frac{\Sigma p}{k} = 0.0355$$

$$\text{Control limits} = \bar{p} \pm 3\sqrt{\frac{\bar{p}(1 - \bar{p})}{n}}$$

$$= 0.0355 \pm 3\sqrt{\frac{0.0355(0.9645)}{100}}$$

$$= 0.0355 \pm 3(0.0185039)$$

$$= 0.0355 \pm 0.05551$$

$$= -0.02001 \text{ and } 0.09101$$

$= 0$ and 0.09101 (The lower control limit is set equal to zero because a negative

sample proportion is not possible, nor is it relevant for this one-sided test.)

19.25 Using Minitab, obtain the p chart for the data in Problem 19.22 based on the sample data only, without the process proportion having been specified. Compare the centerline and control limits in the chart with those calculated in Problem 19.24, above. Identify any test failures that occurred with respect to the first four standard tests for special causes, as described in Section 19.6, which are the only tests that are applied to p charts.

Figure 19-9 is the p chart obtained with Minitab. The centerline and control limits correspond to those calculated in Problem 19.24. As can be observed in the figure, only common-cause variation is included in the chart, and the process appears to be stable.

The Minitab output given in Fig. 19-9 was obtained as follows:

(1) Open Minitab. In the column-name cell for C1 enter: Errors. Enter the error data into C1.

(2) Click **Stat → Control Charts → P**.

(3) In the dialog box, for **Variable** enter: C1. For **Subgroup size** enter: 100. Do not enter any value for **Historical**
     p. Click **OK**.

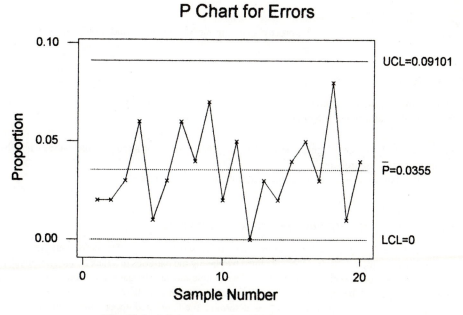

Fig. 19-9 Minitab output for Problem 19.25.

Supplementary Problems

TOTAL QUALITY MANAGEMENT

19.26   Historically, process control has focused on *product* outputs. With respect to the perspective of Total Quality Management (TQM), give several examples of the *other* major category of outputs that is also now the focus of process control.
Ans.   Examples of *service* output should be given.

19.27   Traditionally, it seemed that the best inspector would be an objective person not directly involved in creating the product or service output. Consider the flaw associated with this point of view.
Ans.   This issue is at the heart of TQM, as discussed in Section 19.1.

STATISTICAL QUALITY CONTROL

19.28   What particular set of events during the 1970s and 1980s led to national awareness of the need for higher product quality?
Ans.   The high quality of Japanese imports to the United States, and the balance of trade problem with Japan.

19.29   Who was the American statistician after whom a national award for quality was named in Japan?
Ans.   W. Edwards Deming

TYPES OF VARIATION IN PROCESSES

19.30   What is a *process*?
Ans.   It is a sequence of operations by which such inputs as labor, materials, and methods are transformed into either product or service outputs.

19.31   When is a process considered to be "out of control," and how can it be brought under control?
Ans.   A process is "out of control," or unstable, when there is assignable-cause variation in the quality of the output. Improvement can be achieved by identifying and removing the assignable cause(s).

19.32   What is *tampering* in the context of process control?
Ans.   It is the attempt to adjust a process that is in fact stable and includes only common-cause variation.

CONTROL CHARTS

19.33   What is the statistical sampling method by which the data analyzed by control charts are collected?
Ans.   Method of rational subgroups.

19.34   Other than applying the 3-sigma rule for detecting the presence of an assignable cause, what else do we look for when studying a control chart?
Ans.   The existence of a *pattern* in the sequence of sample results.

CONTROL CHARTS FOR THE PROCESS MEAN: $\bar{X}$ CHARTS

19.35   Table 19.4 presents the battery life, in minutes, for 12 sequential samples of AA batteries, with a sample size of $n = 6$ for each sample. The data were obtained by placing the batteries in a rack that systematically drains the power from them to simulate typical battery usage. The sample means, standard deviations, and ranges also are reported. Suppose that the AA battery specifications require a mean battery life of $\mu = 450$ min with a standard deviation of $\sigma = 15$ min. Using these parameter values, determine the lower and upper control limits for the $\bar{X}$ chart.
Ans.   431.6 and 468.4

Table 19.4 Battey Life

Sample No.	Battery life (min)						$\bar{X}$	s	R
1	445.4	470.3	466.5	432.3	445.5	425.4	447.6	17.94	44.9
2	479.7	466.1	439.2	442.0	432.1	429.4	448.1	20.22	50.3
3	449.7	450.1	432.2	468.1	446.3	452.6	449.8	11.53	35.9
4	467.6	427.9	453.9	445.4	467.9	449.3	452.0	15.04	40.0
5	484.5	436.8	458.6	465.2	437.1	445.1	454.6	18.63	47.7
6	470.5	469.3	435.9	438.1	461.0	431.4	451.0	17.85	39.1
7	411.6	459.7	450.9	449.6	444.9	467.5	447.4	19.29	55.9
8	458.8	442.5	462.2	417.2	424.6	463.9	444.9	20.19	46.7
9	435.4	435.6	451.2	434.7	465.9	425.2	441.3	14.65	40.7
10	448.2	449.7	435.7	438.4	432.7	426.5	438.5	9.00	23.2
11	458.5	436.7	455.5	449.2	440.6	424.0	444.1	12.92	34.5
12	444.6	430.8	463.6	458.2	436.2	458.8	448.7	13.47	32.8

19.36 Prepare the $\bar{X}$ chart for the data in Table 19.4 using the parameter values and control limits from the preceding problem. Interpret any test failures that occurred with respect to the eight standard tests that are used with $\bar{X}$ charts.
Ans.   Test 3 failed at point 10.

19.37 Suppose that the process mean and standard deviation are *not* specified for the battery-life data in Table 19.4. Determine the centerline and control limits for the $\bar{X}$ chart.
Ans.   Centerline $= \bar{\bar{X}} = 447.3$; control limits $= 427.3$ and 467.3.

19.38 Prepare the $\bar{X}$ chart for the data in Table 19.4 using the sample statistics and control limits determined in the preceding problem. Interpret the results associated with the eight standard tests for $\bar{X}$ charts.
Ans.   Test 3 failed at point 10.

CONTROL CHARTS FOR THE PROCESS STANDARD DEVIATION: s CHARTS

19.39 For the battery-life data in Table 19.4, suppose that the process specifications require that $\sigma = 15$ mm. Determine the centerline and the lower and upper control limits for the s chart.
Ans.   Centerline $= 14.27$; control limits $= 0.4334$ and 28.11.

19.40 Prepare the s chart for the battery-life data in Table 19.4 using the centerline and control limits determined in the preceding problem. Interpret the chart.
Ans.   There appears to be no assignable cause associated with the variation in the sample standard deviations.

19.41 Suppose that the process standard deviation was not specified for the battery-life data in Table 19.4. Determine the centerline and control limits for the s chart.
Ans.   Centerline $= \bar{s}15.55$; control limits $= 0.4723$ and 30.64.

19.42 Prepare the s chart for the data in Table 19.4 using the centerline and control limits determined in the preceding problem. Interpret the chart.
Ans.   There appears to be no assignable cause associated with the variation in the sample standard deviations.

CONTROL CHARTS FOR THE PROCESS RANGE: R CHARTS

19.43 Prepare the R chart for the battery-life data in Table 19.4 using computer software. Interpret the chart.
Ans.   From Minitab: Centerline $= 41.42$; control limits $= 0$ and 83.00. There appears to be no assignable cause associated with the variation in the sample ranges.

CONTROL CHARTS FOR THE PROCESS PROPORTION: *p* CHARTS

19.44   A health maintenance organization (HMO) has established the standard that no more than 8 percent of the patients should have to wait more than 20 minutes beyond the appointed time to see the medical provider. For 20 sequential samples of 80 patients, the number of patients who had to wait more than 20 minutes was: 3, 4, 10, 10, 9, 7, 9, 7, 8, 9, 7, 10, 8, 4, 8, 5, 2, 8, 8, and 6. Determine the centerline and the upper control limit for the *p* chart that would be used to monitor this process.
   Ans.   Centerline = π = 0.08; upper control limit = 0.1710

19.45   Prepare the *p* chart by using the centerline and upper control limit determined in the preceding problem. Apply and interpret the result associated with the four standard tests for proportions.
   Ans.   Test 2 failed at samples 11, 12, and 13.

19.46   With respect to the patient waiting times in Problem 19.44, suppose no standard had been set regarding the proportion of patients who are required to wait more than 20 minutes to see the medical provider. Determine the centerline and the upper control limit for the *p* chart.
   Ans.   Centerline = $\bar{p}$ = 0.08875; upper control limit = 0.1841

19.47   Prepare the *p* chart for the waiting times in Problem 19.44, but using the centerline and control limits determined in Problem 19.46, above. Apply and interpret the result associated with the four standard tests for proportions.
   Ans.   No test failures occurred. Using the mean of the sample proportions as the basis for the centerline, there is no assignable-cause variation in the series of proportions.

Table of Random Numbers

10097	85017	84532	13618	23157	86952	02438	76520	91499	38631	79430	62421	97959	67422	69992	68479
37542	16719	82789	69041	05545	44109	05403	64894	80336	49172	16332	44670	35089	17691	89246	26940
08422	65842	27672	82186	14871	22115	86529	19645	44104	89232	57327	34679	62235	79655	81336	85157
99019	76875	20684	39187	38976	94324	43204	09376	12550	02844	15026	32439	58537	48274	81330	11100
12807	93640	39160	41453	97312	41548	93137	80157	63606	40387	65406	37920	08709	60623	2237	16505
66065	99478	70086	71265	11742	18226	29004	34072	61196	80240	44177	51171	08723	39323	05798	26457
31060	65119	26486	47353	43361	99436	42753	45571	15474	44910	99321	72173	56239	04595	10836	95270
85269	70322	21592	48233	93806	32584	21828	02051	94557	33663	86347	00926	44915	34823	51770	67897
63573	58133	41278	11697	49540	61777	67954	05325	42481	86430	19102	37420	41976	76559	24358	97344
73796	44655	81255	31133	36768	60452	38537	03529	23523	31379	68588	81675	15694	43438	36879	73208
98520	02295	13487	98662	07092	44673	61303	14905	04493	98086	32533	17767	14523	52494	24826	75246
11805	85035	54881	35587	43310	48897	48493	39808	00549	33185	04805	05431	94598	97654	16232	64051
83452	01197	86935	28021	61570	23350	65710	06288	35963	80951	68953	99634	81949	15307	00406	26898
88685	97907	19078	40646	31352	48625	44369	86507	59808	79752	02529	40200	73742	08391	49140	45427
99594	63268	96905	28797	57048	46359	74294	87517	46058	18633	99970	67348	49329	95236	32537	01390
65481	52841	59684	67411	09243	56092	84369	17468	32179	74029	74717	17674	90446	00597	45240	87379
80124	53722	71399	10916	07959	21225	13018	17727	69234	54178	10805	35635	45266	61406	41941	20117
74350	11434	51908	62171	93732	26958	02400	77402	19565	11664	77602	99817	28573	41430	96382	01758
69916	62375	99292	21177	72721	66995	07289	66252	45155	48324	32135	26803	16213	14938	71961	19476
09893	28337	20923	87929	61020	62841	31374	14225	94864	69074	45753	20505	78317	31994	98145	36168

Binomial Probabilities

.50	.45	.40	.35	.30	.25 (p)	.20	.15	.10	.05	.01	n	x
.1641	.2119	.2508	.2716	.2668	.2336	.1762	.1069	.0446	.0077	.0001	9	3
.2461	.2600	.2508	.2194	.1715	.1168	.0661	.0283	.0074	.0006	.0000		4
.2461	.2128	.1672	.1181	.0735	.0389	.0165	.0050	.0008	.0000	.0000		5
.1641	.1160	.0743	.0424	.0210	.0087	.0028	.0006	.0001	.0000	.0000		6
.0703	.0407	.0212	.0098	.0039	.0012	.0003	.0000	.0000	.0000	.0000		7
.0176	.0083	.0035	.0013	.0004	.0001	.0000	.0000	.0000	.0000	.0000		8
.0020	.0008	.0003	.0001	.0000	.0000	.0000	.0000	.0000	.0000	.0000		9
.0010	.0025	.0060	.0135	.0282	.0563	.1074	.1969	.3487	.5987	.9044	10	0
.0098	.0207	.0403	.0725	.1211	.1877	.2684	.3474	.3874	.3151	.0914		1
.0439	.0763	.1209	.1757	.2335	.2816	.3020	.2759	.1937	.0746	.0042		2
.1172	.1665	.2150	.2522	.2668	.2503	.2013	.1298	.0574	.0105	.0001		3
.2051	.2384	.2508	.2377	.2001	.1460	.0881	.0401	.0112	.0010	.0000		4
.2461	.2340	.2007	.1536	.1029	.0584	.0264	.0085	.0015	.0001	.0000		5
.2051	.1596	.1115	.0689	.0368	.0162	.0055	.0012	.0001	.0000	.0000		6
.1172	.0746	.0425	.0212	.0090	.0031	.0008	.0001	.0000	.0000	.0000		7
.0439	.0229	.0106	.0043	.0014	.0004	.0001	.0000	.0000	.0000	.0000		8
.0098	.0042	.0016	.0005	.0001	.0000	.0000	.0000	.0000	.0000	.0000		9
.0010	.0003	.0001	.0000	.0000	.0000	.0000	.0000	.0000	.0000	.0000		10
.0005	.0014	.0036	.0088	.0198	.0422	.0859	.1673	.3138	.5688	.8953	11	0
.0054	.0125	.0266	.0518	.0932	.1549	.2362	.3248	.3835	.3293	.0995		1
.0269	.0513	.0887	.1395	.1998	.2581	.2953	.2866	.2131	.0867	.0050		2
.0806	.1259	.1774	.2254	.2568	.2581	.2215	.1517	.0710	.0137	.0002		3
.1611	.2060	.2365	.2428	.2201	.1721	.1107	.0536	.0158	.0014	.0000		4
.2256	.2360	.2207	.1830	.1321	.0803	.0388	.0132	.0025	.0001	.0000		5
.2256	.1931	.1471	.0985	.0566	.0268	.0097	.0023	.0003	.0000	.0000		6
.1611	.1128	.0701	.0379	.0173	.0064	.0017	.0003	.0000	.0000	.0000		7
.0806	.0462	.0234	.0102	.0037	.0011	.0002	.0000	.0000	.0000	.0000		8
.0269	.0126	.0052	.0018	.0005	.0001	.0000	.0000	.0000	.0000	.0000		9
.0054	.0021	.0007	.0002	.0000	.0000	.0000	.0000	.0000	.0000	.0000		10
.0005	.0002	.0000	.0000	.0000	.0000	.0000	.0000	.0000	.0000	.0000		11
.0002	.0008	.0022	.0057	.0138	.0317	.0687	.1422	.2824	.5404	.8864	12	0
.0029	.0075	.0174	.0368	.0712	.1267	.2062	.3012	.3766	.3413	.1074		1
.0161	.0339	.0639	.1088	.1678	.2323	.2835	.2924	.2301	.0988	.0060		2
.0537	.0923	.1419	.1954	.2397	.2581	.2362	.1720	.0852	.0173	.0002		3
.1208	.1700	.2128	.2367	.2311	.1936	.1329	.0683	.0213	.0021	.0000		4
.1934	.2225	.2270	.2039	.1585	.1032	.0532	.0193	.0038	.0002	.0000		5
.2256	.2124	.1766	.1281	.0792	.0401	.0155	.0040	.0005	.0000	.0000		6
.1934	.1489	.1009	.0591	.0291	.0115	.0033	.0006	.0000	.0000	.0000		7
.1208	.0762	.0420	.0199	.0078	.0024	.0005	.0001	.0000	.0000	.0000		8
.0537	.0277	.0125	.0048	.0015	.0004	.0001	.0000	.0000	.0000	.0000		9
.0161	.0068	.0025	.0008	.0002	.0000	.0000	.0000	.0000	.0000	.0000		10
.0029	.0010	.0003	.0001	.0000	.0000	.0000	.0000	.0000	.0000	.0000		11
.0002	.0001	.0000	.0000	.0000	.0000	.0000	.0000	.0000	.0000	.0000		12
.0001	.0004	.0013	.0037	.0097	.0238	.0550	.1209	.2542	.5133	.8775	13	0
.0016	.0045	.0113	.0259	.0540	.1029	.1787	.2774	.3672	.3512	.1152		1
.0095	.0220	.0453	.0836	.1388	.2059	.2680	.2937	.2448	.1109	.0070		2
.0349	.0660	.1107	.1651	.2181	.2517	.2457	.1900	.0997	.0214	.0003		3
.0873	.1350	.1845	.2222	.2337	.2097	.1535	.0838	.0277	.0028	.0000		4

n	x	.01	.05	.10	.15	.20	.25	.30 (p)	.35	.40	.45	.50
1	0	.9900	.9500	.9000	.8500	.8000	.7500	.7000	.6500	.6000	.5500	.5000
	1	.0100	.0500	.1000	.1500	.2000	.2500	.3000	.3500	.4000	.4500	.5000
2	0	.9801	.9025	.8100	.7225	.6400	.5625	.4900	.4225	.3600	.3025	.2500
	1	.0198	.0950	.1800	.2550	.3200	.3750	.4200	.4550	.4800	.4950	.5000
	2	.0001	.0025	.0100	.0225	.0400	.0625	.0900	.1225	.1600	.2025	.2500
3	0	.9703	.8574	.7290	.6141	.5120	.4219	.3430	.2746	.2160	.1664	.1250
	1	.0294	.1354	.2430	.3251	.3840	.4219	.4410	.4436	.4320	.4084	.3750
	2	.0003	.0071	.0270	.0574	.0960	.1406	.1890	.2389	.2880	.3341	.3750
	3	.0000	.0001	.0010	.0034	.0080	.0156	.0270	.0429	.0640	.0911	.1250
4	0	.9606	.8145	.6561	.5220	.4096	.3164	.2401	.1785	.1296	.0915	.0625
	1	.0388	.1715	.2916	.3685	.4096	.4219	.4116	.3845	.3456	.2995	.2500
	2	.0006	.0135	.0486	.0975	.1536	.2109	.2646	.3105	.3456	.3675	.3750
	3	.0000	.0005	.0036	.0115	.0256	.0469	.0756	.1115	.1536	.2005	.2500
	4	.0000	.0000	.0001	.0005	.0016	.0039	.0081	.0150	.0256	.0410	.0625
5	0	.9510	.7738	.5905	.4437	.3277	.2373	.1681	.1160	.0778	.0503	.0312
	1	.0480	.2036	.3280	.3915	.4096	.3955	.3602	.3124	.2592	.2059	.1562
	2	.0010	.0214	.0729	.1382	.2048	.2637	.3087	.3364	.3456	.3369	.3125
	3	.0000	.0011	.0081	.0244	.0512	.0879	.1323	.1811	.2304	.2757	.3125
	4	.0000	.0000	.0004	.0022	.0064	.0146	.0284	.0488	.0768	.1128	.1562
	5	.0000	.0000	.0000	.0001	.0003	.0010	.0024	.0053	.0102	.0185	.0312
6	0	.9415	.7351	.5314	.3771	.2621	.1780	.1176	.0754	.0467	.0277	.0156
	1	.0571	.2321	.3543	.3993	.3932	.3560	.3025	.2437	.1866	.1359	.0938
	2	.0014	.0305	.0984	.1762	.2458	.2966	.3241	.3280	.3110	.2780	.2344
	3	.0000	.0021	.0146	.0415	.0819	.1318	.1852	.2355	.2765	.3032	.3125
	4	.0000	.0001	.0012	.0055	.0154	.0330	.0595	.0951	.1382	.1861	.2344
	5	.0000	.0000	.0001	.0004	.0015	.0044	.0102	.0205	.0369	.0609	.0938
	6	.0000	.0000	.0000	.0000	.0001	.0002	.0007	.0018	.0041	.0083	.0156
7	0	.9321	.6983	.4783	.3206	.2097	.1335	.0824	.0490	.0280	.0152	.0078
	1	.0659	.2573	.3720	.3960	.3670	.3115	.2471	.1848	.1306	.0872	.0547
	2	.0020	.0406	.1240	.2097	.2753	.3115	.3177	.2985	.2613	.2140	.1641
	3	.0000	.0036	.0230	.0617	.1147	.1730	.2269	.2679	.2903	.2918	.2734
	4	.0000	.0002	.0026	.0109	.0287	.0577	.0972	.1442	.1935	.2388	.2734
	5	.0000	.0000	.0002	.0012	.0043	.0115	.0250	.0466	.0774	.1172	.1641
	6	.0000	.0000	.0000	.0001	.0004	.0013	.0036	.0084	.0172	.0320	.0547
	7	.0000	.0000	.0000	.0000	.0000	.0001	.0002	.0006	.0016	.0037	.0078
8	0	.9227	.6634	.4305	.2725	.1678	.1002	.0576	.0319	.0168	.0084	.0039
	1	.0746	.2793	.3826	.3847	.3355	.2670	.1977	.1373	.0896	.0548	.0312
	2	.0026	.0515	.1488	.2376	.2936	.3115	.2965	.2587	.2090	.1569	.1094
	3	.0001	.0054	.0331	.0839	.1468	.2076	.2541	.2786	.2787	.2568	.2188
	4	.0000	.0004	.0046	.0185	.0459	.0865	.1361	.1875	.2322	.2627	.2734
	5	.0000	.0000	.0004	.0026	.0092	.0231	.0467	.0808	.1239	.1719	.2188
	6	.0000	.0000	.0000	.0002	.0011	.0038	.0100	.0217	.0413	.0703	.1094
	7	.0000	.0000	.0000	.0000	.0001	.0004	.0012	.0033	.0079	.0164	.0312
	8	.0000	.0000	.0000	.0000	.0000	.0000	.0001	.0002	.0007	.0017	.0039
9	0	.9135	.6302	.3874	.2316	.1342	.0751	.0404	.0207	.0101	.0046	.0020
	1	.0830	.2985	.3874	.3679	.3020	.2253	.1556	.1004	.0605	.0339	.0176
	2	.0034	.0629	.1722	.2597	.3020	.3003	.2668	.2162	.1612	.1110	.0703

Example: $p(x = 3 \mid n = 6, p = 0.50) = 0.3125$

n	x	.01	.05	.10	.15	.20	.25	.30	.35	.40	.45	.50
13	5	.0000	.0003	.0055	.0266	.0691	.1258	.1803	.2154	.2214	.1989	.1571
	6	.0000	.0000	.0008	.0063	.0230	.0559	.1030	.1546	.1968	.2169	.2095
	7	.0000	.0000	.0001	.0011	.0058	.0186	.0442	.0833	.1312	.1775	.2095
	8	.0000	.0000	.0000	.0001	.0011	.0047	.0142	.0336	.0656	.1089	.1571
	9	.0000	.0000	.0000	.0000	.0001	.0009	.0034	.0101	.0243	.0495	.0873
	10	.0000	.0000	.0000	.0000	.0000	.0001	.0006	.0022	.0065	.0162	.0349
	11	.0000	.0000	.0000	.0000	.0000	.0000	.0001	.0003	.0012	.0036	.0095
	12	.0000	.0000	.0000	.0000	.0000	.0000	.0000	.0000	.0001	.0005	.0016
	13	.0000	.0000	.0000	.0000	.0000	.0000	.0000	.0000	.0000	.0001	.0001
14	0	.8687	.4877	.2288	.1028	.0440	.0178	.0068	.0024	.0008	.0002	.0001
	1	.1229	.3593	.3559	.2539	.1539	.0832	.0407	.0181	.0073	.0027	.0009
	2	.0081	.1229	.2570	.2912	.2501	.1802	.1134	.0634	.0317	.0141	.0056
	3	.0003	.0259	.1142	.2056	.2501	.2402	.1943	.1366	.0845	.0462	.0222
	4	.0000	.0037	.0349	.0998	.1720	.2202	.2290	.2022	.1549	.1040	.0611
	5	.0000	.0004	.0078	.0352	.0860	.1468	.1963	.2178	.2066	.1701	.1222
	6	.0000	.0000	.0013	.0093	.0322	.0734	.1262	.1759	.2066	.2088	.1833
	7	.0000	.0000	.0002	.0019	.0092	.0280	.0618	.1082	.1574	.1952	.2095
	8	.0000	.0000	.0000	.0003	.0020	.0082	.0232	.0510	.0918	.1398	.1833
	9	.0000	.0000	.0000	.0000	.0003	.0018	.0066	.0183	.0408	.0762	.1222
	10	.0000	.0000	.0000	.0000	.0000	.0003	.0014	.0049	.0136	.0312	.0611
	11	.0000	.0000	.0000	.0000	.0000	.0000	.0002	.0010	.0033	.0093	.0222
	12	.0000	.0000	.0000	.0000	.0000	.0000	.0000	.0001	.0005	.0019	.0056
	13	.0000	.0000	.0000	.0000	.0000	.0000	.0000	.0000	.0001	.0002	.0009
	14	.0000	.0000	.0000	.0000	.0000	.0000	.0000	.0000	.0000	.0000	.0001
15	0	.8601	.4633	.2059	.0874	.0352	.0134	.0047	.0016	.0005	.0001	.0000
	1	.1303	.3658	.3432	.2312	.1319	.0668	.0305	.0126	.0047	.0016	.0005
	2	.0092	.1348	.2669	.2856	.2309	.1559	.0916	.0476	.0219	.0090	.0032
	3	.0004	.0307	.1285	.2184	.2501	.2252	.1700	.1110	.0634	.0318	.0139
	4	.0000	.0049	.0428	.1156	.1876	.2252	.2186	.1792	.1268	.0780	.0417
	5	.0000	.0006	.0105	.0449	.1032	.1651	.2061	.2123	.1859	.1404	.0916
	6	.0000	.0000	.0019	.0132	.0430	.0917	.1472	.1906	.2066	.1914	.1527
	7	.0000	.0000	.0003	.0030	.0138	.0393	.0811	.1319	.1771	.2013	.1964
	8	.0000	.0000	.0000	.0005	.0035	.0131	.0348	.0710	.1181	.1647	.1964
	9	.0000	.0000	.0000	.0001	.0007	.0034	.0116	.0298	.0612	.1048	.1527
	10	.0000	.0000	.0000	.0000	.0001	.0007	.0030	.0096	.0245	.0515	.0916
	11	.0000	.0000	.0000	.0000	.0000	.0001	.0006	.0024	.0074	.0191	.0417
	12	.0000	.0000	.0000	.0000	.0000	.0000	.0001	.0004	.0016	.0052	.0139
	13	.0000	.0000	.0000	.0000	.0000	.0000	.0000	.0001	.0003	.0010	.0032
	14	.0000	.0000	.0000	.0000	.0000	.0000	.0000	.0000	.0000	.0001	.0005
	15	.0000	.0000	.0000	.0000	.0000	.0000	.0000	.0000	.0000	.0000	.0000
16	0	.8515	.4401	.1853	.0743	.0281	.0100	.0033	.0010	.0003	.0001	.0000
	1	.1376	.3706	.3294	.2097	.1126	.0535	.0228	.0087	.0030	.0009	.0002
	2	.0104	.1463	.2745	.2775	.2111	.1336	.0732	.0353	.0150	.0056	.0018
	3	.0005	.0359	.1423	.2285	.2463	.2079	.1465	.0888	.0468	.0215	.0085
	4	.0000	.0061	.0514	.1311	.2001	.2252	.2040	.1553	.1014	.0572	.0278
	5	.0000	.0008	.0137	.0555	.1201	.1802	.2099	.2008	.1623	.1123	.0667
	6	.0000	.0001	.0028	.0180	.0550	.1101	.1649	.1982	.1983	.1684	.1222
	7	.0000	.0000	.0004	.0045	.0197	.0524	.1010	.1524	.1889	.1969	.1746
	8	.0000	.0000	.0001	.0009	.0055	.0197	.0487	.0923	.1417	.1812	.1964
	9	.0000	.0000	.0000	.0001	.0012	.0058	.0185	.0442	.0840	.1318	.1746
	10	.0000	.0000	.0000	.0000	.0002	.0014	.0056	.0167	.0392	.0755	.1222
	11	.0000	.0000	.0000	.0000	.0000	.0002	.0013	.0049	.0142	.0337	.0667
	12	.0000	.0000	.0000	.0000	.0000	.0000	.0002	.0011	.0040	.0115	.0278
	13	.0000	.0000	.0000	.0000	.0000	.0000	.0000	.0002	.0008	.0029	.0085
	14	.0000	.0000	.0000	.0000	.0000	.0000	.0000	.0000	.0001	.0005	.0018
	15	.0000	.0000	.0000	.0000	.0000	.0000	.0000	.0000	.0000	.0001	.0002
	16	.0000	.0000	.0000	.0000	.0000	.0000	.0000	.0000	.0000	.0000	.0000
17	0	.8429	.4181	.1668	.0631	.0225	.0075	.0023	.0007	.0002	.0000	.0000
	1	.1447	.3741	.3150	.1893	.0957	.0426	.0169	.0060	.0019	.0005	.0001
	2	.0117	.1575	.2800	.2673	.1914	.1136	.0581	.0260	.0102	.0035	.0010
	3	.0006	.0415	.1556	.2359	.2393	.1893	.1245	.0701	.0341	.0144	.0052
	4	.0000	.0076	.0605	.1457	.2093	.2209	.1868	.1320	.0796	.0411	.0182
	5	.0000	.0010	.0175	.0668	.1361	.1914	.2081	.1849	.1379	.0875	.0472
	6	.0000	.0001	.0039	.0236	.0680	.1276	.1784	.1991	.1839	.1432	.0944
	7	.0000	.0000	.0007	.0065	.0267	.0668	.1201	.1685	.1927	.1841	.1484
	8	.0000	.0000	.0001	.0014	.0084	.0279	.0644	.1134	.1606	.1883	.1855
	9	.0000	.0000	.0000	.0003	.0021	.0093	.0276	.0611	.1070	.1540	.1855
	10	.0000	.0000	.0000	.0000	.0004	.0025	.0095	.0263	.0571	.1008	.1484
	11	.0000	.0000	.0000	.0000	.0001	.0005	.0026	.0090	.0242	.0525	.0944
	12	.0000	.0000	.0000	.0000	.0000	.0001	.0006	.0024	.0081	.0215	.0472
	13	.0000	.0000	.0000	.0000	.0000	.0000	.0001	.0005	.0021	.0068	.0182
	14	.0000	.0000	.0000	.0000	.0000	.0000	.0000	.0001	.0004	.0016	.0052
	15	.0000	.0000	.0000	.0000	.0000	.0000	.0000	.0000	.0000	.0003	.0010
	16	.0000	.0000	.0000	.0000	.0000	.0000	.0000	.0000	.0000	.0000	.0001
	17	.0000	.0000	.0000	.0000	.0000	.0000	.0000	.0000	.0000	.0000	.0000
18	0	.8345	.3972	.1501	.0536	.0180	.0056	.0016	.0004	.0001	.0000	.0000
	1	.1517	.3763	.3002	.1704	.0811	.0338	.0126	.0042	.0012	.0003	.0001
	2	.0130	.1683	.2835	.2556	.1723	.0958	.0458	.0190	.0069	.0022	.0006
	3	.0007	.0473	.1680	.2406	.2297	.1704	.1046	.0547	.0246	.0095	.0031
	4	.0000	.0093	.0700	.1592	.2153	.2130	.1681	.1104	.0614	.0291	.0117
	5	.0000	.0014	.0218	.0787	.1507	.1988	.2017	.1664	.1146	.0666	.0327
	6	.0000	.0002	.0052	.0301	.0816	.1436	.1873	.1941	.1655	.1181	.0708
	7	.0000	.0000	.0010	.0091	.0350	.0820	.1376	.1792	.1892	.1657	.1214
	8	.0000	.0000	.0002	.0022	.0120	.0376	.0811	.1327	.1734	.1864	.1669
	9	.0000	.0000	.0000	.0004	.0033	.0139	.0386	.0794	.1284	.1694	.1855
	10	.0000	.0000	.0000	.0001	.0008	.0042	.0149	.0385	.0771	.1248	.1669
	11	.0000	.0000	.0000	.0000	.0001	.0010	.0046	.0151	.0374	.0742	.1214
	12	.0000	.0000	.0000	.0000	.0000	.0002	.0012	.0047	.0145	.0354	.0708
	13	.0000	.0000	.0000	.0000	.0000	.0000	.0002	.0012	.0045	.0134	.0327
	14	.0000	.0000	.0000	.0000	.0000	.0000	.0000	.0002	.0011	.0039	.0117
	15	.0000	.0000	.0000	.0000	.0000	.0000	.0000	.0000	.0002	.0009	.0031
	16	.0000	.0000	.0000	.0000	.0000	.0000	.0000	.0000	.0000	.0001	.0006
	17	.0000	.0000	.0000	.0000	.0000	.0000	.0000	.0000	.0000	.0000	.0001
	18	.0000	.0000	.0000	.0000	.0000	.0000	.0000	.0000	.0000	.0000	.0000

Table (upper/right block), probabilities by p:

.50	.45	.40	.35	.30	.25	.20	.15	.10	.05	.01	x	n
.0016	.0063	.0199	.0506	.1030	.1645	.1960	.1564	.0646	.0060	.0000	5	25
.0053	.0172	.0442	.0908	.1472	.1828	.1633	.0920	.0239	.0010	.0000	6	
.0143	.0381	.0800	.1327	.1712	.1654	.1108	.0441	.0072	.0001	.0000	7	
.0322	.0701	.1200	.1607	.1651	.1241	.0623	.0175	.0018	.0000	.0000	8	
.0609	.1084	.1511	.1635	.1336	.0781	.0294	.0058	.0004	.0000	.0000	9	
.0974	.1419	.1612	.1409	.0916	.0417	.0118	.0016	.0000	.0000	.0000	10	
.1328	.1583	.1465	.1034	.0536	.0189	.0040	.0004	.0000	.0000	.0000	11	
.1550	.1511	.1140	.0650	.0268	.0074	.0012	.0000	.0000	.0000	.0000	12	
.1550	.1236	.0760	.0350	.0115	.0025	.0003	.0000	.0000	.0000	.0000	13	
.1328	.0867	.0434	.0161	.0042	.0007	.0000	.0000	.0000	.0000	.0000	14	
.0974	.0520	.0212	.0064	.0013	.0002	.0000	.0000	.0000	.0000	.0000	15	
.0609	.0266	.0088	.0021	.0004	.0000	.0000	.0000	.0000	.0000	.0000	16	
.0322	.0115	.0031	.0006	.0001	.0000	.0000	.0000	.0000	.0000	.0000	17	
.0143	.0042	.0009	.0001	.0000	.0000	.0000	.0000	.0000	.0000	.0000	18	
.0053	.0013	.0002	.0000	.0000	.0000	.0000	.0000	.0000	.0000	.0000	19	
.0016	.0001	.0000	.0000	.0000	.0000	.0000	.0000	.0000	.0000	.0000	20	
.0004	.0000	.0000	.0000	.0000	.0000	.0000	.0000	.0000	.0000	.0000	21	
.0001	.0000	.0000	.0000	.0000	.0000	.0000	.0000	.0000	.0000	.0000	22	
.0000	.0000	.0000	.0000	.0000	.0002	.0012	.0076	.0424	.2146	.7397	0	30
.0000	.0000	.0000	.0000	.0003	.0018	.0093	.0404	.1413	.3389	.2242	1	
.0000	.0000	.0000	.0003	.0018	.0086	.0337	.1034	.2277	.2586	.0328	2	
.0000	.0000	.0003	.0015	.0072	.0269	.0785	.1703	.2361	.1270	.0031	3	
.0000	.0002	.0012	.0056	.0208	.0604	.1325	.2028	.1771	.0451	.0002	4	
.0001	.0008	.0041	.0157	.0464	.1047	.1723	.1861	.1023	.0124	.0000	5	
.0006	.0029	.0115	.0353	.0829	.1455	.1795	.1368	.0474	.0027	.0000	6	
.0019	.0081	.0263	.0652	.1219	.1662	.1538	.0828	.0180	.0005	.0000	7	
.0055	.0191	.0505	.1009	.1501	.1593	.1106	.0420	.0058	.0001	.0000	8	
.0133	.0382	.0823	.1328	.1573	.1298	.0676	.0181	.0016	.0000	.0000	9	
.0280	.0656	.1152	.1502	.1416	.0909	.0355	.0067	.0004	.0000	.0000	10	
.0509	.0976	.1396	.1471	.1103	.0551	.0161	.0022	.0001	.0000	.0000	11	
.0806	.1265	.1474	.1254	.0749	.0291	.0064	.0006	.0000	.0000	.0000	12	
.1115	.1433	.1360	.0935	.0444	.0134	.0022	.0001	.0000	.0000	.0000	13	
.1354	.1424	.1101	.0611	.0231	.0054	.0007	.0000	.0000	.0000	.0000	14	
.1445	.1242	.0783	.0351	.0106	.0019	.0002	.0000	.0000	.0000	.0000	15	
.1354	.0953	.0489	.0177	.0042	.0006	.0000	.0000	.0000	.0000	.0000	16	
.1115	.0642	.0269	.0079	.0015	.0002	.0000	.0000	.0000	.0000	.0000	17	
.0806	.0379	.0129	.0031	.0005	.0000	.0000	.0000	.0000	.0000	.0000	18	
.0509	.0196	.0054	.0010	.0001	.0000	.0000	.0000	.0000	.0000	.0000	19	
.0280	.0088	.0020	.0003	.0000	.0000	.0000	.0000	.0000	.0000	.0000	20	
.0133	.0034	.0006	.0001	.0000	.0000	.0000	.0000	.0000	.0000	.0000	21	
.0055	.0012	.0002	.0000	.0000	.0000	.0000	.0000	.0000	.0000	.0000	22	
.0019	.0003	.0000	.0000	.0000	.0000	.0000	.0000	.0000	.0000	.0000	23	
.0006	.0001	.0000	.0000	.0000	.0000	.0000	.0000	.0000	.0000	.0000	24	
.0001	.0000	.0000	.0000	.0000	.0000	.0000	.0000	.0000	.0000	.0000	25	

Table (lower/left block), probabilities by p:

n	x	.01	.05	.10	.15	.20	.25	.30	.35	.40	.45	.50
19	0	.8262	.3774	.1351	.0456	.0144	.0042	.0011	.0003	.0001	.0000	.0000
	1	.1586	.3774	.2852	.1529	.0685	.0268	.0093	.0029	.0008	.0002	.0000
	2	.0144	.1787	.2852	.2428	.1540	.0803	.0358	.0138	.0046	.0013	.0003
	3	.0008	.0533	.1796	.2428	.2182	.1517	.0869	.0422	.0175	.0062	.0018
	4	.0000	.0112	.0798	.1714	.2182	.2023	.1491	.0909	.0467	.0203	.0074
	5	.0000	.0018	.0266	.0907	.1636	.2023	.1916	.1468	.0933	.0497	.0222
	6	.0000	.0002	.0069	.0374	.0955	.1574	.1916	.1844	.1451	.0949	.0518
	7	.0000	.0000	.0014	.0122	.0443	.0974	.1525	.1844	.1797	.1443	.0961
	8	.0000	.0000	.0002	.0032	.0166	.0487	.0981	.1489	.1797	.1771	.1442
	9	.0000	.0000	.0000	.0007	.0051	.0198	.0514	.0980	.1464	.1771	.1762
	10	.0000	.0000	.0000	.0001	.0013	.0066	.0220	.0528	.0976	.1449	.1762
	11	.0000	.0000	.0000	.0000	.0003	.0018	.0077	.0233	.0532	.0970	.1442
	12	.0000	.0000	.0000	.0000	.0000	.0004	.0022	.0083	.0237	.0529	.0961
	13	.0000	.0000	.0000	.0000	.0000	.0001	.0005	.0024	.0085	.0233	.0518
	14	.0000	.0000	.0000	.0000	.0000	.0000	.0001	.0006	.0024	.0082	.0222
	15	.0000	.0000	.0000	.0000	.0000	.0000	.0000	.0001	.0005	.0022	.0074
	16	.0000	.0000	.0000	.0000	.0000	.0000	.0000	.0000	.0001	.0005	.0018
	17	.0000	.0000	.0000	.0000	.0000	.0000	.0000	.0000	.0000	.0001	.0003
	18	.0000	.0000	.0000	.0000	.0000	.0000	.0000	.0000	.0000	.0000	.0000
	19	.0000	.0000	.0000	.0000	.0000	.0000	.0000	.0000	.0000	.0000	.0000
20	0	.8179	.3585	.1216	.0388	.0115	.0032	.0008	.0002	.0000	.0000	.0000
	1	.1652	.3774	.2702	.1368	.0576	.0211	.0068	.0020	.0005	.0001	.0000
	2	.0159	.1887	.2852	.2293	.1369	.0669	.0278	.0100	.0031	.0008	.0002
	3	.0010	.0596	.1901	.2428	.2054	.1339	.0716	.0323	.0123	.0040	.0011
	4	.0000	.0133	.0898	.1821	.2182	.1897	.1304	.0738	.0350	.0139	.0046
	5	.0000	.0022	.0319	.1028	.1746	.2023	.1789	.1272	.0746	.0365	.0148
	6	.0000	.0003	.0089	.0454	.1091	.1686	.1916	.1712	.1244	.0746	.0370
	7	.0000	.0000	.0020	.0160	.0545	.1124	.1643	.1844	.1659	.1221	.0739
	8	.0000	.0000	.0004	.0046	.0222	.0609	.1144	.1614	.1797	.1623	.1201
	9	.0000	.0000	.0001	.0011	.0074	.0271	.0654	.1158	.1597	.1771	.1602
	10	.0000	.0000	.0000	.0002	.0020	.0099	.0308	.0686	.1171	.1593	.1762
	11	.0000	.0000	.0000	.0000	.0005	.0030	.0120	.0336	.0710	.1185	.1602
	12	.0000	.0000	.0000	.0000	.0001	.0008	.0039	.0136	.0355	.0727	.1201
	13	.0000	.0000	.0000	.0000	.0000	.0002	.0010	.0045	.0146	.0366	.0739
	14	.0000	.0000	.0000	.0000	.0000	.0000	.0002	.0012	.0049	.0150	.0370
	15	.0000	.0000	.0000	.0000	.0000	.0000	.0000	.0003	.0013	.0049	.0148
	16	.0000	.0000	.0000	.0000	.0000	.0000	.0000	.0000	.0003	.0013	.0046
	17	.0000	.0000	.0000	.0000	.0000	.0000	.0000	.0000	.0000	.0002	.0011
	18	.0000	.0000	.0000	.0000	.0000	.0000	.0000	.0000	.0000	.0000	.0002
	19	.0000	.0000	.0000	.0000	.0000	.0000	.0000	.0000	.0000	.0000	.0000
	20	.0000	.0000	.0000	.0000	.0000	.0000	.0000	.0000	.0000	.0000	.0000
25	0	.7778	.2774	.0718	.0172	.0038	.0008	.0001	.0000	.0000	.0000	.0000
	1	.1964	.3650	.1994	.0759	.0236	.0063	.0014	.0003	.0000	.0000	.0000
	2	.0238	.2305	.2659	.1607	.0708	.0251	.0074	.0018	.0004	.0001	.0001
	3	.0018	.0930	.2265	.2174	.1358	.0641	.0243	.0076	.0019	.0004	.0001
	4	.0001	.0269	.1384	.2110	.1867	.1175	.0572	.0224	.0071	.0018	.0004

APPENDIX 3

Values of $e^{-\lambda}$

λ	$e^{-\lambda}$	λ	$e^{-\lambda}$
0.0	1.00000	2.5	.08208
0.1	.90484	2.6	.07427
0.2	.81873	2.7	.06721
0.3	.74082	2.8	.06081
0.4	.67032	2.9	.05502
0.5	.60653	3.0	.04979
0.6	.54881	3.2	.04076
0.7	.49659	3.4	.03337
0.8	.44933	3.6	.02732
0.9	.40657	3.8	.02237
1.0	.36788	4.0	.01832
1.1	.33287	4.2	.01500
1.2	.30119	4.4	.01228
1.3	.27253	4.6	.01005
1.4	.24660	4.8	.00823
1.5	.22313	5.0	.00674
1.6	.20190	5.5	.00409
1.7	.18268	6.0	.00248
1.8	.16530	6.5	.00150
1.9	.14957	7.0	.00091
2.0	.13534	7.5	.00055
2.1	.12246	8.0	.00034
2.2	.00180	8.5	.00020
2.3	.10026	9.0	.00012
2.4	.09072	10.0	.00005

Poisson Probabilities

	λ									
X	0.1	0.2	0.3	0.4	0.5	0.6	0.7	0.8	0.9	1.0
0	.9048	.8187	.7408	.6703	.6065	.5488	.4966	.4493	.4066	.3679
1	.0905	.1637	.2222	.2681	.3033	.3293	.3476	.3595	.3659	.3679
2	.0045	.0164	.0333	.0536	.0758	.0988	.1217	.1438	.1647	.1839
3	.0002	.0011	.0033	.0072	.0126	.0198	.0284	.0383	.0494	.0613
4	.0000	.0001	.0002	.0007	.0016	.0030	.0050	.0077	.0111	.0153
5	.0000	.0000	.0000	.0001	.0002	.0004	.0007	.0012	.0020	.0031
6	.0000	.0000	.0000	.0000	.0000	.0000	.0001	.0002	.0003	.0005
7	.0000	.0000	.0000	.0000	.0000	.0000	.0000	.0000	.0000	.0001

	λ									
X	1.1	1.2	1.3	1.4	1.5	1.6	1.7	1.8	1.9	2.0
0	.3329	.3012	.2725	.2466	.2231	.2019	.1827	.1653	.1496	.1353
1	.3662	.3614	.3543	.3452	.3347	.3230	.3106	.2975	.2842	.2707
2	.2014	.2169	.2303	.2417	.2510	.2584	.2640	.2678	.2700	.2707
3	.0738	.0867	.0998	.1128	.1255	.1378	.1496	.1607	.1710	.1804
4	.0203	.0260	.0324	.0395	.0471	.0551	.0636	.0723	.0812	.0902
5	.0045	.0062	.0084	.0111	.0141	.0176	.0216	.0260	.0309	.0361
6	.0008	.0012	.0018	.0026	.0035	.0047	.0061	.0078	.0098	.0120
7	.0001	.0002	.0003	.0005	.0008	.0011	.0015	.0020	.0027	.0034
8	.0000	.0000	.0001	.0001	.0001	.0002	.0003	.0005	.0006	.0009
9	.0000	.0000	.0000	.0000	.0000	.0000	.0001	.0001	.0001	.0002

	λ									
X	2.1	2.2	2.3	2.4	2.5	2.6	2.7	2.8	2.9	3.0
0	.1225	.1108	.1003	.0907	.0821	.0743	.0672	.0608	.0550	.0498
1	.2572	.2438	.2306	.2177	.2052	.1931	.1815	.1703	.1396	.1494
2	.2700	.2681	.2652	.2613	.2565	.2510	.2450	.2384	.2314	.2240

Example: $P(X = 2 | \lambda = 2.5) = 0.2565$

					λ					
X	2.1	2.2	2.3	2.4	2.5	2.6	2.7	2.8	2.9	3.0
3	.1890	.1966	.2033	.2090	.2138	.2176	.2205	.2225	.2237	.2240
4	.0992	.1082	.1169	.1254	.1336	.1414	.1488	.1557	.1622	.1680
5	.0417	.0476	.0538	.0602	.0668	.0735	.0804	.0872	.0940	.1008
6	.0146	.0174	.0206	.0241	.0278	.0319	.0362	.0407	.0455	.0504
7	.0044	.0055	.0068	.0083	.0099	.0118	.0139	.0163	.0188	.0216
8	.0011	.0015	.0019	.0025	.0031	.0038	.0047	.0057	.0068	.0081
9	.0003	.0004	.0005	.0007	.0009	.0011	.0014	.0018	.0022	.0027
10	.0001	.0001	.0001	.0002	.0002	.0003	.0004	.0005	.0006	.0008
11	.0000	.0000	.0000	.0000	.0000	.0001	.0001	.0001	.0002	.0002
12	.0000	.0000	.0000	.0000	.0000	.0000	.0000	.0000	.0000	.0001

					λ					
X	3.1	3.2	3.3	3.4	3.5	3.6	3.7	3.8	3.9	4.0
0	.0450	.0408	.0369	.0334	.0302	.0273	.0247	.0224	.0202	.0183
1	.1397	.1304	.1217	.1135	.1057	.0984	.0915	.0850	.0789	.0733
2	.2165	.2087	.2008	.1929	.1850	.1771	.1692	.1615	.1539	.1465
3	.2237	.2226	.2209	.2186	.2158	.2125	.2087	.2046	.2001	.1954
4	.1734	.1781	.1823	.1858	.1888	.1912	.1931	.1944	.1951	.1954
5	.1075	.1140	.1203	.1264	.1322	.1377	.1429	.1477	.1522	.1563
6	.0555	.0608	.0662	.0716	.0771	.0826	.0881	.0936	.0989	.1042
7	.0246	.0278	.0312	.0348	.0385	.0425	.0466	.0508	.0551	.0595
8	.0095	.0111	.0129	.0148	.0169	.0191	.0215	.0241	.0269	.0298
9	.0033	.0040	.0047	.0056	.0066	.0076	.0089	.0102	.0116	.0132
10	.0010	.0013	.0016	.0019	.0023	.0028	.0033	.0039	.0045	.0053
11	.0003	.0004	.0005	.0006	.0007	.0009	.0011	.0013	.0016	.0019
12	.0001	.0001	.0001	.0002	.0002	.0003	.0003	.0004	.0005	.0006
13	.0000	.0000	.0000	.0000	.0001	.0001	.0001	.0001	.0002	.0002
14	.0000	.0000	.0000	.0000	.0000	.0000	.0000	.0000	.0000	.0001

					λ					
X	4.1	4.2	4.3	4.4	4.5	4.6	4.7	4.8	4.9	5.0
0	.0166	.0150	.0136	.0123	.0111	.0101	.0091	.0082	.0074	.0067
1	.0679	.0630	.0583	.0540	.0500	.0462	.0427	.0395	.0365	.0337
2	.1393	.1323	.1254	.1188	.1125	.1063	.1005	.0948	.0894	.0842
3	.1904	.1852	.1798	.1743	.1687	.1631	.1574	.1517	.1460	.1404
4	.1951	.1944	.1933	.1917	.1898	.1875	.1849	.1820	.1789	.1755
5	.1600	.1633	.1662	.1687	.1708	.1725	.1738	.1747	.1753	.1755
6	.1093	.1143	.1191	.1237	.1281	.1323	.1362	.1398	.1432	.1462
7	.0640	.0686	.0732	.0778	.0824	.0869	.0914	.0959	.1002	.1044
8	.0328	.0360	.0393	.0428	.0463	.0500	.0537	.0575	.0614	.0653
9	.0150	.0168	.0188	.0209	.0232	.0255	.0280	.0307	.0334	.0363
10	.0061	.0071	.0081	.0092	.0104	.0118	.0132	.0147	.0164	.0181
11	.0023	.0027	.0032	.0037	.0043	.0049	.0056	.0064	.0073	.0082
12	.0008	.0009	.0011	.0014	.0016	.0019	.0022	.0026	.0030	.0034

X	λ 4.1	4.2	4.3	4.4	4.5	λ 4.6	4.7	4.8	4.9	5.0
13	.0002	.0003	.0004	.0005	.0006	.0007	.0008	.0009	.0011	.0013
14	.0001	.0001	.0001	.0001	.0002	.0002	.0003	.0003	.0004	.0005
15	.0000	.0000	.0000	.0000	.0001	.0001	.0001	.0001	.0001	.0002

X	λ 5.1	5.2	5.3	5.4	5.5	λ 5.6	5.7	5.8	5.9	6.0
0	.0061	.0055	.0050	.0045	.0041	.0037	.0033	.0030	.0027	.0025
1	.0311	.0287	.0265	.0244	0255	.0207	.0191	.0176	.0162	.0149
2	.0793	.0746	.0701	.0659	.0618	.0580	.0544	.0509	.0477	.0446
3	.1348	.1293	.1239	.1185	.1133	.1082	.1033	.0985	.0938	.0892
4	.1719	.1681	.1641	.1600	.1558	.1515	.1472	.1428	.1383	.1339
5	.1753	.1748	.1740	.1728	.1714	.1697	.1678	.1656	.1632	.1606
6	.1490	.1515	.1537	.1555	.1571	.1584	.1594	.1601	.1605	.1606
7	.1086	.1125	.1163	.1200	.1234	.1267	.1298	.1326	.1353	.1377
8	.0692	.0731	.0771	.0810	.0849	.0887	.0925	.0962	.0998	.1033
9	.0392	.0423	.0454	.0486	.0519	.0552	.0586	.0620	.0654	.0688
10	.0200	.0220	.0241	.0262	.0285	.0309	.0334	.0359	.0386	.0413
11	.0093	.0104	.0116	.0129	.0143	.0157	.0173	.0190	.0207	.0225
12	.0039	.0045	.0051	.0058	.0065	.0073	.0082	.0092	.0102	.0113
13	.0015	.0018	.0021	.0024	.0028	.0032	.0036	.0041	.0046	.0052
14	.0006	.0007	.0008	.0009	.0011	.0013	.0015	.0017	.0019	.0022
15	.0002	.0002	.0003	.0003	.0004	.0005	.0006	.0007	.0008	.0009
16	.0001	.0001	.0001	.0001	.0001	.0002	.0002	.0002	.0003	.0003
17	.0000	.0000	.0000	.0000	.0000	.0001	.0001	.0001	.0001	.0001

X	λ 6.1	6.2	6.3	6.4	6.5	λ 6.6	6.7	6.8	6.9	7.0
0	.0022	.0020	.0018	.0017	.0015	.0014	.0012	.0011	.0010	.0009
1	.0137	.0126	.0116	.0106	.0098	.0090	.0082	.0076	.0070	.0064
2	.0417	.0390	.0364	.0340	.0318	.0296	.0276	.0258	.0240	.0223
3	.0848	.0806	.0765	.0726	.0688	.0652	.0617	.0584	.0552	.0521
4	.1294	.1249	.1205	.1162	.1118	.1076	.1034	.0992	.0952	.0912
5	.1579	.1549	.1519	.1487	.1454	.1420	.1385	.1349	.1314	.1277
6	.1605	.1601	.1595	.1586	.1575	.1562	.1546	.1529	.1511	.1490
7	.1399	.1418	.1435	.1450	.1462	.1472	.1480	.1486	.1489	.1490
8	.1066	.1099	.1130	.1160	.1188	.1215	.1240	.1263	.1284	.1304
9	.0723	.0757	.0791	.0825	.0858	.0891	.0923	.0954	.0985	.1014
10	.0441	.0469	.0498	.0528	.0558	.0558	.0618	.0649	.0679	.0710
11	.0245	.0265	.0285	.0307	.0330	.0353	.0377	.0401	.0426	.0452
12	.0124	.0137	.0150	.0164	.0179	.0194	.0210	.0227	.0245	.0262
13	.0058	.0065	.0073	.0081	.0089	.0098	.0108	.0119	.0130	.0142
14	.0025	.0029	.0033	.0037	.0041	.0046	.0052	.0058	.0064	.0071
15	.0010	.0012	.0014	.0016	.0018	.0020	.0023	.0026	.0029	.0033
16	.0004	.0005	.0005	.0006	.0007	.0008	.0010	.0011	.0013	.0014
17	.0001	.0002	.0002	.0002	.0003	.0003	.0004	.0004	.0005	.0006
18	.0000	.0001	.0001	.0001	.0001	.0001	.0001	.0002	.0002	.0002
19	.0000	.0000	.0000	.0000	.0000	.0000	.0000	.0001	.0001	.0001

X	7.1	7.2	7.3	7.4	λ 7.5	7.6	7.7	7.8	7.9	8.0
0	.0008	.0007	.0007	.0006	.0006	.0005	.0005	.0004	.0004	.0003
1	.0059	.0054	.0049	.0045	.0041	.0038	.0035	.0032	.0029	.0027
2	.0208	.0194	.0180	.0167	.0156	.0145	.0134	.0125	.0116	.0107
3	.0492	.0464	.0438	.0413	.0389	.0366	.0345	.0324	.0305	.0286
4	.0874	.0836	.0799	.0764	.0729	.0696	.0663	.0632	.0602	.0573
5	.1241	.1204	.1167	.1130	.1094	.1057	.1021	.0986	.0951	.0916
6	.1468	.1445	.1420	.1394	.1367	.1339	.1311	.1282	.1252	.1221
7	.1489	.1486	.1481	.1474	.1465	.1454	.1442	.1428	.1413	.1396
8	.1321	.1337	.1351	.1363	.1373	.1382	.1388	.1392	.1395	.1396
9	.1042	.1070	.1096	.1121	.1144	.1167	.1187	.1207	.1224	.1241
10	.0740	.0770	.0800	.0829	.0858	.0887	.0914	.0941	.0967	.0993
11	.0478	.0504	.0531	.0558	.0585	.0613	.0640	.0667	.0695	.0722
12	.0283	.0303	.0323	.0344	.0366	.0388	.0411	.0434	.0457	.0481
13	.0154	.0168	.0181	.0196	.0211	.0227	.0243	.0260	.0278	.0296
14	.0078	.0086	.0095	.0104	.0113	.0123	.0134	.0145	.0157	.0169
15	.0037	.0041	.0046	.0051	.0057	.0062	.0069	.0075	.0083	.0090
16	.0016	.0019	.0021	.0024	.0026	.0030	.0033	.0037	.0041	.0045
17	.0007	.0008	.0009	.0010	.0012	.0013	.0015	.0017	.0019	.0021
18	.0003	.0003	.0004	.0004	.0005	.0006	.0006	.0007	.0008	.0009
19	.0001	.0001	.0001	.0002	.0002	.0002	.0003	.0003	.0003	.0004
20	.0000	.0000	.0001	.0001	.0001	.0001	.0001	.0001	.0001	.0002
21	.0000	.0000	.0000	.0000	.0000	.0000	.0000	.0000	.0001	.0001

X	8.1	8.2	8.3	8.4	λ 8.5	8.6	8.7	8.8	8.9	9.0
0	.0003	.0003	.0002	.0002	.0002	.0002	.0002	.0002	.0001	.0001
1	.0025	.0023	.0021	.0019	.0017	.0016	.0014	.0013	.0012	.0011
2	.0100	.0092	.0086	.0079	.0074	.0068	.0063	.0058	.0054	.0050
3	.0269	.0252	.0237	.0222	.0208	.0195	.0183	.0171	.0160	.0150
4	.0544	.0517	.0491	.0466	.0443	.0420	.0398	.0377	.0357	.0337
5	.0882	.0849	.0816	.0784	.0752	.0722	.0692	.0663	.0635	.0607
6	.1191	.1160	.1128	.1097	.1066	.1034	.1003	.0972	.0941	.0911
7	.1378	.1358	.1338	.1317	.1294	.1271	.1247	.1222	.1197	.1171
8	.1395	.1392	.1388	.1382	.1375	.1366	.1356	.1344	.1332	.1318
9	1256	.1269	.1280	.1290	.1299	.1306	.1311	.1315	.1317	.1318
10	.1017	.1040	.1063	.1084	.1104	.1123	.1140	.1157	.1172	.1186
11	.0749	.0776	.0802	.0828	.0853	.0878	.0902	.0925	.0948	.0970
12	.0505	.0530	.0555	.0579	.0604	.0629	.0654	.0679	.0703	.0728
13	.0315	.0334	.0354	.0374	.0395	.0416	.0438	.0459	.0481	.0504
14	.0182	.0196	.0210	.0225	.0240	.0256	.0272	.0289	.0306	.0324
15	.0098	.0107	.0116	.0126	.0136	.0147	.0158	.0169	.0182	.0194
16	.0050	.0055	.0060	.0066	.0072	.0079	.0086	.0093	.0101	.0109
17	.0024	.0026	.0029	.0033	.0036	.0040	.0044	.0048	.0053	.0058
18	.0011	.0012	.0014	.0015	.0017	.0019	.0021	.0024	.0026	.0029
19	.0005	.0005	.0006	.0007	.0008	.0009	.0010	.0011	.0012	.0014

X	8.1	8.2	8.3	8.4	8.5	λ 8.6	8.7	8.8	8.9	9.0
20	.0002	.0002	.0002	.0003	.0003	.0004	.0004	.0005	.0005	.0006
21	.0001	.0001	.0001	.0001	.0001	.0002	.0002	.0002	.0002	.0003
22	.0000	.0000	.0000	.0000	.0001	.0001	.0001	.0001	.0001	.0001

X	9.1	9.2	9.3	9.4	9.5	λ 9.6	9.7	9.8	9.9	10.0
0	.0001	.0001	.0001	.0001	.0001	.0001	.0001	.0001	.0001	.0000
1	.0010	.0009	.0009	.0008	.0007	.0007	.0006	.0005	.0005	.0005
2	.0046	.0043	.0040	.0037	.0034	.0031	.0029	.0027	.0025	.0023
3	.0140	.0131	.0123	.0115	.0107	.0100	.0093	.0087	.0081	.0076
4	.0319	.0302	.0285	.0269	.0254	.0240	.0226	.0213	.0201	.0189
5	.0581	.0555	.0530	.0506	.0483	.0460	.0439	.0418	.0398	.0378
6	.0881	.0851	.0822	.0793	.0764	.0736	.0709	.0682	.0656	.0631
7	.1145	.1118	.1091	.1064	.1037	.1010	.0982	.0955	.0928	.0901
8	.1302	.1286	.1269	.1251	.1232	.1212	.1191	.1170	.1148	.1126
9	.1317	.1315	.1311	.1306	.1300	.1293	.1284	.1274	.1263	.1251
10	.1198	.1210	.1219	.1228	.1235	.1241	.1245	.1249	.1250	.1251
11	.0991	.1012	.1031	.1049	.1067	.1083	.1098	.1112	.1125	.1137
12	.0752	.0776	.0779	.0822	.0844	.0866	.0888	.0908	.0928	.0948
13	.0526	.0549	.0572	.0594	.0617	.0640	.0662	.0685	.0707	.0729
14	.0342	.0361	.0380	.0399	.0419	.0439	.0459	.0479	.0500	.0521
15	.0208	.0221	.0235	.0250	.0265	.0281	.0297	.0313	.0330	.0347
16	.0118	.0127	.0137	.0147	.0157	.0168	.0180	.0192	.0204	.0217
17	.0063	.0069	.0075	.0081	.0088	.0095	.0103	.0111	.0119	.0128
18	.0032	.0053	.0039	.0042	.0046	.0051	.0055	.0060	.0065	.0071
19	.0015	.0017	.0019	.0021	.0023	.0026	.0028	.0031	.0034	.0037
20	.0007	.0008	.0009	.0010	.0011	.0012	.0014	.0015	.0017	.0019
21	.0003	.0003	.0004	.0004	.0005	.0006	.0006	.0007	.0008	.0009
22	.0001	.0001	.0002	.0002	.0002	.0002	.0003	.0003	.0004	.0004
23	.0000	.0001	.0001	.0001	.0001	.0001	.0001	.0001	.0002	.0002
24	.0000	.0000	.0000	.0000	.0000	.0000	.0000	.0001	.0001	.0001

Proportions of Area for the Standard Normal Distribution

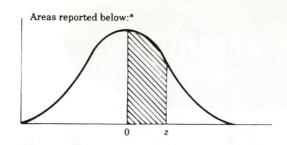

Areas reported below:*

z	.00	.01	.02	.03	.04	.05	.06	.07	.08	.09
0.0	.0000	.0040	.0080	.0120	.0160	.0199	.0239	.0279	.0319	.0359
0.1	.0398	.0438	.0478	.0517	.0557	.0596	.0636	.0675	.0714	.0753
0.2	.0793	.0832	.0871	.0910	.0948	.0987	.1026	.1064	.1103	.1141
0.3	.1179	.1217	.1255	.1293	.1331	.1368	.1406	.1443	.1480	.1517
0.4	.1554	.1591	.1628	.1664	.1700	.1736	.1772	.1808	.1844	.1879
0.5	.1915	.1950	.1985	.2019	.2054	.2088	.2123	.2157	.2190	.2224
0.6	.2257	.2291	.2324	.2357	.2389	.2422	.2454	.2486	.2518	.2549
0.7	.2580	.2612	.2642	.2673	.2704	.2734	.2764	.2794	.2823	.2852
0.8	.2881	.2910	.2939	.2967	.2995	.3023	.3051	.3078	.3106	.3133
0.9	.3159	.3186	.3212	.3238	.3264	.3289	.3315	.3340	.3365	.3389
1.0	.3413	.3438	.3461	.3485	.3508	.3531	.3554	.3577	.3599	.3621
1.1	.3643	.3665	.3686	.3708	.3729	.3749	.3770	.3790	.3810	.3830
1.2	.3849	.3869	.3888	.3907	.3925	.3944	.3962	.3980	.3997	.4014
1.3	.4032	.4049	.4066	.4082	.4099	.4115	.4131	.4147	.4162	.4177
1.4	.4192	.4207	.4222	.4236	.4251	.4265	.4279	.4292	.4306	.4319
1.5	.4332	.4345	.4357	.4370	.4382	.4394	.4406	.4418	.4429	.4441
1.6	.4452	.4463	.4474	.4484	.4495	.4505	.4515	.4525	.4535	.4545
1.7	.4554	.4564	.4573	.4582	.4591	.4599	.4608	.4616	.4625	.4633
1.8	.4641	.4649	.4656	.4664	.4671	.4678	.4686	.4693	.4699	.4706
1.9	.4713	.4719	.4725	.4732	.4738	.4744	.4750	.4756	.4761	.4767
2.0	.4772	.4778	.4783	.4788	.4793	.4798	.4803	.4808	.4812	.4817
2.1	.4821	.4826	.4830	.4834	.4838	.4842	.4846	.4850	.4854	.4857
2.2	.4861	.4864	.4868	.4871	.4875	.4878	.4881	.4884	.4887	.4890
2.3	.4893	.4896	.4898	.4901	.4904	.4906	.4909	.4911	.4913	.4916
2.4	.4918	.4920	.4922	.4925	.4927	.4929	.4931	.4932	.4934	.4936
2.5	.4938	.4940	.4941	.4943	.4945	.4946	.4948	.4949	.4951	.4952
2.6	.4953	.4955	.4956	.4957	.4959	.4960	.4961	.4962	.4963	.4964
2.7	.4965	.4966	.4967	.4968	.4969	.4970	.4971	.4972	.4973	.4974
2.8	.4974	.4975	.4976	.4977	.4977	.4978	.4979	.4979	.4980	.4981
2.9	.4981	.4982	.4983	.4983	.4984	.4984	.4985	.4985	.4986	.4986
3.0	.4987									
3.5	.4997									
4.0	.4999									

*Example: for $z = 1.96$, shaded area is 0.4750 out of the total area of 1.0000

Proportions of Area for the *t* Distribution

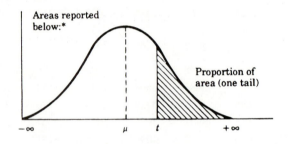

Areas reported below:*

Proportion of area (one tail)

$-\infty$ μ t $+\infty$

df	0.10	0.05	0.025	0.01	0.005	df	0.10	0.05	0.025	0.01	0.005
1	3.078	6.314	12.706	31.821	63.657	18	1.330	1.734	2.101	2.552	2.878
2	1.886	2.920	4.303	6.965	9.925	19	1.328	1.729	2.093	2.539	2.861
3	1.638	2.353	3.182	4.541	5.841	20	1.325	1.725	2.086	2.528	2.845
4	1.533	2.132	2.776	3.747	4.604	21	1.323	1.721	2.080	2.518	2.831
5	1.476	2.015	2.571	3.365	4.032	22	1.321	1.717	2.074	2.508	2.819
6	1.440	1.943	2.447	3.143	3.707	23	1.319	1.714	2.069	2.500	2.807
7	1.415	1.895	2.365	2.998	3.499	24	1.318	1.711	2.064	2.492	2.797
8	1.397	1.860	2.306	2.896	2.355	25	1.316	1.708	2.060	2.485	2.787
9	1.383	1.833	2.262	2.821	3.250	26	1.315	1.706	2.056	2.479	2.779
10	1.372	1.812	2.228	2.764	3.169	27	1.314	1.703	2.052	2.473	2.771
11	1.363	1.796	2.201	2.718	3.106	28	1.313	1.701	2.048	2.467	2.763
12	1.356	1.782	2.179	2.681	3.055	29	1.311	1.699	2.045	2.462	2.756
13	1.350	1.771	2.160	2.650	3.012	30	1.310	1.697	2.042	2.457	2.750
14	1.345	1.761	2.145	2.624	2.977	40	1.303	1.684	2.021	2.423	2.704
15	1.341	1.753	2.131	2.602	2.947	60	1.296	1.671	2.000	2.390	2.660
16	1.337	1.746	2.120	2.583	2.921	120	1.289	1.658	1.980	2.358	2.617
17	1.333	1.740	2.110	2.567	2.898	∞	1.282	1.645	1.960	2.326	2.576

*Example: For the shaded area to represent 0.05 of the total area of 1.0, value of *t* with 10 degrees of freedom is 1.812.

APPENDIX 7

Proportions of Area for the χ^2 Distribution

Areas reported below:*

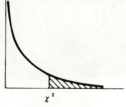 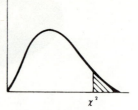

For df = 1,2   For $df \geq 3$

df	Proportion of area										
	0.995	0.990	0.975	0.950	0.900	0.500	0.100	0.050	0.025	0.010	0.005
1	0.00004	0.00016	0.00098	0.00393	0.0158	0.455	2.71	3.84	5.02	6.63	7.88
2	0.0100	0.0201	0.0506	0.103	0.211	1.386	4.61	5.99	7.38	9.21	10.60
3	0.072	0.115	0.216	0.352	0.584	2.366	6.25	7.81	9.35	11.34	12.84
4	0.207	0.297	0.484	0.711	1.064	3.357	7.78	9.49	11.14	13.28	14.86
5	0.412	0.554	0.831	1.145	1.61	4.251	9.24	11.07	12.83	15.09	16.75
6	0.676	0.872	1.24	1.64	2.20	5.35	10.64	12.59	14.45	16.81	18.55
7	0.989	1.24	1.69	2.17	2.83	6.35	12.02	14.07	16.01	18.48	20.28
8	1.34	1.65	2.18	2.73	3.49	7.34	13.36	15.51	17.53	20.09	21.96
9	1.73	2.09	2.70	3.33	4.17	8.34	14.68	16.92	19.02	21.67	23.59
10	2.16	2.56	3.25	3.94	4.87	9.34	15.99	18.31	20.48	23.21	25.19
11	2.60	3.05	3.82	4.57	5.58	10.34	17.28	19.68	21.92	24.73	26.76
12	3.07	3.57	4.40	5.23	6.30	11.34	18.55	21.03	23.34	26.22	28.30
13	3.57	4.11	5.01	5.89	7.04	12.34	19.81	22.36	24.74	27.69	29.82
14	4.07	4.66	5.63	6.57	7.79	13.34	21.06	23.68	26.12	29.14	31.32
15	4.60	5.23	6.26	7.26	8.55	14.34	22.31	25.00	27.49	30.58	32.80
16	5.14	5.81	6.91	7.96	9.31	15.34	23.54	26.30	28.85	32.00	34.27
17	5.70	6.41	7.56	8.67	10.09	16.34	24.77	27.59	30.19	33.41	35.72
18	6.26	7.01	8.23	9.39	10.86	17.34	25.99	28.87	31.53	34.81	37.16
19	6.84	7.63	8.91	10.12	11.65	18.34	27.20	30.14	32.85	36.19	38.58
20	7.43	8.26	9.59	10.85	12.44	19.34	28.41	31.41	34.17	37.57	40.00
21	8.03	8.90	10.28	11.59	13.24	20.34	29.62	32.67	35.48	38.93	41.40
22	8.64	9.54	10.98	12.34	14.04	21.34	30.81	33.92	36.78	40.29	42.80
23	9.26	10.20	11.69	13.09	14.85	22.34	32.01	35.17	38.08	41.64	44.18
24	9.89	10.86	12.40	13.85	15.66	23.34	33.20	36.42	39.36	42.98	45.56
25	10.52	11.52	13.12	14.61	16.47	24.34	34.38	37.65	40.65	44.31	46.93
26	11.16	12.20	13.84	15.38	17.29	25.34	35.56	38.89	41.92	45.64	48.29
27	11.81	12.83	14.57	16.15	18.11	26.34	36.74	40.11	43.19	46.96	49.64
28	12.46	13.56	15.31	16.93	18.94	27.34	37.92	41.34	44.46	48.28	50.99
29	13.12	14.26	16.05	17.71	19.77	28.34	39.09	42.56	45.72	49.59	52.34
30	13.79	14.95	16.79	18.49	20.60	29.34	40.26	43.77	46.98	50.89	53.67
40	20.71	22.16	24.43	26.51	29.05	39.34	51.81	55.76	59.34	63.69	66.77
50	27.99	29.71	32.36	34.76	37.69	49.33	63.17	67.50	71.42	76.15	79.49
60	35.53	37.43	40.48	43.19	46.46	59.33	74.40	79.08	83.30	88.38	91.95
70	43.28	45.44	48.76	51.74	55.33	69.33	85.53	90.53	95.02	100.4	104.2
80	51.17	53.54	51.17	60.39	64.28	79.33	98.58	101.9	106.6	112.3	116.3
90	59.20	61.75	65.65	69.13	73.29	89.33	107.6	113.1	118.1	124.1	128.3
100	67.33	70.06	74.22	77.93	82.36	99.33	118.5	124.3	129.6	135.8	140.2

*Example: For the shaded area to represent 0.05 of the total area of 1.0 under the density function, the value of χ^2 is 18.31 when $df = 10$.

Values of *F* Exceeded with Probabilities of 5% and 1%

df (numerator)

df (denom.)	1	2	3	4	5	6	7	8	9	10	11	12	14	16	20	24	30	40	50	75	100	200	500	∞
1	161	200	216	225	230	234	237	239	241	242	243	244	245	246	248	249	250	251	252	253	253	254	254	254
	4,052	**4,999**	**5,403**	**5,625**	**5,764**	**5,859**	**5,928**	**5,981**	**6,022**	**6,056**	**6,082**	**6,106**	**6,142**	**6,169**	**6,208**	**6,234**	**6,261**	**6,286**	**6,302**	**6,323**	**6,334**	**6,352**	**6,361**	**6,366**
2	18.51	19.00	19.16	19.25	19.30	19.33	19.36	19.37	19.38	19.39	19.40	19.41	19.42	19.43	19.44	19.45	19.46	19.47	19.47	19.48	19.49	19.49	19.50	19.50
	98.49	**99.00**	**99.17**	**99.25**	**99.30**	**99.33**	**99.36**	**99.37**	**99.39**	**99.40**	**99.41**	**99.42**	**99.43**	**99.44**	**99.45**	**99.46**	**99.47**	**99.48**	**99.48**	**99.49**	**99.49**	**99.49**	**99.50**	**99.50**
3	10.13	9.55	9.28	9.12	9.01	8.94	8.88	8.84	8.81	8.78	8.76	8.74	8.71	8.69	8.66	8.64	8.62	8.60	8.58	8.57	8.56	8.54	8.54	8.53
	34.12	**30.82**	**29.46**	**28.71**	**28.24**	**27.91**	**27.67**	**27.49**	**27.34**	**27.23**	**27.13**	**27.05**	**26.92**	**26.83**	**26.69**	**26.60**	**26.50**	**26.41**	**26.35**	**26.27**	**26.23**	**26.18**	**26.14**	**26.12**
4	7.71	6.94	6.59	6.39	6.26	6.16	6.09	6.04	6.00	5.96	5.93	5.91	5.87	5.84	5.80	5.77	5.74	5.71	5.70	5.68	5.66	5.65	5.64	5.63
	21.20	**18.00**	**16.69**	**15.98**	**15.52**	**15.21**	**14.98**	**14.80**	**14.66**	**14.54**	**14.45**	**14.37**	**14.24**	**14.15**	**14.02**	**13.93**	**13.83**	**13.74**	**13.69**	**13.61**	**13.57**	**13.52**	**13.48**	**13.46**
5	6.61	5.79	5.41	5.19	5.05	4.95	4.88	4.82	4.78	4.74	4.70	4.68	4.64	4.60	4.56	4.53	4.50	4.46	4.44	4.42	4.40	4.38	4.37	4.36
	16.26	**13.27**	**12.06**	**11.39**	**10.97**	**10.67**	**10.45**	**10.29**	**10.15**	**10.05**	**9.96**	**9.89**	**9.77**	**9.68**	**9.55**	**9.47**	**9.38**	**9.29**	**9.24**	**9.17**	**9.13**	**9.07**	**9.04**	**9.02**
6	5.99	5.14	4.76	4.53	4.39	4.28	4.21	4.15	4.10	4.06	4.03	4.00	3.96	3.92	3.87	3.84	3.81	3.77	3.75	3.72	3.71	3.69	3.68	3.67
	13.74	**10.92**	**9.78**	**9.15**	**8.75**	**8.47**	**8.26**	**8.10**	**7.98**	**7.87**	**7.79**	**7.72**	**7.60**	**7.52**	**7.39**	**7.31**	**7.23**	**7.14**	**7.09**	**7.02**	**6.99**	**6.94**	**6.90**	**6.88**
7	5.59	4.74	4.34	4.12	3.97	3.87	3.79	3.73	3.68	3.63	3.60	3.57	3.52	3.49	3.44	3.41	3.38	3.34	3.32	3.29	3.28	3.25	3.24	3.23
	12.25	**9.55**	**8.45**	**7.85**	**7.46**	**7.19**	**7.00**	**6.84**	**6.71**	**6.62**	**6.54**	**6.47**	**6.35**	**6.27**	**6.15**	**6.07**	**5.98**	**5.90**	**5.85**	**5.78**	**5.75**	**5.70**	**5.67**	**5.65**
8	5.32	4.46	4.07	3.84	3.69	3.58	3.50	3.44	3.39	3.34	3.31	3.28	3.23	3.20	3.15	3.12	3.08	3.05	3.03	3.00	2.98	2.96	2.94	2.93
	11.26	**8.65**	**7.59**	**7.01**	**6.63**	**6.37**	**6.19**	**6.03**	**5.91**	**5.82**	**5.74**	**5.67**	**5.56**	**5.48**	**5.36**	**5.28**	**5.20**	**5.11**	**5.06**	**5.00**	**4.96**	**4.91**	**4.88**	**4.86**
9	5.12	4.26	3.86	3.63	3.48	3.37	3.29	3.23	3.18	3.13	3.10	3.07	3.02	2.98	2.93	2.90	2.86	2.82	2.80	2.77	2.76	2.73	2.72	2.71
	10.56	**8.02**	**6.99**	**6.42**	**6.06**	**5.80**	**5.62**	**5.47**	**5.35**	**5.26**	**5.18**	**5.11**	**5.00**	**4.92**	**4.80**	**4.73**	**4.64**	**4.56**	**4.51**	**4.45**	**4.41**	**4.36**	**4.33**	**4.31**
10	4.96	4.10	3.71	3.48	3.33	3.22	3.14	3.07	3.02	2.97	2.94	2.91	2.86	2.82	2.77	2.74	2.70	2.67	2.64	2.61	2.59	2.56	2.55	2.54
	10.04	**7.56**	**6.55**	**5.99**	**5.64**	**5.39**	**5.21**	**5.06**	**4.95**	**4.85**	**4.78**	**4.71**	**4.60**	**4.52**	**4.41**	**4.33**	**4.25**	**4.17**	**4.12**	**4.05**	**4.01**	**3.96**	**3.93**	**3.91**
11	4.84	3.98	3.59	3.36	3.20	3.09	3.01	2.95	2.90	2.86	2.82	2.79	2.74	2.70	2.65	2.61	2.57	2.53	2.50	2.47	2.45	2.42	2.41	2.40
	9.65	**7.20**	**6.22**	**5.67**	**5.32**	**5.07**	**4.88**	**4.74**	**4.63**	**4.54**	**4.46**	**4.40**	**4.29**	**4.21**	**4.10**	**4.02**	**3.94**	**3.86**	**3.80**	**3.74**	**3.70**	**3.66**	**3.62**	**3.60**
12	4.75	3.88	3.49	3.26	3.11	3.00	2.92	2.85	2.80	2.76	2.72	2.69	2.64	2.60	2.54	2.50	2.46	2.42	2.40	2.36	2.35	2.32	2.31	2.30
	9.33	**6.93**	**5.95**	**5.41**	**5.06**	**4.82**	**4.65**	**4.50**	**4.39**	**4.30**	**4.22**	**4.16**	**4.05**	**3.98**	**3.86**	**3.78**	**3.70**	**3.61**	**3.56**	**3.49**	**3.46**	**3.41**	**3.38**	**3.36**
13	4.67	3.80	3.41	3.18	3.02	2.92	2.84	2.77	2.72	2.67	2.63	2.60	2.55	2.51	2.46	2.42	2.38	2.34	2.32	2.28	2.26	2.24	2.22	2.21
	9.07	**6.70**	**5.74**	**5.20**	**4.86**	**4.62**	**4.44**	**4.30**	**4.19**	**4.10**	**4.02**	**3.96**	**3.85**	**3.78**	**3.67**	**3.59**	**3.51**	**3.42**	**3.37**	**3.30**	**3.27**	**3.21**	**3.18**	**3.16**
14	4.60	3.74	3.34	3.11	2.96	2.85	2.77	2.70	2.65	2.60	2.56	2.53	2.48	2.44	2.39	2.35	2.31	2.27	2.24	2.21	2.19	2.16	2.14	2.13
	8.86	**6.51**	**5.56**	**5.03**	**4.69**	**4.46**	**4.28**	**4.14**	**4.03**	**3.94**	**3.86**	**3.80**	**3.70**	**3.62**	**3.51**	**3.43**	**3.34**	**3.26**	**3.21**	**3.14**	**3.11**	**3.06**	**3.02**	**3.00**
15	4.54	3.68	3.29	3.06	2.90	2.79	2.70	2.64	2.59	2.55	2.51	2.48	2.43	2.39	2.33	2.29	2.25	2.21	2.18	2.15	2.12	2.10	2.08	2.07
	8.68	**6.36**	**5.42**	**4.89**	**4.56**	**4.32**	**4.14**	**4.00**	**3.89**	**3.80**	**3.73**	**3.67**	**3.56**	**3.48**	**3.36**	**3.29**	**3.20**	**3.12**	**3.07**	**3.00**	**2.97**	**2.92**	**2.89**	**2.87**
16	4.49	3.63	3.24	3.01	2.85	2.74	2.66	2.59	2.54	2.49	2.45	2.42	2.37	2.33	2.28	2.24	2.20	2.16	2.13	2.09	2.07	2.04	2.02	2.01
	8.53	**6.23**	**5.29**	**4.77**	**4.44**	**4.20**	**4.03**	**3.89**	**3.78**	**3.69**	**3.61**	**3.55**	**3.45**	**3.37**	**3.25**	**3.18**	**3.10**	**3.01**	**2.96**	**2.88**	**2.86**	**2.80**	**2.77**	**2.75**
17	4.45	3.59	3.20	2.96	2.81	2.70	2.62	2.55	2.50	2.45	2.41	2.38	2.33	2.29	2.23	2.19	2.15	2.11	2.08	2.04	2.02	1.99	1.97	1.96
	8.40	**6.11**	**5.18**	**4.67**	**4.34**	**4.10**	**3.93**	**3.79**	**3.68**	**3.59**	**3.52**	**3.45**	**3.35**	**3.27**	**3.16**	**3.08**	**3.00**	**2.92**	**2.86**	**2.79**	**2.76**	**2.70**	**2.67**	**2.65**
18	4.41	3.55	3.16	2.93	2.77	2.66	2.58	2.51	2.46	2.41	2.37	2.34	2.29	2.25	2.19	2.15	2.11	2.07	2.04	2.00	1.98	1.95	1.93	1.92
	8.28	**6.01**	**5.09**	**4.58**	**4.25**	**4.01**	**3.85**	**3.71**	**3.60**	**3.51**	**3.44**	**3.37**	**3.27**	**3.19**	**3.07**	**3.00**	**2.91**	**2.83**	**2.78**	**2.71**	**2.68**	**2.62**	**2.59**	**2.57**

df (denominator)

(*continued*)

df (numerator)

df (denom.)	1	2	3	4	5	6	7	8	9	10	11	12	14	16	20	24	30	40	50	75	100	200	500	∞
19	4.38	3.52	3.13	2.90	2.74	2.63	2.55	2.48	2.43	2.38	2.34	2.31	2.26	2.21	2.15	2.11	2.07	2.02	2.00	1.96	1.94	1.91	1.90	1.88
	8.18	**5.93**	**5.01**	**4.50**	**4.17**	**3.94**	**3.77**	**3.63**	**3.52**	**3.43**	**3.36**	**3.30**	**3.19**	**3.12**	**3.00**	**2.92**	**2.84**	**2.76**	**2.70**	**2.63**	**2.60**	**2.54**	**2.51**	**2.49**
20	4.35	3.49	3.10	2.87	2.71	2.60	2.52	2.45	2.40	2.35	2.31	2.28	2.23	2.18	2.12	2.08	2.04	1.99	1.96	1.92	1.90	1.87	1.85	1.84
	8.10	**5.85**	**4.94**	**4.43**	**4.10**	**3.87**	**3.71**	**3.56**	**3.45**	**3.37**	**3.30**	**3.23**	**3.13**	**3.05**	**2.94**	**2.86**	**2.77**	**2.69**	**2.63**	**2.56**	**2.53**	**2.47**	**2.44**	**2.42**
21	4.32	3.47	3.07	2.84	2.68	2.57	2.49	2.42	2.37	2.32	2.28	2.25	2.20	2.15	2.09	2.05	2.00	1.96	1.93	1.89	1.87	1.84	1.82	1.81
	8.02	**5.78**	**4.87**	**4.37**	**4.04**	**3.81**	**3.65**	**3.51**	**3.40**	**3.31**	**3.24**	**3.17**	**3.07**	**2.99**	**2.88**	**2.80**	**2.72**	**2.63**	**2.58**	**2.51**	**2.47**	**2.42**	**2.38**	**2.36**
22	4.30	3.44	3.05	2.82	2.66	2.55	2.47	2.40	2.35	2.30	2.26	2.23	2.18	2.13	2.07	2.03	1.98	1.93	1.91	1.87	1.84	1.81	1.80	1.78
	7.94	**5.72**	**4.82**	**4.31**	**3.99**	**3.76**	**3.59**	**3.45**	**3.35**	**3.26**	**3.18**	**3.12**	**3.02**	**2.94**	**2.83**	**2.75**	**2.67**	**2.58**	**2.53**	**2.46**	**2.42**	**2.37**	**2.33**	**2.31**
23	4.28	3.42	3.03	2.80	2.64	2.53	2.45	2.38	2.32	2.28	2.24	2.20	2.14	2.10	2.04	2.00	1.96	1.91	1.88	1.84	1.82	1.79	1.77	1.76
	7.88	**5.66**	**4.76**	**4.26**	**3.94**	**3.71**	**3.54**	**3.41**	**3.30**	**3.21**	**3.14**	**3.07**	**2.97**	**2.89**	**2.78**	**2.70**	**2.62**	**2.53**	**2.48**	**2.41**	**2.37**	**2.32**	**2.28**	**2.26**
24	4.26	3.40	3.01	2.78	2.62	2.51	2.43	2.36	2.30	2.26	2.22	2.18	2.13	2.09	2.02	1.98	1.94	1.89	1.86	1.82	1.80	1.76	1.74	1.73
	7.82	**5.61**	**4.72**	**4.22**	**3.90**	**3.67**	**3.50**	**3.36**	**3.25**	**3.17**	**3.09**	**3.03**	**2.93**	**2.85**	**2.74**	**2.66**	**2.58**	**2.49**	**2.44**	**2.36**	**2.33**	**2.27**	**2.23**	**2.21**
25	4.24	3.38	2.99	2.76	2.60	2.49	2.41	2.34	2.28	2.24	2.20	2.16	2.11	2.06	2.00	1.96	1.92	1.87	1.84	1.80	1.77	1.74	1.72	1.71
	7.77	**5.57**	**4.68**	**4.18**	**3.86**	**3.63**	**3.46**	**3.32**	**3.21**	**3.13**	**3.05**	**2.99**	**2.89**	**2.81**	**2.70**	**2.62**	**2.54**	**2.45**	**2.40**	**2.32**	**2.29**	**2.23**	**2.19**	**2.17**
26	4.22	3.37	2.98	2.74	2.59	2.47	2.39	2.32	2.27	2.22	2.18	2.15	2.10	2.05	1.99	1.95	1.90	1.85	1.82	1.78	1.76	1.72	1.70	1.69
	7.72	**5.53**	**4.64**	**4.14**	**3.82**	**3.59**	**3.42**	**3.29**	**3.17**	**3.09**	**3.02**	**2.96**	**2.86**	**2.77**	**2.66**	**2.58**	**2.50**	**2.41**	**2.36**	**2.28**	**2.25**	**2.19**	**2.15**	**2.13**
27	4.21	3.35	2.96	2.73	2.57	2.46	2.37	2.30	2.25	2.20	2.16	2.13	2.08	2.03	1.97	1.93	1.88	1.84	1.80	1.76	1.74	1.71	1.68	1.67
	7.68	**5.49**	**4.60**	**4.11**	**3.79**	**3.56**	**3.39**	**3.26**	**3.14**	**3.06**	**2.98**	**2.93**	**2.83**	**2.74**	**2.63**	**2.55**	**2.47**	**2.38**	**2.33**	**2.25**	**2.21**	**2.16**	**2.12**	**2.10**
28	4.20	3.34	2.95	2.71	2.56	2.44	2.36	2.29	2.24	2.19	2.15	2.12	2.06	2.02	1.96	1.91	1.87	1.81	1.78	1.75	1.72	1.69	1.67	1.65
	7.64	**5.45**	**4.57**	**4.07**	**3.76**	**3.53**	**3.36**	**3.23**	**3.11**	**3.03**	**2.95**	**2.90**	**2.80**	**2.71**	**2.60**	**2.52**	**2.44**	**2.35**	**2.30**	**2.22**	**2.18**	**2.13**	**2.09**	**2.06**
29	4.18	3.33	2.93	2.70	2.54	2.43	2.35	2.28	2.22	2.18	2.14	2.10	2.05	2.00	1.94	1.90	1.85	1.80	1.77	1.73	1.71	1.68	1.65	1.64
	7.60	**5.42**	**4.54**	**4.04**	**3.73**	**3.50**	**3.33**	**3.20**	**3.08**	**3.00**	**2.92**	**2.87**	**2.77**	**2.68**	**2.57**	**2.49**	**2.41**	**2.32**	**2.27**	**2.19**	**2.15**	**2.10**	**2.06**	**2.03**
30	4.17	3.32	2.92	2.69	2.53	2.42	2.34	2.27	2.21	2.16	2.12	2.09	2.04	1.99	1.93	1.89	1.84	1.79	1.76	1.72	1.69	1.66	1.64	1.62
	7.56	**5.39**	**4.51**	**4.02**	**3.70**	**3.47**	**3.30**	**3.17**	**3.06**	**2.98**	**2.90**	**2.84**	**2.74**	**2.66**	**2.55**	**2.47**	**2.38**	**2.29**	**2.24**	**2.16**	**2.13**	**2.07**	**2.03**	**2.01**
32	4.15	3.30	2.90	2.67	2.51	2.40	2.32	2.25	2.19	2.14	2.10	2.07	2.02	1.97	1.91	1.86	1.82	1.76	1.74	1.69	1.67	1.64	1.61	1.59
	7.50	**5.34**	**4.46**	**3.97**	**3.66**	**3.42**	**3.25**	**3.12**	**3.01**	**2.94**	**2.86**	**2.80**	**2.70**	**2.62**	**2.51**	**2.42**	**2.34**	**2.25**	**2.20**	**2.12**	**2.08**	**2.02**	**1.98**	**1.96**
34	4.13	3.28	2.88	2.65	2.49	2.38	2.30	2.23	2.17	2.12	2.08	2.05	2.00	1.95	1.89	1.84	1.80	1.74	1.71	1.67	1.64	1.61	1.59	1.57
	7.44	**5.29**	**4.42**	**3.93**	**3.61**	**3.38**	**3.21**	**3.08**	**2.97**	**2.89**	**2.82**	**2.76**	**2.66**	**2.58**	**2.47**	**2.38**	**2.30**	**2.21**	**2.15**	**2.08**	**2.04**	**1.98**	**1.94**	**1.91**
36	4.11	3.26	2.86	2.63	2.48	2.36	2.28	2.21	2.15	2.10	2.06	2.03	1.98	1.93	1.87	1.82	1.78	1.72	1.69	1.65	1.62	1.59	1.56	1.55
	7.39	**5.25**	**4.38**	**3.89**	**3.58**	**3.35**	**3.18**	**3.04**	**2.94**	**2.86**	**2.78**	**2.72**	**2.62**	**2.54**	**2.43**	**2.35**	**2.26**	**2.17**	**2.12**	**2.04**	**2.00**	**1.94**	**1.90**	**1.87**
38	4.10	3.25	2.85	2.62	2.46	2.35	2.26	2.19	2.14	2.09	2.05	2.02	1.96	1.92	1.85	1.80	1.76	1.71	1.67	1.63	1.60	1.57	1.54	1.53
	7.35	**5.21**	**4.34**	**3.86**	**3.54**	**3.32**	**3.15**	**3.02**	**2.91**	**2.82**	**2.75**	**2.69**	**2.59**	**2.51**	**2.40**	**2.32**	**2.22**	**2.14**	**2.08**	**2.00**	**1.97**	**1.90**	**1.86**	**1.84**
40	4.07	3.23	2.84	2.61	2.45	2.34	2.25	2.18	2.12	2.07	2.04	2.00	1.95	1.90	1.84	1.79	1.74	1.69	1.66	1.61	1.59	1.55	1.53	1.51
	7.31	**5.18**	**4.31**	**3.83**	**3.51**	**3.29**	**3.12**	**2.99**	**2.88**	**2.80**	**2.73**	**2.66**	**2.56**	**2.49**	**2.37**	**2.29**	**2.20**	**2.11**	**2.05**	**1.97**	**1.94**	**1.88**	**1.84**	**1.81**

(continued)

df (numerator)

df (denom.)	1	2	3	4	5	6	7	8	9	10	11	12	14	16	20	24	30	40	50	75	100	200	500	∞
42	4.07 **7.27**	3.22 **5.15**	2.83 **4.29**	2.59 **3.80**	2.44 **3.49**	2.32 **3.26**	2.24 **3.10**	2.17 **2.96**	2.11 **2.86**	2.06 **2.77**	2.02 **2.70**	1.99 **2.64**	1.94 **2.54**	1.89 **2.46**	1.82 **2.35**	1.78 **2.26**	1.73 **2.17**	1.68 **2.08**	1.64 **2.02**	1.60 **1.94**	1.57 **1.91**	1.54 **1.85**	1.51 **1.80**	1.49 **1.78**
44	4.06 **7.24**	3.21 **5.12**	2.82 **4.26**	2.58 **3.78**	2.43 **3.46**	2.31 **3.24**	2.23 **3.07**	2.16 **2.94**	2.10 **2.84**	2.05 **2.75**	2.01 **2.68**	1.98 **2.62**	1.92 **2.52**	1.88 **2.44**	1.81 **2.32**	1.76 **2.24**	1.72 **2.15**	1.66 **2.06**	1.63 **2.00**	1.58 **1.92**	1.56 **1.88**	1.52 **1.82**	1.50 **1.78**	1.48 **1.75**
46	4.05 **7.21**	3.20 **5.10**	2.81 **4.24**	2.57 **3.76**	2.42 **3.44**	2.30 **3.22**	2.22 **3.05**	2.14 **2.92**	2.09 **2.82**	2.04 **2.73**	2.00 **2.66**	1.97 **2.60**	1.91 **2.50**	1.87 **2.42**	1.80 **2.30**	1.75 **2.22**	1.71 **2.13**	1.65 **2.04**	1.62 **1.98**	1.57 **1.90**	1.54 **1.86**	1.51 **1.80**	1.48 **1.76**	1.46 **1.72**
48	4.04 **7.19**	3.19 **5.08**	2.80 **4.22**	2.56 **3.74**	2.41 **3.42**	2.30 **3.20**	2.21 **3.04**	2.14 **2.90**	2.08 **2.80**	2.03 **2.71**	1.99 **2.64**	1.96 **2.58**	1.90 **2.48**	1.86 **2.40**	1.79 **2.28**	1.74 **2.20**	1.70 **2.11**	1.64 **2.02**	1.61 **1.96**	1.56 **1.88**	1.53 **1.84**	1.50 **1.78**	1.47 **1.73**	1.45 **1.70**
50	4.03 **7.17**	3.18 **5.06**	2.79 **4.20**	2.56 **3.72**	2.40 **3.41**	2.29 **3.18**	2.20 **3.02**	2.13 **2.88**	2.07 **2.78**	2.02 **2.70**	1.98 **2.62**	1.95 **2.56**	1.90 **2.46**	1.85 **2.39**	1.78 **2.26**	1.74 **2.18**	1.69 **2.10**	1.63 **2.00**	1.60 **1.94**	1.55 **1.86**	1.52 **1.82**	1.48 **1.76**	1.46 **1.71**	1.44 **1.68**
55	4.02 **7.12**	3.17 **5.01**	2.78 **4.16**	2.54 **3.68**	2.38 **3.37**	2.27 **3.15**	2.18 **2.98**	2.11 **2.85**	2.05 **2.75**	2.00 **2.66**	1.97 **2.59**	1.93 **2.53**	1.88 **2.43**	1.83 **2.35**	1.76 **2.23**	1.72 **2.15**	1.67 **2.06**	1.61 **1.96**	1.58 **1.90**	1.52 **1.82**	1.50 **1.78**	1.46 **1.71**	1.43 **1.66**	1.41 **1.64**
60	4.00 **7.08**	3.15 **4.98**	2.76 **4.13**	2.52 **3.65**	2.37 **3.34**	2.25 **3.12**	2.17 **2.95**	2.10 **2.82**	2.04 **2.72**	1.99 **2.63**	1.95 **2.56**	1.92 **2.50**	1.86 **2.40**	1.81 **2.32**	1.75 **2.20**	1.70 **2.12**	1.65 **2.03**	1.59 **1.93**	1.56 **1.87**	1.50 **1.79**	1.48 **1.74**	1.44 **1.68**	1.41 **1.63**	1.39 **1.60**
65	3.99 **7.04**	3.14 **4.95**	2.75 **4.10**	2.51 **3.62**	2.36 **3.31**	2.24 **3.09**	2.15 **2.93**	2.08 **2.79**	2.02 **2.70**	1.98 **2.61**	1.94 **2.54**	1.90 **2.47**	1.85 **2.37**	1.80 **2.30**	1.73 **2.18**	1.68 **2.09**	1.63 **2.00**	1.57 **1.90**	1.54 **1.84**	1.49 **1.76**	1.46 **1.71**	1.42 **1.64**	1.39 **1.60**	1.37 **1.56**
70	3.98 **7.01**	3.13 **4.92**	2.74 **4.08**	2.50 **3.60**	2.35 **3.29**	2.23 **3.07**	2.14 **2.91**	2.07 **2.77**	2.01 **2.67**	1.97 **2.59**	1.93 **2.51**	1.89 **2.45**	1.84 **2.35**	1.79 **2.28**	1.72 **2.15**	1.67 **2.07**	1.62 **1.98**	1.56 **1.88**	1.53 **1.82**	1.47 **1.74**	1.45 **1.69**	1.40 **1.62**	1.37 **1.56**	1.35 **1.53**
80	3.96 **6.96**	3.11 **4.88**	2.72 **4.04**	2.48 **3.56**	2.33 **3.25**	2.21 **3.04**	2.12 **2.87**	2.05 **2.74**	1.99 **2.64**	1.95 **2.55**	1.91 **2.48**	1.88 **2.41**	1.82 **2.32**	1.77 **2.24**	1.70 **2.11**	1.65 **2.03**	1.60 **1.94**	1.54 **1.84**	1.51 **1.78**	1.45 **1.70**	1.42 **1.65**	1.38 **1.57**	1.35 **1.52**	1.32 **1.49**
100	3.94 **6.90**	3.09 **4.82**	2.70 **3.98**	2.46 **3.51**	2.30 **3.20**	2.19 **2.99**	2.10 **2.82**	2.03 **2.69**	1.97 **2.59**	1.92 **2.51**	1.88 **2.43**	1.85 **2.36**	1.79 **2.26**	1.75 **2.19**	1.68 **2.06**	1.63 **1.98**	1.57 **1.89**	1.51 **1.79**	1.48 **1.73**	1.42 **1.64**	1.39 **1.59**	1.34 **1.51**	1.30 **1.46**	1.28 **1.43**
125	3.92 **6.84**	3.07 **4.78**	2.68 **3.94**	2.44 **3.47**	2.29 **3.17**	2.17 **2.95**	2.08 **2.79**	2.01 **2.65**	1.95 **2.56**	1.90 **2.47**	1.86 **2.40**	1.83 **2.33**	1.77 **2.23**	1.72 **2.15**	1.65 **2.03**	1.60 **1.94**	1.55 **1.85**	1.49 **1.75**	1.45 **1.68**	1.39 **1.59**	1.36 **1.54**	1.31 **1.46**	1.27 **1.40**	1.25 **1.37**
150	3.91 **6.81**	3.06 **4.75**	2.67 **3.91**	2.43 **3.44**	2.27 **3.14**	2.16 **2.92**	2.07 **2.76**	2.00 **2.62**	1.94 **2.53**	1.89 **2.44**	1.85 **2.37**	1.82 **2.30**	1.76 **2.20**	1.71 **2.12**	1.64 **2.00**	1.59 **1.91**	1.54 **1.83**	1.47 **1.72**	1.44 **1.66**	1.37 **1.56**	1.34 **1.51**	1.29 **1.43**	1.25 **1.37**	1.22 **1.33**
200	3.89 **6.76**	3.04 **4.71**	2.65 **3.88**	2.41 **3.41**	2.26 **3.11**	2.14 **2.90**	2.05 **2.73**	1.98 **2.60**	1.92 **2.50**	1.87 **2.41**	1.83 **2.34**	1.80 **2.28**	1.74 **2.17**	1.69 **2.09**	1.62 **1.97**	1.57 **1.88**	1.52 **1.79**	1.45 **1.69**	1.42 **1.62**	1.35 **1.53**	1.32 **1.48**	1.26 **1.39**	1.22 **1.33**	1.19 **1.28**
400	3.86 **6.70**	3.02 **4.66**	2.62 **3.83**	2.39 **3.36**	2.23 **3.06**	2.12 **2.85**	2.03 **2.69**	1.96 **2.55**	1.90 **2.46**	1.85 **2.37**	1.91 **2.29**	1.78 **2.23**	1.72 **2.12**	1.67 **2.04**	1.60 **1.92**	1.54 **1.84**	1.49 **1.74**	1.42 **1.64**	1.38 **1.57**	1.32 **1.47**	1.28 **1.42**	1.22 **1.32**	1.16 **1.24**	1.13 **1.19**
1000	3.85 **6.66**	3.00 **4.62**	2.61 **3.80**	2.38 **3.34**	2.22 **3.04**	2.10 **2.82**	2.02 **2.66**	1.95 **2.53**	1.89 **2.43**	1.84 **2.34**	1.80 **2.26**	1.76 **2.20**	1.70 **2.09**	1.65 **2.01**	1.58 **1.89**	1.53 **1.81**	1.47 **1.71**	1.41 **1.61**	1.36 **1.54**	1.30 **1.44**	1.26 **1.38**	1.19 **1.28**	1.13 **1.19**	1.08 **1.11**
∞	3.84 **6.64**	2.99 **4.60**	2.60 **3.78**	2.37 **3.32**	2.21 **3.02**	2.09 **2.80**	2.01 **2.64**	1.94 **2.51**	1.88 **2.41**	1.83 **2.32**	1.79 **2.24**	1.75 **2.18**	1.69 **2.07**	1.64 **1.99**	1.57 **1.87**	1.52 **1.79**	1.46 **1.69**	1.40 **1.59**	1.35 **1.52**	1.28 **1.41**	1.24 **1.36**	1.17 **1.25**	1.11 **1.15**	1.00 **1.00**

Factors for Control Charts

Sample size n	c_4	c_5	d_2	d_3	D_3	D_4
2	0.7979	0.6028	1.128	0.853	0	3.267
3	0.8862	0.4633	1.693	0.888	0	2.574
4	0.9213	0.3889	2.059	0.880	0	2.282
5	0.9400	0.3412	2.326	0.864	0	2.114
6	0.9515	0.3076	2.534	0.848	0	2.004
7	0.9594	0.2820	2.704	0.833	0.076	1.924
8	0.9650	0.2622	2.847	0.820	0.136	1.864
9	0.9693	0.2459	2.970	0.808	0.184	1.816
10	0.9727	0.2321	3.078	0.797	0.223	1.777
11	0.9754	0.2204	3.173	0.787	0.256	1.744
12	0.9776	0.2105	3.258	0.778	0.283	1.717
13	0.9794	0.2019	3.336	0.770	0.307	1.693
14	0.9810	0.1940	3.407	0.763	0.328	1.672
15	0.9823	0.1873	3.472	0.756	0.347	1.653
16	0.9835	0.1809	3.532	0.750	0.363	1.637
17	0.9845	0.1754	3.588	0.744	0.378	1.622
18	0.9854	0.1703	3.640	0.739	0.391	1.608
19	0.9862	0.1656	3.689	0.734	0.403	1.597
20	0.9869	0.1613	3.735	0.729	0.415	1.585
21	0.9876	0.1570	3.778	0.724	0.425	1.575
22	0.9882	0.1532	3.819	0.720	0.434	1.566
23	0.9887	0.1499	3.858	0.716	0.443	1.557
24	0.9892	0.1466	3.895	0.712	0.451	1.548
25	0.9896	0.1438	3.931	0.708	0.459	1.541

Critical Values of *T* in the Wilcoxon Test

1-sided	2-sided	n = 5	n = 6	n = 7	n = 8	n = 9	n = 10
P = 0.05	P = 0.10	1	2	4	6	8	11
P = 0.025	P = 0.05		1	2	4	6	8
P = 0.01	P = 0.02			0	2	3	5
P = 0.005	P = 0.01				0	2	3

1-sided	2-sided	n = 11	n = 12	n = 13	n = 14	n = 15	n = 16
P = 0.05	P = 0.10	14	17	21	26	30	36
P = 0.025	P = 0.05	11	14	17	21	25	30
P = 0.01	P = 0.02	7	10	13	16	20	24
P = 0.005	P = 0.01	5	7	10	13	16	19

1-sided	2-sided	n = 17	n = 18	n = 19	n = 20	n = 21	n = 22
P = 0.05	P = 0.10	41	47	54	60	68	75
P = 0.025	P = 0.05	35	40	46	52	59	66
P = 0.01	P = 0.02	28	33	38	43	49	56
P = 0.005	P = 0.01	23	28	32	37	43	49

1-sided	2-sided	n = 23	n = 24	n = 25	n = 26	n = 27	n = 28
P = 0.05	P = 0.10	83	92	101	110	120	130
P = 0.025	P = 0.05	73	81	90	98	107	117
P = 0.01	P = 0.02	62	69	77	85	93	102
P = 0.005	P = 0.01	55	68	68	75	84	92

1-sided	2-sided	n = 29	n = 30	n = 31	n = 32	n = 33	n = 34
P = 0.05	P = 0.10	141	152	163	175	188	201
P = 0.025	P = 0.05	127	137	148	159	171	183
P = 0.01	P = 0.02	111	120	130	141	151	162
P = 0.005	P = 0.01	100	109	118	128	138	149

1-sided	2-sided	$n = 35$	$n = 36$	$n = 37$	$n = 38$	$n = 39$	$n = 40$
$P = 0.05$	$P = 0.10$	214	228	242	256	271	287
$P = 0.025$	$P = 0.05$	195	208	222	235	250	264
$P = 0.01$	$P = 0.02$	174	186	198	211	224	238
$P = 0.005$	$P = 0.01$	160	171	183	195	208	221
1-sided	2-sided	$n = 41$	$n = 42$	$n = 43$	$n = 44$	$n = 45$	
$P = 0.05$	$P = 0.10$	303	319	336	353	371	
$P = 0.025$	$P = 0.05$	279	295	311	327	344	
$P = 0.01$	$P = 0.02$	252	267	281	297	313	
$P = 0.005$	$P = 0.01$	234	248	262	277	292	
1-sided	2-sided	$n = 46$	$n = 47$	$n = 48$	$n = 49$	$n = 50$	
$P = 0.05$	$P = 0.10$	389	408	427	446	466	
$P = 0.025$	$P = 0.05$	361	379	397	415	434	
$P = 0.01$	$P = 0.02$	329	345	362	380	398	
$P = 0.005$	$P = 0.01$	307	323	339	356	373	

INDEX